The USENET Book

Finding, Using, and Surviving Newsgroups on the Internet

Bryan Pfaffenberger, Ph.D.

Addison-Wesley Publishing Company

Reading, Massachusetts • Menlo Park, California • New York
Don Mills, Ontario • Wokingham, England • Amsterdam
Bonn • Sydney • Singapore • Tokyo • Madrid • San Juan
Paris • Seoul • Milan • Mexico City • Taipei

Many of the designations used by manufacturers and sellers to distinguish their products are claimed as trademarks. Where those designations appear in this book, and Addison-Wesley was aware of a trademark claim, the designations have been printed in initial capital letters or all capital letters.

The authors and publishers have taken care in preparation of this book, but make no expressed or implied warranty of any kind and assume no responsibility for errors or omissions. No liability is assumed for incidental or consequential damages in connection with or arising out of the use of the information or programs contained herein.

Library of Congress Cataloging-in-Publication Data

Pfaffenberger, Bryan, 1949–
  The USENET book : finding, using, and surviving
newsgroups on the Internet / Bryan Pfaffenberger.
      p.   cm.
  Includes index.
  ISBN 0-201-40978-X (pbk.)
  1. Internet (Computer network)   2. USENET.   I. Title.
TK5105.875.I57P485 1995
004.69—dc20

Sponsoring Editor: David J. Clark
Project Editor: Joanne Clapp Fullagar
Production Coordinator: Deborah McKenna
Techical Reviewer: Gina Bull
Cover design: Jean Seal
Text design: Joyce C. Weston
Set in 11 point Minion by Gex

1 2 3 4 5 6 7 8 9 -MA- 9897969594
First printing, November 1994

Addison-Wesley books are available for bulk purchases by corporations, institutions, and other organizations. For more information please contact the Corporate, Government, and Special Sales Department at (800) 238-9682.

Acknowledgments

To write a book on so monumental a subject as USENET, one needs lots of help! First and foremost, I'd like to thank the netizens, too numerous to name here, who encouraged this project and provided helpful information. In particular, Judy Haldemann bouyed up my sagging spirits on more than one occasion, and forwarded a steady stream of Net delights for my perusal. My assistant, Kit Riddle, spent many long hours entering data for the humongous Chapter 18, and David Seaman, director of UVA's pathbreaking Electronic Text Center, aided in the preparation of the newsgroup subject index, one of this book's most useful tools. I'd like to thank my acquistions editor, David Clark, for inspiration throughout. Joanne Clapp Fullagar and her excellent staff—Deborah McKenna, Susan Riley, and Sharon Hilgenberg—provided the ideal mix of editorial acumen and creative freedom.

Most of all, I'd like to thank my wife, Suzanne, and two children, Michael and Julia, for putting up with my long hours at the keyboard...when we could have been doing more fun things. By the time I was done, though, all three demanded their own modems—so they could log on to USENET!

For Suzanne, always

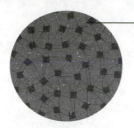

This is a book about USENET, which—next to electronic mail—is the computer's most impressive and exciting contribution to mass communication.

It's also one of the toughest to use effectively. USENET is overwhelmingly complex, and a superficial look might put you off. Here's a pretty typical first reaction to USENET: "Whoa—five thousand newsgroups! I don't have time for this." (A *newsgroup* is a named discussion group that focuses on a particular topic, such as backpacking, the politics of health reform, or sound systems for Windows computers.) Or maybe you'll come across a newsgroup that's in the throes of a *flame war* (a protracted and often vitriolic dispute over something) and thought that USENET's just a waste of time— a meaningless diversion, as a friend of mine put it rather caustically, "for people who like to shoot their mouths off."

This book's basic message is that both of these impressions are wrong. There *is* a way to find your way through the USENET maze and find the information—and most of all, the *people*—who can help you grow both professionally and personally. USENET has certainly changed me. It's my business to understand technology, and USENET has become an indispensable part of my professional life. USENET is equally vital for my hobbies, too— backpacking, classical music, gardening, and science fiction. Even more important to me, though,

are the people I've come to know through USENET discussions. I've never met them in *Real Life (RL)*, but I think of some of them as my friends. They are extraordinary, one-in-a-million people. I wouldn't have "met" them if I hadn't plowed into USENET, despite my own initial misgivings.

This book is an invitation to make USENET part of your life. It presents a *strategy* for coping with USENET's complexity and verbiage. You'll learn how to transform it into a tool of vital personal and professional importance.

DO I REALLY NEED TO READ A *BOOK* ABOUT USENET?

A lot of people log on to USENET, have a look, get overwhelmed, and log off. Others try to use their newsreaders, only to find that they can't figure out the obtuse, UNIX-style documentation—and give up. Still others try to post an article, make a mistake, get flamed, and won't touch USENET again. If you want to learn how to make USENET part of your life in a productive way, there's easily a book's worth of knowledge and skills to learn.

All those "Getting Started with Internet" books, with their one-chapter USENET tantalizers, just don't devote enough space to USENET to give you anything more than a superficial introduction. For example, all of them show you only one newsreader—say, nn—and tell you, cavalierly, that if you *aren't* using nn, you *should* be. But these authors know perfectly well, or should know, that most of the people logging into USENET via *shell accounts* (accounts on computer systems accessed via the telephone system) don't have any control over which newsreader they're using—the system administrator chooses, and everyone's stuck with the choice. And good luck with the on-line *man pages* (computer-accessible documentation), which were written *by* the UNIX hacker and *for* the UNIX hacker. It's no wonder that most people have no idea how to use their newsreader well! This book fully documents the top newsreaders. Even if you're using a newsreader that's not on this list, this book will help you master *any* newsreader in short order.

SO WHAT'S IN THIS BOOK?

Everything you need to make USENET a productive addition to your professional and personal life.

- You'll begin with a thorough grounding in USENET's history, culture, and organization—knowledge that's necessary if you want to become a full-fledged member of the USENET community. That's the purpose of Part I, "Introducing USENET."
- You'll learn how to master a *newsreader* (a program used to read USENET). Most newsreaders are very poorly documented, and many of the people using them don't have a clue how these powerful programs could save them time and help them get the most out of USENET. Part II, "Reading the news," fully documents nine of the top newsreading programs and teaches you how to get the most out of any other newsreader you'll encounter.
- You'll learn how to write your own USENET articles and participate fully in USENET newsgroups, without finding yourself on the wrong end of a flame war for violating USENET *netiquette*, the Net's informal rules for on-line comportment. That's the job of Part III of this book, "Now it's your turn."

- You'll learn how to find high-quality newsgroups that are loaded with information and contacts pertaining to your personal and professional interests. A unique feature of this book is its original reviews of the top USENET newsgroups, selected on the basis of the richness of their informational resources, the quality of their dialogue, and the knowledge of their participants. And to help you find your way through the more than 5,000 newsgroups, you'll also find a subject index. Curious to know which newsgroups pertain to Macintoshes, photography, or Nordic skiing? You'll find the answer fast.
- If you'd like to go further with USENET, you'll learn how you can create a newsgroup and even how to become a USENET site. You'll also learn how to think your way through some of the compelling issues of USENET—issues that will shape the future not only of USENET, but more broadly of computer-based communications generally in the century to come.

AW, C'MON. DOESN'T USENET = ALT.WASTE.TIME?

I don't think so, obviously, or I wouldn't have written this book. Here are some ways you can put USENET to good use

- **Finding people who are experts in an area.** Want to hobnob with the some of the best pilots, mountain climbers, writers, or biologists in the world? You'll find them as well as experts in every conceivable field of knowledge in USENET newsgroups. And if you approach them in the right way, you'll discover that most of them are very willing to share their knowledge and experience.
- **Locating others who share your interests.** OK, so there aren't that many people interested in recording your community's history—or so you think. Try posting an article on a local newsgroup, and see what happens. Not infrequently, contacts made through USENET lead to meetings in Real Life (RL), resulting in lasting friendships—and not a few marriages!

- **Learning how to look at an issue from multiple viewpoints.** Perhaps the most valuable skill you can learn in today's complex, global economy is the ability to examine difficult issues from all sides and form judgments that are enriched by a wide diversity of opinion. USENET's disagreements aren't always congenial, but they're certainly wide open!

- **Looking for answers to specific problems.** Can't get your LaserWriter to work with your PC? Can't figure out why your cat's fur looks listless? Don't know whether you can get parts for a 1974 Fiat Spyder? These are just some of the thousands of questions that get answered every day on USENET.

- **Discovering knowledge.** Many of USENET's best newsgroups maintain documents called *Frequently Asked Questions* (*FAQs*) that sum up the accumulated knowledge of the group's participants. (If a newsgroup has a FAQ, you should read it before you post a question that's been answered time and again!) These and other informational resources are periodically posted to relevant newsgroups, and they add up to an astonishing amount of knowledge, on hundreds of subjects. Just two examples: From rec.gardens, you can read everything participants have learned—sometimes the hard way—about ordering plants by mail; from soc.cultural.thai, you'll find seven huge documents that contain a rich tapestry of knowledge concerning Thailand's culture, language, history, economy, and tourism.

- **Obtaining free software and shareware.** USENET is an excellent source of *binary files* (files that are ready to run, or execute, on a particular computer) as well as *source code* (program instructions that haven't been compiled into executable code yet). If you're using Microsoft Windows or a Macintosh, for example, you'll find hundreds of utilities, applications, sounds, icons, and more.

- **Finding jobs.** Many people have found jobs through USENET connections. In highly specialized or technical areas, it isn't easy to find knowledgeable, competent employees. The person who's discovered that you're a treasure-trove of knowledge on a subject might have a job offer in mind.

- **Getting the most out of your computer.** No matter what kind of computer you're using, USENET can help you improve your system's performance. It's an invaluable source of tips, hints, information on hard-to-get supplies, ways to work around problems, the latest computer viruses, and fixes for bugs.

Admittedly, there are lots of ways you can waste time with USENET, but the same's true of television. Kept in proportion, USENET can be lots of fun—and there's nothing inherently wrong with that. Every day, I get laughs from alt.humor.best-of-internet. I love the discussions of the San Francisco 49ers, my favorite football team (although I do wish the Cowboys fans would stay out of it). If this is a waste of time, then so is the break around the water cooler at the office, where people crack jokes and trade the latest scores—and return to work refreshed.

WHAT DO I NEED TO EXPLORE USENET?

You'll need access to a computer, of course—but it needn't be anything fancy, as explained in Chapter 3. The computer must either be equipped with a *modem* (a device that allows your computer to "talk" to other computers via the telephone system) or connected to a *local area network (LAN)* that permits you to access USENET. (A local area network connects as many as several dozen computers within a department or building, allowing them to share data and printers. Some LANs have external Internet connections.) You'll also need an *account* (a subscription) to a computer system that makes USENET available.

Chapter 3, "Connecting to USENET," covers the many ways you can connect to USENET, including on-line services such as CompuServe and Delphi and bulletin board systems (BBSs). As you'll learn, connecting to USENET isn't the same thing as connecting to Internet, although it's certainly possible to do both at the same time.

> **TIP:** Do you already subscribe to America Online, Delphi, or CompuServe? If so, you've already got access to USENET. If not, a good way to explore USENET, at least initially, is to try one of these service's freebie sign-up deals; at this writing, for instance, Delphi is offering five hours of free Internet access (including USENET) if you accept their trial offer. If you don't like the service, you can cancel after using up your free time. For more information, see Chapter 3.

SUMMARY

USENET can be overwhelming and exasperating, but there's a way to transform it into a powerful tool for your personal and professional enrichment. You need to understand USENET's culture and traditions, and you need to learn how to use your newsreader software correctly. In addition, you need to learn how to post without finding yourself on the wrong end of a flame war. Finally, you need to identify the newsgroups that contain discussions and resources relevant to the topics in which you're interested. This book is organized to help you achieve all of these goals. Welcome to USENET!

FROM HERE

- **Flip to Chapter 1**, "USENET fundamentals," for explanations of the basics of USENET
- **Never seen USENET in action?** Take a look at Chapter 2, "A quick USENET tour."
- **Ready to start learning your newsreader?** Look for your newsreader software in Part II, "Reading the news." If it's not treated in depth, you'll learn how to master *any* newsreader in Chapter 6, "Understanding newsreaders."

PART I
INTRODUCING
USENET

For generations of people accustomed to top-down broadcast media such as radio and television, USENET is a refreshing, even revolutionary change: It doesn't feed you predigested pap based on some marketer's idea of what you're *supposed* to consume. In contrast to broadcast media, with information producers on one end and information consumers on the other, USENET enables anyone with access to a suitably connected computer to *originate* information and make it available, potentially, to an audience that currently numbers 7 million people. What's in USENET, in short, depends on what ordinary people put into it.

A community product, a people's medium, a global letters-to-the-editor column, an electronic soapbox—that's USENET (or the Net, as net.denizens like to abbreviate it). The Net's democracy explains its extraordinary vitality. When you explore USENET, you find out what all kinds of people want to say about every conceivable subject, rather than what some media magnate or government agency *thinks* you should read. Organized into more than 5,000 topically differentiated newsgroups, USENET is the world's first truly democratic mass medium, a place where birds-of-a-feather, even if separated by continental or even global distances, can congregate. And when they do, a community develops—a *virtual* community, as author Howard Rheingold puts it, of people who may have

never actually met in person. They share resources, exchange knowledge, develop a sense of common identity, and—yes—argue like hell, sometimes. USENET's sometimes destructive flame wars are as legendary as its revealing, wide-open discussion—but that's part of the Net, too.

For USENET's many critics, of course, the medium's bottom-up democracy is also its weakness—how could the rantings and ravings of millions of people add up to anything other than a waste of time? And indeed, there are facetious, juvenile, malicious, misleading, self-serving, obscene, idiotic, and even illegal USENET postings. Whether we like to admit it or not, the unsavory aspects of USENET reflect what's unsavory about our society. There's racism to be found on USENET, and sexism too—more than a few women have found themselves hounded out of discussions. To avoid USENET because some of its participants are jerks, however, is to miss the work of some of the finest people you'll ever encounter—knowledgeable in their fields, eloquent in their opinions, tolerant of diverse viewpoints, dedicated to USENET's democratic ideals. Just like a high-quality speaker system that reproduces the pianist Glenn Gould's groans and grunts as well as his trills and arpeggios, USENET digitally reproduces the trash as well as the treasures—but I hope you'll agree that the treasures make USENET worth the effort.

WHAT IS USENET?

This question is surprisingly difficult to answer—which helps to explain why USENET is so widely misunderstood. There's a strong temptation to begin negatively, by saying what USENET isn't:

- USENET isn't a computer network (a collection of physically connected computers). USENET traverses virtually every kind of computer network in existence.

- It isn't the Internet, although the Internet plays a big role in disseminating USENET throughout the world.

- It isn't a gigantic computer bulletin board system (BBS) or an on-line service, both of which require a centralized computer system to store messages and receive calls. USENET's literally all over the place.

So what *is* USENET? Before you can understand the answer to this surprisingly complex question, you need to grasp that a revolution in computer technology has occurred during the past twenty years. As you're surely aware, different brands of computers can exchange data only with difficulty—try getting that Macintosh disk into your Microsoft Windows system. (It *can* be done, but only with special equipment.) The people who have tried to hook computers together into networks have experienced similar problems—and they've solved them. They've come up with ways to make dissimilar computer networks *interoperate* (work with each other) so that a user of one kind of computer can actually exchange data with and even control another, distant computer somewhere else on the network—even if it's made by a different manufacturer.

What makes interoperability possible is the widespread acceptance of *protocols* (published standards for computer communications). An *open protocol* is a public domain (free) standard that any hardware manufacturer or software publisher can use. What makes the Internet possible is the widespread acceptance of the TCP/IP protocols. Any computer that conforms to the TCP/IP protocols can be hooked up to the Internet.

The same goes for USENET. What makes USENET possible is the existence of a well-defined protocol for the format and the distribution of *articles* (USENET messages). By "format," I mean the organization of each article into two distinct parts, the *header* (the part that contains information about the article's subject, where it came from, and other things) and the *body* (the part that contains the text somebody wrote). So far as this part of the USENET standard goes, it's not that much different than electronic mail. It's the distribution part that differs—and radically. Basically, USENET is set up so that any message you contribute to the network gets sent out and copied repeatedly until every USENET site—currently 180,000 of them!—has a copy of it. Talk about self-publishing!

This might be easier to understand if you can relate it to something in your personal experience. Remember Valentine's Day in grade school? To make sure no one's feelings got hurt, the teacher asks every student to get as many cards as the number of other students in the class—if there are 25 students besides yourself, you get 25 cards. In the end, everyone in the class gets a card from everyone else. A full set of the cards, to put it in tech-speak, has *propagated* to each individual in the class.

Basically, USENET works the same way—when you post a message, the software distributes the text and keeps making copies of it, until eventually every participating computer can access a copy of the message. When a new message arrives at a USENET *site* (a computer that receives USENET messages), the message goes into a topically differentiated newsgroup, each with its own name (such as rec.backcountry or alt.cd-rom). When someone replies to one of the posted messages, the reply propagates in the same way that an original posting does, going to the correct cubbyhole—the named newsgroup—from which the reply originated.

WHY DO THEY CALL IT "NEWS"?

USENET postings aren't newspaper articles, with a "who-what-where-when-why" structure. Most of them are brief messages from individuals who wish to contribute to the discussion on a topic, and in a number of ways—by providing opinion, of course, but also by providing facts, additional information resources, and suggestions on how to improve the discussion. What makes them "news" is the fact that the discussion is up-to-the-minute, often referring to ongoing events. For example, within a couple of days of the famous 1994 O.J. Simpson cavalcade on the Los Angeles freeways, several newsgroups were full of discussion of the legal and social issues involved. The newsgroup called rec.humor had already accumulated dozens of O.J. Simpson jokes (in varying degrees of poor taste), and a new alt newsgroup had been formed: alt.fan.o-j-simpson.

USENET postings are "news" in another sense, too: They remain accessible for only a brief time—as little as a week—before they're erased. With as much as 170 MB of new postings coming in every day, even a large USENET site can't afford to keep articles stored on the disk for longer than a week or so. To make room for new articles, the old ones are deleted.

Does this mean USENET articles are lost to history? Some newsgroups maintain archives of all the postings that have been made to the group, but this is the exception rather than the rule.

IS USENET PART OF THE INTERNET?

This is a sore point for old USENET hands. Newspaper and magazine articles tend to equate USENET with the Internet, as if they were one and the same. The short answer is, yes, USENET *is* part of the Internet, but USENET isn't limited to the Internet—and originally, it was conceived as a low-cost alternative to the Internet's predecessor, the ARPANET (see "Where did USENET come from?").

The Internet, in case you've been in the back woods for the last two years, is a global *internetwork* (a network of linked networks). Its foundation laid by the widespread acceptance of the TCP/IP protocols, the Internet's formed through the linkage of thousands of formerly separate networks.

The Internet provides a large part of USENET's distribution system, but there are other internet-working standards (such as the *Unix-to-Unix Copy Program [UUCP]*) at work in disseminating USENET articles. USENET is organized so that it doesn't really matter which networks transport the news—in fact, there are several networks involved in relaying and duplicating USENET postings; the Internet is just one of them. On-line information services such as CompuServe, bulletin board systems (BBSs), and freenets provide additional points of entry for USENET messages. You've heard about the Internet, how huge it is, and how fast it's growing. Potentially, USENET is even bigger, because it's not limited to networks that employ the Internet's TCP/IP protocols.

How many people use USENET?

No one knows for sure. But the Network Measurement Project at the DEC System Laboratory, Palo Alto, CA, has used automated analytical tools and statistical analysis to make some good guesses, summarized in Table 1-1. At this book's writing, there were 180,000 USENET sites—that is, computer systems with sufficient disk space to store the enormous amount of data generated by USENET activity and make this data available to the very much larger population of people who have accounts on these computers—21 million in all. And of these 21 million, about one third — 7 million or so—read the news.

Does this mean that your USENET postings will be read by 7 million people? Nope. Very few people subscribe to more than one or two dozen of the thousands of newsgroups, and their subscription lists differ. This fragments the audience. The readership of a reasonably popular newsgroup, such as rec.foods.cooking, is about that of a large town or a small city—between 100,000 and 200,000.

TABLE 1-1. USENET'S READERSHIP (JUNE, 1994)

Total number of USENET sites: 180,000

Total number of USENET readers: 7,126,000

Average traffic per day (megabytes): 172MB

Average traffic per day (number of messages): 67,344

USENET Readership Summary Report, June 1994

Thousands of newsgroups have readerships equal to a town or suburb (25,000 to 100,000).

By any standard, USENET's on the up side of a phenomenal growth curve. In 1979, there were only three USENET sites, circulating an average of two articles per day. During the early 1980s, growth was slow; by 1983, for instance, there were 600 USENET sites, exchanging an average of 120 articles per day. But growth soon accelerated beyond anyone's wildest expectations. By 1988, 11,000 sites exchanged 1,800 articles per day; the number of articles per day was to grow to 26,000 in 1993, and 67,344 in 1994—with 180,000 sites! Even mentioning these numbers threatens to date this book horribly, since they're likely to double by the time this book reaches your hands.

For this book, though, the real question isn't how many people access USENET—it's how many people access USENET *well*. How many hundreds of thousands of them log on out of curiosity, have a few laughs, and retreat in confusion, without grasping how useful USENET can be? The answer to that question is surely "far too many." Like most Internet applications, learning how to exploit USENET fully isn't an easy or trivial task. We're talking about 170 MB of new data daily—that's enough to fill about 250 paperback novels—per day! This is it, folks: "information overload." To turn USENET into a useful tool, you need guidance, tutorials, documentation, reference information, and newsgroup reviews—and that's exactly what this book is for.

WHERE IS THE CENTRAL OFFICE OF USENET, INC.?

There isn't one. USENET isn't a formal organization. It's a loose collection of system administrators, united in what has been termed a "cooperative anarchy." No one's in control of USENET. The technical standards, the software, the administration, the distribution—they're all the results of strictly volunteer effort and generous contributrions of system resources. There's no formal USENET organization (although USENET system administrators regularly meet at the Usenix conference), no formal rules—and no formal enforcement procedure for such rules, anyway. To be sure, the system administrators at USENET sites can and do exercise control over which newsgroups and newsgroup *hierarchies* the site carries—for this reason, USENET's structure might quite accurately be described as a collection of baronies without a king. (*Hierarchy* is the USENET term for a category of newsgroups that cover a general topic, such as recreation or computers.) But there's no firm consensus on just what role system administrators should play in controlling USENET's content, and the matter remains controversial (see Chapter 21, "USENET issues and futures"). And because there are now so many different ways that USENET messages can traverse the Internet, one site's decision to omit a specific newsgroup probably won't affect the ability of "downstream" sites to receive the newsgroup, as was once the case. As long as USENET's software is operating, it will distribute USENET messages to every site that's willing to accept them.

WHAT'S A NEWSGROUP?

A newsgroup is the basic unit of USENET's organization. Each newsgroup has a name such as rec.backcountry that captures the newsgroup's focus; all the rec.* groups (any group whose name begins with "rec") are recreation-oriented newsgroups. Rec.backcountry is a recreation-oriented newsgroup that's concerned with backpacking, climbing, mountain biking, and other backcountry activities.

WHAT'S AN ARTICLE?

Within a newsgroup, you'll find articles—contributions from people who read, and respond, to USENET news. Here's what an article looks like:

```
Newsgroups:sci.astronomy
Subject:Is there an archive of Jupiter
pix?
Date:July 25, 1994
Organization:Free Union School
Does anyone know whether there's an
archive of Hubble shots of Jupiter,
including the comet collision? I could
really use them for a science class I'm
teaching. TIA, Jennifer
=======================================
Jennifer A. Smith
Free Union School
Free Union, VA
jas@albemarle.county.va.us
"If you can read and write, thank a
teacher"
=======================================
```

An article has three parts:

- **Header.** The beginning lines of the article, which begin with titles such as "Newsgroups" and "Date," provide important information to the computer programs that process USENET messages. This information includes the name of the newsgroup (or newsgroups) to which the message has been posted and the subject of the message.

- **Body.** Contains the message that the contributor has written.

- **Signature.** At the end of the message, the contributer can optionally include personal information. Sometimes, people like to include a memorable or witty quotation in their signatures, but this is frowned on if it takes up too much room.

Follow-up postings (replies) frequently post the text of the original article, as in the following example:

```
Newsgroups: sci.astronomy
Subject:Re: Is there an archive of
Jupiter pix?
Date:July 28, 1994
Organization:Chesapeake Bay College

Jennifer Smith wrote,
>Does anyone know whether there's an
>archive of Hubble shots of Jupiter,
>including the comet collision? I could
>really use them for a science class
>I'm teaching. TIA, Jennifer

Try subscribing to alt.binaries.pictures—
I've seen lots of Jupiter pix there in
the past couple of days. Good luck,
John Chesterson
+++++++++++++++++++++++++++++++++++++++++
```

HOW DO YOU READ THE ARTICLES IN A NEWSGROUP?

USENET is a prime example of the *client-server model* of network application design in which client programs—running on the user's machine—obtain information from server programs running on a computer located elsewhere. You use a *client program* (newsreader) that runs on the machine you're using. The client program is designed to help you navigate the network—in this case, USENET. The client program contacts a *server,* a program that accepts requests from the client, processes them, and displays the result. Hundreds or even thousands of clients may access the server simultaneously. Each USENET site has one or more servers; it's not known how many USENET clients are in existence, but the number is surely in the millions.

USENET's server software is briefly described in Chapter 20, "Becoming a USENET site", but it isn't something you'll need to worry about. Choosing a newsreader, however, is another matter (see Chapter 6, "Understanding newsreaders"). There are many newsreaders in existence and some are better than others. A good newsreader helps you do some or all of the following:

- Choose the newsgroup you want to read

- Display an organized list of the article's subjects

- Follow the thread of the discussion by grouping articles on the same subject

- Display, print, and save articles

- Mark articles as read so you don't see them again the next time you start the newsreader program

- Reply to an article's author by mail

- Post a *follow-up article* (a response to a posted article) to the newsgroup

- Post an article on a new subject

- Kill (ignore) articles with certain subjects or authors that you don't want to read

To see what a USENET session looks like on-screen, flip to Chapter 2, "A quick USENET tour."

One of the down sides of USENET is that there's no "market-leading" newsreader, a sure bet that you can choose to ensure that you're getting high-quality software. With *dialup access* (see Chapter 3, "Connecting to USENET"), the type of access with which you're most likely to start, you'll be stuck with the newsreader that's been selected for you. In dialup access, you use a communication program and a modem to contact a distant computer, which you operate by remote control. You must use the software this computer provides. Good luck! By shopping selectively among the on-line serves such as CompuServe, America Online, and Delphi, though, you can exercise some choice. You have much more choice if you achieve the connection of the future, called *dialup IP*, a method of directly accessing the Internet through telephone connections. For dialup IP, your computer requires software that supports the Internet's data-handling standards. Such software is included free with the latest version of the Macintosh system software and will be included in the forthcoming Microsoft Windows 9.5 (called "Chicago" in its beta version). Chapter 3 goes into all these subjects in more detail; but as you'll see, dialup IP bears consideration, if only because you can choose your own newsreader, which you install and run on your computer. The quality of the newsreader you'll use determines in no small measure how much you'll enjoy Internet and how much you'll get out of it.

WHERE DID USENET COME FROM?

USENET has its origins in a 1976 program called Unix-to-Unix Copy (UUCP), created at AT&T's Bell Laboratories. Written by Mike Lesk, UUCP provided the technical means by which geographically separated UNIX sites could exchange information and files by means of long-distance telephone connections—and thereby realize one of UNIX's design goals: to foster the growth of a UNIX community. Incorporated into UNIX Version 7 and later released in other popular UNIX versions as well, UUCP provided wide-area network (WAN) technology to many colleges, universities, and companies that, at the time, could not participate in the Internet's predecessor, the ARPANET. Access to the ARPANET was restricted to colleges and universities that had Department of Defense contracts. Utilizing the telephone system, UUCP allowed UNIX sites previously shut out of the ARPANET to exchange mail, transfer files, and execute commands on a remote system.

In 1979, two graduate students at Duke University, Tom Truscott and James Ellis, conceived of USENET as a way of linking departments within a university and with nearby universities. Working with Steve Bellovin, a graduate student at the University of North Carolina (UNC) in nearby Chapel Hill, they developed a program that would allow UNIX computer users to exchange messages in a fashion similar to the subject-organized mailing lists that had developed on the ARPANET. They coined the term "USENET," short for "UNIX User's Network," for their new network idea. They described USENET as a "distributed decentralized news system," a "poor man's ARPANET" that would assist UNIX users with the peculiarities of the UNIX operating system (at the time, AT&T, kept out of the computer business by federal anti-trust regulations, offered no UNIX support). The system was first tested by linking UNC with a computer at nearby Duke University. The public domain system software that supported the first version of USENET news, called A-News, was released to the UNIX community at the 1980 winter meetings of USENIX, a professional association of UNIX users and developers. The program created a sensation at the conference.

USENET surprised its creators. They thought the software would be used to link the various computers in different departments within a university, perhaps adding a few computers at nearby universities. But they underestimated, as they later observed, the "human hunger for communication." To their amazement, USENET soon blossomed into a national, and then an international network. And with USENET's rapid growth came another surprise: Users weren't content to restrict themselves to computer-related subjects. Popular from an early date were the "Human-Net" mailing lists imported from the ARPANET, and many human interest USENET newsgroups were soon to follow.

As the number of newsgroups proliferated, the limitations of the early USENET's structure and software became clear. New versions of the supporting software—B-News, subsequently followed by the current C-News, dealt with the challenges posed by thousands of newsgroups and millions of users. A reorganization of newsgroup names, dubbed the "Great Renaming," resulted in today's hierarchical newsgroup names, which are functioning reasonably well—despite some evident inconsistencies. For instance, there's an alt.beer and a rec.foods.drink.beer *and* a rec.arts.brewing. See Chapter 4, "How USENET is organized," for more information on finding your way though USENET's complexities.

Today, USENET is growing at an amazing rate—about 10 to 15 percent per month. At these rates, the Net's current 7 million users will grow to approximately 12 million just in the time it takes to get this book printed!

Can USENET cope with its current explosive growth? Throughout USENET's history, the "old timers" (defined as anyone who's been on the Net longer than you!) have lamented the coming destruction of USENET as hordes of new users come online—users who don't know anything about the Net's traditions, customs, lore, and etiquette. In the throes of the blues, they post articles proclaiming the "Imminent death of the Net." Since the Net's death has been predicted so many times, and obviously the predictions have proven false, this has become something of a joke—at the end of an article lamenting one of USENET's many shortcomings, you'll see the one-liner, "Imminent death of the Net—film at 11."

Surely, the Net's growth poses considerable problems. USENET exists only because system administrators are willing to provide part of their system's disk space and processing capacity for USENET—but the magnitude of USENET postings is causing growing difficulties. On the other hand, the cost of primary storage—hard disks—is dropping almost as fast as the demand for USENET is growing. There are bound to be some bumps along the way, but USENET has survived every technical challenge it's faced thus far. USENET is well on its way to becoming a truly mass medium—right now, its audience is larger than Roseanne's (a fact that, for me, tends to restore my faith in humanity).

FROM HERE

• Want to see what USENET looks like on-screen? Flip to Chapter 2, "A quick USENET tour."

• In the dark about what those newsgroup names mean? Flip to Chapter 4, "How USENET is organized."

• Like to learn more about USENET's customs and traditions? Flip to Chapter 5, "USENET's values, customs, and lore."

Although there are many ways to access USENET and the dozens of newsreaders available, the basic processes of reading the news are the same: You subscribe to newsgroups, view a list of article subjects, and read the selected articles. You may also post articles on new subjects or reply to a current article. This chapter provides an overview of these basic processes, enabling you to understand what reading the news is all about.

A visual introduction to USENET is also an introduction to newsreading software, which is the software you use to navigate USENET, read the news, and post your articles. This chapter begins by briefly describing the basic structure of all USENET newsreaders, a topic that is explored in greater detail in Chapter 6, "Understanding newsreaders."

ABOUT NEWSREADER LEVELS

Newsreaders vary in details, but they all have the same basic structure: They're like a layer cake.

The newsgroup selector (the newsreader's top layer) has tools to help you *subscribe to* (select) newsgroups. A newsgroup subscription, incidentally, isn't like a magazine subscription. The newsgroup isn't notified in any way that you've subscribed—the "subscription" is just a setting in the newsreader program that indicates which newsgroups you want to read on a regular basis. After you've subscribed to a newsgroup, the newsreader

will make this newsgroup accessible to you in some way, such as by putting it at the top of the newsgroup list or asking whether you want to read it when you log on. With the newsgroup selector's help, you can choose the group you want to read, which takes you to the next layer.

In the *thread selector* (the newsreader's second layer "down") are the subjects of the articles currently available in the newsgroup you've chosen to read, grouped (ideally) by subject. With the subjects grouped this way, it is easy to follow the "thread" of a discussion—hence the term *thread* (a group of articles that all contain replies and commentary on one original article). A *threaded newsreader* is a newsreader that groups articles by subject in this way—and believe me, you won't want to settle for anything less. (Many of the newsreaders offered by BBS systems and freenets aren't threaded.) When you've found a "hot" topic, the thread selector lets you choose the articles you want to read—and it also lets you move to the next layer.

The *article selector* (the third level down) contains the articles you want to read. At this layer, you can post new articles to the group or reply to existing ones. After you read an article, the newsreader deletes the article from the list so that you don't see it the next time you log on. (If you want to re-read the article, though, you can do so—as long as it hasn't expired.)

Much of what you'll do with a newsreader involves going down (subscribing to a group, choosing a newsgroup to read, viewing the threads, selecting articles to read, and reading the articles), as well as going back up (redisplaying the thread list, or going to a different newsgroup). A good newsreader lets you do this easily and with a minimum of confusion.

Featured in this chapter is an *NNTP newsreader,* WinVN, which I've chosen to illustrate the mechanics of reading the news. An NNTP newsreader is a client program, one that runs on your computer and makes contact with an NNTP server. This is a program that conforms to the Network News Transport Protocol, the standard by which USENET news is disseminated. The program is a nights-and-weekends effort of Mark Riordan, a systems programmer at Michigan State University, who started the program's development in 1989. In Fall of 1992, Sam Rushing and Jim Dumoulin took over the program's development. The program is currently in the public domain; you can obtain it via anonymous FTP from many sites, including ftp.ksc.nasa.gov, in the directory /pub/win3/winvn. In anonymous FTP, you use a client program to obtain files from another computer on the Internet. It's called anonymous FTP because you type "anonymous" when you make contact with the remote file server and because the file transfer makes use of the File Transfer Protocol. Let's take a look at WinVN to see how this newsreader handles these procedures.

USING THE NEWSGROUP SELECTOR

When you start WinVN for the first time, the program downloads the names of all the newsgroups available from your NNTP server. The result is a very lengthy list, the top of which is shown in Figure 2-1. (The NNTP server to which WinVN is connected in this figure offers only 3,307 newsgroups; your server may offer as many as 5,000.) When you log in subsequent sessions, the program will detect any new newsgroups that may have been added and ask you whether you want to subscribe to them.

With WinVN, you can subscribe to a newsgroup in two ways: You can scroll the window to look for the newsgroup's name—or, if the idea of hunting through 3,307 newsgroups daunts you, you can search for a newsgroup by typing part or all of its name. Once you find the name of the newsgroup to which you want to subscribe, you highlight it and choose the Subscribe command from the Group menu. WinVN places the group at the top of your list (Figure 2-2) and changes its color, indicating that you've subscribed to the group. (The window bar still says "0 Subscribed"—and it will until you save your newsgroup list, which is accomplished only by quitting WinVN. The next time you log on, the number will be correct.)

The first time you access USENET, you'll want to build your *subscription list,* a list of the newsgroups you want to read regularly. With WinVN, you can do

```
0 alt.3d
0 alt.abortion.inequity
0 alt.activism
0 alt.activism.d
0 alt.activism.death-penalty
0 alt.adoption
0 alt.aldus.pagemaker
0 alt.alien.visitors
0 alt.amiga.demos
0 alt.angst
0 alt.animation.warner-bros
0 alt.answers
0 alt.appalachian
0 alt.aquaria
0 alt.archery
0 alt.architecture
0 alt.artcom
0 alt.arts.ballet
0 alt.ascii-art
0 alt.astrology
0 alt.atheism
0 alt.autos.antique
0 alt.autos.rod-n-custom
0 alt.bacchus
0 alt.backrubs
0 alt.bbs
0 alt.bbs.ads
0 alt.bbs.allsysop
0 alt.bbs.internet
0 alt.bbs.lists
```

Figure 2-1. At the newsgroup selector level, you can subscribe to newsgroups and choose the newsgroups you want to read.

so by repeating the procedure just described until you've added the groups you think you'll read on a regular basis. You can also reorganize the subscribed newsgroups until they're arranged in the order you like. In Figure 2-3, you see my subscription list, organized the way I like it—with current news and sports at the top, followed by newsgroups tracking my professional interests (telecommunications and book publishing) and some hobbies (backpacking and music). Incidentally, the zeros in front of the newsgroup name will be replaced by the number of available articles, but only after you've opened the newsgroup (as described in the next section).

USING THE THREAD SELECTOR

When you've finished your subscription list, it's time to read the news! To do so, you just select the group you want to read, and press Enter. You'll see the thread selector, shown in Figure 2-4.

In the thread selector window, you see the two basic kinds of USENET postings you'll encounter:

- **Original articles.** A post on a new subject; the article's subject doesn't have the word "Re:" (regarding).

- **Follow-up articles.** An article written in response to a previous original article. Follow-up articles are grouped together so that you can follow the thread of the discussion. You don't see the subject of the article, since it's the same as the original article.

As you just learned, a threaded newsreader can't group all the articles on the same subject if some of them don't quote previous posts. That's why WinVN offers a very useful feature, the ability to group articles by subject (see Figure 2-5). With the articles grouped by subject, you'll be sure that you haven't missed any of the responses to a thread, including those reponses that didn't quote any previous articles.

WinVN can sort the articles in other ways—and this is a very nice feature. For example, you can sort

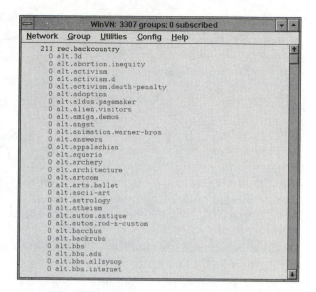

Figure 2-2. After you subscribe to a newsgroup, WinVN places the group at the top of the newsgroup list.

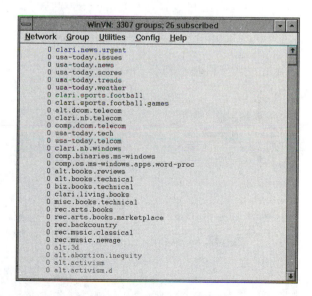

Figure 2-3. Organize your subscription list so that the newsgroups are listed in the order you want to read them.

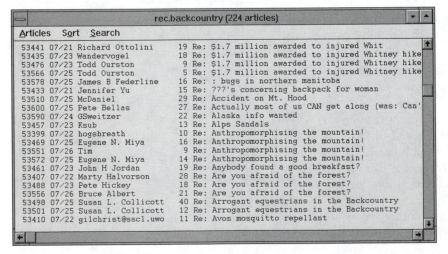

```
┌───────────────────────────────────────────────────────────────────────┐
│ ─                     rec.backcountry (224 articles)            ▼ ▲    │
├───────────────────────────────────────────────────────────────────────┤
│ Articles   Sort   Search                                               │
├───────────────────────────────────────────────────────────────────────┤
│ 53449 07/25 David Paul          10 Fires in Colorado                 ↑ │
│ 53450 07/25 Bill Tuthill        11 Re: Whisplight vs. Peak1: Which is better? │
│ 53451 07/22 Harriet Roberts     12 Re: Can't we all get along? (was: Multiple-use T │
│ 53452 07/22 Bill Tuthill        18 Re: E. coli in the High Country     │
│ 53453 07/25 Steve Helle         40 Needle Mtns. Trip Rpt. - CO         │
│ 53454 07/23 Alan Silverstein    13 Re: stop airplane noise in parks!   │
│ 53455 07/23 Alan Silverstein    25 Re: Trip report:  Grand Canyon, North Rim to riv │
│ 53465 07/25 Dave Medlicott      34  ▌                                  │
│ 53456 07/22 Bill Tuthill         6 Re: CAR CAMPING TENT                │
│ 53457 07/23 Ksub                13 Re: Alps Sandals                    │
│ 53458 07/25 Rocky Waters        14 Re: Rogue River Jet Boats?          │
│ 53459 07/22 Wilbur Luo/DCOM     20 Re: Compeed (sp?) for blisters?     │
│ 53460 07/25 John H Jordan       17 Re: Avon mosquitto repellant        │
│ 53422 07/24 Rob Bidleman         6  ▌                                  │
│ 53553 07/25 Tom Moser           17  ▌                                  │
│ 53461 07/22 John H Jordan       19 Re: Anybody found a good breakfast? │
│ 53462 07/22 Dan Yurman         649 Idaho Rivers United: Summer 94      │
│ 53464 07/23 David Stepp          7 Gratitude                          │
│ 53466 07/25 Joe Ehrlich         21 Re: Remington Tents-Thumbs up or down? │
│ 53467 07/25 Cynthia S. Lammert  11 Is High Adventure=Coleman brand?    │
│ 53469 07/25 Eugene N. Miya      16 Re: Anthropomorphising the mountain! ↓ │
│ ←                                                                    → │
└───────────────────────────────────────────────────────────────────────┘
```

Figure 2-4. The thread selector shows you the topics of the group's current articles, grouped by subject.

OK, the program finds the next article that contains this word in its subject line.

USING THE ARTICLE SELECTOR

In the article selector, you read articles that look interesting. With WinVN, it's simple to do so: Just double-click the article's subject in the thread selector, and you'll see the article selector window shown in Figure 2-6.

In this window, you can do any of the following:

the articles by author so that all the contributions by a favorite contributor are grouped for your perusal. You can sort the articles by date, by size, and by article number, as well.

To find articles of interest, just browse through the list by clicking the down arrow or dragging the scroll box down. If you're reading a newsgroup with lots of articles, though, you may find it faster to search for an article. To search with WinVN, choose Find from the Search menu, and type a word in the dialog box that appears. After you click

- Search the article's text for passages containing a word you specify.

- Save or print the article. If it contains *uuencoded* binary information, you can decode this information into a file. In uuencoding, binary data—such as a program or a graphic—is translated into ASCII (text) data so that it can be conveyed via the Internet's text-only communication pathways.

- Respond to the article's author by email.

```
┌───────────────────────────────────────────────────────────────────────┐
│ ─                     rec.backcountry (224 articles)            ▼ ▲    │
├───────────────────────────────────────────────────────────────────────┤
│ Articles   Sort   Search                                               │
├───────────────────────────────────────────────────────────────────────┤
│ 53441 07/21 Richard Ottolini    19 Re: $1.7 million awarded to injured Whit ↑ │
│ 53435 07/23 Wandervogel         18 Re: $1.7 million awarded to injured Whitney hike │
│ 53476 07/25 Todd Ourston         9 Re: $1.7 million awarded to injured Whitney hike │
│ 53566 07/25 Todd Ourston         5 Re: $1.7 million awarded to injured Whitney hike │
│ 53578 07/25 James B Federline   16 Re: : bugs in northern manitoba     │
│ 53433 07/21 Jennifer Yu         15 Re: ???'s concerning backpack for woman │
│ 53510 07/25 McDaniel            29 Re: Accident on Mt. Hood            │
│ 53600 07/25 Pete Bellas         27 Re: Actually most of us CAN get along (was: Can' │
│ 53590 07/24 GSweitzer           22 Re: Alaska info wanted              │
│ 53457 07/23 Ksub                13 Re: Alps Sandals                    │
│ 53399 07/22 hogsbreath          10 Re: Anthropomorphising the mountain! │
│ 53469 07/25 Eugene N. Miya      16 Re: Anthropomorphising the mountain! │
│ 53551 07/26 Tim                  9 Re: Anthropomorphising the mountain! │
│ 53572 07/25 Eugene N. Miya      14 Re: Anthropomorphising the mountain! │
│ 53461 07/23 John H Jordan       19 Re: Anybody found a good breakfast? │
│ 53407 07/22 Marty Halvorson     28 Re: Are you afraid of the forest?   │
│ 53488 07/23 Pete Hickey         18 Re: Are you afraid of the forest?   │
│ 53556 07/26 Bruce Albert        21 Re: Are you afraid of the forest?   │
│ 53498 07/25 Susan L. Collicott  40 Re: Arrogant equestrians in the Backcountry │
│ 53501 07/25 Susan L. Collicott  12 Re: Arrogant equestrians in the Backcountry │
│ 53410 07/22 gilchrist@sscl.uwo  11 Re: Avon mosquitto repellant       ↓ │
│ ←                                                                    → │
└───────────────────────────────────────────────────────────────────────┘
```

Figure 2-5. Grouping articles by subject ensures that you won't miss any of the responses to an article, even if some of these responses don't quote preceding articles.

Figure 2-6. The article selector window lets you read the text of the article.

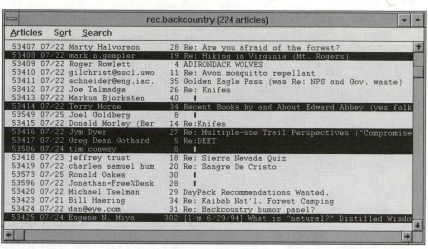

- Post a follow-up message to the group.

- Forward the article to an email address.

- View the next article that's listed in the article selector window.

- View the next article with the same subject.

In addition to these options, you can go back "up" one layer to the thread selector, and use the thread selector to choose another article to read.

WRITING YOUR OWN MESSAGES

You can write your own USENET messages in three ways:

- **Replying to an article by email.** Your message doesn't appear in the newsgroup; it just goes to the author of the posting to which you're replying. You should choose this option if you have something to say to the author that wouldn't interest the group.

- **Posting a follow-up message.** Your reply to an article is posted to the group and becomes part of the thread.

- **Posting with a new subject.** This message starts a new subject rather than replying to an existing one.

The following sections illustrate these procedures with WinVN. Please note that my purpose here is to illustrate the basic procedures of using a newsreader; there's plenty more to say about writing for USENET (and that's why a whole section of

this book, Part III, "Now it's your turn," is devoted to the subject).

Replying to an article by email

Often, it's best to reply by responding directly to the author of an article rather than to the newsgroup as a whole. For example, suppose you're responding to a request in rec.backcountry for specific information, such as the name of a good backpacking trail in the Dolly Sods Wilderness of West Virginia. Since this information is of great interest to the person who posted the query but of little interest to the group as a whole—rec.backcountry is read internationally, after all—you should reply by email.

To reply by email with WinVN, choose the Compose Mail command from the Respond menu. WinVN opens a Composing Reply Message window and automatically quotes the text of the article to which you're replying. In addition, the program adds an *attribution,* (an opening line that says "In article such-and-such, you say:"). You can and should edit the quoted text down to just the passage to which you want to respond (see Figure 2-7). After you've edited the quoted text, you can add your message (see Figure 2-8).

For more information on replying to articles via email, see Chapter 16, "Posting your own messages."

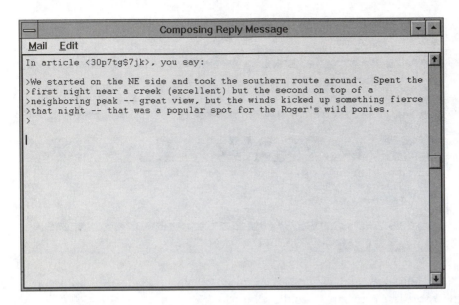

Figure 2-7. When you reply via email, your reply goes only to the article's author.

follow-up articles, see Chapter 16, "Posting your own messages."

Posting an article with a new subject

With most newsreaders, you can post articles with new subjects at just about any level of the program. If you're within a newsgroup at the time, the program assumes that you want to post your message to that newsgroup. If you're looking at the newsgroup selector, you'll be prompted to type the name of the newsgroup or newsgroups to which you want to post. Most newsreaders let you *crosspost* articles—(post articles in more than one newsgroup). Although you shouldn't crosspost to unrelated groups, there are sometimes valid reasons for crossposting (for more information, see Chapter 16, "Posting your own messages").

With WinVN, you can post a new message at any level of the program: In the newsgroup selector, for example, you can choose New Article from the Utilities menu; in the

Posting a follow-up article

The procedure you follow to post a follow-up article is usually the same one you used to reply via email, except that your response is posted to the newsgroup. As with an email response, you can quote (and edit) the text of the article to which you're replying. For more information on writing

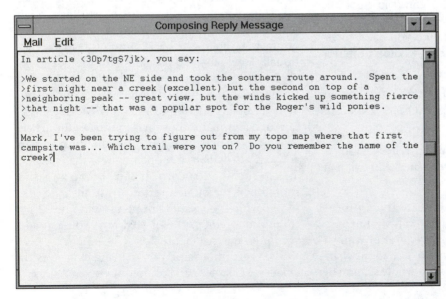

Figure 2-8. The relationship between the quoted text and your comment or question should be obvious, as in this example.

Figure 2-9. When you post a new message, the newsreader automatically creates the header.

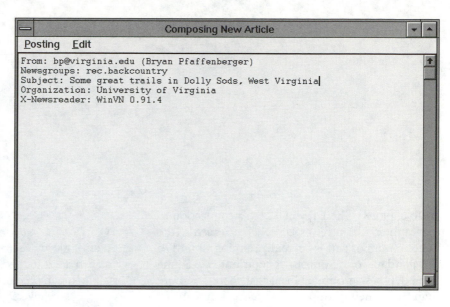

thread selector, you choose the same command from the Article menu. After dealing with dialog boxes prompting you to specify the target newsgroup(s) and a subject, you see a window where you can type your message. As shown in Figure 2-9, the newsreading software automatically creates a header for your article. You can then type your message and choose the command that posts the messge to the group.

Don't be disappointed if your post doesn't show up immediately, even on your own server. It takes time to disseminate USENET messages. A busy server may take an hour or more to incorporate your article into the USENET newsgroup. You'll probably see it the next time you log on.

SUMMARY

There are many newsreaders available, but their basic functions are the same: They give you tools to subscribe to newsgroups, view and organize articles, read selected articles, and respond with your own messages. For this reason, most newsreaders resemble a layer cake in their use of three levels—the newsgroup selector, the thread selector, and the article selector. A good newsreader provides obvious, intuitive ways to move among these levels, read the news, and write your own messages.

FROM HERE...

- For more information on newsgroups and how they're named and organized, see Chapter 4, "How USENET is organized."

- To learn more about newsreader features, see Chapter 6, "Understanding newsreaders."

- For more information on specific newsreaders, see Part II, "Reading the news."

To explore USENET, you'll need a connection to a computer that receives USENET *news feeds* (the huge amount of data—currently running about 170 MB per day—of new postings contributed to all the USENET newsgroups). Given that there are more than 5,000 newsgroups in existence, you can lay down good money that it's going to be a *big* computer. Anything less than a minicomputer or mainframe will almost certainly offer less than the full selection of newsgroups.

You can make such a connection in a variety of ways—more, probably, than you'd imagined. Chances are good that you have several options available, running the gamut from the few newsgroups available on some college kid's *bulletin board system (BBS)* to national and even international computer services, including CompuServe and America Online (AOL). (A BBS is a computer hobbyist's on-line system, usually running on a PC, that offers games, files, and discussion to dialup users.)

This chapter surveys all the ways you can connect to USENET, assessing each connection method's strengths, weaknesses, and costs. Please note that this chapter is specifically about connecting to USENET; this often involves connecting to the Internet, but, as you'll see, sometimes it doesn't.

We'll start with an overview of the three basic methods of USENET connectivity. The chapter then burrows down into the two dialup methods you're most likely to use: dialup access (shell accounts) and dialup IP (SLIP/PPP). It closes with an exploration of the hardware and software you'll need.

TIP: Don't sign up for fee-based USENET access until you've investigated the many ways you can get it for free. If you're a student, a staff member, or a teacher at a college or university, your university may offer free dialup access to USENET; the same goes for workers at many large corporations. In many large cities, you can take advantage of *freenets,* which are municipal information systems (often based in the local library). Some of them offer USENET access. These and other free or low-cost USENET access options are surveyed in this chapter.

Please note that this chapter focuses on the ways personal computer users can connect to USENET *servers* (computers that receive USENET news feeds); it's not concerned, therefore, with the very much more technical matter of receiving the news feeds yourself and becoming a USENET site through such means as the Unix-to-Unix Copy Program (UUCP). This isn't something you'd want to do with a personal computer, anyway; you'd be getting so much data every day that there wouldn't be any room on your hard disk for your applications! To illustrate: A USENET site in New Zealand currently requires 750 MB of disk space just to store one and one-half day's worth of USENET traffic—and that's up 50% from just six months ago. To find out what's involved in becoming a USENET site, see Chapter 20.

THE THREE BASIC WAYS TO CONNECT TO USENET

From a technical standpoint, your options boil down to three categories: dialup access using a modem, network access using a network interface card, and dialup IP access using a modem or ISDN. The following sections introduce these three connection methods.

Understanding dialup access

In dialup access, you equip your computer with a *modem* and *communications software,* a program that transforms your computer into a terminal (screen and keyboard) of a remote computer. (Modems and communications softwware are discussed in the sections titled "What hardware do you need" and "What software do you need," later in this chapter). You then dial a distant computer that offers USENET. This computer might be a UNIX minicomputer lodged in a college's academic computing center, a huge computer system at the headquarters of an on-line information service such as CompuServe, or a PC running bulletin board software in a computer hobbyist's den.

Dialup access is inexpensive (and sometimes free), but it has some major drawbacks—for instance, you're stuck with the newsreader software that the remote computer uses. For example, if you access USENET through America Online, you're stuck with AOL's newsreading software, surveyed in Chapter 7, "Reading the news with America Online." It's easy to use, but it lacks some key features that regular news readers deem essential.

In general, dialup access gives you a way of controlling a distant computer remotely, and that's why it's so inconvenient. If you decide to decode a *binary file* (a program or graphic) or save a particularly interesting USENET article, the result is a saved file on the distant computer, not on yours. To get the file to your computer, you'll have to go through a separate, tedious procedure called *downloading.* In downloading, you transfer a file from a remote computer to your own, a process that can take several minutes for a lengthy file. Dialup access is widely available, though, and chances are you'll first access USENET by means of dialup access.

Understanding dialup IP

This connection method also uses a modem, but it does so with a twist: You connect to an Internet computer using special software that conforms to the SLIP or PPP standards, which are explained in the section titled "Connecting to USENET through dialup IP (SUP/PPP)" later in this chapter. This software makes your phone connection appear to the network as if it were an honest-to-goodness LAN connection—your computer actually becomes part of the Internet. That's why it's called dialup IP. The IP is short for "Internet Protocol," the name for the set of standards that governs the exchange of data among Internet-compatible computers. You can use dialup IP for any Internet application, including *FTP* (a standard for exchanging files via the Internet), *Gopher* (a menu-based information retrieval system), and the *World Wide Web* (another Internet information retrieval system based on hypertext principles). To connect to USENET, however, the Internet computer you're contacting must offer USENET access by means of the Network News Transport Protocol (NNTP)—again, this is explained in more detail in the section titled "Connecting to USENET through dialup IP" later in this chapter. Dialup IP using Plain Old Telephone Service (POTS) isn't any faster than dialup access—you're still limited by the top speed of your modem—but it gives you the same benefits as a LAN connection: You can choose your own newsreader, and you don't have to download the files you save. What's more, you're not limited to just one application at a time, as you are with dialup access: You can run a USENET newsreader in one window, your electronic mail in another, and Mosaic (a World Wide Web navigator) in a third.

Does dialup IP have a down side? You bet. It's not widely available yet. And in general, it's more expensive and more difficult to implement than dialup access.

But dialup IP's day is coming, and coming fast. To be sure, dialup IP at 14.4 Kbps modem speeds is a far cry from the experience of using USENET on a LAN operating at 10 Mbps. But unbeknownst to most people, noise-free digital telephone lines have been snaking their way closer and closer to your home. Thanks to a major standardization agreement by the telephone companies in 1991, digital telephone service—at speeds of 64 Kbps—is now available in many cities, and more are added every day. The service, called Integrated Digital Services Network (ISDN), is discussed in the following box.

IS THERE A DIGITAL TELEPHONE SUBSCRIPTION IN YOUR FUTURE?

ISDN is a set of standards for high-speed digital communications that can make use of existing twisted-pair telephone lines. For Internet and USENET users, ISDN opens the potential for you to connect with an Internet service provider at a cool 64,000 bits per second (64 Kbps)—and without even tying up your phone line. Sound good? Read on.

ISDN is a proven digital telephone standard that is already widely implemented in Europe and Japan. The standard was originally proposed in 1984 by the Comité Consultiv International de Télégraphique et Téléphonique (CCITT), a United Nations organization that coordinates international telecommunications (the CCITT is now known as the ITU-TSS, the same organization that sets the modem standards discussed previously). In the United States, the regional Bell companies adopted incompatible standards, leading to slow progress ("ISDN? It means, 'It Still Does Nothing,'" as one wag put it.). But a 1991 agreement settled the matter: Thanks to this agreement, the regional Bell ISDN offerings finally are compatible not only with each other but also with foreign ISDN systems. More than 50% of regional Bell system lines were expected to have ISDN capability by the end of 1994. But fair warning—you may have heard about the "telephone mentality," dead set against innovation, and it's still in evidence in laggard markets: A Centel marketing person in Charlottesville, Virginia, told an interested party that the office just "wasn't in the mood" to sell ISDN.

ISDN services fall into three categories: Basic Rate ISDN (BRI), Primary Rate ISDN (PRI), and Broadband ISDN (B-ISDN). Designed as the basic option for consumers, Basic Rate ISDN offers two 64,000 bit per second channels for voice, graphics, and data, plus one 16,000 bit per second channel for signalling purposes. Primary Rate ISDN, for businesses, provides twenty-three channels with 64,000 bits per second capacity. Broadband ISDN, still under development, could handle 150 Mbps, but only if you've got optical fiber cables running to your home or office.

What will ISDN cost you? It's more expensive than your current Plain Old Telephone Service (POTS) line, but not by much—in one area, $29 per month. To put this into perspective, that's about the same as two analog lines—but with ISDN, one line gives you two channels with separate numbers, so ISDN isn't any more expensive for two-line households. There are some hidden costs, however, beyond replacing all your phones with newer digital models. To connect your PC to an ISDN line, you'll need about $500 worth of equipment. For more information, see the section titled "Equipment for ISDN connectivity," later in this chapter. These prices are sure to take nose dives as the market ramps up.

Understanding local area network access

If you're using a computer at work that's connected to a local area network (LAN), it's possible that this network is connected to the Internet. If it is, you're in luck because you can probably access USENET this way. A big plus: You can choose your own newsreader program from the likes of Trumpet (see Chapter 13, "Trumpet for Windows"), or Newswatcher (see Chapter 14, "Newswatcher for Macintosh") and install it on your computer. Another big plus: Because you can run the news-reading software on your PC, there's no need for the tedious downloading procedure; the files are saved to your PC's hard disk. The biggest plus of all: speed. Local area networks operate at speeds of at least ten million bits per second (10 Mbps), which is a heck of a lot faster than any modem is ever going to be (modems have a theoretical limit of 56,000 bits per second (56 Kbps). Unfortunately, LAN access is available only if your office computer is connected to an Internet-linked LAN. And for those lucky souls, there are network administrators to help with software installation and network connectivity. For this reason, this book focuses on the two dialup methods: dialup access and dialup IP. The next two sections survey these two methods in detail.

Here's a quick review of the basic points about connecting to USENET:

- If your office computer is connected to a local area network, find out if you can use the network to access USENET.

- Most readers of this book will start out with dialup access. It's cheap and widely available.

- Dialup IP via SLIP/PPP is the coming thing. Prices are dropping and services are becoming more widely available. If you're serious about the USENET and Internet, you'll soon "graduate" to dialup IP.

- In the coming decade (or maybe longer, if your phone company's like mine), your telephone line will change from analog to digital (ISDN), opening up the possibility of 64 Kbps connectivity to homes, schools, and offices.

The next two sections of this chapter explore in detail the techniques you're most likely to use: dialup access and dialup IP.

CONNECTING TO USENET THROUGH DIALUP ACCESS

Dialup access is probably the least desirable way to connect to USENET because you're stuck with the newsreader or newsreaders the service provider gives you, and you'll have to download any articles or files you save. But it's cheap, and for this reason alone it's a good place to start your USENET exploration. To understand dialup access, it's helpful to distinguish between the three basic types of shell accounts, as explained in the next section. Following that is a survey of the service providers that can hook you up to USENET.

The three types of shell accounts

When you connect to USENET via dialup access, you're using a *shell account* (a program that masks the internal intricacies of a computer operating system, such as UNIX, and allows the user to give commands). With regard to USENET access, there are three different kinds of shell accounts :

- **"Dumped at the UNIX prompt."** The simplest shell account "dumps you at the UNIX prompt," a phrase you'll appreciate after you've experienced it: As with MS-DOS, you're looking at an arcane symbol and a blinking cursor, but there isn't a clue on-screen about what to do next. Most university and some service provider shell accounts work this way. The drawback to being dumped at the UNIX prompt is that you'll have to learn how to use a few UNIX commands. On the plus side, once you learn these commands you will be able to manipulate and download files with ease.

- **Menu-driven systems.** You see an on-screen menu of options from which you can choose. That's nice, but what if the programmer left out options you need? Menu-driven systems are easy to use but constraining. One system I tried while researching this book lets you save USENET articles in a News directory, but didn't let you access the directory so you could copy or download the file. (I'm not making this up—security paranoia, which I'm sorry to say is well-founded, sometimes leads system administrators to do things like this.)

- **Graphical user interface (GUI) front ends.** A front end is a program that runs on your PC, providing an easy-to-use interface to the computer service you're contacting. The best of these employ GUI principles, with on-screen mousable windows, pull-down menus, and graphics galore. This approach is exemplified by CompuServe Information Manager (CIM).

Bulletin board systems (BBS)

A BBS is a do-it-yourself computer information system that is created with a personal computer, a modem, and BBS software. It generally offers a menu-driven or even a graphical user interface. Usually operated on a volunteer basis by computer hobbyists, BBS systems typically offer hundreds or even thousands of programs and graphics files to download, local electronic mail, games. Some BBS systems are free, but most charge a modest fee, such as $25 per year, for unrestricted access. Increasingly, they're offering access to USENET.

Is the BBS route for you? Bear in mind that most BBS systems use PCs, and for this reason they can't handle the massive influx of data in a full USENET feed. Chances are that a BBS advertising "USENET access" is really offering only a handful of newsgroups (as few as two or three, in fact). The limitation, to be sure, may be legitimate: Some BBSs specialize in a particular field and carry only USENET newsgroups that pertain to that field. For instance, a BBS in Georgia specializes in computer-

aided design (CAD) and carries several CAD- and engineering-related USENET groups.

Another down side to the BBS route to USENET: the newsreaders. The newsreading software has to be built into the BBS's Internet-access package, and from what I've seen, it's little more than an afterthought. Compared to the richly featured newsreaders available for UNIX and Windows systems, BBS newsreaders are difficult to use and may lack features crucial to effective newsreading, such as subject threading.

This gloomy scenario is sure to change, though. Doubtless, you'll see BBSs advertising hundreds of the top USENET groups and full-featured newsreaders. And many BBS systems offer a trial period during which you can explore the system without subscribing. If you find a local BBS that offers the newsgroups you want, it might just do the trick for you.

> **TIP:** Not sure what a "real" newsreader can do? Check out Chapter 2, "A quick USENET tour." You'll see a very nice Microsoft Windows program called WinVN in action. Match WinVN up against the BBS newsreaders you're examining, and don't settle for less.

Freenets

A freenet is a community-based bulletin board system (BBS) that's designed to serve the citizens of a city, county, or region. Typically, you can access the catalog of the municipal library, leave email messages for local politicos, and, increasingly, access the Internet. Some freenets offer access to USENET, too. Most freenets are, as the name implies, free for citizens of the locality; others might have to pay a modest fee.

Don't expect miracles from freenets; most are underfunded and overutilized, hardly a winning combination. You may find it very difficult to log on to a popular freenet. Moreover, it costs money to get USENET feeds, so you shouldn't expect a full selection of newsgroups—and, as with bulletin board systems, the newsreader software may leave a great deal to be desired. However, if there's a freenet in your area that's offering USENET access, by all means check it out.

On-line information services

An on-line information service is a centralized computer system, accessible through dialup access, that makes services such as current stock quotes, news, sport scores, weather, and downloadable files available to home computer users. The leading service, Prodigy, doesn't offer USENET access, but its competitors (America Online, Delphi, and CompuServe) have developed USENET newsreaders and offer a full selection of newsgroups. To see what these services look like, flip to Chapter 7, "Reading the news with America Online," Chapter 8, "Reading the news with Delphi," and Chapter 9, "Reading the news with CompuServe."

These three services let you access thousands of newsgroups. America Online and CompuServe do so by means of easy-to-use navigation programs, best exemplified by CompuServe Information Manager (CIM). Costs are low to moderate. America Online, for example, charges a flat monthly fee for unlimited access, but you'd be wise to watch the clock while you're using CompuServe! So what's the down side? Generally, the newsreading software. You're stuck with the software that the service provides, and, as Chapters 7 through 9 attest, you'll miss out on many of the features that USENET aficionados regularly enjoy. Still, an on-line information service might be a good place to start—and that's particularly true if you're already a subscriber to one of these services.

University and organizational computer systems

If you're affiliated with a university or an organization of some kind, it's possible that you can get free dialup access to USENET: Call your organization's computer center to find out. Chances are good that

you'll be accessing a UNIX computer system and using a UNIX newsreader, such as tin (see Chapter 10, "Reading the news with tin"), nn (see Chapter 11, "Reading the news with nn"), or rn and trn (see "Reading the news with rn and trn," Chapter 12). The plus side: You'll be using a newsreader that can do just about anything that a true USENET junkie would want to do, such as decoding uuencoded files, creating *kill files* (lists of subject words and authors that a newsreader uses to delete articles so

THE CLEVELAND FREENET

One of the largest and most successful freenets, the Cleveland Freenet serves northeastern Ohio from its base at Case Western Reserve University (The Cleveland Free-Net Project, Case Western Reserve University, 10900 Euclid Avenue, Cleveland, OH 44106-7072). With 64 modem lines and Internet connections, the Cleveland Freenet serves more than 4000 users a day with a total of 250 computer services, including multi-user chat lines, huge resources of community information, news, and limited USENET access. There's no charge for an account, and you don't have to be a Cleveland—or even an Ohio—resident to register.

Developed by Dr. Tom Grundner, the Cleveland Freenet pioneered the idea of a community computer service based on free access. A key theme: public participation in local political processes, including direct access to government officials. Affiliated with the Cleveland Freenet is the National Public Telecomputing Network (NPTN), a non-profit organization that helps freenets get started. On-line, the service is organized like a municipal center, with a post office, a courthouse and government center, a school house, a business and industrial park, an arts building, and a communications center.

that you never ever see them), and quoting the text of original articles in your follow-up postings. The down side: Dumped at the UNIX prompt, you'll be using the UNIX operating system and UNIX programs, which were written by and for genius computer scientists with pointy heads, white coats, and Mensa memberships. Still, millions of people who couldn't even program their VCR have learned to read the news with the likes of tin, trn, and nn, and so can you if you're willing to spend a bit of time learning—and you'll find plenty of guidance in this book.

ON-LINE SERVICES OFFERING USENET ACCESS

America Online (America Online, Inc., 8619 Westwood Center Drive, Vienna, VA 22182-2285; 800-827-6364) stresses ease of use. Like its nearest competitor, Prodigy, AOL targets home computer users; you'll find on-line versions of popular magazines, news, stock quotes, weather, discussions of current affairs, and reference works that kids can use for schoolwork. You install AOL's software on your Macintosh or Windows system, and you'll access the service by means of familiar, mousable windows and menus. Offering an impressive suite of USENET newsgroups, AOL has another plus: It's cheap, as on-line services go: A flat monthly fee gives you unlimited access time to explore the USENET world (but note that you'll pay a timed connection fee of $3.50 per hour). So what's the catch? The newsreading software leaves a great deal to be desired, as Chapter 7, "Reading the news with America Online," explains. Currently, AOL is available only in North America.

CompuServe (CompuServe, Inc., P.O. Box 20212, Columbus, OH 43320; 800-848-8199) offers a full suite of services, including news, stock quotes, general reference works, travel services, on-line shopping, interactive games, and topic-related forums. Currently, CompuServe is available in 135 countries. Unlike AOL or Prodigy, CompuServe targets the adult computer hobbyist—there's a wealth of computer-related information available, including dozens of vendor forums that contain up-to-the-

minute bug fixes and software updates. In the fall of 1994, the service plans to introduce access to a full suite of USENET newsgroups, which you can read using CompuServe's default ASCII (text) interface or—better—the Windows-based CompuServe Information Manager (CIM). In addition, CompuServe has done a good job of implementing high-speed modem access; in most cities, you can connect to the service at 14.4 Kbps. A negative, and a big one: USENET access isn't part of the basic services you get as part of CompuServe's not-so-flat monthly fee—you'll pay up to $16 an hour to explore USENET.

Delphi (1030 Massachusetts Avenue, Cambridge, MA 02138, 1-800-695-4005) was the first on-line service to offer a full suite of Internet services (including electronic mail, Telnet, FTP, and WAIS) and it's still one of the least expensive ways to access USENET. You'll find the usual mix of news, sports results, travel services, on-line shopping, travel services, and discussion groups. Currently, Delphi is offered in more than 40 countries. But don't expect the graphical user interfaces that CompuServe (with WinCIM) and AOL offer; you'll be using a text-based interface. But that's not such a bad thing: People have been reading USENET with text-based UNIX newsreaders for a long time. To read the news with Delphi, you can use Delphi's own user-friendly newsreader, or you can use nn, one of the most powerful and full-featured UNIX newsreaders (see Chapter 11).

Internet service providers

Increasingly, dialup access to the Internet and USENET is available from commercial Internet *service providers,* such as Performance Systems International (PSI). A service provider sells Internet access in a number of ways, generally including dialup access, dialup IP, and much more expensive dedicated connections involving a permanently installed, leased telephone line. For as little as $9 per month, you get unlimited dialup access to an Internet-linked UNIX computer, where, in general, you'll encounter the same software you'd find on a university computer system, with some of the sting taken out, perhaps, by an on-screen menu system.

To access the service provider, you'll dial a local number. If you're lucky, you'll access the provider directly, meaning that there are no per-hour communication fees to pay. Elsewhere, the local number you dial will connect you to a *public data network (PDN),* (network that provides long-distance access to the service provider). This is going to cost you money, ranging from $2.50 per hour nights and weekends to as much as $18 per hour during peak usage hours.

What do you see on-screen? If the service provider offers a shell account, you'll probably find yourself looking at a menu of options, including USENET— but you might just see the UNIX prompt.

CONNECTING TO USENET THROUGH DIALUP IP (SLIP/PPP)

And now for the future: dialup IP. To understand why, let me get technical for a moment.

The big problem with dialup access is that your computer isn't really connected to the Internet. Basically, the Internet is a method of dividing data into *datagrams* (little addressed packets) that can be efficiently and reliably transmitted over a variety of networks and shared by just about any kind of computer. When you're working with a shell account, the little datagrams don't come to your computer. They stop at the remote computer, where you see the results—for USENET, displayed articles—on the screen. To get them to your computer, you have to carry out that tedious downloading procedure I mentioned earlier.

What's so cool about dialup IP is that your computer actually becomes part of the Internet—it joins in the give-and-take flow of datagrams. When you're looking at an article on-screen, you're looking at data that has already arrived at your computer. It's a snap to save it or print it.

Cool it may be, but dialup IP has a way of giving people fits: It isn't easy to install or configure a SLIP or PPP connection, as many would-be

SELECTED USENET SERVICE PROVIDERS

CNS Internet Express (719-592-1240), based in Colorado, offers continental U.S. dialup access to USENET and other Internet services by means of the company's 800 number. You'll pay $2.75 per hour, with a $10 monthly minumum and a $35 sign-up fee.

PSILink (703-709-0300) offers USENET and Internet access throughout the world using public data network (PDN) access at rates as low as $2.50 per hour, plus the service's monthly access charge (currently, $29 per month for a 9600 bps modem). But you'll have to use PSI's software; the newsreader can best be regarded as primitive.

Vnet Internet Access, Inc. (800-377-3282) offers dialup USENET and Internet access locally in North Carolina cities and nationally at rates as low as $2.75 per hour at off-peak times. You'll pay a flat $24.95 monthly fee for 80 hours of access; if you actually go over this amount, each additional hour costs just $1. You'll find yourself dumped at the UNIX prompt, but here's the good news: You can choose among the top three UNIX newsreaders, tin, rn, and trn.

Internet users have discovered to their dismay. Happily, things are getting easier (see the box entitled "Interamp points the way").

What's SLIP?

Serial Line Interface Protocol (SLIP) is one of the older Internet protocols (standards). Basically, it specifies the procedure that's used to transform the stream of Internet datagrams so that they can be sent over a point-to-point, two-wire connection. It also pulls off a neat trick: It hoodwinks the Internet into thinking that your temporary connection, achieved by means of a modem housed at the service provider's headquarters, is actually an Ethernet port with a permanent *IP address* (a number that uniquely identifies the location of each of the millions of computers linked to the Internet). Your computer can exchange datagrams with other Internet computers only if it has, or the Internet "thinks" it has, a permanent IP address.

INTERAMP POINTS THE WAY

Interamp (800-827-7482), offered by Performance Systems International (PSI), is the wave of the future: For the $200 sign-up fee, you get Netmanage Chameleon, a high-quality commercial Windows socket and PPP package that's already configured to access the service. You just pop in the disk, install the software, click the icon, and you're connected. Rather than locking you into their software choice, you can use the newsreader you want, such as Trumpet for Windows (Chapter 13) or WinVN(Chapter 2). The signup fee includes three months of unlimited access. One drawback: PSINet currently has 80 *points of presence (POPs)* throughout the country, an area where the service is accessible by dialing a local number. But if you're not near one of these, you'll have to pay long distance fees to access the service.

TIP: SLIP pulls off a neat trick, but it's an antiquated protocol. Although SLIP is still widely offered, it does not provide any error correction for noisy telephone lines. A noisy telephone line can bollix a SLIP connection, resulting in a frozen or hung connection that will make you think one of your programs has crashed. The more recent *Point-to-Point Protocol* (*PPP*) offers superior performance. Still, SLIP has its adherents. Today's modems come with built-in error-correction controls, and as long as the modem at the other end conforms to the same error-correction standards, a SLIP connection can work as well as PPP.

What's PPP?

Point-to-Point Protocol (PPP) is a more recent Internet standard governing the transfer of Internet datagrams via modems and telephone lines. Like SLIP, PPP hoodwinks the Internet into thinking your computer has a permanent IP address, enabling your computer to exchange Internet datagrams with other Internet computers. But it's more up-to-date: It offers data compression, data negotiation, greater efficiency, and error correction to make the connection work much more smoothly. The new version of Microsoft Windows, Windows 95, will include PPP suppport.

WHAT HARDWARE DO YOU NEED?

If you're planning to explore USENET with dialup access, the most likely starting point for beginners, you'll need a PC and a fast modem. For dialup IP, you'll need a PC and a *very* fast modem. Trendsetters contemplating ISDN connections will need an ISDN card and a terminal adaptor. The following sections elaborate.

Just about any PC will do

Unless you're working in a high-tech office with a professional workstation, you'll need a personal computer to access USENET—but it needn't be the latest, fastest, and snazziest screamer in town. In fact, you can read the news with just about any existing PC, Macintosh, or Amiga system, as long as you can equip it with a reasonably high-speed modem or a network interface card (NIC), as explained in the following sections.

Modems—The faster, the better

To access USENET by means of Plain Old Telephone Service (POTS), you'll need a modem. As you recall, a modem is a computer accessory that permits your computer to communicate with other computers via the telephone system, which can't handle computer signals unless they're altered. The phone system, after all, was designed for the human voice, so it's optimized to carry the sound frequencies the human voice uses. To send computer signals, a modem modulates (changes) these signals into sounds within the frequency range of the human voice; it also demodulates incoming signals. The term "modem" is an abbreviation of MOdulator/DEModulator.

Modems transfer information far more slowly than computers. Those little telephone cables just can't handle much data, as you'll learn to your dismay when trying to transfer a huge graphics file. The effect is very much, as one frustrated user was heard to remark, like trying to push an elephant through a straw.

Part of the problem has to do with the paucity of wires in the standard POTS telephone setup—there are just two. Inside your computer, communications take place on an electronic freeway, with as many as 64 lanes. A unit of data can be transmitted with all those little yes-no nuggets of information (bits) traveling side-by-side at high speeds. To put this same data through a modem is like forcing this traffic on to a two-lane country road, with all the data bits having to follow each other in a sequence. Slows it down a bit, as you can imagine.

The POTS line causes other problems, too. Inside the computer, the bits traveling along those data freeways depart and arrive at precise intervals measured by your computer's internal clock. But there are no clock pulses available on telephone lines. For this reason, modems must communicate using *asynchronous communication* (untimed communication). The question here is that, lacking the synchronization of clock beats, how does the receiving modem know when one unit of data ends and the other begins? The clever solution to this problem is to add a start bit at the beginning of a unit of data and a stop bit at the end of the unit of data. With most PCs, the standard unit of data is eight bits or one byte. (One byte is needed to represent one character, such as a letter or number.) All these start and stop bits add 20% *overhead* (extra information that has to be transmitted to make sure the data arrives intact); but hey—the miracle is that it works at all.

Now that you know you'll be pushing elephants through straws and adding two extraneous bits for every byte of data as well, you'll understand my next point: Although you can get away with a clunker of a PC, you'll be very wise to get the fastest modem you can afford. And that needn't involve big bucks—you can get a reasonably fast (14.4 Kbps) modem for less than $100. For dialup access, I'd suggest that you consider 14.4 Kbps to be the minimum speed you'd tolerate, unless you just love sitting around waiting for the screen to update. To be sure, you can experiment with a 2400 bps modem, but I'll bet you order a faster one in short order.

What is "fast," modem-wise? Let's begin by clearing up some confusion: Don't measure a modem's performance by its *baud rate* (the number of switching operations it can perform in one second; thus a 600-baud modem can perform 600 switching operations). Yes, I know, you see it all the time in ads—and even in the screens of communication programs. Early modems transmitted one bit of information per baud, but that's no longer true. Today's modems can transmit four or more bits of information for each switching event. For this reason, the only meaningful measurement of a modem's performance is the number of *bits per second (bps)* the modem can transmit. Today's high-speed modems operate at speeds of 14,400 bps (14.4 Kbps)—that's reasonably fast—and

28,800 bps (28.8 Kbps), which is very fast. In general, you'll need a 14.4 Kbps modem for any form of dialup access, but you should go for a 28.8 Kbps modem if you're contemplating dialup IP. Note, though, that your modem can go only as fast as the one at the other end. If your service provider offers 14.4 Kbps access and has no plans to upgrade, don't waste your money on a 28.8 Kbps modem.

But speed isn't everything. To communicate with each other, the modems at the sending and receiving ends of the line must obey the same *modulation protocol* (a standard that specifies the modulation method). (When you see the word "protocol," just think "standard," and you'll understand the concept just fine.) It's very wise to stick with modems that conform to the international protocols (standards) maintained by the International Telecommunications Union–Telecommunications Standards Section (ITU-TSS), an agency of the United Nations. The ITU-TSS, formerly called the CCITT (Comité Consultiv International de Télégraphique et Téléphonique), is responsible for all those "V-dot" standards you've probably encountered, such as V.32bis and V.42. An ITU–TSS compatible modem can "talk" to another ITU–TSS compatible modem, even if it's made by a different manufacturer.

> **TIP:** If you're looking for a 14.4 Kbps modem, look for one that conforms to the V.32bis standard. (Incidentally, "bis" means "the second," so V.32bis is the second version of the V.32 protocol.) For 28.8 Kbps modems, look for V.34 compatibility—and don't settle for anything else (see the box entitled "Modems to avoid").

You've probably had enough of this "V-dot" talk, but there are two additional matters to consider when selecting a modem: hardware-based data compression and error correction. By "hardware-based," I mean that the compression and error correction are built into the modem's hardware, rather than a program you run on your computer. The advantage of hardware-based data compression and error correction is that they're "on" all the time—all the data you send, and all the data you receive, are compressed and checked for errors. Like modulation protocols, hardware-based data compression and error correction conform to ITU–TSS standards—here, V.42 and V.42bis:

- v.42 is an error correction protocol that is implemented within the modem, rather than in the communications software. When both the sending and receiving modems conform to the v.42 standard, errors are automatically detected and the sending modem is instructed to repeat the transmission until the information is received intact. What's cool about V.42 is that it all but eliminates *garbage characters,* those irritating, extraneous letters and punctuation marks that appear out of nowhere when you're connecting via dialup access. This really comes in handy when you're posting USENET articles—after all, you don't want your *signature* to be followed by "#@@#%(&#@%^." An extra plus: V.42 eliminates the need for start bits and stop bits, so your modem seems to work about 20% faster; with a 14.4 Kbps modem, you'll get data transfer rates of up to 16 Kbps.

- The V.42bis standard regulates the compression of data that's sent via the modem. By compressing the data on one end of the transmission and decompressing the data on the other, V.42 produces the effect of speeding transmission because there is less data to transmit. The protocol specifies how data should be compressed on the sending end and decompressed on the other. If the data is not already compressed, gains in effective transmission speeds of up to 400% can be realized.

Computer people will say that V.42 and V.42bis aren't that big of a deal, but they're thinking of the standard on-line application: downloading compressed files from on-line services such as CompuServe or a bulletin board system (BBS).

There are two reasons why a modem capable of error correction and data compression can't improve downloading performance: When you download, you use a *file transfer protocol* (such as Zmodem or Kermit) to ensure the exact transmission of the file, and the file's probably already compressed—further compression could actually make the file bigger, not smaller. (A file transfer protocol is a standard for error-free data transmission.) You don't often use file transfer protocols when you're reading USENET; you'll be dealing with a lot of uncompressed, uncorrected on-screen text. So V.42 and V42bis are very nice things to have when you're reading USENET with dialup access. Hardware-based error correction and data compression can significantly improve your enjoyment and use of USENET.

Modems come in two basic physical designs: the external modem and the internal modem. An external modem has its own case and power supply; you plug it into one of your computer's serial ports by means of a cable that's usually provided with the modem. An internal modem is designed to fit into one of your computer's expansion slots. Because it does not require its own power supply or case, an internal modem is usually cheaper than an external modem.

Equipment for ISDN connectivity

If you're lucky enough to have an ISDN line running to your home and office, you can dispense with the modem—but you'll need other equipment:

- A **Network Terminator-1** (NT-1) that deals with mixing the signals on the ISDN line. With some NT-1s, you can connect as many as eight digital devices to the line, including computers and digital telephones. The cost is about $300.

- **Digital telephones** will be needed to replace their analog predecessors; count on spending a minimum of $125 per phone.

- An **ISDN adapter** for your PC. This is an expansion board that fits into one of your computer's expansion slots; it will put you back about $200.

TIP: If you're using an IBM PC or PC-compatible computer, there's a very good argument for getting an external modem: It's easier to configure your system. You just plug your modem into an available serial port on the back of your computer's case, and tell your communication program which port you've used (it's probably COM1 or COM2; if you're not sure, check your computer's documentation). If you use an internal modem, you're in for a hassle. You'll have to figure out which of the four possible serial ports are available, and you'll have to set jumpers (little pin connectors) on the modem board that tell the modem which port to use. But that's not all. You'll also have to choose an unoccupied IRQ. Basically, an IRQ is a line directly to the processor that enables the modem to say, "Hey, I need your attention." There are only a limited number of IRQ lines available. Other expansion boards in your system, such as a sound card, may have already laid claim to the IRQ that your modem is preconfigured to use, leading to an unsavory problem known as an *IRQ conflict,* a computer crash caused by two devices trying to access the same IRQ line. Such problems can be resolved; sadly, they often require hours of time talking to technical assistance people. The new Plug 'n' Play technology jointly developed by Intel, Microsoft, and Compaq promises to put an end to these hassles, but Plug 'n' Play-compatible modems aren't expected to appear until the release of Microsoft Windows 95.

WHAT SOFTWARE DO YOU NEED?

Communications software for dialup access

A communications program transforms your PC into a remote terminal (a keyboard and screen that are linked to another computer located elsewhere) that can be linked to another computer by means of your modem and the telephone system. Ideally, a communications program eases you through all the following various tasks of linking to a remote computer:

- **Identifying your modem and choosing the port.** After you've installed your communications program, you'll need to tell it which modem you're using, the modem's speed (in bits per second), and the serial port to which you've connected the modem. The better programs let you do this by clicking options in a dialog box.

MODEMS TO AVOID

You may run into spectacular deals on modems that are described as if they're ITU–TSS compatible, when in fact they're not. Two examples: V.32terbo (19.2 Kbps) and V.Fast Class (V.FC) modems. Neither of these standards stems from the ITU-TSS. V.32terbo is a proprietary standard developed in 1993 by AT&T. The word "terbo," incidentally, is a rather blatant play on the similarities between the ITU-TSS's official term for some of its standards, ter ("the third"), and the old let's-make-it-sound-souped-up standby from junk advertising, turbo. Now that the ITU-TSS V.34 standard has been published, V.32terbo modems will fade quickly away.

If you're shopping for a 28.8 Kbps modem, you may find good deals on modems that conform to the "V.Fast Class" standard. Developed jointly by several modem manufacturers in anticipation of the long-delayed V.34 standard, V.FC will fall by the wayside now that the official ITU-TSS standard for 28.8 Kbps transmission has been published. Many of these modems can be upgraded to the official V.34 standard, but you'll be wise to avoid this hassle: Just get yourself a V.34 modem.

- **Setting communications parameters.** To establish a connection with a remote computer via dialup access, you must use the same asynchronous communications options that the remote computer is using—the same number of data bits (usually 8), the *parity checking* (error checking) method (usually no parity), and the same number of stop bits (usually one). If you're trying dialup access to a computer and don't know the communications parameters, N81 is a very good bet.

- **Dialing the remote computer.** Your communications program knows how to "talk" to your modem by means of a *command set* (a programming language that your modem recognizes). You type the number in a dialog box, and the program tells the modem, "Hey, dial the number."

- **Handling login.** To work with a distant computer by means of dialup access, you'll need an *account* (a subscription that allows you to access the computer)—which might be free, if it's a perk of your job or university affiliation. Whether or not you're charged a fee, the account comes with a *login name* (such as your initials) and a *password* (a secret code that you type to gain access to the system). The better communications programs can record your login procedure and do it for you automatically the next time.

- **Emulating a remote terminal.** When you make the connection with the remote computer and log on successfully, your communications program tells your computer to pretend that it's a remote terminal of the distant computer you've contacted. You see messages from the distant computer on your screen, and the responses you make—such as typing **y** for "yes" or **n** for "no"—are sent to the remote computer. Essentially, you'll be operating a program that's running on the remote computer—all the real action is far away.

- **Capturing incoming text to a disk file.** Like to have a record of what's transpired on-screen? Communications programs let you "capture" incoming text to a disk file—replete with all the unwanted menus and extraneous garbage that goes along with an on-line session, I might add. To be usable, capture files need quite a lot of editing.

- **Downloading files.** If you save articles or files on the remote system, you'll need to download them to your computer. This procedure involves transferring the file by means of a file transfer protocol, such as Zmodem, which ensures error-free transfer of the information. Popular file transfer protocols include Zmodem and Kermit. If you're planning to subscribe to CompuServe, look for a modem that recognizes the CompuServe B file transfer protocol.

> **TIP:** Just about any communications program will suffice for reading USENET with dialup access. The key thing is to get a program that fully supports the specific brand and model of modem you're using. If the program doesn't provide such support, you may not be able to take full advantage of valuable features such as V.42 error correction and V.42bis data compression. Ask, "Does this program support my SuperSnazzy 14.4 Deluxe?"

Do you really need to buy a communications program for dialup access? It depends. If you're subscribing to a bulletin board system (BBS) or a UNIX shell account, you'll have to get one. If you're subscribing to America Online, CompuServe (via CompuServe Information Manager), or other services that provide their access disks, you'll find that these disks provide everything you need to get your modem going, log on, and enjoy USENET.

Software for dialup IP

If you're planning to go the dialup IP route, you'll need to equip your computer with software that enables direct *TCP/IP* (Internet) connectivity. To access USENET, you'll use SLIP or PPP to contact a computer that can function as a *Network News Transport Protocol (NNTP)* server, the standard that governs the distribution of USENET news via the Internet.

Fair warning: Installing and configuring this software is at present a formidable task that's beyond the skill level of most home personal computer users. Here's what's involved:

- You'll need software for TCP/IP connectivity—that is, a program that gives your PC or Macintosh the ability to "converse" with other computers running TCP/IP (the Internet protocols).

- You'll need software that enables your modem to communicate with a USENET server by means of the SLIP or PPP protocols.

- You'll need a compatible *client program* (a newsreader that can run on your computer). A client program helps you contact and receive information from a server program that makes information available. For reading the news, you'll need an NNTP client that runs on your PC or Mac system.

> **TIP:** Unless you're a computer programmer or a very experienced user, your best option here is to subscribe to a SLIP or PPP service provider and get the necessary software from them (see the box titled "Interramp points the way" earlier in this chapter for an example). Ideally, the software has been completely preconfigured so that it dials the correct number, enables the SLIP or PPP connection, and accesses the NNTP server. You just install the software, click the icon, and read the news. You may still need to select and install an NNTP client such as Trumpet for Windows or WinVN, but that's a snap once TCP/IP connectivity and SLIP or PPP have been achieved.

Dialup IP software for Microsoft Windows

As you just learned, you need three kinds of programs to access an NNTP server via SLIP or PPP—a utility that gives your computer TCP/IP connectivity, a program that enables SLIP or PPP, and a newsreader compatible with your program. We'll start with the utility that gives Windows systems TCP/IP connectivity.

Happily, there's a very clear picture here. For Microsoft Windows, TCP/IP connectivity is best achieved by means of a program that conforms to the *Winsock* specification (an open standard that defines TCP/IP (Internet) connectivity for computers running Microsoft Windows). This specification outlines how Windows applications can "talk" to the Internet and exchange data with other Internet computers—in other words, it's an *application program interface (API)* (interface that provides the resources necessary for applications to communicate with other Internet-capable computers). Specifically, the specification calls for a utility file, a *dynamic link library (DLL)* called WINSOCK.DLL to be placed on your hard disk. A DLL contains resources that more than one program can access. This file contains the procedures

---

CHICAGO, CHICAGO

Microsoft's forthcoming Windows 95, code-named Chicago during its development, will feature TCP/IP support—including full support for PPP dialup IP connectivity. And now for the good news: Chicago supports the Winsock specification, meaning that Winsock-compatible newsreaders such as WinVN and Trumpet for Windows will work with Chicago. Windows 95 support for TCP/IP connectivity, and especially for Winsock and PPP, will lay the foundation for continued migration from dialup access to dialup IP.

---

needed to link your Windows computer to the Internet, whether this link is achieved through a network interface card or dialup IP.

What's so great about the Winsock specification? Some companies that make Windows-compatible Internet software design their own proprietary standards for handling TCP/IP connectivity, but it comes with a price: Other applications can't run while you're using such a program. That's a drag, and here's why. One of the ultra-cool things about SLIP and PPP is that you can run two more Internet applications at a time—for instance, you can read the news in one window while you're checking your email in another. If you use nothing but Winsock-compatible applications, you'll have no problem. A program that uses a proprietary TCP/IP interface, however, will tie up your system and prevent you from using your Winsock-compatible clients.

The WINSOCK.DLL file can be accessed by any Winsock-compatible application: It provides a standard Internet interface that several applications can use, even if they're published by different software companies. At this writing, the most widely recommended Winsock package is Trumpet Winsock (Trumpet Software International), a shareware package that's widely available via ftp. A plus: This package includes the second crucial piece of the dialup IP software puzzle, the SLIP support.

Concerning newsreaders, the third level of dialup IP software for Windows, there's very good news indeed: Some of the best newsreaders available anywhere are among those available for Windows. I've chosen one of them, WinVN, to illustrate USENET in Chapter 2; it's a free program that's in the public domain. Another newsreader, Trumpet for Windows, is a shareware program; it's discussed in Chapter 13.

TIP: To find the latest information on Winsock-compatible Windows clients, check out Craig Larsen's Winsock Application FAQ. It's available by sending email to info@LCS.com; be sure to put FAQ in the subject line. You can also retrieve the file through the World Wide Web at http://www.ramp.com/~lcs.

Dialup IP software for Macintoshes

If you're using a Macintosh, you'll need TCP/IP support too; popular options include Apple's pricey MacTCP package and the freeware NCSA Telnet package, which includes TCP/IP connectivity. In addition, you'll need SLIP or PPP support. A popular SLIP package is InterSLIP. Popular newsreaders include Newswatcher and Nuntius.

SUMMARY

This chapter explored the many ways you can connect your home or office computer to USENET, including some low-cost and "freebie" options such as bulletin board systems (BBSs) and freenets. A quick and inexpensive way to get started with USENET is to subscribe to an on-line service that offers USENET newsgroups, such as America Online or CompuServe. Although dialup access (shell accounts) are cheap and readily available, it's clear that the dialup IP via SLIP and PPP represent the wave of the future. Microsoft Windows users are positioned to reap the benefits here, thanks to Windows 4.0's Winsock-compatible TCP/IP and PPP support and the existence of excellent NNTP newsreader clients, including WinVP and Trumpet for Windows.

FROM HERE...

- For an overview of what you'll do when you read the news, see Chapter 2, "A quick USENET tour."

- If you've decided to subscribe to an on-line service, check out Chapter 7, "Reading the news with America Online," Chapter 8, "Reading the news with Delphi," or Chapter 9, "Reading the news with CompuServe Information Manager."

- If you've a shell account on a UNIX machine, check out the chapters on UNIX newsreaders: See Chapter 10, "Reading the news with tin", Chapter 11, "Reading the news with nn", and Chapter 12, "Reading the news with rn and trn".

- If you've decided to go the NNTP client route, check out Chapter 13, "Trumpet for Windows," or, for you Macintosh users, Chapter 14, "Newswatcher for Macintosh." Chapter 4 illustrates the basics of newsreading using WinVN, a very nice Windows NNTP client.

4

How USENET is
ORGANIZED

With many servers offering 5,000 newsgroups or more, it's easy to get lost in the jungle of newsgroups. Fortunately, USENET isn't just one huge undifferentiated mass of information—it's organized in a logical way, as this chapter explains.

THE HIERARCHY CONCEPT

Basic to the naming of USENET newsgroups is the concept of *hierarchy* (a succession of things, one after the other, in which each level is subordinate to the one above). In nature, for example, there are animals called *marsupials*—the ones with a pouch for the young. An example of a North American marsupial is the opossum. If animals had Net names, the opossum would be named "marsupial.opossum."

At the beginning of a newsgroup name, you find the *top-level hierarchies,* such as alt, comp, or rec. This name indicates in the most general way what a specific newsgroup is about. The rec.* newsgroups, for instance, are concerned with recreational activities and hobbies. The term *rec hierarchy* refers collectively to all the rec newsgroups. Within the rec hierarchy, you'll find these *second-level hierarchies,* each of which contains several newsgroups:

- **rec.arts.*** Literature, art, film, theatre, and television (but not music).

- **rec.audio.*** Audio equipment—where to buy it, what's best, how to enjoy it.

- **rec.autos.*** Cars—antique automobiles, buying and selling cars, sports cars, and racing.

- **rec.aviation.*** Flying—everything about civil and military aviation.

- **rec.bicycles.*** Bikes—racing, riding, buying and selling, and even the sociology of bicycling.

- **rec.crafts.*** Making beer, jewelry, quilts, wine, and more.

- **rec.food.*** Everything about cooking and serving a fine meal, including drinks.

- **rec.games.*** Games of all types, including board games and computer games.

- **rec.humor.*** Various aspects of humor.

- **rec.models.*** All kinds of models, including radio control.

- **rec.music.*** All kinds of music, from classical to the latest pop fad.

- **rec.pets.*** Cats, dogs, birds, and snakes.

- **rec.photo.*** Everything about amateur photography: cameras, lenses, darkrooms, buying and selling.

- **rec.radio.*** All about radio, both commercial and amateur.

- **rec.skiing.*** Skiing, both nordic and downhill.

34

- **rec.sport.** Baseball, basketball, boxing, cricket, fencing, football, hockey, rugby, table-tennis—you name it.

- **rec.travel.** Everything about traveling—including getting tickets, choosing destinations, and what it's like when you're there.

- **rec.video.** Amateur and professional video production.

Within a second-level hierarchy such as rec.arts, you'll find two or more *third-level hierarchies,* such as the following (selected) rec.arts newsgroups:

- **rec.arts.books.** About books generally, including authors, publishers, the marketplace.

- **rec.arts.dance.** All about dance.

- **rec.arts.poems.** Every aspect of poetry, including original poems to read on-line.

And there are even a few fourth-level hierarchies, such as rec.arts.sf.tv.*, concerning science fiction shows on TV. This hierarchy contains the following newsgroups.

- **rec.arts.sf.tv.babylon-5.** Discussion concerning the TV series Babylon 5.

- **rec.arts.sf.tv.quantum-leap.** Discussion concerning the TV series Quantum Leap.

Is USENET naming really all that systematic? Ideally, yes, but this picture of neatly organized newsgroups breaks down on closer examination. Just a sampling of idiosyncracies:

- **rec.arts.cinema** and **rec.arts.movies.** Uh, what's the difference? Turns out that one is *moderated* (see the sec-

tion titled "Moderated newsgroups" later in this chapter for more information).

- **rec.arts.theatre** and **rec.arts.theatre.misc.** Where do you post an article that's about some general aspect of theatre?

- **rec.birds** and **rec.pets.birds.** This makes sense, actually, although it's not immediately obvious from the names: rec.birds is about birdwatching, while rec.pets.birds is about keeping birds as pets.

The appearance of order breaks down further when you consider the *alternative newsgroups,* the subject of the next section.

THE STANDARD AND ALTERNATIVE NEWSGROUP HIERARCHIES

The more than 5,000 newsgroups that are distributed to all or most USENET sites fall into two categories: the *standard newsgroup hierarchies* and the alternative newsgroup hierarchies.

The standard newsgroup hierarchies

Listed in Table 4-1, these hierarchies contain newsgroups that were created by a formal voting procedure (see Chapter 19, "Creating a newsgroup"). One criterion for inclusion is that the newsgroup

TABLE 4-1. THE STANDARD NEWSGROUP HIERARCHIES

HIERARCHY NAME	SUBJECT
comp	Every aspect of computers and computer use
misc	Miscellaneous
news	Usenet—its administration and use
rec	Recreation, hobbies, sports
sci	The sciences
soc	Social issues
talk	No-holds-barred dialogue on controversial topics

must be named in a way that fits into the logical hierarchy of newsgroup names. USENET sites are expected to carry all of the standard newsgroup hierarchies (with the exception of talk).

The alternative newsgroup hierarchies

Listed in Table 4-2, these hierarchies bypass the formal voting procedure—it's not necessary to win a vote to add newsgroups to these hierarchies. On the other hand, sites aren't obliged to carry them.

It's a mixed bag, with newsgroups coming from a variety of sources. You'll find *echoes* (automatic copies) of *mailing lists* carried on BITNET, an academic network composed of IBM mainframes at North American and European colleges and universities. (A mailing list is a means of distributing a discussion by electronic mail; all subscribers receive a copy of each message.) You'll also find the ClariNet and usa-today newsgroups, which contain the full text of the same stories you'll see in tomorrow's newspaper. (The clari and usa-today newsgroups are carried only by sites that have paid the necessary licensing fees.) The K12 and bionet hierarchies contain a wealth of useful information for people with professional interests. You'll find foreign language newsgroups in the fr (French), de (German), and relcom (Russian) hierarchies. Users of DEC computer systems will find items of interest in the vmsnet groups, while the gnu hierarchy offers newsgroups that deal with the products of the Free Software Foundation.

These hierarchies aside, it's the alt hierarchy that comes to mind when people think about the alternative newsgroups. The alt hierarchy was deliberately

TABLE 4-2. USENET'S ALTERNATIVE NEWSGROUP HIERARCHIES (SELECTED)

HIERARCHY NAME	SUBJECT
alt	Wide-open discussion on hundreds of subjects
bionet	Biology, biochemistry, biophysics, and more
bit	Usenet echoes of BITNET mailing lists
biz	Newsgroups providing information about businesses
clari	Usenet echoes of wire service stories
de	German newsgroups
fr	French newsgroups
K12	Elementary and secondary education
gnu	Discussion of products of the Free Software Foundation
ieee	Newsgroups created by the Institute of Electrical and Electronics Engineers (IEEE)
relcom	Russian newsgroups
usa-today	The full text of USA Today
vmsnet	The fine points of DEC computers

created to encourage the creative and spontaneous side of USENET, even if doing so also encourages the silly side. Among the alt newsgroups are some of the best groups on the Net, such as alt.folklore.urban, and some of the most pathetic, stupid, and juvenile.

The alt hierarchy isn't all chaos and anarchy; there are some well-developed subject hierarchies. Here's a sampler:

- **alt.bbs.*** Bulletin board systems (BBS), including lists of bulletin boards in your area and discussions of specific BBS programs.

- **alt.binaries.*** Binary files, including multimedia, pictures, and sounds.

- **alt.comics.*** Comic books, including ElfQuest, Superman, Batman, and—of course—alternative comics.

- **alt.culture.*** Discussions of specific human cultures, from Alaska to USENET.

- **alt.current-events.*** What's happening right now.

- **alt.fan.*** Everything from the Addams Family's murderous Wednesday to Woody Allen, with stops along the way for the likes of Rush Limbaugh and Noam Chomsky.

- **alt.folklore.*** Legends and tales of the computer industry, ghost stories, urban folklore, and more.

- **alt.food.*** Some things the rec.food hierarchy forgot, including McDonald's and pancakes.

- **alt.games.*** Specific games, such as Netrek and Street Fighter 2.

- **alt.music.*** Specific groups, artists, and genres.

- **alt.online-service.*** Discussions of Genie, Prodigy, America Online, and the like.

- **alt.paranet.*** Alien abductions, telephathic experiences, and other things that aren't scientifically explicable.

- **alt.personals.*** If you're into bondage, spanking, bisexuality, or just romantic evenings with Mantovani, you'll find like-minded people here.

- **alt.politics.*** Discussions of specific political issues, such as the Information Superhighway, green politics, and political correctness.

- **alt.religion.*** Discussions of specific religions, including Islam, Eckankar, Christianity, and shamanism.

- **alt.sex.*** Every aspect of sex, plus some you haven't heard of (yet).

- **alt.sources.*** Source code (uncompiled computer programs) for a wide variety of computer systems.

- **alt.sport.*** Discussion of sports not covered in the rec.sports.* hierarchy, plus newsgroups devoted to specific professional baseball, basketball, football, and hockey teams.

- **alt.support.*** Help for people with specific problems, ranging from arthritis to tinnitus.

- **alt.tv.*** Discussions of specific television programs.

LOCAL AND REGIONAL NEWSGROUPS

Not all newsgroups are flung to the far corners of the Internet, and beyond. Local and regional newsgroups have more limited distributions, as the following explains:

- **Local newsgroups.** These newsgroups are created to benefit a specific organization, such as a company or a university. See Table 4-3 for examples of local newsgroups.

- **Regional newsgroups.** These newsgroups are created to benefit a city, metropolitan area, a broader regional area, a state, or a country other than the U.S. See Table 4-4 for examples of regional newsgroups.

THE GREAT RENAMING

Among the most traumatic events in USENET's history was The Great Renaming, a newsgroup reorganization that was completed by 1987. The Great Renaming has its origins in the Backbone Cabal, an informal consortium of system administrators positioned at privileged distribution points. At the time, there was only one world newsgroup hierarchy, the Net hierarchy, within which every newsgroup had an equal claim to fame: Respectable groups took their place on the same list with "noisy" groups given to flame wars. The list was poorly organized, but there was an additional justification for the Great Renaming: System administrators had no means by which they could selectively exclude a whole category of unwanted newsgroups from their sites. The result of the Great Renaming was the creation of the current standard newsgroup hierarchies, the so-called Seven Sisters (comp, misc, news, rec, sci, soc, and talk). But one of the underlying motivations of the Great Renaming was to move the "noisy" groups to the talk hierarchy—which, not surprisingly, was excluded at many sites. This brought on what was doubtless the greatest uproar in the Net's history, replete with flame wars, accusations of censorship, and proclamations of the Imminent Death of the Net. In retrospect, it seems like a pretty good idea.

This nice, neat picture is sullied somewhat by the following exceptions. For one thing, USENET sites located outside of a local or regional newsgroup's area can carry the newsgroup, if they wish. America Online, for instance, carries the local newsgroups for many U.S. colleges and universities —not a bad idea, considering that AOL is hoping to sign up lots of college students.

What are local and regional newsgroups for? Lots of things that are of great interest to people in a given locality (but not of much interest outside of it). Here are some examples:

- **Items for sale.** Sooner or later, you'll run into a posting like the famous one, posted to a world newsgroup, about a mattress set for sale in New Jersey. Such postings belong in local and regional newsgroups, not the world ones.

TABLE 4-3. SOME LOCAL NEWSGROUPS AT THE UNIVERSITY OF VIRGINIA

NEWSGROUP NAME	PURPOSE
uva.cd-swap	Tired of those CDs?
uva.chat.student-media	Gripes and whining about student newspapers
uva.flame	Where to post when the glamour wears off
uva.rec.sci-fi	Meet other local sci-fi enthusiasts here
uva.test	Test-post here
uva.want-ads	For sale, cheap

TABLE 4-4. SELECTED REGIONAL NEWSGROUPS

AB	Alberta, Canada	NJ	New Jersey
AUS	Australia	NLNET	Netherlands
AUSTIN	Austin, TX	NO	Norway
BA	San Francisco Bay Area, CA	NZ	New Zealand
BOULDER	Boulder, CO	OH	Ohio
CA	California (state-wide)	PDX	Portland, Oregon
CAN	Canada	PBX	Pittsburgh, PA
CHI	Chicago, IL	PNW	Pacific Northwest (Oregon and Washington)
CHV	Charlottesville, VA		
CLE	Cleveland, OH	SAC	Sacramento, CA
COS	Colorado Springs, CO	SAT	San Antonio, TX
DC	Washington, DC	SDNET	San Diego, CA
DK	Denmark	STL	St. Louis, MO
FJ	Japan	TN	Tennessee
GTB	Gothenberg, Sweden	TOR	Toronto, Ontario, Canada
HSV	Huntsville, AL	TX	Texas
LA	Los Angeles, CA	UK	United Kingdon
MELB	Melbourne, Victoria, Australia	VA	Virginia
MTL	Montreal, Canada	WI	Wisconsin
NE	New England		

- **Reviews of local restaurants.** Where's the best Thai restaurant in town?

- **Discussion groups for local issues.** At many colleges and universities, a professor can set up a local newsgroup for a class.

MODERATED NEWSGROUPS

One of the most frequent complaints about USENET is the low *signal-to-noise ratio* to be found in the typical newgroup. In electrical engineering, the term "signal to noise ratio" refers to the loudness of the signal as against background noise. By extension, a group with a low "signal to noise ratio" has relatively few valuable postings, as against the "noise"—useless postings full of uninformed opinion, pointless rage, and misdirected venom.

One way of dispensing with the noise is to create a *moderated newsgroup*, in which articles aren't posted directly to the group. Instead, they're sent to the email address of the group's *moderator*, a person who has agreed to take on the task of screening the articles (and replies made to these articles). Only those postings that conform to the group's stated mission appear in the newsgroup.

Improving the signal-to-noise ratio isn't the only motivation for creating a moderated group. Some groups exist for the sole purpose of providing information, such as news.lists (this newsgroup publishes analytical reports concerning USENET usage, such as the Top 40 Newsgroups). The entire ClariNet hierarchy falls into this category (with the exception of one group that's intended for discussion of ClariNet); the clari newsgroups provide the full text of UPI, AP, and other wire service reports.

Leaving aside many obscure moderated groups in the comp hierarchy, there aren't that many moderated newsgroups. Table 4-5 lists the moderated

TABLE 4-5. MODERATED NEWSGROUPS (SELECTED)	
alt.atheism.moderated	rec.arts.cinema
alt.binaries.pictures.fine-art.d	rec.arts.comics.info
alt.binaries.pictures.fine-art.digitized	rec.arts.erotica
alt.binaries.pictures.fine-art.graphics	rec.arts.movies.reviews
alt.gourmand	rec.arts.sf.announce
misc.activism.progressive	rec.arts.sf.reviews
misc.answers	rec.arts.startrek.info
misc.education.multimedia	rec.arts.startrek.reviews
misc.handicap	rec.audio.high-end
misc.legal.moderated	rec.autos.sport.info
misc.news.east-europe.rferl	rec.aviation.announce
misc.news.southasia	rec.aviation.answers
misc.test.moderated	rec.aviation.questions
rec.arts.anime.info	rec.aviation.stories
rec.arts.anime.stories	rec.food.recipes
rec.arts.ascii	rec.food.veg.cooking

TABLE 4-5. MODERATED NEWSGROUPS (SELECTED) (CONTINUED)

rec.games.mud.announce	sci.nanotech
rec.guns	sci.physics.plasma
rec.humor.funny	sci.physics.research
rec.humor.oracle	sci.psychology.digest
rec.hunting	sci.psychology.research
rec.mag.fsfnet	sci.space.news
rec.music.gaffa	sci.space.science
rec.music.info	sci.space.tech
rec.music.reviews	sci.virtual-worlds
rec.radio.broadcasting	sci.virtual-worlds.apps
rec.radio.info	soc.answers
rec.skiing.announce	soc.culture.indian.info
rec.sport.cricket.info	soc.culture.jewish.holocaust
rec.sport.cricket.scores	soc.feminism
sci.aeronautics	soc.history.moderated
sci.aeronautics.airliners	soc.history.war.world-war-ii
sci.answers	soc.politics
sci.astro.hubble	soc.politics.arms-d
sci.astro.research	soc.religion.bahai
sci.bio.evolution	soc.religion.christian
sci.econ.research	soc.religion.christian.bible-study
sci.math.research	soc.religion.eastern
sci.med.aids	soc.religion.islam
sci.military	soc.religion.shamanism

newsgroups found in the alt, misc, rec, sci, and soc hierarchies. This table is well worth examining because many of USENET's best newsgroups are moderated.

MAILING LISTS

A mailing list resembles a moderated newsgroup in that participants send messages to a central point, where they're collected and disseminated. (Sometimes they're screened, sometimes they're not.) But here's the difference. From the central collection point, postings to the mailing list are sent to the electronic mailboxes of everyone who has subscribed to the list. It was once thought that USENET would replace mailing lists, since it's a hassle to read your mail when your personal correspondence is mixed in with mailing list postings. But that hasn't happened; in fact, the number of mailing lists is growing as quickly as the number of USENET newsgroups.

Why do mailing lists remain popular? Part of the reason, again, is the low signal-to-noise ratio of so many USENET newsgroups. Somebody who wants to start a new, serious USENET newsgroup on a technical or advanced subject must accept that, sooner or later, the newsgroup will become littered with postings from people who just don't know what they're talking about. Given such concerns, it might seem wiser to create a mailing list.

Some mailing lists are effectively kept secret: Only those who are invited to join the group receive the moderator's electronic mail address. Others are *publicly accessible* (anyone can join them merely by sending an email message to the moderator). An example: A.Word.A.Day mails you an English vocabulary word every day, complete with a definition. To subscribe, you send an email message to wordsmith@viper.elp.cwru.edu. In the Subject: line of your message, type **Subscribe** followed by your full name. Leave the body of the message blank.

> **TIP:** For a list of current mailing lists, check out Stephanie De Silva's *Publicly Accessible Mailing Lists,* a fourteen-part compendium published monthly in news.lists and news.answers. Alternatively, you can access the list though anonymous FTP to a Usenet FAQ archive (such as rtfm.mit.edu, in the directory /pub/usenet/news.lists).

Some of the moderated newsgroups that you'll find on USENET are USENET versions, or echoes, of mailing lists. That's true of the entire bit hierarchy; all the groups are echoes of mailing lists from BITNET, an academic network of universities and colleges working with antiquated IBM mainframe systems. Reversing this pattern, some USENET newsgroups are reflected as mailing lists for the benefit of people who don't have access to USENET.

When a mailing list and USENET newsgroup are linked, there are three possible *gateways* through which messages can be disseminated:

- **Fully bidirectional gateway.** You can post a message to the newsgroup or send it to the mailing list manager's address; either way, it appears both in the mailing list and on the newsgroup. All of the BITNET mailing lists echoed in the bit hierarchy have fully bidirectional gateways.

- **One-way gateway.** The mailing list reflects the newsgroup and doesn't accept postings; alternatively, the newsgroup reflects the mailing list and doesn't accept postings.

- **Digest format.** Postings to the mailing list and/or the newsgroup go to a moderator, who periodically summarizes the contributions in the form of a *digest,* (a document, often fairly lengthy, in which contributions are grouped by subject and often edited). For examples of a digest, see comp.risks.

SUMMARY

A newsgroup's name can tell you a lot about its contents. The name itself reflects a hierarchy of inclusiveness, with the most inclusive part of the name (such as comp or rec) coming first. The second part of the name indicates a subcategory, as in rec.foods.*, and there may be additional subcategories.

The core of USENET is the set of seven standard newsgroup hierarchies (comp, misc, news, rec, sci, soc, and talk). Most sites carry these hierarchies. They're not obligated to carry the alternative newsgroup hierarchies (containing the alternative newsgroup hierarchy *par excellence*, alt), but many do. Alternative newsgroup hierarchies are diverse and include foreign language groups and commercial services such as ClariNet. At most sites, you'll find a smattering of local and regional newsgroups.

If you're distressed by the low signal-to-noise ratio in many USENET discussion groups, check out the moderated newsgroups: A human moderator screens all the postings to make sure they conform to the group's stated mission. The continued popularity of private and public mailing lists attests to the vulnerability of USENET newsgroups to uninformed postings and other forms of net.abuse.

FROM HERE

- For more information on finding newsgroups, see Chapter 18, "USENET's best: the top newsgroups reviewed."

- For information on how newsgroups are created, see Chapter 19, "Creating a newsgroup."

- For an exploration of USENET culture and values, see Chapter 5, "USENET's values, customs, and lore."

USENET isn't a physical computer network or a formal organization with a headquarters and leadership. More than anything else, it's a community—and what's more, it's a community that has developed a unique and characteristic culture. To be sure, there's a bewildering variety of values and lifestyle choices to be found among net.people. Yet, when the Net comes under real or perceived attack, these same people tend to express core USENET values, including a bias against blatant commercialism and a Libertarian-like concept of free expression.

Understanding USENET's core values is an essential part of USENET literacy and lays the foundation for a successful USENET experience. Violating them, intentionally or not, will subject you to reprisals at the hands of self-styled *net.police*, USENET participants who have anointed themselves to be the preservers of USENET customs. They'll surely send you abusive email and, if the violation is considered especially severe, they may even attempt to hound you off the network.

It's wise, then, to understand USENET's values—and fun, too, as this chapter suggests. USENET's culture includes a well-developed tradition of wacky, satirical, and often self-referential humor, replete with pranks, lampoons, and devastating one-liners. Some of this is just pure silliness, but it's still important to understand: net.people poke fun at everything, including themselves, and sooner or later they'll poke fun at you. Approached with a healthy sense of humor, a respect for core USENET values, and a bit of humility, USENET's a lot more fun.

USENET's culture is sometimes summed up by the term netiquette, a neologism contracting "network" and "etiquette," but I define netiquette more narrowly: The term refers to the specific things one ought to do while posting to respect the rights and feelings of other users of the network. For more information, see Chapter 15, "Working with a virtual community."

THE BIAS AGAINST BLATANT COMMERCIALISM

Anyone who wishes to work successfully with the USENET community must clearly realize that blatant commercialism isn't welcome, and it's sure to be sanctioned with formidable punitive measures. At the minimum, this includes *mail bombing* (filling your electronic mailbox with huge amounts of garbage data). At the extreme, it will include computer-programmed salvos on your fax machine that will tie it up for days or weeks, and even virus-like programs that roam USENET looking for your posts and canceling them before they appear. For a particularly compelling example of a blatantly commercial post and the net.police's response, see the section on the Green Card flame war in Chapter 21, "USENET issues and futures."

What's blatant commercialism, as net.people see it? Certainly, it isn't the use of the Net for business reasons. Many businesses use the Net successfully—and they even advertise and sell, without arousing the ire of the net.police. You have to be blatant.

Although there's no hard-and-fast definition of "blatant" commercialism, the following are sure to arouse the net.police's ire:

- **Carpet bombing newsgroups** with advertising unrelated to the newsgroup's mission. In *carpet bombing,* an article is crossposted to two or more newsgroups whose topics bear no relation to the posted article. This is extremely irritating to people who are seriously trying to read the newsgroup; it's like finding junk mail in the middle of a book you're trying to read.

- **Active commercial advertising** in newsgroups other than the various newsgroups in the biz hierarchy or local/regional for-sale newsgroups. It's quite OK, though, to reply to a post—preferably by email—if you think you have a product or service that a poster can use.

- **Solicitation** based on dishonest or illegal pyramid schemes, chain letters, or scams of any kind.

The Hacker Ethic

What's the source of the Net's anti-commercial ethos? It goes back, in part, to the Hacker Ethic, ably described by Stephen Levy in his *Hackers: Heroes of the Computer Revolution* (1984). Hackers, properly speaking, are computer enthusiasts who revel in finding original, even unorthodox, solutions to technical problems in computing. Within the computing community, the term "hacker" and the hacker tradition are very positively viewed, in contrast to the negative connotation of criminality that the press has long tried to attach to the term. Hacking has a distinguished history in computing and is responsible for some of the technology's most impressive technical advances; it has

---

A GUIDE TO USENET HUMOR

As one of the wittier genres of contemporary writing, USENET all but forces one to the dictionary to master the nuances of humor. You're sure to run into USENET postings that can be described in the following terms:

- **caricature**—Deliberately exaggerating some prominent characteristic for humorous effect ("If you wouldn't SHOUT with your CAPITAL LETTERS, someone might actually READ WHAT YOU'RE SAYING.") Closely related is **parody**, the sustained use of imitation to expose an author's stylistic deficiencies or poverty of thought.

- **irony**—Using terms that are the opposite of the meaning actually intended ("Sure, the Macintosh is a great computer. Just like Sri Lanka's a great naval power.")

- **irreverence**—Lacking in respect; disdainful of convention ("My university? A diploma factory mired in pretense.")

- **lampoon**—A work that exposes the folly in something by using humor and especially irony, saying the opposite of what's really intended ("Everyone on USENET just loves long signature files. Don't stop at four lines— take 20, or 30, and don't forget to add a pretty picture and a long quotation.")

- **sarcasm**—Bitter, cutting, biting mockery ("I'm glad you thought you were serious— for a distressing minute there, I thought it was self-parody.")

- **sardonicism**—Contemptuous mocking of the motives of others ("I'm sure you had no ulterior motives in posting that advertisement. . . . And by the way, I just bought the Brooklyn Bridge last week.")

- **satire**—The use of humor to expose folly or wrongdoing ("The next time I post, I'm going to think like you do—which is to say not at all.")

absolutely nothing to do with computer crime (in fact, one of hacking's core premises is that it is never defensible to destroy or misuse computer data).

The culture of hacking has its origins in bizarre college pranks, such as the covert substitution of the colored cards held up by Washington fans at the 1961 Rose Bowl so that the cards read "Cal Tech" instead; from such elaborate pranks arose the notion of the hack as an astonishing feat that is both devilishly clever and technically sophisticated. In computing, the culture of hacking matured in the computing laboratories of MIT, Berkeley, and other large universities during the late 1960s and early 1970s. Computers weren't all that easy to come by in those days, particularly for 17-year-old programming geniuses who knew perfectly well that they could do things *right*. Viewing the computer establishment as a technologically retrograde, profit-oriented abomination that only functioned to keep computers away from the people who knew what to do with them, hackers developed an ethic that stressed three key philosophical points:

- Access to computers should be absolutely open to everyone who can make intelligent use of them.

- Access to information related to computers should be available to any interested person, free of charge.

- Any person in a position of authority should be mistrusted, and their influence should be countered by creating systems that ensure decentralization.

UNIX and the tradition of open software exchange

Hackers became graduate students, and then professors of computer science. And as they did, an accident of history put into their hands a very powerful set of public-domain computer tools, the UNIX operating system and its utility programs. As will be seen, the availability of freely distributable versions of UNIX, coupled with the anti-commercial ethos of academic, were to deepen the anti-commercial biases that are so evidently manifest in today's USENET.

In the late 1970s, federal antitrust regulations prohibited AT&T from entering the computer business, and so the UNIX operating system—an innovation stemming from AT&T's Bell Laboratories—was distributed free of charge to colleges and universities throughout the U.S. There soon arose a tradition of free and open exchange of UNIX-related software, bug fixes, configuration files, and documentation, one that parallels and was obviously informed by the academic community's preference for the open and free exchange of scientific and technical information. USENET's creators envisioned the network as a means of distributing UNIX-related information in an environment of free and open exchange.

The UNIX users' community's traditions deeply affected an entire generation of computer science students and faculty and has led to some extreme positions. For example, a Cambridge, MA–based organization called the Free Software Foundation (FSF) is dedicated to eliminating restrictions on the copying, redistribution, and modification of computer programs. To promote this goal, the organization offers an integrated, UNIX-like software system called GNU (short for "GNUs Not UNIX"). The software is made available under the organization's General Public License, which specifies that the software is freely redistributable provided no commercial use is made of it.

In many ways, USENET can be viewed as a technological realization of the Hacker Ethic's core premises. It's available without time-based billing or other barriers to just about anyone who can get access to an Internet-linked computer system. Knowledge regarding the use of USENET is freely available within USENET itself, in the form of the various .answers newsgroups. These newsgroups serve as repositories for helpful documents known as frequently asked questions (FAQs), as well as tutorials and usage information. The many newsgroups in the gnu hierarchy, to cite another example, provide documentation and knowledge-sharing resources for the Free Software Foundation's products. And USENET's technical structure "wires in" decentralization, particularly now that so many sites have multiple Internet connections: A newsgroup that's banned at one site can easily reach other sites by worming its way through the Internet's mazeway of interconnections.

Acceptable Use Policies (AUP) and government subsidies

Yet another source of the bias against blatant commercialism lies in the *Acceptable Use Policies (AUP)* maintained by NSFNET, the backbone network that provides much of the Internet's transcontinental bandwidth. Because the NSFNET is partly funded by U.S. taxpayers, the National Science Foundation (NSF)—the organization that administers NSFNET—stipulates that the purpose of the network is to advance research communication in and among U.S. research and educational institutions. Business participation is restricted to non-proprietary uses carried out in a spirit of open scientific collaboration. The guidelines permit announcements of new products, but only if they pertain to research or instruction. Specifically excluded are uses motivated by profit or extensive use of the network for private or personal business.

NSFNET's Acceptable Use Policies are frequently criticized for their vagueness; for example, just when does a business's USENET post cross the line between an "instructional" or "research-related" announcement and one that's frankly motivated by profit? Yet the guidelines aren't as vague as they might appear, once one gets to know USENET a bit better. In a newsgroup that focuses on a specific technical area, such as software for displaying graphics, carefully worded commercial posts are often welcome in that they provide precisely the kind of information that people are looking for. That same post might be deemed inappropriate, however, if it's posted to unrelated newsgroups.

Increasingly, the bulk of the Internet's bandwidth—and that includes USENET—is being carried on for-profit commercial backbone networks that do not have AUP policies. It's not often realized that the NSFNET backbone itself isn't owned by the U.S. government; it's leased from a commercial service provider. Just how this transition will affect USENET in the coming years is an open question, to which this book returns in Chapter 21, "USENET issues and futures." For now, it's safe to say that USENET's biases against blatant commercialism are still very strong and likely to remain so even if the AUP restrictions become even more irrelevant than they already are.

THE LIBERTARIAN TILT

USENET's biases against blatant commercialism have been shaped, in part, by the network's origins in the hacker community. Not surprisingly, USENET's politics have followed suit. To be sure, you'll find every shade of political affiliation on the Net, from ultra-conservative Christian fundamentalists on the right to Maoists and anarchists on the left. When it comes to Net-related issues, however, you'll find a middle-ground consensus that's remarkably in accord with the basic tenets of Libertarianism—a doctrine that resonates perfectly with the anti-authoritarianism biases of the hacker tradition. Here's a quick review of basic Libertarian premises.

Libertarians believe that the left-right political split locks us into a lose-lose situation. Leftists want social justice but seek to achieve this by imposing constraints on economic freedoms. On the right, conservatives offer economic freedoms, but want to impose limits on your individual freedom. Libertarians believe that social justice and economic progress can be achieved only when governments abandon their aspirations to regulate individual behavior. People should be free to develop their potential to the maximum, Libertarians believe. Any law or regulation that interferes with this freedom is wrong and will inevitably produce negative results: Convincingly, they cite Prohibition and the welfare system, two equally disastrous chapters in American history, in support of their claims. Getting specific, Libertarians endorse the right to bear arms, demand absolute press freedom and oppose censorship of any kind, favor the decriminalization of drugs, oppose restrictions on abortion, and advocate the weakening of immigration restrictions. They favor the restoration of a decentralized democracy that will permit people to flower, not grind them into the dirt.

You'll find plenty of people on the Net, to be sure, who advocate gun control and oppose abortion. But when it comes down to freedom of expression, USENET's tilt toward Libertarianism is very much in evidence. Suppose you run across a posting that offends you in some way, such as a graphic featuring child pornography. You'll find ready agreement that the material is offensive and even illegal, but calls to remove such postings from the Net will bring out the net.police in droves. You'll be told, "If something offends you, there's a very simple solution: Don't read it."

To make sure that you don't read something that might offend you, experienced posters preface articles containing potentially offensive material with a description of the contents and a warning that you shouldn't continue if such material offends you; alternatively, the text may be encrypted through *rot-13* (a simple mechanism that moves each letter down the alphabet 13 spaces). Most readers can decrypt the text by means of a simple command. In the compass of Net values, if you read an offensive article or rotate the encrypted text and get upset, it's *your* fault, not the fault of the person who posted the offensive material.

It need hardly be stated that this position exposes USENET to danger—sooner or later, some USENET participants fear, some politically ambitious district attorney is going to bust a USENET site. Worse, the behavior of net.police makes it very difficult to resolve this problem through dialogue with the people who post potentially actionable material. A person who posts pictures involving sex-ual depictions of children or sexual acts of violence toward women, for instance, may receive little or no criticism; however, a person who posts a message critical of such postings finds a barrage of hysterical email messages in his or her mailbox the next morning. For further discussion of this and related issues, see Chapter 21, "USENET issues and futures."

HOLY WARS, FLAME WARS, AND EGREGIOUS PUBLIC DISAGREEMENTS

Most people who have used computer-mediated communication readily agree that it seems to foster acrimony. Face to face, we timidly nod our head and smile, even though we're thinking, "This is bullshit." On-line, however, the constraints of face-to-face interaction disappear, and out comes what people really think—and all too often, without any consideration for the feelings of people at the other end of the message. The results are three regrettable USENET phenomena that I've termed *holy wars, flame wars,* and *egregious public disagreements.*

The Net's holy wars don't involve religion, though there are plenty of religion-related flame wars to be found on the Net. Rather, it's a disagreement over the right way to implement computer technology, a topic dear to the heart of the computer enthusiasts and professionals who number prominently among USENET's denizens. A holy war takes on the attributes of a religious controversy in that the various positions boil down to very deeply held, irreducible propositions about the correct way to design and implement computing technology. Classic holy wars include the old one concerning whether the most significant bit in a unit of data should come first or last, and the more recent one concerning the merits and desirability of the IBM PC as against the Apple Macintosh.

The problem with holy wars is that, ultimately, they never reach any consensus or resolution—if you've tried convincing a Macintosh person to try using MS-DOS, you'll know what I mean. In many newsgroups, you'll find FAQs that beg newcomers not to post positions related to holy war issues; the result could very well be a re-ignition of a bandwidth-consuming debate that's never likely to produce a consensus.

> **TIP:** Be sure to read a newsgroup's FAQ, if there is one, before posting an article to a newsgroup. For more information on FAQs, see Chapter 16, "Posting your own messages."

Flame wars resemble holy wars in that they involve protracted disagreements—but it's a disagreement in which one or more of the parties involved has lost his or her cool and started *flaming*. In email, a *flame* is a poorly considered message that's conceived in anger and ridden (usually) with profanities. Flames appear on USENET, too—all too often, as you'll find.

A recent example of a flame war: The proposal to create the newsgroup soc.religion.unitarian-univ, a moderated newsgroup for Unitarians, received little notice until an unidentified *sysop* (a system administrator of a USENET site) posted a message proclaiming that the Unitarians are an "anti-Christian cult" and urged all Christians to vote against the creation of the group.

The sysop's post was a classic example of *flame bait* (a message so deeply in contravention of USENET's norms that it sends people through the roof). For one thing, the person who sent the message lacked sufficient courage of conviction to have signed his or her name. But most of all, the post ran counter to the core of the USENET ethos: Intelligent participation in civic life requires the full and free exchange of opinion and information.

Yet another variant on the flame war is the *dictionary flame* (a battle concerning the proper meaning of some term that's come up in the discussion). People can be surprisingly uptight about superficial matters of spelling, grammar, and usage on the Net (for someone who teaches English, as I do, this ought to be gratifying, but it leads to such repulsive ends that I take no joy in it). Ultimately, the contestants will pull out their dictionaries—and *then* they'll argue about which dictionary is best. Time to set up a kill file!

A particularly unpleasant variety of the flame war is what I term the *public personal disagreement (PPD)* (two warring individuals taking their battle to the newsgroup in an attempt to elicit support and sympathy for their side). A typical PPD posting begins something like this:

"So-and-so sent me an email message claiming that I was a misinformed jerk who should take a hike! Well I'll tell you who's a jerk! And stupid! He can't even spell! Look at this: [long quotation deleted]...."

The poster of such a message is clueless in every way, but especially regarding one of the canons of netiquette: You're not supposed to post email messages without the writer's permission (see Chapter 15, "Working with a virtual community").

All kidding aside, you'll be wise to stay out of flame wars of any kind, ranging from the holy to the egregious. Generally, they're a waste of time and contribute significantly to the reduction of a newsgroup's signal to noise ratio. Sometimes, just staying silent—not biting the bait—is a much more effective way of dealing with obnoxious people and their obnoxious opinions. To be sure, sometimes a flame war does lead to the resolution of an issue; more often, flame wars drive a wedge between the warring parties rather than fostering any kind of resolution. In time, the war just fades away.

> **TIP:** There is an elegant technical remedy for holy wars, flame wars, and PPDs: It's called the *kill file,* and it can help you identify specific subjects and authors that you'd like to ignore. Subsequently, the unwanted posts don't appear in the list of articles you see on-screen. The kill file is introduced in Chapter 3, "Connecting to USENET." Be sure to read that chapter carefully!

PRANKS

Hacking had its origins in elaborate practical jokes, and the tradition continues on USENET. You'll be wise to watch out for *trolling* and forged postings, unless you like having someone try to make you look like a fool.

Trolling refers to the practice of posting an apparently serious article that contains an obvious factual mistake, such as the assertion (posted to rec.music.classical) that Seiji Ozawa is one of the greatest tuba players of his generation (he's a conductor). Rising to this bait will be a conceited nitpicker who, by failing to perceive what is obvious to others—namely, that the post is a troll—reveals himself to be quite the fool. Moral of the story: USENET isn't wisely approached with a know-it-all or self-righteous attitude.

Forged postings make their appearance on April Fool's Day, naturally. Ostensibly posted by a net.god (a well-known network personality), they make some kind of outrageous pronouncement. Inevitably, this is taken seriously by some, who post messages that (in retrospect) make them look rather silly. Look at the calendar before biting *this* bait.

> **TIP:** Prank postings—trolls and forgeries—are common enough to warrant caution: If an article sounds like it's too good or too weird to be true, it probably isn't.

Sooner or later, you'll run in to the famous Nieman-Marcus Cookie post. Supposedly, a Nieman-Marcus customer liked the firm's chocolate chip cookies so much that he requested the recipe. He was told the cost was "250," which he took to mean $2.50. However, when he got his Visa bill, he found the actual charge to be $250. But Nieman-Marcus refused to refund his money. In revenge, he decided to post the recipe to the Net. It's a hoax; the recipe, which calls for huge amounts of ingredients, doesn't produce anything that comes even close to a chocolate chip cookie.

URBAN FOLKLORE

The telling of tall tales and the making of legends hasn't ended with the passing of agrarian society; in fact, today's communications technologies—fax machines, email, television, and (especially!) USENET—are ideally suited to the dissemination of *urban folklore* (myths and legends of modern society). From an anthropological standpoint, this is a fascinating phenomenon—but it can pose problems, too, as the "dying child" post amply illustrates.

A recurrent USENET post, the "dying child" article describes the touching tale of the dying boy who has requested postcards so that he can get into the *Guinness Book of World Records*. Like much folklore, this has some basis in fact: seven-year-old Craig Shergold, diagnosed with a terminal brain tumor, did indeed request that people worldwide send him postcards so he could make the record books. The British public health care service, which prioritizes and rations care for terminally ill patients, refused to operate on Craig. But Craig didn't die. Hearing about his plight, an American billionaire flew him to Charlottesville, Virginia, where physicians successfully extracted the tumor—which turned out to be benign. The only problem is that, thanks to repeated postings of the story, Craig is still getting postcards—an estimated 33 million of them, at last count, and the repeated posting of this article has become an expensive nightmare for the British postal service.

The "dying child" article may well have descended from folklore to prank—and if so, it's a particularly mean-spirited one. But all too many people continue to contribute false or misleading information to USENET—a fact that led to the formation of alt.urban.folklore, a newsgroup devoted to collecting and exposing the myths that USENET and other electronic media help to disseminate (see the box titled "Things that sound like they might be true, but aren't"). Before you post an article describing that great story about the car thief who was squashed dead in a stolen BMW during the '89 San Francisco Bay Area earthquake, you'd be wise to take a look at the alt.urban.folklore FAQ—it isn't true. Posting an article containing an urban myth that's known or believed to be false is a sure-fire way to get yourself flamed.

NEWBIES, CLUELESS AND OTHERWISE

In Piers Anthony's Xanth novels, the mysterious land called Xanth is a delightful, hard to find place that seems to be adjacent to every known country. And it brings out magic powers in whomever dwells there. Each new generation, believing Xanth to be a very special place, fears outside colonization from the denizens of Mundania, whom they presume to

---

THINGS THAT SOUND LIKE THEY MIGHT BE TRUE, BUT AREN'T

According to the alt.folklore.urban FAQ, the following urban myths are false:

• Fluorescent lights rob your body of essential vitamins.

• The words to "Louie, Louie" are dirty.

• People sometimes spontaneously explode and burn up.

• A well-known obscene word is an old acronym for "Fornication Under Consent of the King."

• Koalas are always stoned because of intoxicants in the eucalyptus leaves they eat.

• Mommy birds will not sit on their nests after you touch their eggs.

• A worker at an auto parts store, over a period of years, stole Cadillac parts one-by-one until he had a whole car.

• The Prodigy on-line service secretly reads your computer's hard disk and uploads your personal information to IBM.

---

pose a dire threat to Xanth's special qualities. But inevitably, the colonizations occur, and in the end it turns out to be a Good Thing: The colonizers become magical themselves, and the whole cycle repeats itself.

Anthony must have been thinking of USENET, which has been through several colonization waves of its own. Each time, a flood of *newbies* (new users) arrives on the scene, unaware of USENET's customs, netiquette, and traditions, and makes every conceivable on-line gaffe, you'll see countless postings proclaiming the "imminent death of the Net," generally due to USENET's supposed inability to handle the massive influx of people who just don't understand what the Net's supposed to be about. Such postings usually decry the "obvious" decline in the quality of dialogue over the past n years, which is attributed to the arrival of all these horrible newcomers.

Don't buy it. There seems to be some kind of psychological payoff to thinking that you were a pioneer, and everything used to be just wonderful, but it's now being spoiled by newcomers who didn't have to slog through six miles of deep snow to get to an ASCII terminal. One of the best innovations of the Great Renaming (see the box titled "The Great Renaming" in Chapter 4) was the notion of newsgroup subhierarchies (the division of a newsgroup such as rec.music into as many as several dozen newsgroups such as rec.music.classical and rec.music.reggae); there's no reason that this process cannot continue even as the Net scales up massively, preserving a sense of intimacy in the increasingly specialized newsgroups.

There's no foundation to the old-timer's belief that newbies are destroying the Net, but that's little consolation when you find yourself getting flamed for some trivial misdeed. Learn what you can from the helpful people who offer advice, and ignore the jerks who call you names. Remember that, despite beliefs about the Imminent Death of the Net, most net.people are genuinely helpful of newcomers—especially when those newcomers show respect for the Net's culture and traditions.

GIVE SOMETHING BACK

Perhaps the most fundamental of USENET values is the notion that, having read USENET and profited personally and professionally from the information and resources you've retrieved, you should contribute in some way. If you're not sure how, here are some suggestions:

- Do all you can to learn the specifics of USENET netiquette (see Chapter 15, "Working with a virtual community") and don't post to newsgroups until you're sure you understand what the newsgroup's all about.

- If you think you can help someone who has posted an article requesting assistance, do it—preferably by email.

- Once you become experienced with USENET, don't flame newcomers for the mistakes they make. Just remember that you were a newbie too, once.

- Post only when you've got something constructive and substantive to offer.

- If you have some information or knowledge that's pertinent to a newsgroup's topic, offer to help with the FAQ.

- If you've written something that's full of information useful to readers of a newsgroup, offer to include it among the newsgroup's *periodic informational postings* (documents that are posted at set intervals, such as once or twice per month, to the newsgroup).

SUMMARY

Although net.people disagree on just about everything, there are some core values that tend to come to the fore when the Net is under real or perceived attack: a deep distaste for blatant commercialism and an equally strong preference for absolute freedom of expression. These values have their origins in the old and praiseworthy tradition of hacking, which has made a distinguished contribution to the history of computing technology. The more you understand USENET's history, the hacker tradition, and the Net's Libertarian tilt, the more you'll understand what tends to anger net.people—and the less likely it is that you'll find your mailbox full of flames the morning after you post.

Watch out for flame wars and pranks—the former indicating too little humor, and the latter a little too much! The same advice goes for both: Don't bite the bait. Ignore the whining you'll see about how newcomers are destroying the Net—it's just not true (remember Xanth!). USENET has survived every crisis it's faced and grown in quality, diversity, and breadth. You're about to become a part of this process! Just remember to give something back.

FROM HERE

- If you'd like to learn more about the specifics of netiquette, flip to Chapter 15, "Working with a virtual community."

- Don't want to get flamed as a "clueless newbie"? Master your newsreader software before posting—and understand its limitations. Get started with the next chapter.

PART II

READING

THE NEWS

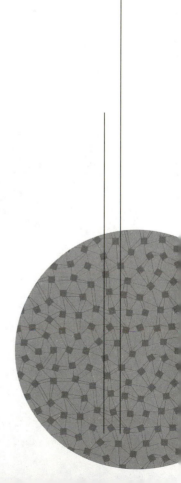

6

UNDERSTANDING
NEWSREADERS

To read USENET articles, you'll use a news-reader. A newsreader is a client program that accesses a USENET *server* (a computer that regularly receives the latest USENET postings and makes them accessible for you and others to read).

Unfortunately, there's no single, dominant newsreader in widespread use. That's not true for another common application of the Internet, the World Wide Web (WWW); a program called Mosaic, created by the National Center for Supercomputer Applications (NCSA), is far and away the most popular Web navigator. For USENET, though, there are literally dozens of newsreaders in existence. They include the newsreading functions of on-line service software, such as the newsreader built into CompuServe Information Manager (CIM). Most of the rest of them are public domain or shareware programs. And, for the most part, they're very poorly documented—or there's no documentation at all. Perhaps the worst news of all is that there's a general inverse relationship between power (the ability to customize your newsreading procedures) and ease of use: The easiest newsreaders to use, such as those offered by America Online and CompuServe as well as the NNTP-based newsreaders such as WinVN, are also lacking in certain key features. The most powerful newsreaders, full-featured UNIX programs such as trn and nn, are far from easy to learn. Some programs come close to offering a compromise—tin (see Chapter 10, "Reading the news with tin") is a good example—but the USENET world is still waiting for its "killer application."

A GUIDE TO PART II OF THIS BOOK

The purpose of Part II, "Reading the news," is to help you master newsreader software. The following chapters teach you how to get the most out of the nine most popular newsreaders for USENET access. Chapters 7 through 9 explore the newsreading capabilities of the top three on-line services that provide USENET access:

- **America Online** (Chapter 7). AOL's newsreader software is easy to use, as you'll see, but it omits crucial features.

- **Delphi** (Chapter 8). Delphi's newsreader is good for reading the news, but clunky for posting your own articles. But it's cheap, and if you like you can use the full-featured nn newsread (for details on using nn with Delphi, see Chapter 11).

- **CompuServe** (Chapter 9). CompuServe's USENET access offers most of the features you'll want, but the service is pricey.

Chapters 10 through 12 cover the most popular UNIX newsreaders, which you're very likely to encounter if you're using dialup access:

- **tin** (Chapter 10). This is an easy-to-use program that also has lots of powerful features—a great choice.

- **nn** (Chapter 11). A hacker's program, and tolerable once you're used to its idiosyncracies, but best avoided if you're new to USENET and to Unix.

- **rn and trn** (Chapter 12). The older version, rn, can't be recommended with much enthusiasm, but the new one—trn—is outstanding.

Chapters 13 and 14 cover the most popular newsreaders for users who access USENET through local area networks (LANs) or dialup IP:

- **Trumpet for Windows** (Chapter 13). The leading Microsoft Windows newsreader.

- **Newswatcher** (Chapter 14). The leading Macintosh newsreader.

Note that Chapter 2, "A quick USENET tour," covers WinVN, another popular Windows newsreader. If you've chosen WinVN—not a bad choice, incidentally—you can use this chapter as a guide to learning the program.

You should read this chapter before going on to the coverage of your newsreader elsewhere in Part II; it introduces fundamental concepts of newsreader usage.

WHAT IF MY NEWSREADER ISN'T COVERED HERE?

Read on, read on. The purpose of this chapter is partly to help you evaluate the strengths and weaknesses of any newsreader, including the ones this book covers and any other newsreader you're likely to encounter. So be sure to read this chapter so that you can judge the quality of newsreaders other than the ones I've covered. A second purpose of this chapter is to help you learn any newsreader that's not documented here. For specifics on learning a newsreader, see the section titled "Learning an undocumented newsreader," later in this chapter.

WHAT'S ".NEWSRC"?

Sooner or later, you'll run across a reference to something called *.newsrc* (it's a file that keeps a record of your subscribed and unsubscribed newsgroups).

IS THERE A "DREAM" NEWSREADER?

No. Not yet, anyway.

A "dream" newsreader would provide powerful tools to help you fully participate in USENET. It would organize information on-screen in an easy-to-understand way, provide convenient procedures for performing newsreading tasks, perform all the tasks that experienced net.people want to perform, and work in such an intuitively sensible way that you wouldn't *need* the documentation. All nine of the most popular newsreaders, the ones covered in this book, fall down in one or more of these departments.

In UNIX systems, .newsrc is stored in your home directory. On other systems, .newsrc—or its equivalent—is also stored in your personal area. It's *your* file: It contains a record of the newsgroups to which you've subscribed, and even which articles you've read.

TIP: Can someone tell which newsgroups you're reading? You bet. All they have to do is access your .newsrc file—and on UNIX systems, that's pretty easy to do. If you're concerned that someone might make untoward use of your newsgroup preferences, don't use dialup access; read the news with an NNTP newsreader and dialup IP (see Chapter 3, "Connecting to USENET"). With this combination, your .newsrc file is stored on your own computer, where it's relatively secure (as long as you keep your room locked—or your computer secured—when you're not around).

The cruder UNIX newsreaders require you to edit .newsrc directly—it's the only way you can subscribe or unsubscribe to newsgroups. If you're instructed to do this, open the file with the system's default text editor, usually vi. Note that this procedure isn't necessary with most newsreaders.

To open .newsrc with vi, type the following:

```
vi .newsrc
```

To type an unsubscribed newsgroup's name, use an exclamation mark after the name:

```
rec.arts.sf.reviews!
```

To subscribe to a newsgroup, delete the exclamation mark and type a colon:

```
rec.arts.sf.reviews:
```

With vi, you do this by positioning the cursor on the exclamation point and typing the following:

```
r:
```

Now save the file. With vi, you do this by typing **ZZ**.

New and bogus newsgroups

Your .newsrc file (or its equivalent for non-UNIX systems) isn't the same thing as the list of current newsgroups maintained by your site's server. When you start your newsreader, the program checks for discrepancies between .newsrc and the current (correct) newsgroup list. There are two possible kinds of discrepancies:

- **New newsgroups.** If new newsgroups have been created since you last logged on, the newsreader will prompt you to determine whether you want to add the newsgroups to your subscription list.

- **Bogus newsgroups.** If the newsreader determines that there's a newsgroup listed in your .newsrc file that's *not* listed in the current (correct) newsgroup list, you'll be informed that your .newsrc file contains a *bogus newsgroup* (a newsgroup that has been determined to be invalid for some reason). For example, it may have been created in violation of the voting procedures or its

name may contain a misspelling that's been corrected. If you're asked whether you want to delete bogus newsgroups, by all means do so.

Understanding newsreader levels

As explained in Chapter 2, "A quick USENET tour" (see the section titled "About newsreader levels"), all newsreaders are designed to fit the procedures of reading the news, and that means they have distinct *levels* (modes of operation). Here's a quick review of the levels you'll find in a full-featured newsreader:

- **Newsgroup selector.** At this level, you can subscribe to newsgroups to create your *subscription list* (the list of newsgroups that you want to read regularly). You'll find out about any new newsgroups that have been created since you last logged on, and you'll have an opportunity to subscribe to one or more of them. This level also provides tools that help you choose the particular newsgroup you want to read right now. You can also unsubscribe to groups you've found uninteresting. In some newsreaders, you can post articles at this level.

- **Thread selector.** At this level, you see a newsgroup's current articles. Ideally, they're grouped by threads (subjects) so you can "follow the thread" of the discussion. Some newsreaders let you sort the articles in other ways, such as by author, by date, or by article title. The worst newsreaders just show you the list of articles in the order they came into the server (ugh!). At this level, you can choose which articles you want to read.

- **Article selector.** At this level, you see the article or articles that you've chosen to read. You can page through the article and, when you're finished, mark the article as read and move on to the next one, reply to the article or post an article on a new subject, forward the article to someone, save the article, or print the article. Some newsreaders give you tools to search the text of lengthy articles.

As you read the news, you move down and up the levels—for example, when you're done reading an article, you go back to the article selector, choose a different article, and return to the pager. When you're done with a newsgroup, you go back to the newsgroup selector to choose a different newsgroup or to log off.

That's the basic structure of a newsreader. Every newsreader surveyed in this book has this structure, and any newsreader not covered here is very likely to have it too. The structure's dictated by the nature of newsreading tasks.

WHAT TO LOOK FOR IN A NEWSREADER

Newsreaders vary widely in quality, and even the best newsreaders, at this writing, have their drawbacks. The worst ones are all but unusable, at least for sustained, in-depth USENET involvement.

Most newsreaders do an acceptable job of performing the basic tasks described in the preceding section, "Understanding newsreader levels." Yet most fall down in the thread-selecting and article-viewing levels, discussed in the following sections. If you've a choice in your newsreading software, keep the following checklists in mind when you're examining your options.

At the newsgroup selector level

A good newsreader gives you easy-to-use tools for managing your subscription list and subscribing to newsgroups.

- **Subscription list management.** You should be able to view the list of newsgroups to which you've subscribed and organize it to your liking. It should be easy to navigate the list—you shouldn't have to remember bizarre or arcane keyboard commands. Windows, Mac, CompuServe, and America Online do the best job here, which isn't surprising, considering that they offer *graphical user interfaces (GUI)*. A GUI is a user-friendly design for program control that lets you choose most operations with a mouse by pointing at

on-screen pictures or choosing items from menus. If you plan to subscribe to lots of newsgroups and to change your subscription list often, you'll appreciate good performance here.

- **Subscribe to newsgroups by pattern.** Suppose you're interested in subscribing to all the newsgroups that mention "mail" in their names. With a newsreader that offers this feature, you can do so easily. This is a nice feature to have, but you can still subscribe to the same newsgroups manually if the newsreader you're using lacks this feature.

- **Virtual newsgroups.** An advanced newsreader feature is the ability to concatenate (join) two or more related newsgroups (for example, comp.mail.multimedia and comp.mail.mime, which both pertain to multimedia electronic mail). After concatenation, the newsgroups appear as if they were just one (larger) newsgroup. This is an attractive feature if your interests demand that you read all the USENET postings pertaining to a particular subject.

At the thread selector level

When you've chosen a newsgroup to read, your newsreader should quickly display a list of the current articles, sorted by thread. If possible, avoid unthreaded newsreaders, such as rn and most of the readers you'll find running on bulletin board systems (BBSs), unless they can at least group articles by subject. You should be able to navigate this list easily as you choose articles to read. Look for the following:

- **Quick response.** The best newsreaders, such as trn, use a built-in database of indexed articles, so the article list appears very quickly. Otherwise, you'll have to wait while the newsreader compiles its own index; for a lengthy article list, this can take as much as a minute. **Note:** If you're using dialup IP, you'll have to put up with slow response because the article headers must be downloaded from the NNTP server.

- **True threads.** A newsreader that groups articles by threads doesn't just sort the articles by subject. It actually detects which articles are in response to which other ones, so you can navigate the thread of the discussion with ease.

- **Sorting options.** It's nice to be able to sort the article list in various ways—by date of submission, author, alphabetical order by title, or grouped by subject, in addition to thread sorting.

- **Selecting more than one article at a time.** It's very convenient to be able to select two or more threads and then switch to the article selector to read just these threads (and no others).

- **Decoding of multi-part binary files.** If you plan to access binary files (such as graphics or software) through USENET, this feature is all but indispensable. To distribute a binary file via the Internet, it must coded by the uuencode utility, which transforms all the file's binary information into the coded ASCII characters that the Internet can convey. Because there are article length limitations on many systems, these files must then be broken down into two or more articles, which are named in a way that shows the sequence and the total

number of articles (for example, 1/3, 2/3, and 3/3). A newsreader that's equipped to decode multi-part files makes the decoding process a snap: You just select the files and choose the command.

At the article selector level

A good newsreader displays the current article and gives you easy-to-use tools for reading it. If the article turns out to be uninteresting, you should be able to mark the article as read before you reach the end; you should also be able to forward it, reply to it, save it, or print it. These are the basic features; here are some desirable things to look for.

- **rot-13 encryption and decryption.** Rot-13 is a simple encryption technique that moves each letter down the alphabet 13 spaces. It's used to encrypt text that might be offensive or unsuitable

for younger readers. To read rot-13 text, you need a newsreader that's capable of decrypting the ciphertext.

- **Search for text within an article.** If you're reading a lengthy article such as a FAQ, it's very convenient to be able to search forward and backward for text that matches a pattern you specify.

- **Easy to use, built-in text editor for your posts.** You shouldn't have to memorize complicated commands or procedures to write, edit, and send a reply or a new post. The cruder UNIX newsreaders (rn and nn) dump you into the system's default text editor such as vi, which is difficult to use and cumbersome to learn.

- **Automatic quoting when you reply to an article.** This is a very helpful feature; it automatically copies the text of an article and puts in the attribution, or source, of the article as well as the quotation markers (the colons or greater-than signs that indicate that you're quoting someone's text).

- **Crossposting.** It's a violation of network etiquette (see Chapter 15, "Working with a virtual community") to crosspost to inappropriate groups—but it's also a violation, if considerably less severe, to *fail* to crosspost when doing so makes sense. On-line service newsreaders disable crossposting in an effort to prevent net.abuses such as *spamming* (posting irrelevant articles to dozens or even hundreds of newsgroups). You can get around this limitation by posting the same message manually to two or more newsgroups, but this wastes network bandwidth: It's more economical (in terms of disk storage and transmission bandwidth) to store and relay a crossposted message than to post two or more copies of the same message. In addition, a good newsreader will stop displaying a properly crossposted article once it has been read in one newsgroup. A manually crossposted article still appears in other groups even though it has been read in one—and that brings out the net.police.

- **Header editing.** You should be able to edit the header. If you can't, you won't be able to control where your follow-up posts go, and you could find yourself getting flamed for not crossposting to the right groups or using the follow-up line incorrectly (see Chapter 16, "Posting your own messages").

- **Kill capabilities.** Many newsreaders omit this feature, but I wouldn't use USENET without it: You can exclude ("kill") unwanted articles by subject, by author, and by site of origin. You'll enjoy USENET much more when you've prevented the juvenile jerks from showing up in your article lists. The best newsreaders let you set up a *global kill* (a setting that works in all the newsgroups).

LEARNING AN UNDOCUMENTED NEWSREADER

Once you understand the way newsreaders work, it's easy to learn a new one—even if there's no documentation (or it's written in TechSpeak, which is just as bad). You know that the program must distinguish between the newsgroup, thread, and article selector levels—unless it's missing one or more of these features (in which case you'd be wise to avoid it). You know which tasks the newsreader ought to perform. It's just a matter of finding out how this particular newsreader performs these tasks.

To help you learn an undocumented newsreader, I've included the following form, which you can fill out for your own use. Use the on-line help and what documentation is available to make your own newsreader "cheat sheet." Note that your newsreader may not have all of the features listed here.

SUMMARY

No single newsreader dominates the market; there are dozens in existence. If you're using dialup access, chances are you'll be stuck with whatever newsreader the service offers; a few service providers let you choose. If you're using network access or dialup IP, you can choose your own newsreader. Choose one that has the features you want.

The remaining chapers in Part II survey the nine most popular newsreaders. If your newsreader isn't included, you can use the "cheat sheets" in this chapter to help you learn how to use it.

Your newsreader uses a file to keep track of your subscription list. If there's a discrepancy between this file and your server's current newsgroup list, you'll be asked whether you want to subscribe to new groups or delete bogus newsgroups.

When you evaluate a newsreader, find out if it allows crossposting, header editing, and kill files; these are very desirable features if you want to make full use of USENET.

If you want to read all the newsgroups on a subject, look for a reader that can construct a virtual newsgroup from two or more newsgroups pertaining to the same topic.

If you want to decode multi-part binary files, look for a reader that can automatically extract this information to a binary file.

FROM HERE

- If you're still in the dark about how to connect to USENET, see Chapter 3, "Connecting to USENET."

- If your newsreader is among those documented in Part II, flip to its chapter to learn how to use your software. If you're using WinVN, take a look at Chapter 2, "A quick USENET tour."

- If you've already learned how to use your newsreader at a basic level and you're anxious to post your first article, flip to Part III, "Now it's your turn."

NAVIGATION BASICS

TO ACCOMPLISH THIS:	DO THE FOLLOWING:
Start the program	
View on-screen help	
Move the cursor or highlight down one line	
Move the cursor or highlight up one line	
Display the next screen down	
Display the next screen up	
Quit the program	

SUBSCRIPTION SELECTOR

TO ACCOMPLISH THIS:	DO THE FOLLOWING:
View list of new newsgroups (newsgroups added to server's list since you last logged on)	
View list of subscribed newsgroups	

SUBSCRIPTION SELECTOR (CONTINUED)

TO ACCOMPLISH THIS:	DO THE FOLLOWING:
Go to a newsgroup by typing its name	
Search for a newsgroup by typing part of its name	
Search for all the newsgroups that match a text pattern you type	
Display all the unsubscribed groups	
Unsubscribe to uninteresting groups	
Change the order of groups in the subscription list	
Mark the currently selected newsgroup as read	
Select a newsgroup to read and go to the thread selector	

THREAD SELECTOR LEVEL

TO ACCOMPLISH THIS:	DO THE FOLLOWING:
Change the sort order of the article list	

THREAD SELECTOR LEVEL (CONTINUED)

TO ACCOMPLISH THIS:	DO THE FOLLOWING:
Search forward for an author matching a pattern you specify	
Search forward for a subject matching a pattern you specify	
Mark a thread as read so that it doesn't appear in the article list again	
Extract (uudecode) the binary information in a multi-part file	
Choose a thread to read and move down to the article selector	
Go back up to the newsgroup selector	

ARTICLE SELECTOR LEVEL

TO ACCOMPLISH THIS:	DO THE FOLLOWING:
Display the next page of the article	
Redisplay the article's first page	

ARTICLE SELECTOR LEVEL (CONTINUED)

TO ACCOMPLISH THIS:	DO THE FOLLOWING:
Mark the article as read even though you haven't finished reading it, and display the next article	
Kill this subject in this newsgroup	
Kill this author in this newsgroup	
Kill this subject in all newsgroups (global kill)	
Kill this author in all newsgroups (global kill)	
Search the article for text matching a pattern you specify	
Print the article	
Forward the article to an email address you specify	
Save the article to a file	
Extract (uudecode) the binary information in an article	

ARTICLE SELECTOR LEVEL (CONTINUED)

TO ACCOMPLISH THIS:	DO THE FOLLOWING:
Display the next article in the thread	
Display the previous article in the thread	
Display the first article in the next thread	
Reply to the article via email	
Reply to the article via a follow-up post	
Post an article on a new subject	
Move up to the thread selector	

America Online (AOL), an on-line information service, offers dialup access to a central computing facility, located in Vienna, VA, where you commingle with about one million other AOL subscribers. Focusing on home personal computer users, AOL offers the usual on-line mix of news, sports, weather, stock quotes, on-line vendor support, and downloadable files. What's of interest here, though, is the fact that AOL offers easy-to-use, inexpensive access to USENET. In the absence of other alternatives, it's a good place to start your exploration of the USENET community.

I can almost see the flames arriving in my mailbox. OK, netters, I admit that AOL's USENET software has significant shortcomings—for instance, it doesn't include any facilities for including quoted text in follow-up postings; if you want to include such text, you must do so by manually cutting and pasting. Worse, you can't crosspost: Your postings go to the group you're reading, and that's that. In addition, AOL has been slow to implement high-speed service; in many areas, you're restricted to 2400 bps. Most damning of all are AOL's length limitations; you're limited to postings of about five single-spaced pages, and there's also a limit, if less severe, on incoming messages—if a post is lengthy, you may find, maddeningly, that it has been truncated. Still, AOL's ease of use makes it a reasonable choice for anyone who's just getting started with USENET, and that's especially true if you're new to computers as well. If your needs don't go beyond exchanging short text messages with other net.people on a few newsgroups, AOL isn't a bad choice. Just be sure you're aware of the service's limitations, and learn how to work around them.

As you're reading this chapter, bear in mind that AOL's USENET software is still evolving; the company plans to add new features, which may well be in place by the time you read this book. (One of them, according to an AOL on-line notice, is quotation capabilities, and there's talk of adding signatures, as

IT'S THE SOFTWARE

What makes AOL so easy to use? The secret's in the software. To subscribe to AOL, you need a copy of the AOL disk, which is available in Windows, DOS, and Macintosh versions. (To get a copy of the disk, call 1-800-827-6364.) After you install the software on your computer, you use this software to call AOL (in most cities, there's a toll-free local access number). On-screen, you'll see pull-down menus, dialog boxes, icons, and help screens just like the ones in your other applications. Even though AOL doesn't (at this writing) support 14.4 Kbps access, the service seems faster than it is. That's because much of the information, such as the dialog boxes and menus, loads almost instantaneously from your computer's hard disk.

well.) I'm assuming you've installed AOL's software and opened your AOL account; go straight to AOL's Internet Center, where you'll find the USENET options. This chapter teaches the fundamentals of AOL's Microsoft Windows software, but the DOS and Macintosh versions are virtually identical.

ACCESSING THE INTERNET CENTER

You're logged on to AOL and ready to go; ignore the news (bad) and stocks (worse), and head straight for USENET. From the Go To menu, choose Keyword (or just use the Ctrl + K shortcut). You'll see the Go To Keyword dialog box. Type **Internet**, and click OK (or press Enter). You'll see the Internet Center window, shown in Figure 7-1.

If you've used AOL for a while, you're already familiar with its easy, point-and-click icons (pictures of computer resources). The Newsgroups icon depicts a globe with a pushpin-affixed note (global bulletin board, get it?)—although, if you're a bit nearsighted like me, you could mistake the icon for a bomb with a threatening letter attached.

Leaving aside the Internet Center's Internet options, such as WAIS, click the Newsgroups icon. AOL displays the Newsgroups window, shown in Figure 7-2. In the list, you can choose documents that explain how AOL's newsreader software works. The icons provide access to the basic newsreader functions, which

the following pages survey in detail. Table 7-1 summarizes AOL's keyboard shortcuts.

SUBSCRIBING AND UNSUBSCRIBING TO NEWSGROUPS

Like all newsreaders, AOL's software lets you create and maintain a subscription list. This list contains the names of the newsgroups you want to read regularly. To get you started, AOL sets up a "newbie" subscription list that includes several newsgroups from the news.* hierarchy (including news.announce.newusers, a good place to start). You can subscribe to additional newsgroups by adding names to the list. And as you'll learn in this section, you can unsubscribe to unwanted groups by removing names. (After you've read news.announce.newusers, for example, you'll probably want to remove this newsgroup from your subscription list. The shorter the list, the easier it is to locate the group you want to read.)

You'll see your subscription list after you click the Read My Newsgroups icon, so give it a try. This window is shown in Figure 7-3. At the bottom of

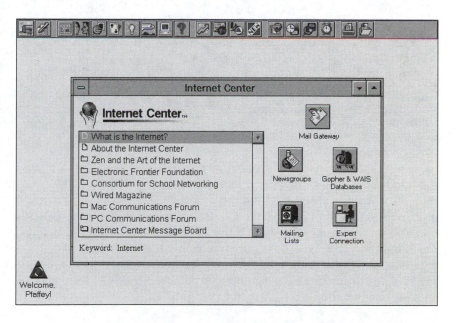

Figure 7-1. The Internet Center provides access to America Online's USENET software.

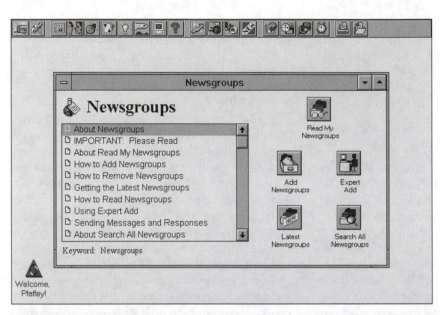

Figure 7-2. The Newsgroups window lets you choose general USENET information and basic newsreader functions.

TABLE 7-1. QUICK REFERENCE: AOL'S KEYBOARD SHORTCUTS

PRESS THIS KEY:	TO DO THIS:	PRESS THIS KEY:	TO DO THIS:
Ctrl + F4	Close a window	Control + M	Open Mail window
Ctrl+ C	Copy	Control + V	Paste
Ctrl + X	Cut	Control + S	Print a message
Shift + Tab	Move to previous button	Control + S	Save a message
Tab	Move to next button	Page Up	Scroll up a page
Control + F6	Next window	Page Down	Scroll down a page
Control + K	Open Keyword window	Esc	Stop incoming text

the window are two buttons that let you display subjects (threads), a Remove button that lets you unsubscribe to a newsgroup, and a More button that lets you see additional entries. If the More button is dimmed, as it is in this figure, there are no more entries. To the right are icons; one lets you mark all the articles in a newsgroup as read, and another provides the USENET (dotted) versions of

AOL's newsgroup names. The question mark displays a window of helpful information.

For now, close the Read My Newsgroups window (to do so, just click the Control menu icon—the dash—in the window's upper-left corner). You'll see the Newsgroups window again. This window's icons give you four ways to subscribe to newsgroups:

Figure 7-3. The Read My Newsgroups window shows the newsgroups to which you're currently subscribed.

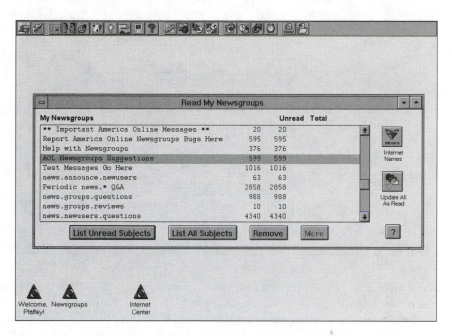

• **Add Newsgroups icon.** AOL groups the newsgroups by categories, allowing you to explore the list using windows. After you've displayed and selected the name of the group you want to add, you click the Add button to add it to your subscription list.

• **Expert Add icon.** If you already know the dotted name (such as alt.folk-lore.urban) of the newsgroup you want to add, this is by far the easiest way to add a newsgroup to your subscription list.

• **Search All Newsgroups icon.** This icon displays a search window, which lets you type words that AOL tries to match in its list of newsgroup names. For example, if you type "back-country," AOL will find rec.backcountry, and you can add this group to your list by clicking the Add button.

• **Latest Newsgroups icon.** This icon displays a list of the new groups that AOL has named using its "English" translations of dotted names. If you wish, you can select and add one or more of the new newsgroups.

Subscribing to newsgroups with the Add Newsgroups icon

I'm sure you've developed a list of the newsgroups you'd like to read, so here's your chance to subscribe. In the Newsgroups window, click the Add Newsgroups icon. (If you can't see the Newsgroups window, click the minimize button in the Read My Newsgroups window.) You'll see the Add Newsgroups window, shown in Figure 7-4.

In just one little window, you can see only a few names—the Alternative Newsgroups (alt.*), the BITNET mailing lists echoed in the bit hierarchy,

---

AMERICA ONLINE'S "FRIENDLY" VERSION OF USENET NAMES

How do you make USENET warmer, friend-lier, more cuddly? Apparently, America Online's designers felt that the dot-based USENET names ought to go. In place of aol.messages.test, for instance, you'll see a group called "Test messages go here." The renaming isn't done consistently, though; news.announce.newusers is still news.announce.newusers. Don't like the AOL "translations" of net.names? Just click the Internet Names icon. You'll see a window showing the net.name for each of AOL's monikers.

69

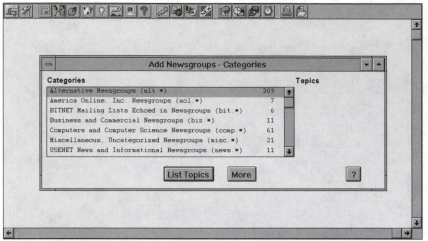

Figure 7-4. The Add Newsgroups window lets you subscribe to newsgroups.

Among the local newsgroups are hierarchies from dozens of colleges and universities, towns and cities, corporations and networks. Table 7.2 provides a representative sampling. Note that the number of topics for each hierarchy doesn't represent the number of newsgroups available; AOL further groups the newsgroups within these categories, as you'll see shortly.

and a few more. To save on-line time, AOL doesn't download a lengthy list unless you click the More button. If you keep clicking More until it's dimmed, indicating that there isn't any more data to download, you'll have an impressive list indeed—a list of more than 100 newsgroup categories, drawn not only from the *world newsgroups* and the *alternative newsgroups* but also from dozens of *local newsgroups*—it's a truly interesting smorgasbord.

Now add an "Alternative newsgroup," as AOL puts it. To display the list of alt.* newsgroups, you can select the Alternative newsgroup option and click List Topics, or you can just double-click the option. After doing so, you see the Alternative Newsgroups (alt.*)—Topics window, shown in Figure 7-5. This window, the newsgroup selector window, lists newsgroups and groups of newsgroups.

To add a specific newsgroup, we'll need to tunnel down a bit deeper into AOL's windows. In the Alternative Newsgroups (alt.*)—Topics window, click the down arrow until you see the Automobile newsgroups (alt.auto.*) option. Then click the List

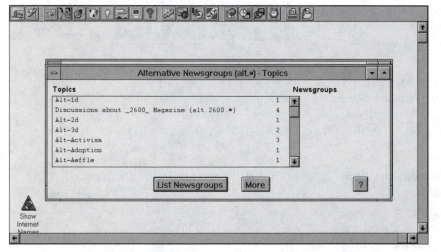

Figure 7-5. The newsgroup selector window lists America Online's alt* newsgroup categories.

Table 7-2. Selected America Online newsgroup hierarchies

HIERARCHY NAME	NUMBER OF TOPICS
Alternative newsgroups (alt.*)	389
Austin, TX newsgroups (austin.*)	13
Biology-related newsgroups (bionet.*)	28
Boston Computer Society newsgroups (bcs.*)	8
Business and commercial newsgroups (biz.*)	11
California newsgroups (ca.*)	45
Chicago, Il newsgroups (chi.*)	31
Computers and computer science newsgroups (comp.*)	61
Denmark newsgroups (dk.*)	8
E-mail systems and related newsgroups (mail.*)	22
FidoNet-echoed newsgroups (fido.*)	34
Florida newsgroups (fl.*)	14
HEPnet newsgroups (hepnet.*)	10
HIV-issues newsgroups (hiv.*)	17
Mailing lists echoed to USENET (list.*)	32
NASA newsgroups (nasa.*)	1
New York University newsgroups (nyu.*)	18
Recreational and hobby newsgroups (rec.*)	55
Science and research newsgroups (sci.*)	45
Social issues and socializing newsgroups (soc.*)	19
Talk/debate and issues newsgroups (talk.*)	10
University of California newsgroups (uc.*)	39

*America Online, July 1994

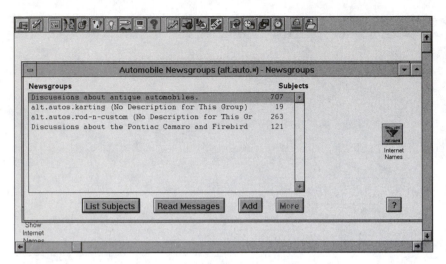

Figure 7-6. This window shows the alt.auto.* newsgroups.

see in Figure 7-7, the newsgroup names are shown in parentheses.

Now subscribe to alt.autos.antique. To do so, highlight this item and click the Add button. You'll see a dialog box asking you whether you want to add "Discussions about antique automobiles" to your subscription list. Just click OK. In a moment,

Newsgroups button to see the newsgroups that AOL has grouped under this category. They're shown in Figure 7-6.

AOL's user-friendly newsgroup names may leave you wondering just which newsgroup they're talking about. If you would like to see the real USENET name of the group, you can do so by clicking the Internet names button. Doing so produces the Show Internet Names window, which lists the names of the groups shown in the current window; as you can

you'll see an information box informing you that your request has been accepted.

Note that you can read newsgroups without subscribing to them; the window shown in Figure 7-7 includes a Read Messages button. To get an idea what the newsgroup's like before subscribing, skip to the section titled "Reading Articles," later in this chapter. Note, however, that you can't post new messages to the group or create follow-up postings; you can do that only after you've subscribed.

To see your subscription list again, close all those windows until you can see the Newsgroups window again, and click Read My Newsgroups. (I'm assuming you know the basic Windows commands, but here's a reminder: To close a window quickly, just click the window's Control menu icon—the big dash

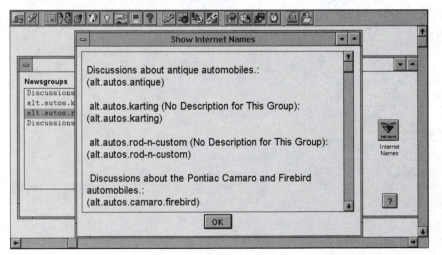

Figure 7-7. The Show Internet Names window lets you see the newsgroups' real USENET names.

Figure 7-8. After you subscribe to a newsgroup, you see the newsgroup's name in the Read My Newsgroups window.

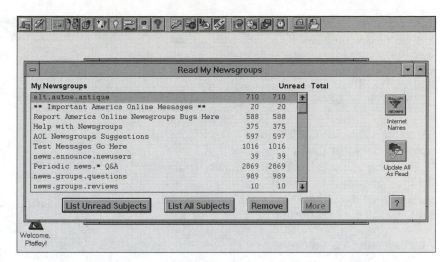

in the box located in the window's upper-left corner.) As you can see in Figure 7-8, the Read My Newsgroups window now contains the name of the newsgroup to which you've just subscribed.

Subscribing to newsgroups with Expert Add

If you know the name of the newsgroup you want to join, don't fuss with AOL's subject categories and windows: Use Expert Add instead. To use Expert Add, display the Newsgroups window and click the Expert Add icon. You'll see a dialog box asking you to type the name of the newsgroup to which you'd like to subscribe. Click OK, and you'll see a confirmation message; click OK again, and you'll see a message confirming that the group has been added to your subscription list. If you typed the name wrong, or if AOL doesn't get a feed for that group, you'll see an alert box informing you that the name isn't valid.

Searching for newsgroups

If you can't find the newsgroup you're looking for, AOL includes a feature

Figure 7-9. To search for newsgroups, type one or more groups separated by the OR, AND, or NOT operators.

(called Search All Newsgroups) that matches words you type to the newsgroup's USENET names (but not AOL's "English" translations). To search for newsgroups, click the Search All Newsgroups icon. You'll see the Search Newsgroup Titles window shown in Figure 7-9.

In the Search Newsgroup Titles window, you can type one or more words separated by *logical operators* (AND, OR, and NOT), which indicate the breadth of narrowness of the search. If you type

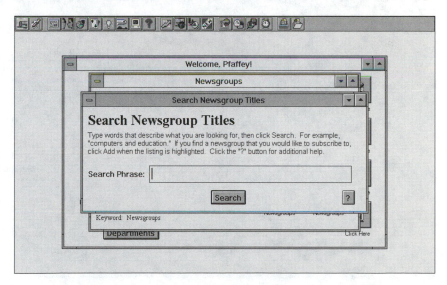

"Mac and binaries," you'll retrieve only those news-groups in which both "Mac" and "binaries" appear in the newsgroup's name (such as comp.binaries.mac). An AND search is restrictive. If you type "Mac or binaries," you'll get a very much longer list of every newsgroup that includes either "Mac" or "binaries." If you type "binaries not Mac," you'll get a list of the newsgroups that include "binaries" in their names, except the ones that also include "Mac."

The result of a search is a Search Results window, like the one shown in Figure 7-10. To add one or more of the newsgroups to your subscription list, just highlight the newsgroup name and click Add.

Unsubscribing to newsgroups

Unsubscribing to newsgroups is a lot less compli-cated than subscribing—there's only one window involved, the Read My Newsgroups window. To unsubscribe to any of the newsgroups in the win-dow, just select it and click the Remove button. You'll see a dialog box asking you to confirm this, and another informing you that the deletion has been accepted. The newsgroup to which you've unsubscribed no longer appears in the list.

VIEWING SUBJECTS

America Online's USENET newsreading software is threaded, meaning that articles are grouped by subject. To view subjects, display the Read My Newsgroups window, and select the newsgroup you want to read. Then click List Unread Subjects. (To re-read articles you've already read, click List All Subjects.) You'll see a subject selector window such as the one shown in Figure 7-11, which lists the subjects and the number of articles for each one. Remember, if the More button is available, you can display additional articles by clicking it.

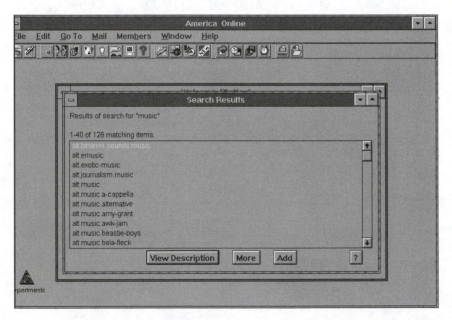

Figure 7-10. This window shows the names of all the newsgroups that match your search request.

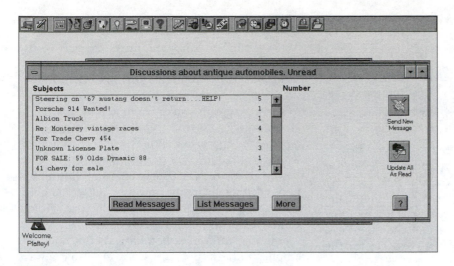

Figure 7-11. The subject selector window shows the articles grouped by subject.

READING ARTICLES

Once you've displayed the subject list, you can do two things: Display a list of the articles within a subject, or go directly to the articles and read them.

If you've selected a subject with more than one article, you can see a list of the articles within a subject by clicking the List Message button; the next window lists the email address of each article's author and the time of the article's creation. But this information isn't of much value, unless you're looking for articles by a specific person.

Normally, the best way to start reading is to skip the message list. Just select the subject you want to read, and click Read Messages. You'll see the article selector window, titled with the name of the

Figure 7-12. When you read a message with the article selector, the window's title reflects the name of the subject you're reading.

subject you're reading, as shown in Figure 7-12.

At the bottom of the article selector window, you'll see the following buttons:

- **Previous.** Click here to see the previous article in the subject. If you're now reading the first article in the subject, clicking this button will display the last article in the previous subject.

- **More.** If this button is available (not dimmed), click here to see more of the current article's text.

- **Send Response.** Click here to create a follow-up posting (see "Posting a follow-up message," later in this chapter).

- **Next.** Click here to see the next article in the subject. If you're now reading the last article in the

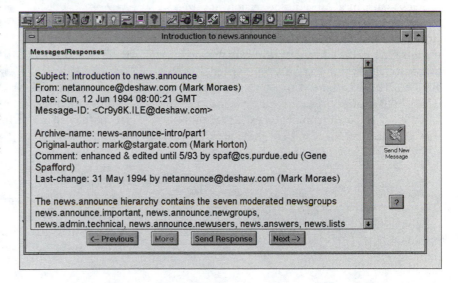

75

subject, clicking this button will display the first article in the next subject.

> **TIP:** If you've selected a lengthy article that turns out to be uninteresting, you can stop the flow of incoming text by pressing Esc.

When you've finished reading articles in this subject and adjacent ones, you may wish to view the subject selector window again. To do so, just close the window in which you've been reading the articles. You'll see the subject selector window again. Choose a new subject, and click the Read Messages button; you'll see the messages for the subject you've selected.

> **TIP:** If the article's lines don't fit within the window, make the window bigger by dragging the right border.

MARKING ARTICLES AS READ

You probably won't read all the articles posted to a newsgroup. Unless you would like to see these articles again in a subsequent session, it's a good idea to mark them all as read. Having done so, you won't have to scroll through all those subjects again using AOL's clunky More button, which—at 2400 bps—downloads subjects at a glacial pace. To mark all the articles in a newsgroup as read, open the newsgroup's subject selector window, and click the Update All As Read icon. The next time you open this newsgroup, you won't see these articles when you click the List Unread Subjects button.

> **TIP:** Want to read an article that you've actually read or marked as read? In the subject selector window, click the List All Subjects button.

NO CROSSPOSTINGS, PLEASE

AOL's USENET software provides easy-to-use tools for posting new messages and follow-up messages. But this software has one important limitation: You can't crosspost. Your message always goes to the newsgroup you're reading, and that newsgroup only. That's true even if you're replying to a crossposted message that lists several newsgroups within its header.

According to an AOL spokesperson, this limitation is deliberate: It's the only way AOL could guarantee that its subscribers would not violate USENET norms that forbid excessive crossposting, spamming, and carpet bombing. As this book has emphasized, though, crossposting isn't always bad—in fact, it's a violation of USENET norms to *fail* to crosspost when doing so makes sense. For example, readers of rec.aquaria might find your sci.aquaria posting of interest. What's more, crossposting a message consumes less bandwidth than posting separate messages to each group. A reasonable compromise, and one currently under consideration at AOL, is to permit subscribers to crosspost to as many as five groups. This feature may have been implemented by the time you read this book.

POSTING NEW MESSAGES

Before you post your own articles, please read Part III, "Now it's your turn," with care (especially Chapters 15 and 17). Under no circumstances you should post to USENET until you fully understand the fundamentals of network etiquette and the special characteristics of the newsgroup to which you want to post.

You can post new messages (as opposed to follow-up messages) at two different levels, at the subject selector level or the article selector level. At both levels, you'll see the same button, called Send New Message. To post a new message to a newsgroup, select the newsgroup in the Read My Newsgroups window, and display the subject or article selector.

Figure 7-13. In this window, you type a new posting.

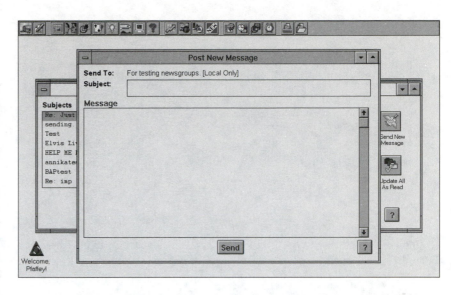

Then click Send New Message. You'll see the Post New Message window, shown in Figure 7-13.

This window has three areas:

- **Send To.** This area shows the name of the newsgroup to which this message will be posted. **Note:** At this writing, this area is not editable, making cross-posting impossible.

- **Subject.** Here, you type a short description of your message's subject.

- **Message.** In this area, you type your message.

To send your message, just click the Send button. To cancel the message without sending it, just close the window by clicking the Control menu icon (the dash in the upper-left corner of the window).

POSTING A FOLLOW-UP MESSAGE

To post a follow-up message, you must display the article to which you want to reply (see "Reading Articles," earlier in this chapter). Click the Send Response button, and you'll see the Post Response window shown in Figure 7-14.

Note that the AOL software has started a quotation for you. But it's up to you to add the text. Don't bother retyping it; this is Windows, after all, and you can use the Clipboard. To quote specific text from the article you were reading, activate the article selector window by clicking it or choosing it from the Window menu. Then select the text you want to quote, and use the Edit Copy command (or Ctrl + C) to copy it to the Clipboard. Now, activate the Post Response window again, and position the

insertion point where you want the quoted text to appear. Use the Edit Paste command (or Ctrl + P) to paste the text from the Clipboard (see Figure 7-15).

SAVE $$$ BY COMPOSING YOUR POSTINGS OFF-LINE

Rather than composing your message on-screen, create it before logging with your word processing program. Be sure to save the file as plain ASCII text. Now log on to America Online. When you've displayed the Post New Message window, click open the File menu and choose Open, or just use the Ctrl + O keyboard shortcut. In the Open dialog box, select your file, and click OK. AOL will open your file in a new window. In the Edit menu, choose Select All, or just use the Ctrl + A keyboard shortcut. From the Edit menu, choose Copy, or just press Ctrl + C. Now close this window, and position the insertion point within the Message area of the Post New Messages window. To insert your file into this window, click open the Edit menu and choose Paste, or just press Ctrl + V.

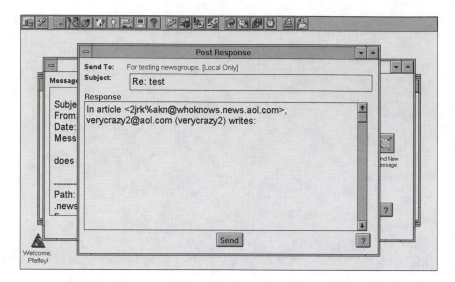

Figure 7-14. In this window, you type a follow-up posting.

ally, as shown in Figure 7-16. This is a serious shortcoming of the AOL software; a fix is reportedly in the works.

PRINTING AND SAVING MESSAGES

As explained in Chapter 2, "A quick USENET Tour," dialup access has many shortcomings; with most systems, it's very difficult to save or print your messages. Not so with AOL. Anything that's displayed in a text window—a message you're reading, or one you've written—can be saved or printed with ease. To print a message, click open the File menu and choose Print (or just use the Ctrl-P shortcut). To save a message, click open the File menu and choose the Save option (or just press Ctrl + S).

This Clipboard quoting technique isn't difficult to use. Compared to traditional newsreaders, though, it has one gigantic drawback: It violates the USENET customary practice of marking the quoted lines (usually with a greater-than sign) so readers can easily tell what's been quoted. Moreover, other newsreaders depend on these marks to indicate *cascaded quotations* (quotations of quotations). So, you'll have to type them manu-

SUMMARY

America Online's USENET software is exceptionally easy to use. Anyone who is new both to USENET and to computers should check out AOL; in no time at all, you'll be participating in USENET discussions. And compared to other methods of dialup access, AOL

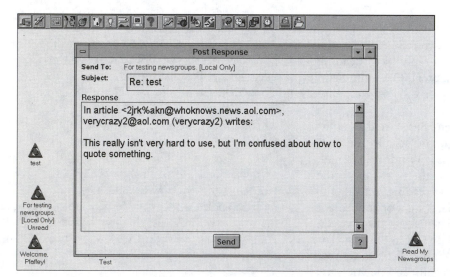

Figure 7-15. To quote an article's text, copy the text to the Clipboard and insert the text in the Post Response window.

Figure 7-16. Adding greater-than marks to indicate quoted material.

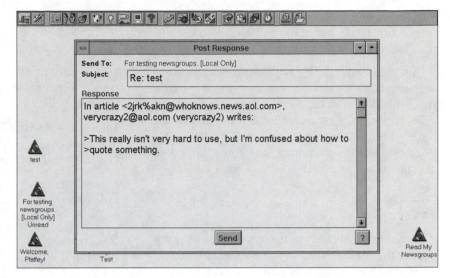

provides very convenient tools for saving and printing USENET postings. At this writing, though, AOL's user-friendliness comes at the price of features found in most other newsreaders. Here's a quick list of the more conspicuous omissions, just so you'll know what you're missing:

- **Crossposting.** As already mentioned, you can't crosspost with AOL's software (at least at this writing). The new or follow-up messages you post go to the current newsgroup, and no others.

- **Automatic quotation.** Most newsreaders give you the option of automatically adding the text of a posting to your follow-up posting; this text is clearly and correctly marked with greater-than signs (>).

- **Email reply by default.** Most newsreaders are preset to send your replies to the original poster via email, rather than posting them to the newsgroup. In addition, the software automatically inserts the original poster's email address.

- **Kill files.** There's no way you can kill unwanted threads so that they don't appear in the subject selector.

REPLY BY EMAIL? THERE'S NO BUTTON!

A serious shortcoming of AOL's USENET software is the lack of an email reply button. In AOL's (unfortunate) nomenclature, "reply" means "post a follow-up message"—and that's just what the Reply button does. According to experienced USENET readers, some AOL users seem to have been confused by this nomenclature, judging from the fact that they have publicly posted messages that were clearly intended as private email replies. If you want to send an email reply, you use AOL's standard mail capabilities. Here's how to avoid having to retype the poster's email address. In the postage message, select the poster's email address (you'll find it in the From line at the beginning of the messge), and copy it to the Clipboard. Then, click open the Mail menu and choose the Compose Mail option (or just press Ctrl + M). Position the insertion point in the address area, and paste the address from the Clipboard. You can then compose and send your message, which will go to the original poster only (and not to the newsgroup).

• **Extraction.** AOL provides no software for encoding or decoding binary files; you'll have to do this on your PC.

America Online's USENET capabilities, in sum, are adequate for somebody who wants to participate in USENET discussions, reading and posting brief messages. Computer hobbyists looking for binary files or researchers who deal with lengthy documents will soon look elsewhere for more capable newsreader software.

FROM HERE

• For an introduction to netiquette and working with the USENET community, see Chapter 15, "Working with a virtual community."

• For tips and pointers on writing for a USENET audience, see Chapter 16, "Posting your own messages."

• To make sure you've learned all you can about a newsgroup before you post, see Chapter 16, "Posting your own messages."

• To ensure that you don't make posting mistakes that could get you flamed, see Chapter 16, "Posting your own messages."

• For pointers on handling replies via email and follow-up postings, see Chapter 16, "Posting your own messages."

• Need help finding the right newsgroups? See Part IV, "Building your subscription list."

Delphi, one of the smallest on-line services, is also the first to offer a full suite of Internet services, including USENET access. Like other on-line services, Delphi offers a wide range of services, including the latest news, weather, and sports results, forums for users of specific computer systems and programs, on-line shopping, travel services, games, email, and more. Internet offerings include WAIS databases, FTP, Gopher, Internet Relay Chat (IRC), and all of the USENET newsgroups.

Delphi gives you a choice of newsreaders—you can use Delphi's own newsreading software (described in this chapter) or the full-featured nn newsreader (described in Chapter 11, "Reading the news with nn"). Because nn is the more difficult of the UNIX newsreaders to learn and use, you'd be wise to start with Delphi's software, and then move up to nn when you're ready to take advantage of its advanced features.

No matter which newsreader you choose, though, you'll find that Delphi has one serious disadvantage, compared to other ways to connect to USENET through dialup access: When the time comes to post your own messages or write replies, you're stuck with a *line editor* (a text-editing program that lets you work with only one line at a time). As you can imagine, a line editor isn't very convenient to work with. To edit a previous line of text, for example, you must use a command that makes that line accessible again, and you can make corrections—but only on that line. Still, people do get used to using line editors, and Delphi might be a good choice if you contemplate writing only short posts and replies.

DELPHI BASICS

Delphi uses a *menu-driven interface* (menus of selectable items appear on the screen). To select an item, you type its name (or number), and press Enter. You then see a submenu, with more options. To navigate Delphi, you'll go "down" into submenus, and then back up to the previous menu.

To use Delphi effectively, you need to master the keyboard commands that let you navigate the menus. Although there are menu equivalents for some of these, they take longer to type. Table 8-1 sums up the keyboard commands you'll use most frequently when navigating Delphi. In particular, remember Ctrl-Z; you'll use it often.

SELECTING THE USENET AREA

When you log on to Delphi, you type your user name and password, and you see Delphi's Main menu:

```
MAIN Menu:
Business and Finance  Mail
Computing Groups      Member Directory
Conference            News,Weather,and
Custom Forums           Sports
Entertainment and     Reference and
Games                   Education
Groups and Clubs      Shopping
Internet Services     Travel and Leisure
```

```
Using DELPHI          HELP
Workspace             EXIT
```

To access the Internet services area, type **Internet** and press Enter. (It's not necessary to type the whole phrase "Internet services.") You'll see the Internet Services title screen; just press Enter to continue, and you'll see the menu of Internet offerings, as shown here:

```
About the Internet    FTP-File Transfer
                      Protocol
Conference            Gopher
Databases (Files)     IRC-Internet
                      Relay Chat
EMail                 Telnet
Forum (Messages)      Utilities
                      (finger,
                      traceroute,
                      ping)
Guides (Books)        USENET Newsgroups
Register/Cancel
Who's Here            Help
Workspace             Exit
```

Internet SIG>Enter your selection:

To access USENET, type **USENET** and press Enter. You'll see the USENET menu, as shown here:

```
USENET Menu:

About USENET Discussion Groups
USENET (Delphi Newsreader)
NN Newsreader (USENET)
Instructions for the NN Newsreader
Exit
```

USENET>Enter your selection:

You should begin by accessing the option titled "About USENET Discussion Groups," which contains valuable information about USENET in general and Delphi's service in particular. Type **About** and press Enter. You'll see the following menu:

```
New User Topics and FAQS (NEW USERS,
START HERE!)
Page 1 of 1

1 HELP File for the DELPHI newsreader
  Text
2 READ BEFORE POSTING!!              Text
3 News Announce Newusers
  (news.announce.newusers)         USENET
4 Newusers Questions
  (news.newusers.questions)        USENET
5 FAQ—Frequently Asked
  Questions in Delphi Internet
  SIG                                Menu
```

TABLE 8-1. BASIC NAVIGATION COMMANDS (DELPHI)	
TO DO THIS:	PRESS THIS KEY:
Enter	Confirm the choice you've just typed
Ctrl + Z	Return to the previous menu
Ctrl + S	Pause the display
Ctrl + Q	Resume scrolling the display
Ctrl + C	Cancel and return to previous prompt
q	Quit viewing a lengthy document

```
6  ===FAQ FILES FROM USENET===        Text
7  NOTE: The items below are
   files from rtfm.mit.edu            Text
8  FAQ: What is USENET?               Text
9  FAQ: Answers to Frequently
   Asked Questions about USENET       Text
10 FAQ: A Primer on How to Work
   with the USENET Community          Text
11 FAQ: Rules for Posting to
   USENET                             Text
12 FAQ: Emily Postnews Answers
   Your Questions on Netiquette       Text
13 FAQ: Hints on Writing Style
   for USENET                         Text
14 FAQ: Welcome to
   news.newusers.questions!           Text

Enter Item Number, SAVE, ?, or BACK:
```

To select item 2, type **2** and press Enter. You'll see a document containing some excellent advice about posting articles; please read it carefully (and before you post, please read Part III of this book as well). To see an additional screenful of text, just press Enter. When you're finished viewing the document, press Ctrl + Z (or type **Back**) to return to the menu shown above.

Now press Ctrl + Z (or type **Back** again) to return to the USENET Main menu, and select USENET (Delphi newsreader). To do so, just type **USENET** and press Enter. You'll see the following menu:

```
USENET Discussion Groups
Page 1 of 3

1 PERSONAL FAVORITES               Menu
2 Access Any Newsgroup (by
  typing its name)                 USENET
3 DELPHI Newsreader Help           Text
4 READ BEFORE POSTING TO ANY
  NEWSGROUP!!!!                    Text
5 New User Topics and FAQS
  (NEW USERS, START HERE!)         Menu
6 How to Create Signature,
  Edit Personal Favorites         Text
7 How to Create New Newsgroups
  (FAQs)                          Menu
```

```
8  USENET FAQs (Frequently Asked
   Questions Files)                   Menu
9  USENET by Gopher (works better
   in Gopher GRAB BAG menu)           Menu
10 DELPHI Command Summary             Menu
11                                    Text
12 ===NEWSGROUP LISTS ===             Text
13 Search for (but not connect
   to) Newsgroups, Mailing Lists      Menu
14 Newsgroup Lists (Delphi lists:
   8/03/94, others: 08/01/94)         Menu
15                                    Text
16 ===SELECTED NEWSGROUPS===          Text
17 Best of Internet—DON'T POST!
   See FAQ (alt.best.of.internet) USENET
18 Comet Shoemaker-Levy 9
   (alt.sl9)                          USENET
19 Commercial Online Services
   (alt.online-service)               USENET

Enter Item Number, MORE, ?, or EXIT:
```

At this stage, you may want to see the list of newsgroups that Delphi makes available. See the following section for details.

VIEWING THE NEWSGROUP LIST

To view Delphi's newsgroup list, display the USENET Discussion Groups menu shown in the preceding illustration, if necessary. Then type **14** and press Enter. You'll see the Newsgroup lists menu, shown here:

```
Newsgroup Lists (Delphi lists: 8/03/94,
   others: 08/01/94)
Page 1 of 1

1 Delphi Newsgroups (alt. thru
  cle.) as of 8/03/94               Text
2 Delphi Newsgroups (comp. thru
  za.) as of 8/03/94                Text
3 List of New and Deleted
  Newsgroups This Week              Text
4 List of Active Newsgroups,
  Part I (comp, misc,news)         Text
```

```
5  List of Active Newsgroups,
   Part II (rec, sci, soc, talk)    Text
6  Alternative Newsgroup List,
   Part I (alt thru bit)            Text
7  Alternative Newsgroup List,
   Part II (clarinet thru vmsnet)   Text
8  Mailing Lists Available in
   USENET                           Text
9  List of Lists (Mailing Lists)    Menu
10 Bogus Newsgroups List
   (3/10/94)                        Text

Enter Item Number, SAVE, ?, or BACK:
```

The options of interest are 1, 2, and 3, which contain information about Delphi's newsgroups; the other options are USENET postings accessible in news.answers and news.lists. Type **1** and press Enter, and you'll see the following prompt:

```
Press ENTER to display, D to
Download, C to Cancel:
```

If you'd like to download the list to a file on your computer, type **D** and press Enter; you'll be asked to supply a file name and to choose a *file transfer protocol* (a method to ensure error-free transmission of the file to your computer). Your communications program probably recognizes all or most of the options, but Zmodem is the best for most purposes. If you'd prefer to view the file on-screen, just press Enter. You'll see a list such as the following:

```
Delphi Newsgroups (alt. thru cle.):
   8/03/94
=====================================
alt.0d
alt.1d
alt.2600
alt.2600.hope.announce
alt.2600.hope.d
alt.2600.hope.tech
alt.2d
alt.3d
alt.59.79.99
alt.abortion.inequity
alt.abuse-recovery
alt.abuse.offender.recovery
```

```
alt.abuse.recovery
alt.activism
alt.activism.d
alt.activism.death-penalty
alt.adoption
alt.aeffle.und.pferdle
alt.agriculture.fruit
More?
```

To see another page, just press Enter. If you don't want to continue, type **n** and press Enter (or just press Ctrl + C). You'll see the Newsgroups Lists menu again. To return to the USENET Discussion Groups menu, type **BACK** and press Enter (or just press Ctrl + Z).

SUBSCRIBING TO NEWSGROUPS

In Delphi, you subscribe to newsgroups by creating a "Personal Favorites" list. Initially, this list contains no newsgroups. To add newsgroups to this list, you must display the thread selector for the newsgroup, and use the SAVE command, as explained in the following sections. To access a newsgroup's thread selector, you can go to the newsgroup by typing its name, or you can search for a group.

Subscribing to a newsgroup by typing its name

To subscribe to a newsgroup by typing its name, display the USENET Discussion Groups menu, type 2 if necessary, and press Enter. You'll see the following prompt:

```
Please enter a USENET discussion
topic, such as alt.online-service.
Topic:
```

Type the newsgroup name, and press Enter. If you make a typing mistake, you'll see a message such as the following:

```
Unable to access "alt.cl1". It is
either spelled incorrectly or not
currently carried by Delphi.
```

If you made a spelling mistake, just repeat the entire procedure from the beginning.

Assuming you typed the name correctly and Delphi carries the group, you'll see a prompt such as the following:

```
45 messages have been posted in the
last 14 days; You've read none of them.
Select which messages: Unread, All,
Date or ?> [unread]
```

Just press Enter to see the thread selector, as in the following example:

```
alt.s19
Page 1 of 2 [45 messages in 22
discussion threads]
1  Add funniest comment by Carl
   Sagan... We MUST TAKE STEPS TO --
   (11 msgs)
2  Could we predict??? (2 msgs)
3  Alien spacecraft taking a peek at
   Jupiter.. (9 msgs)
4  CARL SAGAN's comments (3 msgs)
5  SL9 fragment W impact image, SPIREX
   infra-red, small jpg
6  SPIREX infrared impacts summary
   (long, but much smaller than source)
7  Hubble Image of Jupiter and Io
   Available
8  Smog hypothesis (Why are SL9 impact
   spots black?)
9  s19 images and info sites (3 msgs)
10 Technical difficulties remain
   (sci.space.tech,.science)
11 450 Comet Shoemaker-Levy Impact
   Images Available
12 Near InfraRed image just after SL9
   impact, with Io
13 SL9 - Radio Observations, Taunton
   School, Somerset, UK
14 SL9 Impact Site Longitudes
15 Actual (observed) Times of Comet
   Strikes Needed
16 SL9 fragment U very small B&W gif
17 Total Mass of SL9 ?
```

```
18 JPL Radio Observations of Comet
   Shoemaker-Levy
19 Galileo Update - 08/01/94
```

```
Enter Thread Number, MORE, ADD, ?, or
EXIT:
```

To add the group to your subscription lists ("Favorites List"), type **save** and press Enter. You'll see a confirmation message such as the following:

```
Confirm: Save "rec.music.classical" to
your Personal Favorites area? (y or n)
```

To add the group, type **y** and press Enter. You'll see the thread selector again. If you would like to read the group, you can do so now (see the section titled "Reading the news," later in this chapter). To add more newsgroups to your subscription list, press Ctrl + Z until you see the USENET Discussion Groups menu again. Then repeat this procedure, or search for a newsgroup, as described in the following section.

Searching for a newsgroup

If you're not sure how to type the exact name of a newsgroup, or if you'd like to see a list of all the newsgroups that contain a word you specify, you can search for newsgroups—but note that Delphi doesn't include the alt newsgroups in the search. To search the list of the standard newsgroups, choose option 13 from the USENET Discussion Groups menu (type **13** and press Enter). You'll see the following menu:

```
Search for (but not connect to)
Newsgroups, Mailing Lists
Page 1 of 1

1 Search for Specific Newsgroups
  (excludes alt. groups)        Search
2 Search Educator's Guide to E-Mail
  Lists                          Search
3 Search Academic email lists
  (Kovacs)                       Search
4 Search Academic email lists (alt.
  Kovacs)                        Search
```

```
5 Search Academic email lists
  (another approach)           Search

Enter Item Number, SAVE, ?, or BACK:
```

As this menu indicates, you can search for *mailing lists* as well as newsgroups. To search for a standard USENET newsgroup, type **1** and press Enter. You'll see the following prompt:

```
Search for:
```

Type a word or part of a word, and press Enter. The following shows the results of a search for "classical":

```
Search for: classical
Search for Specific Newsgroups
(excludes alt. groups)
Page 1 of 1
1 rec.music.classical           Text
2 rec.music.classical.guitar    Text
3 rec.music.indian.classical    Text
4 rec.music.early               Text
5 sci.classics                  Text

Enter Item Number, SAVE, ?, or BACK:
```

To subscribe to one of these groups, type its number and press Enter, and press Enter again to display the thread selector. Then type **save** and press Enter to add the newsgroup to your subscription list. Press Ctrl + Z until you see the Search for Specific Newsgroups menu again; from here, you can subscribe to another of the newsgroups on the list of newsgroups matching the word you specify, or you can press Ctrl + Z again to return to the USENET Discussion Groups menu.

READING ARTICLES

Delphi's newsreader provides convenient tools for reading the news. The newsreader groups messages by subject, making it easy and enjoyable to follow the thread of a discussion.

To begin reading the news, display the USENET Discussion Groups menu, if necessary, and select option 1 (PERSONAL FAVORITES). You'll see a menu such as the following, which lists the groups to which you've subscribed:

```
PERSONAL FAVORITES
Page 1 of 1

1 rec.music.classical           USENET
2 rec.backcountry               USENET
3 rec.music.early               USENET
4 alt.sl9                       USENET

Enter Item Number, ?, or BACK:
```

To choose one of the subscribed newsgroups, type the number and press Enter. You'll see Delphi's thread selector, discussed in the following section.

Navigating the thread selector

Delphi's thread selector groups articles by subject, as shown, with the number of articles in a thread noted in parentheses at the end of the title.

```
alt.sl9
Page 1 of 2 [45 messages in 22
discussion threads]

1   Add funniest comment by Carl
    Sagan... We MUST TAKE STEPS TO --
    (11 msgs)
2   Could we predict??? (2 msgs)
3   Alien spacecraft taking a peek at
    Jupiter.. (9 msgs)
4   CARL SAGAN's comments (3 msgs)
5   SL9 fragment W impact image, SPIREX
    infra-red, small jpg
6   SPIREX infrared impacts summary
    (long, but much smaller than
    source)
7   Hubble Image of Jupiter and Io
    Available
8   Smog hypothesis (Why are SL9 impact
    spots black?)
9   sl9 images and info sites (3 msgs)
10  Technical difficulties remain
    (sci.space.tech,.science)
11  450 Comet Shoemaker-Levy Impact
    Images Available
```

```
12 Near InfraRed image just after SL9
   impact, with Io
13 SL9 - Radio Observations, Taunton
   School, Somerset, UK
14 SL9 Impact Site Longitudes
15 Actual (observed) Times of Comet
   Strikes Needed
16 SL9 fragment U very small B&W gif
17 Total Mass of SL9 ?
18 JPL Radio Observations of Comet
   Shoemaker-Levy
19 Galileo Update - 08/01/94
```

```
Enter Thread Number, MORE, ADD, ?, or
EXIT:
```

If you see a thread you want to read, you can display the first article in the thread by typing the thread's number and pressing Enter, as explained in the next section. For now, learn how to navigate in the thread selector.

Delphi's thread selector is organized by pages; at the top of the screen, you're told how many pages of thread titles there are (here, just 2). Table 8-2 shows the options for displaying a different page.

Displaying articles

When you've displayed a page containing threads you want to read, you move down to the article selector to display them. Here, Delphi's newsreader has an excellent feature: You can select just the threads you want to read, and when you move down to the article selector, you see just these threads, arranged in numerical sequence. For example, you can tell the newsreader that you want to read threads 1-3,5,13,15. When you press Enter, you'll see the first article in the first thread; as you continue to read, you see the articles in threads 2, 3, 5, 13, and 15, but no others.

To tell the newsreader which threads you want to read, type one or more numbers at the following prompt:

```
Enter Thread Number, MORE, ADD, ?, or
EXIT:
```

To read just one thread, type a number and press Enter. To type a range of threads, type the beginning number, a hyphen (-), and the end number (as in this example: 13-19). You can also combine single numbers and ranges, as in this example: 1-3,5,13,15. Just press Enter to confirm your choice, and you'll see the first article in the first thread you selected.

Reading and disposing of articles

At the article selector level, Delphi's newsreader begins by displaying the first article in the first thread you selected, as in the following example:

```
[Message 1 of 1 in thread 19 of 19]
alt.sl9

NASA Creates Near-Earth Object Search
Committee
```

TABLE 8-2. DISPLAYING A DIFFERENT PAGE		
TYPE THIS:	THEN PRESS THIS KEY:	TO DO THIS:
MORE	Enter	See the next page
PREV	Enter	See the previous page
PAGE	Spacebar, then type the page you want	Go to a specific page
PAGE LAST	Enter	Go to the last page in the thread selector list
PAGE 1	Enter	Return to the first page in the thread selector

```
From: Ron Baalke
<baalke@kelvin.jpl.nasa.gov>
Date: 3 Aug 1994 20:35 UT (3 screens)
Donald L. Savage
Headquarters, Washington, D.C.
August 3, 1994
(Phone: 202/358-1547)
RELEASE: 94-128
NASA APPOINTS NEAR-EARTH OBJECT SEARCH
  COMMITTEE
NASA today announced the establishment
of a committee which will develop a
plan to identify and catalogue, to the
extent practicable within 10 years, all
comets and asteroids which may threaten
Earth.

Dr. Eugene Shoemaker was appointed as
Chairman of the eight-member Near-Earth
Object Search Committee. Shoemaker, an
astronomer with the Lowell Observatory
and professor
More?
```

If the article's longer than one page, you see the prompt "More," as just shown. To see more, just press Enter. To quit reading the article, type **n** and press Enter (or just press Ctrl + Z). You'll see the prompt that appears at the end of a message:

```
Next thread [Return], Reply, or ?>
```

At this point, you can do the following:

- To see the article's full header, type **HEADER** and press Enter.

- To reread the message, type **CURRENT** and press Enter.

- To reread the previous message in the thread (if any), type **LAST** and press Enter.

- To reread the first article in the current thread, type **TOP** and press Enter.

- To read the original article in the thread, the one to which the current message is replying, type **ORIGINAL** and press Enter. Note that the original message may not be available if it has expired.

- To forward the article to an email address you specify, type **FORWARD** and press Enter. You'll be asked to type the email address.

- To save the article to a downloaded file, type **FILE** and press Enter. You'll be asked to specify the name of the file.

- To go to the next newsgroup in your favorites list, type **GROUP** and press Enter.

- To return to the thread selector, type **BACK** and press Enter, or just press Ctrl + Z.

Displaying articles non-stop

Delphi's newsread offers a very convenient news-reading method for anyone who would like to capture the articles on-screen at high speeds, log off, and them read them later (when Delphi's time billing clock isn't adding to your Visa bill).

To display messages non-stop, use the thread selector to display the threads you want to capture. Then turn on your communication program's *file capture* feature (this feature captures all the incoming text to a file name you specify). Type the numbers of the threads you want to capture, followed by the word **NONSTOP,** as in the following example:

```
1-3,6-10 NONSTOP
```

Then press Enter. The articles will whiz by, probably too fast for you to read them—but that's the point. By doing this you're minimizing your on-line charges! You can use your word processing program later to read the articles, at your leisure.

> **TIP:** Most communications programs are set up to append new incoming data to the capture file you've opened. If that's true of your communications program, you can select additional threads for capturing, and your program will add them at the end of the previous set of articles.

POSTING YOUR OWN MESSAGES

Before you post your own articles, please read Part III, "Now it's your turn," with care (especially Chapters 15 and 17). Under no circumstances should you post to USENET until you fully understand the fundamentals of network etiquette and the special characteristics of the newsgroup to which you want to post.

Delphi's newsreader is excellent for reading articles, but very poor for posting them. Not only are you forced to use a line editor, as explained at the beginning of the chapter, but the reader violates USENET norms by posting your replies to the newsgroup by default. (The newsreader should post your replies via email by default.) As the following sections indicate, however, you can work around these flaws.

Posting replies via email

USENET norms call for you to reply via email, rather than posting to the newsgroup, if you just want to say something to the author of an article. You can do this with Delphi's newsreader, but you have to remember to type a command that's not listed in the prompt. (This shortcoming may have been corrected by the time you read this.)

To reply via email, display the article to which you want to reply. At the end of the article, you'll see the following prompt:

```
Next thread [Return], Reply, or ?>
```

Type **MAIL REPLY** and press Enter. You'll see the following, which shows the header of your message:

```
From: Bryan Pfaffenberger
<pfaffey@delphi.com>
To: Ralph Cornbread Jr.
<ralphc@xanth.florida.edu>
Subject: Re: Cheap CDs by mail order
Reference ID:
<310dga$31e@xanth.forida.edu>
```

```
Would you like to quote sections of
message <310dga$31e@pipe1.pipeline.com>
in your reply (y or n)? [n]
```

If you'd like to quote some of the text of the article, type **y** and press Enter. You'll see the message to which you're replying, with each of the lines numbered. At the bottom of the screen, you see the following prompt:

```
Enter a range of lines you wish to
quote. For example, if you want to
quote the text in lines 7 through 15,
you would type "7-15". Please limit the
range to 10 lines maximum. After you
respond to the range, you can enter
another range.
```

Type the range of lines you want to quote, and press Enter. The newsreader shows the lines you've quoted, as in the following example:

```
>Consider XYZ CD Express. I've been a
>"member" for three years and now I
>NEVER buy anything unless I get 3 for
>1 (nearly every other month). Even the
>starter offer is good. 8 or 10 for the
>price of 1.
```

At the bottom of the quoted text, you'll see the following:

```
Enter your response to the quote.
Control-Z when Complete. /HELP for
Help.
```

Here, Delphi has started its rather primitive on-screen editor, which forces you to work with just one line at a time. You can just start typing; if you make a mistake, you can use the Backspace key to rub out the error (on some systems, you may have to press Delete instead). When you come to the end of the line, press Enter to start a new line, and continue.

The problems come when you need to make a correction on a line other than the one you're working with. Here's a list of what you can do with the editor:

- To list all the lines you've typed, type **/LIST.**

- To delete the last line you typed, type **/DELETE.**

As you probably have concluded, you can't do much with the default editor. There's a somewhat more complex editor available, which you can invoke by typing **/EDIT,** but it's not much better.

When you've finished typing your reply, press Ctrl + Z. You'll see a message asking you to confirm the message:

```
Post, List, or Cancel?
```

If you'd like to check your message one more time, type **List** and press Enter. To send the message, type **post** and press Enter. To abandon the message without sending it, type **Cancel** and press Enter.

Writing a follow-up post

To reply with a follow-up post, display the article to which you want to reply, type **REPLY**, and press Enter. The procedure you follow subsequently is identical to the procedure described in the previous section, "Posting replies via email."

Posting an article on a new subject

To post an article on a new subject, display the thread selector, type **ADD**, and press Enter. You'll see a prompt asking you to type a subject. Type the subject, and press Enter. You then see a screen showing the header of the new post, as in the following example:

```
From: Toulouse La Trek
<.trekkie@delphi.com>
Subject: performance
Please enter your message below.
Control-Z when Complete. /HELP for
Help.
```

Type your message, pressing Enter at the end of each line. When you're finished with your message, press Ctrl + Z. You'll see the following:

```
Post, List, or Cancel?
```

If you'd like to check your message one more time, type **List** and press Enter. To send the message, type **post** and press Enter. To abandon the message without sending it, type **Cancel** and press Enter.

SUMMARY

Apart from its clunky text editor, Delphi's newsreader provides reasonably good features for reading the news. The newsreader lacks many features, though, such as kill files, which you're sure to prefer once you progress beyond the newbie stage. Then, you should contemplate switching to nn, a much more powerful newsreader that's described in Chapter 11, "Reading the news with nn."

FROM HERE

- For an introduction to netiquette and working with the USENET community, see Chapter 15, "Working with a virtual community."

- For tips and pointers on writing for a USENET audience, see Chapter 16, "Posting your own messages."

- To make sure you've learned all you can about a newsgroup before you post, see Chapter 16, "Posting your own messages."

- For pointers on handling replies via email and follow-up postings, see Chapter 16, "Posting your own messages."

- To ensure that you don't make posting mistakes that could get you flamed, see Chapter 17, "Dealing with USENET problems."

- Need help finding the right newsgroups? See Part IV, "Building your subscription list."

Like America Online (AOL), CompuServe is an on-line information service that offers dialup access to a central computing facility. At this writing, CompuServe subscribers number more than two million. By the time you read this book, CompuServe will have made available a well-conceived USENET newsreader that will meet the needs of most readers of this book. But be forewarned: Of all the on-line services discussed in this book, CompuServe has the stiffest fees—you'll pay a basic rate for unlimited connect time per month, but that only applies to CompuServe's basic services. Unfortunately, USENET isn't among the basic services. In addition, you may have to pay communication fees and other surcharges. For more information on current rates, contact CompuServe's customer service center (currently 1-800-848-8990).

Cost issues aside, CompuServe's USENET newsreader is a good choice for anyone who wants to read USENET discussions and post text replies—as long as you keep its shortcomings in mind. Like America Online's newsreader software, CompuServe's newsreader doesn't let you crosspost and doesn't automatically quote the text to which you're replying. In addition, there are no facilities for extracting and decoding multi-part binary files. For this reason, CompuServe's USENET software isn't the best choice if you're hoping to obtain and exchange binary files. For this purpose, you'll be much better off with a UNIX newsreader such as trn (see Chapter 12, "Reading the news with rn and

trn") or a SLIP/PPP-compatible newsreader such as Trumpet for Windows (see Chapter 13, "Trumpet for Windows"). In contrast to AOL's offering, CompuServe's newsreader lets you create signatures and kill files—and these are big pluses. In general, CompuServe's USENET software is richer in features, more logical in its organization, and more convenient to use than America Online's offerings.

When you access CompuServe, you can do so in two ways: using the ASCII interface or the CompuServe Information Manager (CIM) interface. The ASCII interface receives deserved criticism; the cryptic menus and hard-to-remember commands will send you scurrying for reference information. In reply to these criticisms, CompuServe introduced CIM, a *front end* program for CompuServe access. A front end program runs on your computer, providing resources (such as menus and indexes) that would otherwise have to be downloaded from the service. CIM is a graphical user interface (GUI) program that makes CompuServe much easier to use. You install CIM on your computer, and it handles all the details of connecting you to CompuServe and guiding you through the service's features.

This chapter teaches the fundamentals of reading USENET with WinCIM, the version of CompuServe Information Manager (version 1.3) that runs on Microsoft Windows–equipped PCs. (To find out which version of WinCIM you're using, open the Help menu, and choose About CIM.) Similar versions of CIM are available for MS-DOS and

Macintosh computers; if you're using one of these computers, you can still use this chapter as a guide to accessing USENET via CompuServe, although some commands are differently worded. As you're reading this chapter, please bear in mind that additional features may have been added or existing ones may have been altered in the many months that it takes a book such as this one to find its way to the bookstores. In addition, I'm assuming that you've successfully installed and started WinCIM, that you're connected to CompuServe, and you're ready to go—so let's get started!

GETTING STARTED

To access CompuServe's USENET software, open the Services menu and choose Go. If you prefer, you can use the Ctrl + G keyboard shortcut. You'll see a dialog box asking you which service you want to access. Type use. You'll see a dialog box informing you that, because USENET messages originate from the wide world beyond CompuServe, these messages may contain offensive material that isn't suitable for kids. After you acknowledge this message by pressing Enter, you'll see the Internet window shown in Figure 9-1.

To access the USENET newsreader, press the down arrow key until you've highlighted USENET Newsgroups. Then choose Select by clicking this button or

just pressing Enter (you can quickly choose any highlighted button by pressing Enter). You'll see the USENET Newsgroups window, shown in Figure 9-2. In this window, you can read documents about USENET (such as "Newsgroup etiquette") and access the ASCII and CIM newsreaders.

> **TIP:** To choose any option quickly with CIM, just move the mouse pointer to the option and double-click the left mouse button.

To access the CIM newsreader from the USENET Newsgroups window, select USENET News Reader (CIM) and click Select. You'll see the second USENET Newsgroups window, shown in Figure 9-3. From this window, you can subscribe to newsgroups and access your subscription list. In addition, you can post new messages (see the section titled "Writing replies" later in this chapter) and you can choose USENET options.

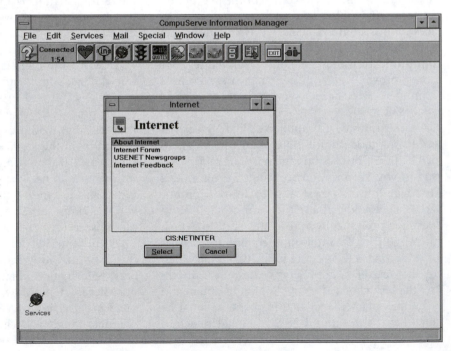

Figure 9-1. You access CompuServe's USENET newsreader through the Internet window.

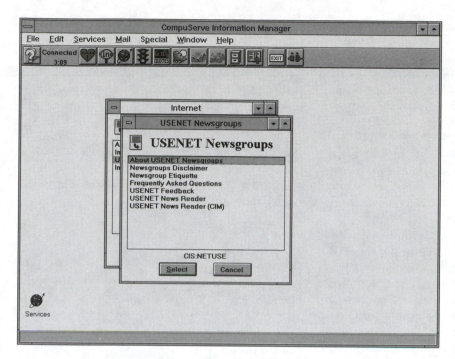

Figure 9-2. This window provides access to all of CompuServe's USENET services.

four lines. CIM will automatically add this signature to your postings and email replies. Additionally, the Ignore button lets you create kill settings (see the section titled "Killing unwanted articles," later in this chapter), and the Get Message by Id button lets you retrieve an article by typing its ID number. When you're finished typing your name, organization, and signature, choose OK. You'll see the USENET Newsgroups window again (the one that's shown in Figure 9-3).

Let's start by choosing Set USENET Options. You'll see the Options window, shown in Figure 9-4. In this window, you type your name and organization, precisely the way you want them to appear in the headings of the USENET messages you create. In addition, you can type a signature of up to

> **TIP:** Don't let the four-line signature restriction irritate you—it's not an unreasonable limitation. USENET netiquette discourages lengthy signatures, which are considered wasteful of network *bandwidth* (the data-carrying capacity of the network). Most of the UNIX newsreaders automatically truncate signatures longer than four lines. CompuServe's design is in accord with long-established USENET principles.

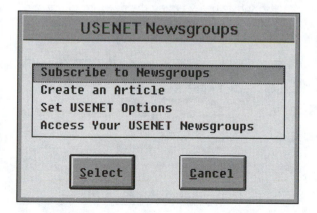

Figure 9-3. This window provides access to the newsreader's newsgroup selector and subscription list.

SUBSCRIBING TO NEWSGROUPS

Now that you've set your USENET options with your name, organization, and signature, it's time to subscribe to some newsgroups! From the USENET Newsgroups window shown in Figure 9-3, choose Subscribe to Newsgroups. You'll see the Subscribe to Newsgroups window, shown in Figure 9-5. At the left of the window is a list box, which lets you browse for newsgroups by selecting a newsgroup hierarchy from the list. You can also search for newsgroups by typing a key word, such as *music*. If you know the exact name of the group to which you want to subscribe, you can do so by typing the name.

Subscribing to newsgroups by browsing

Let's start subscribing by browsing in the Browse for Newsgroups list box. To see more of the hierarchy names, just click the down arrow key or drag the scroll box down. When you see a hierarchy in which you'd like to browse, select the hierarchy name and click Select—or just double-click the name. You'll see a window such as the one shown in Figure 9-6, which lists the newsgroups available in the rec hierarchy. To see more of the groups, just click the down arrow or drag the scroll box down.

Note: CompuServe's newsgroup lists don't contain newsgroups that might contain adult-oriented material—and rightly so, considering that lots of kids use CompuServe. You can still subscribe to such groups, however, if you know the group's exact (dotted) name. For more information on adding groups by name, see "Subscribing to news groups by typing the newsgroup's name," later in this section.

If you see a group that looks interesting, you can preview it, if you wish, by clicking the Preview button. You'll see the Access Newsgroups window, which lets you browse the thread subjects and view articles. When you're finished browsing the group, click Cancel until you see the newsgroup browsing window again.

To subscribe to a newsgroup, just move the mouse pointer to one of the check boxes, and click the mouse within the check box so that an "X" appears. Subscribe to as many groups as you wish. When you're done, click Subscribe. You'll see a dialog box confirming your subscription, and you'll see the Subscribe to Newsgroups window again.

At this point, you can select another hierarchy and subscribe to more groups, if you like. You'll find a full selection of the standard newsgroup hierarchies, but the alternative newsgroup hierarchies are

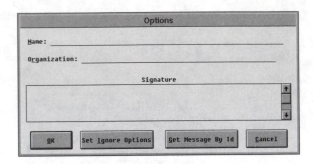

Figure 9-4. In this window, you type your name, organization, and signature.

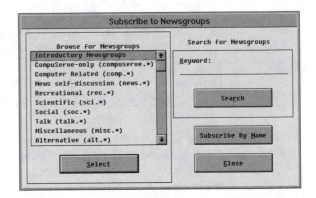

Figure 9-5. In this window, you can subscribe to newsgroups by browsing or searching for them. You can also subscribe by typing the newsgroup's name.

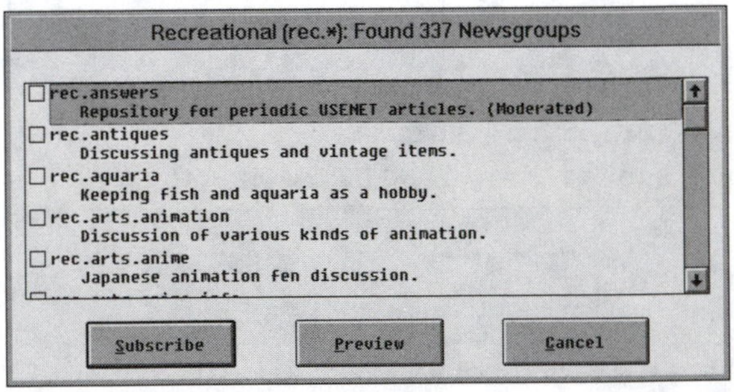

Figure 9-6. To subscribe to a newsgroup, just click the check box so that an "X" appears.

represented (at this writing) only by the alt.* groups. When you're done subscribing to news-groups, click Close, and you'll see the USENET Newsgroups window again (see Figure 9-3).

Subscribing to newsgroups by searching

Let's say you're interested in music, and you're not sure which music-related newsgroups CompuServe offers. You can find out fast using the Search for Newsgroups area, the second area of the Subscribe to Newsgroups window (see Figure 9-6). This com-mand searches all the newsgroup hierarchies, and it isn't restricted to the newsgroup names: It also searches a short description of the newsgroup (for example, alt.fan.shostakovich has the description, "Fans of the music of Shostakovich").

To perform a search, you use the Keyword area. Type a word that describes your interest, and click Search. Don't worry about capitalization, which the search software ignores.

If CompuServe can't find any newsgroups, you'll see a dialog box informing you that the search turned up nothing; try searching again with a different word. A successful search produces a window such as the following, shown in Figure 9-7.

This window works just like the newsgroup browsing window (see Figure 9-6). You can pre-view groups by clicking the Preview button, and you can subscribe to groups by clicking the check

box next to the group's name. Subscribe to as many groups as you wish. When you're done, click Subscribe. You'll see a dialog box confirming your subscription, and you'll see the Subscribe to Newsgroups window again.

> **TIP:** Keep the search word short. If you're interested in music, type **music** instead of "musical" or "music-related"; CompuServe's search software (like all computer search soft-ware) is very literal and will try to match exactly what you've typed. "Music" matches many newsgroups, but "musical" and "music-related" retrieve few or none.

You can repeat this procedure to subscribe to additional newsgroups, if you wish. When you're done subscribing to newsgroups, click Close, and you'll see the USENET Newsgroups window again (see Figure 9-3).

Subscribing to newsgroups by typing the newsgroup's name

You can also subscribe to newsgroups by typing the newsgroup's exact (dotted) name, such as "rec.backcountry" or "alt.binaries.sounds.misc." For groups that might contain objectionable or adult material, this is the *only* way you can add the groups to your subscrip-tion list.

To subscribe to a group by typing its name, click the Subscribe By Name button, which you'll find in the Subscribe to News-groups window (see Fig-ure 9-5). You'll see a dialog box containing an area in

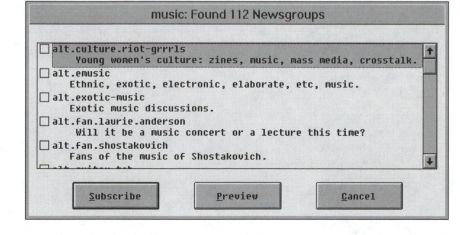

Figure 9-7. A search for "music" retrieved 112 music-related newsgroups!

which you can type the newsgroup name. Type the name, and choose OK. If CompuServe receives this group, you'll see a dialog box informing you that the group has been added to your subscription list. If not, you'll see an alert box informing you that no such group exists.

You can repeat this command, if you like, to subscribe to additional newsgroups by name. When you're done subscribing to newsgroups, click Close, and you'll see the USENET Newsgroups window again (see Figure 9-3).

ACCESSING YOUR SUBSCRIPTION LIST

Now that you're finished subscribing to newsgroups, it's time to access your subscription list. From the USENET Newsgroups window (see Figure 9-3), choose Access Your USENET Newsgroups. You'll see the Access Newsgroups window, shown in Figure 9-8. From this window, you select the newsgroup you want to read by highlighting the group's name on-screen. Then you can browse the threads or search for threads using a key word, as explained in the following sections.

Selecting threads by browsing

To browse a newsgroup's threads, choose Browse in the Access Newsgroups window. You'll see the Browse window, shown in Figure 9-9. As the figure illustrates, you see the threads in alphabetical order (except that threads starting with numbers or punctuation marks come

first). To the right of the thread title, you see the number of articles for each thread. The buttons at the bottom of the window sum up what you can do: You can read articles (Get), mark articles as read (Clear), post a new article (Create), or close this window and return to the Access Newsgroups window (Cancel). For now, choose Cancel so that you can learn how to choose threads by searching.

Selecting threads by searching

If your time is limited—and considering CompuServe's rates, it *is* limited—consider searching for threads by subject. Here, you limit the thread display to just those articles within the selected newsgroup that contain a key word you specify. For example, suppose you're interested in reading what rec.music.classical posters think of the most recent Haydn recordings, or what rec.backcountry folks think about Yosemite. With the Search command in the Access Newsgroups window, you can quickly search the selected newsgroup and display just those threads that contain the key word you typed. The search isn't case sensitive.

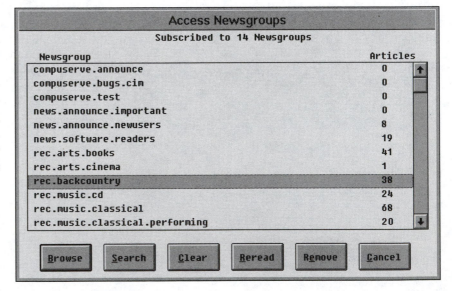

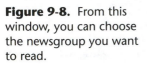

Figure 9-8. From this window, you can choose the newsgroup you want to read.

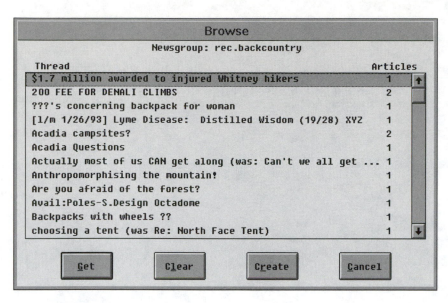

Figure 9-9. This window shows you the threads (subjects) in the current newsgroup.

clicking the Clear button in the Browse window. You won't see this thread again the next time you access the newsgroup.

Sometimes none of the threads look interesting. Rather than clicking them one by one and choosing Clear, just click Cancel to close this window and redisplay the Access Newsgroups dialog box (see Figure 9-8). Select the newsgroup, and click Clear.

To select threads by searching, choose Search in the Access Newsgroups window. You'll see the Search by Topic dialog box, shown in Figure 9-10. Type the word, and choose OK.

Figure 9-11 shows the results of a search by topic. You see a Browse window, just like the one in Figure 9-9. However, this one lists only those threads that contain the key word you typed—here, "Haydn." As you can see, this is a quick way to reduce the number of threads you must go through in order to find an interesting thread.

Clearing uninteresting threads

If a thread doesn't look interesting, you can clear it without reading it by selecting the thread and

Figure 9-10. When you type a word in this dialog box, CompuServe limits the thread display to just those threads containing this word.

READING THE NEWS

When you see a list of threads in the Browse window, you can read articles. To do so, just select the thread you want to read, and choose Get. You'll see the Display Article Contents window, shown in Figure 9-12. This window shows the first article in the thread you've selected. From here, you can navigate to additional articles in the thread, and to articles in different threads. You can also mark articles as unread by clicking Hold, forward articles to an address you specify, and download articles. These tasks are explained in this section. For information on posting your own articles, see the section titled "Writing replies," later in this chapter.

Navigation basics

In the Display Article Contents window (see Figure 9-12), you see the first article in the thread you selected. Take a moment now to learn the features of this window.

In the upper-right corner of the window, there's an indicator that shows how many articles there are in the thread you're viewing—here, there's just

Figure 9-11. The result of a search by topic is a thread list containing only those threads that contain the key word.

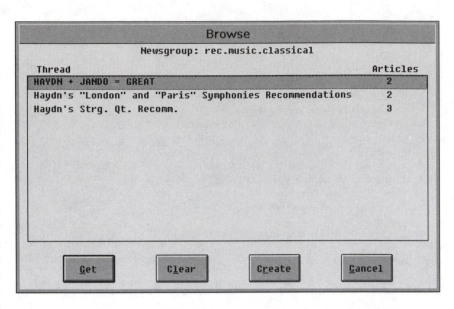

one, so the indicator says "Article 1 of 1." If there were more than one article in this thread, you'd see something like "Article 1 of 7."

The scroll bars give you the tools needed to display the current article. To see more of the text, click the down arrow or drag the scroll box down. If necessary, you can click the right arrow (or drag the scroll box to the right in the horizontal scroll bar) to view lines that the window has truncated.

At the bottom of the window, you see two Thread buttons. If you choose the < button, you see the first article in the previous thread. If you choose the > button, you see the first article in the next thread.

Holding articles

As you'll quickly discover while reading the news with CompuServe's newsreader, any article that you've displayed disappears from the thread list—in other words, the

Figure 9-12. In this window, you can read and manage the articles in a newsgroup.

software marks it as read. Unlike most other USENET newsreaders, you don't have to page through the article to the end to mark the article as read; viewing any part of it is enough to do the job.

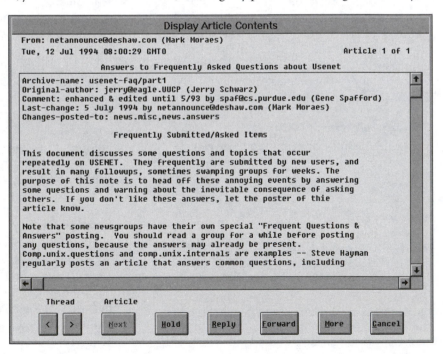

TIP: The <u>M</u>ore button doesn't show you more of the article; instead, it brings up a dialog box with further options (see the section titled "Killing unwanted articles" later in this chapter).

To prevent the software from marking the article as read, click the <u>H</u>old button. The next time you access this group's thread list in the Browse window, you'll see this article in the list.

TIP: If you forget to choose <u>H</u>old, don't despair—you can still redisplay the article (see the section titled "Rereading Articles" later in this chapter).

Forwarding articles

You can forward an article that you've displayed in the Display Article Contents window. To do so, choose the <u>F</u>orward button. You'll see a dialog box in which you can type the email address of the person to whom you'd like to forward the message. In addition, there's an area in which you can type some additional text, if you wish. To forward the message, choose <u>O</u>K.

Printing and saving articles

If you've scrolled to the end of an article, you can print or save the text using WinCIM's <u>F</u>ile menu commands. To print the current article, choose

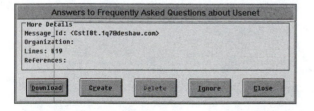

Figure 9-13. This window gives you more options concerning the article that's currently displayed in the Display Article Contents window.

Print (or press Ctrl + P). To save the current article, choose <u>S</u>ave (or press Ctrl + S), and type a file name.

Downloading articles

Sometimes the articles you view are so long that it would be faster—and cheaper!—to download the article to a file on your computer rather than reading it on-screen. To do so, display the article and click the <u>M</u>ore button. You'll see a window such as the one shown in Figure 9-13. This window shows you additional header information about the article and lets you choose from several options. The one we'll discuss now is <u>D</u>ownload.

To download the current article to your computer, choose <u>D</u>ownload. You'll see a dialog box asking whether you want to include the quoting in the article. If so, choose <u>Y</u>es. To delete the quoted material, choose <u>N</u>o. Next, you'll see a Save As dialog box, in which you type a file name for the file. When you click OK, CompuServe downloads the article's text to the file name you've specified.

KILLING UNWANTED ARTICLES

You can increase your enjoyment of USENET by killing unwanted postings so that they never appear in the thread list. With CompuServe's software, you can kill by subject and by author within a newsgroup; there's no global kill capability at this writing.

To kill unwanted postings, you use the Ignore Criteria window, shown in Figure 9-14. You can access this window in two ways:

• In the USENET Newsgroups window that you see when you begin your USENET session (see Figure 9-3), choose Set USENET options. In the Options window (see Figure 9-4), choose Set Ignore Options. You'll see a dialog box asking you to select the newsgroup for which you'd like to set the ignore options. Select the group, and choose OK. You'll see the Ignore Criteria window.

• In the Display Article Contents window (see Figure 9-12), click More. In the window that appears after you click the More button (see Figure 9-13), click Ignore. You'll see the Ignore Criteria window.

Killing articles by subject

When you kill articles by subject, you type a word or phrase. The newsreader then ignores any article that contains this word or phrase in its subject line. You won't see these articles in your Browse window.

To kill articles by subject, click Subject, if necessary, in the Ignore by area, and then click the OK button. You'll see the Ignore by dialog box shown in Figure 9-15. In the Subject area, type the word or phrase. If you would like to kill the subject only for a certain number of days, type the number of days in the area called Number of days to ignore. After the number of days you type, you'll start seeing articles with this subject again. If you would prefer to exclude this subject permanently, click the Non_Expiring check box. When you're finished, click OK. You return to the Ignore Criteria window, and you'll see your kill criteria in the Subject area.

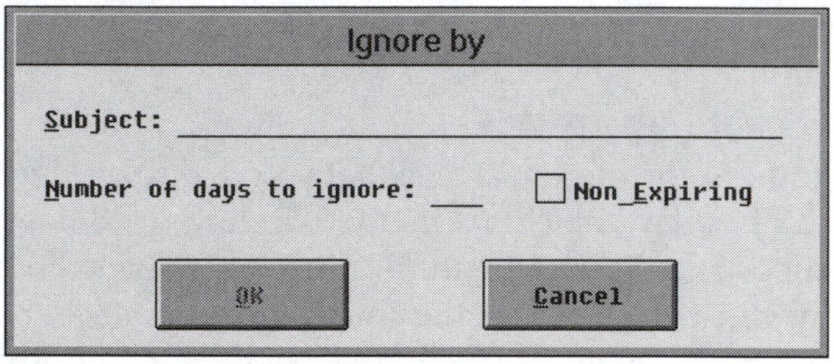

Killing articles by author

When you kill articles by author, you type the author's email address. CompuServe intercepts any postings to the current group by this author and ignores them; you won't see them in the Browse or Display Article Contents windows.

To kill articles by author, click the Author button in the Ignore by area, and choose OK. Then click Insert. You'll see the Ignore by dialog box shown in Figure 9-16. In the Author area, type the author's email address. If you would like to kill the author only for a certain number of days, type the number of days in the area called Number of days to ignore. After the number of days you type, you'll start seeing this author's articles again. If you would prefer to banish this author for all time, click the Non_Expiring check box. When you're finished, click OK. You return to the Ignore Criteria

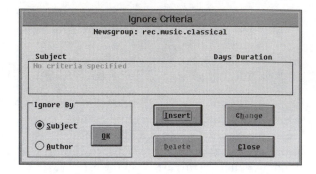

Figure 9-14. In this window, you tell CompuServe to ignore articles containing certain names or subject words.

Figure 9-15. In this dialog box, you type a word or phrase to be used in killing articles by subject.

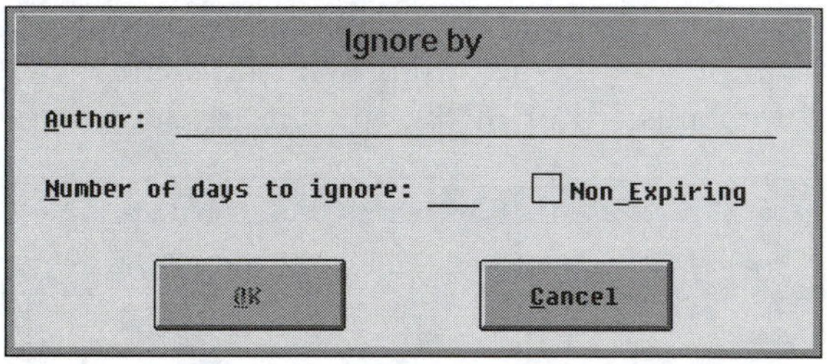

Figure 9-16. In this dialog box, you type the email address of an author whose postings you don't want to see.

window, and you'll see your kill criteria in the Author area.

> **TIP:** You can kill all the articles coming from a certain site, if you wish. Proceed as if you were killing by author, but type just the portion of the address that comes after the @ sign, as in the following example:
> badboys.miscreant.org.

Editing your kill criteria

If you change your mind about your kill criteria, you can edit or delete your kill settings. Just display the Ignore Criteria window again, and click Subject or Author to display the kill criterion you want to change. Select the criterion in the list, and choose Change to alter the criterion (you'll see the Ignore By dialog box again). Choose Delete to remove the criterion.

REREADING ARTICLES

As you've seen, CompuServe's newsreader software is trigger-happy when it comes to marking articles as read; just a peek at an article, and it's cleared from the newsgroup. If you forgot to click the Hold button, you can recover a cleared article by displaying the Access Newsgroups window again (see Figure 9-8). Click the Reread button, and you'll see a dialog box asking how many articles you want to restore to the group. Type at least the number of articles you read in the last section, and click OK. CompuServe restores the articles to the newsgroup.

POSTING NEW ARTICLES

Before you post your own articles, please read Part III, "Now it's your turn," with care (especially Chapters 15 and 17). Under no circumstances should you post to USENET until you fully understand the fundamentals of network etiquette and the special characteristics of the newsgroup to which you want to post.

You can post your own new messages in two different ways:

• In the USENET Newsgroups window (Figure 9-3), you can choose Create an Article. This is a good option for posting a new article to a newsgroup.

• In the Browse window (see Figure 9-9), you can click Create. This is also a good option for posting a new article to a newsgroup.

Either way you choose, you'll see the Create USENET Message window, shown in Figure 9-17. In the Newsgroups area, choose the newsgroup to which you want to post the message. In the Subject area, type a descriptive subject. Making sure the Post to Newsgroup option is selected, type your message in the Message Contents area. If you prefer, you can upload a message from your PC using the Upload button. Choose Send to send the message to the newsgroup you've selected.

WRITING REPLIES

You can reply to an article in two ways:

• By replying via email to the article's author. In accord with standard USENET procedures, this is the default option in CompuServe's newsreader.

• By posting a followup article to the group.

To write a reply, display the article in the Display Article Contents window (see Figure 9-12), and choose the Reply button. You'll see the Reply to USENET Message window, shown in Figure 9-18. Note that the newsreader software has filled in the subject line for you; if you wish, you can change this. By default, the software selects the Send via E-mail check box. If you would like to send an email reply, just leave this box checked. To send a followup posting, click the Send via E-mail check box to remove the "X," and click the Post to Newsgroup check box so that an "X" appears. Type or upload your message in the Message Contents area, and click Send.

Figure 9-17. You see this window (with these settings) when you choose Create to post a new message.

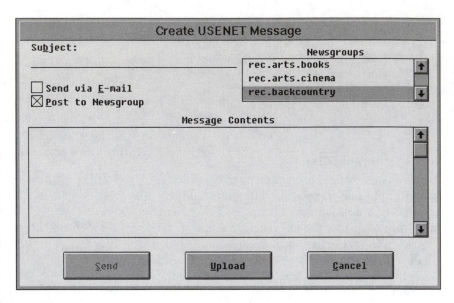

SUMMARY

CompuServe's USENET newsreader is the best currently offered by on-line information services. Like the better UNIX newsreaders, it offers powerful tools for managing subscription lists, subscribing to groups by key words, viewing articles by threads, and killing unwanted postings by author and subject. And thanks to WinCIM, printing and saving USENET articles is a cinch. Many USENET readers will find this software to be more than adequate for their purposes. Still, it's worth knowing what you're missing. Here are some features that you'll find in the most powerful UNIX newsreaders, such as trn:

- Global kill settings, so that unwanted subjects and articles do not appear in any of your subscribed newsgroups. (CompuServe's kill features apply only to one newsgroup at a time.)

- Automatic decoding and extraction of multi-part

Figure 9-18. In this window, you reply via email or a follow-up posting to the article you're viewing.

binary files. With CompuServe's newsreader, you'll have to download each section of the file and decode them on your PC.

- Crossposting to two or more groups. Although excessive crossposting is a violation of USENET norms, the failure to crosspost under some

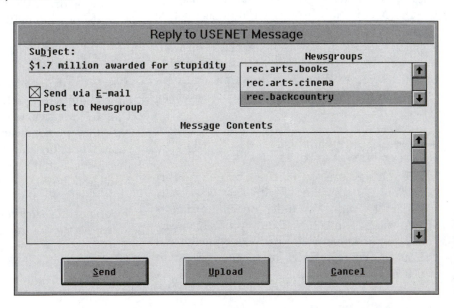

conditions is *also* a violation of USENET norms. For example, one should crosspost an article about a Disneyland visit to misc.kids and rec.arts.disney.

FROM HERE

- For an introduction to netiquette and working with the USENET community, see Chapter 15, "Working with a virtual community."

- For tips and pointers on writing for a USENET audience, see Chapter 16, "Posting your own messages."

- To make sure you've learned all you can about a newsgroup before you post, see Chapter 16, "Posting your own messages."

- To ensure that you don't make posting mistakes that could get you flamed, see Chapter 17, "Dealing with USENET problems."

- For pointers on handling replies via email and follow-up postings, see Chapter 16, "Posting your own messages."

- Need help finding the right newsgroups? See Part IV, "Building your subscription list."

10

The first of the full-featured UNIX newsreaders to be discussed in this book, tin is also by far the easiest to use. A threaded newsreader, it groups postings by topics, permitting you to scan easily for relevant subjects. If you can't find what you're looking for, an easy-to-use search command lets you search for words or phrases in newsgroup names, thread titles, and even article text. Want to search the unsubscribed newsgroups, just to make sure you haven't missed anything? You can *yank in* (display) all the unsubscribed groups—all those thousands of them—and search them too, and *yank out* (eliminate those groups from your subscription list) when you're done.

As you'll see in this chapter, tin combines ease of use with some powerful capabilities—for example, you can kill unwanted postings in virtually any conceivable way (by subject, by author, by site, or by text patterns you specify). To be sure, there are newsreaders with more features, but they're more difficult to use. If you're just getting started with UNIX and tin's one of the available readers, it's a very good choice. You'll find tin on a variety of UNIX machines, including NeXT computers and Macintoshes running AUX (Apple's version of the UNIX operating system); tin also runs on Amiga computers.

Tin's author is Iain Lea, a native of Britain who's now living in Germany, where he handles Internet gateways for Siemens AG, the European computer and telecommunications giant. Besides maintaining tin, Iain divides his time between working out, riding his motorcycle, and running a beer garden. Iain based

tin on a newsreader called tass, which was developed by Rich Skrenta in 1991; tass, in turn, was influenced by NOTES, a 1982 newsreader developed at the University of Illinois by Ray Essick and Rob Kolstad.

This chapter covers the fundamentals of using tin for reading the news; certain advanced commands, such as the ability to pipe articles to a UNIX function, aren't discussed. Note, too, that there are several versions of tin in common use; the latest version (at this writing) is 1.3, but you may encounter version 1.2 or 1.1 on many systems that haven't got around to upgrading.

> **TIP:** To find out what version of tin you're using, start tin (as described in the next section) and press **v.** At the bottom of the screen, you'll see the version number.

STARTING TIN

The method you use to start tin depends on which system you're using. In some systems, you choose tin from a menu, such as the one shown here:

```
USENET newsgroups
nn      -     Read the news with nn
tin     -     Read the news with tin
trn     -     Read the news with trn
<CR>    -     Return to the main menu
```

<CR>, incidentally, is the way computer people refer to the Enter key on your keyboard (its official

name is carriage return, a holdover from typewriter days).

On other systems, you start tin by typing the following and pressing Enter:

`tin`

Just what you see when you start tin for the first time depends on how your system administrator installed the software. For example, you may see a question asking whether you want to subscribe automatically to new newsgroups. Each new day brings at least one new newsgroup, and sometimes as many as three or four. Chances are good that few of them will prove of interest to you, so you should answer "No" (type **n**) to this question. If you don't see this question, tin will automatically subscribe you to new newsgroups, and you'll see them in the subscription list. For information on how to unsubscribe to these newsgroups, see the section titled "Unsubscribing and deleting unwanted newsgroups," later in this chapter.

> **TIP:** If you find that you're subscribed to all the newsgroups when you start tin for the first time, type U, and when you see the prompt asking which newsgroups you'd like to unsubscribe, type *, and press Enter.

Another possibility: You may see a brief introduction to tin. This is worth reading. When you're done, just press Enter to continue.

GETTING HELP

To get help at any time in tin, just press **h.** You'll see a screen that lists the commands available at the current level. At the bottom of the screen, you'll see the following:

TABLE 10-1. MOVING THE CURSOR IN TIN	
PRESS THIS KEY:	TO MOVE TO:
Down arrow (or j)	Down one line
Up arrow (or k)	Up one line
PgDn (or Ctrl + D or Ctrl + F or space bar)	Down one screen
PgUp (or Ctrl + U or Ctrl + B or b)	Up one screen
End (or $)	End of list or end of article
Home (or Ctrl + R)	Beginning of list or article

```
PgD,End,<SPACE>,^D - page down. PgUp,
Home,b,^U - page up. <CR>,q - quit.
```

To see another screen of help, press PgDn, End, the space bar, or Ctrl + D. To see the previous screen, press b, Ctrl + U, or PgUp. To exit the help screen and return to tin, press q or Enter. Table 10-1 summarizes how to move the cursor in tin.

USING THE NEWSGROUP SELECTOR

Like all newsreaders, tin has several levels. The first, the newsgroup selector (called Group Selection), lets you choose newsgroups (see Figure 10-1). Following this screen's title, you see the number of newsgroups to which you're currently subscribed. For each newsgroup, there's a number that indicates how many articles are currently available to read. (If there's no number, it may mean that there are no articles—but that's not necessarily true. The names of some newsgroups are so long—american.automobile.breakdown.breakdown.breakdown comes to mind—that the name covers up the space where the number of articles would appear.)

On most systems, your system administrator has chosen a few newsgroups to get you started. You'll learn how to add more in a moment, but first you should learn a few basics of using tin.

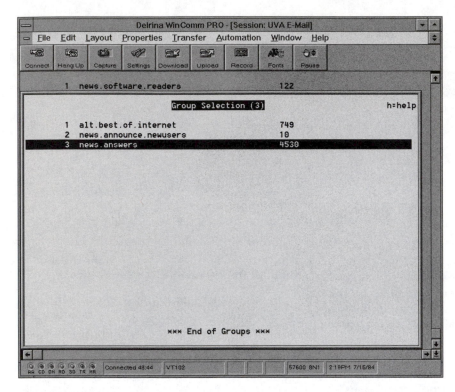

Figure 10-1. In tin's startup screen you see the names of the newsgroups to which you're subscribed.

name, and tin will find the group and ask you where you want to position the group in your subscription list.

To select a group by name, type **g** (lowercase). You see the following message at the bottom of the screen:

`Newsgroup>`

Type the newsgroup name. Type the newsgroup's name without any spaces, and don't forget the dots! If you make a typing mistake, just press Backspace to rub out the error, and retype. When you're sure you've typed the command correctly, press Enter. To cancel this command, press Esc.

Note: If you type the name of the newsgroup incorrectly, or if your site doesn't receive that group, you'll see the message, "Newsgroup such-and-such not found in active file." Look at this message to see if you've typed the name of the newsgroup incorrectly. Did you include the periods?

Assuming that you typed the name correctly and your site receives the group, you see the following message:

`Position news.software.readers in group list [1,2,..,$]>`

Here, tin's asking you where you want the newsgroup to appear in your subscription list. If you type 3, for instance, tin will place the newsgroup in

SUBSCRIBING AND UNSUBSCRIBING TO NEWSGROUPS

The chief function of the newsgroup selector is to let you subscribe to newsgroups that you want to read, as well as to unsubscribe to groups you no longer want to read. The simplest way to subscribe to a newsgroup is to select the group by name, as described in the following section. If you'd like to search the list of available newsgroups for groups that match a pattern you specify, such as "aviation" or "backcountry," you'll need to yank in the unsubscribed groups, as described later in this section.

Selecting a group by name

Now it's time to subscribe to some newsgroups! If you know the name of the newsgroup to which you want to subscribe, you can select the group by the third position in your list. (Don't worry about wiping out the newsgroup that's currently in that position; tin will move it down to make room.) To place the newsgroup at the end of the list, type a dollar sign ($).

After you select a newsgroup by name, you see the newly subscribed newsgroup in the position you indicated. In Figure 10-2, for instance, you see the selected group, alt.folklore.urban, in the No. 1 position.

About yanking

One of tin's strong points is its ability to search for newsgroups that conform to text patterns you specify. You can use these capabilities to build a tailored subscription list very quickly.

The procedure you use is, admittedly, a little confusing at first. You begin by yanking in all the newsgroups known to your system. The result of yanking in all the newsgroups is a very long list of 5,000 or more newsgroups—far more than you could conveniently use or manage. But that's where tin's powerful searching and selection tools come in handy.

Once you've subscribed to all the newsgroups you want to read, you yank out the unsubscribed groups. You can then move newsgroups so that they appear in the order you want. So let's give it a try!

Yanking in the unsubscribed groups

To yank in all the unsubscribed groups, type **y**. You'll see the following message:

```
Yanking in all groups...
```

After you type **y,** tin adds the newsgroups to the list—which is now very long, as you can see in Figure 10-3. The yanked-in newsgroups are automatically unsubscribed, as indicated by the letter "u" at the beginning of each line. The newsgroups to which you're currently subscribed—in Figure 10-3, for example, alt.best.of.internet—lack this "u," which means that you've subscribed to this newsgroup. The other newsgroups to which you're subscribed are buried somewhere in this lengthy list, taking the position they normally occupy in your .newsrc file.

Note: Capitalization matters in tin commands. The **c** command, for instance, differs from the **C**

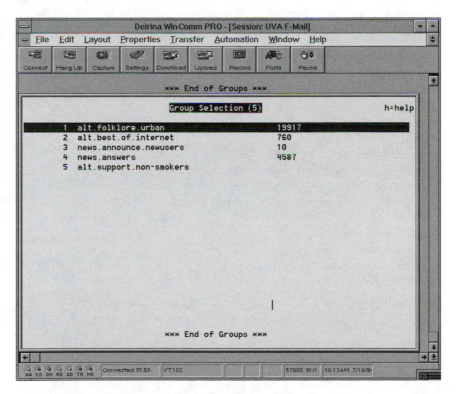

Figure 10-2. After you select a newsgroup by name, you see the newsgroup in your subscription list.

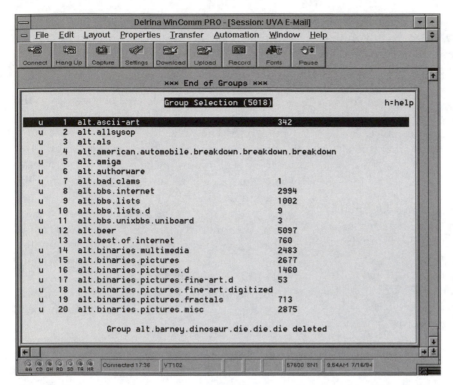

Figure 10-3. When tin yanks in the newsgroups, the reader adds all the new and unsubscribed newsgroups to your subscription list.

subscribe to this group, type **s.** You'll see a message confirming that you've subscribed to this group.

To continue the search, just press the slash key (/) again. You'll see the following message, indicating that tin intends to proceed using the same pattern you typed previously:

```
Search forwards
[bbs]>
```

command. When you type tin's one-letter commands, be sure to do so using the case (uppercase or lowercase) that's indicated.

Searching for newsgroups

You don't have to know the exact name of a newsgroup to subscribe. A search command lets you search forward (down in the list) or backward (up in the list) for newsgroups that conform to a pattern you specify, such as a word (like "teenagers").

To search for groups, yank in all the unsubscribed newsgroups, if necessary, by typing **y.** Now press the forward slash key (/). You'll see the following message:

```
Search forwards [?]<>
```

Type the pattern, and press Enter. Assuming tin can find a match, the program scrolls to the newsgroup containing the match and selects it. To

To search with the same pattern, just press Enter. To change the search pattern, type a new pattern and press Enter.

If you've been searching and want to return to the top of the subscription list so that your search will proceed from the beginning, just type **1** and press Enter.

You can also search backwards (up in the subscription list). To search backwards, type a question mark (**?**). You'll see the following message:

```
Search backwards [?]>
```

Type the pattern for which you want to search, and press Enter.

TIP: You can press Esc to cancel any tin command. To cancel a search after pressing the slash key, for instance, just press Esc.

Subscribing to a newsgroup by pattern searching

Let's say you're interested in subscribing to *every* newsgroup that's related to your interests, such as biking or aviation. If so, tin offers a very convenient feature that subscribes you to all the groups matching a pattern. You could use this command, for instance, to subscribe to all the newsgroups whose names contain the word "aviation." In tin versions prior to 1.3, this command searches your .newsrc file, so it doesn't include new groups that haven't been incorporated into .newsrc. With version 1.3, this command searches all groups.

To subscribe to all the newsgroups matching a pattern, type **S** (capital S). You see the following message:

```
Enter regex subscribe pattern>
```

To use this command, you must type the *regex* pattern correctly. A regex pattern, short for "regular expression," must conform to rigid rules of syntax. For example, unlike the search command discussed in the previous section, this command does not automatically search for *substrings* (patterns occurring within other text; for example, "internet" in alt.best.of.internet). To search for a substring, you must use one or more asterisks as wildcards. To search for all the groups containing "cd-rom" somewhere in their titles, for instance, type *cd-rom*.

After you type the pattern and press Enter, you'll see a message informing you how many groups match the pattern; tin automatically subscribes you to these groups, as in the following:

```
subscribed to 3 groups
```

If no groups match the pattern, you'll see the "No matches" message. Try again, making sure to surround the pattern with asterisks, and check your spelling carefully.

TIP: If you find that this command subscribes you to many more groups than you had expected, you can undo the command by typing **U** (capital U). You'll see a message asking you to type a pattern. Type exactly the same pattern you used to subscribe to the newsgroups. Tin will use this pattern to unsubscribe the same groups.

Yanking out the unsubscribed groups

Once you're finished adding newsgroups to your subscription list, you'll want to yank out the unsubscribed groups. To do so, just type **y** again. You'll see the following message:

```
Yanking in subscribed groups...
```

This message is confusing; what tin is really doing is yanking *out* the unsubscribed groups. But the effect is pretty obvious—the unsubscribed groups are gone, and you're left with a nice, compact list of the groups to which you've subscribed (see Figure 10-4).

TIP: If you see the message, "Yanking in unsubscribed groups," type **y** again. The y command is a toggle command: The first time you press it, the command yanks in the unsubscribed groups; the second time you press it, the command yanks out the unsubscribed groups. You may have to press the key twice to get the effect you want.

MANAGING YOUR SUBSCRIPTION LIST

Once you've created your subscription list, you'll need to keep it in good shape by listing the groups in the order you want. In addition, you'll want to eliminate groups you're not reading. To do so, you first select a group so that its name is highlighted in reverse video, as described in the following section. Then you can move it or delete it, as described in subsequent sections.

Selecting a newsgroup

To select a newsgroup means to highlight the group's name in reverse video (highlighted). When a group name is highlighted, tin knows that the next command you give should affect this group and no other.

Selecting a group is easy. You can simply use the arrow keys to move the highlight. Alternatively, you can type the group's number. You'll see the following message:

```
Select group> 4
```

If the number is correct, just press Enter to select the group. To change the number, press the Backspace key and retype the number. Then press Enter to select the group.

Moving newsgroups in the subscription list

Now it's time to tailor your subscription list by moving the newsgroups so that they're listed in the order you want. To move groups, you use the m command.

> **TIP:** When you read your newsgroups, tin automatically goes to the next group containing unread news. For this reason, you should begin your list with the groups you read every time you log on. Put less frequently read groups in the middle, and groups you're not likely to read at the bottom. You can then begin reading with the groups you read all the time, proceeding to less important groups, and quitting when you wish.

```
Position comp.bbs.misc in group list
[1,2,..,$]>
```

Just type the number corresponding to the position in which you want the newsgroup to appear. To put the newsgroup at the end of the list, type a dollar sign ($).

Unsubscribing and deleting unwanted newsgroups

You can unsubscribe to a group by selecting it and typing **u** (unsubscribe). You'll see a u to the left of the group's name, indicating that it's unsubscribed. But the u command leaves the group's name in the list; to remove it, you'll have to go through a whole cycle of yanking in and yanking out, a tedious business at best. It's better to use the Ctrl + K command. Hold down the Ctrl key and press K; here, it

Figure 10-4. After yanking out the unsubscribed groups, you see your subscription list.

```
Delrina WinComm PRO - [Session: UVA E-Mail]
File   Edit   Layout   Properties   Transfer   Automation   Window   Help

Connect  Hang Up  Capture  Settings  Download  Upload  Record  Fonts  Pause

                    Group Selection (12)                        h=help

     1   alt.folklore.urban                19917
     2   alt.best.of.internet                760
     3   news.announce.newusers               10
     4   news.answers                       4587
     5   alt.cd-rom                         5431
     6   alt.privacy                        2642
     7   comp.society.privacy                 26
     8   rec.backcountry                     570
     9   alt.usenet.offline-reader            84
    10   alt.privacy.clipper                 706
    11   rec.crafts.winemaking                39
    12   comp.sys.ibm.pc.hardware.cd-rom    2184




                    *** End of Groups ***

AA CD DH RD SD TR HR   Connected 1:34:27  VT102        57600 8N1  11:11AM 7/16/9
```

doesn't matter whether you press uppercase or lowercase, though it's easier to press Ctrl + k (lowercase). This command removes the newsgroup from your .newsrc file. After you press Ctrl + K, you see a message such as the following one, except that it will include the newsgroup you're deleting:

```
Delete news.lists.ps-maps from .newsrc?
(y/n): y
```

Just press Enter to delete the group.

If you used Ctrl + K on the wrong newsgroup by accident, you can undo the deletion: You can type **Z** (capital Z) to restore the newsgroup to your subscription list. Table 10-2 summarizes how to use the newsgroup selector.

TABLE 10-2. NEWSGROUP SELECTOR QUICK REFERENCE (TIN)	
PRESS THIS KEY:	TO DO THIS:
/	Search forward for a newsgroup matching a pattern you specify
?	Search backward for a newsgroup matching a pattern you specify
C	Mark the current group as read and go to the next unread group
c	Mark the selected group as read
Ctrl + K	Delete the selected newsgroup from .newsrc
Ctrl + L	Redraw the screen
g	Subscribe to a newsgroup by typing its name
h	View a help screen of commands at this level
m	Move the selected group within the subscription list
q	Quit tin
S	Subscribe to groups matching a pattern you type
s	Subscribe to the selected group
U	Unsubscribe to groups matching a pattern you type
u	Unsubscribe to the selected group
y	Yank in unsubscribed newsgroups or yank out unsubscribed newsgroups (toggle)
w	Post a new article to the selected group
W	View a list of the articles you've posted
z	Mark all the articles in the selected group as unread
Z	Undelete group previously deleted with Ctrl + K

VIEWING SUBJECTS (THREADS)

Once you've created your subscription list, you're ready to read newsgroups! At the beginning of a tin session, the program automatically selects the first newsgroup in the list. You have the following options:

- **You can read the selected newsgroup.** To do so, just press Enter. Because tin is a threaded newsreader, you next see a list of the subjects (threads) that this newsgroup contains.

- **You can mark all the articles in the selected newsgroup as read.** If you really don't want to read the new articles that have come in, type **c.** You'll see a message asking you to confirm this action; to do so, type **y.** To mark all the articles as read without confirmation, type **C.** Used the c or C command on the wrong group? Just select the group, and type **z** to mark all the articles as unread.

- **You can skip the selected newsgroup and go on to the next one.** To do so, just press the down arrow key. Alternatively, type the newsgroup's number, or search for a newsgroup using the / or ? keys.

Once you've selected a newsgroup to read and pressed Enter (or Tab), you'll see the thread selector (called the Group Index, in tin's nomenclature). At this level, you can view the thread topics currently available in the selected newsgroup. You can then view a list of the articles in the thread, mark the thread as read, kill the thread, or read the thread. Additionally, you can search for a subject you specify or for threads containing articles by an author whose name you specify. The following sections detail these procedures.

Opening the thread selector

To work with the thread selector, you first select a newsgroup. To view the thread selector, just press Enter. Optionally, you can press Tab, which opens the next newsgroup that contains unread news. You'll see the thread title index, illustrated in Figure 10-5. At the top of the screen, after the newsgroup's name, you see the number of threads (here, 14) and the number of articles within all the threads (39). The threads are listed in numerical order.

Each thread is listed on its own line, beginning with the number. Here's thread No. 6:

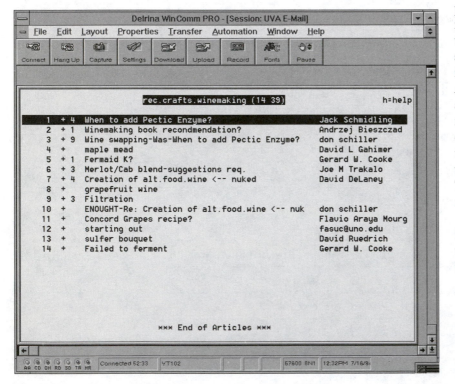

Figure 10-5. The thread title index lets you see the subjects of articles in the selected newsgroup.

```
6 + 3 Merlot/Cab blend-suggestions req.
Joe M Trakalo
```

Here's what this line means:

- The plus sign (+) indicates that the article is unread. After you've read the article (or marked it as read), the plus sign disappears.

- The number following the plus sign tells you how many articles you'll find in the thread.

- The thread's title is listed next.

- At the end of the line, you find the name of the article's author.

Controlling the display

At the thread selector level, you have two options for controlling the display. If you aren't interested in seeing the authors' names, type **d.** After you press this key, tin removes the authors' names from the list. If you would like to see these names again, just type **d** again.

The second option concerns the grouping of articles in threads. If you would rather see a list of each article's subjects, grouped in the order in which they were posted to the group, type **u.** You'll see the subjects, as if you were using an unthreaded newsreader (such as rn). To see the threads again, just type **u** again.

Marking the thread as read

If you're not interested in reading the articles in a thread, you should mark the thread as read. The next time you start tin, you won't see this thread again.

To mark a thread as read, type **K** (capital K). After you press K, tin marks the thread as read by removing the plus sign and advances the selection to the next unread thread. If you change your mind, you can mark the thread as unread by selecting it again and typing **Z.**

If you would like to mark all the threads as read, type **c.** You'll see the newsgroup selector.

Reading the thread

To read a thread, simply press Enter. You'll see the first article in the thread. If you've already read some of them, you can optionally press Tab, which displays the next unread article in the thread. For more information on what you can do at the article level, see the section titled "Using the article selector," later in this chapter.

Searching for subjects

If a newsgroup has many pages of unread threads, you may wish to search for a thread whose title contains words matching a pattern. The method you use is exactly the same one you use in the newsgroup selector. To search forward (down in the thread title index), type a forward slash (/), type the pattern, and press Enter. To search backward (up in the thread title index), type a question mark (**?**), type the pattern, and press Enter.

Assuming the search is successful, tin selects the first thread that matches the pattern you typed. If you would like to continue the search, type / or ? again. To search with the same pattern, just press Enter. To search for a different pattern, type the new pattern and press Enter.

Note: These two searching commands search only the text of the thread's titles, not the text of the articles themselves.

Searching the threads for authors

Suppose you're looking for a posting by a specific author. With tin, you can quickly locate the next posting by a specific author in the text by typing **a** for a forward search (type **A** for a backward search). You'll see the following message:

```
Author search forwards [?]>
```

Type the author's last name, and press Enter. Assuming tin can find this author's name within the newsgroup, the program displays the first posting by this author. For more information on reading articles, see "Using the article selector," later in this chapter.

Viewing a list of the articles in a thread

You can see a list of the articles in the thread. This command may prove useful if you want to read selected articles within the thread (for example, the articles by "Larsen" and "Rosaldo" but not those by "Anderson" or "Lee"). To view the list, type **l**. You'll see a list of the articles and the authors' names. From this screen, you can select an individual article within a thread (to select an article, just use the arrow keys or type the article's number). Once the article is selected, you can read it by pressing Enter. Alternatively, you can return to the thread selector by typing **i** (lowercase i), short for "index").

Tagging threads

You can perform certain operations, such as mailing and saving threads, on more than one thread at a time. To do so, you must first tag the threads. To tag a thread, select the thread and type **T**, after which you'll see a number next to the thread's name, indicating the order in which you've tagged the articles.

Mailing a thread

You can mail one or more threads to an email address you specify. To do so, select the thread you want to mail. Alternatively, tag the threads you want to mail. Then type **m**. You'll see the following message:

```
Mail a)rticle, t)hread, r)egex pattern,
T)agged articles, e)xit: t
```

If you select just one thread, tin will place a "t" after the colon; just press Enter to save the thread. If you tagged more than one thread, tin places a "T" after the colon; just type **T** to save all the tagged threads. You next see the following message:

```
Mail article to [ ]>
```

Type an Internet email address, and press Enter. (If you use this command again in the same tin session, you'll see this email address within the brackets. Just press Enter to mail the selected thread or threads to this address.)

Saving the thread to a file

You can save one or more threads to a file in your *home directory*, the file-storage area that was set up for you when you established your account. To do so, select the thread you want to save. Alternatively, tag the threads you want to save. Then type **s**. You'll see the following message:

```
Save a)rticle, t)hread, r)egex pattern,
T)agged articles, e)xit:
```

If you select just one thread, tin will place a "t" after the colon; just press Enter to save the thread. If you tag more than one thread, tin places a "T" after the colon; just type **T** to save all the tagged threads. You now see the following message:

```
Save filename [ ]>
```

To save the thread or threads to a file in your home directory, type a file name and press Enter.

Returning to the newsgroup selector

At the thread selector level, you'll probably select a thread to read and move down to the article selector level (described in the next section). To return to the newsgroup selector level, type **i** or **t**.

> **TIP:** If tin doesn't redraw the screen after you move back to the newsgroup selector, just press Ctrl + L. Table 10-3 summarizes how to use the thread selector in tin.

USING THE ARTICLE SELECTOR

When you've found a thread you want to read, press Enter or Tab to move to the article selector, and you see an article (see Figure 10-6). The article's title is shown in reverse video at the top of the screen. To the right of the title, you see the number of the thread, and the number of responses, if any, to the current article.

TABLE 10-3. THREAD SELECTOR QUICK REFERENCE (TIN)

PRESS THIS KEY:	TO DO THIS:
/	Search forward for a thread matching a pattern you specify
?	Search backward for a thread matching a pattern you specify
a	Search forward for an author matching a name you specify
A	Search backward for an author matching a name you specify
c	Mark the selected group as read and return to the newsgroup selector
m	Mail the selected thread to an Internet email address
q	Quit tin
s	Save the selected thread to a file
t	Return to the newsgroup selector
T	Tag a thread
w	Post a new article to the selected group
W	View a list of the articles you've posted
Z	Mark the selected thread as unread

At the article selector level, you can use commands to help you navigate the list of articles, control the display, and dispose of articles once you've looked at them. In addition, you can search an article for text matching a pattern you specify; you can also search for authors and mail or save one or more articles.

Navigating the article selector

It's easy to move around the article selector. Table 10-4 provides a quick overview of the commands you use.

In addition to these commands, you can just type a number to go to a specific article in a thread. For example, if you type **4,** tin displays the fourth article in the thread.

Article display options

While you are reading articles, you can make use of display options that enable you to display or hide header information and to display rot-13 (rotated) text.

To see all the header information associated with an article, press Ctrl + H.

To decrypt text encoded with rot-13, type **d.** To encrypt the text again, type **d** again.

Disposing of articles

If you display an article's last page and exit the article, tin assumes you've read the article and marks it as read. To mark the article as read even before you've reached the end, type **k;** tin then displays the next unread article in the thread. If there

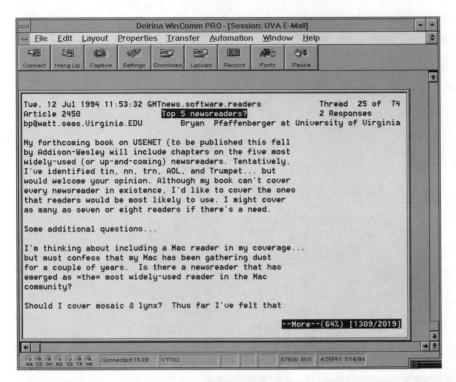

Figure 10-6. At the article selector level, you view the articles in a thread.

TABLE 10-4. NAVIGATION COMMANDS IN THE ARTICLE SELECTOR

PRESS THIS KEY:	TO DO THIS:
Space bar	Display the next page of an article
Ctrl + R	Redisplay the article's first page
Ctrl + $	Redisplay the article's last page
n	Display the next article in the thread
N	Display the next unread article in the thread
p	Display the previous article
>	Display the last article in the thread
<	Display the first article in the thread
Enter	Go to the first article in the next thread
i	Return to the thread selector index

are no more unread articles in the thread, tin displays the first unread article in the next thread.

A bit of reading within a thread may convince you that all of the articles are uninteresting. If so, you can mark the whole thread as read by typing **K.** This command is very useful if you've read a couple of articles, aren't interested in what you're seeing, and want to move on to the next thread.

If all the current articles in the newsgroup seem uninteresting, you can mark them all as read by typing **c.** You'll see the newsgroup selector again.

While displaying articles, you can also reply to the article (via email) or create a follow-up posting. For more information, see the section titled "Posting a follow-up message" later in this chapter.

Searching article text

If you're reading a lengthy article, you can search forward for text that matches a pattern you specify. To do so, press the forward slash (/) key. You'll see the following message:

```
Search forwards [?]>
```

Type the pattern you want to match, and press Enter. If tin can match the text, the program displays the page of the article that contains the text you typed.

Searching the articles for authors

At the article selector level, you can search for authors. This command works precisely the same way that the corresponding command works at the thread selector level; flip back to the section titled "Searching the threads for authors" for details.

Tagging articles

As with threads, you can perform certain operations such as mailing and saving on more than one article at a time. To do so, you must first tag the articles. To tag an article, display the article and type **T,** after which you'll see the following message, indicating that the article has been tagged:

```
tagged article
```

Repeat this operation until you've tagged all the articles that you want to mail or save.

Mailing articles

As with threads, you can mail one or more articles to an email address you specify. To do so, select the thread you want to mail. Alternatively, tag the threads you want to mail. Then type **m.** You'll see the following message:

```
Mail a)rticle, t)hread, r)egex pattern,
T)agged articles, e)xit: a
```

If you select just one article, tin will place an "a" after the colon; just press Enter to save the article. If you tag more than one article, tin places a "T" after the colon; just type **T** to save all the tagged threads. You'll see the following message:

```
Mail article to [ ]>
```

Type an Internet email address, and press Enter. (If you use this command again in the same tin session, you'll see this email address within the brackets. Just press Enter to mail the selected thread or threads to this address.)

Saving articles to a file

You can save one or more articles to a file in your home directory. To do so, display the article you want to save. Alternatively, tag the articles you want to save. Then type **s.** You'll see the following message:

```
Save a)rticle, t)hread, r)egex pattern,
T)agged articles, e)xit:
```

If you select just one article, tin will place an "a" after the colon; just press Enter to save the article. If you tag more than one article, tin places a "T" after the colon; just type T to save all the tagged articles. You'll then see this message:

```
Save filename [ ]>
```

To save the article or articles to a file in your home directory, type a file name and press Enter.

Table 10-5 summarizes how to use the article selector in tin.

TABLE 10-5. ARTICLE SELECTOR QUICK REFERENCE (TIN)

PRESS THIS KEY:	TO DO THIS:
/	Search forward in an article for text matching a pattern you specify
?	Search backward in an article for text matching a pattern you specify
>	Go to the last article in the thread
<`	Go to the first article in the thread
a	Search forward for an author matching a name you specify
A	Search backward for an author matching a name you specify
c	Mark this group as read and return to the newsgroup selector
d	Toggle rot-13 coding on and off
f	Post a follow-up message without quoting the original article's text
F	Post a follow-up message and quote the original article's text
i	Return to the thread selector index
k	Mark the current article as read and display the next unread article
K	Mark the current thread as read and display the first unread article in the next thread
m	Mail the current article (or tagged articles) to an Internet electronic mail address
p	Display the previous article
q	Quit tin
s	Save the current article (or tagged articles) to a file
t	Return to the newsgroup selector
T	Tag an article
w	Post a new article to the selected group
W	View a list of the articles you've posted
z	Mark an article as unread

POSTING NEW MESSAGES

Before you post your own articles, please read Part III, "Now it's your turn," with care (especially Chapters 15 and 17). Under no circumstances should you post to USENET until you fully understand the fundamentals of network etiquette and the special characteristics of the newsgroup to which you want to post.

You can post new messages at any level of tin—the newsgroup selector, the thread selector, or the article selector. If tin is currently displaying the newsgroup selector, you must first select the newsgroup to which you would like to post.

To post a new message, type **w.** You'll see the following message:

```
Post Subject [?]>
```

Type a brief but descriptive subject line, and press Enter. Next, you'll see the default editor for your system—probably vi, but possibly emacs or jove (Figure 10-7). See Appendix A for quick reference guides for these commonly used text editors.

On the distribution line, type a *distribution* (the default is world). Carefully consider whether world distribution is necessary; you can reduce Internet costs and bandwidth by limiting the distribution.

> **TIP:** Want to crosspost your message? To do so, type a comma after the newsgroup name that's currently entered on the newsgroups line, and type an additional newsgroup name. If you wish to crosspost to more newsgroups, type the name of each group to which you want to post your message, separating the names by commas.

When you're finished typing your post, choose the command that exits the text editor (see Appendix A for the command required by the text editor you're using). You'll see the following message:

```
a)bort, e)dit,
p)ost: p
```

To post your message, just press Enter. To work on the message some more, type **e.** To cancel the message without posting it, type **a.**

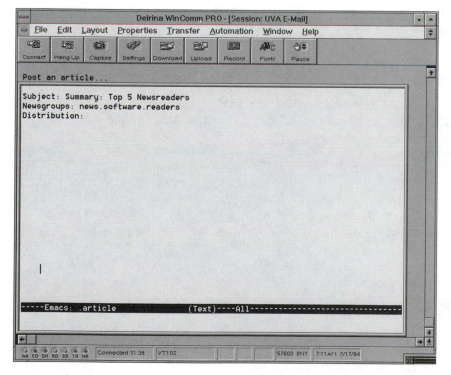

Figure 10-7. When you post a new message, tin automatically starts the default text editor for your system.

WRITING A RESPONSE

You can write a response to the article that's currently displayed in the article selector. Like all good newsreaders, tin gives you two options for responding. You can reply directly to the author via email, or you can post a follow-up message to the newsgroup.

Whether you reply via email or post a follow-up message, you can choose to quote the text of the original article, if you like.

Sending a reply via email

To send a reply to the article's author through email, type **r.** (To quote the text of the article in your reply, type **R.**) When you're finished typing your reply, choose the exit command for your text editor (see Appendix A). You'll see the following message:

```
a)bort, e)dit, s)end: s
```

To send your message, just press Enter. Your reply goes only to the article's author and won't appear in the newsgroup. To work on the message some more, type **e.** To cancel the message without posting it, type **a.**

Posting a follow-up message

To post a follow-up message, type **f.** (To quote the text of the article in your reply, type **F.**) On the distribution line, type a distribution (the default is world).

By default, tin proposes to post your message only to the current newsgroup, even if the original article was crossposted. To crosspost to more newsgroups, type the name of each group to which you want to post your message, separating the names by commas.

When you're finished typing your reply, choose the exit command for your text editor (see Appendix A). You'll see the following message:

```
a)bort, e)dit, p)ost: p
```

To post your reply, just press Enter. To work on the message some more, type **e.** To cancel the message without posting it, type **a.**

KILLING UNWANTED POSTINGS

A good newsreader provides the means to screen out unwanted postings from net.abusers. With tin, you can kill all the postings with a specific subject. You can also kill all the postings from a particular author. Additionally, you can kill any posting that contains any text pattern you specify within the Subject line, the From line, or both. You can also kill within the currently selected newsgroups, or in all newsgroups. With these options, you can kill just about any type of message you don't want to see.

Using the kill menu

To access the kill menu, display the thread selector. To kill a specific subject or author, select the article that contains the subject line or author's name that you want to kill. Then press Ctrl + K. You'll see the kill menu, shown in Figure 10-8.

Automatically, tin fills in the Kill Subject and Kill From areas with settings drawn from the article that was selected when you pressed Ctrl + K. Note, however, that these settings are very restrictive: They

Figure 10-8. You can use the kill menu to prevent unwanted postings from appearing in one or more newsgroups.

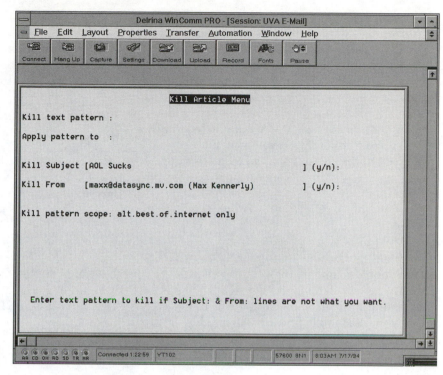

would only kill another posting by the same author with the same subject line.

At the bottom of the screen, you see the following message:

```
Enter text pattern
to kill if Subject:
& From: lines are
not what you want.
```

And that's just what you should do. With the cursor in the Kill text pattern area, type a text pattern. Be sure to use wildcards if you want to kill any subject line that contains an unwanted word or phrase. Typing *scum*, for instance, will kill any posting in which the word "scum" appears anywhere in the subject line. When you are finished typing the text, press Enter. The cursor is now positioned in the area labeled Apply pattern to. You'll see the following message:

```
Select where text pattern should be
applied. <SPACE> toggles & <CR> sets.
```

Here, you select the part of the posting to which tin will apply the text pattern. By default, tin looks at the subject line when the program tries to match the pattern text. By changing the setting in this area, you can tell tin to search only the From line or both lines (the Subject line and the From line). To change the setting, press the space bar. To confirm your choice, press Enter. You'll see the following message:

```
Apply kill to current group only or all
groups. <SPACE> toggles & <CR> sets.
```

Here, you choose the scope of the kill: just the selected newsgroup, or all groups. To change the setting, press the space bar. To confirm your choice, press Enter. Now you see the following message:

```
a)bort e)dit s)ave killfile: s
```

To save your choices, just press Enter. To cancel your choices, type **a.** To edit the kill file directly with your default editor, type **e.**

Kill tips

The Kill menu lets you ignore articles by author and by site, if you use the following tricks:

- To kill all the posts by a specific author, select one of this author's messages, and press Ctrl + K. Press Enter to activate the Kill Subject area, and type **n.** Then type **y** to activate the Kill From area. In the Kill pattern scope area, select the scope of the kill, and press Enter. Press Enter again to save your choices.

- To kill all the posts from a specific site, select a message that comes from this site, and press Ctrl + K. In the Kill From area, carefully note the site's *domain name* (the part of the email address after the @ sign). In the Kill text pattern area, carefully type the domain name surrounded by asterisks (such as *ddt.com*), and press Enter. In the Apply pattern to area, press the space bar to choose From line only. Press Enter, and choose the scope of the kill (just the selected newsgroup, or all newsgroups). Press Enter again to save your choices.

SUMMARY

A powerful newsreader that emphasizes ease of use, tin should figure among your top choices. As with any newsreader, you'll have to spend some time setting up your subscription list, but once you've done so, you'll find tin remarkably easy to use.

FROM HERE

- For an introduction to netiquette and working with the USENET community, see Chapter 15, "Working with a virtual community."

- For tips and pointers on writing for a USENET audience, see Chapter 16, "Posting your own messages."

- To make sure you've learned all you can about a newsgroup before you post, see Chapter 16, "Posting your own messages."

- For pointers on handling replies via email and follow-up postings, see Chapter 16, "Posting your own messages."

- To ensure that you don't make posting mistakes that could get you flamed, see Chapter 17, "Dealing with USENET problems."

- Need help finding the right newsgroups? See Part IV, "Building your subscription list."

One of the premier UNIX newsreaders, the nn program is *menu-driven* (options are chosen from a menu). It's also a threaded newsreader, (articles are grouped by thread). In these respects, it resembles tin, the subject of the previous chapter. But nn represents a level of power beyond any of the previously discussed newsreaders. A few examples:

- A built-in uudecode function lets you quickly and automatically decompress, concatenate (join together), and decode multi-part binary files, such as executable program and graphics files.

- There's no waiting for the list of unread articles to appear on-screen, even if there are thousands of them, since nn employs its own super-fast database.

- You can merge related newsgroups (such as alt.rock-n-roll.*) so that they appear on-screen as if they were a single newsgroup.

But be forewarned: All this power comes at a price. If you're not familiar with UNIX, nn can be a pain to learn. In keeping with UNIX's minimalist philosophy, nn strives for economy and efficiency—but sometimes at the expense of transparency and ease of use. You'll find that some of nn's trickier commands assume knowledge of tacit UNIX conventions; if you're not familiar with them, there's a steep initial learning curve. For instance, in the version of nn currently in widespread use there's no newsgroup selector level, making it very inconvenient to subscribe and unsubscribe to newsgroups.

(Note, however, that version 6.5 will remedy this deficiency.) If you're new to UNIX and USENET, I recommend that, if possible, you start with tin (see Chapter 10, "Reading the news with tin"), the easiest of all the UNIX newsreaders to learn and use. Still, nn's powerful capabilities amply repay the time and effort you put into learning the program.

A European effort, nn has 1986 origins in the work of a programmer at Texas Instruments' Denmark office, Kim F. Storm. Storm maintained the program through version 6.4, the one commonly found at UNIX sites throughout the world. In the early 1990s, Peter Wemm, a German programmer who works for an Internet service provider, took over nn's development in concert with a mailing list of about 70 active participants who called themselves the "nn development group." Whether we'll see a Version 6.5 depends on this group's ability to put in volunteer time, a scarce commodity in their busy lives.

In case you're curious, "nn" stands for "No News is Good News." If you choose a newsgroup that has no unread news, you see the message, "No news is good news." Well, maybe, but I do sort of enjoy reading USENET, Kim....

This chapter covers the fundamentals of using nn for reading the news. As with other powerful UNIX newsreaders, I haven't discussed all the advanced features of the program (just the ones you're likely to use on a regular basis). Covered in this chapter is Kim Storm's version of nn, version 6.4, with notes on the improved features in the forthcoming version 6.5. If you're not sure which version you're using, start nn, as described in the section titled "Starting nn" and type **V**. You'll see the current version number at the bottom of the screen.

> **TIP:** Be careful about capitalization when typing nn's commands—to nn, **G** and **g** mean two totally different things.

DEFINING YOUR SUBSCRIPTION LIST

One of nn's least-loved qualities is the fact that, by default, it subscribes you to all the USENET newsgroups available at your site. If you have a kind sys-

tem administrator, this list may have been narrowed down to a more manageable number; Delphi, for example, narrows the list down to 35 newsgroups (see Table 11-1).

Otherwise, you'll be subscribed to about ten zillion newsgroups—and when you start nn, you'll be forced to read these groups in the default presentation order (the order they're listed in .newsrc). This is very inconvenient; in order to read the groups you're interested in, you'll have to use the G command (discussed in a later section), and type the name of the next group you want to read. Sooner or later, you'll want to edit your .newsrc file so that you can read your favorite newsgroups in the order you want—so why not do it right now?

TABLE 11-1. INITIAL nn SUBSCRIPTION LIST (DELPHI)

alt.answers	comp.windows.s
alt.bbs	news.announce.important
alt.fan.dave_barry	news.announce.users
alt.internet.services	news.answers
alt.irc	news.groups
alt.politics.clinton	news.lists
alt.rock-n-roll	news.users.questions
alt.sources	rec.arts.movies
comp.graphics	rec.arts.startrek.current
comp.multimedia	rec.games.trivia
comp.music	rec.humor
comp.os.ms-windows.apps	rec.humor.funny
comp.programming	rec.sport.baseball
comp.sys.ibm.pc.misc	soc.politics
comp.sys.mac.announce	

Creating .newsrc

The first step you take to create your subscription list involves starting nn and immediately quitting the program; this puts all the available newsgroups into your .newsrc file. For information on starting the program, see the following section titled "Starting nn." Remember to exit immediately by typing **Q** (a capital Q, not a lowercase q).

Editing .newsrc

To edit .newsrc, you'll need to know how to use your system's default editor (probably vi, but possibly another text editor such as emacs). To open the file with vi, you type the following:

```
vi .newsrc
```

On-screen, you'll see a list of newsgroup names, such as the one shown in Figure 11-1. Note that each newsgroup name ends in a colon (:). The colon indicates that you're subscribed to the newsgroup. As you can see, you're currently subscribed to *all* the newsgroups.

Now you'll do a global replace, in which your text editor replaces all the colons with exclamation marks (!). The exclamation mark indicates that you're unsubscribed to the current group. After performing the global replace operation, you'll be unsubscribed to all of the newsgroups.

To perform the global replace with vi, carefully type the following and press Enter:

```
:s/:/!/
```

Figure 11-1. .newsrc is a text file containing the names of available USENET newsgroups.

This command tells vi to go through the file and replace all the colons with exclamation marks.

When your text editor has finished performing the global replace, search for the newsgroups you want to read on a regular basis, and change the exclamation points back to colons. With vi, you can search for a group by typing a forward slash (/) followed by the newsgroup name, as in the following:

```
/news.announce.newusers
```

When you've located the group to which you want to subscribe, change the exclamation point back to a colon. With vi, you do this by positioning the cursor on the exclamation point and typing the following:

```
r:
```

Now save the file. With vi, you do this by typing **ZZ**. You've trimmed down your subscription list to a manageable size, and now you're ready to enjoy nn.

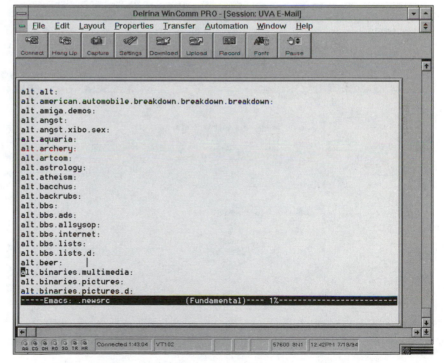

125

STARTING NN

The method you use to start nn depends on which system you're using. In some systems, you choose nn from a menu, such as the one shown here:

```
Welcome to the nn news reader
Release 6.4.18

Unlike the other news readers you might
be familiar with, the ultimate goal of
nn is "not to read news"; actually,
"nn" is an acronym for "No News," and
the motto of nn is:

No news is good news, but nn is better.

I hope that you will enjoy using nn.

Three levels of online help are available:
? gives a quick reference guide for the
current mode.
```

```
:help explains how to get help on
specific subjects.
:man opens the online manual.

Use Q to quit nn.

Have fun,

Kim Fabricius Storm
Texas Instruments A/S
Denmark<
```

On other systems, you start nn by typing the following and pressing Enter:

```
nn
```

You'll see a message such as the following, except that nn will list the first subscribed newsgroup in your .newsrc file:

```
Enter news.announce.newusers (29
unread)?
```

You can type **n** for "no," or **y** for "yes." Go ahead and type **y**, and you'll get your first look at nn on-screen (Figure 11-2). As you can see, you're looking at nn's thread selector (nn's term for this level is selection mode). At this level, you can do the following:

- Display the next or previous newsgroup
- Subscribe to a newsgroup
- Browse through the thread list
- Switch to the article selector and read articles

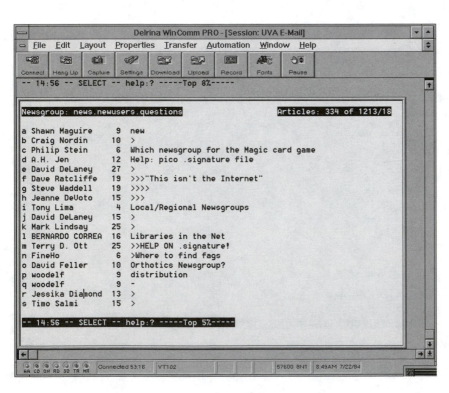

Figure 11-2. Since there's no newsgroup selector in nn, the program starts at the thread selector level.

126

Figure 11-3. Type a question mark (?) to display a help screen such as this one (for nn's thread selector).

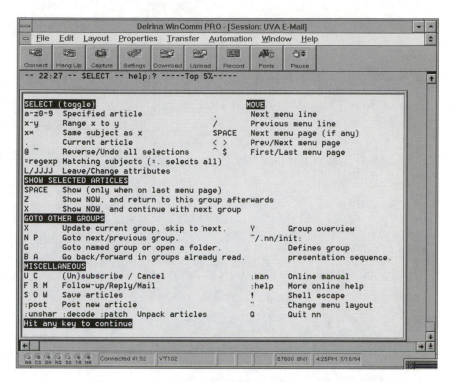

Following a brief section on getting on-screen help with nn, subsequent sections discuss each of these in detail.

GETTING HELP

To get help with whatever you're doing in nn (such as using the thread selector), just type a question mark (?). You'll see a screen such as the one shown in Figure 11-3. To return to nn, just press any key.

Table 11-2 summarizes how to use the cursor in nn.

NEWSGROUP NAVIGATION BASICS

Although nn doesn't have a newsgroup selector level, you can display a list of subscribed newsgroups, move up or down in the subscription list, and subscribe or unsubscribe to newsgroups. The following sections detail these procedures.

Displaying a list of subscribed newsgroups

To see a list of the newsgroups to which you've subscribed, type **Y**. You'll see a list such as the following:

```
320  news.answers
219*news.newusers.questions
29   news.software.nn
```

For each newsgroup, the number of unread articles is shown. The asterisk shows your current position in the list. To continue with nn, just press any key.

TABLE 11-2. MOVING THE CURSOR IN NN

PRESS THIS KEY:	TO MOVE TO:
Down arrow (or ,)	Down one line
Up arrow (or /)	Up one line
Space bar	Next page and mark read articles as read
Enter (or >)	Next page without marking read articles as read
<	Previous page
$	Last (bottom) page of articles
^	First (top) page of articles

Displaying the next or previous newsgroup

Your subscription list consists of the newsgroups within .newsrc that you've marked with a colon (:), and you see these groups in the order in which they're listed in .newsrc. To move to other newsgroups, you have the following command options:

- To mark all the articles in the current newsgroup as read and move to the next newsgroup in the list, type **X**.

- To display the next subscribed newsgroup that contains unread news, type **N**. If you're on the last page of the newsgroup, just press the space bar.

- To display the previous newsgroup, type **P**.

> **TIP:** When you're reading the last newsgroup in your subscription list, remember that nn will dump you out of the program if you type N to go to the next newsgroup. If you don't want to quit nn, go to another newsgroup by typing its name, as explained next.

Going to a newsgroup by name

To jump to a newsgroup by typing its name, press **G**. You'll see the following message:

```
Group or Folder (+./~ %=sneN)
```

Within the parentheses, you see options pertaining to folders (files containing stored articles) and various search options, which aren't relevant here. Just type the newsgroup name, and press Enter. You then see the following message:

```
Number of articles (juasne) (j)
Use: j)ump u)nread a)ll @)archive
s)ubject n)ame e)ither or number
```

The default option, j, is the one you want. It means jump to the newsgroup. Just press Enter, and you'll see the newsgroup's thread selector.

Unsubscribing to Newsgroups

If you've decided that you don't want to read a newsgroup regularly, you can unsubscribe easily. With the newsgroup's thread selector on-screen, type **U**. You'll see a message such as the following:

```
Unsubscribe to alt.net-
abusers.flame.flame.flame ?
```

Type **y** to confirm unsubscribing to this group.

If you change your mind, just type **U** again. You'll see this message:

```
Already unsubscribed. Resubscribe to
alt.net-abusers.flame.flame.flame?
```

Type **y** if you really want to resubscribe; otherwise, type **n**.

Table 11-3 summarizes how to use the newsgroup selector in nn.

USING THE THREAD SELECTOR

By default, nn displays the current newsgroup's subjects (threads). You can change the display, change the sort order, and select articles for reading. The following sections detail these procedures.

Understanding the thread selector

Helpful features make nn's thread selector easy to use. At the top of the screen, you see the newsgroup name and the total number of articles in the newsgroup. At the bottom of the screen, you see a status line such as the following:

```
-- 17:16 -- SELECT -- help:? -----Top
6%-----
```

Indicated from left to right are the current time, the current mode (SELECT, the mode in which you select articles to read), a reminder that you can display a help screen by typing a question mark (?), and an indication of where the currently displayed page of articles stands among the articles available for display (here, you're viewing the top of the first page of the articles, which shows the first 6% of the articles available to read).

TABLE 11-3. NEWSGROUP SELECTOR QUICK REFERENCE (NN)

PRESS THIS KEY:	TO DO THIS:
?	View a help screen of commands at this level
G	Subscribe to a newsgroup by typing its name
N	Go to the next subscribed group
P	Go to the last group you displayed
Q	Quit nn
U	Unsubscribe to the current group
Y	Display a list of subscribed groups

This is the best choice for most situations. Sometimes, though, you may wish to group articles in other ways. Here's a quick overview of your sort options:

- **Arrival time.** Articles are sorted by the time they arrived at your site.

- **Subject.** This is the default sort order. Threads are grouped by subject, with the earliest-arriving articles shown first.

Changing the display

If you press the open double quotes (") key, nn cycles among four different display modes:

```
Jonny Jetson    26 Short introduction

26   Short introduction

Short introduction

Jonny Jetson    Short introduction +26
```

The number (in this example, "26,") refers to the number of lines in the listed article.

> **TIP:** If the current screen shows some follow-up articles, you will see greater-than signs (>)—sometimes three or four of them. One greater-than sign (>) indicates that the article is a direct reply to the original posting. Two signs (>>) indicate a reply to the first follow-up posting; three (>>>) indicate a reply to the second follow-up posting, and so on.

Sorting the display

One of nn's powerful features is the ability to sort the display. By default, nn sorts the articles by subject, allowing you to follow the threads with ease.

- **Lexical.** Threads are shown in alphabetical order.

- **Age.** Threads are sorted by the article's age (the creation date), with the oldest articles first.

- **Sender.** Threads are sorted by author, with all of an author's posts grouped together.

To sort the display, type a colon (:) to enter nn's command mode. Then type **sort** followed by a space and the sort option you want, as in the following example:

```
:sort lexical
```

Press Enter to confirm your choice.

If you make a mistake, such as leaving out the space or spelling part of the command wrong, you see a message such as the following:

```
unknown command: "SORTSSER"
```

Just try again.

Selecting and deselecting articles

You can select more than one article to read a time. The articles you've selected appear in reverse video (highlighted). When you move to the article selector, you'll see the articles you've selected, one after the other, with no unselected articles between them. The status line changes to show the number of selected articles left to read, as in the following:

```
-- 20:11 --alt.etext-- 2 MORE+next --
help:?--Top 3%-
```

It pays to learn the selection commands. You can use them to create a tailored selection list of just those articles you want to read.

To select the article on which the cursor is selected, just type a period (.). Remember that you can also type an asterisk (*), which automatically selects all the articles with the same subject. If you change your mind, just use the same command again.

To select an article other than the one on which the cursor is positioned, just type the article's letter.

You can also select articles by typing a *regular expression*, such as FAQ (this expression will select all the articles that contain the word "FAQ" in their subject lines). It isn't necessary to use wildcards with this command. To select using an expression, type an equals sign (**=**). You'll see the following message:

```
Select regexp:
```

Type the word you want to use as a basis for selection, and press Enter.

> **TIP:** If you want to deselect the articles you selected with an expression, just type two tildes (~~).

Table 11-4 summarizes the use of the thread selection in nn.

READING ARTICLES

Once you've selected the articles you want to read, it's easy to read them: Just type **Z**. You'll see the first selected article on-screen. Once you've displayed an article, you can page through it, change the display, encrypt it or decrypt it, decode it, and search for text within it. When you've reached the end of the

TABLE 11-4. THREAD SELECTOR QUICK REFERENCE (NN)	
PRESS THIS KEY:	TO DO THIS:
"	Cycles through display formats
$	Display the last article in the menu
*	Select entire thread
,	Move cursor down one line
.	Select article
/	Move cursor up one line
:sort	Change the way the articles are grouped
<	View the previous page
=	Select all the articles matching a pattern you specify
>	View the next page without marking articles as read
^	Display the first article in the menu
~~	Deselect articles selected by pattern searching
Down arrow	Move cursor down one line
Q	Quit nn
space bar	View the next page
Up arrow	Move cursor up one line
Z	Read selected article(s)

article, you can leave it for later action (mark it as unread), mark the article as read and go on to the next (or previous), save the article, or mail it to someone. (Of course, you can also reply via email or post a followup message, as explained later in this chapter.) The following sections explain in detail what you can do while you're reading the news.

Changing the display

To see the article's full header, just type **h**. Should you encounter an article with lots of extra spaces and unneeded tabs, you can compress this white space by typing **c** (if the command doesn't work as you expected).

Encrypting or decrypting with rot-13

Occasionally, you'll encounter an article that's been encrypted with rot-13, which hides objectionable material from those who might be offended by it. To decrypt an article containing rot-13 text, type **D**. To encrypt an article that contains ordinary text, use the same command (**D**).

Decoding an article

If you're viewing an article that was encoded with uuencode, you can decode it using the :decode command. To use this command, type **:decode** and press Enter. You'll see the following message:

```
Decode Directory:
```

Type the directory in which you want to store the decoded file, and press Enter. When the decoding is complete, you'll see the name of the file.

> **TIP:** To decode a multi-part file, return to the thread selector by typing **Z**. Then select all the files, and use the :decode command.

Searching for text

If you're reading a lengthy article, such as a FAQ, you may wish to search forward in the article for text matching characters you specify. For example, suppose you're interested in the section of the FAQ that deals with file compression. You can search for "file compression," and nn will take you to the next occurrence of that text, skipping as many screens as necessary.

To search forward for text, just type a forward slash (/) followed by the text you want to find. To continue the search for another instance of the same term, type a period.

Marking articles as read

When you've looked at an article, you need to tell nn what to do with it—hold it for later rereading, mark it as read, or kill the whole subject for this session.

To hold the article for later rereading, type **l**. You'll see this article again in the thread selector.

To mark the article as read (whether or not you've actually reached the end of it), type **n**. You'll see the next selected article.

To kill the article's subject (and other articles with the same subject) for the current session, type **k**. You'll see the first selected article in the next thread. This is a good option if the thread turns out to be uninteresting—why bother going through the rest of the articles in the thread?

Saving articles

To save the article with a full header, type **s**. To save the article with a short header, type **o**. Either way, you'll see a message such as the following:

```
Save on (+~|) +alt.activism
```

This message tells you that nn is proposing to save the article in a file named after the newsgroup you're reading. To save the article to a file with a name you specify, press Del to wipe out the newsgroup's name, and type the file name you want. Then press Enter.

Forwarding articles

To mail the article to an email address you specify, type **m**. You'll see the message:

```
Include original article?
```

Type **y** to include the text of the original article in the thread, if it's available; type **n** to send just the article you're displaying. You're then prompted to type an email address. Type the address, and press Enter. Next, you're prompted to enter a subject.

Type the subject, and press Enter. The next section gives you the opportunity to edit the forwarded message; type **y** to edit the message with your default text editor. If you type **n**, nn sends the message to the address you've specified. Table 11-5 summarizes how to use the article selector in nn.

POSTING NEW MESSAGES

Before you post your own articles, please read Part III, "Now it's your turn," with care (especially Chapters 15 and 17). Under no circumstances should you post to USENET until you fully understand the fundamentals of network etiquette and the special characteristics of the newsgroup to which you want to post.

You can post new messages at either level of nn—the thread selector or the article selector.

TIP: Want to crosspost your message? To do so, type a comma after the newsgroup name that's currently entered on the newsgroups line, and type an additional newsgroup name. If you wish to crosspost to more newsgroups, type the name of each group to which you want to post your message, separating the names by commas.

TABLE 11-5. ARTICLE SELECTOR QUICK REFERENCE (NN)

PRESS THIS KEY:	TO DO THIS:
/	Search forward in an article for text matching a pattern you specify
?	Display help
D	Toggle rot-13 coding on and off
f	Post a follow-up message
K	Kill the current thread for this session and display the first unread article in the next thread
I	Mark an article as unread
m	Mail the current article to an Internet electronic mail address
n	Mark the current article as read and display the next unread article
o	Save the current article without full header to a file
p	Display the previous article
Q	Quit nn
s	Save the current article with full header to a file
Z	Return to the thread selector

To post a new message, type **:post**. You'll see the following message:

```
POST to group
```

Type the name of the newsgroup or newsgroups to which you want to post, and press Enter. You'll see the following message:

```
Subject:
```

Type a brief, descriptive subject, and press Enter. You'll then see the following message:

```
Keywords:
```

Type three or four words that describe your message's content, and press Enter. You'll see the following:

```
Summary:
```

Briefly summarize your message, and press Enter. You'll see the following message:

```
Distribution: (default 'world')
```

If it makes sense, type a narrower distribution and press Enter; otherwise, just press Enter to choose the default world distribution.

Next, you see your default editor—probably vi. Compose your message and save it. You'll then see the following message:

```
a)bort e)dit h)old m)ail r)eedit s)end
v)iew w)rite
Action: (post article)
```

Just press Enter to post the article to the newsgroup. To cancel the post, type **a** and press Enter.

> **TIP:** Want to include a signature with your posts? Like most newsreaders, nn automatically appends a file named .signature, if such a file is found in your home directory. You can create the file with a text editor.

WRITING A RESPONSE

You can write a response to the article that's currently displayed in the article selector. Like all good newsreaders, nn gives you two options for responding. You can reply directly to the author via email, or you can post a follow-up message to the newsgroup.

Whether you reply via email or post a follow-up message, you can choose to quote the text of the original article, if you like.

Sending a reply via email

To send a reply to the article's author through email, type **r**. You'll see the following message:

```
Include original article?
```

To include the article's text, type **y**. To omit the text, type **n**. Press Enter, and you'll see your default text editor. Type and save your response. When you exit the text editor, you'll see the following message:

```
a)bort e)dit h)old m)ail r)eedit s)end
v)iew w)rite
Action: (send letter)
```

Just press Enter to send the email reply, or type **a** to cancel. The mail is automatically sent to the email address in the original message's header.

Posting a follow-up message

To post a follow-up message, type **f**. You'll see the following message:

```
Include original article?
```

To include the article's text, type **y**. To omit the text, type **n**. Press Enter, and you'll see your default text editor. Type and save your response. When you exit the text editor, you'll see the following message:

```
a)bort c)c e)dit h)old m)ail r)eedit
s)end v)iew w)rite
Action: (post article)
```

Just press Enter to send the email reply, or type **a** to cancel. The mail is automatically sent to the email address in the original message's header.

KILLING UNWANTED POSTINGS

A good newsreader provides the means to screen out unwanted postings from net.abusers. With nn, you can kill all the postings with a specific subject. You can also kill all the postings from a particular author. Additionally, you can kill any posting that contains any text pattern you specify within the Subject line, the From line, or both. And you can kill within the currently selected newsgroups, or in all newsgroups. With these options, you can kill just about any type of message you don't want to see.

Killing the current subject

It's a simple matter to kill the current subject for a period of 30 days, which ought to be enough for the hue and cry to die down. To do so, display the article and type **K**. You'll see the following message:

```
AUTO (k)ill or (s)elect (CR => Kill
subject 30 days)
```

Just press Enter. You'll see a message asking you to type the number of the article that contains the subject line; type the number, and press Enter. You won't see this subject in the current newsgroup's subject list for 30 days.

Killing by subject

To kill articles by subject, type **K**. You'll see the following message:

```
AUTO (k)ill or (s)elect (CR => Kill
subject 30 days)
```

Type **k**, and you'll see the following:

```
AUTO KILL on (s)ubject or (n)ame (s)
```

To kill by subject, type **s**. You'll see a message such as the following:

```
KILL Subject: (=/)
```

To kill the subject of the current article, type the equals sign (**=**). To type a regular expression, type the forward slash (**/**), and then type the expression and press Enter. Alternatively, just type the exact subject line you want to kill.

> **TIP:** Here's an example of killing with a regular expression. To kill the words "must die" within any subject, use the regular expression *must die* (this will eliminate all messages of the sort "all <such-and-suches> must die," a favorite subject line of net.abusers.

You'll see the following message:

```
KILL in (g)roup 'alt.test' or in (a)ll
groups (g)
```

Type **g** to kill in the current newsgroup, or type **a** to kill globally (in all newsgroups). Next, you see the following message:

```
Lifetime of entry in days (p)ermanent
(30)
```

To kill the subject for a specified number of days, type the days and press Enter, or just press Enter to accept the default (30 days). To kill the subject permanently, type **p**. You'll be asked for confirmation; if you're serious about this, type **y**; otherwise, type **n**.

Killing by author

You use almost exactly the same procedure to kill by author. To kill articles by author, type **K**. You'll see the following message:

```
AUTO (k)ill or (s)elect (CR => Kill
subject 30 days)
```

Type **k**, and you'll see the following:

```
AUTO KILL on (s)ubject or (n)ame (s)
```

To kill by author, type **n**. You'll see a message such as the following:

```
KILL Subject: (=/)
```

To kill the author of the current article, type the equals sign (**=**); you'll be asked to confirm the kill name. To type a regular expression, type the forward slash (**/**), and then type the expression and press Enter. Alternatively, just type the exact name you want to kill.

Whatever kill option you choose, you'll see the following message:

```
KILL in (g)roup 'alt.test' or in (a)ll
groups (g)
```

Type **g** to kill in the current newsgroup, or type **a** to kill globally (in all newsgroups). Next, you see the following message:

```
Lifetime of entry in days (p)ermanent
(30)
```

To kill the subject for a specified number of days, type the days and press Enter, or just press Enter to accept the default (30 days). To kill the subject permanently, type **p**. You'll be asked for confirmation; if you're serious about this, type **y**; otherwise, type **n**.

AUTO-SELECTING "HOT" ARTICLES

With nn, you can use a variation of the kill procedures to do precisely the opposite: auto-select certain articles when you enter the newsgroup. This is a very convenient feature in that articles from "hot" authors or pertaining to "hot" topics are preselected; you just type **Z** to read them. (You can still select additional articles manually.)

To auto-select subjects and authors, type **K**, as you would for killing, as described in the previous section. You'll see the following menu:

```
AUTO (k)ill or (s)elect (CR => Kill
    subject 30 days)
```

Type **s**. From here, the procedures you use to auto-select subjects or authors are exactly the same as the ones you use to kill them; see the previous section for details.

SUMMARY

Not the easiest program to learn and use, nn seems rather long in the tooth—not too surprising, considering that it's over ten years old, an eternity in Internet terms. Once you get used to its peculiarities, though, it isn't a bad newsreader—it can do just about everything you'd want a newsreader to do.

FROM HERE

- For an introduction to netiquette and working with the USENET community, see Chapter 15, "Working with a virtual community."

- For tips and pointers on writing for a USENET audience, see Chapter 16, "Posting your own messages."

- To make sure you've learned all you can about a newsgroup before you post, see Chapter 16, "Posting your own messages."

- For pointers on handling replies via email and follow-up postings, see Chapter 16, "Posting your own messages."

- To ensure that you don't make posting mistakes that could get you flamed, see Chapter 17, "Dealing with USENET problems."

- Need help finding the right newsgroups? See Part IV, "Building your subscription list."

This chapter teaches you how to use two of the most widely used UNIX newsreaders: rn and trn. The two are virtually identical, except that trn is a threaded newsreader—and that fact alone makes it preferable to rn by a large margin. Still, rn is the only choice on many systems, so you may get stuck with it.

If you're stuck with rn, though, don't despair. You can still follow threads, but you'll have to use a keyboard command to do so. You'll find rn very powerful and reasonably easy to use—it's easier than nn (see Chapter 11, "Reading the news with nn"), though not as easy as tin (see Chapter 10, "Reading the news with tin").

This chapter covers the fundamentals of using rn and trn for reading the news. For this reason, many of rn's advanced commands, such as macros and startup options, aren't discussed. If you're lucky enough to have trn, start by reading what follows concerning rn; except for the thread selector, trn works exactly the same way.

STARTING RN OR TRN

The method you use to start rn or trn depends on which system you're using. In some systems, such as the one shown here, you choose rn or trn from a menu:

```
USENET newsgroups

nn    -      Read the news with nn
tin   -      Read the news with tin
```

```
rn    -      Read the news with rn
trn   -      Read the news with trn
<CR>  -      Return to the main menu
```

On other systems, you start rn or trn by typing the following and pressing Enter:

```
rn
```

   or

```
trn
```

When you start rn or trn, the program looks for your .newsrc file, which contains your list of subscribed newsgroups. On some systems, your system administrator may have set up this file for you so that it contains several newsgroups pertinent to new users, such as news.newusers.announce. If rn or trn doesn't find a .newsrc file, it creates one.

The program also checks your .newsrc file to make sure your newsgroup list is up-to-date. If your .newsrc file contains the names of newsgroups that have since been declared invalid, you may see a message informing you that your .newsrc file contains a bogus newsgroup. Just type **y** to remove the group.

If any new newsgroups have arrived at your site since you last logged on, you'll see a query telling you the group's name and asking whether you want to add the group. Type **y** to add the group to your subscription list, or **n** to leave the group unsubscribed.

Next, rn or trn displays a list of the number of unread messages in the first five newsgroups:

```
Unread news in clari.news.urgent 8
articles
Unread news in clari.nb.trends 9
articles
Unread news in clari.tw.computers 89
articles
Unread news in news.groups.reviews 1
article
Unread news in usa-today.news 5
articles
etc.
```

You then see the name of the first subscribed newsgroup, and rn or trn asks whether you want to read it. You see a message such as the following:

```
8 unread articles in clari.news.urgent
-- read now? [ynq]
```

At this point, you can do one of the following things:

- Read the first subscribed newsgroup. You'll see the article selector and the first unread article. For information on using the article selector, see the section titled "Reading articles," later in this chapter.

- Subscribe or unsubscribe to newsgroups. The next section covers the two programs' newsgroup selector.

> **TIP:** As you'll quickly learn, rn or trn is set up so that you can just press the space bar to accomplish the next action. If you're in doubt about what to do, try pressing the space bar. When you see command options in parentheses, you can press the space bar to choose the first option in the parentheses. For example, if you see (npq), pressing the space bar chooses "n."

GETTING HELP

It's easy to get help in rn or trn: Just type **h** at any time. You'll see a screen that lists the commands available at the current level. At the bottom of the screen, you'll see the following message:

```
[Type space to continue]
```

To see another screen of help, press the space bar. To quit help and return to rn or trn, type **q**.

USING THE NEWSGROUP SELECTOR

The newsgroup selector in rn or trn is crude by comparison to tin (see Chapter 10, "Reading the news with tin")—you don't see an on-screen list of subscribed newsgroups. To navigate among newsgroups, as well as to subscribe or unsubscribe to them, you must type commands when you see a prompt such as the following:

```
****** 10 unread articles in
clari.living.consumer -- read now?
[ynq]
```

The following sections describe your newsgroup selector options in detail.

Navigating among subscribed newsgroups

By default, rn or trn presents your subscribed newsgroups in the order they're listed in your .newsrc file—although, as you'll see, you can alter the newsgroup order without editing .newsrc. When you're asked whether you want to enter a newsgroup, you can use any of the following commands in Table 12-1 to navigate among your subscribed newsgroups:

When you reach the end of the subscription list, you see the following message:

```
****** End of newsgroups -- what next?
[npq]
```

To see the first newsgroup in your subscription list that still has unread news, type **n,** or type **p** to see the previous group with unread news. To exit rn or trn, just type **q**.

Unsubscribing to a newsgroup

When you see the prompt asking whether you want to enter a newsgroup, you can unsubscribe. Use the newsgroup navigation commands discussed in the previous section to display the prompt, such as the following:

TABLE 12-1. NAVIGATING AMONG YOUR SUBSCRIBED NEWSGROUPS

PRESS THIS KEY:	TO DO THIS:
n	Go to the next newsgroup with unread news
N	Go to the next newsgroup, whether or not it has unread news
p	Go to the previous newsgroup with unread news
P	Go to the previous newsgroup, whether or not it has unread news
- (hyphen)	Go to the previously displayed newsgroup, no matter where it stands in your subscription list
1	Go to the first newsgroup in your subscription list
^ (caret)	Go to the first newsgroup that contains unread news
$	Go to the end of the subscription list
g followed by a space and the newsgroup's name, and press Enter	Go to a subscribed newsgroup by typing its name
/ followed by the word (for example, /privacy finds comp.privacy), then press Enter	Search forward (down in the subscription list) for a subscribed newsgroup containing a word or pattern
? followed by the word, then press Enter	Search backward (up in the subscription list) for a subscribed newsgroup containing a word or pattern

```
54 unread articles in sci.aquaria --
read now? [ynq]
```

Just type **u** to unsubscribe to the newsgroup. You'll see a message such as the following:

```
Unsubscribed to newsgroup sci.aquaria
```

Restricting the display of newsgroups

To focus your reading on just those newsgroups whose names match a particular word such as "privacy," use the **o** (restriction) command (that's the letter o, not the number zero). For example, if you type **o privacy** and press Enter, rn or trn will restrict the display of groups to just those groups that contain "privacy" in their names. The restriction

remains in effect until you've finished reading all the unread articles in the newsgroups. To end the restriction before finishing all the unread articles, type **o** by itself and press Enter.

> **TIP:** Use the restriction command frequently—it's a great way to make temporary groups of subscribed newsgroups so that it's easy to move among them. For example, typing **O news** groups together the two newsgroups containing the word "news": usa-today.news and clari.news.urgent, which I like to read at the beginning of a USENET session.

Subscribing to newsgroups

With rn or trn, you can subscribe to a newsgroup by typing its name. If you can't remember the newsgroup's exact name you can search your .newsrc file for both subscribed and unsubscribed groups that match the pattern. This search procedure is discussed in the following section.

To subscribe to a newsgroup by typing its name, type **g** followed by a space and the newsgroup's name. If you aren't currently subscribed to the newsgroup, you'll see a message such as the following:

```
Newsgroup alt.flame is unsubscribed --
resubscribe? [yn]
```

To subscribe to the newsgroup, type **y**. If you change your mind, type **n**.

Searching for a newsgroup's name

If you can't remember the exact name of the newsgroup to which you want to subscribe, you can see an on-screen list. To see this list, type **l** followed by the part of the newsgroup's name you remember. For example, typing "**l feminism**" searches for all the newsgroups that contain "feminism" in their titles. You'll see the following message:

```
Completely unsubscribed newsgroups:
```

After this message you'll see the names of groups, if any, that are known to the server but aren't contained in your .newsrc file. After being prompted to press Enter, you then see the following:

```
Unsubscribed but mentioned in
/home/.newsrc:
alt.feminism
soc.feminism
```

To subscribe to one of these groups, you can use the g command, as discussed previously. To subscribe to all of them, see the next section.

Subscribing to newsgroups that match a pattern

To build your subscription list quickly, you can subscribe to all the groups matching a pattern you specify. Type **a** followed by the pattern you want.

For example, typing "**a bicycle**" tells rn or trn to search for all the unsubscribed newsgroups that contain the word "bicycle." If rn or trn finds any matching newsgroups, you'll see one or more queries, such as the following:

```
Newsgroup rec.bicycles.marketplace is
unsubscribed -- resubscribe? [yn]
```

Type **y** to subscribe to the newsgroup, or type **n** to reject the group and move on to the next query, if there is one.

Moving newsgroups

With rn or trn, you can move newsgroups in your subscription list without editing .newsrc. To do so, type **m** and press Enter. You'll see the following:

```
Put newsgroup where? [$^Lq]
```

At this point, you have the options shown in Table 12-2.

Table 12-3 provides a quick overview of working with the newsgroup selector.

READING ARTICLES

To read the news with rn or trn, use the newsgroup selection level's navigation commands to display the prompt for the newsgroup you want to read, such as the following:

```
54 unread articles in sci.aquaria --
read now? [ynq]
```

Just type **y** to read the first unread article in this group. If the article doesn't fit on one page, press the space bar to continue. Keep going until you reach the end of the article. When you come to the end of an article, you'll see the following message:

```
End of article 51923 (of 52245) -- what
next? [npq]
```

> **TIP:** To mark an article as read without having to page through the whole article, just type **n**. You'll see the next unread article.

TABLE 12-2. POSITIONING NEWSGROUPS

PRESS THIS KEY:	TO DO THIS:
^	Put the newsgroup first
$	Put the newsgroup last
.	Put the newsgroup before the current one
- followed by a subscribed newsgroup's name	Put it before that newsgroup
+ followed by a subscribed newsgroup's name	Put it after that newsgroup
L	See a list of your currently subscribed newsgroups, showing the order in which they're currently arranged
q	Cancel this command

The following sections discuss what you can do at the article selector level.

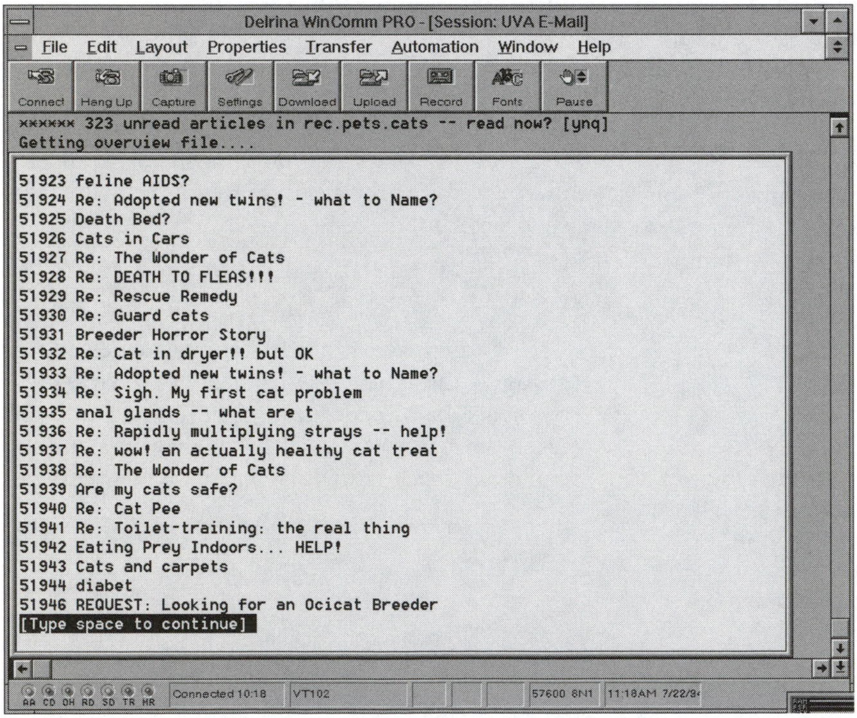
Delrina WinComm PRO - [Session: UVA E-Mail]
File Edit Layout Properties Transfer Automation Window Help
Connect Hang Up Capture Settings Download Upload Record Fonts Pause
****** 323 unread articles in rec.pets.cats -- read now? [ynq]
Getting overview file....
51923 feline AIDS?
51924 Re: Adopted new twins! - what to Name?
51925 Death Bed?
51926 Cats in Cars
51927 Re: The Wonder of Cats
51928 Re: DEATH TO FLEAS!!!
51929 Re: Rescue Remedy
51930 Re: Guard cats
51931 Breeder Horror Story
51932 Re: Cat in dryer!! but OK
51933 Re: Adopted new twins! - what to Name?
51934 Re: Sigh. My first cat problem
51935 anal glands -- what are t
51936 Re: Rapidly multiplying strays -- help!
51937 Re: wow! an actually healthy cat treat
51938 Re: The Wonder of Cats
51939 Are my cats safe?
51940 Re: Cat Pee
51941 Re: Toilet-training: the real thing
51942 Eating Prey Indoors... HELP!
51943 Cats and carpets
51944 diabet
51946 REQUEST: Looking for an Ocicat Breeder
[Type space to continue]
Connected 10:18
VT102
57600 8N1
11:18AM 7/22/9

Figure 12-1. With rn, you can view a list of the subjects in the current newsgroup; just press the equals sign (=) to enter the group.

Viewing a list of subjects (rn)

Although rn isn't a threaded newsreader, you can still view a list of subjects. To view this list, type an equals sign **(=);** you'll see a subject list similar to the one shown in Figure 12-1. Press the space bar to continue. (To quit displaying the subject list, type **q**.)

Viewing the threads (trn only)

When you enter a newsgroup in trn's threaded (+) mode, you see a list of articles grouped by thread (see Figure 12-2). As you can see, articles are grouped so that all the responses are

TABLE 12-3. NEWSGROUP SELECTOR QUICK REFERENCE (RN OR TRN)

PRESS THIS KEY:	TO DO THIS:
$	Go to the end of the subscription list
-	Go to the previously displayed newsgroup
/	Search forward for a newsgroup matching a pattern you specify
?	Search backward for a newsgroup matching a pattern you specify
^	Go to the first newsgroup with unread news
1	Go to the first newsgroup, whether or not it has unread news
c	Mark the current group as read and go to the next unread group
g	Subscribe to a newsgroup by typing its name
h	View a help screen of commands at this level
l	Type a pattern and press Enter to see a list of newsgroups containing text that matches the pattern
m	Move the current newsgroup—type **h** to see a list of moving options
m	Move the selected group within the subscription list
n	Go to the next newsgroup with unread news
N	Go to the next newsgroup, whether or not it has unread news
o	Type a pattern and press Enter to set up a newsgroup display restriction. To end the restriction, just type o and press Enter
P	Go to the previous newsgroup, whether or not it has unread news
p	Go to the previous newsgroup
q	Quit rn or trn
u	Unsubscribe to the current group
y	Read the current group now

shown after the article they quote. Note that some-times the subject changes during the discussion; trn still groups the articles that were written in response to the thread, even if the subject name changes. The number at the beginning of the thread indicates the number of articles in the group.

Article navigation options

When viewing an article with rn or trn, you can use any of the navigation commands in Table 12-4 to navigate within the article.

Article display options

While reading articles, you can use display options that enable you to display both header information and rot-13 (rotated) text. To see all the header information associated with an article, type **v**. To decrypt text encoded with rot-13, type **X**. To encrypt the text again, just repeat the command. To restart the article and decrypt the text, press **Ctrl + X**.

Disposing of articles

When you've decided to stop reading an article, you have the options shown in Table 12-5.

Marking all the articles in a group as read

If all the current articles in the newsgroup seem uninteresting, you can mark them all as read by typing **c**. You'll see the following message:

```
Do you really want to mark everything
as read? [yn]
```

Type **y** to confirm marking all the articles as read, or type **n** to return to the article selector.

Reading the next article on the same subject (rn only)

Although rn isn't a threaded newsreader, you can still follow a discussion by using the Ctrl + N command. This command scans forward for the same subject and makes ^N (Ctrl + N) the default command choice for the next article; you can choose it by just pressing the space bar. Try it!

To cancel the threaded reading mode, just use another of the article selector commands, such as n or p.

Note this command works in trn, too—but I can't imagine that you'd want to hunt for threads this way when you can use trn's thread selector.

Searching for a subject

To search for the next article with a subject that contains a pattern you specify, press the forward

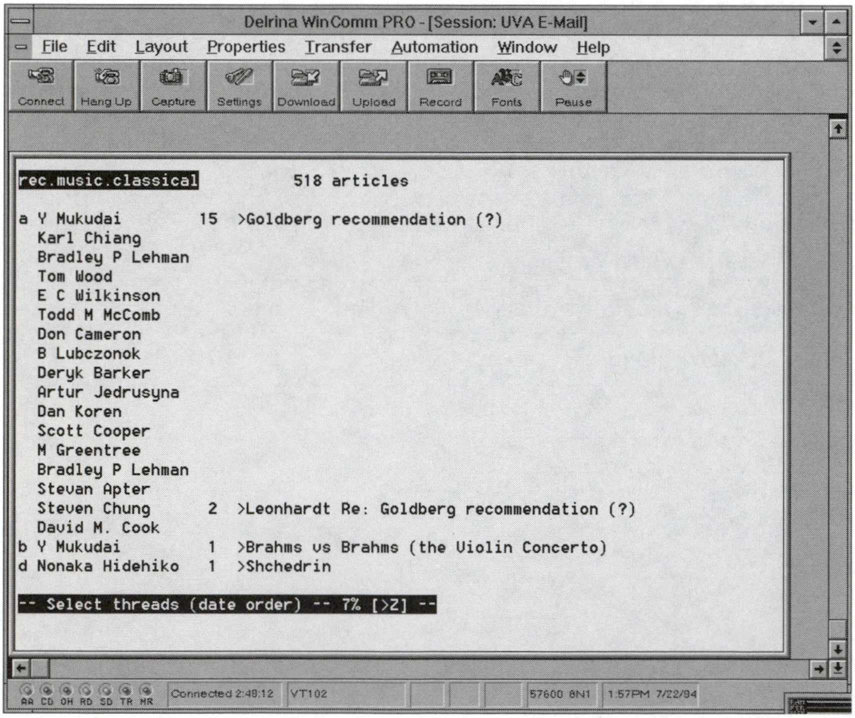

Figure 12-2. trn sorts the article list by threads.

TABLE 12-4. NAVIGATION COMMAND QUICK REFERENCE (RN OR TRN)

PRESS THIS KEY:	TO DO THIS:
b	Back up a page
Enter	Display one more line of the article
d	Display another half page of the article
Ctrl + R	Restart the current article
q	Go to the end of the current article without marking it as read or unread

slash (/) key followed by the pattern you want to match. Then press Enter. If rn or trn can match the text, the program displays the page of the article that contains the text you typed. If not, you see the message "Not found."

Searching headers

You can also search for text within headers. This command can be used to search for authors, origination sites, organizations, and other infor-

mation that appears within an article's header. To do so, press the forward slash (/) key followed by the pattern you want to match. Then press the slash key again and type **h.** Finally, press Enter. Your command looks something like this:

`/esmith@barney.dinosaur.com/h`

If rn or trn can match the text, the program displays the page of the article that contains the text you typed. If not, you see the message "Not found."

TABLE 12-5. NAVIGATING ARTICLES IN RN AND TRN

PRESS THIS KEY:	TO DO THIS:
j	Mark the article as read and go to the end of the article
m	Mark the article as unread and go to the end of the article
k	Mark as read all articles with the same subject as the current article
n	Go to the next unread article
N	Go to the next article, whether or not it's read
p	Go to the previous article
P	Go to the previous article, whether or not it's read
-	Go to the previously displayed article, no matter where it stands in the article sequence
the number and press Enter	Go to the number of the article (as displayed in the subject list)

Searching article text

An advanced feature of rn or trn is its ability to search for article text. To do so, press the forward slash (/) key followed by the pattern you want to match. Then press the slash key again and type **a**. Finally, press Enter. Your command looks something like this:

```
/veterinarian/a
```

If rn or trn can match the text, the program displays the page of the article that contains the text you typed. If not, you see the message "Not found."

Extracting binary files

If the article you're reading contains a binary file encoded with uuencode, you can easily and quickly decode it by typing **e**.

> **TIP:** To decode a binary file posted in two or more articles, display each article in sequence, type e in each of them. Be sure to follow the sequence exactly; for example, decode the article named "1/3" first, followed by "2/3" and "3/3."

Saving articles to a file

You can save one or more articles to a file in your home directory. To do so, display the article you want to save. Then type **s** followed by a space and the name of the file in which you want to save the article. Then press Enter.

Table 12-6 summarizes the use of the article selector in rn and trn.

POSTING NEW MESSAGES

Before you post your own articles, please read Part III, "Now it's your turn," with care (especially Chapters 15 and 17). Under no circumstances should you post to USENET until you fully under-

stand the fundamentals of network etiquette and the special characteristics of the newsgroup to which you want to post.

To post a message on a new subject, switch to the article selector, if necessary, and type **f**. You'll see the following:

```
Are you starting an unrelated topic?
[ynq]
```

Type **y** to post a new message. You'll see the following:

```
Subject:
```

Type a brief, descriptive subject, and press Enter. You'll see the following:

```
distribution
```

Type a distribution and press Enter. To choose world distribution, just press Enter without typing anything.

You'll see a message warning you that this program posts messages that many will receive; type **y** if you're sure you want to proceed, or **n** to cancel. You're then prompted to type the name of a file to include, if any; just press Enter to skip this step.

Now Pnews starts your default editor as shown in Figure 12-3. At the top of the screen, note that you can edit the header lines, if you wish; you can add additional newsgroups for crossposting. Just separate the groups using commas.

When you're finished typing your post, choose the command that exits the text editor. For information on what to do next, see the section titled "Sending options," later in this section.

Note: Pnews isn't needed if you're using trn, which lets you post articles by using your default editor.

Sending a reply via email

To send a reply to the article's author through email, type **r**. You'll see the following message:

```
Prepared file to include [none]?
```

TABLE 12-6. ARTICLE SELECTOR QUICK REFERENCE (RN AND TRN)

TYPE THIS:	TO DO THIS:
-	Display the previously viewed article
/pattern	Search forward for a subject matching a pattern you specify
/pattern/a	Search forward for article text matching the pattern you specify
/pattern/h	Search forward for a pattern matching the pattern you specify
c	Mark this group as read and return to the newsgroup selector
Ctrl + n	Search forward for the next article with the same subject as the current article, and make ^N the default mode
e	Extract a uuencoded binary file
F	Post a follow-up message and quote the original article's text
f	Post a follow-up message without quoting the original article's text
j	Mark the article as read and go to the end of the article
k	Mark the current thread as read and display the first unread article in the next thread
m	Mark the article as unread and go to the end of the article
N	Mark the article as read and go to the next article, whether or not it's read
n	Mark the current article as read and display the next unread article
p	Display the previous article with unread text
P	Display the previous article, whether or not it has unread text
s	Save the current article (or tagged articles) to a file
X	Toggle rot-13 coding on and off

If you want to include a file, type its name and press Enter. Otherwise, just press Enter without typing anything else, and you'll see your default text editor (see Appendix A for quick reference guides to the most common default editors).

When you're finished typing your post, choose the command that exits the text editor, and turn to "Sending options," later in this section.

Posting a follow-up message

To post a follow-up message, display the article, and type **f** to post without quoting, or **F** to post with the article's text quoted. You'll see a message asking you to confirm that you want to do this; type **y.** You'll see the following message:

`Prepared file to include [none]?`

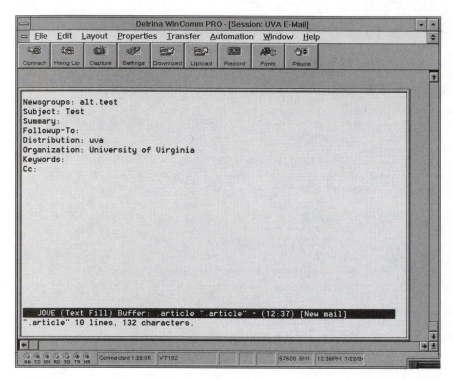

```
Delrina WinComm PRO - [Session: UVA E-Mail]
 File   Edit   Layout   Properties   Transfer   Automation   Window   Help

 Connect  Hang Up  Capture  Settings  Download  Upload  Record  Fonts  Pause


Newsgroups: alt.test
Subject: Test
Summary:
Followup-To:
Distribution: uva
Organization: University of Virginia
Keywords:
Cc:







  JOVE (Text Fill) Buffer: .article ".article" - (12:37) [New mail]
".article" 10 lines, 132 characters.

AA CD OH RD SD TR HR   Connected 1:28:05   VT102          57600 8N1  12:38PM 7/22/9
```

Figure 12-3. By default, rn or trn posts new messages to the newsgroup that's active when you type the f command.

message when you exit your text editor:

```
Check spelling,
Send, Abort, Edit,
or List?
```

To see what your message will look like, type **l**. At the bottom of the message, you'll see the same menu again.

To check the spelling in your article, type **c** and press Enter. If there are any misspellings, you'll see a screen with the mis-spelling highlighted; at the top you'll see possible correction words. If one of the correction words is the correct spelling, type its number. If not, press the space bar. You'll see the same menu again; type **e** to edit the document and correct the error. To cancel your message, type **a**. To send your message, type **s**.

To include a file, type its name and press Enter. Otherwise, just press Enter without typing anything else, and you'll see your default text editor (see Appendix A for quick reference guides to the most common default editors).

> **TIP:** If you're responding to a cross-posted message, consider whether you really want your article to go to all the crossposted groups. If not, please edit the newsgroups line in the article's header.

When you're finished typing your post, choose the command that exits the text editor, and turn to "Sending options," later in this section.

Sending options

Whether you're posting a new message, an email reply, or a follow-up message, you'll see the following

KILLING UNWANTED POSTINGS

Of all the UNIX newsreaders, rn or trn offers what are perhaps the most sophisticated capabilities for killing unwanted articles. However, they're also the most difficult to use—to get the most killing power, you'll have to edit a kill file directly.

Killing the easy way

The easiest way to kill is to display an article that contains a subject you want to kill, and type **K**. For example, suppose you are very sick of seeing articles with the subject "Macs Suck." One little letter—a K—will delete them from the current newsgroup permanently.

Using a kill file

Every newsgroup to which you're subscribed can have its own kill file, an ordinary text file that contains kill commands. To open this file, display an article within the newsgroup and press Ctrl + K. You'll see your default editor and a new, blank file. (If you use the K command just described, this file may already have a kill command within it.)

Each kill command must be typed on its own line and follow the following pattern exactly:

```
/: pattern/:j
```

In place of "pattern," you type a word or characters that you want to exclude. The j tells rn or trn to mark the article matching this pattern as read. Here's an example: To get rid of any article with a subject such as "All cat lovers must die," press Ctrl + K and type the following:

```
/:*die*/:j
```

Then save the file and exit your text editor. The killing doesn't take place until the next time you enter the newsgroup.

A kill command written like the preceding one kills articles that contain the pattern in the subject line. You can also kill articles based on text anywhere in the header, as well as within the article itself.

To kill any article from esmith@barney.dinosaur.com, for instance, type the following in the newsgroup's kill file:

```
/:*esmith@barney.dinosaur.com*/h:j
```

To kill any article containing the phrase "make money fast" in the article's text, type the following in the newsgroup's kill file:

```
/: *make money fast*/a:j
```

Save the kill file text; the killing will occur the next time you enter the group.

SUMMARY

The threaded version of rn, called trn, is one of the best UNIX newsreaders, offering a good combination of features. It's weak at the newsgroup selector level, though. If you're stuck with the older version, rn, you can still follow threads using the Ctrl + N keyboard command.

FROM HERE

- For an introduction to netiquette and working with the USENET community, see Chapter 15, "Working with a virtual community."

- For tips and pointers on writing for a USENET audience, see Chapter 16, "Posting your own messages."

- To make sure you've learned all you can about a newsgroup before you post, see Chapter 16, "Posting your own messages."

- For pointers on handling replies via email and follow-up postings, see Chapter 16, "Posting your own messages."

- To ensure that you don't make posting mistakes that could get you flamed, see Chapter 17, "Dealing with USENET problems."

- Need help finding the right newsgroups? See Part IV, "Building your subscription list."

READING THE NEWS WITH TRUMPET FOR WINDOWS

The first of the NNTP newsreaders to be thoroughly documented in this book, Trumpet for Windows is designed to work with Microsoft Windows in both dialup IP and local area network (LAN) settings. (Another NNTP newsreader for Microsoft Windows, the public domain reader WinVN, was featured in Chapter 2.) A shareware product, WinTrumpet is a far cry from the most powerful UNIX newsreaders—although it can group articles by subject, for example, there's no true threading, and no facilities are available for killing subjects or authors, whether globally or within a newsgroup. Still, WinTrumpet takes full advantage of the Microsoft Windows environment. As a result, it's considerably easier to use than any of the UNIX newsreaders, and this fact alone gives WinTrumpet an enthusiastic following.

You can use WinTrumpet on a Windows system that's connected to the Internet via dialup IP or a local area network (LAN). (For more information on connecting to the Internet, see Chapter 3.) In addition to providing USENET access, WinTrumpet also includes an email management program similar to Eudora. However, this chapter focuses on WinTrumpet's USENET capabilities.

WinTrumpet is the creation of Peter Tattam, a programmer in the Department of Psychology at the University of Tasmania, in Tasmania, Australia. A tireless worker, Tattam created Trumpet during late-night sessions. Incidently, Peter is a musician and plays—you guessed it—the trumpet.

OBTAINING AND INSTALLING WINTRUMPET

You can obtain WinTrumpet using anonymous FTP to the following address:

`ftp.utas.edu.au`

Please note that this site is located on a low-bandwidth network in a remote location. To avoid placing undue stress on this network, please download the WinTrumpet software during evening and weekend hours (Tasmania's time zone is ten hours ahead of GMT.)

There are four versions of WinTrumpet, but by far the most frequently used—and the one this book recommends—is WTWSK, the version designed to work with a Winsock-compliant TCP/IP driver for Microsoft Windows. The WTWSK file will be named in a way that indicates the current version (such as WTWSK10A.ZIP, the file for Version 1.0 A of WinTrumpet). Note that this file is compressed using PKZIP, a standard DOS/Windows file compression utility. You will need a copy of PKUNZIP.EXE, freely available in FTP sites throughout the Internet, to decompress the file. You also need the files WINTRUMP.HLP, NEWS.INI and NEWS.PRM.

After you've obtained WinTrumpet, make a directory called WINTRUMP, and store the files there. Run PKUNZIP.EXE to decompresss the *.ZIP file or files. Using Program Manager, create a WinTrumpet program group and add an icon for Trumpet for Windows.

TIP: Before installing WinTrumpet, you will need the following information: The full domain name of your NNTP server, the full domain name of the computer that houses your *SMTP* (electronic mail) *server,* your email address, and the *domain name* of your time server. (A domain name is an Internet address, such as Watt.seas.Virginia.edu.) If you're not sure what all this information is about, don't worry: You just have to type it in a dialog box when you configure WinTrumpet. If you don't have this information, get it from your service provider.

ABOUT SHAREWARE

WinTrumpet is distributed as shareware, which means—specifically—that you can use the program without charge for a 30-day evaluation period. If you decide to keep using the program after this period expires, you must register the program by sending the registration fee to Trumpet Software International (GPO Box 1649, Hobart, Tasmania, Australia 7001).

You're probably thinking, "Why bother sending the registration fee?" After all, you've got the software, and TSI is very unlikely to discover that you're using it without having paid the registration fee. Doubtless, many people use this and other shareware programs without paying the fee, but remember this: If no one pays registration fees, shareware authors will have no incentive to continue producing outstanding programs such as WinTrumpet and making them available at low cost. When you pay your registration fee, you are not only doing something that is decent and honest in its own right; you are also contributing positively to the computer-user community.

STARTING AND CONFIGURING WINTRUMPET

Before starting Trumpet, use your word processing program to create a signature file. Many servers cut off signatures longer than four lines, so keep yours short. Save the file in WinTrumpet's directory (WINTRUMP) as a plain (ASCII) text file named SIG.TXT, and quit your word processing program.

Before starting WinTrumpet, you should be logged on to your local area network. If you're using dialup IP, use your SLIP or PPP driver to establish a connection with your service provider.

If you've installed WinTrumpet as described in the previous section, you can start the program by double-clicking its icon in Program Manager. Win-Trumpet will automatically display the Trumpet Setup dialog box, shown in Figure 13-1. You need to supply Trumpet with the following information (ask your service provider or network administrator for this information if you don't have it):

- **NNTP Host Name.** Type the host name of the NNTP server here. You can type either the domain name (such as jefferson.cad.vua.edu) or an IP address, but it's preferable to type the domain name.

- **SMTP Host Name.** Type the name of the computer that houses the mail server you use. This information is needed so that you can send electronic mail replies to articles you read.

- **Email Address.** Type the first part of your email address before the @ sign, and the second part after the @ sign. For example, if your email address is teddy@jurassic.dinosaur.com, type "teddy" before the @ sign and "jurassic.dinosour.com" after the @ sign. This information is needed so that people can reply to you via email.

- **Organization.** If you wish, you can type the name of your organization here. Leave this blank if you're posting from a home computer or you don't want to associate your postings with your organization.

- **Full Name.** Type your full name in this area.

149

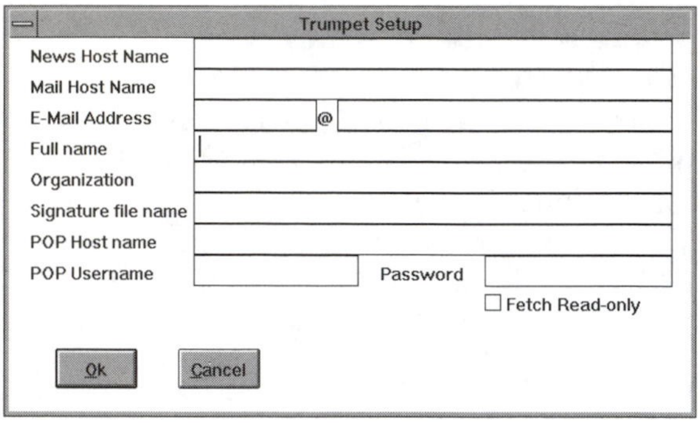

Figure 13-1. You see this dialog box when you start WinTrumpet for the first time.

- **Signature File Name.** If you want WinTrumpet to automatically append a signature file to your posts, type the name of your signature file (such as SIG.TXT) here.

The other fields are relevant only if you're using WinTrumpet's email capabilities, which are not covered in this chapter. When you're finished with the Trumpet Setup dialog box, choose OK.

Next, you see the Network Setup dialog box. If you're using the recommended WinSock version of WinTrumpet, you need only type the domain name of your local time server (this is optional). From this information, WinTrumpet derives the exact GMT, which it uses to record the time on your posts. If you leave this area blank, WinTrumpet uses the time from your computer's system clock. Choose OK to confirm your choices in this dialog box.

> **TIP:** Like using the keyboard? There are short-cut keys for most of WinTrumpet's commands, as indicated later in this chapter. Moreover, you can use standard Windows techniques to access menu items. For example, to open the Article menu and choose Append to File, hold down the Alt key and type **a** (for Article), and then type **a** one more time to select the Append to File option.

Using the newsgroup selector

After you finish configuring WinTrumpet, the program logs on to the NNTP server and downloads the lengthy list of newsgroup names. On a slow SLIP connection, this may take a few minutes. Assuming all goes well, your screen should look like the one in Figure 13-2.

> **TIP:** If you see a message that WinTrumpet cannot find the name of your server, choose Setup from the File menu, and try typing the actual IP address of the NNTP server. This bypasses the DNS lookup, which is prone to failure under certain conditions. Choose Reconnect from the File menu to reestablish the connection.

Understanding WinTrumpet's window

Like all Microsoft Windows applications, WinTrumpet runs in a standard window containing pull-down menus at the top of the screen. In the panel below the menu bar, you see the News window. **Note:** WinTrumpet also has a Mail window; if you see this window instead, the title bar will contain "[Mail]" instead of "[News]". To display the News window, choose 1 News from the Window menu.

Below the menu bar is a blank line that's used for status information, and below this is a box containing the names of subscribed newsgroups. You can use the scroll bar to display additional names.

Below the newsgroup box, you see another box—blank, at this point—that's used to display the text of articles.

At the bottom of the screen is a bar of buttons, which you'll use to control WinTrumpet. You learn more about these buttons in the section titled "Using the article selector" later in this chapter.

Unsubscribing ("zapping") all the newsgroups

When you log on with WinTrumpet the first time, the program automatically subscribes you to all the newsgroups available from your server. This is very inconvenient, since you'd have to scroll interminably

Figure 13-2. After you finish configuring WinTrumpet, the program establishes a connection with the NNTP server and downloads the newsgroup names.

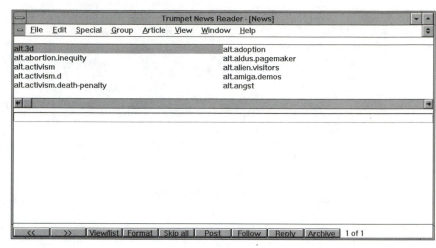

to find the group you want in the lengthy list. It's best to unsubscribe to all the groups and then subscribe selectively to just the ones you want to read on a regular basis.

To unsubscribe to all the groups, choose Zap All Subscribed Groups from the Special menu. You'll see an alert box asking you to confirm this command. **Note:** "Zapping" the groups doesn't delete them or make them inaccessible to you. It just removes their names from the subscription list. You can easily resubscribe to the groups you've "zapped."

Subscribing to newsgroups

Once you've "zapped" all those newsgroups' names, you can subscribe to just the groups you want. To do so, choose Subscribe from the Group menu. You

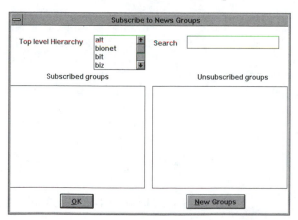

Figure 13-3. This dialog box provides tools for subscribing to newsgroups.

see the Subscribe to News Groups dialog box, shown in Figure 13-3.

To subscribe to newsgroups by scrolling, click the hierarchy to which you want to subscribe, and use the scroll bar to display the name of the newsgroup you want. Then just click the name. You'll see the newsgroup name in the left side of the dialog box.

To subscribe to a newsgroup by pattern-matching, type a word or part of a word (such as "music") in the Search box. In the Unsubscribed Groups area, WinTrumpet will display the names of the newsgroups that match this pattern, if any. To subscribe to a group, just click its name.

TIP: You can combine these subscription procedures to build your subscription list quickly. For instance, you could subscribe to all the groups pertaining to rock-n-roll.

USING THE SUBJECT SELECTOR

Trumpet isn't a true threaded newsreader, like trn (see Chapter 12, "Reading the news with rn and trn"), but it can group articles by subject. To display the subjects in a newsgroup, double-click the newsgroup's name in the subscription list. You'll see a dialog box informing you that WinTrumpet is scanning the group, and then the subjects appear in the lower half of the window, as shown in Figure 13-4.

If a scroll bar appears at the right of the box in which the subject names are displayed, you can scroll the window to see additional subjects.

USING THE ARTICLE SELECTOR

When you've identified an article that you want to read, just double-click the article's subject to display the article in the article window, as shown in Figure 13-5. At the bottom of the window are the following buttons:

• << Display the previous article

• >> Display the next article

• **View/List.** Toggle the display between the subject selector and the article selector windows.

• **Format.** Toggle the display between formatted text (with the currently chosen font) or plain text (using a system font). To change the font, choose Font from the Special menu.

• **Skip all.** Skip all the articles in the current newsgroup and go to the next newsgroup in your subscription list.

• **Post.** Post an article on a new subject to the current newsgroup.

• **Follow.** Post a follow-up article to the article that's currently displayed in the article window.

• **Archive.** Save the current article in a folder named after the current newsgroup. You can access this folder using the Mail window, as described later in this chapter.

Navigating in the article selector

It's easy to navigate from article to article in the article selector; just click the >> to see the next article, or << to see the previous one. To return to the subject selector, click the View/List button.

Article display options

The View menu offers three options—Full headers, Word Wrap, and Rot-13, which come in handy while you're viewing articles. These are toggle options; if the option has a check beside it, it's turned on, and choosing it will turn it off. If the option doesn't have a check besides it, it's off, and choosing it will turn it on.

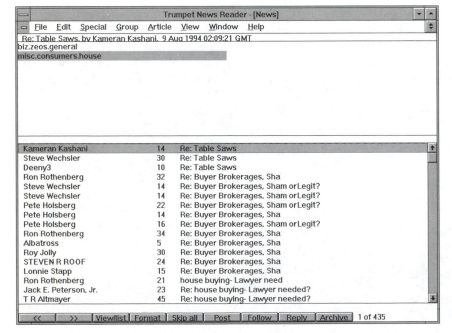

Figure 13-4. To display the subjects in a newsgroup, just double-click the newsgroup's name.

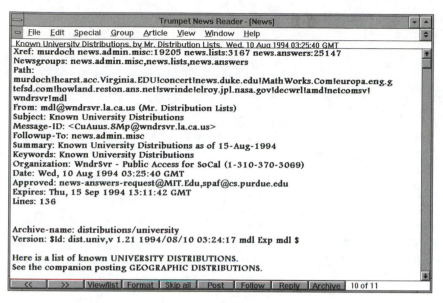

Figure 13-5. WinTrumpet displays an article in a full-sized window; the buttons at the bottom let you navigate with ease.

You can dispose of an article in the following ways:

- **Forwarding the article.** To forward the article to an email address you specify, choose Forward from the Article menu. In the window that appears, type the email address to which you want to send the article, and click the Send button.

- **Full Header.** By default, this option is turned off. To see the full header of an article you're reading, turn this option on.

- **Word Wrap.** By default, this option is turned on so that WinTrumpet automatically fits the text to the window in which you're viewing the article. To see the line breaks that the article's author used, turn this item off.

- **Rot-13.** By default, this option is turned off. If you're viewing an article that has been encrypted with Rot-13, turn this option on so that you can read the text.

Disposing of articles

When you've finished reading an article, Win-Trumpet automatically marks the article as read. When you display the subject list, you'll see that the program placed a mark (>>) next to the article's name. The article remains on the subject list until you close this newsgroup; after that, you don't see the article again unless you "unread" the read articles, as described in the next section.

- **Storing the article in a folder.** WinTrumpet lets you store articles in a folder, which is similar to an email folder. The folder is named after the newsgroup and contains only the articles that you've stored in the folder. To store an article in a folder, click the Folder button. If no folder for that newsgroup exists, WinTrumpet creates one automatically. To read the articles in a folder, choose Mail from the Window menu, and double-click the newsgroup name.

- **Saving the article to a file.** To save the current article to a file, choose Save to File from the Article menu. To add the article to the end of an existing file, choose Append to File from the Article menu.

UNREADING AND READING ARTICLES

When you read an article, WinTrumpet marks the article as read, and you won't see this article the next time you open the newsgroup. But the program gives you many options for reversing this by "unreading" the articles. You can also mark articles as read even though you haven't read them. The following sections detail these procedures.

Unreading articles

In the subject selector window, you have the following options for unreading articles:

- **Unreading an article you've read in this session.** To mark as unread an article that has the "read" mark (>>) next to it, select the article and choose Toggle from the Article menu.

- **Unreading all the articles in the group.** To unread all the articles, including ones that you've read in this or previous sessions, switch to the newsgroup selector, and select the newsgroup's name. Then select Unread All from the Groups menu. To unread just the last ten or twenty articles you read, choose Unread ten or Unread twenty from the same menu.

Marking articles as read

If you would like to mark articles as read even though you haven't read them, you can do so in the following ways:

- **Marking a single article as read.** To mark an article as read, select the article in the subject selector and click the Skip button. Alternatively, choose Toggle from the Article menu so that a "read" mark (>>) appears next to the article's name.

- **Marking all the articles in a group as read.** To mark all the retrieved articles as read, choose Read All from the Group menu.

- **Marking all the articles in a group as read without opening the subject selector.** If you've been away on vacation for a couple of weeks or more, you may find hundreds or thousands of articles in your newsgroup. Retrieving all these articles will take a few minutes. To mark all the articles in a newsgroup as read without retrieving them, choose Catch Up from the Group menu.

WRITING YOUR OWN MESSAGES

Before you post your own articles, please read Part III, "Now it's your turn," with care. Under no circumstances should you post to USENET until you fully understand the fundamentals of network etiquette and the special characteristics of the newsgroup to which you want to post.

With WinTrumpet, you can write your own messages in the following ways:

- **Posting a message on a new subject.** You can do this at any level of the program.

- **Replying via email.** You can do this in the subject or the article selector levels.

- **Posting a follow-up message.** You can do this in the subject or the article selector levels.

The following sections detail the procedure you use to write your own messages.

Posting an article on a new subject

To post an article on a new subject, select the newsgroup to which you want to post—or just display its subjects or an article. Then click the Post button, or choose Post from the Article menu. You'll see the Post Article dialog box, shown in Figure 13-6.

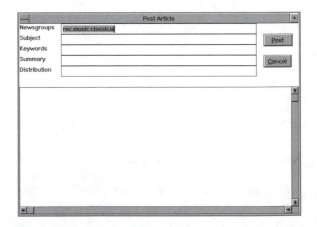

Figure 13-6. In this dialog box, you create a post on a new subject.

Fill out each of the header areas carefully. To crosspost your article, type one or more additional newsgroup names, with each newsgroup separated by a comma. Write your message in the space provided, and click Post when you're done. To cancel your message, click Cancel.

> **TIP:** To create a post free from spelling errors, write your message in your word processing program, and check the spelling. Copy the message to the Clipboard, and paste it into the Post Article dialog box.

Replying by email

To reply by email, select the article in the subject selector, or display the article. Then click the Reply button, or choose Reply from the Article menu. You'll see the dialog box shown in Figure 13-7. Note that WinTrumpet automatically copies the text from the article and fills out the To, Subject, and Cc boxes automatically. Be sure to delete the header and other quoted material that's not needed for your reply. Then type your message, and click Send. To cancel your message, click Cancel.

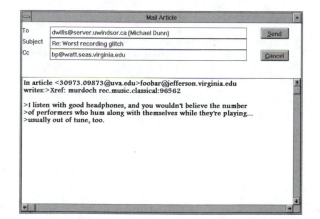

Figure 13-7. In this window, you reply to articles via email.

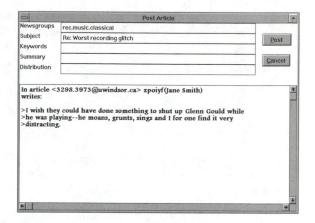

Figure 13-8. In this dialog box, you create a follow-up article.

> **TIP:** To reply via email without quoting the original article, choose Mail from the Article menu.

Creating a follow-up post

To create a follow-up post, select the article in the subject selector, or display the article. Then click the Follow button, or choose Follow from the Article menu. You'll see the dialog box shown in Figure 13-8. Note that WinTrumpet has filled in the Newsgroups and Subject areas. You can edit these areas, if you wish. If you're replying to a cross-posted article, consider whether you really want to crosspost to all the mentioned groups. Add information to the Keywords, Summary, and Distribution boxes. Remove from the quoted text anything that's not pertinent to your reply, including the quoted header, and type your message. When you're done, click Post. To cancel your message, click Cancel.

Table 13-1 summarizes the WinTrumpet keyboard shortcuts.

Cancelling your article

To cancel an article that you've posted, use the subject selector to display the article, and choose

TABLE 13-1. WINTRUMPET KEYBOARD SHORTCUTS

Press this key:	To do this:
Ctrl + F	Post a follow-up article
Ctrl + M	Reply by electronic mail (no quoting)
Ctrl + P	Post article on new subject
Ctrl + R	Reply by electronic mail
Ctrl + S	Mark article as read (skip)
Ctrl + T	Toggle selected article read/unread
Ctrl + U	Unread the last 20 articles
Ctrl + V	Move article to folder

Cancel from the Article menu. You can't cancel articles other than the ones you posted. Note that it takes time for the cancel message to propagate through USENET, so some people will have a chance to read your post even after you've cancelled it.

SUMMARY

WinTrumpet is easy to use and takes good advantage of the Microsoft Windows environment. The program lacks certain important features such as subject/author killing and threading, but these features are scheduled to be included in the next version of the program.

FROM HERE

• For an introduction to netiquette and working with the USENET community, see Chapter 15, "Working with a virtual community."

• For tips and pointers on writing for a USENET audience, see Chapter 16, "Posting your own messages."

• To make sure you've learned all you can about a newsgroup before you post, see Chapter 16, "Posting your own messages."

• For pointers on handling replies via email and follow-up postings, see Chapter 16, "Posting your own messages."

• To ensure that you don't make posting mistakes that could get you flamed, see Chapter 17, "Dealing with USENET problems."

• Need help finding the right newsgroups? See Part IV, "Building your subscription list."

14

The first of the Macintosh NNTP newsreaders to be documented in this book, Newswatcher takes full advantage of the Macintosh user interface and provides full-featured newsreading capabilities. A copyrighted product that is made widely available on *copyleft* principles (you can use it as long as you don't sell it), Newswatcher was written by John Norstad of Northwestern University.

Newswatcher requires a Mac equipped with System 7 and at least 2.5MB of memory. Also required is an Internet connection—dialup IP or TCP/IP network access—and the Apple MacTCP package.

OBTAINING AND INSTALLING NEWSWATCHER

You can obtain Newswatcher using anonymous FTP to the following address:

`ftp//:ftp.acns.nwu.edu/pub/newswatcher`

After you've obtained Newswatcher, make a folder called Newswatcher, and store the Newswatcher file there.

> **TIP:** Before installing Newswatcher, you will need the following information: The full domain name of your NNTP server, the full domain name of the computer that houses your SMTP (electronic mail) server, your electronic mail address, and the domain name of your time server. If you're not sure what all this information is about, don't worry: You just have to type it in a dialog box when you configure Newswatcher. If you don't have this information, get it from your service provider.

NUNTIUS

Another copylefted newsreader for the Macintosh is Nuntius, a creation of Peter Speck of Denmark. Nuntius is a Macintosh version of nn, the popular UNIX newsreader, but it lacks nn's advanced kill file capabilities. Otherwise, it's similar in features to Newswatcher, but it's not as logically laid out or as easy to use. Since both are available at no cost, I'd recommend Newswatcher.

STARTING AND CONFIGURING NEWSWATCHER

If you've installed Newswatcher as described in the previous section, you can start the program by double-clicking its icon. Newswatcher doesn't know how to contact your NNTP server yet, so all you see is a blank Untitled window and the program's menu bar.

To contact your NNTP server, Newswatcher needs the following information from you. Some of this information must be obtained from your system administrator.

- **NNTP news server.** You can supply Newswatcher with either the domain name (such as jefferson.cad.vua.edu) or an IP address, but it's preferable to type the domain name.

- **SMTP mail server.** Type the name of the computer that houses the mail server you use. This information is needed so that you can send email replies to articles you read.

- **Email address.** This information is needed so that people can reply to you via email.

- **Organization.** If you wish, you can tell Newswatcher the name of your organization here. Leave this blank if you're posting from a home computer.

- **Signature.** Think about what you want to include in your signature. Remember, you don't need to include your name or email address because this information is in the header of your posts.

> **TIP:** Before configuring Newswatcher, create folders called Saved Messages and Extracted Binaries. Place these folders in your Newswatcher folder.

To configure Newswatcher, choose Preferences from the File menu. You'll see the Preferences dialog box, shown in Figure 14-1. To configure Newswatcher, you choose the topic you want in the Topic list box. Currently, you're seeing the General Options. Several of them are already selected. You can choose additional options, if you like. When you're done, you choose OK. To select the next set of options, you choose a different topic in the Topic list box and make new selections. Here's how to configure Newswatcher (note that I've skipped some of the topics that you don't need to worry about):

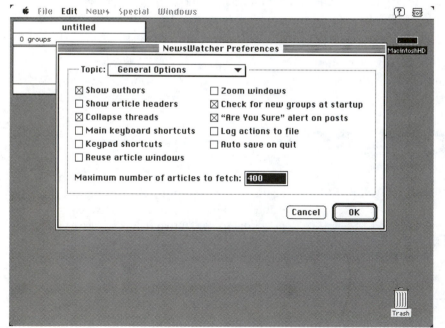

Figure 14-1. To configure Newswatcher, you use the Preferences dialog box.

- **General Options.** These options are mainly a matter of preference, but I like to show authors, collapse threads, check for new groups on startup, and autosave on quit. My network connection is fast, so I'm willing to fetch 500 articles at the maximum.

- **Server Addresses.** In this dialog box, you type the name of your NNTP news server and your SMTP mail server. Obtain this information, if necessary, from your system administrator.

- **Personal Information.** Supply your full name (first name first), your organization (optional), and your email address.

- **Signature.** No more than four lines, please, and don't repeat your name, organization, or email address.

- **Message Options.** Please select Reply via email, and deselect Reply via posting (you can still post followup articles, as explained later). Important: Choose Show Details so that you can see and edit all the header information. Don't use tabs, since many terminals can't display them.

- **Remote Host Information.** If you need to supply a username and password to access your NNTP server, type them here.

- **Font and Size.** Surely you'll want to choose a font other than Monaco!

- **Saved Messages.** Choose a default folder.

- **FTP Helper Program.** If you have an FTP client program such as Fetch,

indicate its location here so that you can use Newswatcher's Option-click command to retrieve highlighted files from archives.

- **Extracting Binaries.** If you want to decode binary files, enter the name of the folder here.

GETTING THE GROUP LIST

After you finish configuring Newswatcher, choose Rebuild Group List from the Special menu. The program logs on to the NNTP server and downloads the lengthy list of newsgroup names. On a slow SLIP connection, this may take a few minutes. To see the Full Group List, choose Show Full Group List from the Windows menu. Your screen should look like the one in Figure 14-2.

SUBSCRIBING TO NEWSGROUPS

A unique feature of Newswatcher is its ability to let you define more than one subscription list. For example, you could define one list for

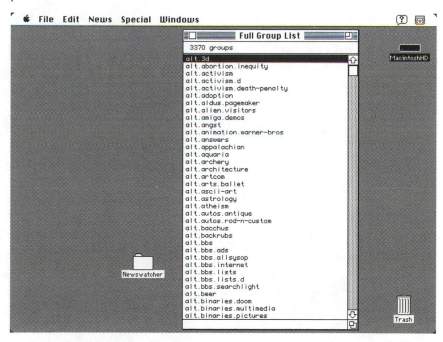

Figure 14-2. The Full Group list contains all the newsgroups available at your server.

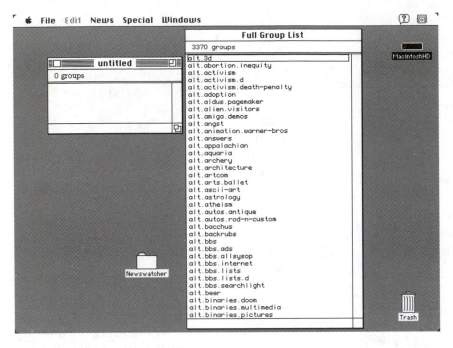

Figure 14-3. This dialog box provides tools for subscribing to new groups.

aviation-related topics and another for current events. To create your first subscription list, choose New Group Window from the File menu. You'll see an Untitled window like the one in Figure 14-3.

To subscribe to newsgroups, scroll through the Full Group List. To select a group to add to your subscription list, just click it. To select two or more groups that are positioned together in the list, click the first one and then Shift-click the last one. To select additional groups without deselecting previously selected groups, hold down the Command key when you click. When you're finished selecting groups, drag them to the Untitled window. You'll see the subscribed groups in the window, as shown in Figure 14-4. Note that Newswatcher determines how many articles are available and displays them next to the newsgroup name.

When you're finished adding groups to the Group

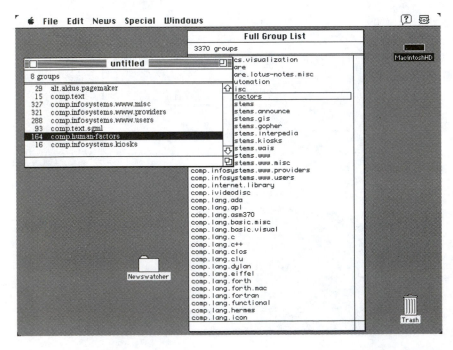

Figure 14-4. To subscribe to newsgroups, just drag them from the Full Group List to the new Group Window (Untitled) that you're creating.

Window, open the File menu and choose Save. Give the window a distinctive name, such as "Desktop Publishing" or "Aviation," and store the newly named Group Window in the Newswatcher folder.

You can create additional Group Folders, if you like. Give each a distinctive name and store it in the Newswatcher folder.

If you would like to unsubscribe to a newsgroup, just select the newsgroup and choose Cut. To get rid of an entire Group Window, just drag it to the Trash. (This doesn't erase the newsgroups on the server, naturally, and it's a good thing—if it did, you'd have lots of people out to skin you alive.)

USING THE THREAD SELECTOR

Newswatcher is a true threaded newsreader, like trn (see Chapter 12, "Reading the news with rn and trn"), so it groups articles based on the article references contained in the article's headers. To display the subjects in a newsgroup, double-click the newsgroup's name in the Group Window. The thread selector appears in a new window, as shown in Figure 14-5. Note the triangle at the beginning of some of the lines; this indicates that there is more than one article in the thread. To see the names of all the authors who have contributed the articles to the thread, just click the triangle. Figure 14-6 shows a thread that's been opened by clicking its triangle. To hide the names and collapse the thread list, just click the triangle again.

Figure 14-5. To display the subjects in a newsgroup, just double-click the newsgroup's name.

USING THE ARTICLE SELECTOR

When you've identified an article that you want to read, just double-click the article's subject to display the article in the article window, as shown in Figure 14-7. You see the header information at the top of the window; use the scroll bar to display more of the text, if you wish.

Navigating in the article selector

To see the next article in the thread, open the News menu and choose Next Article, or just use the Command-I shortcut. To see the first article in the next thread, open the news menu and choose Next Thread, or just use the Control-T command. To see the first article in the next newsgroup, open the News menu and choose Next Group, or use the Control-J shortcut. Note that you can open any article by selecting the thread selector window and double-clicking the article you want to read.

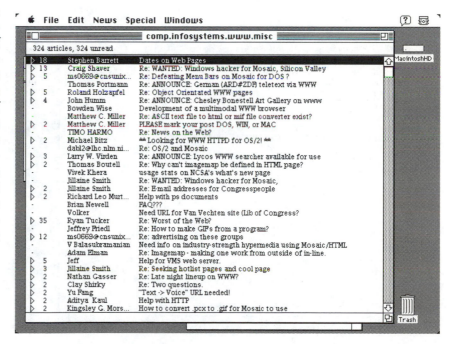

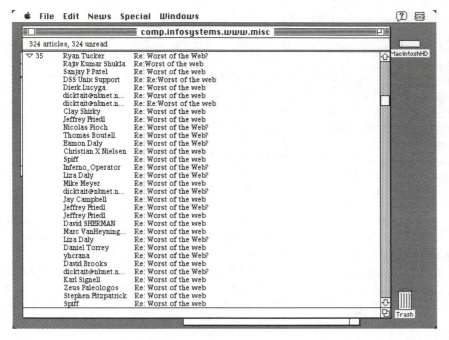

Figure 14-6. To view the names of the authors who have contributed articles to a thread, just click the triangle.

Article display options

While you're viewing an article, you can choose display options to change its on-screen appearance:

- **Headers.** To view full header information, open the Edit menu and choose Show Details (or use the Command-H shortcut). To hide the full header information, choose Hide Details from the Edit menu or press Command-H again.

- **Rot-13.** By default, this option is turned off. If you're viewing an article that has been encrypted with Rot-13, turn this option on by choosing Rot-13 from the Edit menu. To turn Rot-13 off, choose the command again.

Disposing of articles

When you've finished reading an article, Newswatcher automatically marks the article as read (you'll see a

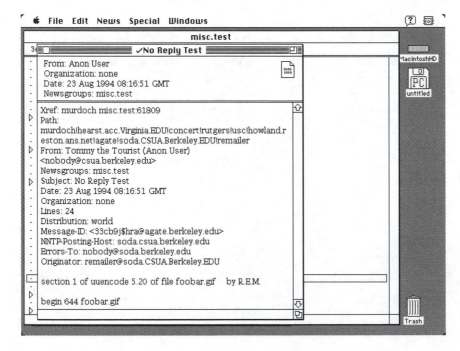

Figure 14-7. Newswatcher displays an article in a window, with the header information shown at the top.

check mark next to the article's name in the thread selector window).

Besides reading the article and closing it (which marks it as read), you can dispose of an article in the following ways:

- **Marking an article as read.** To mark an article as read even though you haven't opened it, select it and choose Mark Read from the News menu (or press Command-M).

- **Marking an article as unread.** To mark a read article as unread, choose Mark Unread from the News menu or press Command-U.

- **Forwarding the article.** To forward the article to an email address you specify, choose Forward from the News menu. In the window that appears (Figure 14-8), type the email address to which you want to send the article. Make sure the email icon is selected (the little letter), and click the Send button. **Note:** To send a copy to yourself, just click the little head.

- **Saving the article to a file.** To save the current article to a file, choose Save from the File menu. You'll see a standard Save dialog box that lets you name the file and choose its storage location.

- **Printing the article.** Just choose Print from the File menu or press Command-P.

You can also reply to the article by email or a followup post, as explained in the sections titled

"Replying by email" and "Creating a follow-up post," respectively.

WRITING YOUR OWN MESSAGES

Before you post your own articles, please read Part III, "Now it's your turn," with care. Under no circumstances should you post to USENET until you fully understand the fundamentals of network etiquette and the special characteristics of the newsgroup to which you want to post.

With Newswatcher, you can write your own messages in the following ways:

- **Posting a message on a new subject.** You can do this at any level of the program.

- **Replying via electronic mail.** You can do this in the thread or the article selector levels.

- **Posting a follow-up message.** You can do this in the thread or the article selector levels.

The following sections detail the procedure you use to write your own messages.

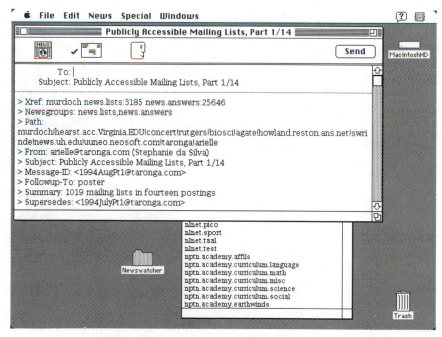

Figure 14-8. Click the letter icon to email the article.

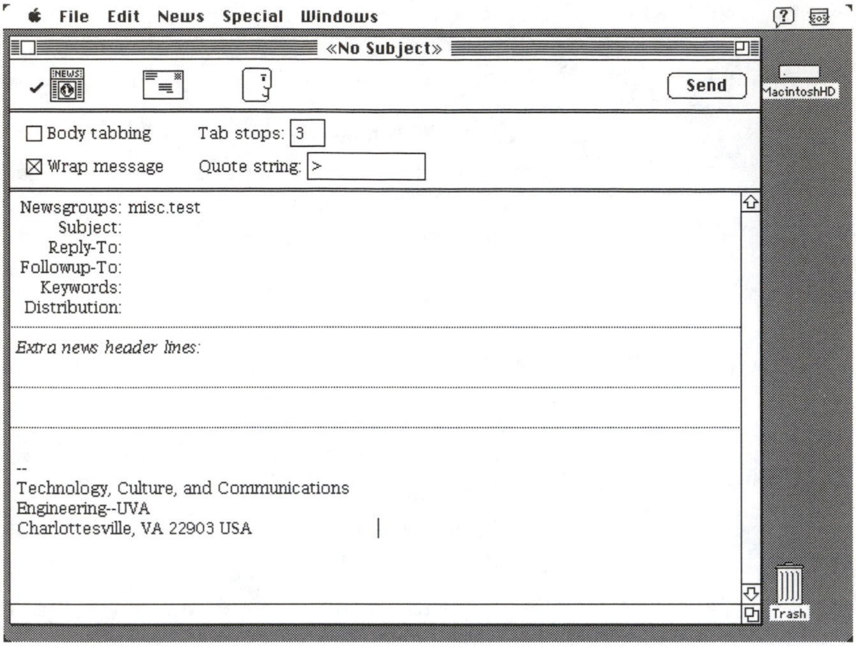

Figure 14-9. In this window, you create a post on a new subject.

Posting an article on a new subject

To post an article on a new subject, select the news-group to which you want to post—or just display its subjects or an article. Then click the Post button, or choose Post from the Article menu. You'll see the Post Article dialog box. **Note:** If you don't see all the header information, choose Show Details from the Edit menu to display all the header information, shown in Figure 14-9.

Fill out each of the header areas carefully. To crosspost your article, type one or more additional newsgroup names, with each newsgroup separated by a comma. Be sure to specify where your readers should follow up by typing one of the newsgroup's names in the Followup-To: line. Note that News-watcher automatically adds your signature.

Write your message between the two blank lines above your signature (Figure 14-10). When you're done

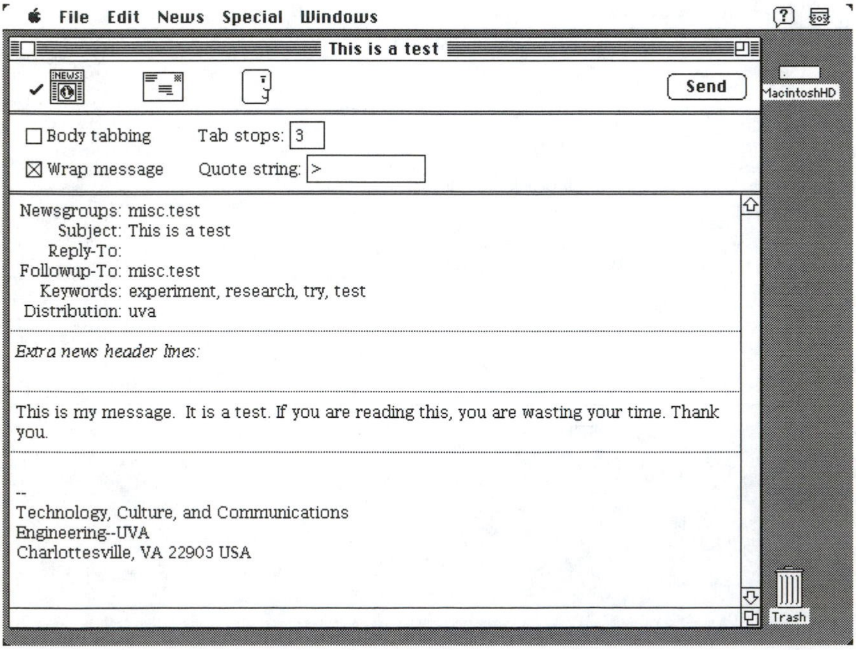

Figure 14-10. Write your new post in the space provided, and click Send when you're done.

writing, make sure the News icon is selected so that this item will be posted to the newsgroup, and click Send.

> **TIP:** To create a post free from spelling errors, write your message in your word processing program, and check the spelling. Copy the message to the Clipboard, and paste it into the New Message window.

Replying by email

To reply by electronic mail, select the article in the thread selector, or display the article. Then choose Reply from the News menu. You'll see the window shown in Figure 14-11. Note that Newswatcher automatically copies the text from the article and fills out the Newsgroups and Subject lines automatically.

To reply to the article via email, click the letter icon. Be sure the followup post icon (the News icon) is deleted (no check mark). Click the little head (the Self) if you want a copy. Note that Newswatcher automatically adds the email address. Type your message between the two lines at the bottom (above your signature).

Creating a follow-up post

To create a follow-up post, you use exactly the same procedure you used to create an email reply, except that you click the follow-up post icon (the one that says "News") instead of the mail icon. You'll see different

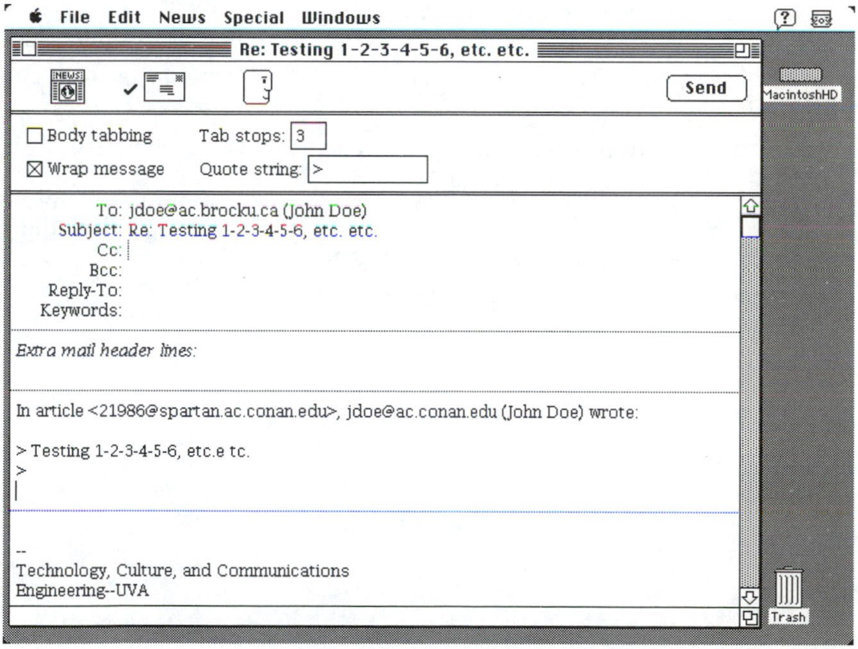

Figure 14-11. In this window, you reply to articles via email or follow-up posting.

headers, too, as shown in Figure 14-11. If you're responding to a crossposted article, please be sure to respond only to the newsgroup listed in the Followup-To: line. Edit the header information if necessary. Click Send when you're ready to send your article.

To cancel a post without sending it, just click the close box. You'll see a dialog box asking whether you really want to cancel the article. Click Discard to cancel your post.

Table 14-1 summarizes the Newswatcher keyboard shortcuts.

EXTRACTING BINARIES

To extract binary files (pictures, sounds, and programs) from uuencoded posts, select the article that contains the file. If the picture is split into two or more articles, select all the articles that contain parts of the file. Then choose Extract Binaries.

Note: In order to extract binary files, you'll need the helper program called uuUndo, which is widely found at anonymous FTP sites.

TABLE 14-1. NEWSWATCHER KEYBOARD SHORTCUTS

PRESS THIS KEY:	TO DO THIS:
Ctrl + F	Post a follow-up article
Ctrl + M	Reply by electronic mail (no quoting)
Ctrl + P	Post article on new subject
Ctrl + R	Reply by electronic mail
Ctrl + S	Mark article as read (skip)
Ctrl + T	Toggle selected article read/unread
Ctrl + U	Unread the last 20 articles
Ctrl + V	Move article to folder

SUMMARY

Although Newswatcher is easy to use, it offers an unusually strong selection of features for a GUI newsreader. The only feature that's missing is the ability to kill articles by author, subject, and site.

FROM HERE

- For an introduction to netiquette and working with the USENET community, see Chapter 15, "Working with a virtual community."

- For tips and pointers on writing for a USENET audience, see Chapter 16, "Posting your own messages."

- To make sure you've learned all you can about a newsgroup before you post, see Chapter 16, "Posting your own messages."

- For pointers on handling replies via email and follow-up postings, see Chapter 16, "Posting your own messages."

- To ensure that you don't make posting mistakes that could get you flamed, see Chapter 17, "Dealing with USENET problems."

- Need help finding the right newsgroups? See Part IV, "Building your subscription list."

PART III

NOW IT'S YOUR TURN

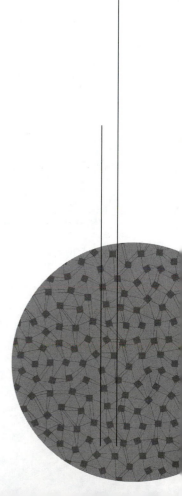

15

You've surely heard of netiquette, the rules of proper on-line comportment—and you've also heard that you should understand the rules of netiquette before you post. And it's true. But netiquette isn't just a matter of rules, which you can learn by rote and apply one by one. To be sure, there are some hard-and-fast rules that you'd better learn, like replying only to the follow-up address in a crossposted article, if you don't want to get flamed! But more broadly, the specific rules of netiquette testify to a broader underlying conception of the USENET community's identity and moral values. If you want to write successfully for USENET, begin by understanding the general concepts, and then move on to the specifics.

This chapter introduces these fundamental concepts about USENET as a moral community—concepts that you must understand clearly if you wish to participate fully in the USENET community. Chapter 16 goes on to the specific rules you should follow when posting.

SOME THINGS TO REMEMBER

It's pretty simple: When you get involved in USENET, you join a human community—a global one, at that—and you'll thrive if you can show consideration for others. It's a community in which you're a guest, enjoying benefits someone else is paying for; USENET is a privilege, not a right, and you should understand that others are taking risks to give you the freedom to express yourself. It's a

computer network, to be sure, but ultimately it links *people,* not computers, and that means people's feelings are inevitably involved. Those people deserve the same consideration you give the people you interact with in your daily life. Be aware that "friendly sarcasm" can come across the wrong way in a USENET posting. And don't waste people's time: Write concisely, and get to your point immediately—unless, of course, that would involve spoiling their fun by giving away the ending of a movie! As for your opinions, they're really not of much interest to anyone unless you can back them up with some solid facts or reasoning. If there's something of substance that you can contribute, you certainly should—but restrain the impulse to advertise in inappropriate places. If you can understand these points, you'll do fine on USENET. The following sections elaborate.

It's a global community

USENET embraces all of North America, growing parts of Central America, most of Europe, much of the former Soviet Union, and increasing numbers of Asian countries—and it's accessible via UUCP in more out-of-the-way places. That's its strength. On any given subject, you'll run across perspectives and opinions that differ radically from your own. From this encounter you'll emerge incomparably enriched; you'll have brought your own views up against very different ways of seeing things, and you'll learn what lies behind—and how best to defend—the views that you choose to express.

Imagine what Latin Americans would have to say about the U.S. invasion of Grenada, for instance, or how EuroDisneyland comes across to tradition-minded Europeans. You'll find out, on USENET.

This fact alone calls for tolerance of opinion, but there's something else to bear in mind. Many of the people posting to the Net don't speak English as their primary tongue. Although there are French, German, and other foreign-language newsgroups on USENET, many of the posts you're reading come from non-English speakers who perceive that USENET is a valuable resource. Take a look at the headers and names in a typical newsgroup, and you'll see what I mean—lots of Changs, Ramachandrans, Fernandos, and more. Many such posts come from the increasingly cosmopolitan North American nations, of course, but many more wend their way to USENET from far-away places. Don't flame them if they make grammatical errors or spelling mistakes!

You're a guest

More than a few USENET participants mistakenly believe that USENET is a public utility, like the telephone system, and that they therefore have the right to post anything they want. But it's not so simple. Individual Americans have the freedom to express any view they wish to express, so long as it is not slanderous, obscene, or dangerous to public safety. But you *don't* have the freedom to force someone else to publish your views at their expense.

Most USENET sites are *privately owned* computers found at colleges and universities, corporations, non-profit organizations, and the headquarters of Internet service providers. If these computers are construed as privately owned printing presses, then it is clear beyond doubt that a USENET participant does *not* possess an absolute freedom of speech, any more than you have the right to publish anything you want in your local newspaper. In the U.S., the federal government and the states can make no law abridging the freedom of a newspaper to publish anything it wants so long as it is not obscene, but nobody has the right to

force the newspaper to publish something it *doesn't* want to publish, for whatever reason.

Again, it's not quite so simple. Technology has a way of pushing the law into new, unknown realms, which will ultimately require an expensive court challenge to establish a precedent. For instance: Suppose my system administrator, overloaded with complaints, tells me to stop posting those flames to alt.politics.european. So I take an old 386, boot up Linux (a version of UNIX that runs on PCs), pay for a USENET feed and a high-bandwidth connection, and start up my posts again. Do I now own a printing press? Maybe.

The confusion posed by such matters lends credence to the view that the USENET as a whole *does* constitute a public utility, a service so crucial to the public welfare that—despite its private ownership—it is in the people's vital interest that the government regulate the utility and insist on free public access. To promote capital investment in public utility infrastructure, the U.S. government as well as federal and state courts have taken the view that a public utility cannot be held responsible for an individual's use of this utility to send obscene, slanderous, or publicly dangerous messages. In a recent and important court case, a federal court ruled that the on-line service CompuServe could not be held liable for a slanderous message that had been posted on one of the service's bulletin boards. (The liability of the individual who posted the message was never in doubt.)

Resolving such matters is going to take further clarification in court, with consequences that are sure to be unfortunate for the individuals involved. The U.S. legal system works by precedent, but this comes at the expense of ruining the lives of just about everyone involved—houses are lost, companies are bankrupted. Don't force someone else into losing everything in the defense of your freedom. If you really want to push the freedom issues, get your own USENET site and post all you like—and *you* take the full responsibility. Until the legal status of USENET receives clarification, you should avoid posting any messages *on someone else's system* that could be construed to be obscene, defamatory, seditious, or an infringement on a copyright. For more information on these issues, see Chapter 21, "USENET issues and futures."

It's not free

If you're using USENET at a college or university or a large organization, you might get the idea that it's free—but it isn't. Just because you're not paying a fee to use USENET doesn't mean that it's free from cost. Organizations pay for USENET feeds, high-bandwidth transmission lines, long-distance telephone charges, disk storage space, and processor time. According to one estimate, it costs roughly $0.0025 to disseminate 1K (1,024 characters) throughout USENET. The larger the file, the higher the cost—so it's not too surprising that USENET's more expensive groups consist of binary files postings (graphics and sound files). Table 15-1 lists some of the worst offenders.

Given that posting to USENET costs money, experienced USENET posters do all they can to lower costs by conserving bandwidth (in the USENET context, "the amount of network resources consumed by postings")—and the less, the better. Many of the rules of netiquette follow from the bandwidth-preservation dictum, such as keeping messages short and concise, avoiding lengthy signatures, and condensing quoted material. For further discussion of bandwidth preservation issues, see Chapter 17, "Dealing with USENET problems."

There's a human being at the other end of the wire

When you're working with a computer network, it's easy to forget that there are other people involved because you just see lifeless symbols on the screen. Unfortunately, this leads some people to write things that they'd never say in person—things that can hurt.

There's no easy cure for this, as networked organizations all over the world have learned to their dismay. It's easy to lose your cool, write a flame, and hit the Enter key—and only later do you realize that you've sent an ill-considered, possibly defamatory message to everyone in your organization. The ultimate victim of such behavior is you—*you're* the one who, at the end of the day, is going to be seen as the irritating, irascible jerk.

Here's the best cure: If you see something on USENET that rattles your cage, log off—and sleep on it. Chances are, tomorrow morning it won't seem like such a big deal. If you decide to post or reply, you'll be able to do so in a reasonable, non-emotional way.

TABLE 15-1. SEVERAL OF USENET'S MORE EXPENSIVE GROUPS	
NEWSGROUP NAME	COST PER MONTH
alt.binaries.pictures.erotica	$286,000.00
alt.binaries.sounds.misc	$54,760.00
alt.binaries.sounds.tv	$30,400.00
alt.binaries.pictures.erotica.male	$25,230.00
de.alt.binaries.pictures.female	$24,070.00
alt.binaries.sounds.mods	$17,600.00

Sarcasm may not come across the way you intended

Be aware that it's very difficult to take what you think is an affectionately sarcastic remark and make it come across that way in a USENET posting. Here's an example:

```
This is another one
of your pet schemes,
isn't it?
```

The person on the other end of this message can

very well take this in the wrong way and think you mean it as a genuine put-down. For this reason, some use *smileys* (also called *emoticons)* to help contextualize messages. A smiley is formed from ordinary ASCII characters, and it's supposed to look like a face. When you look at a smiley, turn your head sideways, and you'll get the idea:

```
This is another one of your pet
schemes, isn't it? :-)
```

I think you'll agree that the smiley does soften this statement somewhat, but be aware that smileys have come into no small disrepute. Computer columnist John Dvorak blasted them recently: For Dvorak, smileys are nothing more than contrivances used to shore up feeble writing skills—skills too undeveloped to convey the nuances of friendly sarcasm in writing. And on USENET, the use of smileys suggests to some that the writer is a newbie, mindlessly copying traits that the press has associated with USENET writing.

You'll run across long lists of smileys, but many of these are actually *ASCII art:*

```
@:-)   I'm wearing a turban
```

Very few smileys are in common use (see the box entitled "Smileys you're likely to encounter"), and I see them very infrequently these days.

How would one soften the sarcasm of "This is another one of your pet schemes, isn't it?" You could write, "Your critics might say that this is another of your 'pet schemes'—but they don't know you like I do!" Or you could just take the best advice: Skip the sarcasm altogether, and save it for face-to-face meetings, where it's more easily put into context with smiles and pats on the back.

Please don't waste people's time

Part of your consideration for others involves taking steps to avoid wasting their time. You'll know exactly what I mean the next time you read a lengthy follow-up post, which turns out to contain nothing but a verbatim quotation from the previous article you read and the words "Me too" or "I agree" at the bottom. You'll find more specific suggestions for quoting effectively and writing tight, concise articles in the next chapter.

Don't spoil people's fun

Here's a very good reason to disobey the last section's dictum about putting your message on the first screen that appears: People *hate* having their fun spoiled. It's fine to post a movie review, but if you must reveal the ending, put the words "Spoiler" on the subject line (see Chapter 17, "Dealing with USENET problems"), and *don't* reveal the information on the first screen. Here's an acceptable spoiler:

```
Xref: murdoch rec.movies.horror
Path:Murdoch!hearst.acc.Virginia.EDU!
concert!gatech!swrinde!pipex!
From: 96nim@suz.ic.sp.uk (Nimrod
Magnifico)
Newsgroups: rec.music.horror
Subject: Death So Angelic--
***SPOILER!!!***
Date: 16 Aug 1994 12:18:43 GMT
Organization: Department of
Gerontology, University of London
Lines: 49
Distribution: world


Here's a review of Death So Angelic,
but please note that this post contains
a SPOILER! If you don't want to find
out when Darlene confronts Henry after
the incident in the graveyard, *stop
reading now*!

MORE....
```

SMILEYS YOU'RE LIKELY TO ENCOUNTER	
:-)	I'm making a joke; don't take this seriously.
;-)	I'm winking or flirting with you.
:-(	This makes me sad.
:`-(	I'm crying!
:-0	I'm overjoyed!

Let's *please* not start *that* again

While we're on the subject of avoiding wasting people's time, here's another point. There are some subjects on which people aren't ever going to agree, and it's better not to bring them up in a USENET newsgroup. Here's a more or less random list: abortion, affirmative action, radical feminism, civil rights for homosexuals, evolutionism vs. creationism, the merits of Zionism, rape, burning the American flag, and handgun control. Bringing up any of these subjects can ignite a flame war that can consume bandwidth for days or weeks, pushing out intelligent discussion—and ultimately convincing people that reading a particular newsgroup isn't worth it. If you feel that you must raise one of these divisive issues, do so in one of the talk∗ groups—that's what they're for.

SUBJECT LINES EVERYONE'S SICK OF SEEING

Make money fast! This is a chain letter that's recurrently posted, most likely as a prank, but it can have serious consequences—chain letters and pyramid schemes are illegal and posting or forwarding this message can lead to the loss of your USENET privileges.

Help dying child make the Guinness Book of Records! This has some basis in fact: seven-year-old Craig Shergold, diagnosed with a brain tumor, did indeed request that people world wide send him postcards so that he could make the record books. He received 33 million postcards and did make the record books. But there's just one problem: Craig recovered. An American billionare flew him to Charlottesville, Virginia, where physicians successfully extracted the non-malignant tumor. The only problem is that, thanks to repeated postings of the story, Craig is still getting postcards—hundreds of thousands of them, an expensive nightmare for the British postal service.

Free Neiman-Marcus chocolate cookie recipe! According to the nicely written story, a Neiman-Marcus customer liked the firm's chocolate chip cookies so much that he requested the recipe. He was told the cost was "250," which he took to mean $2.50. However, when he got his Visa bill, he found the actual charge to be $250. But Neiman-Marcus refused to refund his money. In revenge, he decided to post the recipe to the Net. It's a hoax; the recipe, which calls for huge amounts of ingredients, doesn't produce anything that comes even close to a chocolate chip cookie.

FCC to implement modem tax soon! Call your congressman! A modem tax was in fact proposed years ago, but it was quickly defeated.

Used microwave oven for sale in South Bend, Indiana. This is posted for world distribution, naturally.

Imminent death of the Net predicted! Gloomy prognostications regarding the future of USENET have appeared since soon after its inception; meanwhile, it has grown by leaps and bounds.

Survey—Please Respond! Amateur and student sociologists, please take note: USENET is a *terrible* place to post a survey. This has been done so often and so ham-handedly that the few people who *do* respond will go to some length to make up completely ridiculous answers. (A reporter recently posted a query to alt.binaries.pictures.erotica: "Please help with my article! Why do you like these pictures?" I'd hate to see her electronic mailbox—it's probably full of several megabytes' worth of scanned porn, on the theory that "a picture is worth a thousand words.")

Opinions are like rear ends—everybody has one

Who cares what you think? You, naturally, but chances are that few other people do. Sorry, that's the way the world works. But here's some good news. People *do* care, and care very much, about your opinion if you're able to back it up with facts and figures. Philosophically speaking (for a moment), the difference lies in an *opinion* (not backed up) and a *proposition*. A proposition is an opinion that contains a statement regarding the conditions that would have to be true for the proposition to be broadly accepted.

This is really pretty simple. Here's an opinion:

```
The state forestry department in this
state doesn't care about preserving the
forests.
```

Here's the same statement, recast as a proposition:

```
Any state forestry service that
permits public forests to be sold to
loggers faster than the trees can be
replenished has lost sight of its
public responsibility.
```

The second sentence is a proposition—it specifies the conditions under which a state forestry service can be described as "irresponsible." Now that's something we can sink our teeth into. We can debate this proposition. Some people are going to agree, and some people might disagree, but you've provided the grounds for what I think will be a *very* interesting discussion.

You can contribute—just do so substantively

USENET needs more than well-informed opinion. It needs your experience, whatever information is at your disposal, facts that you're aware of but others aren't, and pointers to rich sources of information that you've discovered and want to share. Here's an example of the type of posting that everyone would like to see more of:

```
Xref: murdoch rec.music.classical
Path:Murdoch!hearst.acc.Virginia.EDU!
swindle!heaven!palace9!pipey!
From: janinek@scasss.uu.se (Janine
Knowbot)
Newsgroups: rec.music.classical
Subject: More delicious Oxons
recordings
Date: 18 Aug 1994 02:43 GMT
Organization: University of Uppsala
Lines: 9
Distribution: world
```

A WORD TO THE DEVOUT

Few USENET newsgroups are free from posts, often completely out of context or even irrelevant to the newsgroup's topic, from evangelical Christians out to save souls (whether they want to be saved or not). Like unwanted and inappropriate advertising, such posts are probably more effective in doing the opposite of what they intend—that is, they may persuade some people that evangelical Christians are tiresome, narrow-minded jerks bent on pushing their ideas down everyone's throats. If you're really serious about spreading the Word, you'll do a lot better by engaging people in reasoned, polite discussion that's open to the perspectives and feelings of others. Very few people would object to a well-reasoned, well-written contribution to an ongoing discussion that's informed by a deep understanding of Christian perspectives. A suggestion: If you see something on USENET that's bothering you, talk to your clergy person—chances are, he or she will be able to suggest something that's truly substantive, such as a relevant biblical passage and some suggestions for sharing it in a positive way.

The following Oxons disks offer exceptional sound and performance quality, IMHO:

```
Spectre de la Nuit  4.550750
Haydn concertos      4.550713
Rameau (harpsichord)     4.550465
```

What's so great? Masterful musician-ship, near-perfect ensemble playing, resonant recording with beautiful spatial depth—a joy.
You can order directly from Oxons by calling 1-800-555-1234 but B&R Discounters has them on sale for just $5.90 (call 1-800-555-4321). If you're on the Web, check out the Oxons home page at http://muse.oxons.com/ pub/web/home. Enjoy!

Don't peddle in USENET newsgroups

The USENET community's norms strongly discourage the use of USENET for advertising purposes. Sure to raise the wrath of the net.police are chain letter scams (Make Money Fast!), ads posted indiscriminately to dozens, hundreds, or even—in the famous "Green Card" incident—to thousands of newsgroups, or any blatantly self-aggrandizing post that ignores the discussion and traditions of a newsgroup. That said, there are ways to sell (and buy) on the Net that are accepted as a matter of course:

- It's fine to post advertisements in any local or regional "for-sale" newsgroup.

- Newsgroups in the biz.* hierarchy are specifically intended for new product announcements, press releases, and other promotional material.

- If you can offer a service or product that directly addresses a need that's come up in a newsgroup thread, there's nothing wrong with a post that describes what you have to offer. Just be sure to emphasize that you're doing so in response to the thread of discussion, and adopt a humble, apologetic tone.

SUMMARY

USENET isn't so much a way of connecting computers as it is a way of connecting people. For this reason, anyone capable of basic, elementary consideration for others is likely to do pretty well. That consideration should extend to the people who make USENET available by committing huge amounts of disk space, processing time, and network bandwidth to support USENET's hue and cry.

FROM HERE

- For the specifics of netiquette when it comes time to post, see Chapter 15, "Dealing with a virtual community."

- For help with USENET problems, such as unwanted electronic mail, see Chapter 17, "Dealing with USENET problems."

CONTRIBUTING TO USENET

Here's a checklist of ways you can enrich USENET through your own contributions:

- **Summarize information that's appeared in other media.** If you're reading rec.birds, for example, you might want to share with the group the *Wall Street Journal*'s recent estimate that Americans spend $2 billion annually on birdseed, birdhouses, and other birdwatching equipment. **Note:** Please do not post copyrighted material verbatim—put it in your own words and summarize.

- **Share resources you've compiled or created.** If you're reading rec.backcountry, for example, why not share that backpacking checklist that you've spent years developing?

- **Report experiences with products or services other group members are likely to use.** If you've found something that's just right for your needs—or doesn't work as claimed—share the information with the appropriate group.

- **Provide pointers to information sources that are of interest to members of the group.** Found an ftp site loaded with neat stuff? Let the group know.

- **Point out a new perspective or a new way of examining a problem that hasn't yet been offered.** You don't even have to claim the perspective for your own—you can say, "Just for the sake of looking at this from another angle, here's how such-and-such a person might view this," or "I'm just playing the devil's advocate here, but...."

- **Ask detailed, specific questions that aren't answered in the newsgroup's FAQ ("Frequently Asked Questions").** No, you're not pestering the group—far from it. It's very rare to see a well-formulated question, one that provides enough background information so that people can try to answer it intelligently. What's more, your question—and the best answer—may make it into the FAQ's next edition!

16

POSTING YOUR OWN MESSAGES

Your first post should be a successful one—and it will be, if you read this chapter carefully! In it, you'll learn how to prepare for posting by creating a tolerable signature file, choosing the right newsgroup, reconnoitering the group to make sure you understand its mission, and reading the group's FAQ. You'll also learn what *not* to post, and how to type your post so that it will look fine on any USENET terminal. Next, you'll try a test posting, which is entirely acceptable—if you do it correctly. Finally, you'll learn the mechanics of replying via email, posting a follow-up article, and posting an article to a new subject—and how to avoid the numerous pitfalls that could get you flamed if you're not careful.

THE PRELIMINARIES

A successful USENET post—particularly your first one—isn't a spur-of-the-moment, impulsive response to something you see on-screen. It's the result of careful preparation and planning, as this section explains.

Creating your signature file

A signature file is a brief text file, no more than four lines in length, that your newsreader automatically appends to your posts and email replies. Ideally, a signature file tells the reader more about you—for instance, your address and (optionally) telephone number, and perhaps a very brief snip-

pet or quotation that indicates something about your philosophy of life (or lack of it). Here's mine (one line!):

```
TCC|Sci/Eng|UVA|Charlottesville|VA
22903|804-924-6095
```

> **TIP:** Please note that you do *not* need to include your full name, your organization's full name, or your email address in your signature, because this information is available in the header of every post you write.

Lots of people break the four-line limit, but lengthy signatures are considered wasteful of USENET bandwidth—and flamed accordingly. In attempt to enforce the four-line limit, many newsreaders are set up to truncate your signature if it's longer than four lines. Even if you're tempted to create a "slightly" longer one, you'd be well advised to keep it to four lines—unless you're comfortable with sending out posts with half your personal information cut off.

If you plan on doing most of your posting to just one or two newsgroups, and effectively becoming part of a community, consider omitting the signature file—just sign your posts with your first name. People will get to know you from your posts, and if anyone's interested in learning more about you, they'll contact you.

In posts originating from corporate or organizational sites, you'll frequently encounter a statement such as this one: "The opinions in this post are mine alone, and not those of Big Bucks, Inc." If you plan to post from work, it's a good idea to include a phrase such as this one, and here's why. Sooner or later, something you post is going to rattle someone's cage, and that someone might assume that you were speaking for your company—and write to your boss! (Experienced Net people know that the opinions expressed in USENET are those of the posters alone, but newbies may not realize this.)

Just how you create a signature file depends on the newsreader you're using.

- **UNIX newsreaders.** If you're using any of the UNIX newsreaders with a shell account, use the default text editor (usually vi) to create the file.

THE EVER-ENIGMATIC USENET SIG QUOTATION

Sig quotations vary, but compiling a long list of them persuades one that there's a coherent, underlying theme: an urbane, cynical sense of detachment, angst, and purposelessness. Take a look:

"Attack life, it's going to kill you anyway!"

"The Enemy of the Good is the Better."

"When I die I want to go like my granddad, peaceful and in his sleep, not like his passengers, yelling and hysterical."

"By the time you make ends meet, they move the ends."

"Have angst, will travel."

"Chaos is continual creation."

"I would rather live in a society which treated children as adults than one which treated adults as children."

"de-moc-ra-cy (di mok' ra see) n. Three wolves and a sheep voting on what's for dinner."

Name it .signature, and place the file in your home directory. **Note:** Be sure to place a period before "signature."

- **On-line service, Windows, and Macintosh newsreaders.** Look for a menu item called "Signature." You'll see a window in which you'll be able to create and save your signature file.

Read the newsgroup for a while

Before posting, read the newsgroup for at least a week—preferably two. You'll get a sense of what kinds of topics come up and what currently interests people.

Obtaining a newsgroup's FAQ

One of USENET's many unique characteristics is the availability of FAQs—documents containing answers to frequently asked questions. FAQs are of practical interest, of course, since it's expected that you won't post queries about any of the questions the FAQ answers. People get tired of seeing the same questions over and over! If you post such a question, you'll get a terse—and often angry—email response (or several of them!) directing you to "read the FAQ."

There's another good reason for reading FAQs: They assemble an amazing amount of knowledge on their topics. FAQs aren't just a set of rules for using the newsgroup; they contain answers, often very reliable and authoritative ones, on the questions people typically ask about a subject. If you were to assemble all of USENET's FAQs into a volume, you'd have a very rich collection of reference information, almost encyclopedic in scope.

> **TIP:** Does a given newsgroup have a FAQ? Check Appendix A, which lists the FAQs available in mid-summer 1994 at rtfm.mit.edu.

If you can't find the FAQ in the newsgroup or the *.answers groups, there's a FAQ archive at rtfm.mit.edu. The following is an anonymous FTP session that you can use as a model for retrieving FAQs from this archive.

At the UNIX prompt ($), type the following:

```
$ ftp rtfm.mit.edu
```

Assuming all goes well, you'll see the following:

```
Connected to BLOOM-PICAYUNE.MIT.EDU.
220 rtfm ftpd (wu-2.4(24) with built-in
ls); bugs to ftp-bugs@rtfm.mit.edu
```

You're prompted to type a login name. Here, you should type "anonymous," as shown in the following:

```
Name (rtfm.mit.edu:bp): anonymous
```

You'll see the following confirmation message, plus a request for your email address:

```
331 Guest login ok, send your complete
e-mail address as password.
Password:bp@virginia.edu
```

If there are too many people trying to access the archive, you'll see a screen listing other FTP sites that maintain FAQ archives. If everything goes well, you'll see the following:

```
230 Guest login ok, access restrictions
apply.
```

Type the following directory command to access the USENET directory:

```
ftp> cd /pub/usenet
```

You'll see a confirmation, as shown here:

```
250 CWD command successful.
```

Now type another directory command to access the newsgroup archive you want. Here's the command for the group soc.net-people:

```
ftp> cd soc.net-people
```

To access a different newsgroup, just type **cd** followed by the name of the newsgroup (for example, "cd rec.backcountry").

If an archive for this group exists, you'll see the message:

```
250 CWD command successful.
```

If not, you'll see a message informing you that there's no such directory. Check your spelling and typing carefully, and try again. If you still can't access the directory, this means the newsgroup doesn't have a FAQ or any informational resources, so type **bye** to log off.

To see a listing of the files in the directory you've just accessed, type **ls**.

```
ftp> ls
200 PORT command successful.
150 Opening ASCII mode data connection
for file list.
FAQ:_How_to_find_people_s_E-
mail_addresses
FAQ:_College_Email_Addresses_3_3_
[Monthly_posting]
FAQ:_College_Email_Addresses_1_3_
[Monthly_posting]
FAQ:_College_Email_Addresses_2_3_
[Monthly_posting]
Tips_on_using_soc.net-
people_[1.m._07_15_94]
226 Transfer complete.
```

To retrieve one or more files, I suggest that you use the mget command. This command lets you use wildcards to retrieve the files, so you don't have to type those lengthy, difficult file names precisely, as you would have to do with the get command. Here's an example:

```
ftp> mget FAQ*
```

This command retrieves any of the listed files that start with FAQ. Note: UNIX is case-sensitive, so you must type the uppercase (capital) and lowercase letters correctly. You'll see a prompt such as the following, which you answer by typing **y** (yes) or **n** (no):

```
mget FAQ:_College_Email_Addresses_1_3_
[Monthly_posting]? y
200 PORT command successful.
150 Opening ASCII mode data connection
for FAQ:_College_Email_Addresses_1_3_
[Monthly_posting] (59859 bytes).
226 Transfer complete.
```

```
61218 bytes received in 4.435 seconds
(13.48 Kbytes/s)
```

If you've used mget, you'll be asked whether you want to transfer any additional files that match the pattern you typed. To transfer a file, type **y;** if you don't want the file, type **n.**

When you've obtained all the files you want, you can switch to another newsgroup's archive, if you wish. To do so, type **cd** followed by a space and two dots, as in the following:

```
>ftp:cd
250 CWD command successful.
```

Now you're back at the /pub/usenet directory level. You can switch to another newsgroup's archive, as in the following example:

```
ftp> cd rec.music.classical
250 CWD command successful.
```

When you're finished transferring the FAQs you want, log off by typing **bye:**

```
ftp> bye
221 Goodbye.
```

> **TIP:** If you're using a shell account, you'll need to transfer the files to your computer in order to print them. Find out from the system's help desk how to transfer these files to your computer using a file transfer protocol such as Zmodem or Kermit. But here's a faster way: If your communications program has a capture mode, turn it on, and type **cat** followed by the name of the FAQ you just transferred. Note that you can use the asterisk (*) wildcard to avoid having to type the whole file name:
>
> ```
> cat Tips*
> ```
>
> The file will whiz by on-screen, but your communications program is capturing the file to your hard disk. When you see the end of the FAQ, turn off the capture file.

Reading the FAQ

Not all FAQs are organized the same way, but typically they begin with a list of the topics the FAQ covers, as in the following selection from the soc.culture.canada FAQ:

```
UPCOMING EVENTS


ABOUT SOC.CULTURE.CANADA
1.1 Where can I get an update of this
FAQ?
1.2 Why are so many posts on
soc.culture.canada of political
nature?
```

You can scroll or search forward to the section that interests you:

```
UPCOMING EVENTS


1.1 Where can I get an update of
this FAQ?
This FAQ is updated monthly and
posted on the USENET newsgroup
soc.culture.canada.
```

> **TIP:** Be sure to scan the list of questions at the beginning of the FAQ—and don't post these questions to the group!

Understanding a newsgroup's peculiarities

One good reason for reading the newsgroup for a while and obtaining the FAQ is that each newsgroup tends to have its own, distinct culture and rules of comportment. Here's a list of things to watch out for:

- **Binary newsgroups.** Please don't post discussion articles to binary newsgroups, which almost always have a newsgroup named .d (short for "discussion") that's intended for this purpose. An example: alt.binaries.pictures.sounds is supposed to be for binary sound files only, while alt.binaries.sounds.d is for discussion of these sounds. Note that this rule is very seldom observed, to the chagrin of experienced posters, who post messages urging discussion articles to be posted to the .d group; but this is itself an infringement of the rule!

- **Moderated newsgroups.** Don't try to post directly to these newsgroups; send an email message to the moderator.

- **Movie and fiction newsgroups.** In any of the groups that review movies or fiction, you can post a review that reveals the ending—but please use a subject line with the word "Spoiler," and don't reveal the ending on the first screen of your post. People will get very upset with you if you don't follow these rules.

- **"Wanted" newsgroups.** Don't post any discussion articles to these newsgroups, such as comp.sources.wanted. They're for people's requests only.

- **"For sale" and "marketplace" newsgroups.** These newsgroups are intended to help individuals—not firms—to sell items to other individuals. If you post to one of these groups, please be specific about what you have to sell, post to the correct group, and cancel your article after you sell your item. Ship your item COD.

UNDERSTANDING THE STRUCTURE OF USENET HEADERS

To post messages to USENET without committing errors, it's necessary to understand the structure of an article's header. (An article consists of two parts, the header and the body.) Here's an example of a header:

```
From: tomj@furball.cmsx.COM (Tom
Jackson)
Path: cbosgd!eoha!duh!dliu!tomj
Newsgroups: news.software.readers
Subject: New Windows newsreader
announced
```

```
Message-ID: <642@tomj@furball.cmsx.COM>
Date: Fri, 19 Nov 94 16:14:55 GMT
Followup-To: news.software.readers
Expires: Sat, 1 Jan 95 00:00:00 -0500
Organization: Confederated Marketing
Services eXpress
```

Some of the headers are required, while others are optional, as explained in the following sections. Take a couple of minutes to skim over this information; you'll find it very valuable in learning how to avoid the gaffes that newbies so often make!

Required headers

The following indicates the purpose of the required headers:

- **From.** This line contains the email address of the person who sent the message, in the Internet syntax. It may also contain the full name of the person, in parentheses.

- **Date.** The date and time that the message was originally posted to the network. Generally, the date is indicated in Greenwich Mean Time (GMT).

- **Newsgroups.** The newsgroup or newsgroups to which the article will be posted. Multiple newsgroups may be specified, separated by a comma.

- **Subject.** Tells what the message is about. It should suggest the content well enough that the reader can decide whether to read the message. If the message is submitted in response to another message (for example, a follow-up) the default subject should begin with the four characters "Re:", and the "References" line is required.

- **Message-ID.** This line gives the message a unique identifier. The identification code may not be reused during the lifetime of the message.

- **Path.** The path through USENET sites that the message took to arrive at the current site. Each forwarding system adds its name to the path.

Optional headers

The following headers are optional:

- **Reply-To.** This line has the same format as "From". If present, mailed replies to the author should be sent to the name given here. Otherwise, replies are mailed to the name on the "From" line.

- **Sender.** This field is present only if the submitter manually enters a "From" line. It is intended to record the entity responsible for submitting the message to the network.

- **Followup-To.** This line has the same format as "Newsgroups". If present, follow-up messages are to be posted to the newsgroup or newsgroups listed here. If this line is not present, follow-ups are posted to the newsgroup or newsgroups listed in the "Newsgroups" line.

- **Expires.** This line, if present, is in a legal USENET date format. It specifies a suggested expiration date for the message. If not present, the local default expiration date is used.

- **References.** This field lists the Message-IDs of any messages prompting the submission of this message. It is required for all follow-up messages but forbidden when a new subject is raised. The purpose of the "References" header is to allow messages to be grouped into threads by the newsreader program.

- **Distribution.** This line is used to define the distribution scope of the message. More than one distribution can be entered, separated by commas.

- **Organization.** The text of this line is a short phrase describing the organization to which the sender or the machine belongs. This line is needed to help identify the person posting the message because host names are so cryptic that it's difficult to recognize the organization's name from the email address alone.

- **Keywords.** This line can contain a few key words that describe the message's content, as an aid to someone trying to determine whether it's worth reading.

- **Summary.** This line can contain a brief summary of the message, again as an aid to someone trying to determine whether the message is worth reading.

- **Approved.** This line is required for any message posted to a moderated newsgroup; it indicates the moderator's email address (and, implicitly, his or her approval of the message).

- **Lines.** A count of the number of lines in the body of the message.

- **Xref.** This line contains information about where the host USENET site stores the message.

Typical newbie screw-ups

Now that you're familiar with the required and optional USENET header lines, here's an overview of typical newbie gaffes—the kind of things that really irritate the old-timers. Listed here are the screw-ups that stem from lack of knowledge of USENET's headers; there are other potential screw-ups that I'll discuss later.

- **Crossposting without specifying a follow-up newsgroup.** If you crosspost a message to more than one newsgroup, you should always specify to which of these newsgroups follow-up messages should be sent. *Never* crosspost without specifying a Followup-To newsgroup.

- **Follow-ups to inappropriate newsgroups.** When you reply to a crossposted message, you should *never* reply to all the crossposted groups—this results in duplicate threads appearing in many newsgroups. *Always* reply *only* to the Followup-To newsgroup!

- **Misattributed quotes.** When you reply to an article, the newsreading software automatically adds an attribution line, indicating the Message-ID and

From address of the message that's being quoted. In a forwarded message, or an article that's been replied to many times, the attribution may not correctly identify the text that you go on to quote! You may need to edit the attribution line to make sure that it's correct.

- **Empty messages.** Whoops! You don't know how to use your newsreader yet. Prepare for a few flames in your mailbox—you've just wasted people's time.

- **Multiple posts of the same message.** Here's another version of "I don't know how to use my newsreader." Such messages start with, "I wasn't sure whether my previous message made it, so here's another one...." Prepare for flames.

- **Thinking you're replying by email, when in fact you're posting a follow-up article.** This can be *very* embarrassing, particularly when you're saying something personal. Learn how to use your newsreader!

> **TIP:** The newsreaders supplied with on-line services, as well as graphical user interface (GUI) newsreaders designed to work with Microsoft Windows and the Macintosh, sometimes prevent users from seeing or editing the full header information. This in itself is responsible for some of these gaffes, but bear in mind that the USENET community will hold you, not your newsreader, responsible for any errors you make! If you find that your newsreader boxes you into making one of these errors, *switch newsreaders.*

WHAT NOT TO POST

Some articles just don't belong on USENET at all, and if you post one of them, you can expect criticism—and it may not be gentle. To make USENET useful, people have to wade through huge volumes of unwanted postings. Often, these postings violate common-sense rules that ought to be obvious to anyone with some consideration, but sometimes they're just typical newbie mistakes. Read the following, and you won't make them!

Please **don't** post any of the following:

- **Inappropriate test messages.** Please do not post a test message to a substantive newsgroup with world distribution! There are test newsgroups provided for this purpose. Please read carefully the section titled "Posting test messages" later in this chapter.

- **Questions already answered in the newsgroup's FAQ.** Before posting an article, obtain and read the newsgroup's FAQ, as explained in the previous section.

- **Answers to questions already answered within the thread.** If you see an article that asks a question, don't answer it until you've finished reading the entire thread—someone else may have posted the answer.

- **Reponses that ought to be sent by email.** If someone asks for the name and address of a good antique automobile dealer in Virginia or West Virginia, please don't post the answer to the newsgroup! It isn't of interest to all. Send your response via email to the person who posted the query.

- **Articles that don't pertain to the newsgroup's topic.** The only way you'll know the group's topic for sure is to read the FAQ and read the newsgroup.

- **Advertisements or self-aggrandizing articles.** Advertising, in the form of product announcements, is welcomed only in the biz.* newsgroups. A legitimate exception: Groups in which collectors participate, such as rec.autos.antique, permit and even welcome "for sale" posts that are relevant to the group's topic. Use a specific subject line: for example, "MGB for sale—Beaverton, OR."

- **"Me too!" or "I agree" replies.** These generally quote a previous post in its entirety. If that's all you have to say, *shut up.*

- **Requests for help with USENET or Internet.** You'll get much better results if you ask for help from your local system's help desk. In addition, there are rich informational resources available on the Internet that can answer these questions.

- **Repeat posts just because there weren't any responses the first time.** If they didn't find it interesting the first time, they'll find it even *less* interesting the second!

- **Is John Doe out there?** There's a newsgroup for such requests; it's called soc.net-people. It's used to track down old friends that you've lost contact with. Better: Get the FAQ titled "How to find people's E-mail addresses," which is posted frequently to comp.mail.misc,soc.net-people, news.newusers.questions, comp.answers, soc.answers, and news.answers.

- **My email didn't get through! Help!** You're trying to reach someone on *one* system. So why post a message that people will read around the world? Pick up the phone and call.

- **Current news events.** OK, the space shuttle blew up—but by the time your post about this reaches newsgroups throughout USENET, everyone will know about it anyway. You're just wasting bandwidth.

- **Corrections to egregious factual errors.** Sure, you know that Coppola didn't direct *Star Wars,* as the post you're reading attests. But this is a trick! It's called a troll, and it's designed to lure people into making fools of themselves.

- **Responses to net.abusers.** Please don't bite the bait. People who post obnoxious or inappropriate material to USENET are juvenile misfits who do so for one reason only: They want attention! By responding and pointing out what jerks they are, you're only giving them what they want. By

the way, they already *know* they're jerks. They *like* being jerks. They take satisfaction in annoying other people. Well, did you expect the world to be perfect?

CONSIDERATIONS FOR TYPING AND FORMATTING YOUR POST

People will be reading your posts on all kinds of computers and terminals, so it's important to type and format your post so others will find it easy to read. Here are some points to bear in mind:

- **Line lengths.** On many terminals, people can't read your post if the lines are longer than 72 characters. If you're not sure whether your news-reader formats your line lengths to 72 characters or less, try a test post (see the section titled "Posting test messages," later in this chapter). You may have to end your lines with a carriage return (Enter) keystroke to make sure your lines are short enough—and that's particularly true if you're using a newsreader that doesn't automatically insert hard return characters at the end of each line.

- **Tabs.** Don't use tabs. Many newsreaders can't recognize tab characters. If you want to indent or align text, use spaces.

- **Capitalization.** Please do not type your post, or any part of it, using CAPITAL LETTERS. It's considered to be "shouting" and annoys people. But don't type your post with all lowercase letters either ("i was reading your post and i found it interesting...."); it's harder to read. Just use the normal rules for capitalization, and you'll do fine.

POSTING TEST MESSAGES

In almost every newsgroup, you'll run across messages with subjects that say, "TEST MESSAGE! PLEASE IGNORE!" But you can't ignore such messages—they've already taken up room on your screen, interrupting the flow of discussion. Not only that, such messages have probably been posted with world distribution, wasting network bandwidth for no justifiable reason. If you do this, expect to get flamed—and you'll deserve it. There's a right way to post a test message, as this section explains. Please read it carefully.

Two newsgroups have been set aside for the sole purpose of giving people a place to post test messages: alt.test and misc.test. Please post your test messages to one of these groups (or both, if you want to test crossposting). But there's one other thing to remember: Please use the narrowest possible distribution for your post so that it doesn't propagate beyond your site. At the University of Virginia, for example, we can choose from the following distributions: uva (Univ. of Virginia only), chv (Charlottesville), va (Virginia), us (United States), or world (global distribution). For a test post, one should choose uva—the narrowest distribution.

> **TIP:** Don't get upset if you don't see your post immediately. At many sites, USENET postings are processed only at periodic intervals, such as once every half hour. If you log on several hours later, you'll see your post.

REPLYING TO ARTICLES

Chances are that your first post will be a reply to an article you've read in a newsgroup. You've got something to say or some information to provide, and it's obvious that it would be helpful.

Choosing your reply method (email or follow-up post)

The first question you must answer is whether you should post your reply publicly to the newsgroup (a follow-up posting) or privately (via email). If you're responding to a query for information that the original poster alone is interested in, there's no question: Send your reply via email. Often, though,

it's not so easy to judge whether your response would prove of general interest. It all depends on the context. For example, suppose you're responding to an article in news.software.readers titled "I need a newsreader for Windows?" Here, you'd respond via email—this person is just asking for some suggestions, which wouldn't be of interest to most readers of this group (they very likely know what the leading Windows newsreaders are). But take this example in the same newsgroup: "Windows newsreaders—equal to UNIX readers?" Your answer to this question might be of more general interest—and if you think it would be, respond via a follow-up post.

> **TIP:** Sometimes you'll see a post that asks for information, and says "Reply via email, and I'll summarize." Do what's requested—reply via email. This person is promising to post an article later summarizing all the responses.

There's one general rule you can follow, though, that holds true in all situations: Praise in public (via a posted article), and criticize in private (via email).

Handling quotations

Whether you're responding via email or a follow-up post, a good newsreader will automatically quote the article to which you're responding. It does so by copying the text of the article to the editor you're using, and by placing a disctictive symbol—usually a greater-than (>) symbol—in front of each quoted line.

So that you can see how this works—and what can go wrong—let's take a look at a (fictitious) original posting, and what happens when you quote it:

```
Newsgroups: misc.consumers.house
From: mrocker@ale.frisco.com (May
Rocker)
Subject: Reverse osmosis water
filters???
```

Organization:Schooner Steam Beer
Date: Wed, 15 Aug 1994 00:09:30 GMT
Lines: 13

Whoa, what a hassle building a new
house.... I've had to research all this
stuff that I knew *nothing* about
before we got started!

Here's the latest.... I'm looking for a
reverse osmosis water filter but have
no idea who makes a good one. I want
one that doesn't waste too much water
and gives good water pressure even
when the tank is not completely full.
Does anyone have any suggestions or
experience with these things?

Incidentally, thanks to everyone who
contributed to that great thread on
shingles—I learned a lot.
—May

```
   _____   ____
  / / \ / / \      "There must be some
 / / \ / /\ \      kind of way out of
/__/  \/_ / \__\            here..."
     mrocker@ale.frisco.com <May Rocker>
```

When you reply to this article, your newsreader—if it's equipped to do so—will copy the text
to your editor, and it will look something like this:

In mrocker@ale.frisco.com (Mabelleine
Rocker) writes:

>Whoa, what a hassle building a new
>house.... I've had to research all
>this stuff that I knew *nothing* about
>before we got started!

>Here's the latest.... I'm looking for
>a reverse osmosis water filter but
>have no idea who makes a good one. I
>want one that doesn't waste too much
>water and gives good water pressure
>even when the tank is not completely
>full. Does anyone have any suggestions,
>or experience with these things?

>Incidentally, thanks to everyone who
>contributed to that great thread on
>shingles—I learned a lot.
> —May
>
> _____   ____
> / / \ / / \   "There must be some
> / / \ / /\ \   kind of way out of
>/__/ \/_ / __\   here..."
>   mrocker@ale.frisco.com <May Rocker>

Now here's Point No. 1 about quoting correctly:
Never quote the entire original article. Point No. 1A:
Don't quote the signature!

Use your editor to whittle the quoted text down
to just the point to which you want to respond. If
you don't know how to use your editor to do this,
log off now, get the manual, and read it!

Here's a well-edited version of the quotation.
Note how all the extraneous verbiage has been
removed:

In mrocker@ale.frisco.com (Mabelleine
Rocker) writes:

>I'm looking for a reverse osmosis
>water filter but have no idea
>who makes a good one.

I understand that Home Depot offers one
for $150 that does a good job. It has
2-3 gal capacity and wastes 2 gal for
each pure gallon. It's economical to
run but doesn't have a great warranty.
Some builders I know think it's great.

Replying to cross-posted messages

Please read this section carefully to avoid making a
very common error. If you're replying to an article
that has been crossposted, your newsreader may
post your reply to all the groups mentioned in the
original article's newsgroup line. Some people may
not have been happy about the crosspost in the
first place, and they're going to be even less happy
about your reply!

Here's an example. Suppose you see the following post:

```
Newsgroups: news.software.readers,
alt.flame,
alt.culture.usenet, alt.stupidity,
alt.religion.kibology,soc.feminism,
talk.origins
Followup-to:news.software.readers
From: lbeck@viking.uu.se
Subject: Flame-proofing algorithm?
Organization: Uppsala University
Date: Wed, 15 Aug 1994 00:09:30 GMT
Lines: 13

We're working on a new newsreader and
we're wondering if anyone has given any
thought to a "flame filter"—presumably
this would search for obscenities or
overuse of capital letters ???

Reactions, anyone?

--Lars
```

This post is arguably off-topic for many of the groups listed, but is perhaps justifiable in that some of them are liable to flame wars. But your reply certainly wouldn't be!

Note the follow-up to: line! That's where your reply should go. Depending on the newsreader you're using, you may have to edit the newsgroups line in the header to make sure that your follow-up post goes to just one group rather than the whole crosspost list.

If the subject has drifted, change the subject line!

One of USENET's least appealing characteristics is *subject drift,* the tendency of discussions to move far away from the topic mentioned in the Re: subject line. If you're participating in such a discussion, edit the subject line to reflect the change in the discussion's topic.

Don't start a new thread by posting a follow-up

If you don't know how to use your newsreader to post an article on a new subject (see the next sec-

tion), please do not try to start a new thread by posting a follow-up and then ignoring the subject. People find this very irritating, and you'll get some very testy mail.

POSTING AN ARTICLE ON A NEW SUBJECT

When you post an article to a new group, you must take into consideration whether you're posting to the correct newsgroup, whether you should crosspost, what your subject line should say, and more. This section details the considerations that go into an effective post on a new subject.

Finding the right group

With thousands of newsgroups in existence, this is more than a small challenge! But you'll find plenty of help right here. Check out the Newsgroup Subject Index, at the end of this book, for a keyword-based subject index to more than 5,000 newsgroups! For more information on the top newsgroups in USENET, check out Chapter 18, "USENET's best: the top newsgroups reviewed."

Making crossposting decisions

In general, you shouldn't crosspost at all unless you've a very good reason for doing so. One example: People like to crosspost to alt.aquaria and rec.aquaria, on the theory that some sites have one group, but not the other; a crossposted article reaches almost all USENET sites. But even this generates controversy.

If you do decide to crosspost, by all means use your newsreader's crossposting capabilities rather than posting separate messages to each group. Two reasons support this admonition: Crossposting conserves bandwidth (in comparison to posting separate messages, it's more efficient), and some advanced newsreaders automatically hide crossposted articles that have already been read in another newsgroup (this won't work if you manually post separate copies to more than one group).

Choosing a distribution

Another decision you'll have to make concerns the geographic distribution of your choice. Here's a rundown of your options and examples of when to choose them:

- **Local.** Your post won't propagate beyond your organization. Example: you want to discuss something that affects the people who work for your organization.

- **Regional.** Your post won't propagate beyond your city or metropolitan area. Example: You want to sell something in a regional "for-sale" newsgroup.

- **State.** Your post won't propagate beyond your state. Example: You want to discuss an issue that affects residents of your state, but no other.

- **Country.** Your post won't propagate beyond your country. Example: You want to discuss a product that's available in your country.

- **Global.** Your post will propagate to all USENET sites. USENET will have to bear the expense of duplicating your message hundreds of thousands of times. Example: You want to raise an issue that you're certain will be of interest to people in every country USENET reaches.

Obviously, it makes good sense to think long and hard about your distribution choices. In general, use the smallest geographic distribution that makes sense for your post.

Setting the expiration date

As you've probably noticed, USENET articles don't hang around for long—ten to fourteen days at the maximum. Then they're erased to make room for the incoming flood of new articles. Even so, you can choose an expiration date for your article, if you wish. This would have some effect only if you choose a *shorter* time than the expiration period in effect at most sites; if you try to choose a longer time, such as one or two months, your efforts will go to naught, since your post will be erased anyway!

To set an expiration date for your article, place a line in the header below the Newsgroups line, and type an expiration date such as the following:

```
Expires: 15 Mar 95
```

When would this be useful? Suppose you're about to head off for a vacation, and you don't want the post to remain current while you're gone. Set it to expire a couple of days before you go.

Writing an effective subject line

When you write a follow-up post, you don't have to worry about the subject line: The newsreader automatically quotes the subject line of the article you're quoting and adds "Re:" to it. When you post an article on a new subject, though, you need to devote some thought to writing an effective subject line. If it isn't effective, people won't read your post. Here are some tips:

- **Keep it short.** Most newsreaders allow only 40 spaces for the subject.

- **Be specific.** Vague subjects such as "Help Needed" or "Some Thoughts..." aren't likely to attract much interest.

- **Don't "shout."** Resist the temptation to type something like "!!!READ THIS NOW!!!"; it's annoying, and you'll hear about it.

Additional header fields you can use

The better newsreaders can search forward in a lengthy newsgroup to find articles based on a text pattern the user types. To maximize the chances that your document will be retrieved by such a search, take a moment to type two or three key words in the Key Words field of your article's header. These words should differ from the ones used in your article's subject line, but they should include any words in the article itself that describe the subject of your post. Try to think of general words that put your post into a general category of some kind, as well as specific words that identify the unique content of your post. An article about a great source of parts for antique sports cars, for example, could use the key words *parts, cheap, Turner Classic Cars, Virginia.*

For the benefit of those strapped for time (and who isn't?), you can use the Summary field. Type a one-line summary of the most important point you want to make—and don't try to tease people into actually reading the whole article. *Spill the beans*—make the point.

CANCELLING A MESSAGE

If you just sent out a post and you regret having done so for some reason, you can cancel it. But bear in mind that the Cancel command has to chase down every copy that's been made of your post, so it's likely that many people will have an opportunity to read it before it disappears from view. The sooner you cancel, the better.

To cancel an article with rn, trn, or nn, type **C**. In tin, type **D**. With America Online, Windows, and Macintosh newsreaders, look for a Cancel command on one of the menus.

SUMMARY

To post successfully, begin by creating a brief signature. Read a newsgroup for at least a week or two before posting, get to know the group's peculiarities,

and by all means read the FAQ. You should know by heart the list of things you should never post. When you type your post, remember that some terminals can't display more than 72 characters in a line. If you must post a test message, post to alt.test or misc.test, and choose a local distribution. When replying, reply by email unless you're sure your response is of general interest. Edit the quotation down to the most important sentence or two; be sure to remove the signature! Edit the header line, if necessary, so that you reply only to the follow-up newsgroup. When you post to a new subject, choose the correct group, crosspost only when necessary, choose the smallest geographic distribution that's appropriate for your post, and write an effective subject. If you feel that you'd like to cancel your message, do so as soon as you can.

FROM HERE

- Need help finding a newsgroup? Flip to Chapter 18, "USENET's best: The top newsgroups reviewed," and to the Newsgroup Subject Index, at the back of this book.

- Not sure how to deal with problem posters? See Chapter 17, "Dealing with USENET problems."

DEALING WITH USENET PROBLEMS

USENET is lots of fun, for the most part, and—as this book has argued—it can become an indispensable part of your information-gathering strategy. It doesn't seem like much fun, however, when you run into the irritating, antisocial, or even downright sociopathic behavior of a whole host of net.abusers, including spewers, spammers, trollers, cascaders, and more, who perpetrate various forms of mischief that are explained in this chapter. Much of this behavior is just an irritation, and can even be mildly amusing—until it starts wasting too much of your time. Pranks abound, some of them nasty enough to leave you shaking with rage. It's tough to resist the temptation to flame them back—but, as this chapter argues, flaming back is exactly what you *shouldn't* do.

You should be aware, too, you can get into trouble in USENET—particularly by posting to the alt.sex.* groups, which may result in unwanted email, public embarrassment, and other problems. In short: There are people out there who range from Mildly Irritating to Seriously Not Nice, and this chapter has one overriding aim: to teach you how to keep them out of your life.

A USENET BESTIARY

Beholding the often bizarre phenomena of USENET day after day, one begins to build a taxonomy of the curious and odd beasts that seem to generate the more disagreeable postings. I offer this partly in jest, in that I don't think spewing or cascading makes one into a Spewer or Cascader as I've defined them, as if an occasional thoughtless or even deliberate action could serve to define one's essence. Many of these offenders are, after all, a little tardy in the maturity department, but time may cure that. But I would like to call attention to the conclusions people will draw about anyone who engages in the following antisocial activities.

There's really only one basic point to all that follows, though. All of these people share one characteristic in common: There's something sufficiently pathetic or unsatisfying about their lives that they're trying to get attention by irritating other USENET posters or even trying to trash the Net. For heaven's sake, don't give them what they want—attention!

- Don't post a message taking exception to the behavior of one of these offenders. They're logging on hour by hour, hoping to see posts from the fools they've snared into responding.

- Don't bother sending them critical email messages. You might wake up the next morning to find 15MB of child pornography in your mailbox, together with a note to your system administrator about the horrible things you're storing on his or her disk drive.

- In short: IGNORE THEM! Deprive them of the one thing they want, and they'll find somewhere else to play.

- If you feel you must do something about their posts, you can contact the postmaster at the site from which their posts originated. But *please* don't try to *mail bomb* or flame the postmaster as a means of getting his or her attention about the offending person's activities! It's very possible that the site name is a forgery, as you'll see in this chapter. For more information, see the section titled "Dealing with offensive mail," later in this chapter.

In what follows, I've arranged our beasts in ascending order, based on the gravity of their offenses; the list starts with the mildly irritating and ends with the truly obnoxious.

Cascaders

Here's a truly idiotic game. To understand how it's played, you need to know how newsreaders handle quotations of quoted material. Suppose I post the following:

```
There's a quick remedy--log off.
```

Now somebody quotes it:

```
You wrote,
>There's a quick remedy--log off.
We'd rather *you* logged off.
```

In a subsequent follow-up post, somebody quotes the quote:

```
In a recent post, so-and-so wrote:
>You wrote,
>>There's a quick remedy--log off.
>We'd rather *you* logged off.
We'd rather you *both* logged off.
```

Now here's what cascaders do. The objective is to have the last word in a cascade war:

```
>>>>>>>>Forget I ever said it.
>>>>>>>No, I won't.
>>>>>>Oh, please do.
>>>>>You first.
>>>>Who started this, anyway?
>>>Not me.
>>And who will end it?
```

```
>Me. I win.
No, you don't.
```

Isn't that fun?

Spewers

A spewer won't leave his pet idea alone and posts to as many groups as possible—including many where his ideas aren't welcome or pertinent. An example: Someone violently opposed to affirmative action, who keeps raising this issue in alt.culture.african-american despite repeated protestations that it has nothing to do with the newsgroup's topic.

Snots

A snot—and that's all you see, because he's looking down his nose at you—thinks he knows everything about a subject, and doesn't suffer fools gladly. Give a straight answer to something? That's beneath him:

```
Sanjay Ramachandran
<chandra@petite.cs.njstate.edu writes,

>Would someone mind telling me what all
>this Linux talk is
>about? It's not in my computer
>dictionary.

Take my advice—go back to your Linus
blanket, you're not in this league.
```

Trollers

Here's an interesting reverse on snottiness—it's an attempt to get snots to reveal themselves for what they are, plumped-up phonies with an exaggerated sense of their self-importance. To troll, you post something that is so obviously false that anyone in his or her right mind (supposedly) would recognize it as a troll, and ignore it:

```
Kato the Great
<kato@klingon.ncarts.edu> writes,

>I haven't seen such a great film since
>Francis Ford
```

```
>Coppola directed the Star Wars
>trilogy.
```

```
You idiot! Star Wars—the first film,
anyway—was directed by George Lucas!
```

Spammers

Spammers try to spoil other people's fun, and get attention for themselves, by filling up newsgroups with unwanted junk that's unrelated to the newsgroup's topics. The word itself seems to stem from a Monty Python routine: "We have eggs, spam, eggs and spam, eggs, toast and spam, eggs spam and spam, and spam, spam, spam, spam, spam, spam, spam, and spam." The term "spamming" has its origins in MUD games ("MUD" is short for Multi-user dungeons) and refers to the very unfriendly strategy of keeping someone out of a game by jamming their channel with unwanted verbiage. As applied to USENET, it retains its connotation of spoiling people's fun, and it's equally unwelcome. These days, though, the motives may be more starkly economic than antisocial—in one case, peddlers posted an advertisement to every USENET newsgroup in existence! This topic is examined in Chapter 21, "USENET issues and futures."

Flame Baiters

Flame baiters bombard USENET with deliberately provocative, ultra-obnoxious posts. Their objective? Starting a flame war. A fictitious and egregious but not unlikely example:

```
Brenda Jones <bjones@macrosoft.com.
writes,
```

```
>My kitty is always so glad to see me
>at the end of the day!
>She purrs and noses me. Sometimes I
>wonder if she's my
>best friend!
```

```
Your best friend is a CAT? Get a life—
or maybe just get laid :-)
```

You'll see plenty of flame bait of this sort on the Net—postings with racial and ethnic slurs (usually screaming in ALL UPPERCASE) as their subjects. Before firing off a flame in response, bear in mind that an unknown (but probably large) proportion of such posts are pranks, originating from college campuses. College students are notoriously lax about their accounts: Jane says, "Here's my password, I'm taking the semester off," and before the week is over John has given it to several dozen of his "hacker" friends. And in computer labs, students log on, check their mail, and then leave for the pizza joint, unthinkingly leaving an active session on-screen. Your friendly neighborhood prankster has been waiting patiently for just this to occur—and fifteen minutes later, another offensive edition hits the Net. The student who left the session running will have quite a surprise in his mailbox the next morning.

One of the very real problems with USENET, as Chapter 21 discusses, is the lack of *authentication*—that is, some sort of procedure that verifies just who is responsible for a given message. Lax college students aside, it's almost a trivial task for a knowledgeable hacker to forge a USENET posting, and that's where many of the Net's more disagreeable posts come from.

The consequences of a forgery can be costly for those in whose names the forgery was committed. In August, 1994, a message titled MAKE.MONEY.REAL.FAST was posted to more than 100 newsgroups. The message outlined an illegal pyramid scheme and urged readers to send money to the operator of a computer bulletin board system in New York called Net Access (netaxs.com). In fact, the post originated from Drexel University, as was obvious from the header. The From: line listed an account at netaxs.com, but the Message-ID—added automatically by the system software subsequent to the forgery—indicates that the post came from Drexel. But not very many people noted this fact; they instead bombarded Net Access with more than 1,000 messages, many of them flames.

Net Access officials summed up the lessons posed by this event: In the absence of an authentication method for USENET postings, you should never assume that the ostensible author actually wrote the post.

In sum, there's little point in flaming the ostensible perpetrators of flame bait, because you can't be sure just who was responsible for a given post. A recent case in point: Nearly two dozen newsgroups were hit recently with a 17K post, ostensibly from a Christian family radio network, admonishing the sinful to repent—and in terms that were as obnoxious as they were illiterate. Bombarded with complaints, the radio service claimed that the post had originated from one of their "overly devout" backers, for whom they had recently had a spate of complaints regarding unwanted faxes.

Infectors

USENET is fast becoming one of the chief distribution platforms for some of the latest and most vicious computer viruses. Gullible readers of alt.sex.binaries.pictures.erotica, for instance, were more than a little surprised recently to find that the Sexotica game they had downloaded infected their system with the Kaos 4 virus, which is so new that most virus detection programs can't detect it. Several people reported that the virus had wiped out their vital system files, forcing them to reformat their hard drives with complete and catastrophic loss of everything stored on them.

> **TIP:** *Don't ever download an executable program from USENET*—it's just too dangerous. If you must do so, try to run it on a dual-floppy system, where it can do only limited harm. But don't worry about text and graphics files— despite what you'll hear from the trollers on the Net, they can't infect your system.

I'm sorry if I've made it sound like there's nothing but a bunch of losers and sociopaths on-line.

To be sure, you have to watch out for yourself— that's life. But don't let these jerks blind you to the angels, the big brothers and big sisters, the boosters and counselors and Dutch uncles, the soothsayers and poets and philosophers, the artists and the mystics—USENET is a network of people, and there are highs as well as lows.

THE (UNFORTUNATELY NECESSARY) ART OF THE KILL FILE

The proper remedy for all of the above-mentioned forms of net.abuse is the kill file, a feature of the better newsreaders that lets you delete certain posts before they appear on your thread selector. With the best readers, you can kill in the following ways:

- **By subject.** You'll never see any article again with the words "Die, Sinners," or "Make Money Fast!"

- **By author.** Vexed by a persistently obnoxious participant in a particular newsgroup? Add this person's email address to your kill file—and he or she is history.

- **By site.** If you notice that many undesirable posts come from a particular site, you can add this site to your kill file, and you won't see any more posts from this site. This is a rather extreme measure that cuts out the good as well as the bad.

The best newsreaders can kill globally (for all newsgroups) as well as within a particular newsgroup.

Kill files aren't the most elegant solution in the world. A person who posted something idiotic might repent and start contributing famously, but you'll never know it. In the future, more sophisticated filters might permit statistical analyses of article content, based on some algorithm that nobody's yet thought of. For now, though, the kill file is the only alternative to having these jerks in your face.

STAYING OUT OF TROUBLE

In the computerized role-playing games known as MUDs, it's possible to engage in virtual social relationships with other people that you meet in the game's fantasy space. Now just suppose you run into a member of the opposite sex who seems nice, friendly, and sexy, and one thing leads to another, speaking cybersexually, of course. In a heated, erotic moment, you type romantic and sexy things, and it all seems like lots of fun. What you don't realize is that you've been had. The whole time, your ostensible "partner," who probably isn't of the sex he or she claimed to be, has been recording what you've typed, and you'll find it posted to the Net the next morning—maybe with a copy to your boss, just for extra laughs.

The moral here is that you'd best be wary. You'll meet lots of wonderful people on USENET, to be sure, but remember the saying: "If it sounds too good to be true, it probably isn't." There are lots of pranksters, jokers, and tricksters out there just waiting to bait you into something compromising. If you're approached by someone by email after you've posted something, take it slow and easy—make sure you get to know the person very, very well before revealing personal information or anything that could conceivably be used against you.

It's good to remember the following: Never post anything on USENET—and that includes "private" email replies—that you wouldn't want to have repeated to an assembled audience of your coworkers, your family, and your Sunday School teacher. Some pointers:

- If you're using your computer at work, don't post to the alt.sex.* groups. Someone might think it's funny to send a copy of your posts to your boss.

- Don't cuss. Remember, the audience includes your Sunday School teacher!

- If you're married or seriously involved with someone, please remember that having an on-line "romance" with another person will almost certainly be viewed as cheating. *You* may think it's all for fun, but you could hurt your partner—and the "playful" computer romance could turn out to involve deeper feelings than you'd bargained for.

Posting anonymously

If you feel that you want to post something that could get you in trouble, there's an option: You can send a message to an anonymous posting service. The best services permit anonymous two-way communication; that is, you can post an anonymous article, and people can reply to you—and you'll receive the replies via email—with their identity masked as well. This means, of course, that there's a record of your identity somewhere in the anonymous posting service's computer, so you'd best be sure that you trust the system operator before using such a service.

The longest-running anonymous posting service, located in Finland, is anon.penet.fi, and as you'll quickly discover on USENET, that's where most anonymous posts originate. Receiving over 3,000 messages per day, this site is responsible for approximately 5% of all USENET postings! Send mail to help@anon.penet.fi for information.

> **TIP:** Be aware that many people dislike the whole concept of anonymous posting, believing that one should stand behind one's word. Moreover, anonymous posting services have been badly abused by a very small minority of users who employ such services to intimidate and harass. Still, there are valid reasons for posting anonymously (see alt.whistleblowing in Chapter 18). For more information on the controversy over anonymous postings, see Chapter 21, "USENET issues and futures."

An anonymous service should be used only with the greatest caution. Here are some basic rules, suggested by Larry Detweiler in his FAQ titled "Anonymity on the Internet":

- Anonymity should be used only when it is strictly necessary to permit you to make a valuable and substantive contribution to USENET without fear of retribution or harassment. For instance: A woman might wish to detail her experiences with on-line harassers without the risk of further harassment.

- Never use an anonymous service to harass or attack other USENET users.

- Don't use an anonymous service to break rules, such as posting opinion to a group that forbids discussion.

- Don't post anonymously to the standard newsgroups (comp, misc, news, rec, sci, soc, talk); anonymous postings should be directed to the alt.* groups only.

> **TIP:** There's nothing funnier—or sometimes, sadder—than someone who has posted anonymously, only to forget that their newsreader automatically includes their signature! Before posting anonymously, use the command that turns off adding your signature automatically. To make sure you haven't left any traces of your identity in your post, begin by sending an anonymous message to yourself.

DEALING WITH OFFENSIVE MAIL

If you're receiving unwanted email from someone as a result of a USENET post, the best approach—at least initially—is to ignore it and delete it. Whatever you do, don't respond; you'll do nothing but encourage the person who's harassing you. Should the harassment continue, you do have one avenue of recourse: You can complain to the postmaster—not the system administrator, please!—of the service from which the mail originates. The postmaster is the person responsible for supervising email accounts and ascertaining that account holders are behaving in accordance with the service's guidelines. Almost all systems have explicit procedures for cancelling the accounts of users who abuse their privileges.

When you write to the postmaster, please refrain from blaming the postmaster (or the postmaster's organization) for the behavior of an account holder; the postmaster is almost certainly unaware of the behavior. Remember, the mail might not even be originating from the site, due to a forgery! Describe what has happened in matter-of-fact terms, enclosing samples from the offending messages, and ask for assistance.

SUMMARY

Cascaders, spewers, snots, and trollers are irritating, and they waste bandwidth, but they're basically harmless. More vexing are spammers, who disrupt the flow of discussion with unwanted, and usually voluminous, advertising or proselytizing material. Worse still are flame baiters, whose pranks can hurt—and cause terrible problems for the system administrators at the sites from which their hate-filled posts originate. Of real danger to you are infectors who want to ruin your computer system, and pranksters who may try to lure you into saying things you'll later regret. USENET can be lots of fun, but be wary.

FROM HERE

- To find newsgroups that remain (relatively) devoid of net.abuse, check out the reviews in Chapter 18, "USENET's best: The top newsgroups reviewed."

- For more information on the issues facing USENET, see Chapter 21, "USENET issues and futures."

PART IV

BUILDING YOUR

SUBSCRIPTION

LIST

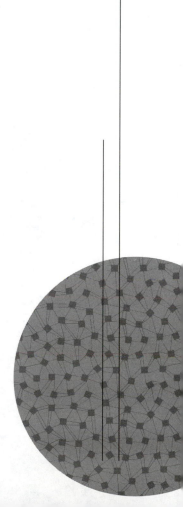

18

USENET'S BEST:
THE TOP
NEWSGROUPS
REVIEWED

With thousands of newsgroups in existence, it's a challenge to build a good subscription list. You're looking for newsgroups of interest, of course, but you'd also like to experience the best of USENET—high-quality discussion carried on by informed, supportive people. But you just don't have time to browse through dozens, let alone hundreds or thousands, looking for the ones that measure up to your standards. And you won't find much help on-line. The brief, one-line newsgroup descriptions found in the newsgroup lists posted to news.lists are too brief—and often, they're flippant or otherwise uninformative. And apart from news.newsgroups.reviews, a new group that hasn't produced many reviews thus far, there hasn't been any way to gauge a group's quality except by plunging in.

Until now, that is. This book offers two original resources designed to help you build an effective subscription list quickly.

- This chapter offers reviews of more than 300 of USENET's top newsgroups. You'll find tons of information about the newsgroups that are most likely to interest you, including typical recent postings, a review of the quality of discussion, lists of information resources, and much more.

- The Newsgroup Subject Index, at the end of this book, provides a key word and topical index to more than 5,000 USENET newsgroups. If you'd like to know which groups pertain to "privacy," for instance, just look it up—you'll find more than a dozen groups that relate to this topic.

WHAT'S A "TOP NEWSGROUP"?

I've used three criteria to decide which newsgroups to include in this chapter:

- **Top newsgroups by volume.** The top 100 newsgroups, by volume of posting. Please note that volume alone is not an indication of quality. Among the groups that receive the most postings are some of USENET's worst (as you'll see).

- **Newsgroups with FAQs.** If people have gone to the trouble to create a FAQ (Frequently-Asked Questions list) for a group, I take this to be a sign of potential quality—such a group is more likely than un-FAQed groups to offer quality discussion. And there's good reason for this supposition: FAQs improve a newsgroup's signal-to-noise ratio by answering the newbie questions that people would otherwise post to the group.

- **Moderated newsgroups.** Most moderated newsgroups were created to cut out the noise and maximize the signal, so they're naturally good candidates for a list of high-quality newsgroups.

To keep this chapter down to a manageable size, I've excluded some of the groups that would have qualified under one of the preceding criteria. Here's an overview of what's excluded:

- **Newsgroups with advanced technical or scientific topics.** My purpose here is to review the newsgroups that will prove of general interest to my readers. I'm assuming that you're using a PC or a Macintosh, for example, so the myriad UNIX hacker groups in the comp.* hierarchy won't be of interest to you.

- **Fan newsgroups** in the alt.fan.*, rec.music.*, and other hierarchies. Again, these newsgroups aren't of general interest—and if you're really a fan, you'll want to jump into a group that's not very good and get things going.

- **"Game" newsgroups** that pertain to specific games. Like the fan newsgroups, these aren't of general interest unless you know how to play the game or would like to learn how.

- **Cultural newsgroups** pertaining to specific cultures, such as soc.culture.swiss or soc.culture.tamil. There are many of these, and many are well worth reading if you've personal or professional interests in their subjects, but they're not of general interest and tend to have low readership levels.

- **Newsgroups with very low distributions or usage levels.** I've excluded some groups that would otherwise qualify, just because they seem pretty dead at this writing. That could change, though.

I know that my sieve has let some jewels slip through unnoticed. If you find a group that you feel belongs among USENET's best, would you please let me know? Send email to bp@virginia.edu, and I'll review the newsgroup for the next edition.

THE RATING STARS EXPLAINED

Using the rules just mentioned, I whittled the newsgroup list down to 300 top newsgroups and subscribed to all of them. I read the posts. I retrieved and read the FAQs. I dug up and analyzed the usage statistics. And I rated them according to the following system:

★★★★★ Here's one of USENET's best, a newsgroup that belongs in just about everyone's subscription list. There's a pattern here: The best groups tend to have well-defined topics, excellent (and often very lengthy) FAQs and tons of additional information resources, high-quality discussion with frequent postings of information as well as opinion, and mature, knowledgeable participants.

★★★★ A good newsgroup that's worth a look even if the topic isn't of personal or professional interest to you.

★★★ good newsgroup for anyone with interests in its topic, but probably wouldn't appeal to others.

★★ Of interest only to those with serious personal or professional interests in the subject matter; marred by some kind of irritating flaw (such as excessive crossposting, flame wars, low signal-to-noise ratio, low frequency, or poor quality of discussion).

★ One of USENET's worst, the sort of thing that the tabloid newspapers write about. Avoid or join a maturity enhancement support group.

A NOTE ON THE STATS

For each newsgroup, I've collected statistics on the following:

- **Readership.** An estimate of the number of people currently reading the group.

- **Rank.** The group's ordinal rank among newsgroups, based on the volume of postings.

- **Messages per month.** The number of articles posted per month.

- **Crossposting Percentage.** The percentage of articles crossposted to other newsgroups.

- **Availability.** The percentage of USENET sites that currently offer this group.

These statistics come from the most recently available posting from the Network Measurement Project at the DEC Network Systems Laboratory, in Palo Alto, CA. They're based on a program called

Arbitron, which is run at each of the participating USENET sites, and subsequently collated. The sites represent only a sample of the total USENET universe, and for this reason alone shouldn't be taken as gospel. Moreover, each of the stats is based on assumptions, which may or may not prove to be erroneous—for example, "Readership" is based on a statistical estimate of the number of users at a given site who open the newsgroup for any reason at all. Still, the Arbitron statistics are better than none, and they're useful for rough-and-ready comparisons among newsgroups.

> **TIP:** For the latest statistics on USENET newsgroups, check out the newsgroup news.lists. If the Arbitron postings aren't there, use anonymous FTP to retrieve the latest lists:
> `ftp://ftp.rtfm.mit.edu/pub/usenet/news.lists`

WHAT'S IN THIS CHAPTER?

You'll find the following sections in this chapter:

- **Newsgroups for beginners.** Here are reviews of the news.* groups that are recommended for newbie USENET users.

- **The top newsgroups reviewed.** Here are the rest of the newsgroup reviews, organized alphabetically. Enjoy!

NEWSGROUPS FOR BEGINNERS

news.announce.newusers ★★★★★

Information of interest to all new users of USENET.

Typical recent postings   How to Become a USENET Site, How to Get Information about Net-

works, What Is USENET?, What Is USENET? A Second Opinion, A Primer on How to Work with the USENET Community, Answers to Frequently Asked Questions about USENET, Emily Postnews Answers Your Questions on Netiquette, Hints on Writing Style for USENET.

Review   Don't miss the informational postings you'll find here! These are essential reading for anyone serious about using USENET well.

Advice to newbies   Don't post to this group; it's for informational postings only.

Adult-oriented?   No.

Readership   800,000.

Rank   1.

Messages per month   37.

Crossposting percentage   43%.

Availability   92% of USENET sites.

Moderated?   Yes.

Special features   Periodic postings of important informational documents.

FAQ title   None.

FAQ location   N/A.

Other information resources   None.

Archive site   rtfm.mit.edu /pub/usenet/news.announce.newusers

Related groups   news.groups, news.admin.misc, news.announce.newgroups

news.answers ★★★★★

FAQs for most of USENET's best newsgroups are posted here at periodic intervals.

Typical recent postings   Netrek FTP List, Rocky Horror Theater List, Book Catalogues and Book Clubs List, soc.feminism References, Law Related Resources on the Internet and Elsewhere.

Review   If you're looking for a FAQ, you might find it more quickly by searching the archive site at rtfm.mit.edu. This group is worth browsing, though, because new FAQs appear all the time.

Advice to newbies   Don't post to this group; it's for FAQs and other informational postings.

Adult-oriented?   No.

Readership   360,000.

Rank   2.

Messages per month   1,584.

Crossposting percentage   100%.

Availability   88% of USENET sites.

Moderated?   Yes.

Special features   Periodic postings of FAQs and other important informational documents.

FAQ title   *.answers submission guidelines

FAQ location   alt.answers, comp.answers, misc.answers, news.answers, soc.answers

Other information resources   None.

Archive site   None.

Related groups   comp.answers, rec.answers, alt.answers, misc.answers, sci.answers, soc.answers, talk.answers

news.lists ★★★★

Statistics about USENET.

Typical recent postings   Top 40 Newsgroups by Crossposting Percentage, Top 40 Newsgroups by Traffic Volume, Top 40 Newsgroups by Per-Reader Cost.

Review   This isn't an essential newsgroup, but the statistics make for fascinating reading.

Advice to newbies: Don't post here; this newsgroup is for informational postings only.

Adult-oriented?   No.

Readership   160,000.

Rank   27.

Messages per month   70.

Crossposting percentage   21%.

Availability   89% of USENET sites.

Moderated?   No.

Special features   None.

FAQ title   None.

FAQ location   N/A.

Other information resources   None.

Archive site   At the FAQ archive (FTP to rtfm.mit.edu /pub/usenet/news.lists).

Related groups   None.

news.misc ★★★

USENET—where it's going, what's wrong with it, and how to cope with its problems.

Typical recent postings   International Free Press, Fallacies about the Internet, Archiving News, Purchasing a Hierarchy, Fluxers: They're Here and More Are Coming.

Review   Here's an excellent introduction to USENET's give-and-take discussion, carried on by some of the Net's top system administrators (as well as an assortment of kooks).

Advice to newbies   You shouldn't post here until you've become very familiar with USENET and feel confident that you are knowledgeable enough to contribute.

Adult-oriented?   No.

Readership   120,000.

Rank   80.

Messages per month   300.

Crossposting percentage   52%.

Availability   87% of USENET sites.

Moderated?   No.

Special features   None.

FAQ title   None.

FAQ location   N/A.

Other information resources   None.

Archive site   None.

Related groups   None.

news.newusers.questions ★★★★★

Questions about USENET posed by newbies and answered by sympathetic old-timers.

Typical recent postings   FTP Manual for New Users, File Transfers Info, Where to Post My First Message, Email Address Lookup, Is There a Test Newsgroup?

Review   A browse through this newsgroup is strongly suggested for newbies; you'll find that many others have the same questions that you do, and they're often answered in a helpful way. (Many of the answers are sent through email, though, so they may not show up in the group.)

Advice to newbies   This newsgroup is for you. You'll make mistakes, but hey, the old-timers did too!

Adult-oriented?   No.

Readership   210,000.

Rank   16.

Messages per month   1,929.

Crossposting percentage   3%.

Availability   89% of USENET sites.

Moderated?   No.

Special features   None.

FAQ title   None.

FAQ location   None.

Other information resources   None.

Archive site   None.

Related groups   news.announce.newusers

THE TOP NEWSGROUPS REVIEWED

alt.activism ★★★★

The struggle for social justice, generally from leftist or Libertarian perspectives—and peppered with occasional conservative broadsides. Of interest to anyone curious about alternative perspectives on current issues and events.

Typical recent postings   This Is Capitalism: Child Labor and Child Death, War on Drugs—War on WHICH Drugs, Do Minimum Wage Laws Cost Jobs, Kim Il Sung: A Story Unknown in U.S., C-SPAN Schedule, McDonalds Pays Health Insurance Overseas.

Review   If you're looking for intelligent discussion from alternative political perspectives, this is the place—typically, you'll find thoughtful exchanges on a variety of issues—and from a variety of political perspectives.

Advice to newbies   Read this group carefully before posting; expect criticism when you post.

Adult-oriented?   No.

Readership   160,000.

Rank   24.

Messages per month   1,700.

Crossposting percentage   59% (a high figure, but mostly due to crossposting with alt.activism.d, which isn't clearly distinguished from this group).

Availability   63% of USENET sites.

Moderated? No.

Special features Regular postings of Conspiracy Nation, an electronic newsletter created by Brian Francis Redman of PrarieNet.

FAQ title There's no FAQ for alt.activism, but you'll find the Anti-War-On-Drugs Activists' List posted frequently to this group.

FAQ location alt.activism, alt.drugs, talk.answers, talk.politics.drugs, news.answers, alt.answers

Other information resources Libertarian FAQ: Frequently Asked Questions, Libertarian FAQ: World's Smallest Political Quiz, Libertarian FAQ: Organizations, Anti-War-On-Drugs Activists

Archive site None.

Related groups alt.activism.d, alt.activism.death-penalty, alt.drugs, alt.politics.reform, alt.society.resistance, alt.society.civil-liberty, soc.rights.human. Above all, try misc.activism.progressive, a moderated newsgroup with lots of informative postings

alt.aldus.pagemaker ★★★

The premier desktop publishing program. Of interest to Aldus PageMaker users.

Typical recent postings Ventura Publisher—How Good?, Printing to a Deskjet 550C, Image Control, Upgrade Cost Ridiculous.

Review A fine resource for anyone working with PageMaker or desktop publishing in general.

Advice to newbies Don't ask this newsgroup to teach you the basics of PageMaker; read your manual to find answers to common new user questions. Please read the group's FAQ before posting to avoid asking questions that have been posed before.

Adult-oriented? No.

Readership 20,000.

Rank 1,299.

Messages per month 384.

Crossposting percentage 5%.

Availability 63% of USENET sites.

Moderated? 46.

Special features None.

FAQ title None.

FAQ location None.

Other information resources Aldus PageMaker FAQ, Desktop Publishing Resources FAQ

Archive site None.

Related groups bit.listserv.pagmaker

alt.angst ★★

Things that hurt very much for a long time, coupled with a thorough conviction that one's life is meaningless. Of interest to those who enjoy pretending to be depressed; if you're really depressed, see alt.support.depression and get help.

Typical recent postings Unrequited Love, The CIA Is Reading My Mind, Dentist Panic—Info Wanted, Help—Modem Struck by Lightning, I Want to Die!

Review If you've got the blues, you'll find plenty of support in alt.angst, the denizens of which seem to revel in lucid descriptions of life's pointlessness. Please read the group's FAQ before posting to avoid asking questions that have been posed before.

Advice to newbies Cheerfulness of any sort is not well tolerated. Above all, do not use those cute smileys. Otherwise: If it feels bad, describe it intelligently, and post it.

Adult-oriented? Infrequently.

Readership 34,000.

Rank 850.

Messages per month   2,180.

Crossposting percentage   17%.

Availability   57% of USENET sites.

Moderated?   No.

Special features   The Angst Calendar, available by anonymous ftp from ftp.mantis.co.uk, in the directory /pub/alt.angst.

FAQ title   The alt.angst FAQ

FAQ location   alt.angst,alt.answers,news.answers (monthly posting).

Other information resources   Who's Not Who on alt.angst (posted monthly).

Archive site   http://www.cs.indiana.edu/hyplan/krawling/angst.html

Related groups   alt.society.generation-x, rec.arts.poems,alt.misanthropy,alt.bitterness—but try alt.support.depression!

alt.aquaria ★★★

Everything about aquaria—the fish, the tanks, the water, the problems. Of interest to anyone who owns or is thinking about buying an aquarium.

Typical recent postings   Hematoma in Bubble-Eyed Goldfish—Help, How Much Do You Pay for Electricity, Black Light for Aquaria, Ammonia Driving Me Nuts, Fishy Feats and Tricks, Feeding Sea-Horses.

Review   Intelligent, useful discussions of all aspects of keeping an aquarium; frequent postings from experts.

Advice to newbies   Read the FAQs to make sure you don't ask a question that's already been answered, and be sure to crosspost to rec.aquaria. (Not all sites receive both groups, so the two groups exist to make sure that all sites receive all the postings.)

Adult-oriented?   No.

Readership   60,000.

Rank   387.

Messages per month   870.

Crossposting percentage   25%.

Moderated?   No.

Special features   Extensive informational resources add up to a superb introductory course in keeping an aquarium.

FAQ title   alt.aquaria FAQ: Beginner Topics and Books

FAQ location   alt.aquaria, rec.aquaria, sci.aquaria (monthly).

Other information resources   AQUARIA FAQ: Filters, AQUARIA FAQ: Magazines and Mail Order Information, AQUARIA FAQ Plants, AQUARIA FAQ: Water.

Archive site   None.

Related groups   rec.aquaria (essentially the same newsgroup) and sci.aquaria (for discussions of scientific research on water-related topics).

alt.archery ★★★

All aspects of the ancient and noble sport of archery. Of interest to archers and anyone thinking about getting involved in archery.

Typical recent postings   Buying a First Target, African Bowhunting, Nocks for Carbon Arrows, Archery Shops in California.

Review   If archery is your sport, subscribe to alt.archery—you'll find lots of kindred spirits in a low-key, mature newsgroup.

Advice to newbies   Don't hesitate to participate if you're interested in archery. Please read the group's FAQ before posting to avoid asking questions that have been posed before.

Signal-to-noise ratio High—most postings are informative and intelligent.

Adult-oriented? No.

Readership 29,000.

Rank 992.

Messages per month 190.

Crossposting percentage 1%.

Availability 55% of USENET sites.

Moderated? No.

Special features A comprehensive series of FAQs presents a fine introduction to the sport of archery (see "Other Information Resources," later in this chapter).

FAQ title The alt.archery FAQ

FAQ location alt.archery (monthly posting).

Other information resources FAQ: Archery Organizations, FAQ: Archery Books, FAQ: Asian Turkish Bow Construction. FAQ: Bowhunting Tips, FAQ: General Archery, FAQ: General Bow Construction,FAQ: Traditional Archery, FAQ: Target Archery, FAQ: Archery History, FAQ: Walkback Tuning, FAQ: Bowfishing Tips, FAQ: Kyudo (Japanese Archery), FAQ: Crossbows

Archive site None.

Related groups None.

alt.ascii.art ★★★

Making pictures composed of nothing but the standard ASCII character set. Of interest to ASCII artists and anyone trying to figure out how they do it.

Typical recent postings Hamburger, Armadillo, Spock, Sheep.

Review An amusing diversion, ASCII art is an old computer craft that has taken on new life in the Internet, which can transmit only ASCII charac-

ters. You'd be amazed by what some ASCII artists have been able to do with nothing more than the resources of the typewriter keyboard! But this newsgroup has much more discussion than art. For the best in ASCII art, see the moderated group rec.arts.ascii.

Advice to newbies Anyone is welcome to contribute, but it's a good idea to read the group's FAQ first.

Adult-oriented? No, although an occasional R-rated nude pops up.

Readership 37,000.

Rank 768.

Messages per month 1,266.

Crossposting percentage 9%.

Availability 45% of USENET sites.

Moderated? No.

Special features The group's FAQ contains many excellent examples of ASCII art.

FAQ title FAQ: ASCII Art Questions and Answers

FAQ location alt.ascii.art, alt.binaries.pictures.ascii

Other information resources The newsgroup alt.binaries.pictures.ascii contains uuencoded files of ASCII art.

Archive site There are numerous archives of ASCII art, including the following which are accessible through anonymous FTP: mordor.ind.wpi.edu (directory: pub/ascii/art/pictures); ftp.mcs.com (directory: mcsnet.users/jorn/ascii-art); ftp.ncsu.edu (directory: pub/ncsu/chking/Archive).

Related groups alt.binaries.pictures.ascii

alt.astrology ★★★

Astrology, from the perspective of astrological practitioners and well-informed enthusiasts.

Of interest to professional or amateur astrologers.

Typical recent postings Skeptics—Get a Life, Virgo Extremism, Retrogrades in Natal Chart, Aquarius with Leo Rising, Outer Planets and 40-Year-Olds, Bad Day for a Wedding.

Review If you're interested in astrology, and especially if you're a practicing astrologer, you'll find many kindred spirits in this newsgroup.

Advice to newbies Please read the FAQ before posting—it's an excellent source of answers to commonly asked questions that don't belong on the newsgroup (such as, "I don't know my exact birth time—how can I find out?"). Note that discussions of the veracity of astrology belong in sci.skeptics.

Adult-oriented? No.

Readership 34,000.

Rank 851.

Messages per month 1,796.

Crossposting percentage 4%.

Availability 57% of USENET sites.

Moderated? No.

Special features None.

FAQ title Alt.Astrology Newcomers Read This: Frequently Asked Questions

FAQ location alt.astrology, alt.answers, news.answers (monthly posting).

Other information resources None.

Archive site None.

Related groups Skeptics should post to sci.skeptics; you'll just get flamed if you post to alt.astrology.

alt.atheism ★★★★

Every aspect of atheism, including whether it is reasonable to pretend to be religious in order to avoid upsetting one's family, what to do about prayer in schools, discrimination against atheists, Sunday trading laws, myths about satanic child abuse, whether an atheist should "stay in the closet," how religious organizations prey on new college students, how to get rid of proselytizers, why people become atheists. Of interest to atheists, agnostics, and religious people who are genuinely curious about atheists' perspectives.

Typical recent postings Psychological Causes of Atheism, What Is Atheism?—Article 1, Questions for the Atheist, Zoroastrian baggage, Do Buddhists consider themselves to be Atheists?

Review Worthy discussions of topics of concern to atheists, but expect constant interruptions from evangelical Christians looking to save souls. Some alt.atheism members wait in anticipation of poorly argued evangelical postings and take evident pleasure in tearing them to shreds. The group's FAQs constitute a treasure-trove of information for the free-thinking individual—as well as religious people who are sincerely trying to understand why others don't share their faith (and don't want it rammed down their throats).

Advice to newbies Don't post to alt.atheism without reading the group's extensive FAQs; chances are, your question has already been answered. Take a look at *Alt.Atheism FAQ: Quick Index of FAQ Topics;* this provides an index to the many topics covered in the group's extensive FAQs.

Adult-oriented? No.

Readership 88,000.

Rank 158.

Messages per month 5,503.

Crossposting percentage 19%.

Availability 62% of USENET sites.

Moderated? No.

Special features Extensive FAQs provide an excellent introduction to atheist perspectives.

FAQ title Alt.Atheism FAQ: Quick Index of FAQ Topics

FAQ location   alt.atheism, alt.atheism.moderated, news.answers, alt.answers

Other information resources   Alt.Atheism FAQ: Introduction to Atheism, Alt.Atheism FAQ: Overview for New Readers, Alt.Atheism FAQ: Constructing a Logical Argument, Alt.Atheism FAQ: Atheist Resources

Archive site   http://www.mantis.co.uk/atheism, http://bigdipper.umd.edu/atheism/

Related groups   alt.atheism.moderated

alt.backrubs ★★

Massage as a legitimate stress-relieving, non-sexual activity. Of interest to anyone who'd like to learn how to employ massage as a stress-relieving technique.

Typical recent postings   Good Way to Massage Feet, Rolfing, National Boards Exam, Deep Tissue.

Review   A low-volume group, but of interest to anyone who's involved in legitimate massage.

Advice to newbies   Anyone is welcome to contribute, but it's a good idea to read the group's FAQ first.

Adult-oriented?   No.

Readership   35,000.

Rank   825.

Messages per month   189.

Crossposting percentage   1%.

Availability   55% of USENET sites.

Moderated?   No.

Special features   The group's four-part FAQ (see next item) is an excellent introduction to the art and science of legitimate massage.

FAQ title   FAQ: alt.backrubs FAQ

FAQ location   alt.backrubs

Other information resources   None.

Archive site   ftp.csd.uwo.ca (directory: /pub/news/alt.backrub)

Related groups   None.

alt.bbs ★★★

General aspects of computer bulletin board systems (BBS). Of interest to BBS enthusiasts and people concerned generally with the social and legal issues they raise.

Typical recent postings   Best shareware CD for BBS?, OJ Simpson BBS, Yeah… but how can I make money with all this stuff?

Review   Good general discussions of BBS technology, marketing, and issues.

Advice to newbies   Don't post a query asking whether there's a BBS in your area; get the National Graphical BBS List or post to alt.bbs.lists.d (*not* to alt.bbs.lists).

Adult-oriented?   No.

Readership   130,000.

Rank   53.

Messages per month   1,075.

Crossposting percentage   8%.

Availability   68% of USENET sites.

Moderated?   No.

Special features   Check out the National Graphical BBS List.

FAQ title   None.

FAQ location   N/A.

Other information resources   National Graphical BBS List

Archive site   rtfm.mit.edu and mirror sites.

Related groups   alt.bbs.allsysop, alt.bbs.lists, alt.bbs.lists.d, alt.bbs.searchlight, comp.bbs.misc

alt.bbs.internet ★★★

Computer bulletin board systems (BBS) and the Internet—how to get them connected, what software is available for handling USENET newsgroups and Internet email, billing issues, BBSs with Internet access. Of interest to anyone looking for inexpensive USENET or Internet access.

Typical recent postings   Japan Internet Access, Free Internet Access in Ann Arbor Area, Internet Access in Las Vegas Area, Affordable Internet Access in NW Indiana, Declaration of War on Satan's BBSs.

Review   If you're looking for inexpensive USENET access, check out this group for news of Internet-linked bulletin board systems (BBS). For more information on this inexpensive means of USENET access, see Chapter 3.

Advice to newbies   If you're aware of a BBS that carries USENET, please post a message to this group so that others can benefit.

Adult-oriented?   No.

Readership   110,000.

Rank   84.

Messages per month   1,013.

Crossposting percentage   14%.

Availability   65% of USENET sites.

Moderated?   No.

Special features   Looking for an Internet-capable BBS in your area? Check out the National Graphical BBS List.

FAQ title   None.

FAQ location   N/A.

Other information resources   National Graphical BBS List

Archive site   rtfm.mit.edu and mirror sites.

Related groups   alt.bbs.allsysop, alt.bbs.lists, alt.bbs.lists.d, alt.bbs.searchlight, comp.bbs.misc

alt.bbs.lists ★★★★

Lists of computer bulletin board systems (BBS). Of interest to anyone looking for a BBS in a specific area.

Typical recent postings   BBS List of Switzerland, Montreal BBS List, Good BBS in the Austin Area, Amazon's Arena BBS, SLIP/PPP Access in Eastern Massachusetts, New Zealand BBS List, 707 area code BBSs.

Review   This is the place to look for lists of computer bulletin board systems (BBS).

Advice to newbies   Please do not post discussion here; the place for discussion of these lists is alt.bbs.lists.d.

Adult-oriented?   No.

Readership   72,000.

Rank   262.

Messages per month   319.

Crossposting percentage   12%.

Availability   62% of USENET sites.

Moderated?   No.

Special features   Check out the National Graphical BBS list.

FAQ title   None.

FAQ location   N/a.

Other information resources   National Graphical BBS List

Archive site   rtfm.mit.edu and mirror sites.

Related groups   alt.bbs, comp.bbs.misc, alt.bbs.internet

alt.bbs.lists.d ★★

Discussion of lists of computer bulletin board systems (BBS). Of interest to anyone looking for a BBS in a specific area.

Typical recent postings   Anatomically Correct BBS Moves to 408 Area, Concord CA BBS Is Free!, Greatest Graphics BBS.

Review   Most people don't seem to get the point that discussion of BBS lists belongs here and not in alt.bbs.lists; frequency is low and contains lists crossposted (inappropriately) from alt.bbs.lists.

Advice to newbies   This is the place for discussion of bbs lists; if you've a list, please post it to alt.bbs.lists.

Adult-oriented?   No.

Readership   72,000.

Rank   822.

Messages per month   319.

Crossposting percentage   12%.

Availability   62% of USENET sites.

Moderated?   No.

Special features   Check out the National Graphical BBS list.

FAQ title   None.

FAQ location   N/a.

Other information resources   National Graphical BBS List

Archive site   rtfm.mit.edu and mirror sites.

Related groups   alt.bbs, comp.bbs.misc, alt.bbs.internet

alt.beer ★★★★

The delights of a fine brew—which is the best, how to make good beer, and what to do about that beer belly. Of interest to anyone who likes fine beers.

Typical recent postings   How to Start a Microbrewery, Molson Beer Tasting—Interesting Results, Rare Flemish Beers, "Romantic" Dinner Beers, Recommend Brew Kit for the Beginner.

Review   Good discussion of the finer points of beer and brewing, with lots of interesting and useful information.

Advice to newbies   Read the FAQ—you'll find answers to just about all the questions people typically ask about beer (for example, "What's the difference between an ale and a beer?").

Adult-oriented?   Yes.

Readership   52,000.

Rank   490.

Messages per month   1,689.

Crossposting percentage   19%.

Availability   58% of USENET sites.

Moderated?   No.

Special features   An "FTP by mail" service is available for alt.beer files; send mail to "ftpmail@exchange.tlh.fl.us". In the body of the message, type **GET FILENAME** where FILENAME is the file that you want. For example, to get ALT_BEER.FAQ type **GET ALT_BEER.FAQ** in the message body. The system will then send it back to you via email. Available files include BEER.NDX (index of alt.beer files), ALT_BEER.FAQ, BEERGAME.TXT (locations of beer-drinking games), and BEERMAGS.TXT (guide to beer-related magazines).

FAQ title   Alt.Beer FAQ

FAQ location   alt.beer, alt.answers, news.answers

Other information resources   None.

Archive site   The alt.beer archives are available via anonymous ftp to ftp.cwru.edu. Change directories to ~/pub/alt.beer. **Note:** This archive is scheduled to be moved and may have done so by the time you read this; check the latest edition of the FAQ.

Related groups   rec.food.drink.beer

alt.best.of.internet ★★★★

This newsgroup contains posts that originally appeared in other newsgroups, but were forwarded here by someone who thought they would prove of general interest. For anyone who's interested in what's lively, funny, and interesting about Internet.

Typical recent postings   Proof That Barney IS Satan, Chicken Nipples, How to Hunt Lions, The Geek Code, What Exactly Is a Robot Fetish?

Review   I'm of two minds about ABOI: On the one hand, there are some very entertaining posts here. On the other hand, they were lifted out of their intended context by persons other than their authors, and sometimes in a way that implicitly mocks the original poster. That's a violation of USENET's own rules of netiquette!

Advice to newbies   Do not post to alt.best.of.internet! This newsgroup is reserved for *forwarded posts*. If you would really like to participate, find a post in another newsgroup that you think is of general interest, and forward the post to alt.best.of.internet.

Adult-oriented?   Yes.

Readership   51,000.

Rank   504.

Messages per month   573.

Crossposting percentage   4%.

Availability   53% of USENET sites.

Moderated?   No.

Special features   None.

FAQ title   alt.best.of.internet Frequently Asked Questions

FAQ location   alt.best.of.internet

Other information resources   None.

Archive site   For the FAQ, see rtfm.mit.edu and mirror sites.

Related groups   None.

alt.binaries.multimedia ★★

Postings of full-motion video files (mainly MPEG); G-rated content. Of interest to computer hobbyists who want to experiment with the display of full-motion video on their computers.

Typical recent postings   The Verstappens Formula 1 Accident, Video for Windows Runtime File, Where Can I Get a DOS MPEG Player That Really Works?

Review   Some interesting MPEG files make this group worth an occasional look.

Advice to newbies   Check out the alt.binaries.pictures.* FAQ for information on how to download multi-part files. For information on MPEG players, see comp.multimedia.

Adult-oriented?   No.

Readership   67,000.

Rank   301.

Messages per month   1,061.

Crossposting percentage   4%.

Availability   45.5% of USENET sites.

Moderated?   No.

Special features   None.

FAQ title   For information on decoding multi-part files, check out the alt.binaries.pictures FAQ. This FAQ comes in three parts, titled alt.binaries.pictures FAQ—General Etiquette, alt.binaries.pictures FAQ—General Info, alt.binaries.pictures FAQ—OS Specific Info. Posted frequently to the newsgroup is THE "WHAT/WHERE/WHY/HOW" FOR

PICTURES (info on picture decoding!), which provides information on obtaining the FAQs. For information on MPEG, see the FAQs for comp.multimedia: MPEG—FAQ: multimedia compression (seven parts).

FAQ location alt.binaries.pictures.d, alt.binaries.pictures.fineart.d, alt.binaries.pictures.erotica.d, alt.sex.pictures.d, news.answers, alt.answers, comp.multimedia

Other information resources See the newsgroup comp.multimedia for up-to-date information on MPEG readers.

Archive site You can obtain the alt.binaries.pictures FAQs from ftp.cadence.com in directory /pictures/FAQ; look for files "part1", "part2", and/or "part3". Another site: ftp.cs.ruu.nl in the directory /pub/NEWS.ANSWERS/ picturesfaq for files "part1", "part2" or "part3". The FAQs are also available at rtfm.mit.edu (in the directory /pub/usenet/alt.binaries.pictures) as are the MPEG FAQs (in the directory /pub/usenet/ comp.multimedia).

Related groups comp.multimedia, comp.os.mswindows.programmer.multimedia, comp.os.os2.multimedia, comp.publish.cdrom.multimedia, comp.sys.amiga.multimedia, misc.education.multimedia

alt.binaries.pictures ★★★★

This newsgroup's posts contain binary graphics files (mainly GIF and JPEG) of "G-rated" subject matter. For anyone with a good color monitor and video card who'd like to display high-quality, high-resolution graphics. Note: This newsgroup is slated to be replaced by alt.binaries.pictures.misc; if this newsgroup doesn't show up on your server's newsgroup list, it has probably been declared to be a bogus newsgroup.

Typical recent postings Comet Images, Halley's Comet, Castle, Pluto and its moon (Charon).

Review If your newsreader can decode multi-part graphics files, take a look: You may find some of the first-rate astronomical images that are posted here occasionally. If your graphics software can save the images to the Windows bitmap format (.bmp), you can use the images as Windows wallpaper.

Advice to newbies Please do not post discussion to alt.binaries.pictures; that's what alt.binaries.pictures.d is for. Above all, don't post an article asking for help decoding pictures; read the FAQ. Please post G-rated pictures to alt.binaries.pictures.misc.

Adult-oriented? No.

Readership 93,000.

Rank 272.

Messages per month 535.

Crossposting percentage 17%.

Availability 60% of USENET sites.

Moderated? No.

Special features None.

FAQ title The alt.binaries.pictures FAQ comes in three parts, titled alt.binaries.pictures FAQ— General Etiquette, alt.binaries.pictures FAQ—General Info, alt.binaries.pictures FAQ— OS Specific Info. Posted frequently to the newsgroup is THE "WHAT/WHERE/WHY/ HOW" FOR PICTURES (info on picture decoding!), which provides information on obtaining the FAQs.

FAQ location All of the alt.binaries.pictures.* newsgroups; news.answers

Other information resources None.

Archive site You can obtain the FAQ from ftp.cadence.com in directory /pictures/FAQ; look for files "part1", "part2", and/or "part3". Another site: ftp.cs.ruu.nl in the directory /pub/ NEWS.ANSWERS/pictures—faq for files "part1", "part2" or "part3". The FAQ is also available at rtfm.mit.edu.

Related groups   alt.binaries.pictures.anime, alt.binaries.pictures.ascii, alt.binaries.pictures.cartoons, alt.binaries.pictures.d, alt.binaries.pictures.erotica, alt.binaries.pictures.female, alt.binaries.pictures.furry, alt.binaries.pictures.male, alt.binaries.pictures. misc, alt.binaries.pictures.erotica.orient, alt.binaries.pictures.fine-art.d, alt.binaries.pictures.fine-art.digitized, alt.binaries.pictures.fine-art.graph, alt.binaries.pictures. fractals, alt.binaries.pictures.furry, alt.binaries.pictures.supermodels, alt.binaries.pictures.tasteless, alt.binaries.pictures.misc, alt.binaries.pictures.utilities

alt.binaries.pictures.d ★★

Discussion of the graphics posted to alt.bina-ries.pictures.misc. Of interest to those with comments, questions, or criticism concerning the pictures posted in alt.binaries.pictures.

Typical recent postings   Problem with Decoded GIFs, Smart Decoder Wanted, UNIX gif2jpg Converter.

Review   This is a low-volume group; people don't seem to get the point that discussion belongs here, not in alt.binaries.pictures.

Advice to newbies   Please don't post discussion articles to alt.binaries.pictures; this is the place for it. If you don't know how to decode graphics files, please read the FAQ.

Adult-oriented?   No.

Readership   93,000.

Rank   142.

Messages per month   535.

Crossposting percentage   17%.

Availability   60% of USENET sites.

Moderated?   No.

Special features   None.

FAQ title   The alt.binaries.pictures FAQ comes in three parts, titled alt.binaries.pictures FAQ—General Etiquette, alt.binaries.pictures FAQ—General Info, alt.binaries.pictures FAQ—OS Specific Info. Posted frequently to the newsgroup is THE "WHAT/WHERE/WHY/HOW" FOR PICTURES (info on picture decoding!), which provides information on obtaining the FAQs.

FAQ location   alt.binaries.pictures.d, alt.binaries.pictures.fine-art.d, alt.binaries.pictures.erotica.d, alt.sex.pictures.d, news.answers,alt.an

Other information resources   None.

Archive site   You can obtain the FAQ from ftp.cadence.com in directory /pictures/FAQ; look for files "part1", "part2", and/or "part3". Another site: ftp.cs.ruu.nl in the directory /pub/ NEWS.ANSWERS/pictures-faq for files "part1", "part2" or "part3". The FAQ is also available at rtfm.mit.edu.

Related groups   alt.binaries.pictures.d, alt.binaries.pictures.fine-art.d, alt.binaries.pictures.erotica.d, alt.sex.pictures.d

alt.binaries.pictures.erotica ★

Erotic pictures—or pornographic pictures, if you prefer. Most of the pictures are of females, or males and females together, although there are occasional male-only postings.

Typical recent postings   A Day at the Park, Do I Get the Job, Applying Sunblock Can Be Fun, Star Trek Nudes, Kim Basinger Topless, Candy Cantaloupes.

Review   Most of this newsgroup's postings consist of scanned versions of published photographs, which in most cases is an outright copyright violation. Whatever else you might think of this newsgroup's content, please remember that participating in it helps to perpetuate illegal activities that could threaten the autonomy of USENET. There are occasional posts of historical erotica (for example, from the 1920s) that are of some historical and aesthetic interest. The group was split some time ago into alt.binaries.pictures.erotica.males and alt.binaries.pictures.erotica.females, but this is still the newsgroup of choice for erotic pictures of females.

Advice to newbies Please do not encourage activity in this newsgroup. If you can't resist it, don't download executable files (such as strip poker games); they're very likely to contain viruses. Note, too, that this newsgroup is *only* for postings of graphics files; for discussion, post to alt.binaries.pictures.erotica.d.

Adult-oriented? Yes.

Readership 260,000.

Rank 10.

Messages per month 8,772.

Crossposting percentage 1%.

Availability 53% of USENET sites.

Moderated? No.

Special features Occasional postings of "sexy" programs, which may contain particularly destructive computer viruses. (Note that graphics files cannot contain viruses unless they're packaged with a program that transforms them into executable files.)

FAQ title The alt.binaries.pictures FAQ comes in three parts, titled alt.binaries.pictures FAQ—General Etiquette, alt.binaries.pictures FAQ—General Info, alt.binaries.pictures FAQ—OS Specific Info. Posted frequently to the newsgroup is THE "WHAT/WHERE/WHY/HOW" FOR PICTURES (info on picture decoding!), which provides information on obtaining the FAQs.

FAQ location alt.binaries.pictures.d, alt.binaries.pictures.fine-art.d,

alt.binaries.pictures.erotica.d, alt.sex.pictures.d, news.answers, alt.an

Other information resources None.

Archive site You can obtain the FAQ from ftp.cadence.com in directory /pictures/FAQ; look for files "part1", "part2", and/or "part3". The FAQ is also available at rtfm.mit.edu.

Related groups alt.binaries.pictures.d, alt.binaries.pictures.fine-art.d, alt.binaries.pictures.erotica.d, alt.sex.pictures.d, alt.sex, alt.sex.bondage

alt.binaries.pictures.erotica.d ★

Discussion of erotic pictures posted to alt.binaries.pictures.erotica.

Typical recent postings Tasteful Female GIFs, Famous Playboys for Sale, Cody Summer (from Penthouse), Tonya Harding Pix in Penthouse.

Review There's no serious discussion here of the graphics posted to alt.binaries.pictures.erotica—just requests for reposts and trolls regarding "erotic ftp sites."

Advice to newbies Skip it.

Adult-oriented? Yes.

Readership 110,000.

Rank 82.

Messages per month 1,309.

Crossposting percentage 9%.

Availability 51% of USENET sites.

Moderated? No.

Special features None.

FAQ title The alt.binaries.pictures FAQ comes in three parts, titled alt.binaries.pictures FAQ—General Etiquette, alt.binaries.pictures FAQ—General Info, alt.binaries.pictures FAQ—

OS Specific Info. Posted frequently to the newsgroup is THE "WHAT/WHERE/WHY/HOW" FOR PICTURES (info on picture decoding!), which provides information on obtaining the FAQs.

FAQ location alt.binaries.pictures.d, alt.binaries.pictures.fine art.d, alt.binaries.pictures.erotica.d, alt.sex.pictures.d,news.answers, alt.an

Other information resources None.

Archive site You can obtain the FAQ from ftp.cadence.com in directory /pictures/FAQ; look for files "part1", "part2", and/or "part3". Another site: ftp.cs.ruu.nl in the directory /pub/ NEWS.ANSWERS/pictures-faq for files "part1", "part2" or "part3". The FAQ is also available at rtfm.mit.edu.

Related groups alt.binaries.pictures.d, alt.binaries.pictures.fine-art.d, alt.binaries.pictures.erotica.d, alt.sex.pictures.d, alt.sex, alt.sex.bondage

alt.binaries.pictures.erotica.male ★

Erotic pictures—or pornographic pictures, if you prefer—of men.

Typical recent postings Hunky Latino, Bearish, Guys in Underwear, Hairy Muscles.

Review Most of this newsgroup's postings consist of scanned versions of published photographs, which in most cases is an outright copyright violation. Whatever else you might think of this newsgroup's content, please remember that participating in it helps to perpetuate illegal activities that could threaten the autonomy of USENET.

Advice to newbies Please do not encourage activity in this newsgroup. If you can't resist it, don't download executable files (such as strip poker games); they're very likely to contain viruses. Note, too, that this newsgroup is *only* for

postings of graphics files; for discussion, post to alt.binaries.pictures.erotica.d.

Adult-oriented? Yes.

Readership 29,000.

Rank 991.

Messages per month 1,504.

Crossposting percentage 4%.

Availability 42% of USENET sites.

Moderated? No.

Special features None.

FAQ title The alt.binaries.pictures FAQ comes in three parts, titled alt.binaries.pictures FAQ— General Etiquette, alt.binaries.pictures FAQ—General Info, alt.binaries.pictures FAQ— OS Specific Info. Posted frequently to the newsgroup is THE "WHAT/WHERE/ WHY/HOW" FOR PICTURES (info on picture decoding!), which provides information on obtaining the FAQs.

FAQ location alt.binaries.pictures.d, alt.binaries.pictures.fine-art.d, alt.binaries.pictures.erotica.d, alt.sex.pictures.d, news.answers, alt.answers

Other information resources None.

Archive site You can obtain the FAQ from ftp.cadence.com in directory /pictures/FAQ; look for files "part1", "part2", and/or "part3". Another site: ftp.cs.ruu.nl in the directory /pub/ NEWS.ANSWERS/pictures-faq for files "part1", "part2" or "part3". The FAQ is also available at rtfm.mit.edu.

Related groups soc.motss

alt.binaries.pictures.misc ★★★★

This newsgroup's posts contain binary graphics files (mainly GIF and JPEG) of "G-rated" subject

matter. **This newsgroup was to have been replaced alt.binaries.pictures, but many postings still go to that newsgroup (so you should read it, too, if you're interested in these graphics). Of interest to anyone with a good color monitor and video card who'd like to display high-quality, high-resolution graphics.**

Typical recent postings Anza-Borrego Park, Deep Space 9 Station, Virgin of Guadalupe, Preliminary List of Sites with Comet SL-9 Jupiter Crash GIFs.

Review If your newsreader can decode multi-part graphics files, take a look: You may find some of the first-rate astronomical images that are posted here occasionally. If your graphics software can save the images to the Windows bitmap format (.bmp), you can use the images as Windows wallpaper.

Advice to newbies Please do not post discussion to alt.binaries.pictures.misc; that's what alt.binaries.pictures.d is for. Above all, don't post an article asking for help decoding pictures; read the FAQ.

Adult-oriented? No, although some of the graphics range in the PG territory.

Readership 130,000.

Rank 49.

Messages per month 1,779.

Crossposting percentage 14%.

Availability 55% of USENET sites.

Moderated No.

Special features None.

FAQ title The alt.binaries.pictures FAQ comes in three parts, titled alt.binaries.pictures FAQ—General Etiquette, alt.binaries.pictures FAQ—General Info, alt.binaries.pictures FAQ—OS Specific Info. Posted frequently to the newsgroup is THE "WHAT/WHERE/WHY/HOW" FOR PICTURES (info on picture decoding!), which provides information on obtaining the FAQs.

FAQ location All of the alt.binaries.pictures.* newsgroups; news.answers

Other information resources None.

Archive site You can obtain the FAQ from ftp.cadence.com in directory /pictures/FAQ; look for files "part1", "part2", and/or "part3". Another site: ftp.cs.ruu.nl in the directory /pub/NEWS.ANSWERS/pictures-faq for files "part1", "part2" or "part3". The FAQ is also available at rtfm.mit.edu.

Related groups alt.binaries.pictures.anime, alt.binaries.pictures.ascii, alt.binaries.pictures.cartoons, alt.binaries.pictures.d, alt.binaries.pictures.erotica, alt.binaries.pictures.female, alt.binaries.pictures.furry, alt.binaries.pictures.male, alt.binaries.pictures, misc, alt.binaries.pictures.erotica.orient, alt.binaries.pictures.fine-art.d, alt.binaries.pictures.fine-art.digitized, alt.binaries.pictures.fine-art.graph, alt.binaries.pictures.fractals, alt.binaries.pictures.furry, alt.binaries.pictures.supermodels, alt.binaries.pictures.tasteless, alt.binaries.pictures.misc, alt.binaries.pictures.utilities

alt.binaries.sounds.d ★

Discussion of binary sound files posted to alt.binaries.sounds.misc. Of interest to those with questions or comments concerning the binary sound files posted to alt.binaries.sounds.misc.

Typical recent postings Mac to WAV Converter, What Is a WRK File, Would Someone Please Post "Hello."

Review A low-volume group for discussion of the sounds posted to alt.binaries.sounds. There's not much meaningful discussion of the sounds—most of the posts are queries for information concerning sound players and requests for reposts.

Advice to newbies Please read the group's FAQ before posting to avoid asking questions that have been posed before.

Adult-oriented?   No.

Readership   49,000.

Rank   536.

Messages per month   170.

Crossposting percentage   11%.

Availability   55% of USENET sites.

Moderated?   No.

Special features   None.

FAQ title   FAQ: Audio File Formats

FAQ location   N/A.

Other information resources   None.

Archive site   You can get the FAQ from rtfm.mit.edu in the directory /pub/usenet/ alt.binaries.sounds.misc.

Related groups   alt.binaries.sounds.misc, alt.binaries.sounds.tv, alt.binaries.sounds.music, comp.dsp, comp.sys.ibm.pc.soundcard, comp.sys.ibm.pc.soundcard.advocacy, comp.sys.ibm.pc.soundcard.games, comp.sys.ibm.pc.soundcard.misc, comp.sys.ibm.pc.soundcard.tech, comp.sys.ibm.pc.soundcard.music

alt.binaries.sounds.misc ★

Binary files containing sounds that you can play on your computer system (if it's equipped with a sound board). Of interest to those wishing to jazz up their computer by assigning sounds to system events, such as system startup or shutdown.

Typical recent postings   Kids in the Hall, Van Down by the River, Warner Bros. Cartoon Music, Theme from Shaft.

Review   Most of this newsgroup's postings consist of pirated versions of recorded music, which in most cases is an outright copyright violation. Please remember that participating in it helps to perpetuate illegal activities that could threaten the autonomy of USENET.

Advice to newbies   Please do not encourage activity in this newsgroup. If you can't resist it, please download only those files that were created by the poster and specifically placed in the public domain for everyone's enjoyment. Note, too, that this newsgroup is *only* for postings of sound files; for discussion, post to alt.binaries.sounds.d.

Adult-oriented?   No.

Readership   74,000.

Rank   248.

Messages per month   1,540.

Crossposting percentage   9%.

Availability   54% of USENET sites.

Moderated?   No.

Special features   None.

FAQ title   FAQ:Audio File Formats

FAQ location   alt.binaries.sounds.misc, news.answers

Other information resources   None.

Archive site   You can get the FAQ from rtfm.mit.edu in the directory /pub/usenet/ alt.binaries.sounds.misc.

Related groups   alt.binaries.sounds.d, alt.binaries.sounds.tv, alt.binaries.sounds.music, comp.dsp, comp.sys.ibm.pc.soundcard, comp.sys.ibm.pc.soundcard.advocacy, comp.sys.ibm.pc.soundcard.games, comp.sys.ibm.pc.soundcard.misc, comp.sys.ibm.pc.soundcard.tech, comp.sys.ibm.pc.soundcard.music

alt.bonsai ★★★

The Oriental art of growing dwarfed trees or bushes in a plate or dish. Of interest to anyone attempting bonsai or interested in its philosophy or history.

Typical recent postings   Sick Juniper Bonsai, Ginkgo Germination, Good Trees for Desert Climate.

Review   This is a low-volume group that will nevertheless prove of interest to bonsai practitioners. Note that rec.bonsai doesn't entirely duplicate the postings to this group; if your site has both, you should read both.

Advice to newbies   Anyone is welcome to contribute, but it's a good idea to read the group's FAQ first.

Adult-oriented?   No.

Readership   15,000.

Rank   1,516.

Messages per month   73.

Crossposting percentage   28% (due to crossposting to rec.arts.bonsai).

Availability   45% of USENET sites.

Moderated?   No.

Special features   The group's five-part FAQ (see next item) is an excellent introduction to the art of bonsai.

FAQ title   The rec.arts.bonsai/alt.bonsai FAQ

FAQ location   alt.bonsai, rec.arts.bonsai

Other information resources   None.

Archive site   An anonymous FTP server for Bonsai GIFS (and other types of pictures) and other bonsai related files is available at bonsai.pass.wayne.edu (IP address 141.217.25.20). Login as anonymous and use guest as a password.

Related groups   rec.arts.bonsai

alt.books.reviews ★★

Reviews (submitted by anyone who's interested) of popular or trade fiction or nonfiction books; see alt.books.reviews.technical for reviews of technical books. Of interest mainly to readers of science fiction and science-oriented books.

Typical recent postings   Review of *How Are We to Live?* by Peter Singer; Book Review *How to BBS for Profit*; Review of *Ethernet Pocket Guide*, by Spinney.

Review   Sometimes worth reading, this newsgroup carries do-it-yourself reviews of books on many topics, but there's a pronounced bias toward technical works (despite the fact that reviews of such works are supposed to be submitted to alt.books.reviews.technical). Unfortunately, authors and publishers don't seem to be able to resist submitting "reviews" of their own works; this group could use a moderator.

Advice to newbies   This group is for reviews of general-interest works; post reviews of technical books to alt.books.reviews.technical.

Adult-oriented?   No.

Readership   37,000.

Rank   771.

Messages per month   361.

Crossposting percentage   16%.

Availability   52% of USENET sites.

Moderated?   No.

Special features   The Book Review Index contains an index of reviews that will be made available at a future archive site; check the FAQ for details.

FAQ title   FAQ for alt.books.reviews

FAQ location   alt.books.reviews, rec.arts.books, rec.answers, news.answers

Other information resources   Book Review Index

Archive site   At this writing, an archive site was planned but details had not been finalized. You can get the Book Review Index via anonymous ftp from rtfm.mit.edu in the directory /pub/usenet/alt.books.reviews.

Related groups   rec.arts.books, biz.books.technical, misc.books.technical

alt.books.technical ★★

Reviews of technical books in computer and computer-related fields. Of interest to anyone learning the Internet or UNIX and looking for good books—but don't bother reading the newsgroup. Just get the Book Review List instead (see later item).

Typical recent postings   *DOS User's Guide to the Internet* (Review), *TeX By Example* (Review), What To Do About Curled Paperback Covers?

Review   This is a low-volume newsgroup with posts that might interest those learning the Internet and UNIX. A drawback: Authors and publishers use the newsgroup to advertise their own works. Many of the posts aren't reviews at all and don't belong in the newsgroup.

Advice to newbies   Post discussion articles to misc.books.technical.

Adult-oriented?   No.

Readership   37,000.

Rank   773.

Messages per month   150.

Crossposting percentage   33%.

Availability   57% of USENET sites.

Moderated?   No.

Special features   None.

FAQ title   FAQ for alt.books.reviews

FAQ location   alt.books.reviews, alt.books.technical, rec.arts.books, rec.answers, news.answers

Other information resources   Book Review Index; Unofficial Internet Book List, A Concise Guide to UNIX Books

Archive site   At this writing, an archive site was planned but details had not been finalized. You can get the Book Review Index via anonymous ftp from rtfm.mit.edu in the directory /pub/usenet/alt.books.reviews.

Related groups   alt.books.reviews, rec.arts.books, biz.books.technical, misc.books.technical

alt.business.multi-level ★★★

Multi-level marketing—or, in plain English, the attempt to get rich by pestering all of your friends and relations to start selling a product (such as detergents) so that you can receive sales commissions. Of interest to any-one who's a distributor for an MLM company, or thinking about becoming one.

Typical recent postings   Gourmet Coffee = $$$!, I've Been Stupid for 20 Years, Amway "Tools" Scam, MLM Reference Material.

Review   Good discussion of the myriad issues facing MLMs—for instance, whether the whole thing's a scam. Essential for anyone involved in MLM or thinking about getting into it.

Advice to newbies   Please read the group's FAQ before posting to avoid asking questions that have been posed before.

Adult-oriented?   No.

Readership   15,000.

Rank   1,538.

Messages per month   1,309 .

Crossposting percentage   2%.

Availability   53% of USENET sites.

Moderated? No.

Special features The group's FAQ is an excellent, even-handed introduction to the issues concerning MLMs and should be read by anyone with interests in this area.

FAQ title alt.business.multi-level FAQ (Frequently Asked Questions)

FAQ location alt.business.multi-level, alt.answers, news.answers

Other information resources None.

Archive site You can get the FAQ from rtfm.mit.edu in the directory /pub/usenet/ alt.business.multi-level.

Related groups None.

alt.callahans ★★★★

The Callahan's Place novels of Spider Robinson. Of interest to anyone who wants to experience gentle and congenial social interaction by means of USENET postings.

Typical recent postings A Shy Hello, Party Pizza for All Newcomers.

Review Callahan's motto is "Shared pain is lessened, shared joy is increased; thus do we refute entropy." Callahan's Place is a sort of fantasy novel's answer to a bar, replete with unicorns and other magical creatures, at which anyone may make a toast to share joy or pain. The postings, properly, are supposed to emulate the fictional space of Robinson's novels through the use of narrative and dialogue. The group's gentle and sociable philosophy is a very nice corrective to the normal hue and cry of USENET dialogue. As you can well imagine, though, lots of posters—particularly crossposters—don't respect the group's traditions, so you'll want to perfect the art of the kill file.

Advice to newbies Unlike most newsgroups, alt.callahans welcomes newbies—and in fact,

prefers to call them newcomers. Please read the New Patron's Guide to Posting.

Adult-oriented? No, although some of the subjects discussed pertain to adult situations.

Readership 50,000.

Rank 519.

Messages per month 4,153.

Crossposting percentage 1%.

Availability 60% of USENET sites.

Moderated? No.

Special features Posts should be phrased in dialogue, capturing the gestalt of Robinson's novels; please read the New Patron's Guide to Posting before posting an article to alt.callahans.

FAQ title All About Callahans

FAQ location alt.callahans

Other information resources New Patron's Guide to Posting

Archive site None.

Related groups None.

alt.cd-rom ★★★

CD-ROM disks and disk drives. Anyone who's using or having trouble with CD ROM disks or CD-ROM drives.

Typical recent postings Cheap prices on CD-ROMS, Good CD-ROM Mail Order Company, Legal Issues Concerning Multimedia, CD-ROM Upgrades, Best Home Health CD-ROM?

Review Not much discussion to be found here— it's mostly a bunch of questions regarding the technical challenges of installing and configuring CD-ROM drives, together with requests for opinions regarding the merits of CD-ROM disks. If you have a CD-ROM–related question, you might try posting it here. If someone else has already asked it, email that person to find out if he or she found the answer. The group is plagued with unwanted advertising.

Advice to newbies   For information on CD-ROM hardware, read the comp.sys.ibm.pc.hardware.cd-rom FAQ.

Adult-oriented?   No, but there are recurrent posts regarding adult CD-ROM disk availability.

Readership   81,000.

Rank   196.

Messages per month   1,858.

Crossposting percentage   6%.

Availability   64% of USENET sites.

Moderated?   No.

Special features   None.

FAQ title   Alt.CD-rom FAQ

FAQ location   alt.cd-rom, comp.multimedia, comp.publish.cdrom.multimedia, comp.publish.cdrom.hardware, comp.publish.cdrom.software, alt.answers, comp.answers, news.answers

Other information resources   T7G Technical FAQ

Archive site   None.

Related groups   comp.multimedia, comp.publish.cdrom.multimedia, comp.publish.cdrom.hardware, comp.publish.cdrom.software

alt.co-ops ★★★

Cooperatives set up according to the Rochdale principles (open, voluntary membership; democratic control; limited return on equity capital; return of net surplus to owner-users; education; cooperation among cooperatives) as well as secular egalitarian communes (intentional communities). Of interest to anyone involved in a cooperative or thinking about setting one up.

Typical recent postings   Dealing with Member Conflicts, What Kind of Lease Form Should I Use in a Co-op Apartment?

Review   A low-volume group, but the postings and discussions are of high quality.

Advice to newbies   Please read the FAQ before posting; it contains information concerning Rochdale co-ops and intentional communities and provides information about books and magazines.

Adult-oriented?   No.

Readership   28,000.

Rank   1,032.

Messages per month   34.

Crossposting percentage   28%.

Availability   57% of USENET sites.

Moderated?   No.

Special features   None.

FAQ title   Co-operatives—Frequently Asked Questions

FAQ location   alt.co-ops, alt.answers, news.answers

Other information resources   None.

Archive site   You can get the group's FAQ from rtfm.mit.edu, in the directory /pub/usenet/alt.co-ops.

Related groups   None.

alt.coffee ★★★

The sublime black beverage—where to get it, how to prepare it. Of interest to gourmet coffee enthusiasts.

Typical recent postings   Los Angeles Coffee Houses, Stronger Than Jolt, Permanent Filters, Brewing Methods, Iced Expresso Drinks.

Review   A healthy group—lots of discussion with a high signal-to-noise ratio, and many tips and recommendations about coffee vendors, brewing techniques. Bound to delight the coffee *aficionado*.

Advice to newbies   Check out the Coffee Resource Guide and Caffeine's Frequently Asked Questions to see whether your question has already been answered there.

Adult-oriented?   No.

Readership   New group; figures not yet available.

Rank   New group; figures not yet available.

Messages per month   New group; figures not yet available.

Crossposting percentage   New group; figures not yet available.

Availability   New group; figures not yet available.

Moderated?   No.

Special features   The Coffee Resources Guide contains a wealth of information on coffee bean and tea vendors, coffee equipment, and coffee-related books and periodicals.

FAQ title   None.

FAQ location   N/A.

Other information resources   Coffee Resources Guide; Caffeine's Frequently Asked Questions (the FAQ for alt.drugs.caffeine).

Archive site   You can get the Coffee Resources Guide, as well as the alt.drugs.caffeine FAQ, via anonymous ftp from rtfm.mit.edu in the directory /pub/usenet/alt.coffee.

Related groups   alt.drugs.caffeine, alt.food.coffee

alt.computer.consultants ★★★

The trials, tribulations, and rewards of going into business as a computer consultant. People who help other people with their computers and get paid for doing it.

Typical recent postings   Which Consulting Organization's Worth It, Who Owns the Source Code, Legal Rights of Software Owner.

Review   A worthwhile discussion group for professional computer consultants, but you'll encounter a lot of noise from posters who think this is the place to post questions about how to hook up their monitors.

Advice to newbies   Please do not post computer-related questions to this group; there are lots of comp.* groups that handle computer-related questions.

Adult-oriented?   No.

Readership   28,000.

Rank   874.

Messages per month   34.

Crossposting percentage   28%.

Availability   57% of USENET sites.

Moderated?   No.

Special features   None.

FAQ title   alt.computer.consultants FAQ

FAQ location   alt.computer.consultants

Other information resources   None.

Archive site   None.

Related groups   None.

alt.config ★★★

Proposals for creation of new alt newgroups and discussions about these proposals. For

anyone interested in the process by which new alt newsgroups are created.

Typical recent postings   Alt.Arts.Storytelling Created, Proposal: Alt.Culture.North-Dakota, Proposal: Alt.Punk.Germany.

Review   If you're thinking of creating an alt newsgroup (see Chapter 19), please post your ideas here first. You'll get plenty of feedback that can help you determine whether the group is really needed, whether system administrators would be likely to carry it, and whether it's logically named.

Advice to newbies   Please do not propose the creation of a new newsgroup until you're familiar with USENET and believe you have determined that there's a legitimate need for a new one; please read Chapter 19 carefully.

Adult-oriented?   No.

Readership   120,000.

Rank   64.

Messages per month   2,048.

Crossposting percentage   15%.

Availability   67% of USENET sites.

Moderated?   No.

Special features   None.

FAQ title   So You Want To Create An Alt Newsgroup

FAQ location   alt.config, alt.answers

Other information resources   Another Listing of Newsgroups in the Alt Hierarchy (Parts 1–3).

Archive site   None.

Related groups   news.config

---

alt.conspiracy ★★★★

Exposés of organized efforts to misrepresent the truth—for example, the assertions by Amer-

ican Nazi organizations that the Holocaust never happened. Of interest to anyone concerned about the organized distortion of truth.

Typical recent postings   LaRouche and Demagoguery, Faked Moon Landings, Baloney Survival Hardware, Clinton Conspiracy.

Review   In this newsgroup, you'll find intelligent discussion regarding some of the crazier conspiracy theories that have been advanced in recent years. Some of the participants are experts in their fields and back up their claims with facts and figures.

Advice to newbies   Read this group carefully before posting—and when you do, make sure you have something substantive to contribute beyond your uninformed opinion.

Adult-oriented?   No.

Readership   98,000.

Rank   130.

Messages per month   3,031.

Crossposting percentage   43%.

Availability   64% of USENET sites.

Moderated?   No.

Special features   The Holocaust FAQ (see "Other information resources") should be required reading for any citizen concerned about the misrepresentation of truth.

FAQ title   None.

FAQ location   N/A.

Other information resources   HOLOCAUST FAQ: Willis Carto & The Institute for Historical Review

Archive site   None.

Related groups   alt.activism, alt.conspiracy.jfk, alt.revisionism

alt.cult-movies ★★★★

The lore and love of cult movies, such as Solaris, An American Werewolf in London, and Plan 9 from Outer Space. Of interest to anyone who loves cult movies.

Typical recent postings Blood-Sucking Freaks, Funny Out-Loud Comments Heard at Horror Films, What's Your Favorite Film Metaphor, Movies That You HATED But Everyone Else Loved.

Review A healthy newsgroup, with lots of intelligent, informative discussion; interesting and fun topics.

Advice to newbies If you're a devotee of the Rocky Horror Picture Show, note that there's a newsgroup devoted to this cult film classic: alt.cult.movies.rocky-horror.

Adult-oriented? No, although some of the postings concern R-rated films and gory scenes.

Readership 79,000.

Rank 210.

Messages per month 3,205.

Crossposting percentage 9%.

Availability 64% of USENET sites.

Moderated? No.

Special features None.

FAQ title None.

FAQ location alt.cult-movies, rec.arts.sf.movies, rec.arts.movies, news.answers, rec.answers, alt.answers

Other information resources Memorable Quotes from Movies; rec.arts.movies Frequently Asked Questions; LIST: MOVIE TRIVIA: in-jokes, cameos, signatures; LIST: Movie Soundtracks; LIST: Crazy Movie Credits; MOVIES: ALIEN FAQ parts 1 through 3; BRAZIL (Movie, 1985) Frequently Asked Questions (FAQ); Movie Database: Frequently Asked Questions List; LIST: Movie BIOGRAPHIES list; Elijah Wood MiniFAQ; Rocky Horror Theater List

Archive site The resources just mentioned are available via anonymous ftp from rtfm.mit.edu, in the directory /pub/usenet/rec.arts.movies.

Related groups alt.cult.movie.rocky-horror, alt.sex.movies, rec.arts.sf.movies, rec.arts.movies

alt.cyberpunk ★★

Cyberpunk, both as a literary movement concerning marginalized people in a technologically advanced society, as well as a contemporary lifestyle—hackers, crackers, and phone phreaks. Of interest to science fiction fans.

Typical recent postings Cyberpunk—The Movie, Comments on *Neuromancer*, Blade Runner, Cyberfonts, Thought Criminals.

Review There's more discussion of cyberpunk literature here than the cyberpunk lifestyle—and given that cyberpunk is dated, it's not too surprising that this newsgroup seems rather listless of late. If you're interested in cyberpunk literature, check out the group's excellent FAQ.

Advice to newbies Please read the FAQ—and read lots of cyberpunk—before you post to this group.

Adult-oriented? No.

Readership 79,000.

Rank 211.

Messages per month 1,280.

Crossposting percentage 6%.

Availability 64% of USENET sites.

Moderated? No.

Special features None.

FAQ title Alt.Cyberpunk Frequently Asked Questions List

FAQ location alt.cyberpunk

Other information resources None.

Archive site None.

Related groups alt.cyberpunk.movement, alt.cyberpunk.tech, alt.hackers

alt.dreams ★★★★

Everything about dreams and dreamings, including nightmares, dream interpretation, out-of-body experiences. Of interest to anyone who has had a puzzling dream and would like some help sorting it out.

Typical recent postings Strange Childhood Night Terrors, Ever Wake Up Laughing, Running from Capture.

Review A very interesting newsgroup with lots of discussion, a high signal-to-noise ratio, and a superb set of FAQs. Everyone dreams, and there's lots of discussion here about what it all means.

Advice to newbies Please read this newsgroup's extensive FAQs before posting—chances are very good that your question has already been answered.

Adult-oriented? Some erotic dreams are described in detail.

Readership 54,000.

Rank 463.

Messages per month 848.

Crossposting percentage 24%.

Availability 59% of USENET sites.

Moderated? No.

Special features This group's multi-part FAQ is one of the most interesting sources you'll encounter on the nature and meaning of dreams.

FAQ title alt.dreams.lucid FAQ

FAQ location alt.dreams, alt.dreams.lucid, alt.answers, news.answers

Other information resources Dreams FAQ Pt. 1/*:General Information, dream interpretation; Dreams FAQ Pt. 2/*:Nightmares, OOBEs, paranormal issues; Dreams FAQ Pt. 3/*:About Lucid Dreaming; Dreams FAQ Pt. 4/*:Research, Help, reading recommendations.

Archive site You can get the FAQs from rtfm.mit.edu in the directory /pub/usenet/alt.dreams.

Related groups alt.dreams.lucid

alt.dreams.lucid ★★

Dreaming while you know that you're dreaming—and controlling the direction the dream takes. For those interested in delving more deeply into the psychic potentialities of lucid dreaming; should appeal as well to fans of Carlos Castaneda.

Typical recent postings Dreamwalker Journal, Keep Waking Up, Violent Lucid Dreams.

Review This is the "fringe" of the alt.dreams set, much influenced by Carlos Castaneda's books about his adventures with a Yaqui Indian sorcerer. To get into this, you'd have to be a true believer in the possibilities of lucid dreaming.

Advice to newbies Please read the alt.dreams FAQ, which contains a section on lucid dreaming, before posting to this group.

Adult-oriented? No.

Readership 14,000.

Rank 1,578.

Messages per month 412.

Crossposting percentage 8%.

225

Availability 44% of USENET sites.

Moderated? No.

Special features None.

FAQ title None.

FAQ location N/A.

Other information resources Alt.dreams FAQ Pt. 3/:About Lucid Dreaming; Shamanism-General_Overview Frequently_Asked_Questions_(FAQ)

Archive site You can get these information resources, including the alt.dreams FAQ, from rtfm.mit.edu in the directory /pub/usenet/ alt.dreams.lucid.

Related groups alt.dreams

alt.drugs ★★

Illegal drugs and drug use—usually from an enthusiastic user's perspective. Of interest to the people who go to Grateful Dead concerts.

Typical recent postings First Acid Trip—What Happened?, Do Drug Dealers Use Internet, Get High on Life, Purity of Pot, Legal Highs.

Review A bore, unless you're a pothead—and even then you'll have to put up with incessant posts from evangelical Christians convinced that Jesus is the greatest high.

Advice to newbies Get counseling.

Adult-oriented? Yes.

Readership 110,000.

Rank 86.

Messages per month 4,001.

Crossposting percentage 13%.

Availability 63% of USENET sites.

Moderated? No.

Special features You'll find the latest pot prices in the Drug Price Report, which comes in U.S. and Non-U.S. versions.

FAQ title None.

FAQ location N/A.

Other information resources Libertarian FAQ: Frequently Asked Questions, Libertarian FAQ: World's Smallest Political Quiz, Libertarian FAQ: Organizations, Anti-War-On-Drugs Activists' Drug Price Report, U.S. Drug Price Report, Non-U.S.

Archive site None.

Related groups alt.drugs.caffeine, alt.drugs.usenet, alt.activism, talk.politics.drugs

alt.drugs.caffeine ★★

The joys of getting completely wired on such things as gourmet coffee and Jolt cola. Of interest to unrepentant caffeine addicts.

Typical recent postings Coffee and Metabolism, Coffee Beans Covered with Chocolate, Losing Weight Without Caffeine.

Review You'd think this group would feature intelligent discussion of the dangers of caffeine. Instead, it's a sort of branch office of alt.coffee. Generally, you'll find a low signal-to-noise ratio and few informative postings. On the other hand, the FAQ (Caffeine's Frequently Asked Questions) is well worth reading.

Advice to newbies Get the FAQ; skip the newsgroup.

Adult-oriented? No.

Readership 11,000.

Rank 1,767.

Messages per month 202.

Crossposting percentage 21%.

Availability   45% of USENET sites.

Moderated?   No.

Special features   None.

FAQ title   Caffeine's Frequently Asked Questions

FAQ location   alt.drugs.caffeine, alt.food.coffee, alt.answers, news.answers

Other information resources   Coffee Resources Guide

Archive site   You can get the FAQ and the Coffee Resources Guide from rtfm.mit.edu, in the directory /pub/usenet/alt.coffee.

Related groups   alt.coffee

alt.etext ★★★

Electronic text generally—electronic 'zines, computer-accessible texts for literary analysis. Of interest to literary scholars and 'zine enthusiasts.

Typical recent postings   Postmodern Parataxis, ANGST—Famous Internet Fanzine, Project Guttenberg Newsletter.

Review   *The* place on the Net for electronic text enthusiasts.

Advice to newbies   If you're not sure what this is all about, please read the FAQ.

Adult-oriented?   No.

Readership   5,900.

Rank   2,206.

Messages per month   42.

Crossposting percentage   13%.

Availability   32% of USENET sites.

Moderated?   No.

Special features   You'll find a periodic newsletter with news of the latest events in the electronic text world.

FAQ title   None.

FAQ location   N/A.

Other information resources   Online Books FAQ, Project Guttenberg List of Etext, Zines_on_the_Internet, Net-Letter_Guide

Archive site   There are several etext archives available on Internet; check out the Project Guttenberg list for a start.

Related groups   rec.arts.books, alt.internet.services, sci.classics

alt.feminism ★

Feminism, real and perceived, but mostly the reaction of various juvenile males who feel threatened but can't really explain why. Of interest to anyone interested in understanding the pathological dimensions of the backlash against the quest for women's rights.

Typical recent postings   Do Nice Girls Speak UNIX?, Is Lesbianism a Turn-On?, Abolishing the Family, Do Women Have Rape Fantasies?

Review   Feminism is a worthy topic for discussion—but it's perhaps too incendiary for USENET. Feminism isn't really the topic here: Most of the posts are from little boys all upset that women are going to take their jobs away. There are some humorous rejoinders from feminists who delight in exposing hypocrisy—of which there's plenty in evidence. Skip alt.feminism; if you're interested in reading intelligent articles on this subject, both pro- and anti-feminist in perspective, check out soc.feminism, a moderated group.

Advice to newbies   Skip this newsgroup.

Adult-oriented?   Yes.

Readership   43,000.

Rank   653.

Messages per month   3,917.

Crossposting percentage 77% (a very high figure, and indicative of frequent trolling and other abuses).

Availability 54% of USENET sites.

Moderated? No.

Special features None.

FAQ title alt.feminism FAQ (monthly posting).

FAQ location alt.feminism, alt.answers, news.answers

Other information resources N/A.

Archive site None.

Related groups soc.feminism (moderated), soc.women, soc.men, talk.abortion

alt.flame ★

Tirades, ranting and raving, carefully contrived put-downs, trolling and other forms of juvenile USENET behavior, interminable fruitless controversy—it's all here. Of interest to the maturity-impaired.

Typical recent postings Barney Loses, Flamers Are Shit, Message to All Faggots.

Review One has to give thanks for the existence of this group—many of USENET's more juvenile posters remain preoccupied with it, so the rest of us can enjoy ourselves undisturbed by their adolescent profanities and ill-considered opinions. A very good reason to check the group periodically: Set up your newsreader's global kill functions to kill any post, in any newsgroup, by anyone who posts a message here.

Advice to newbies Stay out of alt.flame. Repeated use of profanity, attacks on other USENET readers, or the sending of unwanted email could result in the loss of your network access privileges. On the other hand, if this kind of thing appeals to you, would you please post in this group and no others?

Adult-oriented? Profanities are the last resort of the semi-literate and are to be found in abundance.

Readership 120,000.

Rank 63 (and what does this say…).

Messages per month 3,971 completely pointless postings.

Crossposting percentage 36% (a very bad sign; many alt.flame participants are among the network's worst abusers).

Availability 63%.

Moderated? Ha.

Special features Posters appear to have an oversufficiency of testosterone and an insufficiency of dopamine.

FAQ title None.

FAQ location N/A.

Other information resources None.

Archive site None.

Related groups alt.flame.faggots, alt.flame.mud, alt.flame.parents, alt.flame.spelling, alt.stupidity, alt.usenet.kooks

alt.folklore.college ★★★★

The urban folklore of college life—libraries sinking because of the unpredicted weight of the books they contain, student kills self during final examination by putting two pencils up his nose and slamming his head against the desk—the works. Of interest to anyone who cherishes the lore, legends, and foolishness of college life.

Typical recent postings Dorm Designs, Missing Plutonium, Dorm Mistaken for Hospital.

Review A great newsgroup, if lower in volume than the other alt.folklore.* groups; virtually certain to contain some very entertaining posts. An example: A University of Chicago dormitory really *is* named after the guy who invented the zipper.

Advice to newbies Be sure to read the alt.folklore.college FAQ before posting to see whether your myth has already been explored.

Adult-oriented? No.

Readership 39,000.

Rank 729.

Messages per month 311.

Crossposting percentage 15%.

Availability 58% of USENET sites.

Moderated? No.

Special features None.

FAQ title alt.folklore.college Frequently Asked Questions

FAQ location alt.folklore.college

Other information resources FAQ: CSH Coke Machine Information

Archive site None.

Related groups alt.folklore.computers, alt.internet.services, soc.college, soc.college.grad, alt.folklore.urban

alt.folklore.computers ★★★★

The legends, lore, and myths of computing. Of interest to computer users, hobbyists, and anyone interested in the relationship between contemporary culture and technology.

Typical recent postings Hackers in Night Mode, "Hello World" Programs in Different Languages, Stupid UNIX Tricks, Origin of @ Character.

Review One of USENET's best—witty, informed, and often hilarious discussions of the culture of computing. Not to be missed by anyone who enjoys computers and their history.

Advice to newbies This group is generally very tolerant of newcomers and helpful, but be sure to read the group so that you clearly understand the tone and topics of conversation. Contribute only when you've something substantive to add.

Adult-oriented? No.

Readership 100,000.

Rank 108.

Messages per month 2,087.

Crossposting percentage 12%.

Availability 69% of USENET sites.

Moderated? No.

Special features None.

FAQ title Net.Legends.FAQ (Noticeable Phenomena of USENET)

FAQ location alt.folklore.computers, alt.usenet.kooks, alt.answers, news.answers

Other information resources FAQ: CSH Coke Machine Information, Ye Olde Secrete Screene Cheete Sheete

Archive site You can find these resources via anonymous ftp at rtfm.mit.edu in the directory /pub/usenet/alt.folklore.computers.

Related groups comp.society.folklore, alt.folklore.college, alt.folklore.computers, alt.folklore.gemstones, alt.folklore.ghost-stories, alt.folklore.herbs, alt.folklore.info, alt.folklore.science, alt.folklore.suburban

alt.folklore.science ★★★★

Myths presented as if they were scientifically true. Of interest to anyone trying to piece together what's true and what's not.

Typical recent postings 8 Glasses of Water a Day, Nostradamus and the Comet, Electrocution and the Heart, Bigfoot Research Project.

Review A fun exploration of yet another aspect of contemporary myth.

Advice to newbies This group is generally very tolerant of newcomers and helpful, but be sure to read the group so that you clearly understand the tone and topics of conversation.

Adult-oriented? No.

Readership 29,000.

Rank 997.

Messages per month 383.

Crossposting percentage 20%.

Availability 58% of USENET sites.

Moderated? No.

Special features None.

FAQ title alt.folklore.urban Frequently Asked Questions

FAQ location alt.folklore.urban, news.answers, alt.answers

Other information resources Relativity_and_FTL_Travel

Archive site Look for the FAQ and the other resources via anonymous FTP to rtfm.mit.edu in the directory /pub/usenet/alt.folklore.urban.

Related groups alt.folklore.college, alt.folklore.computers, alt.folklore.gemstones, alt.folklore.ghost-stories, alt.folklore.herbs, alt.folklore.info, alt.folklore.suburban, alt.follore.urban, sci.skeptic

alt.folklore.urban ★★★

Urban myths—myths of contemporary life that are disseminated by means of modern communications technologies. Of interest to anyone who enjoys folklore, but check out the other alt.folklore.* groups first.

Typical recent postings Land O' Lakes Butter, Missing Plutonium, Tannin Death (From Washing Coffee Pot in Navy), One Breast Bigger Than the Other, Turtles Illegal in New Jersey.

Review This group may have been the victim of its own success. In the past, it's been one of the most enjoyable newsgroups on USENET, a source for amusing and sometimes hilarious explorations of urban folklore. It's still worth a read, but the group's fame has come at a price—you'll find a lot of juvenile, sarcastic, and pointless silliness scattered amidst the gems.

Advice to newbies This group isn't as friendly as the other alt.folklore.* groups; there's a fair number of trollers and flamers on the lookout for newbies. Be sure to read the group carefully, and above all read the group's FAQ before posting.

Adult-oriented? No.

Readership 140,000.

Rank 35.

Messages per month 6,652.

Crossposting percentage 14%.

Availability 66% of USENET sites.

Moderated? No.

Special features The alt.folklore.urban FAQ is a delight; it's a compendium of urban myths, together with notions about whether they've been found to be true or false.

FAQ title alt.folklore.urban Frequently Asked Questions

FAQ location alt.folklore.urban, news.answers, alt.answers

Other information resources None.

Archive site Get the FAQs and other information resources via anonymous FTP to rtfm.mit.edu in the directory /pub/usenet/.

Related groups alt.folklore.college, alt.folklore.computers, alt.folklore.gemstones, alt.folklore.ghost-stories, alt.folklore.herbs, alt.folklore.info, alt.folklore.science, alt.folklore.suburban

alt.hackers ★★★

The old and estimable art of hacking, the intelligent and often unorthodox rearranging of computer resources to pull off some (preferably spectacular) improvement in a computer system's performance. Of interest to hackers and anyone interested in finding out what hacking's really about (as opposed to the press's misrepresentation of hacking).

Typical recent postings Neat Copy-Protection Hack, My Favorite PDP Hack, Hacking Is Despicable, Tracking Hack—Figure This Out.

Review If you're really interested in knowing what hacking is all about, check this group out. Every post is supposed to report on a neat or unusual hack—and most of the posts are of high quality, since the group is a one-way reflection of a mailing list. The mailing list isn't moderated, but you have to be something of a hacker to figure out how to get your message into it!

Advice to newbies This isn't a place to post unless you consider yourself to be a hacker—and even then, you'll have to prove yourself to gain acceptance from the regulars.

Adult-oriented? No.

Readership 88,000.

Rank 159.

Messages per month 146.

Crossposting percentage 10%.

Availability 62% of USENET sites.

Moderated? In a way—you have to be something of a hacker to figure out how to post to this group!

Special features None.

FAQ title Welcome to Alt.Hackers (Automated Posting).

FAQ location alt.hackers

Other information resources None.

Archive site None.

Related groups alt.cyberpunk

alt.hemp ★

Pot, weed, Mary Jane—call it what you like, it's still marijuana, but this group also deals (if infrequently) with those crusading souls who feel that the free cultivation of hemp is the answer to economic progress. Of interest to two groups, which perhaps overlap a bit: potheads and hemp activists.

Typical recent postings Urine Test in 3 Weeks—Need Help, Male Plants, Brownie Recipe Wanted, That Darned Marijuana Smell.

Review If this group was once envisioned as a hotbed of hemp activism, it's deteriorated lately into a branch outpost of alt.drugs.

Advice to newbies Read the FAQ if you've any questions about pot or hemp.

Adult-oriented? Yes.

Readership 19,000.

Rank 1,329.

Messages per month 956.

Crossposting percentage 22%.

Availability 43% of USENET sites.

Moderated? No.

Special features   None.

FAQ title   alt.hemp CANNABIS/MARIJUANA FAQ

FAQ location   alt.hemp, alt.answers, news.answers

Other information resources   None.

Archive site   None.

Related groups   None.

alt.history.what-if ★★★★

Counterfactual history—what might have happened. Of interest to people with interests in history who would like to explore an interesting line of thought that doesn't sit well with most professional historians.

Typical recent postings   No Oil, No Horses, If the South Had Won the Civil War, Australia Attacked, Tactical Nukes Only.

Review   Fascinating, often witty, and generally intelligent speculations on what might have been, with a focus on historical debate rather than science fiction speculation—posts are expected to concern what might have happened in the past, not what might happen in the future or in science fiction.

Advice to newbies   Please read the FAQ carefully before posting to alt.history.what-if.

Adult-oriented?   No.

Readership   15,000.

Rank   1,513.

Messages per month   649.

Crossposting percentage   7%.

Availability   44% of USENET sites.

Moderated?   No.

Special features   There's a massive (350 page) list of sources for alternate history; see "Other informational resources."

FAQ title   alt.history.what-if FAQ

FAQ location   alt.history.what-if, alt.answers, news.answers

Other information resources   There's a (large) counterfactual history book list at ftp://gandalf.rutgers.edu/pub/sfl/alternatehistories.txt ; it's also to be found via anonymous FTP to rtfm.mit.edu in the directory /pub/usenet/ (look for the files titled LIST).

Archive site   None.

Related groups   alt.history.living, bit.listserv.history, soc.history, soc.history.moderated, soc.history.war.misc, soc.history.war.world-war-ii

alt.housing.nontrad ★★

Alternative housing construction techniques. Of interest to architects, builders, environmentalists.

Typical recent postings   "Underground" Housing, Earthquake-Proof Houses, Architectural Bulletin Board System Available.

Review   A low-volume group that will prove of interest only to those with personal or professional interests in the area.

Advice to newbies   Please read the group's FAQ before posting to avoid asking questions that have been posed before.

Adult-oriented?   No.

Readership   5,200.

Rank   2,311.

Messages per month   126.

Crossposting percentage   9%.

Availability   31% of USENET sites.

Moderated?   No.

Special features   None.

FAQ title   alt.housing.nontrad Frequently Asked Questions

FAQ location   alt.housing.nontrad

Other information resources   None.

Archive site   None.

Related groups   misc.consumers.house

alt.internet.access.wanted ★★★

The quest for free or inexpensive Internet access. Of interest to anyone looking for Internet access.

Typical recent postings   Internet Access Providers in the Ex-Soviet Union, Directory of Internet Access in Europe, Best Access for Atlanta (404) Recommendations.

Review   In this newsgroup, you'll find a mixture of questions ("How Can I Get Internet Access In Cucamonga, CA?") and lots of helpful answers, including some extensive lists of Internet service providers.

Advice to newbies   Please don't post a question about USENET access to this group until you've obtained PDIAL (Public Dialup Internet Access List).

Adult-oriented?   No.

Readership   53,000.

Rank   478.

Messages per month   1,121.

Crossposting percentage   8%.

Availability   58% of USENET sites.

Moderated?   No.

Special features   None.

FAQ title   Public Dialup Internet Access List (PDIAL).

FAQ location   alt.internet.access.wanted, alt.bbs.lists, alt. on-line service

Other information resources   Network Access in Australia FAQ

Archive site   None.

Related groups   alt.bbs.lists, alt.online-service, ba.internet

alt.internet.services ★★★★

Services available through the Internet, including Telnet resources (such as weather reports and library catalogs), FTP resources (file archives), diversions such as MUDs and IRC, and commercial services. Of interest to those wishing to expand their use of the Internet by finding and using new services.

Typical recent postings   Stock Quotes, Senate Addresses, Court Transcripts, Patent Gazette.

Review   A useful newsgroup for queries regarding Internet services and announcements pertaining to such services, but much disturbed by inappropriate postings—the group is too frequently confused with alt.internet.access-wanted.

Advice to newbies   Please do not post questions or announcements here regarding Internet access or general questions regarding how to use Internet. Read the FAQ carefully before posting.

Adult-oriented?   No.

Readership   110,000.

Rank   85.

Messages per month   1,878.

Crossposting percentage   17%.

Availability   62% of USENET sites.

Moderated?   No.

Special features   None.

FAQ title Internet Services FAQ

FAQ location alt.internet.services, alt.answers

Other information resources FAQ: How Can I Send a Fax from the Internet? Unofficial Internet Book List, updated Internet Services List, Internet Mall: Shopping the Information Highway

Archive site None.

Related groups alt.online-service, alt.internet.access-wanted, alt.bbs.lists, alt.bbs.internet

alt.irc ★★

Internet Relay Chat (IRC), a global real-time chat system that used to be lots of fun before it was virtually taken over by some extremely abusive people. Of interest to users of Internet Relay Chat.

Typical recent postings Most Bots Suck, Net Split, Age/Gender Checks, New Server in California.

Review The newsgroup is full of questions from new users—and very few informed responses.

Advice to newbies Skip the newsgroup, and read the FAQ instead.

Adult-oriented? No.

Readership 53,000.

Rank 479.

Messages per month 1,273.

Crossposting percentage 3%.

Availability 57% of USENET sites.

Moderated? No.

Special features None.

FAQ title IRC Frequently Asked Questions (FAQ)

FAQ location alt.irc, alt.ircii, alt.irc.questions, alt.answers, news.answers

Other information resources None.

Archive site None.

Related groups alt.irc, alt.ircii, alt.irc.announce, alt.irc.recovery, alt.irc.questions, alt.irc.undernet

alt.locksmithing ★★★

The art of locksmithing in general, with a pronounced focus on picking locks. Of interest to aspiring locksmiths—and burglars?

Typical recent postings File Cabinets, Cheap Lock-Picking Set, An Old Safe, Home Vaults.

Review Good discussion with lots of well-informed participation. These guys can get into *anything*.

Advice to newbies Please read the group's FAQ before posting to avoid asking questions that have been posed before.

Adult-oriented? No.

Readership 30,000.

Rank 960.

Messages per month 310.

Crossposting percentage 18%.

Availability 55% of USENET sites.

Moderated? No.

Special features None.

FAQ title alt.locksmithing answers to Frequently Asked Questions (FAQ)

FAQ location alt.locksmithing, alt.answers, news.answers

Other information resources None.

Archive site None.

Related groups None.

alt.magic ★★★

Magic, in the sense of stage magicians—entertaining tricks that give the illusion of magic, including—but not limited to—close-up, sleight of hand, platform, stage, and illusion magic. Of interest to practicing magicians, whether professional or amateur.

Typical recent postings   Wristwatch Steals, Flight of the Paper Balls, Houdini Escapes, Card Tricks, Shops in San Francisco.

Review   In this newsgroup, you'll find high-quality discussion of the practice of magicianship and the issues surrounding it—but no step-by-step guides for performing tricks, unless they're posted in contravention of the group's guidelines. As such, it's mostly of interest to practitioners in the field.

Advice to newbies   Please don't reveal how magic tricks are done in this newsgroup. This is a public newsgroup, and professional magicians feel that revealing these tricks undermines the illusion and therefore the audience's pleasure—once you figure out how the tricks are done, the illusion of magic completely collapses. Read the FAQ carefully before contributing.

Adult-oriented?   No.

Readership   27,000.

Rank   1,064.

Messages per month   799.

Crossposting percentage   32%.

Availability   56% of USENET sites.

Moderated?   No.

Special features   The extensive, four-part FAQ is an excellent introduction to magicianship.

FAQ title   alt.magic FAQ (four parts).

FAQ location   alt.magic, alt.answers, news.answers

Other information resources   None.

Archive site   None.

Related groups   alt.magick

alt.magick ★★

Magick, in Aleister Crowley's sense of the term: "the Science and Art of causing Change to occur in conformity with Will," admixed with a good deal of neo-paganism. Of interest to those interested in the occult and things pagan.

Typical recent postings   Evil as Distortion, Magic—Chaos and Otherwise, How To Deal With An Enchantress, The Shadow and the Qlippoth.

Review   Postings to this group tend to be long, rambling disquisitions on matters of "real" magic (as opposed to the "false" magic discussed in alt.magic), with occasional commentaries that strike me as equally obtuse. If you're into Tarot and have more than a passing fancy for the Druids, all of this might mean something to you.

Advice to newbies   Read the group's FAQs and lots of supporting literature carefully before posting.

Adult-oriented?   No.

Readership   40,000.

Rank   706.

Messages per month   2,157.

Crossposting percentage   34%.

Availability   58% of USENET sites.

Moderated?   No.

Special features   None.

FAQ title   alt.magick FAQ

FAQ location   alt.magick, alt.answers, news.answers

Other information resources   Egyptian Gods FAQ, Golden Dawn FAQ, Necromicon FAQ

Archive site ftp.lysator.liu.se /pub/magick

Related groups alt.magic, alt.necromicon

alt.meditation ★★

The art of meditation as a spiritual exercise and a means of stress reduction. Of interest to new age types generally and followers of Eastern religions.

Typical recent postings Happiness Is Inborn in the Self (Retreat), Crystal Meditation/Healing, Ex-Rama Student Describes His Experiences.

Review Lots of posts with news of spiritual retreats, but surprisingly little discussion; it seems there's not much to say in response to a long, obscure post about one's experiences with crystals.

Advice to newbies Please read the group's FAQ before posting to avoid asking questions that have been posed before.

Adult-oriented? No.

Readership 11,000.

Rank 1,761.

Messages per month 441.

Crossposting percentage 10%.

Availability 45% of USENET sites.

Moderated? No.

Special features None.

FAQ title Meditation FAQ

FAQ location alt.meditation, alt.answers, news.answers

Other information resources None.

Archive site None.

Related groups None.

alt.military.cadet ★★★

The cadet experience and the issues facing male-dominated military institutions. Of interest to military cadets, their families, anyone contemplating a military career, and anyone interested in the wider issues raised by military training.

Typical recent postings Homosexuals in the Military, West Point Future, Royal Canadian Air Cadets, Info. on Military Career Possibilities Wanted.

Review Overall, you'll find intelligent and mature discussion of cadet life and related social issues in this newsgroup. Given that these issues have made the news with some frequency of late, this discussion might prove of interest beyond the confines of the cadet corps.

Advice to newbies This group insists on polite discussion and good manners.

Adult-oriented? No.

Readership 6,600.

Rank 2,134.

Messages per month 158.

Crossposting percentage 0%.

Availability 45% of USENET sites.

Moderated? No.

Special features None.

FAQ title Welcome to Alt.Military.Cadet

FAQ location alt.military.cadet

Other information resources None.

Archive site None.

Related groups None.

alt.music.alternative ★★★★

Alternative music—rock, mostly, that's deliberately non-commercial, as a form of protest against Top 40 fodder. For anyone who enjoys listening to alternative music and attending alternative music concerts.

Typical recent postings   Top Ten Albums of Early 90s, Rage Against the Machine, Pioneers of Popular Music, Captain Beefheart, Ultimate Depression Albums.

Review   This is a high-volume group with lots of enthusiastic, good-spirited discussion about alternative music, a topic of importance to the people who post here. People respond to queries with solid information—discographies, upcoming concert dates and appearances, and information about magazine articles in which a group or musician is featured.

Advice to newbies   Please read the group's FAQ before participating; if you love alternative music and have something substantive to offer, you shouldn't be afraid to post.

Adult-oriented?   No.

Readership   99,000.

Rank   126.

Messages per month   7,360.

Crossposting percentage   7%.

Availability   58% of USENET sites.

Moderated?   No.

Special features   Subscribe to rec.music.info for information about all the music-related newsgroups.

FAQ title   alt.music.alternative Frequently Asked Questions

FAQ location   alt.music.alternative, rec.music, rec.answers, news.answers, alt.answers

Other information resources   FAQ Chalkhills The XTC Mailing List. rec.music.info (Monthly Pointer).

Archive site   None.

Related groups   rec.music.info, alt.music.alternative.female

alt.music.progressive ★★★★

Progressive music—music that's deliberately crafted to push the boundaries of musical composition and performance in an intelligent way. Of interest to anyone who enjoys progressive music.

Typical recent postings   Why Do We Like Progressive Music, Pendragon Web Server, Echolyn Info, A Summary of Jon Anderson Albums.

Review   Like alt.music.alternative, you'll find interesting, civilized discussion here. As you'll find when reading the group, much of it is carried on by musicians who appreciate or play progressive music.

Advice to newbies   There's no FAQ, but it's a congenial group that will welcome informed, substantive posts.

Adult-oriented?   No.

Readership   33,000.

Rank   876.

Messages per month   2,784.

Crossposting percentage   4%.

Availability   55% of USENET sites.

Moderated?   No.

Special features   Subscribe to rec.music.info for information about all the music-related newsgroups.

FAQ title   None.

FAQ location   N/A.

Other information resources Marillion and Fish FAQ, rec.music.info (Monthly Pointer).

Archive site None.

Related groups alt.music.hardcore, alt.music.marillion, alt.music.smash-pumpkins, alt.music.techno

alt.pagan ★★★

Paganism, witchcraft, and other pre-Christian religions, particularly as attempts have been made in recent years to strip them of the negative connotations assigned to them during the Christian incursion into Europe and to restore them as living, worthwhile faiths. Included are Wicca, neo-Shamanism, neo-Druidism Asatru and other forms of Norse neopaganism, neo-Native American practices, Women's Spirituality, the Sabaean Religious Order, the Church of All Worlds, Discordianism, and more. Of interest to anyone who finds neo-pagan religions fascinating.

Typical recent postings WARD/Woman Who Lost Her Foster Kids, Veggie Activism, Time To Disorganize, Wearing a Pentacle in Public, Death Threats, Mom and Paganism.

Review Lots of forthright discussion of neopaganism; in particular, the hysterical opposition it engenders, including physical attacks and death threats from fundamentalist Christians.

Advice to newbies Please read the FAQ before posting. Flames by evangelical Christians will be ignored.

Adult-oriented? No.

Readership 76,000.

Rank 236.

Messages per month 2,613.

Crossposting percentage 10%.

Availability 62% of USENET sites.

Moderated? No.

Special features None.

FAQ title alt.pagan Frequently Asked Questions (FAQ)

FAQ location alt.answers, news.answers, alt.pagan

Other information resources None.

Archive site None.

Related groups None.

alt.philosophy.objectivism ★★★★

The philosophy of Ayn Rand (1905–1982), author of *The Fountainhead* (1943), her best-known work. Objectivism is a realist philosophy that endorses moral integrity and free-market capitalism, calls for action based on rational choice, and holds out the promise of happiness in this life. Of interest to anyone interested in Ayn Rand's writings and philosophical perspectives.

Typical recent postings Objectivism and Abortion, Nietszche and Ayn Rand: Separated at Birth, Externalities and Capitalism.

Review If you're interested in Ayn Rand's works, you'll find literate, intelligent, and spirited discussion of her writings and philosophy in this newsgroup.

Advice to newbies Please familiarize yourself with Ayn Rand's philosophy before posting to the group, and read the FAQ.

Adult-oriented? No.

Readership 16,000.

Rank 1,467.

Messages per month 2,085.

Crossposting percentage 26%.

Availability 50% of USENET sites.

Moderated? No.

Special features There's a discussion of Ayn Rand, organized by participants in this newsgroup, to be found on the IRC channel #Aynrand.

FAQ title FAQ: Ayn Rand's Philosophy of Objectivism

FAQ location alt.philosophy.objectivism, sci.philosophy.meta, sci.philosophy.tech, alt.answers, news.answers, sci.answers.

Other information resources Objectivism Resource Guide

Archive site None.

Related groups sci.philosophy.meta, sci.philosophy.tech

alt.politics.ec ★★

The politics and economics of the European union. Of interest to anyone pondering the future of the European union.

Typical recent postings Internet Journal of Government Relations, Euro-Skepticism, France Is a Terrorist Country.

Review A low-volume work that seems to consist mainly of lengthy manifestos, followed by a smattering of replies that are as iconoclastic as they are erudite. No wonder Europeans are having such a tough time unifying their continent!

Advice to newbies Read the FAQ before posting (but frankly, this newsgroup could use some life).

Adult-oriented? No.

Readership 6,700.

Rank 2,118.

Messages per month 127.

Crossposting percentage 58%.

Availability 41% of USENET sites.

Moderated? No.

Special features None.

FAQ title European Union Basics (FAQ)

FAQ location alt.politics.ec, talk.politics.misc, alt.answers, talk.answers, news.answers

Other information resources None.

Archive site None.

Related groups alt.politics.europe, soc.culture.europe

alt.polyamory ★★★

Loving more than one person. Of interest to anyone troubled by polyamorous feelings—or enthusiastic about them.

Typical recent postings Sexual Exclusivity and Ownership, Gender-Neutral Pronouns, From Primary to Secondary.

Review Open discussion of the polyamorous life and the issues it raises, peppered frequently with juvenile posts from clueless college sophomores. (The freshmen are reading alt.sex!).

Advice to newbies Please read the FAQ carefully before posting.

Adult-oriented? There's very little discussion of explicit sex, but very much concerning adult situations.

Readership 21,000.

Rank 1,269.

Messages per month 306.

Crossposting percentage 4%.

Availability 52% of USENET sites.

Moderated? No.

Special features Post personals to alt.polyamory.personals.

FAQ title alt.polyamory Frequently Asked Questions (FAQ)

FAQ location alt.polyamory, alt.answers, news.answers

Other information resources alt.polyamory Frequently Asked Questions (FAQ)—Supplement

Archive site None.

Related groups alt.polyamory.personals

alt.privacy ★★★★

The corporate and governmental abuse of privacy rights in the U.S. Of interest to anyone concerned about the erosion of privacy in the U.S.

Typical recent postings National ID Card Returns, UPS Digital Signature, Weekly SSN Request, Digital Telephony Bill Imminent.

Review One of USENET's better discussion groups, this one often features substantive posts filled with facts, figures, and cogent argument. The discussion is on a high level—with the exception of infrequent idiotic posts from conspiracy nuts—and includes many people who are very well informed concerning the relevant issues.

Advice to newbies Posts are welcome *if* they contain substantive material—describe privacy abuses in detail, and support your contentions with facts and figures.

Adult-oriented? No.

Readership 54,000.

Rank 465.

Messages per month 435.

Crossposting percentage 38%.

Availability 61% of USENET sites.

Moderated? No.

Special features None.

FAQ title Privacy and Anonymity on the Internet (FAQ)

FAQ location alt.privacy, misc.consumers, alt.answers, news.answers, misc.answers

Other information resources Junk Mail FAQ; Anonymity on the Internet (FAQ); The Great USENET Piss List Monthly Posting (list of companies that take regular urine samples for drug abuse).

Archive site None.

Related groups misc.consumers, alt.privacy.anon-server, alt.privacy.clipper, comp.privacy, comp.society.privacy

alt.pub.dragons-inn ★★

An experiment in collective fiction-writing, based on a fantasy setting called Generica (after a role-playing game that proffers a "generic fantasy city"). Each thread in the collective story details one aspect of the narrative, such as the search by the guard Kron for his missing sister. Of interest to those interested in exploring the dynamics of collective storytelling in a very specific fantasy setting.

Typical recent postings Mimi's Story, Introducing MYR ur VINNGLY, Miif's Continuing Journey.

Review An interesting experiment in collective storytelling, but it's definitely an acquired taste: You'd have to do a lot of preparation in order to participate.

Advice to newbies If you're an active RPG player and know the Generica setting well, check out the FAQs and give it a try. Otherwise, forget it.

Adult-oriented? Some of the stories deal with adult situations.

Readership 17,000.

Rank 1,414.

Messages per month 127.

Crossposting percentage 0%.

Availability 50% of USENET sites.

Moderated? No.

Special features This isn't a newsgroup—it's a collective writing experiment.

FAQ title MiniFAQ: New Users Please Read; Frequently Asked Questions

FAQ location alt.pub.dragons-inn

Other information resources Bulletin Board, Character Summaries, History of Nexus, The Directory of Generica

Archive site None.

Related groups alt.pub.amethyst

alt.quotations ★★★★

Quotations of all sorts—quotes from movies, plays, books, TV shows, lectures, literature, and Famous Last Words. Of interest to anyone who appreciates quotations and, especially, writers who can use them in their work.

Typical recent postings Ayn Rand Quotes, Golf Quotes, Rush Limbaugh on Feminism, Birthday Quotes.

Review Here's a great general-interest newsgroup. In an average batch of articles, you'll find several interesting, amusing, and even eye-opening quotes. Food for thought and a few good laughs, to boot.

Advice to newbies Please read the group's FAQ carefully before posting.

Adult-oriented? No.

Readership 27,000.

Rank 1,060.

Messages per month 712.

Crossposting percentage 1%.

Availability 48% of USENET sites.

Moderated? No.

Special features The archive site (see "Archive Site") contains a database of quotations contributed by the group.

FAQ title Quotations Monthly Faq

FAQ location alt.quotations, alt.answers, news.answers

Other information resources List: Movie Quotes (Memorable Quotes from Movies).

Archive site Via anonymous FTP: wilma.cs.brown.edu in the directory pub/alt.quotations/Archive.

Related groups alt.usage.english

alt.religion.all-worlds ★★

The Church of All Worlds (CAW), a neo-pagan organization based loosely on Robert Heinlein's science fiction novel *Stranger in a Strange Land*. CAW emphasizes the eclectic reconstruction of ancient forms of reverence for nature; unlike other forms of neo-Paganism, however, it is future-oriented and actively environmentalist in its politics. Of interest to anyone interested in the neopagan movement.

Typical recent postings Why Are Pagans/Wiccans So Snotty, New Book Listing, What Is All Worlds?

Review The discussion here is undoubtedly of interest to neopagans, but for nonbelievers the impression is of infinite numbers of splinter groups squabbling over trivial points of dogma. For the converted only.

Advice to newbies Please read the newsgroup's FAQ carefully before posting. Flames from evangelical Christians will be ignored.

Adult-oriented? No.

Readership 7,300.

Rank 2,054.

Messages per month 99.

Crossposting percentage 3%.

Availability 42% of USENET sites.

Moderated? No.

Special features None.

FAQ title Church of All Worlds FAQ

FAQ location alt.religion.all-worlds, alt.answers, news.answers

Other information resources None.

Archive site None.

Related groups alt.pagan

alt.romance ★★★★

True love—as distinguished from infatuation on the one hand, and sex on the other. Of interest to anyone who's currently in love, or was once in love, or hopes to be in love.

Typical recent postings Pick-Up Lines List, Flirting Vs. Leering, Lonely, What Women Want, Does An Abusive Father Love You, Worst Movie For A First Date.

Review Lots of good discussion for anyone who's going through the dating scene—and dealing with falling in love.

Advice to newbies Please read the group's FAQ carefully before posting. Flames and juvenile behavior are not welcome.

Adult-oriented? The posts deal with adult situations, but there's very little explicit discussion of sex.

Readership 95,000.

Rank 137.

Messages per month 2,593.

Crossposting percentage 11%.

Availability 62% of USENET sites.

Moderated? No.

Special features The group's multi-part FAQ is an excellent "how-to" manual for establishing and maintaining a loving relationship and should be read by anyone who's been told to Get a Life.

FAQ title alt.romance "FAQ"

FAQ location alt.romance, alt.answers, news.answers

Other information resources None.

Archive site None.

Related groups alt.romance.chat, alt.romance.unhappy

alt.scientology ★★

The Church of Scientology, both pro and con. Of interest to anyone interested in Scientology or, more broadly, the political and legal vicissitudes of an embattled religion.

Typical recent postings Campaign to Ban Scientology in the U.K., Introduction to Scientology Ethics, Gays in Scientology, Scientologist Loses Court Case.

Review In this newsgroup, you'll find discussion of Scientology both pro and con, with some posts providing supporting facts and argumentation—but there's a fair amount of kookiness, too, and irrelevant crossposting.

Advice to newbies Whether you're pro or con when it comes to Scientology, you'd be well advised to read *both* of the FAQs—you'll have a sharper sense of the issues involved, and your participation will be much more valuable.

Adult-oriented? No.

Readership N/A.

Rank N/A.

Messages per month N/A.

Crossposting percentage N/A.

Availability N/A.

Moderated? No.

Special features None.

FAQ title Perhaps indicative of Scientology's controversial nature, there's both a "pro" FAQ (FAQ: alt.religion.scientology Users) and a "skeptics" FAQ (Non-Scientologist FAQ: alt.religion.scientology)

FAQ location alt.religion.scientology, alt.answers, news.answers

Other information resources Books and Tapes on Scientology, Scientology Codes and Creeds, alt.religion.scientology Organizations, alt.religion.scientology User's Catechism, NonScientologist Access FAQ

Archive site None.

Related groups None.

alt.security ★★★★

All aspects of computer security, including preventing snoopers from undeleting files, dealing with crackers, warding off viruses, and encrypting sensitive data. Of interest to anyone who's personally or professionally concerned with computer security issues, broadly defined.

Typical recent postings Win 3.1 and DOS 6.x Security, Pretty Good Privacy, OS Security Ratings, Virus on CD-ROM.

Review This group is well worth reading if you're concerned about security issues: You'll find that among the people posting to this group are some of the most technically astute computer security experts in the world.

Advice to newbies Apart from queries, you'd better know what you're talking about if you post here—the discussions are on a technically sophisticated level.

Adult-oriented? No.

Readership 100,000.

Rank 109.

Messages per month 521.

Crossposting percentage 39%.

Availability 69% of USENET sites.

Moderated? No.

Special features None.

FAQ title None.

FAQ location N/A.

Other information resources computer-security compromise FAQ, computer-security anonymous-ftp FAQ, computer-security vendor-contacts FAQ, computer-security security-patches FAQ, Computer Security Frequently Asked Questions

Archive site None.

Related groups alt.security.index, alt.security.keydist, alt.security.pgp

alt.security.pgp ★★★

Pretty Good Privacy, a freely redistributable encryption technology that's intended to counter the U.S. government's attempts to keep secure encryption technologies out of public hands. Of interest to anyone interested in the issues raised by the public distribution of encryption technologies in general and PGP in particular.

Typical recent postings Security of PGP, France Bans Encryption, PGP and Morality, Clarification of PGP Versions.

Review This is the place to go for intelligent, informed discussion of the PGP algorithm, its potential impact on the Internet, and the issues raised by the public distribution of secure encryption technologies.

Advice to newbies If you're not sure what PGP is, read the group's FAQ before posting.

Adult-oriented? No.

Readership 46,000.

Rank 592.

Messages per month 1,800.

Crossposting percentage 11%.

Availability 60% of USENET sites.

Moderated? No.

Special features None.

FAQ title alt.security.pgp FAQ

FAQ location alt.security.pgp, alt.answers, news.answers

Other information resources Where to Get the Latest PGP

Archive site You can obtain Pretty Good Privacy from an archive at MIT; see "Where to Get the Latest PGP" for details.

Related groups alt.security, alt.security.ripem

alt.sex ★★★★★

Of interest to anyone with questions about sex.

Typical recent postings Low Fat Effects on Libido, Yes—Size Does Matter, Swallowing During Oral Sex, Songs About Masturbation.

Review Here it is, folks—USENET's most popular newsgroup, apart from rec.announce.newusers. Does it derive its popularity from the quality of discussion—or from lurid interest in the subject matter? Both, probably, but the discussion deserves credit, too. This group can do good work in dispelling common myths about sexuality, particularly for people too shy to ask questions in any other forum. Unless you're *very* experienced, there's always something new to learn in alt.sex. One of USENET's best!

Advice to newbies Be careful about posting here—it could have unwanted repercussions—for instance, if you're a female, you could get unwanted email. Try the anonymous posting service if you're worried about the risks. Please read the group's FAQ before posting to avoid asking questions that have been posed before.

Adult-oriented? Yes.

Readership 290,000.

Rank 4.

Messages per month 4,867.

Crossposting percentage 19%.

Availability 60% of USENET sites.

Moderated? No.

Special features Anonymous posting service.

FAQ title alt.sex FAQ

FAQ location alt.sex, alt.answers, news.answers

Other information resources Welcome to alt.sex

Archive site None.

Related groups   alt.binaries.pictures.erotica, alt.sex.bestiality, alt.sex.bondage, alt.sex.homosexual, alt.sex.masturbation, alt.sex.motss, alt.sex.movies, alt.sex.stories, alt.sex.stories.d, alt.sex.wanted, alt.sex.wizards, rec.arts.erotica

alt.sex.bondage ★★★

Kinks: Bondage and discipline, sadism and masochism, dominance and submission. Of interest to anyone curious about BDSM lifestyles—and lots of people are, apparently.

Typical recent postings   About Handcuffs, Japanese Bondage, Tease Tease Pretty Please, Top Ten Unanswered Questions About BDSM.

Review   Another of USENET's most popular groups—and since the proportion of S&M aficionados in the population must be in the single digits, the group's popularity is best explained by sheer voyeurism. There's a fair amount of discussion, though, for anyone who's really interested in such matters.

Advice to newbies   Be careful about posting here—it could have unwanted repercussions. For instance, if you're a female, you could get unwanted email. Try the anonymous posting service if you're worried about the risks. Please read the FAQ before posting—it may answer your question for you.

Adult-oriented?   Yes.

Readership   180,000.

Rank   20.

Messages per month   4,722.

Crossposting percentage   5%.

Availability   57% of USENET sites.

Moderated?   No.

Special features   To post personal ads, use alt.personals.bondage.

FAQ title   The alt.sex.bondage FAQ List

FAQ location   alt.sex.bondage, alt.answers, news.answers

Other information resources   None.

Archive site   None.

Related groups   alt.binaries.pictures.erotica, alt.sex.bestiality, alt.sex.bondage, alt.sex.homosexual, alt.sex.masturbation, alt.sex.motss, alt.sex.movies, alt.sex.stories, alt.sex.stories.d, alt.sex.wanted, alt.sex.wizards, rec.arts.erotica

alt.sex.movies ★★

Adult movies—their miserable plots, laughable acting, and (infrequently) sexy scenes. For fans of adult movies—and if video rental industry figures are accurate, there are lots of them.

Typical recent postings   Fake Breasts, Cindy From Brady Bunch, Porno Satellite Channels, Pornography and Censorship on Larry King.

Review   Hey, I'll save you some time. Are you curious to know whether adult movies are sexy? According to the posts in this group, about 99% of them aren't.

Advice to newbies   Be careful about posting here—it could have unwanted repercussions. Try the anonymous posting service if you're worried about the risks.

Adult-oriented?   Yes.

Readership   110,000.

Rank   83.

Messages per month   1,847.

Crossposting percentage   6%.

Availability   53% of USENET sites.

Moderated?   No.

Special features   Anonymous posting service.

FAQ title   None.

FAQ location   N/A.

Other information resources   None.

Archive site   None.

Related groups   None.

alt.sex.stories ★

Fiction that some apparently find erotic. Of interest to those who appreciate erotic fiction no matter how terrible it is, plus a very sizable (apparently) number of weirdos who get off on stories concerning murder, rape, and cannibalism. Get help.

Typical recent postings   My Sex Slave, Cannibals, Pony Girls, Mary's Last Day.

Review   An unmoderated group for erotic fiction, alt.sex.stories isn't supposed to contain discussion posts (they're supposed to go to alt.sex.stories.d), but the message just hasn't gotten through. As for the fiction, some of it's of passable quality, but there's a very disturbing number of "snuff" stories—there can't be *that* many people who get turned on by this junk, can there? One reader of the newsgroup speculated that this material is being placed in the group as part of a "sting" operation that would shut down the entire alt.sex.* hierarchy.

Advice to newbies   Check out rec.arts.erotica instead—it's a moderated group. There's less noise, and perhaps some of the fiction is of better quality.

Adult-oriented?   Yes.

Readership   270,000.

Rank   9.

Messages per month   2,283.

Crossposting percentage   5%.

Availability   53% of USENET sites.

Moderated?   No.

Special features   None.

FAQ title   FAQ: alt.sex.stories & alt.sex.stories.d

FAQ location   alt.sex.stories, alt.sex.stories.d

Other information resources   None.

Archive site   None.

Related groups   alt.sex.stories.d, alt.sex

alt.sex.wanted ★

Requests for copies of erotic stories, for FTP sites that have erotic GIFS, for email exchanges of a sexual nature, and for real life (RL) sexual contacts. Of interest to those horny to the point of doing something imbecilic.

Typical recent postings   Florida Ladies To Exchange Email, Newbie Slave Mistress, Erotic Email Wanted.

Review   Could anyone possibly get anything other than a lot of prank email from posting here? Personally, I doubt it.

Advice to newbies   Be careful about posting here—it could have unwanted repercussions. For instance, if you're a female, you could get unwanted email (in very large quantities!). Try the anonymous posting service if you're worried about the risks. Please read the group's FAQ before posting to avoid asking questions that have been posed before.

Adult-oriented?   Yes.

Readership   44,000.

Rank   630.

Messages per month   1,182.

Crossposting percentage 7%.

Availability 44% of USENET sites.

Moderated? No.

Special features None.

FAQ title alt.sex.wanted FAQ

FAQ location alt.sex.wanted, alt.answers, news.answers

Other information resources None.

Archive site None.

Related groups alt.sex.services, alt.sex

alt.sexual.abuse.recovery ★★★

All aspects of recovering from sexual abuse, including self-inflicted injuries, multiple personalities, confronting perpetrators, dealing with holidays, self-defense, nightmares, and healing. Of interest to anyone recovering from sexual abuse.

Typical recent postings Jokes Between Friends—How Can I Stop Them Making Me Feel So Upset, A Poem, Feeling Screwed Up, Psychology and Support Groups Newsgroup Pointer, Anger, Poem—Of Hope.

Review This is a valuable and supportive group for anyone who has suffered the torment of sexual abuse.

Advice to newbies Please do not post to this group unless you need the support that it offers. This is not the place for juvenile behavior.

Adult-oriented? No.

Readership 37,000.

Rank 772.

Messages per month 2,063.

Crossposting percentage 1%.

Availability 55% of USENET sites.

Moderated? No.

Special features Anonymous posting service.

FAQ title Bi-Weekly ASAR FAQ list posting

FAQ location alt.sexual.abuse.recovery

Other information resources None.

Archive site None.

Related groups alt.sexual.abuse.recovery.d

alt.shenanigans ★★★★

Harmless practical jokes, tricks, and silliness—shenanigans. If the victim can laugh at it and at himself or herself, it's a shenanigan, not a prank. Of interest to anyone who likes a good laugh—without hurting anyone.

Typical recent postings A Shen for Kids, The World's Best Car Shen, How To Stop Noisy Apartment Neighbors.

Review Great fun. I learned a great trick to play on those telemarketers—bet *they* won't call back!

Advice to newbies Please read the FAQ before posting.

Adult-oriented? No.

Readership 28,000.

Rank 1,029.

Messages per month 983.

Crossposting percentage 3%.

Availability 51% of USENET sites.

Moderated? No.

Special features None.

FAQ title alt.shenanigans—FAQ and guidelines for posting

FAQ location alt.shenanigans, alt.answers, news.answers

Other information resources None

Archive site   Via anonymous FTP to elf.TN.Cornell.EDU, in the /shenanigans directory. **Note:** This archive may have been forced to move by the time this book appears, so check the latest FAQ for the current archive location.

Related groups   None.

alt.sources ★★

Source code—computer programs that have not yet been compiled into executable programs. You'll find source code here for every conceivable computer platform, from PCs to UNIX-based workstations and minicomputers. Unlike the comp.sources.* newsgroups, alt.sources is unmoderated—the programs you're seeing here haven't been approved by anyone. Of interest to programmers, particularly UNIX programmers.

Typical recent postings   USENET Readers, XWD with 24-Bit Support, UNIX Xmodems.

Review   A low-volume group that doesn't have much to offer in these days of freely available binary files; still, a good place to check periodically if you're a programmer—particularly a UNIX programmer—and looking for programming ideas.

Advice to newbies   Please do not post requests for source code here; the proper place for such requests is alt.sources.wanted. For discussion of the posted code, see alt.sources.d.

Adult-oriented?   No.

Readership   130,000.

Rank   56.

Messages per month   217.

Crossposting percentage   15%.

Availability   74% of USENET sites.

Moderated?   No.

Special features   None.

FAQ title   None.

FAQ location   N/A.

Other information resources   Welcome to alt.sources!

Archive site   None.

Related groups   alt.sources, alt.sources.amiga, alt.sources.amiga.d, alt.sources.d, alt.sources.index, alt.sources.mac, alt.sources.mac.d, alt.sources.patches, alt.sources.wanted, aus.sources, bionet.software.sources, comp.sources.b, comp.sources.acorn, comp.sources.amiga, comp.sources.apple, comp.sources.atari.st, comp.sources.bugs, comp.sources.d, comp.sources.games, comp.sources.games.bugs, comp.sources.hp, comp.sources.misc, comp.sources.postscript, comp.sources.Reviewed, comp.sources.testers, comp.sources.unix, comp.sources.wanted, comp.sources.x

alt.sources.mac ★★

Source code—computer programs that have not yet been compiled into executable programs. You'll find source code, including HyperTalk scripts, for Macintosh computers in this newsgroup. Unlike the comp.sources.* newsgroups, alt.sources is unmoderated—the programs you're seeing here haven't been approved by anyone. Of interest to Macintosh programmers and hobbyists.

Typical recent postings   ResFork Utilities, The Game of Life, Laser Prep File.

Review   Like alt.sources, alt.sources.mac seems moribund in these days of freely available binary files, but Macintosh programmers may still find things of interest here.

Advice to newbies   Please do not post requests for source code here; the proper place for such requests is alt.sources.wanted. For discussion of the posted code, see alt.sources.d.

Adult-oriented?   No.

Readership   16,000.

Rank: 1,477.

Messages per month   86.

Crossposting percentage   10%.

Availability   55% of USENET sites.

Moderated?   No.

Special features   None.

FAQ title   alt.sources.mac FAQ

FAQ location   alt.sources.mac, alt.answers, news.answers

Other information resources   None.

Archive site   Several sites archive alt.sources.mac postings: sumex-aim.stanford.edu-/infomac/dev/src; ftp.apple.com - /dts/mac; nic.switch.ch - /software/mac/src; and ftp.acns.nwu.edu (129.105.16.52) - /pub.

Related groups   alt.sources, alt.sources.amiga, alt.sources.amiga.d, alt.sources.d, alt.sources.index, alt.sources.mac, alt.sources.mac.d, alt.sources.patches, alt.sources.wanted, aus.sources, bionet.software.sources, comp.sources.b, comp.sources.acorn, comp.sources.amiga, comp.sources.apple, comp.sources.atari.st, comp.sources.bugs, comp.sources.d, comp.sources.games, comp.sources.games.bugs, comp.sources.hp, comp.sources.misc, comp.sources.postscript, comp.sources.Reviewed, comp.sources.testers, comp.sources.unix, comp.sources.wanted, comp.sources.x

alt.startrek.creative ★★★

Original fiction penned by Star Trek fans, including stories, parodies, poems, "treknology," and timelines. Of interest to Star Trek fans.

Typical recent postings   Star Trek—The Female Perspective, 10 Ways To Bring Back Tasha Yar, BarTrek, ST-The Lousy Generation.

Review   If you're a Star Trek fan, you'll find plenty of fun stuff here. Many of the stories are not terribly well written, since they're amateur efforts—but the price is right!

Advice to newbies   Please read the FAQ before posting. Note that this newsgroup is for stories, not discussion.

Adult-oriented?   No.

Readership   55,000.

Rank   441.

Messages per month   751.

Crossposting percentage   7%.

Availability   59% of USENET sites.

Moderated?   No.

Special features   None.

FAQ title   What is alt.startrek.creative?

FAQ location   alt.startrek.creative

Other information resources   Star Trek Story archive FAQ

Archive site   There's an archive of Star Trek stories, accessible via anonymous FTP, at ftp.cis.ksu.edu (129.130.10.83) in the directory /pub/alt.startrek.creative.

Related groups   rec.arts.startrek.misc, alt.startrek.klingon

alt.suicide.holiday ★★

Not a support group, this newsgroup is better described as a repository for ranting and raving as an alternative to killing yourself—but if you're intent on doing so, you'll probably find clear instructions. Of interest to anyone with an affection for black humor.

Typical recent postings Fear of Dying, Get Yourself Diagnosed Before Considering Suicide, I Can't Go On, Damn It All.

Review If you're looking for the darkest possible humor, look here—and if you're really thinking about doing yourself in, you'll find that there are plenty of good Samaritans lurking around to help.

Advice to newbies Please *don't* read the group's FAQ!

Adult-oriented? No.

Readership 34,000.

Rank 852.

Messages per month 881.

Crossposting percentage 7%.

Availability 57% of USENET sites.

Moderated? No.

Special features None.

FAQ title alt.suicide.holiday periodic Methods File posting

FAQ location alt.suicide.holiday, alt.answers, news.answers

Other information resources None.

Archive site None.

Related groups alt.suicide.finals

alt.support.depression ★★★★

A newsgroup for people who suffer from any form of depression as well as for those who want to learn more about depression. Information posted in the group comes from individuals who have suffered from depression as well as from professionals in the field. Of interest to anyone who is depressed or has a depressed family member or friend.

Typical recent postings Criteria for Depression, I'm Afraid, The Prozac Cowboys, Relationship Breakup.

Review Clinical depression is a very different matter than the ordinary blues, which everyone suffers from now and then. Reading this group can give you a good idea of what that difference entails, enabling you to recognize when you or someone in your family is clinically depressed.

Advice to newbies Please read the group's FAQ before posting to avoid asking questions that have been posed before.

Adult-oriented? No.

Readership 8,800.

Rank 1,923.

Messages per month 1,723.

Crossposting percentage 4%.

Availability 35% of USENET sites.

Moderated? No.

Special features The group's multi-part FAQ contains a wealth of invaluable information on depression and should not be missed by anyone with interest in the subject.

FAQ title Alt.Support.Depression FAQ (five parts).

FAQ location alt.support.depression

Other information resources Depression Book List

Archive site An FTP site at Temple University containing articles related to depression is ftp 129.32.32.98 in the directory /pub/psych.

Related groups alt.support.phobias, sci.psychology, sci.med, sci.med.psychobiology

alt.support.diet ★★★★

This newsgroup provides emotional support, encouragement, and practical advice to those who wish to improve their health, appearance, and self-image image through a weight loss or weight maintenance program.

Typical recent postings I Want to Be a Loser!, Taco Bell Blues, Surgical Options Explored, Nighttime Munchies, Tips to Keep It Off.

Review An extremely valuable newsgroup that should be placed on the subscription list of anyone trying to lose weight.

Advice to newbies Please read the group's FAQ before posting to avoid asking questions that have been posed before.

Adult-oriented? No.

Readership 25,000.

Rank 1,129.

Messages per month 683.

Crossposting percentage 6%.

Availability 54% of USENET sites.

Moderated? No.

Special features The group's multi-part FAQ contains a wealth of important and valuable information.

FAQ title alt.support.diet FAQ

FAQ location alt.support.diet, alt.answers, news.answers

Other information resources None.

Archive site None.

Related groups alt.support.obesity, alt.support.eating-disord

alt.tasteless ★

The gross—the bloodier, the smellier, and the squickier the better. Of interest to those who never grew out of the anal stage.

Typical recent postings The Booger That Refused to Die, A Visit to the Zoo, Boils, Lymph Node Wigs Out, Which Way Would You Like to Be Executed, Shitting at Work, Dick Flop Survey, Renaissance of the Choad.

Review Not for everyone—to put it mildly. Old Guard posters fiercely promote the writing of high-quality—and, above all, original—descriptions of gross events, and viciously flame what they regard to be inferior quality. Speaking of flames, one or more of the individuals involved in this group boast of posting trolls to groups such as rec.pets.cats; it might be wise to obtain the group's Who's Who and add the names therein to your kill file.

Advice to newbies Don't post here until you've read the group for a while and read the FAQ carefully. Even then, expect to be flamed. Get counseling.

Adult-oriented? Yes.

Readership 72,000.

Rank 261.

Messages per month 2,135.

Crossposting percentage 10%.

Availability 57% of USENET sites.

Moderated? No.

Special features Intermittent surveys of alt.tasteless participants, with the none-too-surprising results posted in summaries.

FAQ title Welcome to alt.tasteless! monthly posting.

FAQ location Alt.tasteless, alt. answers, news.answers

Other information resources The alt.tasteless Who's Who (monthly posting).

Archive site Ostensibly, fnovhtu.tu-graz.ac.at /pub/tasteles (yup, just one s at the end). There was nothing in the archive when I logged on.

Related groups alt.binaries.pictures.tasteless

alt.usage.english ★★★★

English, its peculiarities, usage, pitfalls, and many inconsistencies.

Typical recent postings -Able and Ible, Subjunctive, Punctuation In Quotes, Lying vs. Laying.

Review Anyone interested in the English language—writers, editors, readers, speakers, and students—will find this newsgroup interesting, diverting, and sometimes educational.

Advice to newbies This is a friendly group that welcomes any substantive post or follow-up, but please read the group's FAQ to avoid asking questions that have been posed previously.

Adult-oriented? No.

Readership 48,000.

Rank 556.

Messages per month 2,042.

Crossposting percentage 9%.

Availability 60% of USENET sites.

Moderated? No.

Special features None.

FAQ title alt.usage.english FAQ

FAQ location alt.usage.english, alt.answers, news.answers

Other information resources None.

Archive site None.

Related groups misc.education.language.english

alt.usenet.kooks ★★

Quoted examples of some of the weirdest, most offensive, or genuinely crazy stuff that's posted to USENET.

Typical recent postings More Sukru Spoo, What Makes a Kook a Kook.

Review If you're curious about some of the nutcases who pelt the Net with idiocy, here's the place to look. Where else can you run across a post that contains the assertion, "Death is so considerable a gate that it can accomplish everybody?" Use this newsgroup as a means to build a well-proportioned author kill file, but don't kill the people who forward stuff here.

Advice to newbies To post to this group, you need to quote something genuinely nutty that you've run across. Don't forward other people's posts without their permission.

Adult-oriented? No.

Readership 12,000.

Rank 1,680.

Messages per month 1,496.

Crossposting percentage 34%.

Availability 39% of USENET sites.

Moderated? No.

FAQ title Net.Legends.FAQ (Noticeable Phenomena of USENET) Part*/*

FAQ location alt.folklore.computers, alt.usenet.kooks, alt.answers, news.answers

Other information resources None.

Archive site None.

Related groups alt.folklore.computers

alt.uu.future ★★★

The future of the Global Network Academy (GNA), a World Wide Web venture that plans to offer university-level courses online.

Typical recent postings Editor—Course Manual, Tentative Budgets for GNA and MSET, GNA Board of Directors' Election Results.

Review Of interest to anyone concerned about the GNA's direction and future, this newsgroup provides an opportunity for any Internet users to participate in GNA's planning process.

Advice to newbies Please familiarize yourself with GNA and its goals before participating.

Adult-oriented? No.

Readership 12,000.

Rank 1,704.

Messages per month 140.

Crossposting percentage 1%.

Availability 51% of USENET sites.

Moderated? No.

Special features None.

FAQ title Globewide Network Academy FAQ, plain text version.

FAQ location alt.uu.future, alt.education.distance, alt.answers, news.answers

Other information resources GNA on the World Wide Web

Archive site None.

Related groups alt.education.distance, alt.uu.tools

alt.visa.us ★★★

Immigrant and non-immigrant visas to the U.S. Of interest to anyone attempting to obtain a visa to the U.S.

Typical recent postings Canadian Permanent Residence, Parents Sponsoring Children, Hints for Writing a Waiver Application, Alternatives to Employment Based on Green Card, Birth Certificate Info.

Review This newsgroup offers valuable information and discussion for anyone trying to navigate the INS maze; be sure to read the group's FAQ carefully.

Advice to newbies Please read the group's FAQ before posting to avoid asking questions that have been posed before.

Adult-oriented? No.

Readership 22,000.

Rank 1,232.

Messages per month 709.

Crossposting percentage 7%.

Availability 51% of USENET sites.

Moderated? No.

Special features The group's six-part FAQ is a gold mine of information on obtaining U.S. visas.

FAQ title alt.visa.us FAQ

FAQ location alt.visa.us, alt.answers, news.answers

Other information resources None.

Archive site ftp.cs.umd.edu:/pub/cyrillic/us_visas/

Related groups None.

alt.war.civil.usa ★★★

The United States Civil War (1861-65), including military, political, social, economic or other factors that shaped this period of history. This newsgroup also serves as a source of information, assistance, or referral for persons seeking guidance via responses from more knowledgeable contributors.

Typical recent postings Confederate Flag, Alternate histories…, Gettysburg Visit, Grant's Memoirs,

Secession and Morality, Key Confederate Errors at Gettysburg.

Review   If you're interested in the Civil War, this newsgroup will quickly come to the fore in your subscription list. You'll find knowledgeable contributors and intelligent discussion concerning every aspect of the conflict.

Adult-oriented?   No.

Readership   13,000.

Rank   1,655.

Messages per month   893.

Crossposting percentage   0%.

Availability: 53% of USENET sites.

Moderated?   No.

Special features   None.

FAQ title   U.S. Civil War FAQ

FAQ location   alt.war.civil.usa, alt.answers, news.answers

Other information resources   U.S. Civil War Reading List

Archive site   None.

Related groups   alt.war, alt.war.vietnam

alt.wedding ★★★

Getting married—where and when to do it, who to invite, what to serve, what to wear—the works. Of interest to anyone planning a wedding.

Typical recent postings   Gold vs. Silver Rings, Who NOT to Invite to Shower, Received Invitation—Don't Know Them!!!!, Wedding Stress, Videographers.

Review   If you're planning a wedding, this group will form a useful adjunct to the planning process.

You'll share information with lots of people who share your predicament!

Advice to newbies   Please read the group's FAQ before posting to avoid asking questions that have been posed before.

Adult-oriented?   No.

Readership   19,000.

Rank   1,333.

Messages per month   1,840.

Crossposting percentage   0%.

Availability   48% of USENET sites.

Moderated?   No.

Special features   None.

FAQ title   FAQ: alt.wedding

FAQ location   alt.wedding, rec.video, rec.video.production

Other information resources   None.

Archive site   None.

Related groups   rec.video, rec.video.production

alt.whistleblowing

Claims and accusations leveled against individuals or organizations, glorified as a courageous, commendable, and exceedingly dangerous pursuit. Of interest to anyone who's thinking about blowing the whistle on wrongdoing of any kind.

Typical recent postings   Whistleblowing Laws, What Should I Do?

Review   This is the place to raise discussion of scientific fraud, government abuse, and commercial illegalities, whether contributed by USENET posters or published in the mainstream media. You'll find support for whistleblowers here and discussion of the legal, ethical, and political issues raised by whistleblowing.

Advice to newbies   Please read the group's FAQ very carefully before posting. In particular, be aware that defamatory statements in this newsgroup could bring you serious legal problems.

Adult-oriented?   No.

Readership   5,200.

Rank   2,319.

Messages per month   37.

Crossposting percentage   37%.

Availability   37% of USENET sites.

Moderated?   No.

Special features   None.

FAQ title   alt.whistleblowing FAQ

FAQ location   alt.whistleblowing, alt.answers, news.answers

Other information resources   None.

Archive site   None.

Related groups   None.

alt.wired ★★★★★

Wired, the magazine—the articles, the authors, the issues the magazine raises. Not just for fans of the mag; it's of interest to anyone concerned about the cultural, political, and economic issues raised by the development of worldwide computer networking.

Typical recent postings   Libel and the Net, Amiga's Upcoming Advanced Architecture, Neurophone, Cool Web Sites.

Review   Not sponsored by *Wired*, this newsgroup offers entertaining and thought-provoking discussion of the issues raised by the rise of global computer networking. One of USENET's best!

Advice to newbies   Please read the group's FAQ before posting to avoid asking questions that have been posed before.

Adult-oriented?   No.

Readership   27,000.

Rank   1,059.

Messages per month   1,630.

Crossposting percentage   10%.

Availability   47% of USENET sites.

Moderated?   No.

Special features   None.

FAQ title   alt.wired FAQ

FAQ location   alt.wired

Other information resources   None.

Archive site   *Wired* has a World Wide Web home page at http://www.wired.com.

Related groups   None.

alt.zines ★★★★

Zany, often self-published, low-circulation magazines that emphasize the irreverent, the exotic, and the bizarre. Of interest to anyone who finds zines amusing or even important as outlets for alternative writing.

Typical recent postings   Primordial Soup Kitchen Catalog, National Socialist 'zines, Underground Press Convention, Announcing New Edition of Cyberkind.

Review   Many are produced in traditional print media, but many e-zines are available in electronic form. This newsgroup provides news and reviews concerning both types of 'zines.

Adult-oriented?   Yes.

Readership   24,000.

Rank   1,159.

Messages per month   395.

Crossposting percentage   20%.

Availability   52% of USENET sites.

Moderated?   No.

Special features   E-zines are occasionally posted to this group.

FAQ title   Zines on the Internet

FAQ location   alt.zines, alt.answers

Other information resources   Net-Letter Guide

Archive site   None.

Related groups   alt.etext, misc.writing, rec.mag, alt.internet.services

biz.books.technical ★★★

Books on technical subjects, especially UNIX, including reviews and announcements of recent publications. Of interest to those who wish to learn more about UNIX and the Internet.

Typical recent postings   New Unix Book, Cellular Secrets, Copyright Reform Protects Unpublished Work.

Review   This newsgroup contains product announcements from publishers and authors, as well as book reviews, some of which are contributed by the authors themselves!

Advice to newbies   For reviews that at least ought to be unbiased, check out alt.books.reviews.

Adult-oriented?   No.

Readership   20,000.

Rank   1,297.

Messages per month   75.

Crossposting percentage   47%.

Availability   45% of USENET sites.

Moderated?   No.

Special features   The Book Review Index, one of this newsgroup's informational postings, lists the book reviews that will soon be available at an archive site.

FAQ title   None.

FAQ location   N/A.

Other information resources   Book Review Index

Archive site   See "Special features" item.

Related groups   alt.books.reviews, rec.arts.books, misc.books.technical

comp.archives ★★★★★

News regarding new and interesting files accessible through anonymous FTP. Of interest to anyone who wants to find valuable information on the Internet.

Typical recent postings   New Night Bird Screen Saver, Macintosh MOO Distribution, Backgammon for UNIX.

Review   One of USENET's best, this moderated newsgroup contains nothing but announcements of new and interesting files available via anonymous FTP. Don't miss it!

Advice to newbies   For information on FTP, see "Other informational resources" item.

Adult-oriented?   No.

Readership   110,000.

Rank   102.

Messages per month   466.

Crossposting percentage   2%.

Availability   83% of USENET sites.

Moderated?   Yes.

Special features List of anonymous FTP sites (see "Other information resources" item).

FAQ title comp.archives.msdos.announce FAQ (Frequently Asked Questions)

FAQ location comp.archives.msdos.announce, comp.archives.msdos.d, comp.answers, news.answers

Other information resources Anonymous FTP FAQ, and an 11-part Anonymous FTP Site List contains information about FTP sites, and the files they offer.

Archive site None.

Related groups comp.archives.msdos.announce

comp.archives.msdos.announce ★★★★★

FTP-accessible shareware and public domain programs for MS-DOS computers, including upload announcements from site moderators, the MS-DOS sites' periodical summaries, potential policy statements and downtime warnings, and the MS-DOS FTP site moderators' reports about the connectivity problems with their sites. Of interest to anyone looking for shareware or public domain software on the Internet.

Typical recent postings Bootvirus Detection/Repair, Cut and Paste for DOS Text Modes, A List of MS-DOS FTP Sites and Moderators, Virus Information Summary List, Hypertext.

Review This newsgroup is a one-way, moderated newsgroup that's restricted to announcements from FTP site administrators. This newsgroup is not to be missed by anyone looking for MS-DOS freeware or shareware.

Advice to newbies For information on FTP, see the Anonymous FTP FAQ. Discussion about the programs mentioned in this newsgroup should go to comp.archives.msdos.d.

Adult-oriented? No.

Readership 100,000.

Rank 116.

Messages per month 997.

Crossposting percentage 0%.

Availability 78% of USENET sites.

Moderated? Yes.

Special features The SimTel and Oak archives maintain a library of hundreds of useful MS-DOS and Windows programs. See "Archive site" item.

FAQ title comp.archives.msdos.announce FAQ (Frequently Asked Questions)

FAQ location comp.archives.msdos.announce, comp.archives.msdos.d, comp.answers, news.answers

Other information resources None.

Archive site The SimTel and Oak archives of MS-DOS public domain and shareware programs is mirrored at the following sites:

oak.oakland.edu	141.210.10.117
/SimTel/msdos (prev. /pub/msdos)	
wuarchive.wustl.edu	128.252.135.4
/systems/ibmpc/msdos	
archive.orst.edu 1	28.193.2.13
/pub/mirrors/simtel/msdos	
ftp.uu.net	192.48.96.9
/systems/ibmpc/msdos/simtel20	
ftp.funet.fi	128.214.248.6
/pub/msdos/SimTel	
src.doc.ic.ac.uk	146.169.2.1
/pub/packages/simtel	
ftp.switch.ch	130.59.1.40
/mirror/msdos	
ftp.uni-paderborn.de	131.234.2.32
/pcsoft/msdos	
ftp.technion.ac.il	132.68.1.10
/pub/unsupported/dos/simtel	
archie.au	139.130.4.6
/micros/pc/oak	

nctuccca.edu.tw	140.111.1.10
/PC/simtel	
ftp.nectec.or.th	192.150.251.32
/pub/mirrors/msdos	
ftp.cs.cuhk.hk	137.189.4.57
/pub/simtel/msdos	
ftp.cyf-kr.edu.pl	149.156.1.8
/pub/mirror/msdos	
ftp.sunet.se	130.238.127.3
/pub/pc/mirror/SimTel/msdos	
[[gopher: gopher.oakland.edu	
WWW: http://www.acs.oakland.edu]]	
wuarchive.wustl.edu	128.252.135.4
/systems/ibmpc/garbo	
archie.au	139.130.4.6
/micros/pc/garbo	
nctuccca.edu.tw	140.111.1.10
/PC/garbo	

Related groups comp.archives.msdos.d

---

comp.archives.msdos.d ★★★

Discussion, user reports, and debate concerning the software described in comp.archives.msdos.announce. Of interest to anyone who owns or is contemplating downloading this software.

Typical recent postings Telnet for DOS, DOS Beep at POST Time, Paging Software.

Review This newsgroup will interest you if you're thinking about obtaining and using one of the archived MS-DOS or Windows programs announced in comp.archives.msdos.announce or available from the SimTel or Oak archives. You might also scan it to see users' reports of programs of high quality that you wouldn't have otherwise considered.

Advice to newbies Please read the group's FAQ before posting to avoid asking questions that have been posed before.

Adult-oriented? No.

Readership 65,000.

Rank 331.

Messages per month 533.

Crossposting percentage 6%.

Availability 76% of USENET sites.

Moderated? No.

Special features The SimTel and Oak archives maintain a library of hundreds of useful MS-DOS and Windows programs. See "Archive site" item.

FAQ title None.

FAQ location N/A.

Other information resources Useful MS-DOS Programs at SimTel, Garbo, and Cica.

Archive site See comp.archives.msdos.announce for a list of sites mirroring the SimTel and Oak archives.

Related groups comp.archives.msdos.announce, comp.binaries.ibm.pc.wanted, comp.os.msdos.apps, comp.os.msdos.misc, comp.sys.ibm.pc.misc, comp.os.ms-windows

---

comp.benchmarks ★★★

The measurement—and mismeasurement—of computer and network performance. Of interest to computer professionals involved in the benchmarking business, as well as laypersons who'd like to read intelligent, informed opinions regarding this controversial area.

Typical recent postings FP Performance and Spreadsheets, Winmark Benchmark Availability, PowerPC vs. Pentium Benchmark Test, Pentium Math Performance.

Review Although much of the material discussed in this newsgroup is technical in nature, it's fun to read—particularly when you pick up PC magazines only to be inundated with claims based on benchmarks of various kinds. You'll be a lot more skeptical about such claims after reading this newsgroup for a while.

Advice to newbies   You can post questions here, but please do so only after reading the group's several FAQs.

Adult-oriented?   No.

Readership   75,000.

Rank   247.

Messages per month   270.

Crossposting percentage   40%.

Availability   80% of USENET sites.

Moderated?   No.

Special features   Don't miss Eugene Miya's "Twelve Ways to Fool the Masses with Benchmarks"!

FAQ title   comp.benchmarks Frequently Asked Questions (see Other information resources item for a list).

FAQ location   comp.benchmarks

Other information resources   "Twelve Ways to Fool the Masses with Benchmarks, PERFECT CLUB comp.benchmarks FAQ, Network performance measurement tools comp.benchmarks FAQ, Music to benchmark by comp.benchmarks FAQ, References comp.benchmarks FAQ, Good conceptual benchmarking comp.benchmarks FAQ, Benchmark source info-Intro netiquette comp.benchmarks FAQ, Linpack comp.benchmarks FAQ, Measurement environments comp.benchmarks FAQ, Other misc. benchmarks comp.benchmarks FAQ, RFC 1242 terrminology comp.benchmarks FAQ, Equivalence comp.benchmarks FAQ, New FAQ scaffold comp.benchmarks FAQ, Performance metrics comp.benchmarks FAQ, TPC Transaction Processing Council comp.benchmarks FAQ, SLALOM comp.benchmarks FAQ

Archive site   None.

Related groups   None.

comp.compression ★★★

Every aspect of making files smaller and more economical to store and transport, including image and video compression techniques. Of interest to any computer user trying to figure out how to compress or decompress files.

Typical recent postings   Quantum Compression, SunVideo Cell Compression, Document Binary Image Compression, Lossless Chaotic Compression.

Review   If you're professionally interested in data compression of any type, this group belongs on your subscription list. Compression is of interest to most computer users only when they're not sure which technique to use or where to find a decompression program. Questions about them are best answered by reading the group's extensive FAQs rather than pestering regular readers with HELP!!! questions.

Advice to newbies   If you only want to find a particular compression program for a particular operating system, please read first this newgroup's FAQ and the article "How to find sources" which is regularly posted in.news.answers. If you still can't find the program you need, post your request in comp.binaries.ibm.pc.wanted, comp.os.msdos.apps, comp.sources.wanted, comp.sys.mac.wanted, comp.archives.msdos.d, comp.dsp, or alt.graphics.pixutils.

Adult-oriented?   No.

Readership   84,000.

Rank   187.

Messages per month   486.

Crossposting percentage   7%.

Availability   79% of USENET sites.

Moderated?   No.

Special features   Comp.compression is for general discussion of compression-related issues; comp.compression.research contains more technical material of interest to anyone involved in compression-related research.

FAQ title   comp.compression Frequently Asked Questions

FAQ location   comp.compression, comp.compression.research, comp.answers, news.answers

Other information resources
comp.compression FAQ (reminder), Compression Table—How to Decompress Anything (long).

Archive site   None.

Related groups   comp.compression.research, comp.binaries.ibm.pc.wanted, comp.os.msdos.apps, comp.sources.wanted, comp.sys.mac.wanted, comp.archives.msdos.d, comp.dsp, alt.graphics.pixutils

comp.databases ★★

Everything about databases: Database programs, database search techniques, choosing the right database management program.

Typical recent postings   Multi-user Access Databases, Online Stock Databases, Database Programming and Design, Multilevel Security Databases, Catalog of Free Database Systems.

Review   If you're interested in choosing a database program or in general database issues, this group might be of interest. Users of specific database programs will find more detailed information in the program-specific groups listed in "Related groups."

Advice to newbies   There's no FAQ for this group, but see "Other information resources."

Adult-oriented?   No.

Readership   130,000.

Rank   59.

Messages per month   789.

Crossposting percentage   14%.

Availability   84% of USENET sites.

Moderated?   No.

Special features   None.

FAQ title   None.

FAQ location   N/A.

Other information resources   Catalog of free database systems, comp.databases.paradox_FAQ_Monthly_Update, comp.databases.sybase_Frequently_Asked_Questions_(FAQ)

Archive site   None.

Related groups   alt.comp.databases.xbase.clipper, comp.databases, comp.databases.informix, comp.databases.ingres, comp.databases.ms-access, comp.databases.object, comp.databases.oracle, comp.databases.paradox, comp.databases.pick, comp.databases.rdb, comp.databases.sybase, comp.databases.theory, comp.databases.xbase.fox, comp.databases.xbase.misc, comp.sys.mac.databases

comp.dcom.modems ★★★★

Modems—their speed, modulation protocols, conformity to standards, quality, upgradeability, installation, and configuration. Of interest to anyone contemplating the purchase or use of a computer modem.

Typical recent postings   Windows Comm Setting, Mosaic-PPP-mac&fax modem, Connecting 2 Modems on the Same Computer, Modems with Call Progress Analysis, Using a Modem without Disabling Call Waiting.

Review   This newsgroup is packed with information and debate concerning modems and should be read avidly both by anyone contemplating a purchase or having trouble working with a modem. It's too bad there's no FAQ—the group needs one.

Advice to newbies Check out "Other information sources" for FAQs pertinent to specific modem brands.

Adult-oriented? No.

Readership 160,000.

Rank 26.

Messages per month 2,637.

Crossposting percentage 3%.

Availability 87% of USENET sites.

Moderated? No.

Special features None.

FAQ title Fax/Modems: Practical Peripherals PractiFAQ

FAQ location comp.dcom.modems, comp.dcom.fax, comp.answers, news.answers

Other information resources ZyXel modem FAQ list v, AT&T Paradyne modem FAQ, Digicom modem FAQ, ZyXel U1496 series modems resellers FAQ, MS-Windows COM and Ns16550 UART FAQ, Configuring the Telebit Trailblazer for Use with UNIX

Archive site None.

Related groups comp.dcom.fax, comp.dcom.telecom, comp.sys.att, comp.sys.ibm.pc.hardware, alt.dcom.telecom, comp.sys.mac.comm, comp.sys.ibm.pc.comm

comp.fonts ★★★★

Computer typefaces for every brand of computer—their design, use, availability, and aesthetics. Of interest to people who use fonts in their work.

Typical recent postings Times Roman and Times Bold, Classifying Fonts, Truetype Font for Mac, Converting Fonts from Mac to PC and Back.

Review If you're into desktop publishing or just want to get the most out of your system's fonts, this newsgroup belongs in your subscription list. You'll find intelligent discussion of font choices, reviews of new font packages, help with locating obscure fonts (including non-Indo-European language fonts), and more.

Advice to newbies Please read the group's extensive, computer-specific FAQs before posting.

Adult-oriented? No.

Readership 80,000.

Rank 207.

Messages per month 995.

Crossposting percentage 4%.

Availability 81% of USENET sites.

Moderated? No.

Special features Informative FAQs for all popular computer and OS formats; see "Other information resources."

FAQ title comp.fonts FAQ

FAQ location comp.fonts, comp.answers, news.answers

Other information resources Metafont: All fonts available in .mf format, comp.fonts FAQ: Amiga Info., comp.fonts FAQ: Diffs from last posting, comp.fonts FAQ: General Info (1 3), comp.fonts FAQ: General Info (2 3), comp.fonts FAQ: General Info (3 3), comp.fonts FAQ: MS-DOS Info., comp.fonts FAQ: Macintosh Info., comp.fonts FAQ: NeXT Info., comp.fonts FAQ: OS 2 Info., comp.fonts FAQ: Sun Info., comp.fonts FAQ: Unix Info., comp.fonts FAQ: Utilities, comp.fonts FAQ: Vendor List, comp.fonts FAQ: X11 Info

Archive site None.

Related groups None.

comp.graphics ★★★★

Computer graphics, including graphics programs, graphics techniques such as rendering, graphics hardware, and graphics formats. Of interest to anyone who uses computer graphics.

Typical recent postings Editing Animations, Document Image Analysis, Info on Pattern Recognition, Ray Tracing and 3D Graphics, Graphics Package for Mosaics.

Review Solid, valuable information on every aspect of computer graphics, including book reviews and announcements of useful new packages, make this group unusually rich in information resources. If you're trying to figure out all those mysterious acronyms (JPEG, GIF, TIFF, and more), read the FAQs—and read this group.

Advice to newbies Please read the group's FAQ before posting to avoid asking questions that have been posed before.

Adult-oriented? No.

Readership 190,000.

Rank 18.

Messages per month 1,385.

Crossposting percentage 13%.

Availability 84% of USENET sites.

Moderated? No.

Special features None.

FAQ title comp.graphics Frequently Asked Questions (FAQ)

FAQ location comp.graphics, comp.answers, news.answers

Other information resources JPEG Image Compression: Frequently Asked Questions, Computer Resource Listing: BIWEEKLY, MPEG-FAQ: multimedia compression, Color Space FAQ

Archive site None.

Related groups alt.graphics.pixutils, comp.graphics.algorithms, comp.graphics.animation, comp.graphics.avs, comp.graphics.data-explorer, comp.graphics.explorer, comp.graphics.gnuplot, comp.graphics.opengl, comp.graphics.raytracing, comp.graphics.research, comp.graphics.visualization, comp.os.ms-windows.programmer.graphics, comp.sys.amiga.graphics, comp.sys.mac.graphics, comp.sys.sgi.graphics

comp.graphics.animation ★★★

Computer animation—making pictures appear to move on-screen. Of interest to anyone trying to incorporate computer animation into multimedia presentations.

Typical recent postings Animator Relocating, Animation of Human Locomotion, AutoCad to 3Ds, Creating an Animation.

Review This group is for programmers and professional animators who are trying to use animation effectively in their programs and presentations; the discussion is well-informed and requires knowledge of the subject.

Advice to newbies Please read the group's FAQ before posting to avoid asking questions that have been posed before—and especially before posting questions about elementary animation facts or concepts.

Adult-oriented? No.

Readership 88,000.

Rank 161.

Messages per month 580.

Crossposting percentage 9%.

Availability 75% of USENET sites.

Moderated? No.

Special features None.

FAQ title comp.graphics.animation FAQ

FAQ location comp.graphics.animation, comp.answers, news.answers

Other information resources There are extensive archives of program-specific information listed in the FAQ.

Archive site None.

Related groups comp.graphics, alt.graphics.pixutils, comp.graphics.algorithms, comp.graphics.animation, comp.graphics.avs, comp.graphics.data-explorer, comp.graphics.explorer, comp.graphics.gnuplot, comp.graphics.opengl, comp.graphics.raytracing, comp.graphics.research, comp.graphics.visualization, comp.os.ms-windows.programmer.graphics, comp.sys.amiga.graphics, comp.sys.mac.graphics

comp.groupware ★★★

Computer programs and systems that link work groups, such as Lotus Notes. Of interest to professionals in the groupware field.

Typical recent postings Unix and the Problem of Software Production, Microsoft Exchange vs. Lotus Notes, Groupware State of Industry Conference, Real-time Broadcast of Windows Applications.

Review This newsgroup is intended for professional-level discussion of computer groupware.

Advice to newbies Postings from non-professionals are discouraged, but feel free to ask a question (if it's not already answered in the FAQ!).

Adult-oriented? No.

Readership 65,000.

Rank 333.

Messages per month 230.

Crossposting percentage 11%.

Availability 80% of USENET sites.

Moderated? No.

Special features None.

FAQ title comp.groupware FAQ

FAQ location comp.groupware, comp.answers, news.answers

Other information resources Xanadu World Publishing Repository Frequently Asked Question comp.groupware FAQ: Bibliography1: Frequently Asked Question comp.groupware FAQ: Bibliography2: Frequently Asked Question comp.groupware FAQ: Bibliography3: Frequently Asked Question comp.groupware FAQ: Bibliography4: Frequently Asked Question comp.groupware FAQ: Posting guidelines for Comp.groupware. comp.groupware FAQ: Products1: Frequently Asked Questions. comp.groupware FAQ: Products2: Frequently Asked Questions. comp.groupware FAQ: Products3: Frequently Asked Questions.

Archive site None.

Related groups comp.groupware.lotus-notes.misc

comp.home.automation ★★★

Computer techniques for automating the home, with emphasis on the X.10 protocol for home automation. Of interest to anyone planning to use computer technology for home automation purposes.

Typical recent postings X.10 Devices for Ceiling Fan, Home Alarm Communication Formats, New House: Plan for X-10.

Review The X.10 communications protocol for home automation enables homeowners to automate many aspects of a home's function, and the techniques and products of X.10 automation are extensively discussed here. If you're into X.10, this is an indispensable newsgroup.

Advice to newbies If you're not sure what X.10 is all about, please read the group's FAQ before posting to avoid asking questions that have been posed before.

Adult-oriented? No.

Readership 12,000.

Rank 1,696.

Messages per month 483.

Crossposting percentage 6%.

Availability 76% of USENET sites.

Moderated? No.

Special features None.

FAQ title X.10 FAQ

FAQ location comp.home.automation

Other information resources None.

Archive site None.

Related groups None.

---

comp.infosystems.announce ★★

Announcements of new resources accessible through the World Wide Web, Gopher, and WAIS. Of interest to anyone trying to get the most out of Internet connectivity.

Typical recent postings New WWW Guide to Public Health at the University of Arizona, Human-computer Interaction Bibliography, Human Environment Information Kiosk.

Review This moderated group features announcements of rich new information resources, mainly accessible via the World Wide Web but also Gopher and WAIS. Its low volume makes it a poor cousin of the NCSA What's New pages accessible through the World Wide Web.

Advice to newbies This newsgroup is intended for announcements of new information resources on the Internet.

Adult-oriented? No.

Readership 33,000.

Rank 119.

Messages per month 36.

Crossposting percentage 0.9%.

Availability: 59% of USENET sites.

Moderated? Yes.

Special features None.

FAQ title None.

FAQ location comp.infosystems.gopher, comp.answers, news.answers

Other information resources None.

Archive site None.

Related groups comp.infosystems, comp.infosystems.gis, comp.infosystems.gopher, comp.infosystems.interpedia, comp.infosystems.kiosks, comp.infosystems.wais, comp.infosystems.www.misc, comp.infosystems.www.providers, comp.infosystems.www.users

---

comp.infosystems.gopher ★★

The Gopher resource discovery tool—its use, Gopher-accessible resources, new Gopher sites, and the Veronica and Jughead search tools. Of interest to anyone who uses Gopher to retrieve information from the Internet.

Typical recent postings Using Gopher with WWW, Text Viewer for Gopher, Setting Up a Gopher Server, RTF to ASCII Conversion.

Review This is a useful group for anyone who's involved in setting up and maintaining a Gopher site and contains occasional postings of interest to people trying to use Gopher successfully. One gets the feeling, though, that the creative minds and energy are involved in the World Wide Web.

Advice to newbies   Please read the group's FAQ before posting to avoid asking questions that have been posed before.

Adult-oriented?   No.

Readership   55,000.

Rank   453.

Messages per month   541.

Crossposting percentage   8%.

Availability   74% of USENET sites.

Moderated?   No.

Special features   If you're trying to find someone's email address, check out the CSO Nameserver FAQ (see "Other information resources").

FAQ title   Gopher (comp.infosystems.gopher) Frequently Asked Questions

FAQ location   comp.infosystems.gopher, comp.answers, news.answers

Other information resources   CSO Nameserver FAQ

Archive site   None.

Related groups   comp.infosystems, comp.infosystems.announce, comp.infosystems.gis, comp.infosystems.interpedia, comp.infosystems.kiosks, comp.infosystems.wais, comp.infosystems.www, comp.infosystems.www.misc, comp.infosystems.www.providers, comp.infosystems.www.users.

comp.infosystems.www.misc ★★★

The World Wide Web, the emerging world hypertext information system. Topics cover Web navigation tools, creating Web sites, tips and hints. Of interest to anyone hoping to get the most out of the Internet's fastest-growing
information resource. Note: This group replaces comp.infosystems.www.

Typical recent postings   WWW Server over Normal Telephone Lines, Running Executables Off of Mosaic, Economics of Net Presence.

Review   A high-volume group that examines every possible angle of the Web, this group has so many postings that you can't really scan it regularly. Use your newsreader's search capabilities to scan for subjects of interest.

Advice to newbies   Please don't post to comp.infosystems.www, which is slated for removal. Note that comp.infosystems.www.providers is for people who are providing Web services, while comp.infosystems.www.users is for people who are trying to navigate the Web and use Web software. Please read the group's FAQ before posting to avoid asking questions that have been posed before.

Adult-oriented?   No.

Readership   22,000.

Rank   1,225.

Messages per month   927.

Crossposting percentage   16%.

Availability   43% of USENET sites.

Moderated?   No.

Special features   None.

FAQ title   World Wide Web Frequently Asked Questions (FAQ)

FAQ location   comp.infosystems.www.misc, comp.infosystems.www.providers, comp.infosystems.www.users, comp.infosystems.wais, comp.infosystems.gopher

Other information resources   None.

Archive site   None.

Related groups   comp.infosystems.www.providers, comp.infosystems.www.users, comp.infosystems.wais

comp.lang.basic.visual ★★

Microsoft Corporation's Visual Basic, the programming language that is fast emerging as the preferred language for amateur and even professional Windows program development. This newsgroup also covers the application versions of Visual Basic that are packaged with Word and Excel. Of interest to anyone learning Visual Basic or programming competently in that language.

Typical recent postings VBX vs. DLL, Transparent Form, Out of Memory, Does Anyone Really Document?

Review This excessively high-volume group is loaded with useful information and discussion concerning Visual Basic, but it's too much to wade through on a regular basis! Splitting the group into three or four subgroups would help.

Advice to newbies Please read the group's FAQ before posting to avoid asking questions that have been posed before.

Adult-oriented? No.

Readership 34,000.

Rank 855.

Messages per month 3,559.

Crossposting percentage 0.8%.

Availability 63% of USENET sites.

Moderated? No.

Special features Extensive information resources (see "Other information resources").

FAQ title comp.lang.basic.visual General Frequently Asked Questions

FAQ location comp.lang.visual.basic, comp.answers, news.answers

Other information resources FAQ: comp.lang.basic.visual VB DOS Frequently Asked Questions, FAQ: comp.lang.basic.visual VB Win Commercial VBX List, FAQ: comp.lang.basic.visual VB Win Frequently Asked Questions, FAQ: comp.lang.basic.visual VB Win Shareware VBX List

Archive site For Visual Basic materials and resources, use anonymous FTP to contact ftp.cica.indiana.edu in the directory /pub/pc/win3/programr/vbasic.

Related groups None.

comp.lang.postscript ★★★

PostScript, the premier page-description language (PDL) that displays and prints fonts and graphics. Of interest to anyone attempting to program in PostScript or struggling with PostScript devices.

Typical recent postings GhostScript 3.0, Computer Modern Fonts, Halftone Dictionary, Plotting Problem.

Review If you're working with PostScript, this newsgroup belongs in your subscription list. You'll find intelligent and informed discussion regarding programming in PostScript and using PostScript software, such as GhostScript, for displaying and printing PostScript-encoded documents accessible on the Internet.

Advice to newbies Please read the group's unusually informative FAQ before posting.

Adult-oriented? No.

Readership 85,000.

Rank 182.

Messages per month 570.

Crossposting percentage 7%.

Availability 83% of USENET sites.

Moderated? No.

Special features The group's 11 part (!) FAQ is a treasure-trove of information related to PostScript.

FAQ title Postscript Monthly FAQ

FAQ location comp.lang.postscript, comp.answers, news.answers

Other information resources None.

Archive site Sources are available in comp.lang.postscript.sources.

Related groups comp.lang.postscript.sources

comp.mail.mime ★★★

The Multimedia Internet Mail Extensions protocol, which upgrades Internet mail with multimedia capabilities, including fonts, sounds, and video. Of interest to anyone trying to send or receive MIME mail or develop MIME-capable applications.

Typical recent postings Simpler MIME, Mail Program, Gateway Transformations, encoding on-the-fly, Multi-lingual multi-part run on MIME.

Review If you're into MIME, this newsgroup belongs in your subscription list. You'll find informed discussion of MIME techniques, programs, and issues, as well as announcements of new MIME products.

Advice to newbies Please read the group's FAQ before posting to avoid asking questions that have been posed before.

Adult-oriented? No.

Readership 35,000.

Rank 843.

Messages per month 278.

Crossposting percentage 12%.

Availability 75% of USENET sites.

Moderated? No.

Special features None.

FAQ title comp.mail.mime Frequently Asked Questions List (FAQ)

FAQ location comp.mail.mime, comp.answers, news.answers

Other information resources None.

Archive site None.

Related groups None.

comp.mail.misc ★★★

Every aspect of electronic mail—getting access, finding people, sending and receiving messages, dealing with problems. Of interest to email users and email software developers alike.

Typical recent postings External Mail Access, Advice on Email Package, Accessing Mail from Outside a Fire Wall.

Review All of us use email, but it usually doesn't become a topic of concern until it stops working! If you can't get help locally, this newsgroup is a valuable resource. It's also a useful place to find announcements and discussion of new email programs.

Advice to newbies Please read the group's FAQ before posting to avoid asking questions that have been posed before.

Adult-oriented? No.

Readership 110,000.

Rank 105.

Messages per month 394.

Crossposting percentage 15%.

Availability 88% of USENET sites.

Moderated? No.

Special features The group's extensive informational resources provide all the information anyone would need to cope with mail problems, such as sending mail to other networks.

FAQ title   None.

FAQ location   N/A.

Other information resources   Updated Inter-Network Mail Guide; International E-mail Accessibility; Mail Archive Server Software List; Pointer to Mail Archive Servers FAQ; LAN Mail Protocols Summary; FAQ: How to Find People's E-mail Addresses

Archive site   None.

Related groups   alt.bbs.lists, alt.internet.services, comp.misc, comp.mail.uucp, news.newusers.questions, comp.sources.wanted

comp.multimedia ★★★

Every aspect of multimedia presentations on computers: graphics, sound, full-motion video, presentation hardware, programming languages, and aesthetic issues. Of interest to anyone developing multimedia presentations or software.

Typical recent postings   Multimedia Simulations, Multimedia Projector Systems, Multimedia for Unix, Networking a Multimedia Lab, Downsampling 16-bit Audio.

Review   This newsgroup offers interesting, though varied, discussions of multimedia; the newsgroup's lack of focus and high volume raises the cost of reading it regularly, though. I'd suggest using your newsreader's search capabilities to search for specific subjects of interest.

Advice to newbies   There's no FAQ, but please read the JPEG and MPEG FAQs before posting questions concerning these multimedia formats.

Adult-oriented?   No.

Readership   120,000.

Rank   75.

Messages per month   1,185.

Crossposting percentage   10%.

Availability   80% of USENET sites.

Moderated?   No.

Special features   None.

FAQ title   None.

FAQ location   None.

Other information resources   T7G Technical FAQ, JPEG FAQ, MPEG FAQ: Multimedia Compression

Archive site   None.

Related groups   alt.cd-rom, comp.publish.cdrom.multimedia, comp.publish.cdrom.hardware, comp.publish.cdrom.software

comp.music ★★★

Every aspect of computer music, including electronic music, computer-aided music composition, the MIDI interface, synthesizers, and computer music software. Of interest to anyone who's interested in composing electronic music or using the computer as an aid to music composition.

Typical recent postings   Encore's Guitar Capabilities, Yamaha FTP Site, Delay For Synthesis, West Side Story MIDI Music, MIDI And Powerpc 7100 Mac.

Review   If you're into MIDI interfaces, synthesizers, or computer-aided composition, you'll find this group of interest, but be forewarned: The high volume makes it time-consuming to read regularly. On the plus side, there are lots of informed and intelligent contributors.

Advice to newbies Please read the group's FAQ before posting to avoid asking questions that have been posed before.

Adult-oriented? No.

Readership 97,000.

Rank 134.

Messages per month 857.

Crossposting percentage 14%.

Availability 77% of USENET sites.

Moderated? No.

Special features None.

FAQ title Electronic_and_Computer_Music_Frequently-Asked_Questions_(FAQ)

FAQ location comp.music

Other information resources Computer Music Bibliography, Electronic Music Software Price Guide, Midi files software archives on the Internet, Music Notation Programs—a list in answer to a FAQ.

Archive site See the FAQ Title: d MIDI Files: Archive Sources on the Internet.

Related groups rec.music.makers.synth, alt.binaries.sounds.midi

comp.org.eff.news ★★★★★

The official newsgroup of the Electronic Frontier Foundation (EFF), a non-profit organization dedicated to protecting civil liberties in cyberspace.

Typical recent postings This newsgroup posts EFFector Online, the newsletter of the Electronic Frontier Foundation.

Review Anyone interested in the future of USENET in particular and cyberspace communities in general should read the EFF's official organ, and I strongly

recommend joining EFF and supporting its activities. One of USENET's best.

Advice to newbies For EFF-related issues, post to comp.org.eff.talk.

Adult-oriented? No.

Readership 49,000.

Rank 550.

Messages per month 16.

Crossposting percentage 1%.

Availability 60% of USENET sites.

Moderated? Yes.

Special features None.

FAQ title None.

FAQ location N/A.

Other information resources ONLINE OUTPOSTS—Cyberspatial Community Groups—Local, National, International.

Archive site Past issues of EFFector Online are available via anonymous FTP to ftp.eff.org.

Related groups comp.org.eff.talk

comp.org.eff.talk ★★★★

Discussion of issues raised by the work of the Electronic Frontier Foundation in protecting civil liberties in cyberspace. Of interest to anyone concerned about the future of the Internet in general and USENET in particular.

Typical recent postings Libertarianism on the Net, Utah's Suit Against the AA BBS, Privacy in the Workplace, Constitutional Questions—AA BBS.

Review This newsgroup features discussion of issues that pertain directly to USENET, such as copyright, online erotica, legislation affecting the Internet, and much more. The high volume makes the group tedious to read regularly, though, and not everyone who posts knows what they're talking about.

Advice to newbies   If you're not familiar with EFF, please read their materials and familiarize yourself with EFF issues before posting.

Adult-oriented?   No.

Readership   87,000.

Rank   170.

Messages per month   1,309.

Crossposting percentage   56%.

Availability   80% of USENET sites.

Moderated?   No.

Special features   None.

FAQ title   None.

FAQ location   N/a.

Other information resources   ONLINE OUTPOSTS—Cyberspatial Community Groups—Local, National, International.

Archive site   None.

Related groups   comp.org.eff.news

---

comp.os.ms-windows.advocacy ★

Microsoft Windows, both for and against.

Typical recent postings   Netware and OS/2, Insufficient Memory with 32 MB RAM, Turn to the REAL Windows, Lather, Rinse, Repeat.

Review   If you're curious to see what a Holy War is like, take a look at this. Otherwise, forget it.

Advice to newbies   There are better things to do with your time.

Adult-oriented?   No.

Readership   60,000.

Rank   394.

Messages per month   3,162.

Crossposting percentage   54%.

Availability   78% of USENET sites.

Moderated?   No.

Special features   None.

FAQ title   INFO: A Guide to the Windows Newsgroups

FAQ location   You can obtain the Windows FAQs from the following sites:

ftp.nimh.nih.gov	156.40.186.8
/pub/win3/FAQ	
wuarchive.wustl.edu	128.252.135.4
/usenet/comp.binaries.ms-windows/faqs	
ftp.metrics.com	198.133.164.1
/faq	

Other information resources   None.

Archive site   The CICA archive and its mirrors offer numerous Windows shareware and public domain programs. Use anonymous FTP to ftp.cica.indiana edu in the directory /pub/pc/win3, or WWW to http://www.cica.indiana.edu.

Related groups   comp.os.ms-windows.apps, comp.os.ms-windows.setup, comp.os.mswindows.misc, comp.os.mswindows.nt.setup

---

comp.os.ms-windows.apps.misc ★★

Microsoft Windows applications—general issues such as installing, uninstalling, memory allocation, system resource problems, updates. Of interest to anyone concerned about general Windows application issues.

Typical recent postings   Symantec and PC Tools for Windows, WinWord and WP Compatibility, AmiPro vs. Word, Computers in Education, WPWin 6.0 Problems.

Review   If you're using Windows, you might scan this group to see what's up, but the high volume of the posts coupled with their generally low technical level makes the newsgroup less than useful.

Advice to newbies   Please read the group's FAQ before posting to avoid asking questions that have been posed before—but you'd be better off posting in one of the application specific groups, such as comp.os.ms-windows.apps.comm, comp.os.ms-windows.apps.financial, comp.os.mswindows.apps.utilities, and comp.os.ms-windows.apps.word-proc.

Adult-oriented?   No.

Readership   110,000.

Rank   99.

Messages per month   2,032.

Crossposting percentage   5%.

Availability   80% of USENET sites.

Moderated?   No.

Special features   None.

FAQ title   Windows FAQ: How to get it

FAQ location   You obtain the Windows FAQs from the following sites:
ftp.nimh.nih.gov   156.40.186.8
    /pub/win3/FAQ
wuarchive.wustl.edu   128.252.135.4
    /usenet/comp.binaries.ms-windows/faqs
ftp.metrics.com   198.133.164.1
    /faq

Other information resources   None.

Archive site   The CICA archive and its mirrors offer numerous Windows shareware and public domain programs. Use anonymous FTP to ftp.cica.indiana edu in the directory /pub/pc/win3, or WWW to http://www.cica.indiana.edu.

Related groups   comp.os.ms-windows.misc, comp.os.ms-windows.setup, comp.os.mswindows.nt.misc, comp.os.mswindows.nt.setup

comp.os.ms-windows.misc ★★

Microsoft Windows itself—how to install and use it, deal with problems, such as GPFs and running out of system resources, and where it's headed. Of interest to any Windows user.

Typical recent postings   Internal System Fonts, Microsoft to Boost Internet Presence by 3,000 Percent, File Manager Disappeared, Hacking Microsoft TCP/IP.

Review   This group combines a high volume with a high proportion of HELP!!! questions, making it rather tedious to read; it might prove of interest if you're trying to deal with a Windows problem (and who isn't?).

Advice to newbies   Please read the group's FAQ before posting to avoid asking questions that have been posed before—but you'd be better off posting in one of the application specific groups, such as comp.os.ms-windows.apps.comm, comp.os.ms-windows.apps.financial, comp.os.mswindows.apps.utilities, and comp.os.ms-windows.apps.word-proc.

Adult-oriented?   No.

Readership   110,000.

Rank   99.

Messages per month   2,032.

Crossposting percentage   5%.

Availability   80% of USENET sites.

Moderated?   No.

Special features   None.

FAQ title   Windows FAQ: How to get it

FAQ location   You can obtain the Windows FAQs from the following sites:
ftp.nimh.nih.gov   156.40.186.8
    /pub/win3/FAQ
wuarchive.wustl.edu   128.252.135.4
    usenet/comp.binaries.ms-windows/faqs

ftp.metrics.com   198.133.164.1
  /faq

Other information resources   None.

Archive site   The CICA archive and its mirrors offer numerous Windows shareware and public domain programs. Use anonymous FTP to ftp.cica.indiana edu in the directory /pub/pc/win3, or WWW to http://www.cica.indiana.edu.

Related groups   comp.os.ms-windows.misc, comp.os.ms-windows.setup, comp.os.mswindows.nt.misc, comp.os.mswindows.nt.setup

comp.os.ms-windows.word-proc ★★★

Microsoft Windows word-processing applications—the merits of the competing packages, program-specific problems, and questions from users of specific packages. Of interest to those using a Windows word-processing program.

Typical recent postings   File Too Large to Save Error, TIFF File in Word 6.0, Fonts for Mathematical Equations, Anchoring Frames to Columns.

Review   One of the newer (and lower-volume) MS-Windows groups, this one is genuinely valuable for anyone who uses a Windows word-processing program. Marring the group, however, is people's tendency to post questions rather than contributing substantive tips.

Advice to newbies   Please post specific questions and use descriptive subject headers—and please, contribute specific tips and hints, too.

Adult-oriented?   No.

Readership   12,000.

Rank   1,710.

Messages per month   757.

Crossposting percentage   1.9%.

Availability   48% of USENET sites.

Moderated?   No.

Special features   None.

FAQ title   Windows FAQ: How to get it

FAQ location   You can obtain the Windows FAQs from the following sites:
ftp.nimh.nih.gov   56.40.186.8
  /pub/win3/FAQ
wuarchive.wustl.edu   128.252.135.4
  /usenet/comp.binaries.ms-windows/faqs
ftp.metrics.com   198.133.164.1
  /faq

Other information resources   None.

Archive site   The CICA archive and its mirrors offer numerous Windows shareware and public domain programs. Use anonymous FTP to ftp.cica.indiana edu in the directory /pub/pc/win3, or WWW to http://www.cica.indiana.edu.

Related groups   comp.os.ms-windows.apps.comm, comp.os.ms-windows.apps.financial, comp.os.mswindows.apps.utilities

comp.risks ★★★★★

The perils of computer use—security risks, energy consumption, repetitive stress injuries, fraud, illicit commercial use of the Internet. Of interest to anyone who uses a computer.

Typical recent postings   RISKS-FORUM DIGEST (periodic posting in digest format).

Review   One of USENET's best, this newsgroup belongs in every subscription list. You'll find informed, and often disturbing, explorations of every aspect of the risks of computing—but it's not all serious. There's a good dash of computing folklore thrown in, much of it coming from the very people who created modern computing. Always informative, sometimes very entertaining—a "must read."

Advice to newbies Please read comp.risks carefully for a while to decide if you've anything to contribute. And if you do, back it up.

Adult-oriented? No.

Readership 200,000.

Rank 17.

Messages per month 13.

Crossposting percentage 3.7%.

Availability 83% of USENET sites.

Moderated? Yes.

Special features See "Archive sites," for information on the RISKS-FORM DIGEST archive.

FAQ title None.

FAQ location N/A.

Other information resources None.

Archive site There's an archive of comp.risks available via anonymous fpt to ftp crvax.sri.com in the directory /risks. To search back issues with WAIS, use risks-digest.src. With Mosaic, use http://www.wais.com/wais-dbs/risksdigest.html. Review.

comp.society.cu-digest ★★★★★

A vehicle for publication of the Computer Underground Digest, an open forum for the discussion of issues of interest to computer enthusiasts and hackers. Of interest to anyone interested in the social issues raised by computer use.

Typical recent postings This newsgroup publishes the Computer Underground Digest, a weekly electronic magazine.

Review One of USENET's best, this newsgroup belongs on the subscription list of anyone concerned about the social issues of computing—privacy, security, copyright, erotica, encryption, government network surveillance, the works.

Advice to newbies You are encouraged to submit to the editors reasoned essays on the implications and issues of computing; essays are preferred over short articles.

Adult-oriented? No.

Readership 28,000.

Rank 1,050.

Messages per month 16.

Crossposting percentage 0%.

Availability 73% of USENET sites.

Moderated? Yes.

Special features A searchable index of the last five years of Computer Underground Digest was announced at the time of this writing.

FAQ title None.

FAQ location N/A.

Other information resources DOOM FAQ v

Archive site EUROPE: LUXEMBOURG BBS (++352) 466893;

ITALY: Bits against the Empire BBS: +39-461-980493

UNITED STATES: etext.archive.umich.edu (141.211.164.18) in /pub/CuD/; ftp.eff.org (192.88.144.4) in /pub/Publications/CuD; aql.gatech.edu (128.61.10.53) in /pub/eff/ cud/;world.std.com in src/wuarchive/ doc/EFF/Publications/CuD/;uceng.uc.edu in /pub/wuarchive/doc/EFF/Publications/ CuD/;wuarchive.wustl.edu in /doc/EFF/ Publications/CuD/;nic.funet.fi in pub/doc/cud/ (Finland);ftp.warwick.ac.uk in pub/cud/ (United Kingdom);

JAPAN: ftp.glocom.ac.jp /mirror/ftp.eff.org/

Related groups alt.hackers

273

comp.sys.ibm.pc.games.action ★★★

Action and arcade games for IBM PCs and compatibles (DOS, Windows, and OS/2), covering current, past and upcoming games, problems, bugs, hints, companies, reviews, previews, demos, strategies, patches, solutions, FTP-sites, shareware and vaporware. Of interest to any PC game player.

Typical recent postings Some thoughts on the meaning of Doom, Cyberspace and Virtual Reality, Jazzy Jackrabbit Sonic Comparison, Jazz cheat codes, PC versus Console.

Review Help, cheats, secret codes, tricks and tips—it's all here, and if you're a PC game player, you won't be able to resist.

Advice to newbies Please read the Internet PC Games FAQ carefully before posting. In particular, don't ask for codes that are in the manual (thus suggesting you have an illegal copy of the game!), and don't reveal how to do something or what happens without adding SPOILER! to your post.

Adult-oriented? No.

Readership 87,000.

Rank 168.

Messages per month 2,802.

Crossposting percentage 15%.

Availability 71% of USENET sites.

Moderated? No.

Special features If you're interested in DOOM, read alt.doom instead; that's where you'll find most of the discussion of this popular game.

FAQ title PC GAMES FAQ<- Guide to the Gaming World

FAQ location comp.sys.ibm.games.announce, rec.games.misc, comp.answers, news.answers, rec.answers

Other information resources ***NET PC GAMES TOP 100 DOCUMENT***

Archive site The FAQ includes an extensive list of archive sites where shareware and public domain games are available.

Related groups alt.games.doom, alt.games.ibmpc.shadowcaster, alt.games.netrek.paradise, alt.games.vga-planets, alt.games.xpilot, alt.games.xtrek, alt.video.games.reviews, comp.os.os.games, comp.sources.games, comp.sources.games.bugs, comp.sys.amiga.games, comp.sys.ibm.pc.games.adventure, comp.sys.ibm.pc.games.announce, comp.sys.ibm.pc.games.flight-sim, comp.sys.ibm.pc.games.misc, comp.sys.ibm.pc.games.rpg, comp.sys.ibm.pc.games.strategic, comp.sys.ibm.pc.soundcard.games, comp.sys.mac.games, rec.games.corewar, rec.games.netrek, rec.games.video, rec.games.video.do, rec.games.video.advocacy, rec.games.video.arcade, rec.games.video.arcade.collecting, rec.games.video.atari, rec.games.video.classic, rec.games.video.marketplace, rec.games.video.misc, rec.games.video.nintendo, rec.games.video.sega

comp.sys.ibm.pc.games.adventure ★★★

Adventure games for IBM PCs and compatibles (DOS, Windows, and OS/2), covering current, past and upcoming games, problems, bugs, hints, companies, reviews, previews, demos, strategies, patches, solutions, FTP-sites, shareware and vaporware. Of interest to any PC game player.

Typical recent postings Xanth, Alone in the Dark, Genie Stuck, Getting Started with Myst.

Review   Helpful discussion of adventure games, such as King's Quest and Hands of Fate, in which an unchanging character tries to overcome problems, puzzles, and obstacles to obtain a goal.

Advice to newbies   Please read the Internet PC Games FAQ carefully before posting. In particular, don't ask for codes that are in the manual (thus suggesting you have an illegal copy of the game!), and don't reveal how to do something or what happens without adding SPOILER! to your post.

Adult-oriented?   No.

Readership   73,000.

Rank   256.

Messages per month   2,690.

Crossposting percentage   9%.

Availability   71% of USENET sites.

Moderated?   No.

Special features   None.

FAQ title   PC GAMES FAQ<- Guide to the Gaming World

FAQ location   comp.sys.ibm.games.announce, rec.games.misc, comp.answers, news.answers, rec.answers

Other information resources   ***NET PC GAMES TOP 100 DOCUMENT***

Archive site   The FAQ includes an extensive list of archive sites where shareware and public domain games are available.

Related groups   alt.games.doom, alt.games.ibmpc.shadowcaster, alt.games.netrek.paradise, alt.games.vga-planets, alt.games.xpilot, alt.games.xtrek, alt.video.games.reviews, comp.os.os.games, comp.sources.games, comp.sources.games.bugs, comp.sys.amiga.games, comp.sys.ibm.pc.games.action, comp.sys.ibm.pc.games.announce, comp.sys.ibm.pc.games.flight-sim, comp.sys.ibm.pc.games.misc,

comp.sys.ibm.pc.games.rpg, comp.sys.ibm.pc.games.strategic, comp.sys.ibm.pc.soundcard.games, comp.sys.mac.games, rec.games.corewar, rec.games.netrek, rec.games.video, rec.games.video.do, rec.games.video.advocacy, rec.games.video.arcade, rec.games.video.arcade.collecting, rec.games.video.atari, rec.games.video.classic, rec.games.video.marketplace, rec.games.video.misc, rec.games.video.nintendo, rec.games.video.sega

comp.sys.ibm.pc.games.announce ★★★★

Announcements concerning computer games for IBM PC and PC-compatible computers. Coverage includes new release announcements, software publisher news, bug information, reviews, Top 100, and Game Bytes information. Included are any games that run on PCs, including Windows and OS/2 games as well as MS-DOS games.

Typical recent postings   Net PC Games Top 100, Deathmatch WADs Ranked!

Review   If you enjoy PC games, don't miss this newsgroup! The high-quality (if infrequent) postings list information you won't want to miss.

Advice to newbies   This is a moderated group for announcements, FAQs, and informational postings only.

Adult-oriented?   No.

Readership   80,000.

Rank   201.

Messages per month   37.

Crossposting percentage   9%.

Availability   68% of USENET sites.

Moderated?   Yes.

Special features None.

FAQ title PC GAMES FAQ<- Guide to the Gaming World

FAQ location comp.sys.ibm.games.announce, rec.games.misc, comp.answers, news.answers, rec.answers

Other information resources ∗∗∗NET PC GAMES TOP 100 DOCUMENT∗∗∗

Archive site The FAQ includes an extensive list of archive sites where shareware and public domain games are available.

Related groups alt.games.doom, alt.games.ibmpc.shadowcaster, alt.games.netrek.paradise, alt.games.vga-planets, alt.games.xpilot, alt.games.xtrek, alt.video.games.reviews, comp.os.os.games, comp.sources.games, comp.sources.games.bugs, comp.sys.amiga.games, comp.sys.ibm.pc.games.action, comp.sys.ibm.pc.games.adventure, comp.sys.ibm.pc.games.flight-sim, comp.sys.ibm.pc.games.misc, comp.sys.ibm.pc.games.rpg, comp.sys.ibm.pc.games.strategic, comp.sys.ibm.pc.soundcard.games, comp.sys.mac.games, rec.games.corewar, rec.games.netrek, rec.games.video, rec.games.video.do, rec.games.video.advocacy, rec.games.video.arcade, rec.games.video.arcade.collecting, rec.games.video.atari, rec.games.video.classic, rec.games.video.marketplace, rec.games.video.misc, rec.games.video.nintendo, rec.games.video.sega

comp.sys.ibm.pc.games.flight-sim ★★★

Flight simulator games for IBM PCs and compatibles (DOS, Windows, and OS/2), covering current, past and upcoming games, problems, bugs, hints, companies, reviews, previews, demos, strategies, patches, solutions, FTP-sites, shareware and vaporware. Of interest to any PC game player.

Typical recent postings Wing Commander Wingman Commands, Tricky X-Wing Maneuver, Privateer Weirdness.

Review Tips, hints, and discussion regarding flight simulator games, such as Aces over Europe, Falcon 3.0, and Air Warrior. Indispensable for computer air warriors. You won't find much discussion of aviation flight simulators, such as Microsoft Flight Simulator.

Advice to newbies Please read the Internet PC Games FAQ carefully before posting. In particular, don't ask for codes that are in the manual (thus suggesting you have an illegal copy of the game!), and don't reveal how to do something or what happens without adding SPOILER! to your post.

Adult-oriented? No.

Readership 63,000.

Rank 347.

Messages per month 2,524.

Crossposting percentage 9%.

Availability 70% of USENET sites.

Moderated? No.

Special features For discussion of aviation flight simulators, see rec.aviation.simulators.

FAQ title PC GAMES FAQ<- Guide to the Gaming World

FAQ location comp.sys.ibm.games.announce, rec.games.misc, comp.answers, news.answers, rec.answers

Other information resources ∗∗∗NET PC GAMES TOP 100 DOCUMENT∗∗∗

Archive site The FAQ includes an extensive list of archive sites where shareware and public domain games are available.

Related groups alt.games.doom,
alt.games.ibmpc.shadowcaster,
alt.games.netrek.paradise, alt.games.vga-planets,
alt.games.xpilot, alt.games.xtrek,
alt.video.games.reviews, comp.os.os.games,
comp.sources.games, comp.sources.games.bugs,
comp.sys.amiga.games,
comp.sys.ibm.pc.games.action,
comp.sys.ibm.pc.games.adventure,
comp.sys.ibm.pc.games.announce,
comp.sys.ibm.pc.games.misc,
comp.sys.ibm.pc.games.rpg,
comp.sys.ibm.pc.games.strategic,
comp.sys.ibm.pc.soundcard.games,
comp.sys.mac.games, rec.games.corewar,
rec.games.netrek, rec.games.video,
rec.games.video.do, rec.games.video.advocacy,
rec.games.video.arcade,
rec.games.video.arcade.collecting,
rec.games.video.atari, rec.games.video.classic,
rec.games.video.marketplace,
rec.games.video.misc, rec.games.video.nintendo,
rec.games.video.sega

comp.sys.ibm.pc.games.misc. ★★★

Miscellaneous games for IBM PCs and compatibles (DOS, Windows, and OS/2), covering current, past and upcoming games, problems, bugs, hints, companies, reviews, previews, demos, strategies, patches, solutions, FTP-sites, shareware and vaporware. Of interest to any PC game player.

Typical recent postings Looking for a Game Called Hack, Roadrunner Blues, Why Won't Xenka Monk Tell Me about Ashes.

Review Discussion of any games that don't fall into the other comp.sys.ibm.pc.games.* newsgroups, such as golf and car racing games.

Advice to newbies Please read the Internet PC Games FAQ carefully before posting. In particular,

don't ask for codes that are in the manual (thus suggesting you have an illegal copy of the game!), and don't reveal how to do something or what happens without adding SPOILER! to your post.

Adult-oriented? No.

Readership 72,000.

Rank 265.

Messages per month 1,598.

Crossposting percentage 20%.

Availability 72% of USENET sites.

Moderated? No.

Special features None.

FAQ title PC GAMES FAQ<- Guide to the Gaming World

FAQ location comp.sys.ibm.games.announce, rec.games.misc, comp.answers, news.answers, rec.answers

Other information resources ∗∗∗NET PC GAMES TOP 100 DOCUMENT∗∗∗

Archive site The FAQ includes an extensive list of archive sites where shareware and public domain games are available.

Related groups alt.games.doom,
alt.games.ibmpc.shadowcaster,
alt.games.netrek.paradise, alt.games.vga-planets,
alt.games.xpilot, alt.games.xtrek,
alt.video.games.reviews, comp.os.os.games,
comp.sources.games, comp.sources.games.bugs,
comp.sys.amiga.games,
comp.sys.ibm.pc.games.action,
comp.sys.ibm.pc.games.adventure,
comp.sys.ibm.pc.games.announce,
comp.sys.ibm.pc.games.flight-sim,
comp.sys.ibm.pc.games.rpg,
comp.sys.ibm.pc.games.strategic,
comp.sys.ibm.pc.soundcard.games,
comp.sys.mac.games, rec.games.corewar,
rec.games.netrek, rec.games.video,
rec.games.video.do, rec.games.video.advocacy,

rec.games.video.arcade,
rec.games.video.arcade.collecting,
rec.games.video.atari, rec.games.video.classic,
rec.games.video.marketplace,
rec.games.video.misc, rec.games.video.nintendo,
rec.games.video.sega

comp.sys.ibm.pc.games.rpg ★★★

Role-playing games for IBM PCs and compatibles (DOS, Windows, and OS/2), covering current, past and upcoming games, problems, bugs, hints, companies, reviews, previews, demos, strategies, patches, solutions, FTP-sites, shareware and vaporware. Of interest to any PC game player.

Typical recent postings   Some thoughts on the meaning of Doom, Cyberspace and Virtual Reality, Jazz Jackrabbit Sonic Comparison, Jazz Cheat Codes, PC versus Console.

Review   Role playing games, such as Lands of Lore and Ultima VI, set characters in a complex, consistent world; interaction, which involves combat and magic, involves numerical scores such as health points. You'll find plenty of tips and hints here.

Advice to newbies   Please read the Internet PC Games FAQ carefully before posting. In particular, don't ask for codes that are in the manual (thus suggesting you have an illegal copy of the game!), and don't reveal how to do something or what happens without adding SPOILER! to your post.

Adult-oriented?   No.

Readership   51,000.

Rank   347.

Messages per month   2,796.

Crossposting percentage   9%.

Availability   70% of USENET sites.

Moderated?   No.

Special features   None.

FAQ title   PC GAMES FAQ<- Guide to the Gaming World

FAQ location   comp.sys.ibm.games.announce, rec.games.misc, comp.answers, news.answers, rec.answers

Other information resources   ***NET PC GAMES TOP 100 DOCUMENT***

Archive site   The FAQ includes an extensive list of archive sites where shareware and public domain games are available.

Related groups   alt.games.doom, alt.games.ibmpc.shadowcaster, alt.games.netrek.paradise, alt.games.vga-planets, alt.games.xpilot, alt.games.xtrek, alt.video.games.reviews, comp.os.os.games, comp.sources.games, comp.sources.games.bugs, comp.sys.amiga.games, comp.sys.ibm.pc.games.action, comp.sys.ibm.pc.games.adventure, comp.sys.ibm.pc.games.announce, comp.sys.ibm.pc.games.flight-sim, comp.sys.ibm.pc.games.misc, comp.sys.ibm.pc.games.strategic, comp.sys.ibm.pc.soundcard.games, comp.sys.mac.games, rec.games.corewar, rec.games.netrek, rec.games.video, rec.games.video.do, rec.games.video.advocacy, rec.games.video.arcade, rec.games.video.arcade.collecting, rec.games.video.atari, rec.games.video.classic, rec.games.video.marketplace, rec.games.video.misc, rec.games.video.nintendo, rec.games.video.sega

comp.sys.ibm.pc.games.strategic ★★★

Strategy games for IBM PCs and compatibles (DOS, Windows, and OS/2), covering current, past and upcoming games, problems, bugs,

hints, companies, reviews, previews, demos, strategies, patches, solutions, FTP-sites, shareware and vaporware. Of interest to any PC game player.

Typical recent postings   Master of Orion Deluxe, Best Weapon, MultiWar—A New Shareware Game.

Review   Tips, hints, and discussion regarding strategy games, such as Civilization and Master of Orion, which involve the coordination of complex resources.

Advice to newbies   Please read the Internet PC Games FAQ carefully before posting. In particular, don't ask for codes that are in the manual (thus suggesting you have an illegal copy of the game!), and don't reveal how to do something or what happens without adding SPOILER! to your post.

Adult-oriented?   No.

Readership   60,000.

Rank   389.

Messages per month   3,973.

Crossposting percentage   9%.

Availability   71% of USENET sites.

Moderated?   No.

Special features   None.

FAQ title   PC GAMES FAQ<- Guide to the Gaming World

FAQ location   comp.sys.ibm.games.announce, rec.games.misc, comp.answers, news.answers, rec.answers

Other information resources   ∗∗∗NET PC GAMES TOP 100 DOCUMENT∗∗∗

Archive site   The FAQ includes an extensive list of archive sites where shareware and public domain games are available.

Related groups   alt.games.doom, alt.games.ibmpc.shadowcaster, alt.games.netrek.paradise, alt.games.vga-planets, alt.games.xpilot, alt.games.xtrek, alt.video.games.reviews, comp.os.os.games, comp.sources.games, comp.sources.games.bugs, comp.sys.amiga.games, comp.sys.ibm.pc.games.action, comp.sys.ibm.pc.games.adventure, comp.sys.ibm.pc.games.announce, comp.sys.ibm.pc.games.flight-sim, comp.sys.ibm.pc.games.misc, comp.sys.ibm.pc.games.rpg, comp.sys.ibm.pc.soundcard.games, comp.sys.mac.games, rec.games.corewar, rec.games.netrek, rec.games.video, rec.games.video.do, rec.games.video.advocacy, rec.games.video.arcade, rec.games.video.arcade.collecting, rec.games.video.atari, rec.games.video.classic, rec.games.video.marketplace, rec.games.video.misc, rec.games.video.nintendo, rec.games.video.sega

comp.sys.ibm.pc.hardware.misc ★★★

All aspects of IBM PC or PC-compatible hardware that are not covered by one of the other comp.sys.ibm.pc.hardware.∗ (csiph.∗) groups; of interest to those needing assistance with a hardware-related problem. Additional groups in the csiph.∗ hierarchy include comp.sys.ibm.pc.soundcard.tech (Technical topics on PC soundcards), comp.sys.ibm.pc.soundcard.advocacy (Advocacy for a particular soundcard), comp.sys.ibm.pc.soundcard.games (Using soundcards with games), comp.sys.ibm.pc.soundcard.music (Music & sound using soundcards), comp.sys.ibm.pc.soundcard.misc (Soundcards in general), comp.sys.ibm.pc.hardware.video (Monitors/video cards), comp.sys.ibm.pc.hardware.comm

(Modems/fax cards/communication),
comp.sys.ibm.pc.hardware.storage
(Hard/floppy/tape drives & media),
**comp.sys.ibm.pc.hardware.cd-rom (CD-ROM
drives & interfaces)**,
**comp.sys.ibm.pc.hardware.systems (Com-
puter vendors & specific systems)**,
**comp.sys.ibm.pc.hardware.chips (System
chips/RAM chips/cache)**.

Typical recent postings   Write-through or write-back cache modes, Low-Level Format of MFM Drive, Zenon Optimus, AMD 486DX2-66 Chip.

Review   This newsgroup consists mainly of questions on hardware-related issues; there's not much discussion, but some of the questions and answers might be helpful to you.

Advice to newbies   Please read the group's FAQ before posting to avoid asking questions that have been posed before, and take care to post your question to the correct csiph.* group. If you're hoping to sell a computer, post to misc.forsale.computers.pc-clone.

Adult-oriented?   No.

Readership   60,000.

Rank   388.

Messages per month   1,299.

Crossposting percentage   18%.

Availability   69% of USENET sites.

Moderated?   No.

Special features   None.

FAQ title   comp.sys.ibm.pc.hardware.**
Frequently Asked Questions(FAQ)

FAQ location   comp.sys.ibm.pc.hardware,
comp.sys.ibm.pc.hardware.chips,
comp.sys.ibm.pc.hardware.misc

Other information resources   FAQ: The AMI BIOS Survival Guide

Archive site   None.

Related groups   alt.emulators.ibmpc.apple,
alt.games.ibmpc.shadowcaster,

aus.computers.ibm-pc, bit.listserv.ibm,
bit.listserv.ibm-hesc, bit.listserv.ibm-main,
bit.listserv.ibm-nets, bit.listserv.ibmtcp-l,
clari.nb.ibm, comp.binaries.ibm.pc,
comp.binaries.ibm.pc.d,
comp.binaries.ibm.pc.wanted,
comp.protocols.ibm, comp.protocols.tcpip.ibmpc,
comp.sys.ibm.hardware, comp.sys.ibm.pc,
comp.sys.ibm.pc.demos, comp.sys.ibm.pc.digest,
comp.sys.ibm.pc.games.action,
comp.sys.ibm.pc.games.adventure,
comp.sys.ibm.pc.games.announce,
comp.sys.ibm.pc.games.flight-sim,
comp.sys.ibm.pc.games.misc,
comp.sys.ibm.pc.games.rpg,
comp.sys.ibm.pc.games.strategic,
comp.sys.ibm.pc.hardware.cd-rom,
comp.sys.ibm.pc.hardware.chips,
comp.sys.ibm.pc.hardware.comm,
comp.sys.ibm.pc.hardware.misc,
comp.sys.ibm.pc.hardware.networking,
comp.sys.ibm.pc.hardware.storage,
comp.sys.ibm.pc.hardware.systems,
comp.sys.ibm.pc.hardware.video,
comp.sys.ibm.pc.misc, comp.sys.ibm.pc.net,
comp.sys.ibm.pc.programmer,
comp.sys.ibm.pc.rt, comp.sys.ibm.pc.soundcard,
comp.sys.ibm.pc.soundcard.advocacy,
comp.sys.ibm.pc.soundcard.games,
comp.sys.ibm.pc.soundcard.misc,
comp.sys.ibm.pc.soundcard.music,
comp.sys.ibm.pc.soundcard.tech,
comp.sys.ibm.pc.wanted,
comp.sys.ibm.ps.hardware

comp.sys.mac.misc ★★★

All aspects of Macintosh hardware or software that are not covered by any of the other csmm.* newsgroups, including viruses, printing, security, and sound; of interest to those

with questions about Macintoshes, comp.sys.mac.system (Macintosh system software), comp.sys.mac.apps (Macintosh software), comp.sys.mac.wanted (buying Macintosh equipment), comp.sys.mac.hardware (maintenance, problems, repairs, upgrades, video), comp.sys.mac.comm_(modems), comp.sys.mac.games (Macintosh games), comp.sys.mac.games_FAQ, and comp.sys.mac.advocacy (holy wars).

Typical recent postings Excellent Communications, Mac Icon to Windows Icon, Market Research on Notebooks.

Review This newsgroup consists mainly of questions on Macintosh-related issues; there's not much discussion, but some of the questions and answers might be helpful to you.

Advice to newbies Please read the group's FAQ before posting to avoid asking questions that have been posed before, and be sure to post your query to the correct csm.* newsgroup. Don't crosspost; post to one of these newsgroups. If you want to sell a Macintosh, post to comp.sys.mac.wanted and misc.forsale.computers.mac.

Adult-oriented? No.

Readership 130,000.

Rank 60.

Messages per month 2,363.

Crossposting percentage 21%.

Availability 82% of USENET sites.

Moderated? No.

Special features None.

FAQ title Introductory Macintosh Frequently Asked Questions(FAQ)

FAQ location comp.sys.mac.misc, comp.answers, news.answers

Other information resources Macintosh Screensaver Frequently Asked Questions (FAQ). Macintosh application software frequently asked questions (FAQ), comp.sys.mac.comm Frequently Asked Questions

Archive site The two major North American Internet archives of shareware, freeware, and demo software are Info-Mac at sumex-aim.stanford.edu [36.44.0.6], and mac.archive at mac.archive.umich.edu [141.211.120.11]; because these sites are very busy, you may need to try one of the many mirrror sites listed in the newsgroup's FAQ.

Related groups alt.sources.mac, alt.sources.mac.d, aus.mac, comp.binaries.mac, comp.lang.forth.mac, comp.sys.mac, comp.sys.mac.advocacy, comp.sys.mac.announce, comp.sys.mac.apps, comp.sys.mac.comm, comp.sys.mac.databases, comp.sys.mac.digest, comp.sys.mac.games, comp.sys.mac.graphics, comp.sys.mac.hardware, comp.sys.mac.hypercard, comp.sys.mac.misc, comp.sys.mac.oop.macapp, comp.sys.mac.oop.misc, comp.sys.mac.oop.tcl, comp.sys.mac.portables, comp.sys.mac.programmer, comp.sys.mac.scitech, comp.sys.mac.system, comp.sys.mac.wanted, misc.forsale.computers.mac

comp.text ★★

Electronic publishing generally, including desktop publishing, markup languages, and page description languages. Other newsgroups in this hierarchy deal with specific questions related to desktop publishing (comp.text.desktop), FrameMaker (comp.text.frame), InterLeaf (comp.text.interleaf), TeX (comp.text.tex), and SGML (comp.text.SGML).

Typical recent postings PostScript to TIFF, Multilingual Apps, HiTek Report.

Review This newsgroup consists mostly of posted questions; it might be worth reviewing if you're having a desktop publishing-related problem not covered by one of the other newsgroups in the hierarchy.

Advice to newbies Please read the group's FAQ before posting to avoid asking questions that have been posed before.

Adult-oriented? No.

Readership 62,000.

Rank 373.

Messages per month 131.

Crossposting percentage 15%.

Availability 81% of USENET sites.

Moderated? No.

Special features None.

FAQ title comp.text Frequently Asked Questions

FAQ location comp.text, comp.answers, news.answers

Other information resources Desktop Publishing Resources FAQ

Archive site None.

Related groups comp.text.frame, comp.text.interleaf, comp.text.desktop, comp.text.SGML, comp.text.tex

comp.virus ★★★★

Computer viruses, virus detectors, new viruses, Trojan Horses.

Typical recent postings Fixing the Boot Sector of a Floppy, Mosquito Virus, Stoned 4 Mystery.

Review This moderated newsgroup features high-quality discussion of viruses and virus-related topics (such as anti-virus programs).

Advice to newbies Please read the group's FAQ before posting to avoid asking questions that have been posed before—and especially, don't post "Does my system have a virus?" until you've purchased and run an anti-virus checker.

Adult-oriented? No.

Readership 80,000.

Rank 208.

Messages per month 306.

Crossposting percentage 0%.

Availability 81% of USENET sites.

Moderated? Yes.

Special features VALERT-L is a mailing list containing news and alerts about new viruses; it's posted periodically to comp.virus.

FAQ title comp.virus Frequently Asked Questions

FAQ location N/A.

Other information resources Introduction to the Anti-viral archives listing; Antiviral BBS Listing; Antiviral contacts listing; Quick reference antiviral Review chart Amiga Anti-viral archive sites; Anti-viral Documentation archive sites; Apple II Anti-viral archive sites; Archive access without anonymous ftp; Atari ST Anti-viral archive sites; IBMPC Anti-viral archive sites; Introduction to the Anti-viral archives; Macintosh Anti-viral archive sites; Unix security archive sites

Archive site The anonymous FTP archive at cert.org (directory: pub/virus-l) carries all of the VIRUS-L back issues. For more information on archives, see "Other information resources," above.

Related groups None.

rec.aquaria ★★★

Everything about aquaria—the fish, the tanks, the water, the problems. Of interest to anyone who has or is thinking about buying an aquarium.

Typical recent postings Hematoma in Bubble-Eyed Goldfish—Help, How Much Do You Pay for Electricity, Black Light for Aquaria, Ammonia Driving Me Nuts, Fishy Feats and Tricks, Feeding Sea-Horses.

Review Intelligent, useful discussions of all aspects of keeping an aquarium; frequent postings from experts.

Advice to newbies Read the FAQs to make sure you don't ask a question that's already been answered, and be sure to crosspost to alt.aquaria. (Not all sites receive both groups, so the two groups exist to make sure that all sites receive all the postings.)

Adult-oriented? No.

Readership 49,000.

Rank 545.

Messages per month 1,648.

Crossposting percentage 16%.

Availability 73% of USENET sites.

Moderated? No.

Special features Extensive informational resources add up to a superb introductory course in keeping an aquarium.

FAQ title alt.aquaria FAQ: Beginners and Books

FAQ location alt.aquaria, rec.aquaria, sci.aquaria (monthly).

Other information resources AQUARIA FAQ: Filters, AQUARIA FAQ: Magazines and Mail Order Information, AQUARIA FAQ Plants, AQUARIA FAQ Water

Archive site None.

Related groups alt.aquaria (essentially the same newsgroup) and sci.aquaria (for discussions of scientific research on water-related topics).

---

rec.arts.animation ★★★★

Animation and cartoons—how to do it, how to enjoy it.

Typical recent postings Info About Claymation, Disney's Craziest Cartoon, Linus & Lucy, Super-friends.

Review If you're into toons of any kind, either as a fan or a multimedia artist, this is a great newsgroup to read. Postings are of high quality.

Advice to newbies If you're into Japanese comics (anime), see rec.arts.anime.

Adult-oriented? No.

Readership 65,000.

Rank 328.

Messages per month 476.

Crossposting percentage 31%.

Availability 74% of USENET sites.

Moderated? No.

Special features None.

FAQ title rec.arts.animation Frequently Asked Questions

FAQ location rec.arts.animation, rec.answers, news.answers

Other information resources None.

Archive site None.

Related groups alt.animation.warner-bros, alt.tv.animaniacs, alt.tv.tiny-toon, alt.tv.tinytoon.fandom, alt.fan.disney.afternoon, alt.tv.ren-n-stimpy, rec.arts.disney, alt.tv.simpsons

---

rec.arts.anime

Japanese comics, which represent what is perhaps the highest development of comics as an art form.

Typical recent postings Techno Police and Magical Princess Gigi, Anime to Go Mainstream, Siskel and Ebert Like Anime Too, Anime DOOM, Samurai Pizza Cats.

Review None.

Advice to newbies Note that rec.arts.anime is for general discussion of anime; for news and information about anime, see rec.arts.anime.info (moderated). For buying and selling anime-related merchandise, see rec.arts.anime.marketplace. For anime-related stories contributed by USENET authors, see rec.arts.anime.stories (moderated). Please read the group's FAQ before posting to avoid asking questions that have been posed before. Related groups dealing with *manga* (a type of Japanese art that has its roots in Ukiyo-e wood prints; see rec.arts.manga.

Adult-oriented? No.

Readership 80,000.

Rank 203.

Messages per month 4,374.

Crossposting percentage 3%.

Availability 75% of USENET sites.

Moderated? No.

Special features None.

FAQ title rec.arts.anime Frequently Asked Questions

FAQ location rec.arts.anime.info

Other information resources rec.arts.anime: Anime Primer. rec.arts.anime: Anime Resources List. rec.arts.anime: FAQ Availability Info. rec.arts.anime: Frequently Asked Questions. rec.arts.anime: Welcome to rec.arts.anime! rec.arts.manga: Frequently Asked Questions.rec.arts.manga: Manga Guide Part 1 3. rec.arts.manga: Manga Guide Part 2 3. rec.arts.manga: Manga Guide Part 3 3. rec.arts.manga: Manga Resources. rec.arts.manga: Welcome to rec.arts.manga

Archive site See the rec.arts.anime Anime Resources List for information.

Related groups rec.arts.anime.info, rec.arts.anime.marketplace, rec.arts.anime.stories

rec.arts.ascii ★★★★★

ASCII art, but only the best—this is a moderated newsgroup.

Typical recent postings Talk: Light and Dark Effects, Talk: Is It OK to Copy ASCII Art?, For Best Results in Viewing ASCII Art.

Review Maybe it's stupid, but you really don't want to miss this. I'm amazed by what these people are able to do with the standard ASCII characters.

Advice to newbies Practice, practice, practice—and then post, but please read the group's FAQ first!

Adult-oriented? No.

Readership 13,000.

Rank 1,611.

Messages per month 694.

Crossposting percentage 17%.

Availability 39% of USENET sites.

Moderated? Yes.

Special features The FAQ, in two parts, is an electronic library of some remarkable ASCII art.

FAQ title FAQ—ASCII Art Questions & Answers

FAQ location rec.arts.ascii, alt.ascii-art, alt.binaries.pictures, alt.answers, rec.answers, news.answers

Other information resources None.

Archive site None.

Related groups alt.ascii-art, alt.binaries.pictures

rec.arts.bodyart ★★★

Permanent body alteration, in the form of tattoos, body pierces, brandings, and cuttings.

Typical recent postings   Piercing Professional-ism, Tattoo Convention, Genital Piercing and Con-doms, Recoloring Tattoos, Nipple Rings and Dreadlocks.

Review   Not for the general reader, but if you're into body art, you'll find plenty of support and dis-cussion here.

Advice to newbies   The group's unusually exten-sive FAQs should be consulted before posting ques-tions to the group.

Adult-oriented?   No.

Readership   46,000.

Rank   594.

Messages per month   1,107.

Crossposting percentage   1%.

Availability   69% of USENET sites.

Moderated?   No.

Special features   Extensive FAQ libarary.

FAQ title   rec.arts.bodyart piercing FAQ

FAQ location   rec.arts.bodyart

Other information resources   rec.arts.bodyart: Alternative Bodyart FAQ., rec.arts.bodyart: Piercing FAQ—Introduction., rec.arts.bodyart: Piercing FAQ—Piercings & Jewelry., rec.arts.bodyart: Piercing FAQ—Getting a New Pierce., rec.arts.bodyart: Piercing FAQ—Professional Piercers., rec.arts.bodyart: Piercing FAQ—Care of New Pierces., rec.arts.bodyart: Piercing FAQ—Problems & Hazards., rec.arts.bodyart: Piercing FAQ—Healed Pierces., rec.arts.bodyart: Piercing FAQ—Misc. Info., rec.arts.bodyart: Piercing FAQ—Resource List., rec.arts.bodyart: Tattoo FAQ—Introduction., rec.arts.bodyart: Tattoo FAQ—Getting a Tattoo., rec.arts.bodyart: Tattoo FAQ—Sanitation., rec.arts.bodyart: Tattoo FAQ—Conventions., rec.arts.bodyart: Tattoo FAQ—Artist List., rec.arts.bodyart: Tattoo FAQ—Care of New Tattoos., rec.arts.bodyart: Tattoo FAQ—General Care Removal., rec.arts.bodyart: Tattoo FAQ—Misc. Info., rec.arts.bodyart: Tattoo FAQ—Bibliography

Archive site   For the FAQS, use anonymous ftp to the FAQ archive at rtfm.mit.edu. See the FAQ for details regarding other archive sites.

Related groups   alt.sex.bondage

rec.arts.bonsai ★★★

The Oriental art of growing dwarf trees or bushes in a plate or dish.

Typical recent postings   Sick Juniper Bonsai, Ginkgo Germination, Good Trees for Desert Climate.

Review   This group features informed and interest-ing discussion for anyone interested in the art of bonsai; it's a quiet, gentle, and rewarding newsgroup.

Advice to newbies   Anyone is welcome to con-tribute, but it's a good idea to read the group's FAQ first.

Adult-oriented?   No.

Readership   15,000.

Rank   1,516.

Messages per month   73.

Crossposting percentage   28% (due to crossposting to alt.arts.bonsai).

Availability   45% of USENET sites.

Moderated?   No.

Special features   The group's five-part FAQ is an excellent introduction to the art of bonsai.

FAQ title   The rec.arts.bonsai/alt.bonsai FAQ (five parts)

FAQ location   alt.bonsai, rec.arts.bonsai

Other information resources   None.

Archive site   An anonymous FTP server for Bonsai GIFS (and other types of pictures) and other bonsai related files is available at bonsai.pass.wayne.edu (IP address 141.217.25.20). Login as anonymous and use guest as a password.

Related groups   rec.arts.bonsai

rec.arts.books ★★★★

Books—the literary type, not the technical.

Typical recent postings   What's Wrong with Robert Bly, Ayn Rand (arrrrgh!), P.K. Dick's _Do Androids Dream of Electric Sheep_, New Jack Kerouac WWW Site, Shy People's Novels (Silas Marner, Little Dorrit).

Review   Good discussion and quality contributions make this newsgroup worth a look. Be aware that most USENET users are techie types (still), so don't be surprised (or offended) when you find science fiction treated as if it were the high literature that it is.

Advice to newbies   Please read the group's FAQ before posting to avoid asking questions that have been posed before.

Adult-oriented?   No.

Readership   140,000.

Rank   44.

Messages per month   3,429.

Crossposting percentage   10%.

Availability   78% of USENET sites.

Moderated?   No.

Special features   Extensive FAQs list bookstores in major cities. Frequent book reviews.

FAQ title   rec.arts.books Frequently Asked Questions

FAQ location   rec.arts.books, rec.answers, news.answers

Other information resources   FAQ for alt.books.reviews, Book Review Index, Basement Full of Books, Arthurian Booklist, Holmes Booklist, Book Catalogues and Book Clubs List, Robin Hood Booklist, Bookstores in New York City, Books by Mail, Bookstores in Northern North American Cities, Bookstores in Eastern North American Cities, Bookstores in Various Asian Cities, Bookstores in Various European Cities, Bookstores in Western North American Cities

Archive site   Fred Zimmerman (Frederick.Zimmerman@ ciesin.org) maintains the Internet Book Information Center (IBIC)—an experimental project to "provide access to Internet resources related to books." IBIC is available by gophering to sunsite.unc.edu. At the main menu, choose "Worlds of SunSITE by Subject/Internet Book Information Center."

Related groups   alt.books.reviews, biz.books.technical, misc.books.technical, rec.arts.sf.written

rec.arts.comics.misc ★★★

Everything about comic books that isn't appropriately posted to the other rec.arts.comics.* groups—rec.arts.comics.info for announcements and information, rec.arts.comics.marketplace for buying and selling comics, and rec.arts.comics.strips for discussion of newspaper comics.

Typical recent postings   JSA and Waverider, Miracle Man, A Change in Batman's Origin!

Review   This is Grand Central Station for comic book fanatics; lots of fervent discussion from avid fans.

Advice to newbies   Please read the group's FAQs carefully; you'll get seriously flamed if you ask yet another question about how many kinds of Krytonite there are.

Adult-oriented? No.

Readership 19,000.

Rank 1,327.

Messages per month 19.

Crossposting percentage 17%.

Availability 42% of USENET sites.

Moderated? No.

Special features None.

FAQ title Welcome to rec.arts.comics: Introduction

FAQ location rec.arts.comics.info

Other information resources rec.arts.comics.marketplace Frequently Asked Questions List(FAQ), New Weekly Comics Release List, To Protect and Preserve (Protecting Comics), Superman FAQ

Archive site See the FAQs. For the FAQS, use anonymous ftp to the FAQ archive at rtfm.mit.edu.

Related groups rec.arts.comics.info, rec.arts.comics.marketplace, rec.arts.comics.misc, rec.arts.comics.strips

---

rec.arts.comics.info ★★★★

News, announcements, and analysis of the comic book world, with very informative and well-written reviews of the current comic book crop.

Typical recent postings Sandman: WWW Site Now Open!, Pick of the Brown Bag: A Weekly Review: The Prophet's Wisdom.

Review This group's postings are packed with information sure to send any comic book fanatic into the stratosphere—insiders' gossip, interviews with artists, in-depth analysis of the marketplace. But the reviews are of even broader interest. If you're wondering what's going on with this ancient and interesting art form, take a look at the reviews—I won't be surprised if you pay a visit to your local comic book store! (Um, see you there.)

Advice to newbies Post to other groups in the rec.arts.comics.* hierarchy.

Adult-oriented? No.

Readership 26,000.

Rank 1,109.

Messages per month 108.

Crossposting percentage 16%.

Availability 66% of USENET sites.

Moderated? Yes.

Special features None.

FAQ title Welcome to rec.arts.comics

FAQ location rec.arts.comics.info

Other information resources rec.arts.comics.marketplace Frequently Asked Questions List(FAQ), New Weekly Comics Release List, To Protect and Preserve (Protecting Comics), Superman FAQ

Archive site None.

Related groups rec.arts.comics, rec.arts.comics.marketplace, rec.arts.comics.misc, rec.arts.comics.strips

---

rec.arts.comics.strips ★★★

The comics in the daily newspaper.

Typical recent postings New Outland Collection, Calvin and Hobbes Psychotic Snowmen, Strips That Aren't in Your Local Paper, Where Is Gary Trudeau?

Review If you're not content to read them in the paper, but want to talk about them and analyze every last little detail, this is for you. I didn't think

I'd find any *Mary Worth* fans, but by Toutatis, they're in here too.

Advice to newbies   Please read the group's FAQ before posting to avoid asking questions that have been posed before.

Adult-oriented?   No.

Readership   29,000.

Rank   1,012.

Messages per month   319.

Crossposting percentage   6%.

Availability   68% of USENET sites.

Moderated?   No.

Special features   None.

FAQ title   Welcome to rec.arts.comics

FAQ location   rec.arts.comics.info

Other information resources
rec.arts.comics.marketplace Frequently Asked Questions List(FAQ), New Weekly Comics Release List, To Protect and Preserve (Protecting Comics), Superman FAQ

Archive site   For the FAQS, use anonymous ftp to the FAQ archive at rtfm.mit.edu.

Related groups   rec.arts.comics, rec.arts.comics.marketplace, rec.arts.comics.misc, rec.arts.comics.strips

---

rec.arts.disney ★★★

Anything related to the corporate legacies of Walt Disney—including the movies, the theme parks, books, and television shows.

Typical recent postings   Antique Mickey Toy, The Next Disney Flick, Song of the South, Disney Soundtracks, Using Thumbelina to Understand Disney, Disney in VA.

Review   This newsgroup features good, generally friendly discussion, emphasizing Disney's parks and movies. You'll have a chance to debate which of Disney's cartoon classics is the best and—how can you resist this?—you can use Thumbelina to understand Disney, the title of a recent and highly provocative post.

Advice to newbies   Please read the group's FAQ before posting to avoid asking questions that have been posed before.

Adult-oriented?   No.

Readership   78,000.

Rank   228.

Messages per month   3,651.

Crossposting percentage   3%.

Availability   73% of USENET sites.

Moderated?   No.

Special features   None.

FAQ title   rec.arts.disney FAQ

FAQ location   rec.arts.disney, rec.answers, news.answers

Other information resources   Disneyland FAQ, Walt Disney World FAQ

Archive site   For the FAQS, use anonymous ftp to the FAQ archive at rtfm.mit.edu.

Related groups   rec.parks.theme

---

rec.arts.erotica ★★★

Erotic stories and poems, contributed by USENET writers.

Typical recent postings   Fun in the Park, Two Nights, Going Away, Seasons of Change.

Review   Because this group is moderated, there's no discussion, flames, or attacks from the Christian right—but unfortunately, this fact alone can't raise the literary level of most of the contributions, which are for the most part the work of oversexed college students. Once in a very long while there's a work of some literary merit; this newsgroup would probably pass the Supreme Court's old "socially redeeming value" test for the protection of obscenity.

Advice to newbies   Don't try to contribute a story through the anonymous remailer at anon.penet.fi—the moderator won't accept it. Be sure to check your spelling and grammar if you want your contribution to be accepted.

Adult-oriented?   Yes.

Readership   250,000.

Rank   12.

Messages per month   60.

Crossposting percentage   4%.

Availability   70% of USENET sites.

Moderated?   Yes.

Special features   Codes may be assigned to identify the subject material, as follows: admin: administrative announcements, indexes of stories, and so on; animal: bestiality and animals; annc: announcements other than administrative; bond: bondage (physical restraint); dom: domination (primarily psychological); ff: female-female contact; furry: sentient non-human characters; gothic: vampires and other Gothic subjects; group: group sex and threesomes; heavy: "heavy" forms of bdsm; humor: joke posts or amusing stories; incest: incestuous relationships; mf: male-female contact; mild: "mild" forms of bdsm; mm: male-male contact; nc: non-consensual situations; pedo: pedophilia (pre-pubescent); poem: poetry; rape: rape scenes and other violent non-consensual sexuality; scat: scatology and coprophilia; series: long stories split into sections; sf: speculative fiction; sci-fi, heavy fantasy, and the like; sm: sadism and masochism; teen: consensual sex involving teenagers and postpubescents; trans: crossdressing and transgendered material; water: watersports and urophilia.

FAQ title   ADMIN: rec.arts.erotica introduction

FAQ location   rec.arts.erotica, alt.sex, alt.sex.stories.d, rec.arts.prose

Other information resources   None.

Archive site   Rumored to exist, but not made publicly known out of fear of a deluge of FTP requests.

Related groups   alt.sex, alt.sex.stories.d, rec.arts.prose

rec.arts.movies ★★★★★

Typical recent postings   Worst Movie for a First Date, Women Bashing Movies, Movies SO Bad You Walked Out Of, Ten Best Movies This Year So Far.

Review   One of USENET's best, this newsgroup features passionate debate about films by people who obviously love films. The usual exchange of opinion is spiced by reviews, news about favorite actresses and actors, and news from the film industry. Note the richness of the FAQs and the Movie Database; this is one of USENET's most extraordinary accomplishments.

Advice to newbies   Please avoid posting spoilers unless they're clearly marked.

Adult-oriented?   No.

Readership   160,000.

Rank   25.

Messages per month   7,646.

Crossposting percentage   3%.

Availability   77% of USENET sites.

Moderated?   No.

Special features   The movie database is an international volunteer effort coordinated through rec.arts.movies. Currently covering over 32,000 movies, the database has more than 370,000 filmography entries and consumes more than 18 MB of disk space. You'll find filmographies for actors, directors, writers, composers, cinematographers, editors, production designers, costume designers and producers; plot summaries; character names; movie ratings; year of release; running times; movie trivia; quotes; goofs; soundtracks; personal trivia and Academy Award information. Several thousand of the movies are covered completely from the major actors to the minor bit players. For more information, see the Movie Database FAQ (at "Archive Sites").

FAQ title   rec.arts.movies Frequently Asked Questions

FAQ location   rec.arts.movies

Other information resources   LIST: Crazy Movie Credits, LIST: Movie Biographies, Movie Database: Frequently Asked Questions List, Memorable Quotes from Movies [DATABASE LIST], BLADE RUNNER Frequently Asked Questions, BRAZIL Frequently Asked Questions, Movie Goofs and Technical Errors, Elijah Wood Mini-FAQ, LIST: Movie Soundtracks

Archive site   Many questions about movies can be answered by consulting the Movie Database. For information, see the movie database FAQ, which contains full details and is posted weekly to this newsgroup. You can also obtain copies by anonymous ftp to rtfm.mit.edu in the directory /pub/usenet/news.answers/movies; the file is called movie-database-faq.

Related groups   alt.cult-movies, rec.arts.sf.movies, rec.music.movies, rec.arts.tv, rec.arts.movies.reviews

rec.arts.movies.reviews ★★★★★

Typical recent postings: Review: The Slingshot, Review: Andre, Review: Spanking the Monkey.

Review   In-depth reviews, featuring probing and intelligent analyses of every aspect of the film—the script, the acting, the directing, the set, and more. One of USENET's best, and well worth adding to your subscription list.

Advice to newbies   This is a moderated newsgroup featuring in-depth reviews. For discussion, post to rec.arts.movies.misc.

Adult-oriented?   No.

Readership   140,000.

Rank   36.

Messages per month   81.

Crossposting percentage   1%.

Availability   75% of USENET sites.

Moderated?   Yes.

Special features   None.

FAQ title   None.

FAQ location   N/A.

Other information resources   None.

Archive site   None.

Related groups   rec.arts.movies.misc

rec.arts.sf.announce ★★★

Announcements and news of interest to the science fiction community.

Typical recent postings   Where To Find CYBERSPACE VANGUARD 2:3, David Brin Collaborative Project on Kaleidospace, RADIUS Seeks Subscribers.

Review   If you're a science fiction fanatic, you'll want to add this newsgroup to your subscription list. You'll learn about forthcoming books, conventions, journals, and more.

Advice to newbies   This is a moderated newsgroup for announcements only.

Adult-oriented? No.

Readership 40,000.

Rank 712.

Messages per month 21.

Crossposting percentage 10%.

Availability 72% of USENET sites.

Moderated? Yes.

Special features None.

FAQ title rec.arts.sf.groups, an introduction

FAQ location rec.arts.sf.announce, rec.arts.sf.misc, rec.answers, news.answers

Other information resources None.

Archive site There's an SF archive at Lysator, accessible by means of WWW: http://www.lysator.liu.se/sf_archive/sf_main.html; Gopher: gopher.lysator.liu.se, and FTP: ftp.lysator.liu.se, /pub/sf-texts.

Related groups In the rec.arts.sf.* hierarchy: rec.arts.sf.misc, rec.arts.sf.announce, rec.arts.sf.fandom, rec.arts.sf.marketplace, rec.arts.sf.movies, rec.arts.sf.reviews, rec.arts.sf.science, rec.arts.sf.starwars,rec.arts.sf.tv, rec.arts.sf.tv.babylon5,rec.arts.sf.tv.quantum-leap, rec.arts.sf.written. Elsewhere: rec.arts.startrek.info, rec.arts.startrek.tech, alt.books.isaac-asimov, alt.books.deryni, alt.books.m-lackey, alt.cyberpunk, alt.cyberpunk.chatsubo, alt.fan.douglas-adam, alt.fan.eddings, alt.fan.pern, alt.fan.piers-anthony, alt.fan.pratchett, alt.fan.tolkien, alt.fandom.cons, alt.fandom.misc, alt.galactic-guide,alt.music.filk, alt.tv.red-dwarf

rec.arts.sf.misc ★★

Those aspects of science fiction that don't fit into the other rec.arts.sf.* groups.

Typical recent postings Brin a feminist? Sequel to Ringworld Engineers, Xanth Home Page.

Review A goodly amount of crossposting here, because the participants can't figure out what this group is for, either!

Advice to newbies This is a moderated newsgroup for announcements only.

Adult-oriented? No.

Readership 43,000.

Rank 456.

Messages per month 1,035.

Crossposting percentage 19%.

Availability 72% of USENET sites.

Moderated? Yes.

Special features Regular postings of the *Cyberspace Vanguard: News and Views of the Science Fiction and Fantasy Universe.*

FAQ title rec.arts.sf.groups, an introduction

FAQ location rec.arts.sf.announce, rec.arts.sf.misc, rec.answers, news.answers

Other information resources SF-references-in-music_List

Archive site There's an SF archive at Lysator, accessible by means of WWW: http://www.lysator.liu.se/sf_archive/sf_main.html; Gopher: gopher.lysator.liu.se, and FTP: ftp.lysator.liu.se, /pub/sf-texts.

Related groups In the rec.arts.sf.* hierarchy: rec.arts.sf.misc, rec.arts.sf.announce, rec.arts.sf.fandom, rec.arts.sf.marketplace, rec.arts.sf.movies, rec.arts.sf.reviews, rec.arts.sf.science, rec.arts.sf.starwars,rec.arts.sf.tv, rec.arts.sf.tv.babylon5,rec.arts.sf.tv.quantum-leap, rec.arts.sf.written. Elsewhere: rec.arts.startrek.info, rec.arts.startrek.tech, alt.books.isaac-asimov, alt.books.deryni, alt.books.m-lackey, alt.cyberpunk, alt.cyberpunk.chatsubo, alt.fan.douglas-adam, alt.fan.eddings, alt.fan.pern, alt.fan.piers-anthony, alt.fan.pratchett, alt.fan.tolkien, alt.fandom.cons, alt.fandom.misc, alt.galactic-guide, alt.music.filk, alt.tv.red-dwarf

rec.arts.sf.movies ★★★

Science fiction movies other than the ones for which there are separate newsgroups (Star Trek, Star Wars).

Typical recent postings Aliens: The Uncut Version, Star Wars Missing Episodes, Harrison Ford is a replicant.

Review In this newsgroup, you'll find discussion and debate regarding science fiction films, focusing on plots (and plot inconsistencies), trivia, wish lists, critiques, and general ranting and raving about science fiction movies. For the converted only.

Advice to newbies Please read the group's FAQs before posting to avoid asking questions that have been posed before.

Adult-oriented? No.

Readership 58,000.

Rank 408.

Messages per month 1,035.

Crossposting percentage 19%.

Availability 72% of USENET sites.

Moderated? No.

Special features None, but see rec.arts.movies for information about the Movie Database.

FAQ title rec.arts.sf.movies Frequently Asked Questions

FAQ location rec.arts.sf.movies, rec.answers, news.answers

Other information resources LIST: MOVIE TRIVIA: in-jokes, cameos, signatures. LIST: Movie Quotes (Memorable Quotes from Movies. MOVIES: ALIEN FAQ part. MOVIES: ALIEN FAQ part. MOVIES: ALIEN FAQ part. MOVIES: ALIEN FAQ part. Memorable Quotes from Movies [DATABASE LIST]. Movie Database: Frequently Asked Questions List.

Archive site There's an SF archive at Lysator, accessible by means of WWW: http://www.lysator.liu.se/sf_archive/sf_main.html; Gopher: gopher.lysator.liu.se, and FTP: ftp.lysator.liu.se, /pub/sf-texts.

Related groups alt.cult-movies, rec.arts.sf.misc, rec.arts.movies, rec.arts.sf.reviews, rec.arts.sf.announce, rec.arts.sf.science, rec.arts.sf.marketplace

rec.arts.sf.reviews ★★★★★

Probing, interesting review of recent science fiction works.

Typical recent postings OTHERNESS by David Brin, SUMMER OF LOVE by Lisa Mason, Two Anthology Reviews: WEIRD TALES FROM SHAK…BY ELVIS, Review of Effinger's "When Gravity Fails," THE BREATH OF SUSPENSION by Alexander Jablokov.

Review One of USENET's best, this newsgroup features exceptionally well-written and intelligent reviews of recent work in science fiction.

Advice to newbies This is a moderated newsgroup; for discussion, post to rec.arts.sf.misc.

Adult-oriented? No.

Readership 52,000.

Rank 493.

Messages per month 23.

Crossposting percentage 9%.

Availability 69% of USENET sites.

Moderated? Yes.

Special features None.

FAQ title   Welcome to rec.arts.sf.reviews

FAQ location   rec.arts.sf.reviews, rec.answers, news.answers

Other information resources   None.

Archive site   There's an SF archive at Lysator, accessible by means of WWW http// www.lysator.liu.se/sf_archive/sf_main.html; Gopher gopher.lysator.liu.se, and FTP ftp.lysator.liu.se, /pub/sf-texts.

Related groups   In the rec.arts.sf.* hierarchy: rec.arts.sf.misc, rec.arts.sf.announce, rec.arts.sf.fandom, rec.arts.sf.marketplace, rec.arts.sf.movies, rec.arts.sf.reviews, rec.arts.sf.science, rec.arts.sf.starwars,rec.arts.sf.tv, rec.arts.sf.tv.babylon5,rec.arts.sf.tv.quantum-leap, rec.arts.sf.written. Elsewhere: rec.arts.startrek.info, rec.arts.startrek.tech, alt.books.isaac-asimov, alt.books.deryni, alt.books.m-lackey, alt.cyberpunk, alt.cyberpunk.chatsubo, alt.fan.douglas-adam, alt.fan.eddings, alt.fan.pern, alt.fan.piers-anthony, alt.fan.pratchett, alt.fan.tolkien, alt.fandom.cons, alt.fandom.misc, alt.galactic-guide,alt.music.filk, alt.tv.red-dwarf

Adult-oriented?   No.

Readership   63,000.

Rank   350.

Messages per month   4,971.

Crossposting percentage   3%.

Availability   73% of USENET sites.

Moderated?   No.

Special features   None.

FAQ title   rec.arts.sf.written FAQ

FAQ location   rec.arts.sf.written, rec.arts.sf.misc, rec.answers, news.answers

Other information resources   LIST Alternate History Stories

Archive site   There's an SF archive at Lysator, accessible by means of WWW http// www.lysator.liu.se/sf_archive/sf_main.html; Gopher gopher.lysator.liu.se, and FTP ftp.lysator.liu.se, /pub/sf-texts.

Related groups   rec.arts.sf.misc, alt.history.whatif, alt.books.isaac-asimov, alt.books.deryni, alt.books.m-lackey, alt.cyberpunk, alt.cyberpunk.chatsubo, alt.fan.douglas-adam, alt.fan.eddings, alt.fan.pern, alt.fan.piers-anthony, alt.fan.pratchett, alt.fan.tolkien, alt.fandom.misc, alt.galactic-guide

rec.arts.sf.written ★★★★

Published science fiction and fantasy, subjected to high-volume discussion and debate.

Typical recent postings   Science Fiction vs. Fantasy, Worst Science Fiction Novel Ever, Heinlein's Puppet Masters FACTS, The Influence of the Net, Stephen R. Donaldson.

Review   Not to be missed by any SF fan, this newsgroup features volatile—but often informative and interesting—discussion of science fiction novels, with lots of tips about works too good to be missed.

Advice to newbies   Please read the group's FAQ before posting to avoid asking questions that have been posed before.

rec.arts.startrek.current ★★★

Recent Star Trek TV programs, movies, and books (recent = past four months, unless you're talking about an end-of-season cliffhanger).

Typical recent postings   Does Anybody Stay Dead in Star Trek?, Gays in STTNG, Is the Transporter Scientifically Impossible?, Does Anyone Care if Kirk Dies?, English Spoken Everywhere, Star Trek and Religion.

Review Just the thing for the *Star Trek* fan outraged (or delighted) with the last episode—fervent discussion of plots, characterizations, acting, trivia, and bloopers.

Advice to newbies Please read the group's FAQ before posting to avoid asking questions that have been posed before. Above all, don't post spoilers without putting the word SPOILER! in the subject line.

Adult-oriented? No.

Readership 120,000.

Rank 68.

Messages per month 5,901.

Crossposting percentage 6%.

Availability 73% of USENET sites.

Moderated? No.

Special features Frequent information postings.

FAQ title FAQL: Frequently Asked Questions List for rec.arts.startrek.current

FAQ location rec.arts.startrek.current

Other information resources See rec.arts.startrek.info.

Archive site See the FAQ entitled FAQL FTP SITES WITH TREK-RELATED FILES.

Related groups rec.arts.startrek.misc, rec.arts.startrek.fandom, rec.arts.startrek.tech, rec.arts.startrek.info

---

rec.arts.startrek.info ★★★★

Typical recent postings The Dominion—It's Everywhere! Interesting Instrument Approach, New Gene Roddenberry Book Out In Aug., Nimoy Film, Jerry Goldsmith & "Star Trek Voyager."

Review If you're looking for an uncluttered newsgroup to find news about Star Trek, this is the place. This Moderated newsgroup contains nothing but announcements regarding new Star Trek–related conventions, films, magazine articles, archival resources, and much more.

Advice to newbies This is a moderated newsgroup; for discussion, post to other groups in the rec.arts.startrek.* hierarchy.

Adult-oriented? No.

Readership 110,000.

Rank 89.

Messages per month 15.

Crossposting percentage 7%.

Availability 75% of USENET sites.

Moderated? Yes.

Special features USENET's most prodigious library of informational postings.

FAQ title Guidelines for Submitting Articles, Introduction to rec.arts.startrek.info

FAQ location rec.arts.startrek.info

Other information resources List of Upcoming Conventions, Bibliography of ST articles/ books, DIFFs—Star Trek TMS List of Lists, DIFFs—Star Trek TOS/TAS List of Lists, FAQ Star Trek Spelling List, FAQL Acronyms Used in the rec.arts.startrek.* Newsgroups, FAQL FTP Sites with Trek-Related Files, FAQL How to Submit Creative Material, FAQL List of Periodic Postings to r.a.s. Newsgroups, FAQL Multi-Lingual ôStar Trekö, FAQL Names, Ranks, and Serial Numbers (and Crew Data), FAQL Pilto Episodes and Unaired Episodes, FAQL SNAFUs, FAQL Star Trek Abroad, FAQL Star Trek Aliens, FAQL Star Trek Dates and Years, FAQL Star Trek Music, FAQL Time Loops, Yesterday's Enterprise, and Tasha Yar Explained, FAQL diff listing, O'Brien's rank FAQ, ST TNG Canonical Drinking Game, ST TOS Love/ Romance List, Startrek Lists, Shakespeare in Star Trek, Star Trek TOS/ TAS List of Lists, Star Trek Info Lists, Trek Rate Ballot, Trek Rate Results, Star Trek TMS List of Lists, Star Trek Actors' Other Roles FAQ, Star Trek Season Promo Summary, Star Trek Books-On-Tape, FAQ- STTNG

Program Guide, Star Trek Comics Checklist, Star Trek Ships Television and Film, Star Trek Ships Explained, Star Trek Locations

Archive site   See the FAQ entitled FAQL FTP SITES WITH TREK-RELATED FILES.

Related groups   rec.arts.startrek.misc, rec.arts.startrek.current

Other information resources   See rec.arts.startrek.current.

Archive site   See the FAQ entitled FAQL FTP SITES WITH TREK-RELATED FILES.

Related groups   rec.arts.startrek, rec.arts.startrek.current, rec.arts.startrek.fandom, rec.arts.startrek.tech

rec.arts.startrek.reviews ★★★★

Reviews of Star Trek TV shows, books, and movies.

Typical recent postings   DS9 Spoiler: "The Jem'Hadar," DS9 Spoiler: "Tribunal," DS9 Episode Review: IMHO—"Invasive Procedures," DS9 Episode Review: IMHO—"The Siege," ALL Editorial: The Saavik Syndrome.

Review   Here's the place to look, amid the hue and cry of Star Trek discussions, for reviews of Star Trek television shows, books, and movies. A moderated group that accepts only reviews, this group has a refreshingly low volume that enables one to find the reviews easily. And they're worth reading, too.

Advice to newbies   Read all the Star Trek newsgroups, and know your subject well, before submitting a review.

Adult-oriented?   No.

Readership   31,000.

Rank   929.

Messages per month   47.

Crossposting percentage   0%.

Availability   58% of USENET sites.

Moderated?   Yes.

Special features   None.

FAQ title   None.

FAQ location   N/A.

rec.arts.startrek.tech ★★★

The technology of Star Trek—warp speed, transporters, the stuff Scotty (and now Jordy) fools around with.

Typical recent postings   Light Speed, High Gravity Humans, Warp 6 is not Full Impulse!, Enterprise Design Specs, E acceleration.

Review   This is the place for Star Trek technology aficionados to gather and debate; you'll learn, for example, about an obscure physicist who recently argued that Star Trek's warp speed technology just might be possible.

Advice to newbies   Please read the group's FAQ before posting to avoid asking questions that have been posed before.

Adult-oriented?   No.

Readership   73,000.

Rank   257.

Messages per month   967.

Crossposting percentage   10%.

Availability   72% of USENET sites.

Moderated?   No.

Special features   Unusually rich set of FAQs.

FAQ title   FAQL: Frequently Asked Questions List for rec.arts.startrek.tech

FAQ location   rec.arts.startrek.tech

Other information resources   Mini-FAQ Reading List for Rec.arts.startrek.tech., Mini-FAQ Rec.arts.startrek.tech Reading List, Mini-FAQ: Ship Statistics (Absolutely Non-canon), Mini-FAQ: The Holodeck and Computers, Mini-FAQ: Time Travel and Causality Violation, Mini-FAQ: Transporters and Replicators, Mini-FAQ: Warp and Subspace, R.A.S.* NETIQUETTE LIST, R.A.S.* SPOILER LIST, Relativity And FTL Travel, STAR TREK LOCATIONS, STAR TREK SHIPS: EXPANDED, STAR TREK SHIPS: TELEVISION & FILM, STAR TREK SHIPS

Archive site   See the FAQ entitled FAQL: FTP SITES WITH TREK-RELATED FILES.

Related groups   rec.arts.startrek.misc, rec.arts.startrek.current

rec.arts.tv ★★★

The Boob Tube—the shows, the actors and actresses, the advertising, the sublime, the schlock.

Typical recent postings   Forgotten Cartoons, Worst Show on and off the Air, Super Chicken, William S. Burroughs for Nike?, New Really Crummy Show, Anyone Remember Tennessee Tuxedo?

Review   This newsgroup offers lots of fun discussion, but the volume is so high that it's tedious to read on a regular basis. Use your newsreader's search capabilities—or better, read one of the excellent FAQs.

Advice to newbies   Please read the group's posting guidelines and FAQs before posting to avoid asking questions that have been posed before.

Adult-oriented?   No.

Readership   110,000.

Rank   95.

Messages per month   3,010.

Crossposting percentage   11%.

Availability   76% of USENET sites.

Moderated?   No.

Special features   Weekly postings of syndicated ratings.

FAQ title   rec.arts.tv Posting Guidelines

FAQ location   rec.arts.tv, rec.answers, news.answers

Other information resources   Get a Life Program Guide, Married with Children Program Guide, Program Guide, Gilligan's Island FAQ, Soap Episode FAQ, TV Discussion Groups etc., Syndicated Ratings for Week, Mystery Science Theatre FAQ

Archive site   None.

Related groups   rec.arts.sf.tv, rec.arts.tv.uk, rec.arts.tv.soaps, rec.arts.tv.mst3k

rec.audio.misc ★★★

All aspects of high-fidelity systems that don't fit into the other rec.audio.* groups (rec.audio.car, rec.audio.high-end, rec.audio.opinion, rec.audio.pro, and rec.audio.tech).

Typical recent postings   Speaker Wire—The Thicker the Better, Dubbing Quality—Hi vs. Normal Speed, Surround Sound—How Do They Do It?, 50 Watts Better Than 100 Watts?

Review   If you're an audio nut, you'll like this group—the focus is squarely on getting the best possible sound. There are lots of informative postings and reviews along with the inevitable give and take of opinion and hot air.

Advice to newbies   Please read the group's FAQ before posting to avoid asking questions that have been posed before.

Adult-oriented? No.

Readership 100,000.

Rank 113.

Messages per month 1,533.

Crossposting percentage 9%.

Availability 77% of USENET sites.

Moderated? No.

Special features The group's four-part FAQ is an education in audio technology.

FAQ title FAQ: rec.audio

FAQ location rec.audio, rec.music.info, rec.answers, news.answers

Other information resources None.

Archive site None.

Related groups rec.audio.car, rec.audio.misc, rec.audio.tech, rec.audio.high-end

rec.audio.car ★★★

Car stereos—selecting and buying them, installing and maintaining them, protecting them from rip-offs.

Typical recent postings Alpine vs. Eclipse, Superior Sound, Car Audio and Hearing Loss, Replacement Speakers, Small Trucks and Big Speakers.

Review This newsgroup features informed and valuable discussion of car stereos generally, with lots of useful information for anyone thinking about upgrading a car stereo system.

Advice to newbies Please read the group's FAQ before posting to avoid asking questions that have been posed before.

Adult-oriented? No.

Readership 49,000.

Rank 542.

Messages per month 1,119.

Crossposting percentage 2%.

Availability 72% of USENET sites.

Moderated? No.

Special features None.

FAQ title rec.audio.car FAQ

FAQ location rec.audio.car, rec.answers, news.answers

Other information resources None.

Archive site None.

Related groups rec.audio, rec.audio.misc

rec.autos.misc ★★

Wheels, the kind you and I buy (as opposed to antique cars, hot rods, and sport cars, which are dealt with—respectively—in rec.autos.antique, rec.autos.rod-n-custom, and rec.autos.sport).

Typical recent postings Great Dealer Experience, We Bought a Saturn, Exploding Volvo—Am I Paranoid?

Review This newsgroup features lots of discussion about cars, and it might be of interest if you're in the market—but the volume is so high that it's very tedious to read regularly. Use your newsreader's search function to find articles of interest.

Advice to newbies Please don't post "for sale" ads here; they're supposed to be posted in rec.autos.marketplace. Please read the group's FAQ before posting to avoid asking questions that have been posed before.

Adult-oriented? No.

Readership 40,000.

Rank 704.

Messages per month 610.

Crossposting percentage 53%.

Availability 54% of USENET sites.

Moderated? No.

Special features None.

FAQ title rec.autos: Frequently Asked Questions

FAQ location rec.autos, rec.autos.tech, rec.autos.sport, rec.autos.driving, rec.autos.vw, alt.autos.antique

Other information resources The rec.autos Archive Server, rec.autos: Automotive Mailing Lists, rec.autos: Automotive Mailing Lists: how to set up your own, Welcome to the new reader

Archive site None.

Related groups rec.autos.tech, rec.autos.sport, rec.autos.driving, rec.autos.vw, alt.autos.antique

rec.autos.sport ★★★

Racing—the cars, the tracks, the drivers, the pile-ups.

Typical recent postings Pit Fire: Official Cause, Indy Racing League Engine, Maserati Merak SS, INDY: Yellow Flag, Dirty Wheels.

Review This group features high-quality discussion and debate concerning racing matters; if you're a fan, you'll love it.

Advice to newbies Please read the group's FAQ before posting to avoid asking questions that have been posed before.

Adult-oriented No.

Readership 79,000.

Rank 215.

Messages per month 3,146.

Crossposting percentage 3%.

Availability 76% of USENET sites.

Moderated? No.

Special features.

FAQ title rec.autos.sport FAQ

FAQ location rec.autos.sport, rec.autos.sport.info, rec.answers, news.answers

Other information resources rec.autos.sport FAQ 1: Introduction Frequently Asked Questions. rec.autos.sport FAQ 2: Race Schedule Frequently Asked Questions. rec.autos.sport FAQ 3: Single Seater Frequently Asked Questions. rec.autos.sport FAQ 4: NASCAR Frequently Asked Questions. rec.autos.sport FAQ 5: General Autosport Frequently Asked Questions. rec.autos.sport FAQ 6: Other Race Series Frequently Asked Questions. rec.autos.sport FAQ 7: Autosport Addresses.

Archive site None.

Related groups rec.autos.sport.tech, rec.autos.sport.nascar, rec.autos

rec.autos.tech ★★★

The nuts and bolts of automobile technology, from the driver's point of view.

Typical recent postings Jiffy Lube and Synthetic Oil Change, Advice on New Subcompact, Penalty for Pollution Control Violation, Retreaded Tires— Are They Safe?, Warped Rotors.

Review For anyone who enjoys maintaining and repairing cars, this newsgroup will prove of great interest—there's good discussion and lots of information-sharing.

Advice to newbies There's no FAQ, but check out the FAQ for rec.autos.misc before posting.

Adult-oriented? No.

Readership 100,000.

Messages per month 3,360.

Crossposting percentage 18%.

Availability   77% of USENET sites.

Moderated?   No.

Special features   None.

FAQ title   None.

FAQ location   N/A.

Other information resources   None.

Archive site   None.

Related groups   rec.autos, rec.autos.sport

rec.backcountry ★★★★★

Everything about the roadless wilderness— preserving it, exploring it, surviving it.

Typical recent postings   Canoeing in Arkansas, The Badlands, Down vs. Synthetic Fill, Pepper Spray for Bears, Appalachian Trail and Private Land, Places to Buy Equipment in the U.S.

Review   One of USENET's best, the discussion in this newsgroup is on an exceptionally high level. Whether you're interested in mountain climbing or just taking a pleasant hike, there's sure to be something of interest. Posts are informative, discussion is congenial—this is the way USENET is supposed to work.

Advice to newbies   Start with the FAQ titled "Netiquette: Distilled Wisdom," which provides a guide to the rest of the FAQs. Please read these FAQs before posting to avoid asking questions that have been posed before.

Adult-oriented?   No.

Readership   73,000.

Rank   259.

Messages per month   3,196.

Crossposting percentage   2%.

Availability   76% of USENET sites.

Moderated?   No.

Special features   The extensive FAQs add up to a most impressive collection of knowledge about the backcountry.

FAQ title   Netiquette: Distilled Wisdom

FAQ location   rec.backcountry

Other information resources   AMS Distilled Wisdom, Backcountry Ethics Distilled Wisdom, Colin Fletcher Rachel Carson Distilled Wisdom., Eco-warriors Distilled Wisdom., High tech employment, a romantic notion, Information on bears: Distilled Wisdom., Leopolds Land Ethic Distilled Wisdom., Leopolds post Distilled Wisdom., Lyme Disease: Distilled Wisdom., Morbid backcountry memorial: Distilled Wisdom., Netiquette: Distilled Wisdom, Oak Ivy Distilled Wisdom, Phone address list Distilled Wisdom, Questions on conditions and travel DW, rec.backC DISCLAIMER—Distilled wisdom, References Distilled Wisdom, Related news groups: Distilled Wisdom, Snake bite: Distilled Wisdom, Song Distilled Wisdom, summary of one past topic Not Distilled wisdom, Telling questions r.b. Turing test DW:, summary of past topics Distilled non-wisdom, Volunteer Work: Distilled Wisdom, Water filters & Giardia Distilled Wisdom, What is natural? Distilled Wisdom

Archive site   None.

Related groups   rec.climbing.

rec.bicycles.misc ★★★

All aspects of bikes that don't belong in the other rec.bicycles.* newsgroups (rec.bicycles.marketplace, rec.bicycles.racing, rec.bicycles.rides, rec.bicycles.soc, rec.bicycles.tech).

Typical recent postings   Touring Bike vs. Road Bike, Bike Security, Bike Locks/ Liquid Nitrogen, Great Light for Night Riders.

Review   You'll find discussion of the general aspects of cycling in this group, and more specific articles in the other rec.bicycles.* newsgroups; cycling enthusiasts will probably want to add all these groups to their subscriptions lists.

Advice to newbies   Please don't post "for sale" messages in any group other than rec.bicycles.marketplace. Please read the group's FAQ before posting to avoid asking questions that have been posed before.

Adult-oriented?   No.

Readership   42,000.

Rank   676.

Messages per month   2,034.

Crossposting percentage   5%.

Availability   69% of USENET sites.

Moderated?   No.

Special features   None.

FAQ title   Rec.Bicycles Frequently Asked Questions Posting

FAQ location   rec.bicycles.misc, rec.answers, news.answers

Other information resources   FAQ on MTB vs road bike efficiency

Archive site   There's a rec.bicycles FTP archive, which is accessible by gophering to draco.acs.uci.edu (use port 1071).

Related groups   rec.bicycles.marketplace, rec.bicycles.racing, rec.bicycles.rides, rec.bicycles.soc, rec.bicycles.tech

rec.birds ★★★★

Birding—identifying birds in the field by appearance, behavior, and song; attracting wild birds to feeders; behavior of birds in the wild; conservation of wild birds; research into bird life, and more.

Typical recent postings   Ivory-billed Woodpecker, Prairie Falcons, Florida Birding, A Mallard in My Pool, Hawaii Birding Guides/Sites, Osprey—Migrating?

Review   In this newsgroup, you'll find congenial and informed discussion of all aspects of birding. Even if you've never contemplated a birdwatching expedition, you may find this group of interest.

Advice to newbies   Please post discussion of birds as pets to rec.pets.birds. Don't limit your distribution; rec.birds is read around the world. Please read the group's FAQ before posting to avoid asking questions that have been posed before. Please avoid posting on the subject of falconry and domestic cats, subjects that have launched flame wars in the past.

Adult-oriented?   No.

Readership   39,000.

Rank   742.

Messages per month   545.

Crossposting percentage   1%.

Availability   74% of USENET sites.

Moderated?   No.

Special features   None.

FAQ title   rec.birds Frequently Asked Questions

FAQ location   rec.birds, rec.answers, news.answers

Other information resources   rec.birds Monthly Optics for Birding FAQ

Archive site   None.

Related groups   None.

rec.crafts.brewing ★★★★★

Beer—the ancient art of brewing it to perfection. Included are microbreweries as well as home brewing.

Typical recent postings   Book for Beginners, Amber Ale Hopping, I Hate Bottling, Good Head—No Sediment, Non-alcoholic Brew, Blueberry Ale, Anyone?

Review   One of USENET's best, this newsgroup offers the combination of intelligent discussion, rich informational resources, and knowledge-packed posts that show off USENET at its finest.

Advice to newbies   Please read the group's FAQ before posting to avoid asking questions that have been posed before.

Adult-oriented?   No.

Readership   49,000.

Rank   541.

Messages per month   1,775.

Crossposting percentage   1%.

Availability   71% of USENET sites.

Moderated?   No.

Special features   Regular postings of *Homebrew Digest,* a compendium of rich information regarding home beer brewing.

FAQ title   rec.crafts.brewing Frequently Asked Questions(FAQ)

FAQ location   rec.crafts.brewing, rec.answers, news.answers

Other information resources   None.

Archive site   *Homebrew Digest* is archived at sierra.stanford.edu in the pub/homebrew directory.

Related groups   alt.beer

rec.food.cooking ★★★★

Everything about the art and enjoyment of cooking.

Typical recent postings   Cooking Disasters, The Wonderful Eggplant, Attitudes on Food: French vs. American, Boiling Water, Before Steaming a Lobster…, Habanero Hot Sauce.

Review   Mature discussion, lots of information resources, and frequent tips and tricks make this newsgroup especially rewarding.

Advice to newbies   Please read the group's FAQ before posting to avoid asking questions that have been posed before.

Adult-oriented?   No.

Readership   120,000.

Rank   70.

Messages per month   4,351.

Crossposting percentage   3%.

Availability   77% of USENET sites.

Moderated?   No.

Special features   None.

FAQ title   rec.food.cooking Commonly Discussed Topics; rec.food.cooking FAQ and conversion file

FAQ location   rec.food.cooking, rec.food.recipes, rec.answers, news.answers

Other information resources   None.

Archive site   None.

Related groups   rec.food.recipes, rec.food.veg, rec.food.veg.cooking

rec.food.drink ★★★★

This newsgroup should be called rec.food.drink.wine, since that's the subject of most of the discussion.

Typical recent postings Wine Books, Wine Laws, Temecula CA Wines, Wine Tours of San Francisco.

Review Good discussion of matters relating to wines and liqueurs, from the standpoint of the enjoyment of these beverages rather than the snob appeal factor. Lots of tips and reviews in addition to discussion and debate.

Advice to newbies Please read the Wine FAQ before posting to avoid asking questions about wine that have been posed before.

Adult-oriented? No.

Readership N/A.

Rank N/A.

Messages per month N/A.

Crossposting percentage N/A.

Availability N/A.

Moderated? No.

Special features None.

FAQ title Wine FAQ

FAQ location rec.food.drink, rec.answers, news.answers

Other information resources None.

Archive site None.

Related groups rec.food.drink

rec.food.drink.beer ★★★★

Fine beers, especially imported beers and microbrewery beers.

Typical recent postings Czechoslovakian Budweiser, Good Beer in Washington, D.C., Double Diamond, Internet-wide Beer Tasting.

Review This newsgroup features mature discussion of fine beers and offers frequent informational posts and tips on excellent new brews as well as the usual discussion and debate.

Advice to newbies Please read the group's FAQ before posting to avoid asking questions that have been posed before.

Adult-oriented? No.

Readership 20,000.

Rank 1,304.

Messages per month 997.

Crossposting percentage 25%.

Availability 51% of USENET sites.

Moderated? No.

Special features None.

FAQ title rec.food.drink.beer FAQ

FAQ location rec.food.drink.beer, rec.answers, news.answers

Other information resources FAQ Beer Calories, Welcome to rec.food.drink.beer

Archive site ftp://sierra.stanford.edu/pub/homebrew/rfdb

Related groups rec.food.drink

rec.food.drink.coffee ★★

Everything about drinking coffee—where to get good beans, how to grind them, how to brew a good cup.

Typical recent postings Iced Coffee, Price Increase, Guinness and Coffee, Espresso where?, Beans in New York, Espresso Machine.

Review Here's one of those rare cases where the rec.* group doesn't seem as rewarding as its alt.* counterpart (alt.coffee); lots of off-topic posts, spams, and trolls. The caffeine must have gotten to them.

Advice to newbies There's no FAQ, which doesn't help.

Adult-oriented? No.

Readership 6,800.

Rank 2,108.

Messages per month 1,357.

Crossposting percentage 3%.

Availability 40% of USENET sites.

Moderated? No.

Special features None.

FAQ title None.

FAQ location N/A.

Other information resources Coffee Resources Guide, Caffeine's Frequently Asked Questions

Archive site None.

Related groups alt.coffee, alt.drugs.caffeine, alt.food.coffee

---

rec.food.veg ★★

Vegetarianism, pro and con.

Typical recent postings Vegetarian Hypocrisy, Killing, Yuck!!!, Cancer-Meat Connection, Fish-Eaters Are Not Vegetarians, Earthlings' Rights, The Harmful Effects of Eating Animals, Meat-Packing Conspiracy.

Review If you're a vegetarian, you can perhaps glean something of interest from this group, amidst the flames, trolls, and spams. Here's a group crying out for a moderator.

Advice to newbies Please read the group's FAQ before posting to avoid asking questions that have been posed before.

Adult-oriented? No.

Readership 79,000.

Rank 214.

Messages per month 1,697.

Crossposting percentage 8%.

Availability 76% of USENET sites.

Moderated? No.

Special features World Guide to Vegetarianism lists resources by region (see "Other information resources").

FAQ title rec.food.veg Frequently Asked Questions List (FAQ)

FAQ location rec.food.veg, rec.answers, news.answers

Other information resources rec.food.veg World Guide to Vegetarianism (separate lists for California, USA, Canada, and "Other"), Animal Rights FAQ Monthly Posting

Archive site None.

Related groups rec.food.veg.cooking

---

rec.gambling ★★★

Gambling—how to win.

Typical recent postings Louisiana Riverboats, Football Wagering over the Phone, Bookmaker in England, BlackJack Dealer Cheating.

Review This newsgroup features tips and tricks, known only to the computer cognoscenti, about winning at gambling of all kinds—casinos, riverboats, computer slot machines, you name it. I wouldn't bet money on it.

Advice to newbies Please read the group's FAQ before posting to avoid asking questions that have been posed before—if the FAQ still exists (it wasn't in the rftm.mit.edu archive when this book was researched).

Adult-oriented? Yes.

Readership 55,000.

Rank 452.

Messages per month 1,279.

Crossposting percentage 2%.

Availability 73% of USENET sites.

Moderated? No.

Special features None.

FAQ title rec.gambling Frequently Asked Questions (see "Advice to newbies").

FAQ location rec.gambling, rec.answers, news.answers

Other information resources None.

Archive site None.

Related groups None.

---

rec.games.backgammon ★★★

The game of backgammon—the board game, computer versions, clubs, rules, and strategies.

Typical recent postings Chessgammon, FIBS in Vegas, Cube Decision, Spring Tournament.

Review Backgammon fans will find plenty of interest here, and the group's moderate volume makes following the discussion all the more pleasant.

Advice to newbies Please read the group's FAQ before posting to avoid asking questions that have been posed before.

Adult-oriented? No.

Readership 25,000.

Rank 1,155.

Messages per month 309.

Crossposting percentage 1%.

Availability 71% of USENET sites.

Moderated? No.

Special features None.

FAQ title Backgammon— Frequently Asked Questions

FAQ location rec.games.backgammon, rec.answers, news.answers

Other information resources None.

Archive site There's a backgammon WWW page at http://www.statslab.cam.ac.uk/ ~sret1/backgammon/main.html. In addition, there's an anonymous FTP archive at ftp://ftp.netcom./pub/damish.

Related groups rec.games.misc

---

rec.games.board ★★★

Board games such as Scrabble—the ones not dealt with by their own newsgroups (see "Advice to newbies").

Typical recent postings Guerrilla, Board vs. Computer Games, Money Grubbing Game Companies, Nuclear War, Monopoly Card Missing.

Review For questions on Axis and Allies, Talisman, and Scrabble, please read the relevant FAQ before posting to avoid asking questions that have been posed before.

Advice to newbies Several board games have their own newsgroups: Abstract games: rec.games.abstract; rec.games.backgammon; Battletech et alrec.games.mecha; Chess: rec.games.chess; Cosmic Encounter: rec.games.board.ce; Diplomacy: rec.games.diplomacy; Games For Sale: rec.games.board.marketplace; General game design:

rec.games.design; Go: rec.games.go; Magic: The Gathering: rec.games.deckmaster; Miniatures: rec.games.miniatures; Play-by-Mail games: rec.games.pbm; Role-Playing Games: rec.games.frp; Trivia games : rec.games.trivia.

Adult-oriented?   No.

Readership   60,000.

Rank   393.

Messages per month   1,202.

Crossposting percentage   5%.

Availability   76% of USENET sites.

Moderated?   No.

Special features   None.

FAQ title   rec.games.board FAQ and Intro

FAQ location   rec.games.board, rec.answers, news.answers

Other information resources   Axis and Allies FAQ, Talisman boardgame FAQ (Frequently Asked Questions), Scrabble FAQ

Archive site   None.

Related groups   rec.puzzles.crosswords

Advice to newbies   Please read the group's FAQ before posting to avoid asking questions that have been posed before.

Adult-oriented?   No.

Readership   69,000.

Rank   288.

Messages per month   2,163.

Crossposting percentage   0%.

Availability   77% of USENET sites.

Moderated?   No.

Special features   The Internet Chess Server (ICS allows interactive chess games via telnet: ics.uoknor.edu 5000). See the FAQ for more information.

FAQ title   rec.games.chess Answers to Frequently Asked Questions

FAQ location   rec.games.chess, rec.answers, news.answers

Other information resources   None.

Archive site   Several chess games are available via anonymous FTP; see the FAQ for more information.

Related groups   rec.games.chinese-chess

rec.games.chess ★★★★

All aspects of chess, including the game itself, chess organizations, chess bulletin board systems (BBS), ratings, tournaments, supplies, computer chess games, and publications.

Typical recent postings   Complexity Of Chess And Go, Chessbase And OS/2, Derivation Of Terms "Cooks" And Rooks, Chess Master Ratings, Email Chess, Man Killed After Chess Dispute.

Review   Chess aficionados and others will find plenty of interest here—there's a great deal of discussion of the issues posed by chess-playing software, particularly as this software challenges commonly held assumptions about human intelligence.

rec.gardens ★★★★

All aspects of gardening—ordering plants (especially by mail), dealing with pests, fertilizing, designing the garden, keeping it looking nice.

Typical recent postings   Yellow Jackets, Tomatoes! Tomatoes!…Soup?, Maintaining Lawns Organically, Plants That Do Weird Things, Nitrogen in Compost, White Flies.

Review   A great newsgroup for anyone who putters around in the garden—full of tips and advice on all kinds of matters that will instantly interest anyone who gardens occasionally or avidly.

Advice to newbies   Please read the Plants by Mail FAQ before posting to avoid asking questions about mail-order plant firms (the most commonly asked questions in rec.gardens) that have been posed before.

Adult-oriented?   No.

Readership   62,000.

Rank   365.

Messages per month   3,339.

Crossposting percentage   3%.

Availability   76% of USENET sites.

Moderated?   No.

Special features   None.

FAQ title   Plants by Mail FAQ

FAQ location   rec.gardens

Other information resources   None.

Archive site   None.

Related groups   rec.gardens.orchids

rec.guns ★★★

All aspects of firearms laws, buying guns, hunting, skill development, collecting, safety, organized competitions, publications.

Typical recent postings   9mm Cases and Problems, California Gun Carrying Laws, Gun Friendly States, Reloading for Novices, Zeroing Your Rifle Scope, Black Powder.

Review   Intelligent discussion of firearms, with a strong stress on safety and skill development. Not much on collecting, at least in the samples I looked at.

Advice to newbies   This newsgroup isn't the place for discussions on the politics of guns; please post to talk.politics.guns if you have something to say on this.

Adult-oriented?   No.

Readership   61,000.

Rank   380.

Messages per month   4,699.

Crossposting percentage   0%.

Availability   75% of USENET sites.

Moderated?   Yes.

Special features   None.

FAQ title   rec.guns FAQ Pointer

FAQ location   rec.guns, rec.answers, news.answers

Other information resources   The rec.guns FAQ is so voluminous that it's been stored on an anonymous FTP server: flubber.cs.umd.edu (128.8.128.99) in the directory /rec/FAQ.

Archive site   None.

Related group   None.

rec.humor ★★★★

The witty, clever, humorous, droll, hilarious, jocose, but unfortunately also the idiotic, offensive, and juvenile.

Typical recent postings   Humorous Bumper Stickers, Letterman's Top Ten List, Silly but True Lawsuits, Strange but True Names, Stupidest People in the World.

Review   Definitely a mixed bag, rec.humor is a no-holds-barred attempt at humor from widely divergent perspectives on what's funny. Sure to prove offensive to just about anyone, sooner or later.

Advice to newbies   Posting an offensive joke from work could have adverse consequences for your company image.

Adult-oriented?   Yes.

Readership   290,000.

Rank 5.

Messages per month 3,954.

Crossposting percentage 4%.

Availability 79% of USENET sites.

Moderated? No.

Special features None.

FAQ title None.

FAQ location N/a.

Other information resources None.

Archive site None.

Related groups rec.humor.funny

rec.humor.funny ★★★★★

Typical recent postings Flintstone Vitamin Controversy, The Truth About Washington, D.C., How Weather Forecasters Deal with Dreary Forecasts.

Review This moderated newsgroup contains jewels of humor that shouldn't be missed. Although some jokes may prove offensive, they're usually encrypted (with rot-13) so you don't have to read them if you don't like such jokes.

Advice to newbies Please read the Guidelines for Submissions carefully before posting, and be sure to rotate offensive content.

Adult-oriented? No.

Readership One of USENET's top 40 groups: 340,000.

Rank 3.

Messages per month 48.

Crossposting percentage 0%.

Availability 82% of USENET sites.

Moderated? Yes.

Special features None.

FAQ title Introduction to rec.humor.funny

FAQ location rec.humor.funny, rec.answers, news.answers

Other information resources Guidelines for Submissions — Monthly Posting

Archive site Back jokes from RHF are collected into the RHF "TeleJokeBooks." For information on purchasing these volumes, send mail to jokebook@clarinet.com.

Related groups None.

rec.martial-arts ★★★

All aspects of martial arts—the varying disciplines, training, philosophy, schools, equipment, and public service.

Typical recent postings Street Effective Martial Art, World Class Juijitsu, Rare Kata, Taekwon-Do, Women Training in Martial Arts.

Review Martial art enthusiasts will find plenty of material of interest here, peppered occasionally with flamebait from college freshmen and other juvenile types.

Advice to newbies Please don't post the question "What is the best martial art?" in rec.martial-arts.

Adult-oriented? No.

Readership 56,000.

Rank 430.

Messages per month 3,453.

Crossposting percentage 1%.

Availability 74% of USENET sites.

Moderated? No.

Special features None.

FAQ title rec.martial-arts FAQ

FAQ location rec.martial-arts, rec.answers, news.answers

Other information resources   Stretching and Flexibility FAQ

Archive site   Aikido Dojo Directory is available via anonymous ftp from cs.ucsd.edu (132.239.51.3).

Related groups   misc.fitness, rec.arts.dance, alt.arts.ballet, rec.sport.misc

rec.models.rc ★★★

Radio-control models, focusing especially on aircraft—the technology, the organizations, learning to fly, finding (and keeping) places to fly, how to deal with the pain and embarrassment of a crash. Of interest to anyone involved in the rc hobby.

Typical recent postings   Charging Small Capacity Nicads, Hand-Launched Gliders, Big Models—Weird Engines.

Review   RC flying enthusiasts won't want to miss this group; beginners will find the two-part FAQ to provide an excellent introduction to all aspects of RC flying.

Advice to newbies   Please read the group's FAQ before posting to avoid asking questions that have been posed before.

Adult-oriented?   No.

Readership   51,000.

Rank   510.

Messages per month   1,488.

Crossposting percentage   1%.

Availability   75% of USENET sites.

Moderated?   No.

Special features   None.

FAQ title   R/C Flying Part * of * / rec.models.rc FAQ

FAQ location   rec.models.rc, rec.answers, news.answers

Other information resources   None.

Archive site   Programs and other material of interest to rc flyers will be found at bigwig.geology.indiana.edu, in the directory /models.

Related groups   None.

rec.motorcycles ★★★

All aspects of motorcycling—the bikes, helmets, safety, maintenance, repairs, and biker culture.

Typical recent postings   Homicidal Dumptruck, Scratches in Windshields, Harley Horrors, Lane Discipline, Shaft Drive vs. Chain, Freaked Out by Biker.

Review   An ideal enthusiast's newsgroup—lots of discussion on which bike corners best, what to do about routine and bizarre repair problems, how to ride safely. Not to be missed by any motorcyclist.

Advice to newbies   Please read the group's FAQ before posting to avoid asking questions that have been posed before. Note that this newsgroup is intended for posts that wouldn't fit in the rec.motorcycles.dirt, rec.motorcycles.harley, or rec.motorcycles.racing newsgroups.

Adult-oriented?   No.

Readership   84,000.

Rank   186.

Messages per month   6,583.

Crossposting percentage   3%.

Availability   76% of USENET sites.

Moderated?   No.

Special features   None.

FAQ title   rec.motorcycles FAQ

FAQ location   rec.motorcycles

Other information resources Beginner Motorcycle Info: Periodic Post, What is the DoD?—Weekly Micro—FAQ

Archive site None.

Related group rec.motorcycles.dirt, rec.motorcycles.harley, rec.motorcycles.racing

rec.music.bluenote ★★★★

Jazz and blues—the artists, the concerts, the festivals, the clubs, the recordings, the publications, and the music.

Typical recent postings Dizzy?, Bill Evans Recommendations, Coltrane Recommendations, Original Jazz Charts on the Web!, Lee Morgan.

Review Tasteful and often tributory posts regarding the greats of jazz and blues—sure to please anyone who enjoys jazz or blues. You'll find news of concerts, jazz and blues artists, reviews of new recordings and publications, and discussion and debate concerning this musical tradition.

Advice to newbies Please read the rec.music.info FAQ before posting to any music newsgroup. For posts of general interest, please post to rec.music.misc. Please read this group's FAQ before posting to avoid asking questions that have been posed before.

Adult-oriented? No.

Readership 69,000.

Rank 285.

Messages per month 2,589.

Crossposting percentage 5%.

Availability 76% of USENET sites.

Moderated? No.

Special features None.

FAQ title FAQ Rec.music.bluenote

FAQ location rec.music.bluenote, rec.music.info, rec.answers, news.answers

Other information resources Further Sources of Information, List of Open Jam Sessions

Archive site None.

Related groups None.

rec.music.classical ★★★★

Classical music—baroque, classical, romantic, with special emphasis on recordings.

Typical recent postings Comments on the Mahler Recordings, Historical Recordings, Unjustly Neglected Music, Obscure Nationalist Operas, Rossini Overtures.

Review Dave Barry says that the definition of classical music is that it is "not popular," but you'd disagree after reading this high-volume newsgroup! You'll find lots of discussion and debate, with many interesting information postings, reviews of classical recordings, and tips on buying CDs.

Advice to newbies If you're interested in theory or composition, post to rec.music.compose. If you're interested in performance issues, post to rec.music.classical.performing. If you're interested in music prior to 1685, post to rec.music.early.

Adult-oriented? No.

Readership 100,000.

Rank 115.

Messages per month 4,458.

Crossposting percentage 2%.

Availability 77% of USENET sites.

Moderated? No.

Special features None.

FAQ title rec.music.classical

FAQ location   rec.music.classical, rec.music.info, rec.answers, news.answers

Other information resources   None.

Archive site   None.

Related groups   rec.music.classical.performing, rec.music.classical.guitar

rec.music.industrial ★★★

Industrial music, a recent genre of pop music that stresses the alienation of modern society through the exploration of meaningless mechnical sounds and angst-ridden lyrics. Discussed are traditional industrial ensembles (Einstuerzende Neubauten, Throbbing Gristle, Cabaret Voltaire), dance-industrial (Ministry, Skinny Puppy, Front 242, Foetus) and hard techno music (Kraftwerk). Of interest to anyone interested in popular music genres in general and industrial in particular.

Typical recent postings   Experimental Music Shows in NYC, Skinny Puppy Lyrics, Brainchild, SF Club Listings.

Review   Lots of good discussion and plenty of informational postings, such as concert dates and album reviews, though I suspect that most would regard industrial music—and this newsgroup—to be an acquired taste.

Advice to newbies   Please read the group's FAQ before posting to avoid asking questions that have been posed before.

Adult-oriented?   No.

Readership   65,000.

Rank   327.

Messages per month   1,729.

Crossposting percentage   9%.

Availability   72% of USENET sites.

Moderated?   No.

Special features   None.

FAQ title   FAQ: rec.music.industrial

FAQ location   rec.music.industrial, rec.music.info, rec.answers, news.answers

Other information resources   None.

Archive site   None.

Related groups   None.

rec.music.info ★★★★★

Information and announcements pertaining to music (mainly popular) and a guide to the music newsgroups on USENET. Of interest to anyone trying to figure out where to post music-related articles.

Typical recent postings   Release: Recent and Upcoming Album Releases.

Review   One of USENET's best, this moderated newsgroup is the Grand Central Station for all the music newsgroups. You'll find plenty of information on CD sales, concert tour dates, reviews of recent CDs, and FAQs from all the music newsgroups.

Advice to newbies   This is a moderated newsgroup; please read the FAQ to determine where to post.

Adult-oriented?   No.

Readership   65,000.

Rank   323.

Messages per month   183.

Crossposting percentage   35%.

Availability   69% of USENET sites.

Moderated?   Yes.

Special features   None.

FAQ title   rec.music.info FAQ List

FAQ location   rec.music.info

Other information resources   CHART: Bavarian Top 15 Singles, CHART: German Top 10(singles), CHART: Vancouver BC Canada, REC.MUSIC.INFO: no requests for info, *please*, FAQ: Chalkhills, The XTC Mailing List, REC.MUSIC.INFO: List of USENET Musical Newsgroups, REC.MUSIC.INFO: Submission Guidelines for rec.music.info, REC.MUSIC.INFO: Welcome to rec.music.info, INFO: Wanted Disc List, CHART: Dutch Dance, CHART: European Top 20, CHART: UK Indie Charts w/e *, INFO: Musical List of Lists, REC.MUSIC.INFO: List of Internet Musical FTP Sites, REC.MUSIC.INFO: List of Internet Musical Resources, REC.MUSIC.INFO: List of Music-Oriented Fan Clubs, CHART: Dutch Albums, CHART: Dutch Singles

Archive site   None.

Related groups   None.

rec.music.makers ★★★★

Making music, especially with the aid of the new computer tools for synthesis and composition. Software, hardware, supplies, publications, and reviews are included.

Typical recent postings   Music Programs (Mac or PC), Emulating Other Vocalists While Singing, Pursuing the Dream.

Review   Very interesting and thoughtful discussion for anyone who's contemplating a life in music—whether to quit your job, what it takes to make memorable music—the list could go on. Worth a look even if you're not a musician.

Advice to newbies   Please read the group's FAQ before posting to avoid asking questions about synthesizers and electronic music that have been posed before. Note the related newsgroups and be sure to post to the correct group.

Adult-oriented?   No.

Readership   90,000.

Rank   153.

Messages per month   750.

Crossposting percentage   41%.

Availability   77% of USENET sites.

Moderated?   No.

Special features   None.

FAQ title   Electronic_and_Computer_Music_Frequently-Asked_Questions_(FAQ)

FAQ location   N/A.

Other information resources   Listing of open musical jam sessions, MUSENET ordering info, Music Equipment Mail/Phone List, Electronic Music Software Price Guide. Listing of open musical jam sessions, Music Equipment Mail Phone List, Music Notation Programs a list in answer to a FAQ, Music Notation Programs—a list to answer a FAQ.

Archive site   There are numerous archive sites; see the FAQ for details.

Related groups   rec.music.makers.synth, rec.music.makers.guitar, rec.music.makers.bass, rec.music.makers.percussion, rec.music.compose, comp.music, rec.music.industrial, rec.music.makers.builders, rec.music.makers.piano

rec.music.misc ★★

Grand Central Station for general-interest music posts.

Typical recent postings   The Church—New Album?, Songs About Photography, Barry Manilow or Murphy Brown, Unknown Song.

Review   Insufficiently focused to prove of general interest, this newsgroup isn't where the action is—

take a look at the more focused rec.music.* groups instead.

Advice to newbies   Use this newsgroup only for cross-posting general-interest articles, and include a Followup-To header directing replies to a specific rec.music.* newsgroup.

Adult-oriented?   No.

Readership   140,000.

Rank   39.

Messages per month   2,905.

Crossposting percentage   15%.

Availability   77% of USENET sites.

Moderated?   No.

Special features   None.

FAQ title   None.

FAQ location   N/A.

Other information resources   FAQ: Dire Straits Mailing List, CHART: Japanese pop singles/albums, Chart: UK Charts for Week Ending*, SF-references-in-music List, CHART: Austrian Top 20 Singles

Archive site   None.

Related groups   None.

---

rec.music.reviews ★★★★

Reviews of recent pop recordings.

Typical recent postings   China Crisis, Trans-Slovenia Express, TransCom "Evidence" Compilation.

Review   Perhaps too unfocused to prove of general interest, this newsgroup is still worth reading if you're a pop music fan; you may find reviews of disks you've been thinking about buying or find out about promising new artists that you haven't heard of.

Advice to newbies   Please read the group's FAQ before posting to avoid asking questions that have been posed before.

Adult-oriented?   No.

Readership   45,000.

Rank   612.

Messages per month   41.

Crossposting percentage   28%.

Availability   70% of USENET sites.

Moderated?   Yes.

Special features   None.

FAQ title   rec.music.reviews Frequently Asked Questions(FAQ)

FAQ location   rec.music.reviews, rec.answers, news.answers

Other information resources   None.

Archive site   Reviews are archived at ftp.uwp.edu in the directory /pub/music/reviews/. Further subdirectories are organized alphabetically.

Related groups   None.

---

rec.nude ★★★

The naturalist lifestyle— views, news, philosophies, and ideologies.

Typical recent postings   We All Look the Same, Shaved Bodies, Nude Beaches, Naturist Parks, Jamaica Clothing Optional Beaches, A Difficult Time at the Beach.

Review   Discussion of naturalist lifestyles, organizations, and beaches, with periodic pepperings from idiotic juveniles who think they can meet some "hot babe" here.

Advice to newbies   rec.nude isn't a place to pick up a hot girl, freshman. Please don't crosspost to alt.sex.* groups; the naturalist lifestyle isn't (necessarily) about sex.

Adult-oriented? Yes.

Readership 100,000.

Rank 111.

Messages per month 1,355.

Crossposting percentage 2%.

Availability 74% of USENET sites.

Moderated? No.

Special features None.

FAQ title rec.nude FAQ: Naturist Site Reports

FAQ location rec.nude, rec.answers, news.answers

Other information resources Clubs and Publications, Part II of III, REC.NUDE FAQ—electronic Access, Part III of III, REC.NUDE FAQ—The Questions, Part I of III, REC.NUDE FAQ: Naturist Site Reports: Australasia, REC.NUDE FAQ: Naturist Site Reports: California, REC.NUDE FAQ: Naturist Site Reports: Europe, REC.NUDE FAQ: Naturist Site Reports: North America

Archive site None.

Related groups None.

rec.org.mensa ★

Mensa, an organization for those individuals who score in the top 2% of IQ tests. You get a credit card, cuts on insurance, and snob appeal.

Typical recent postings Judicial Idiocy, How to Be an Intellectual Snob, Annual Gatherings, Non-English Languages Spoken in the Home in the USA, Qualifying for Mensa, Gifted African-American Kids.

Review This newsgroup is an obvious target for trollers and flamers; until they get a moderator, skip it.

Advice to newbies Read the FAQ if you like; Mensa may be a worthwhile organization but this newsgroup isn't.

Adult-oriented? No.

Readership 46,000.

Rank 593.

Messages per month 2,239.

Crossposting percentage 3%.

Availability 68% of USENET sites.

Moderated? No.

Special features None.

FAQ title Mensa-FAQ: Do I qualify for Mensa? How do I Join?; Mensa-FAQ: What famous people are members of Mensa?; Mensa-FAQ: What is Mensa?; Mensa-FAQ: What is the Mensa test like?; Mensa-FAQ: What other high-IQ societies are there?

FAQ location rec.org.mensa, rec.answers, news.answers

Other information resources None.

Archive site None.

Related groups None.

rec.org.sca ★★★

The Society for Creative Anachronism (SCA)—or, as SCA aficionados prefer to call it, the Rialto (a marketplace in old Venice in the vicinity of the Rialto bridge, where people met to talk and gossip).

Typical recent postings Desired Crown Qualities and Selection Method, Northern California Renaissance Fair, Plague and Sneezing, Medieval and Renaissance Music.

Review In this newsgroup, you'll find discussion that will prove delicious to SCA enthusiasts and virtually incomprehensible to anyone else—but that's part of SCA's charm and magnetism. Think medieval!

Advice to newbies   Please read the group's FAQ before posting to avoid asking questions that have been posed before.

Adult-oriented?   No.

Readership   50,000.

Rank   527.

Messages per month   3,893.

Crossposting percentage   1%.

Availability   75% of USENET sites.

Moderated?   No.

Special features   None.

FAQ title   rec.org.sca / Rialto Frequently Asked Questions- /

FAQ location   rec.org.sca, rec.answers, news.answers

Other information resources   Come on in—the water's fine, Frequently Asked Questions(FAQ) list available, Intro to the SCA, Consultant List.

Archive site   One of several is located at ftp.nau.edu [134.114.64.24] directory /sca; see the FAQ for more.

Related groups   None.

rec.pets ★★★

Pets generally, but there's a very pronounced ferret bias.

Typical recent postings   Ferret Hiss, Oiling a Hamster Wheel, Glue-eating Rats, My Hedgehog Loves Crispix, What Type of Pet?

Review   This newsgroup isn't well-focused, but if you're a ferret lover, where else can you go?

Advice to newbies   Please note that you should direct posts on birds, dogs, and cats to the appropriate rec.pets.* newsgroup.

Adult-oriented?   No.

Readership   69,000.

Rank   284.

Messages per month   864.

Crossposting percentage   8%.

Availability   75% of USENET sites.

Moderated?   No.

Special features   None.

FAQ title   None.

FAQ location   N/a.

Other information resources   Pet Rat FAQ, Ferret FAQ—General Information, Fleas, Ticks, and Your Pet: FAQ

Archive site   None.

Related groups   rec.pets.birds, rec.pets.cats, rec.pets.dogs, rec.pets.rabbits

rec.pets.birds ★★★

Pet birds (as opposed to birds in nature, discussed in alt.birds)—species, equipment and supplies, care and feeding, illnesses and vets, singing and talking. Of interest to anyone who enjoys pet birds.

Typical recent postings   Sneezing and Stretching, Pet Bird Report, Talking In Sleep, Sounds Birds Hate, Birds For Allergic People.

Review   All aspects of keeping birds as pets are considered and debated in this newsgroup, which features mature and intelligent discussion of pet bird issues. Very interesting discussion; I had no idea, for example, that keeping pet birds has been identified in some studies as a lung cancer risk factor!

Advice to newbies   Please read the group's FAQ before posting to avoid asking questions that have been posed before.

Adult-oriented?   No.

Readership   25,000.

Rank   1,149.

Messages per month   1,115.

Crossposting percentage   2%.

Availability   68% of USENET sites.

Moderated?   No.

Special features   None.

FAQ title   rec.pets.birds FAQ: Monthly Posting.

FAQ location   rec.pets.birds, rec.answers, news.answers

Other information resources   None.

Archive site   None.

Related groups   rec.pets

rec.pets.cats ★★★★★

Cats—the purring, the affection, the fleas, the scratching, the finicky eating... the works.

Typical recent postings   Tomato-eating Cat, Kitties Watching Sex, Cleaning Cat Vomit from Upholstery, Neighbor Lady Wants to Kill My Cats, Need Help, Vaccinating My Own Cats.

Review   One of USENET's best, this newsgroup features the winning combination of interesting discussion, rich informational resources, and an informative FAQ. The newsgroup is occasionally trolled by juveniles; please ignore this.

Advice to newbies   rec.pets.cats is a friendly and helpful group, but is prone to flame wars on three issues: cats on vegetarian diets, declawing cats, and whether to keep cats indoors only or allow them outdoors as well. Please avoid these subjects, and

please read the group's FAQ before posting to avoid asking questions that have been posed before.

Adult-oriented?   No.

Readership   81,000.

Rank   197.

Messages per month   3,094.

Crossposting percentage   4%.

Availability   72% of USENET sites.

Moderated?   No.

Special features   Rich information resources; see that item.

FAQ title   rec.pets.cats FAQ

FAQ location   rec.pets.cats, rec.answers, news.answers

Other information resources   rec.pets.cats: Bombay Breed-FAQ; rec.pets.cats: Chartreux Breed-FAQ; rec.pets.cats: Maine Coon Cats Breed-FAQ, rec.pets.cats: Ragdolls Breed-FAQ; rec.pets.cats: Traditional Siamese Breed-FAQ; rec.pets.cats: Feline Leukemia FAQ

Archive site   None.

Related groups   rec.pets

rec.pets.dogs ★★★★★

Dogs—the breeds, feeds, vets, care, training, affection and loyalty, and much more.

Typical recent postings   Economics of Owning a Puppy, Spouse Hates Our Dog, Intelligence Tests for Dogs, My Blue Heeler is WEIRD!, How to Find a Holistic Vet.

Review   One of USENET's best, this newsgroup—like rec.pets.cats—features the winning combination of interesting discussion, rich informational resources, and an informative FAQ.

Advice to newbies Please read the group's extensive FAQs before posting to avoid asking questions that have been posed before.

Adult-oriented? No.

Readership 79,000.

Rank 212.

Messages per month 5,048.

Crossposting percentage 2%.

Availability 74% of USENET sites.

Moderated? No.

Special features None.

FAQ title Complete List of rec.pets.dogs FAQs

FAQ location rec.pets.dogs

Other information resources rec.pets.dogs: Protection Dogs FAQ; rec.pets.dogs: Breed-FAQ; rec.pets.dogs: *FAQ; rec.pets.dogs: Akitas Breed FAQ; rec.pets.dogs: Basenjis Breed-FAQ; rec.pets.dogs: Border Collies Breed-FAQ; rec.pets.dogs: Bulldogs Breed-FAQ; rec.pets.dogs: Cavalier King Charles Spaniels Breed-FAQ; rec.pets.dogs: Havanese Breed-FAQ; rec.pets.dogs: Kuvaszok Breed-FAQ; rec.pets.dogs: Newfoundlands Breed-FAQ; rec.pets.dogs: Salukis Breed-FAQ; rec.pets.dogs: Samoyeds Breed-FAQ; rec.pets.dogs: Shetland Sheepdogs Breed-FAQ; rec.pets.dogs: Breed Rescue Organizations FAQ

Archive site None.

Related groups rec.pets

rec.photo.misc ★★★★

All aspects of photography not covered in the other rec.photo.* newsgroups (rec.photo.advanced, rec.photo.darkroom, rec.photo.help, rec.photo.marketplace). Of interest to anyone who enjoys photography.

Typical recent postings Rumor About New NIKON Body, Linear vs. Circular Polarizers, Printing Black and White Skin, Extension Tubes, Slides to Photo CD.

Review Very interesting discussion of cameras, films, photographic situations, aesthetics, composition, and much more; intelligent, mature discussion with many well-informed participants.

Advice to newbies Please post "for sale" items to rec.photo.marketplace.

Adult-oriented? No.

Readership 110,000.

Rank 92.

Messages per month 4,620.

Crossposting percentage 2%.

Availability 78% of USENET sites.

Moderated? No.

Special features None.

FAQ title rec.photo FAQ and answers

FAQ location rec.photo

Other information resources Nikon FAQ, Photographic Mail Order Society Survey, Updated CAMERA FEATURE LIST, [Periodic Posting]: Medium Format Digest Info, Photographic Lenses

Archive site moink.nmsu.edu (128.123.1.46)

Related groups None.

rec.radio.amateur.misc ★★★

Grand Central Station for the rec.radio.amateur.* newsgroups; this newsgroup features discussion of topics of general interest and those that don't fit in the other rec.radio.amateur.* newsgroups (rec.radio.amateur.antenna, rec.radio.amateur.digital, rec.radio.amateur.equipment, rec.radio.amateur.homebrew, rec.radio.amateur.space).

Typical recent postings   Crossband Repeating Rigs & Auto IDers, Cable TV Equivalent of 427.25 MHz, Cell RF Characteristics, Building a J-Pole Antenna.

Review   If you're a ham radio aficionado, this newsgroup is essential. You'll find intelligent and informed discussions of equipment, suppliers, frequencies, regulatory issues, and more.

Advice to newbies   Please read the group's FAQ before posting to avoid asking questions that have been posed before, and make sure you post to the correct rec.radio.amateur.* newsgroup.

Adult-oriented?   No.

Readership   86,000.

Rank   173.

Messages per month   1,832.

Crossposting percentage   8%.

Availability   77% of USENET sites.

Moderated?   No.

Special features   None.

FAQ title   rec.radio.amateur.misc Frequently Asked Questions

FAQ location   rec.radio.amateur.misc, rec.radio.info, rec.answers, news.answers

Other information resources   Guide to the Personal Radio Newsgroups, Macintosh Amateur Radio Software, rec.radio.info Submissions Guidelines, Welcome to rec.radio.info, Amateur Radio Newsline, How to Find the Answers to Frequently Asked questions about Ham Radio, US License Examination Opportunities Scheduled, Amateur Radio: Elmers List Info and Administratrivia, Amateur Radio: Elmers List Quick-Search Index, Amateur Radio: Elmers Resource Directory, Index to the rec.radio.amateur.* Supplemental Archives, Radio Amateurs on the

USENET List, Ham Radio FTP area on Oakland, Daily Summary of Solar Geophysical Activity

Archive site   None.

Related groups   rec.radio.amateur.policy, rec.radio.amateur.equipment, rec.radio.amateur.packet, rec.radio.broadcasting

rec.travel.misc ★★★★★

All aspects of travel not specifically covered by the other rec.travel.* groups (rec.travel.air, rec.travel.asia, rec.travel.cruises, rec.travel.europe, rec.travel.marketplace). A common theme: travelers' experiences in specific destinations.

Typical recent postings   Buying Mopeds in India, Travel with a Small Child, Stingers off Australian Coast, European Driving Licenses, Crabs in San Francisco.

Review   One of USENET's best, this group isn't to be missed by anyone who travels. A plus is the group's huge and impressive archive. If you're planning the trip of a lifetime, or just a good summer break, you'll want this group on your subscription list.

Advice to newbies   Please ask travel agents for specific information about destinations, carriers, and the like. Check out the FTP archive for tons of information about popular and out-of-the-way destinations alike.

Adult-oriented?   No.

Readership   150,000.

Rank   28.

Messages per month   5,122.

Crossposting percentage   8%.

Availability   77% of USENET sites.

Moderated?   No.

Special features   None.

FAQ title Simple suggestions for travel (net reminders really).

FAQ location rec.travel

Other information resources None.

Archive site Over 15MB of information contributed by rec.travel posters on travel to many world destinations is available at ftp.cc.umanitoba.ca in the directories under /rec-travel.

Related groups rec.travel.air, alt.internet.services

rec.video ★★★

Home and hobby video cameras, recorders, and image processing, with an emphasis on the technology rather than the aesthetics.

Typical recent postings Wizard's Japanese Laserdisc Update, S-Video—What Are the Technical Advantages?, Viewing Video on the Computer Monitor.

Review The technically oriented discussion tends to focus on the idiosyncracies of specific brands of VCR cameras and recorders, including repair hassles, price breaks, new recording formats, and performance specifications.

Advice to newbies Please read the group's FAQ before posting to avoid asking questions that have been posed before.

Adult-oriented? No.

Readership 180,000.

Rank 21.

Messages per month 1,631.

Crossposting percentage 8%.

Availability 78% of USENET sites.

Moderated? No.

Special features None.

FAQ title rec.video US/ Canada Consumer Video FAQL version *

FAQ location rec.video, alt.answers, news.answers

Other information resources None.

Archive site None.

Related groups rec.video.cable-tv, rec.video.production, rec.video.releases, rec.video.satellite

rec.woodworking ★★★

Working with wood—the materials, the tools, the shop, the traditions, the aesthetics, the safety issues. Of interest to anyone interested in any aspect of woodworking.

Typical recent postings New Tool Scams, Building 18th Century Reproductions, Metric Conversion, Similarities between Sex and Hand Planing, Staining Wood, Quality in Tools.

Review If you work with wood, you won't want to miss this group. The discussion is mature, intelligent, informed, and congenial. You're sure to learn something to repay your time!

Advice to newbies Please read the group's FAQ and the other information resources before posting to avoid asking questions that have been posed before.

Adult-oriented? No.

Readership 61,000.

Rank 381.

Messages per month 2,426.

Crossposting percentage 4%.

Availability 76% of USENET sites.

Moderated? No.

Special features None.

FAQ title rec.woodworking Frequently Asked Questions

FAQ location rec.woodworking, alt.answers, news.answers

Other information resources rec.woodworking Frequently Requested Addresses, rec.woodworking Electric Motors Frequently Asked Questions, rec.woodworking Changes to Frequently Asked Questions, rec.woodworking Frequently Requested Tool Reviews

Archive site None.

Related groups misc.consumers.house

sci.aquaria ★★★

Scientific aspects of aquaria in particular and aquatic life in general. Of interest to anyone interested in the technical or scientific aspects of aquaria or water life.

Typical recent postings Test Kit Recommendations, Mail-Order Mosquito Eaters, Anemone Color Change.

Review This group focuses on the scientific aspects of aquaria and, more broadly, marine biology.

Advice to newbies Like all sci.* newsgroups, this one isn't an appropriate place to post any question that you can look up in a reference work, such as a dictionary or encyclopedia. Read the FAQs to make sure you don't ask a question that's already been answered, and be sure to crosspost to rec.aquaria. (Not all sites receive both groups, so the two groups exist to make sure that all sites receive all the postings.)

Adult-oriented? No.

Readership 31,000.

Rank 950.

Messages per month 420.

Crossposting percentage 60%.

Availability 74% of USENET sites.

Moderated? No.

Special features Extensive information resources add up to a superb introductory course in keeping an aquarium.

FAQ title alt.aquaria FAQ: Beginners and Books

FAQ location alt.aquaria, rec.aquaria, sci.aquaria (monthly).

Other information resources AQUARIA FAQ: Filters; AQUARIA FAQ: Magazines and Mail Order Information; AQUARIA FAQ Plants; AQUARIA FAQ Water

Archive site None.

Related groups rec.aquaria (essentially the same newsgroup) and sci.aquaria (for discussions of scientific research on water-related topics).

sci.astro ★★★

Every aspect of astronomy—selecting and purchasing a telescope, finding objects in space, getting optimum performance, capturing images on film. Of interest to any amateur astronomer.

Typical recent postings Seeing Clearly, Gravity, Carl Sagan—Antichrist?, Time Has Inertia, Equivalence of Time and Mass, Chicken Little, Perseids in Honolulu.

Review Although this group will interest any amateur astronomer, many postings are off-topic (although generally of interest); please read "Advice to newbies" and post to the correct group.

Advice to newbies Like all sci.* newsgroups, this one isn't an appropriate place to post any question that you can look up in a reference work, such as a dictionary or encyclopedia. Please post to the appropriate sci.space.* newsgroup. For astronomy in general, post to sci.astro. For discussion of current research in astronomy and astrophysics, post to sci.astro.research (moderated). For discussion of specific topics in astronomy, post to sci.astro.fits, sci.astro.hubble, or sci.astro.planetarium. For discussion of the Earth Observing System, post to sci.geo.eos. In general, please read the group's FAQ before posting to avoid asking questions that have been posed before.

Adult-oriented?   No.

Readership   120,000.

Rank   74.

Messages per month   3,053.

Crossposting percentage   27%.

Availability   81% of USENET sites.

Moderated?   No.

Special features   Numerous information resources for amateur astronomers.

FAQ title   Space FAQ

FAQ location   sci.astro, sci.space, sci.answers

Other information resources   Purchasing Amateur Telescopes FAQ, Space Calendar, Sky & Telescope Weekly News Bulletin, Electronic Journal of the ASA (EJASA)

Archive site   Back issues of Space Digest (to 1981) are available from ftp://julius.cs.qub.ac.uk/pub/SpaceDigestArchive/.

Related groups   sci.misc, alt.sci.planetary, sci.space.science, sci.space.tech, sci.space.shuttle, sci.astro.hubble

sci.classics ★★★★

Greek and Roman civilization, from Homer to Constantine, and including the impact of these civilizations on the Middle Ages. Encompassed are the Greek and Latin languages, literatures (including poetry, drama, history, philosophy, rhetoric, religion, political theory), art, architecture, and archaeology.

Typical recent postings   Coin Replicas, Trojan Wars, Fourth Century Rome, First Man in Rome.

Review   Classics? Huh? Well, believe it or not, this seemingly conservative subject has just possibly made the most interesting adaptation to global computer networking of any academic subject. You'll find fascinating discussions here of issues in classical scholarship, generally phrased in a way that non-specialists can understand and enjoy. And if you'd like to get your hands on the texts themselves, whether in the original Greek or Latin or in translation, there are marvelous electronic archives of classical texts accessible through the Internet.

Advice to newbies   Like all sci.* newsgroups, this one isn't an appropriate place to post any question that you can look up in a reference work, such as a dictionary or encyclopedia. Please post to the appropriate sci.space.* newsgroup. For astronomy in general, post to sci.astro. For discussion of current research in astronomy and astrophysics, post to sci.astro.research (moderated). For discussion of specific topics in astronomy, post to sci.astro.fits, sci.astro.hubble, or sci.astro.planetarium. For discussion of the Earth Observing System, post to sci.geo.eos. In general, please read the group's FAQ before posting to avoid asking questions that have been posed before.

Adult-oriented?   No.

Readership   31,000.

Rank   942.

Messages per month   233.

Crossposting percentage   0.7%.

Availability   69% of USENET sites.

Moderated?   No.

Special features   None.

FAQ title   sci.classics FAQ

FAQ location   sci.classics, sci.answers

Other information resources   For information on e-text archives, see the FAQ.

Archive site   Among the many electronic text archives is project Libellus, at the University of Washington, Seattle, via anonymous FTP (ftp://ftp.u.washington.edu/public/libellus/texts).

Related groups   None.

sci.crypt ★★★

The science of cryptography—including cryptography, cryptanalysis, and related topics such as one-way hash functions. Of interest to anyone interested in the science of cryptography.

Typical recent postings   UNIX Password Encryption, PGP Vulnerable to Low Exponent Attack, The Theory Behind PGP.

Review   For specialists in the field of crytopgraphy, this is an indispensable newsgroup—but those not conversant with the fundamentals of cryptography may find most of the posts to be unintelligible. Read the FAQ!

Advice to newbies   Like all sci.* newsgroups, this one isn't an appropriate place to post any question that you can look up in a reference work, such as a dictionary or encyclopedia. Please post articles on the politics of cryptography (such as Clipper, Digital Telephony, NSA, RSADSI/PKP, and export controls) to talk.politics.crypto. This newsgroup is for the *science* of cryptography. Please read the group's FAQ before posting to avoid asking questions that have been posed before.

Adult-oriented?   No.

Readership   92,000.

Rank   144.

Messages per month   986.

Crossposting percentage   16%.

Availability   80% of USENET sites.

Moderated?   No.

Special features   The extensive FAQ contains a wealth of knowledge regarding current cryptography knowledge and issues.

FAQ title   sci.crypt Charter: Read Before You Post, Cryptography FAQ (: Overview), Cryptography FAQ (: Net Etiquette), Cryptography FAQ (: Basic Cryptology), Cryptography FAQ (: Mathematical Cryptology), Cryptography FAQ (: Product Ciphers), Cryptography FAQ (: Public Key Cryptography), Cryptography FAQ (: Digital Signatures, Cryptography FAQ (: Technical Miscellany), Cryptography FAQ (: Other Miscellany), Cryptography FAQ (: References)

FAQ location   sci.crypt, alt.privacy, sci.answers, alt.answers, news.answers

Other information resources   RSA Cryptography Today FAQ

Archive site   sci.crypt has been archived since October 1991 on ripem.msu.edu. **Note:** these archives are available only to U.S. and Canadian users. Another site is rpub.cl.msu.edu in /pub/crypt/sci.crypt/ (from Jan 1992).

Related groups   alt.privacy, talk.politics.crypto, alt.security.ripem

sci.electronics ★★★★

All aspects of electronics, with a focus on consumer electronics.

Typical recent postings   Technology for Bar-Code Scanners/ Printers, Uni-Directional Speaker Cable, Tubes vs. Silicon—Let the Debate Begin, An American Microwave in Europe, Remote Interception of Keyboard Data.

Review   An exploration of the possibilities of consumer electronics, from the mundane ("Will my microwave work in Europe?") to the truly weird ("Causing fainting/death over the telephone").

Advice to newbies   Like all sci.* newsgroups, this one isn't an appropriate place to post any question that you can look up in a reference work, such as a dictionary or encyclopedia. There's no FAQ specifically for this newsgroup, but please read the other informational resources to avoid asking questions that have already been answered.

Adult-oriented?   No.

Readership   140,000.

Rank   41.

Messages per month   3,445.

Crossposting percentage   9%.

Availability   81% of USENET sites.

Moderated?   No.

Special features   None.

FAQ title   None.

FAQ location   N/A.

Other information resources   My List of Mail Order Electronics Companies, Electrical Wiring FAQ, Microcontroller FAQ

Archive site   None.

Related groups   rec.radio.amateur.homebrew, rec.radio.amateur.misc, rec.radio.info

---

sci.environment ★★

Environmental science—pollution abatement, site remediation, preventative forest fires, pollution detection and analysis, and more.

Typical recent postings   Nuclear Safety, Energy from the Moon—When the Oil Runs Out, Betting our Lives on Progress, Vegetable Made Paper, HFCs in Printers, Economic vs. Population Growth.

Review   These are worthy subjects, but this newsgroup's value is much reduced by political ranting and raving that does not belong here.

Advice to newbies   Like all sci.* newsgroups, this one isn't an appropriate place to post any question that you can look up in a reference work, such as a dictionary or encyclopedia. *Please* post political discussions to talk.environment.

Adult-oriented?   No.

Readership   87,000.

Rank   169.

Messages per month   1,556.

Crossposting percentage   16%.

Availability   78% of USENET sites.

Moderated?   No.

Special features   None.

FAQ title   None.

FAQ location   N/A.

Other information resources   Electric Vehicles FAQ, Sea Level, Ice, and Greenhouses—FAQ, Ozone Depletion FAQ

Archive site   None.

Related groups   sci.energy, sci.energy.hydrogen, rec.autos.tech, sci.geo.meteorology, sci.geo.geology

---

sci.fractals ★★★

The science and math underlying fractals, which are irregular geometric shapes that can be subdivided in parts, each of which is a miniature copy of the whole. Fractal-based graphics can describe clouds, mountains, and coastlines, and other real-world objects with stunning realism.

Typical recent postings   Fractal Dimension of Turbulent Flow, Box-counting Fractal Dimension, Double Dragon Fractal, Icon Fractals Coloring.

Review Like all sci.* newsgroups, this one isn't an appropriate place to post any question that you can look up in a reference work, such as a dictionary or encyclopedia. This low-volume group is free from noise and sure to please any amateur mathematician with interest in fractals.

Advice to newbies Please read the group's very interesting and informative FAQ before posting to avoid asking questions that have been posed before.

Adult-oriented? No.

Readership 51,000.

Rank 507.

Messages per month 138.

Crossposting percentage 8%.

Availability 67% of USENET sites.

Moderated? No.

Special features Many programs are available via anonymous FTP for generating fractals on your computer. For more information, see the FAQ.

FAQ title Fractal Questions and Answers

FAQ location sci.fractals, news.answers, sci.answers

Other information resources None.

Archive site See the FAQ for information on anonymous FTP archive sites for dozens of fractal-generating programs.

Related groups alt.binaries.pictures.fractals, alt.pictures.fractals

sci.geo.geology ★★★★

The science of the earth—the formation, structure, and dynamics of the earth's crust and interior, volcanoes and earthquakes, rocks, and fossils. Topics for discussion include plate tectonics and tectonophysics, petrology, mineralogy, volcanology, structural geology, paleontology, sedimentary processes, basin analysis, seismic exploration, seismic stratigraphy, petroleum geology, seismology, geochemistry, glaciation, groundwater hydrology, geochronology, paleomagnetism, and paleoclimatology.

Typical recent postings Volcanic Activities and Volcano Images, Geological Music, Geology in Fiction, San Francisco Bay USGS Quake Map, Tides, Phosphorescent Rocks.

Review An interesting newsgroup covering all aspects of geology, this newsgroup is sure to interest anyone fascinated by such phenomena as earthquakes, volcanoes, and continnental drift.

Advice to newbies Like all sci.* newsgroups, this one isn't an appropriate place to post any question that you can look up in a reference work, such as a dictionary or encyclopedia. Please read the group's FAQ before posting to avoid asking questions that have been posed before.

Adult-oriented? No.

Readership 52,000.

Rank 497.

Messages per month 849.

Crossposting percentage 38%.

Availability 75% of USENET sites.

Moderated? No.

Special features

FAQ title sci.geo.geology FAQ

FAQ location sci.geo.geology, sci.answers, news.answers

Other information resources Earth and Sky (a weekly report).

Archive site The On-line Resources for Earth Scientists Guide is available via anonymous ftp at ftp://ftp.csn.org/COGS/ores.txt.

Related groups   sci.geo.eos, sci.geo.fluids, sci.geo.geology, sci.geo.hydrology, sci.geo.meteorology, sci.geo.satellite-nav

sci.geo.meteorology ★★★★

The world's weather—hurricanes, tornados, El Niño, the debate over global warming. Of interest to anyone fascinated by the weather and weather trends.

Typical recent postings   PC Based Computer Models, Forecasting, Northern Lights, Localized Weather Statistics, Spectral Barotropic Model, What's the World's Warmest Spot?

Review   Interesting discussions of metereological phenomena—surely the most common subject in casual conversation—make this newsgroup especially appealing, even for the general-interest reader.

Advice to newbies   Like all sci.* newsgroups, this one isn't an appropriate place to post any question that you can look up in a reference work, such as a dictionary or encyclopedia. Please read the group's FAQ before posting to avoid asking questions that have been posed before. Please post to the appropriate newsgroup. This newsgroup is for general discussions of metereology and oceanography, including current and historic weather patterns, hurricanes, tornados, and so on; for discussions of geophysical fluid dynamics, post to sci.geo.fluids; for discussions of data formats used in the sciences, post to sci.data.formats; for discussions of geographic information systems, post to comp.infosystems.gis; for discussions of nonlinear systems, post to sci.nonlinear; for general flames about the environment, post to talk.environment (but not sci.environment, please).

Adult-oriented?   No.

Readership   45,000.

Rank   621.

Messages per month   440.

Crossposting percentage   7%.

Availability   75% of USENET sites.

Moderated?   No.

Special features   None.

FAQ title   Meteorology Resources FAQ

FAQ location   sci.geo.meteorology

Other information resources   Tropical Cyclone Weekly Summary, Sources of Meteorological Data FAQ, Conferences in the Geosciences FAQ

Archive site   Extensive resources, including data sets and analysis programs, are available via anonymous FTP. For more information, see the Sources of Metereological Data FAQ.

Related groups   sci.geo.eos, sci.geo.fluids, sci.geo.geology, sci.geo.hydrology, sci.geo.meteorology, sci.geo.satellite-nav

sci.lang ★★★★

The scientific study of human languages, present and historical.

Typical recent postings   Name Schemes of the World, Linguistic Dogma, Language Evolution, Mandarin vs. Cantonese, Tonality in Asian Languages.

Review   Interesting, non-technical discussions of linguistics and language make this group of interest to non-specialists.

Advice to newbies   Like all sci.* newsgroups, this one isn't an appropriate place to post any question that you can look up in a reference work, such as a dictionary or encyclopedia. Please read the group's FAQ before posting to avoid asking questions that have been posed before. This newsgroup is for serious discussion of facts or theories related to language; for advice on English usage, see alt.usage.english or misc.writing.

Adult-oriented? No.

Readership 69,000.

Rank 287.

Messages per month 612.

Crossposting percentage 18%.

Availability 77% of USENET sites.

Moderated? No.

Special features None.

FAQ title sci.lang Frequently Asked Questions

FAQ location sci.lang, sci.answers, news.answers

Other information resources None.

Archive site Many Internet-accessible resources are described in the FAQ, but here's a jewel: a 100,000 word English dictionary. It's available via anonymous FTP from ftp.cs.cmu.edu [128.2.206.173] in the directory project/fgdata/dict. Retrieve the files cmudict.0.2.Z (compressed), cmulex.0.1.Z (compressed), phoneset.0.1.

Related groups alt.language.urdu.poetry, misc.education.language.english, sci.lang.japan

sci.math ★★★★★

Mathematics from a layperson's perspective— cunning and debatable proofs, discussion of math teaching in public schools, explorations of intriguing avenues of contemporary mathematics research. Of interest to anyone who enjoys mathematics, even as an occasional diversion.

Typical recent postings Euclid and Proofs, Reality, "New" vs. "Old" Math, Math Humor, The Binomial Identity, Multiple Integral.

Review One of USENET's best, this newsgroup features intelligent, lively, and often amusing dialogue on a wide variety of math-related subjects, many of which are quite accessible to laypeople.

Advice to newbies Like all sci.* newsgroups, this one isn't an appropriate place to post any question that you can look up in a reference work, such as a dictionary or encyclopedia. Please read the group's FAQ before posting to avoid asking questions that have been posed before.

Adult-oriented? No.

Readership 140,000.

Rank 42.

Messages per month 1,771.

Crossposting percentage 17%.

Availability 79% of USENET sites.

Moderated? No.

Special features None.

FAQ title sci.math Frequently Asked Questions

FAQ location sci.math, sci.answers, news.answers

Other information resources sci.math Introduction to Frequently Asked Questions

Archive site None.

Related groups sci.math.num-analysis., sci.math.research, sci.math.symbolic, k12.ed.math, sci.stat.*, sci.physics.*, comp.theory.*, comp.compression.*, comp.arch.arithmetic, sci.engr.*, sci.econ.*, sci.crypt, sci.chaos, sci.fractals, sci.logic, sci.nonlinear, sci.op-research, rec.puzzles, rec.games.chess

sci.med ★★★★

Health, illness, and the practice of medicine.

Typical recent postings Lifestyles of Doctors, Future of Medical Practice, Medical Savings Accounts, Vasectomy vs. Tubal Ligation, Health Reform, Lyme Disease.

Review   Interesting and informative postings about health-related issues make this newsgroup of general interest, despite the occasional flames and fluff.

Advice to newbies   Like all sci.* newsgroups, this one isn't an appropriate place to post any question that you can look up in a reference work, such as a dictionary or encyclopedia. Please read the group's FAQ before posting to avoid asking questions that have been posed before.

Adult-oriented?   No.

Readership   120,000.

Rank   72.

Messages per month   3,396.

Crossposting percentage   17%.

Availability   79% of USENET sites.

Moderated?   No.

Special features   Occasional, informative postings by Net-linked physicians.

FAQ title   None.

FAQ location   N/A.

Other information resources   Cancer—Online Information Sources FAQ, FAQ: Typing Injuries

Archive site   See the group's informational FAQs for related informational resources.

Related groups   sci.med.occupational, alt.support.cancer, sci.med.aids, sci.med.pharmacy, sci.med.dentistry, sci.med.occupational, sci.med.nutrition, sci.med.nursing

sci.physics ★★★★

Physics of interest to the layperson, news of the physics community, physics-related social issues. Of interest to anyone curious about the state of contemporary physics and the implications of current physics theories.

Typical recent postings   Definition of Heat, Ball Lightning, Microtubules and Quantum Mind, Predicting the Future, Dynamics of an Accelerating Car, Buckeyballs!!?!!, Tidal Friction.

Review   Interesting, non-technical discussions of physics theories and their implications make this newsgroup of interest to anyone who's had a basic physics course.

Advice to newbies   Like all sci.* newsgroups, this one isn't an appropriate place to post any question that you can look up in a reference work, such as a dictionary or encyclopedia. Please read the group's FAQ before posting to avoid asking questions that have been posed before. Please post to the appropriate newsgroup. For specialist-level discussions of physics, post to sci.physics.research (moderated). Particle physics is the topic of sci.physics.particle (unmoderated), while new (and wild) physics theories are properly discussed in alt.sci.physics.

Adult-oriented?   No.

Readership   130,000.

Rank   58.

Messages per month   3,332.

Crossposting percentage   17%.

Availability   79% of USENET sites.

Moderated?   No.

Special features   None.

FAQ title   Sci.Physics Frequently Asked Questions

FAQ location   sci.physics, sci.physics.particle, alt.sci.physics.new-theories, sci.answers, news.answers, alt.answers

Other information resources   None.

Archive site   None.

Related groups   sci.physics, sci.physics.accelerators, sci.physics.computational.fluid-dynamics, sci.physics.electromag, sci.physics.particle, sci.physics.fusion, sci.physics.research

sci.skeptic ★★

A place for believers in paranormal phenomena to subject their beliefs to the scrutiny of skeptics.

Typical recent postings   Evolutionism vs. Traditional Christianity, The American Focus on Satanic Crime, Faked Moon Landings, Religion and Politics, Aliens and Atheism.

Review   It's a good idea, but it isn't working out in practice—too many flaky discussions of evolutionism vs. creationism, everlasting lightbulbs, and assassination theories, which belong in other newsgroups.

Advice to newbies   Like all sci.* newsgroups, this one isn't an appropriate place to post any question that you can look up in a reference work, such as a dictionary or encyclopedia. Please read the group's FAQ before posting to avoid asking questions that have been posed before. Please consider whether your post might be better sent to alt.folklore.urban, talk.origins, or alt.conspiracy—and if you decide to post to one of these groups, *don't* crosspost to sci.skeptics.

Adult-oriented?   No.

Readership   95,000.

Rank   139.

Messages per month   4,898.

Crossposting percentage   42%.

Availability   77% of USENET sites.

Moderated?   No.

Special features   None.

FAQ title   sci.skeptic FAQ

FAQ location   sci.skeptic, sci.answers, news.answers

Other information resources   Creation FAQ

Archive site   For a bibliography on skepticism, use FTP to jhuvm.hcf.jhu.edu, log on with **skeptic** and use any non-blank password. Type the command **get skeptic.biblio**.

Related groups   talk.origins, alt.folklore.urban, alt.paranet.paranormal, alt.paranormal, alt.paranormal.channeling

soc.college ★★★★

College issues and college life, from the perspective of current college students and those who remember college days (fondly, generally).

Typical recent postings   Fake IDs/Underage Drinking, Allowance for Freshman, Computer for College, Physics Programs.

Review   Not to be missed by anyone currently connected with a college or university (whether as a student, faculty person, or staff member), this newsgroup features lively discussion of college life, college myths, and college issues (especially Political Correctness).

Advice to newbies   If you're looking for someone's email address, please don't post to the group; see the FAQ: College Email Addresses.

Adult-oriented?   No.

Readership   91,000.

Rank   147.

Messages per month   403.

Crossposting percentage   29%.

Availability   72% of USENET sites.

Moderated?   No.

Special features   None.

FAQ title   alt.folklore.college Frequently Asked Questions

FAQ location   alt.folklore.college

Other information resources FAQ: CSH Coke Machine Information; FAQ: College Email Addresses; List of emailpals living in former Soviet Union area

Archive site None.

Related groups alt.folklore, alt.internet.services, alt.folklore.urban, alt.folklore.computers, soc.netpeople, alt.college.college-bowl, alt.college.food, alt.college.fraternities, alt.college.fraternities.sigma-pi, alt.college.fraternities.theta-tau, alt.college.sororities, alt.college.us, alt.folklore.college, alt.sports.college.ivyleague, clari.sports.basketball.college, clari.sports.football.college, rec.sport.baseball.college, rec.sport.basketball.college, rec.sport.football.college, soc.college, soc.college.grad, soc.college.gradinfo, soc.college.org.aiesec., soc.college.teaching-asst

soc.feminism ★★★★★

The struggle for equal rights for women, with informed commentary (both pro and con).

Typical recent postings Fighting Against Online Harassment, Celebrating Womanhood, Gender Divided Spheres, Differences Between Men and Women, Take Back the Night.

Review One of USENET's best, this moderated newsgroup features informed and intelligent discussion of the issues raised by feminism. It shouldn't be missed by any USENET reader who wishes to be informed about varying women's perspectives on feminist issues. Although the group is moderated, critical posts are welcomed so long as they are reasoned and intelligent.

Advice to newbies Flames won't make it to the group, so don't waste your time.

Adult-oriented? No.

Readership 47,000.

Rank 577.

Messages per month 257.

Crossposting percentage 0%.

Availability 70% of USENET sites.

Moderated? No.

Special features Extensive FAQs are well worth reading for any person who wishes to be informed on feminist issues.

FAQ title soc.feminism Information, soc.feminism References, soc.feminism Resources, soc.feminism Terminologies

FAQ location soc.feminism, soc.answers, news.answers

Other information resources None.

Archive site None.

Related groups alt.feminism—but watch out, it's unmoderated.

soc.motss ★★★

Members of the same sex—that is, gays generally, and gay issues (AIDS, homosexual rights, discrimination). Of interest to gay people.

Typical recent postings Chest Hair, Goldilocks and the Gay Bears, Gay Mormon Email Group.

Review Discussion of gay issues and news related to the gay community will make this newsgroup of interest to gay people internationally.

Advice to newbies Please read the group's FAQ before posting to avoid asking questions that have been posed before.

Adult-oriented? Yes.

Readership 130,000.

Rank 54.

Messages per month 6,768.

Crossposting percentage 12%.

Availability   72% of USENET sites.

Moderated?   No.

Special features   None.

FAQ title   soc.motss FAQ

FAQ location   soc.motss, soc.answers, news.answers

Other information resources   Gay and Lesbian BBS List, Queer Resources Directory FAQ

Archive site   None.

Related groups   alt.homosexual, alt.sex.motss, alt.sex.homosexual, alt.politics.homosexual, soc.bi, alt.bbs.lists, alt.polyamory, alt.transgendered

soc.singles ★★

Light-hearted, sometimes flirtatious discussion for singles, with news of upcoming singles events and discussion of singles-related issues.

Typical recent postings   Opening Lines, Height and Dating, Worst Pickup Line, Random Harassment, Being Single and Depressed.

Review   This newsgroup could be (and has been) lots of fun, but it's much plagued by irrelevant crossposting and personals (in contravention of the group's FAQ).

Advice to newbies   Please read the group's FAQ before posting to avoid asking questions that have been posed before. In particular, don't post personals or requests for sex!

Adult-oriented?   No.

Readership   120,000.

Rank   66.

Messages per month   5,642.

Crossposting percentage   11%.

Availability   72% of USENET sites.

Moderated?   No.

Special features   None.

FAQ title   soc.singles FAQ

FAQ location   soc.singles, soc.answers, news.answers

Other information resources   None.

Archive site   None.

Related groups   soc.singles.nice

PART V

USENET

HORIZONS

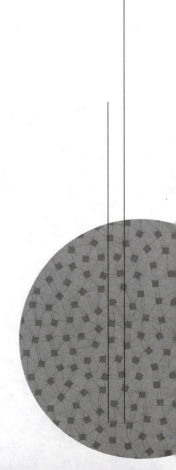

19

With more than 5,000 newsgroups available at many sites, there are plenty of newsgroups in existence, or at least one would think. But hardly a day goes by that your newsreader doesn't report the existence of new newsgroups—sometimes as many as a dozen!

Should you create a new newsgroup? I hope the answer is "no"—I'm having enough trouble keeping up!—but admittedly, you might have a good reason. If you decide to create a new newsgroup, your options are two:

- **Creating a group in the alt.* hierarchy.** There are no restrictions on the creation of new alt.* newsgroups; anyone can do it. On the other hand, sites aren't obligated to carry the new group—and if you don't follow the recommended procedures, they probably won't.

- **Creating a group in the standard hierarchies (comp, misc, news, rec, sci, soc, talk).** To create a new newsgroup in these hierarchies, you must submit your proposal to a formal vote. To win, you must receive more than 200 votes, and you must receive 100 more "yes" votes than "no" votes. If the vote passes, USENET sites are under moral obligation, at least, to carry the group.

This chapter briefly surveys both methods, without going into the technical details of the commands that actually create newsgroups. If you're really serious, see your system administrator.

CREATING AN ALT.* NEWSGROUP

As you browse the alt.* hierarchy, you'll surely agree that there are many successful and valuable newsgroups—just take a look at the four- and five-star selections in Chapter 18, "USENET's best: the top newsgroups reviewed." Groups such as alt.activism, alt.folklore.urban, and alt.history.what-if are fully the equals of the best groups in the standard hierarchy. What does it take to create such a successful group?

Here's the answer: Lots more than just using the UNIX commands that create the group. There are two essential ingredients: You must create enough interest in the group to get high-quality participation, and you must convince system administrators that the group is worth carrying. The following sections elaborate.

Creating interest in your new *.alt group

You should first consider why you want to create a newsgroup in the alt.* hierarchy in the first place. The alt.* hierarchy was created for newsgroups that would probably *not* pass a formal vote for a variety of reasons, including (but not limited to) the controversial nature of the topic. If you think your newsgroup *would* pass a formal vote, you should first consider creating it as a standard newsgroup. By all means, don't advocate the creation of an alt.* newsgroup as a "trial run" for a later standard newsgroup proposal; system administrators will refuse to carry the alt.* group on the grounds that it will lead to bandwidth-wasting duplication.

Your objective here is to build up interest and support for your new group, and the place to start is email. Describe your idea to people who you think might be interested, get their feedback, and profit from it. Chances are they'll have some excellent suggestions to make. Learn from them, reformulate your plans, and send them out again for comments and suggestions. Ask people to forward your message to anyone who might be interested.

Naming your newsgroup

Carefully consider the newsgroup's name. Do you want your newsgroup to fail because it violates some procedural nicety? Here's what to consider:

- There are too many alt.* groups that have two-part names—and the second part is something overly specific or obscure. It's much better to use a three-part name, fitting your new group, if possible, into one of the established second-levels hierarchies (see Table 19-1). (See Chapter 4, "How USENET is organized," for more information on USENET's organization.) If a logical second-level hierarchy doesn't exist, create one.

- Don't use obscure acronyms, such as "adsl" or "4S" or "aaa-cct." Administrators won't be able to tell at a glance what the newsgroup is about, and they may not carry it for that reason alone.

- Don't try to be cute or silly. Names of the type alt.barney.dinosaur.die.die.die try to amuse by replicating the structure of the first newsgroup name of this type (alt.swedish.chefs.bork.bork.bork), but the joke has worn thin.

- Don't create alt.* newsgroups that are based on local or regional concerns. These newsgroups are distributed globally. To create a local, regional, or state newsgroup, see your system administrator for information.

- Don't create alt.* newsgroups based on trendy fads or fashions that will soon be forgotten.

These newgroups are very hard to delete once they're established. An exception: newsgroups in the alt.current-events.* hierarchy.

- Avoid four-part names, unless there's already a well-established third-level hierarchy (an example: the alt.binaries.sounds.* hierarchy). No four-part name should be created if there are no other newsgroups at the third level (for example, don't create alt.food.tacos.hot if there are no other alt.food.tacos.* groups. Use a dash instead: alt.food.tacos-hot).

- Don't use any characters other than the letters a through z and, if necessary for naming purposes, a dash (-).

- No component of the name should be longer than 14 characters, the maximum accepted by the C news software.

Requesting discussion in alt.config

Now it's time to post a call for discussion in alt.config, the newsgroup that's set aside for discussion of new newsgroups. Don't ask for votes; votes have nothing to do with the creation of newsgroups in the alt.* hierarchy. You're asking for *discussion*. It's OK to ask for replies via email, with the promise that you'll summarize later. When you do, please don't post a huge article that just collates all the mail you've received; *summarize* the responses.

To illustrate the value of the discussion process, here's a proposal brought before alt.config:

```
Newsgroups: alt.config,rec.autos.misc,
rec.autos.tech
Date: Wed, 17 Aug 1994 03:23:39 GMT
Lines: 25

I'd like to propose the newsgroup
alt.autos.saturn for discussion of the
Saturn automobile. It's principally
intended for current and future owners,
but everyone is welcome. There is also
a Saturn mailing list (saturn@oar.net),
but I prefer the newsgroup format for
these reasons:
```

TABLE 19-1. SELECTED SECOND-LEVEL ALT.* HIERARCHIES

alt.bbs.*	alt.online-service.*
alt.binaries.*	alt.paranet.*
alt.comics.*	alt.personals.*
alt.culture.*	alt.politics.*
alt.current-events.*	alt.religion.*
alt.fan.*	alt.sex.*
alt.folklore.*	alt.sources.*
alt.food.*	alt.sport.*
alt.games.*	alt.support.*
alt.music.*	alt.tv.*

```
1) There is too much mail. An advanced
   mail reader like elm could handle
   it, but I'd have to go to the
   trouble of installing elm. Even if I
   did that, the mail would collect
   somewhere in my account until I
   deleted it. When I do delete it, I
   have to go to ftp to look back at
   old discussions.

2) The mailing list is small. There are
   a half-million Saturns and there must
   be at least 20,000 Saturn owners on
   the Net, but there are only 500 or so
   mailing list recipients.

3) To each his own. Those who prefer
   mailing lists should have mailing
   lists and those who prefer
   newsgroups should have newsgroups.

4) There are already Harley and VW
   newsgroups and they work.

Many mailing list members doubted the
wisdom of rec.autos.saturn, so I am
```

```
suggesting alt.autos.saturn as a trial
run.

I will wait a week or so for cogent
alternatives to this proposal.
```

Subsequent discussion focused on the problem of proposing the alt.autos.saturn group as a "trial run" for a future rec.autos.saturn move; this is frowned upon by system administrators who will refuse to carry a group for that reason alone. This group's advocate decided to take this good advice and attempt the creation of rec.autos.saturn through the voting procedure.

Please note that system administrators read alt.config—that's part of their job—and make decisions about whether to carry the group. If you want their support, please avoid the following arguments:

- "Other silly newsgroups exist, so why shouldn't I be able to create one?" And make the problem worse?

- "You may think my idea is dumb, but I've got 50 supporting letters!" This isn't convincing. Recently, there was plenty of support for a newsgroup titled alt.destroy.the.internet. Plenty of USENET people are engaged in behaviors that show no concern for the Net's future or the ability of others to use it productively.

- "No one is forced to carry the newsgroup, so what's wrong with creating it?" You'll be causing system administrators everywhere to do the work of evaluating your newsgroups, that's what.

Creating the newsgroup

If you decide to create your newsgroup, see your system administrator. For more information on the newsgroup creation process, see RFC 1036, an Internet "Request for comments" document.

CREATING A STANDARD NEWSGROUP

To create a newsgroup in the standard hierarchies (comp, misc, news, rec, sci, soc, and talk), you must submit your proposal to a formal procedure consisting of a discussion, a vote, a tally, and an announcement. If this procedure is followed correctly and the newsgroup wins approval, system administrators are under a moral obligation to carry the newsgroup. If this procedure is not followed correctly or if the newsgroup loses the vote, system administrators are equally obligated to refuse to carry it, should someone try to create it anyway. The following sections elaborate.

Preliminaries

You should begin the same way you'd begin creating an alt.* newsgroup: Refine your proposal through email discussions, and make sure your proposed name follows established guidelines. Check with your system administrator if you've any doubts about the suitability of the name you've chosen, or send a message explaining your concerns to group-advice@uunet.uu.net.

The discussion

To initiate discussion of your newsgroup, post an article to news.announce.newgroups, as well as to any other newsgroups or mailing lists that pertain to the proposed newsgroup's topic. In your message, use a Followup-to: header that directs discussion to news.groups. news.announce.newgroups is a moderated newsgroup, so don't expect to see your article immediately.

In your proposal, you should indicate the following:

- **The name of the proposed group.** Please make sure you've observed standard newsgroup naming practices (see the selection titled "Naming your newsgroup," earlier in this chapter).

- **Whether it will be moderated or unmoderated.** Indicate the name and qualifications of the moderator.

- **The newsgroup's charter.** This should indicate its purpose, mission, and breadth of topic coverage.

Here's the proposal for rec.autos.saturn:

```
Subject: RFD: rec.autos.saturn
Followup-To: news.groups
Date: 18 Aug 1994 15:19:49 -0400
*****************************************
       REQUEST FOR DISCUSSION (RFD)
            rec.autos.saturn
*****************************************
Group Name:    rec.autos.saturn
Status:        Unmoderated
Summary:       Discussion of all
               aspects of Saturn
               vehicles, especially,
               but not limited to,
               owning and maintaining
               them
Distribution:  World

Proposed Newsgroup line:

rec.autos.saturn    All about Saturn
                    automobiles.


            CHARTER
            -------
The Saturn automobile (actually three
automobiles with two engines: sedan,
```

station wagon, coupe, SOHC, DOHC) is a very popular small car with a devoted customer base. About 500,000 Saturns have been manufactured to date, and Saturn Corp. will soon export to Europe and Japan. There is a fairly large mailing list for Saturn owners (saturn@oar.net, subscription at saturn-request@oar.net), which serves its recipients well.

Unfortunately, most Saturn owners on the Net don't know and will never know that it exists. There is enough interest in Saturn that it should have both a mailing list and a newsgroup.

This newsgroup would be a place to discuss the Saturn that would offer itself to the entire USENET community.

Topics for discussion would include:

How to maintain and repair Saturn vehicles
Performance, efficiency, reliability, and other statistics
The usual enthusiasm and gripes from owners
Reviews and comparisons for shoppers
Price information
All relevant announcements from GM or Saturn Corp.
Shopping for promotional Saturn Corp. items

Please distribute this proposal to anyone who owns or is interested in Saturn vehicles.

This RFD is being submitted to news.announce.newgroups in compliance with the usual guidelines (I hope). I recently posted a proposal to create alt.autos.saturn, but rec.autos.saturn

is simply a better idea. This RFD is being posted to:

    news.announce.newgroups
    news.groups
    rec.autos.misc
    rec.autos.tech
    rec.autos.driving
    rec.autos.marketplace

This RFD will last for 21 to 30 days. Assuming that there are no overwhelming objections to rec.autos.saturn, there will then be a call for votes (CFV) that will last 21 days. As usual, creation of the newsgroup requires 100 more yes votes than no votes and also two yes votes for every no vote.

There follow 21 to 31 days of discussion. At the end of this time, there should be consensus on all of these points; if not, the proposal should be withdrawn for further behind-the-scenes discussion and refining. You can then repeat the discussion procedure with a new proposal.

The vote

Votes for new newsgroups are collected and tallied by an impartial, third-party group known as the USENET Volunteer Votetakers (UVV). Currently coordinating this group is Ron Dippold (rdippold@qualcom.com); you should contact him before issuing a call for votes.

Assuming the group's proposal has met with a positive response, you should immediately issue the Call for Votes (CFV) by posting the request for votes to news.announce.newgroups. Be sure to crosspost the CFV to any newsgroups or mailing lists that pertain to the proposed newsgroup's topic. Please observe the following:

• Clearly indicate how to vote for—and against—the proposal. CFVs that indicate only how one may vote for the proposal are not tolerated and will void the vote.

- State the voting period (at least 21 days but no more than 31 days), as well as the date voting will end. Votes must arrive prior to this date to be counted.

- Remind voters that votes will count only if they're directed to the proper address or addresses (it's OK to have different addresses for "yes" and "no" votes, as long as they're on the same machine). Votes posted to USENET do not count.

- Explain that votes must be explicit: Voters must say "I vote FOR the proposal to create newsgroup such-and-such," or "I vote AGAINST the proposal to create newsgroup such-and-such."

You can repeat the CFV a couple of times, but they must contain the same unbiased voting instructions. But please note that you can't change the *proposal* during the vote—doing so will void the vote.

The Tally

When the voting period is complete, the vote takers post the results to news.announce.newgroups, as well as to the other newsgroups and mailing lists that were crosslisted in the original proposal. A newsgroup passes if:

- There are no serious objections to the voting procedure that might invalidate the vote;

- There are at least 100 more YES than NO votes; *and*

- At least two-thirds of the total votes are favorable.

There follows a five-day waiting period, in which objections to the voting procedure can be brought forth and examined. If no serious objections are raised and the newsgroup passes all three tests, the moderator of news.announce.newgroups announces the creation of the new newsgroup.

What if the proposal fails

An unsuccessful proposal can't be brought up again until six months have elapsed.

SUMMARY

Anyone can create an alt.* newsgroup, but there's no assurance that USENET sites will carry it. To create a successful newsgroup, you must build support, refine your proposal, and observe newsgroup naming guidelines. If you think your group would pass a vote, you should begin by trying to create a standard newsgroup. You must carefully follow the procedures lest your failure to do so invalidate the vote.

FROM HERE

- For information on becoming a USENET site, see Chapter 20, "Becoming a USENET site."

- For an exploration of the issues facing USENET, see Chapter 21, "USENET issues and futures."

20

Creating a new USENET site isn't a trivial decision, and isn't necessary if you just want to read USENET newsgroups. At the mininum, you'll need the following:

- Someone with sufficient time and expertise to cope with the task of administering the USENET site—and that means installing and configuring the software, deciding whether to carry new groups, dealing with problems caused by spammers, trollers, and other net.abusers, and talking to local newspaper people who have heard about "pornography on the Internet."

- Huge amounts of disk space—currently, you'll need (conservatively) about a gigabyte if you'd like to carry all the groups and keep the articles current for a week.

- Fees—as much as $1000 per month—to obtain the news feed, if you can't obtain the feed from a cooperative neighbor. This amount goes up if you don't already have a high-bandwidth Internet connection (forget obtaining all the newsgroups by 14.4 Kbps modem, because it would be on all day and all night).

That said, it costs less—in time, hassles, disk space, and money—to receive fewer newsgroups. A company that wants to provide just a few high-quality newsgroups for employees' use may very well decide that there's justification for becoming a USENET site—you can control which newsgroups your employees access and rest content that they're not reading alt.waste.time.

FINDING A NEWS FEED

Your first step is to determine where you're going to get your *news feed* (automated, periodic updates that carry new articles to your site, and carry your subscribers' responses to the rest of the Net). You've two types of sources for news feeds:

- **NNTP news feeds.** A news feed that employs the Network News Transport Protocol (NNTP) requires Internet connectivity. With an NNTP feed, you can carry all the newsgroups, if you wish.

- **UUCP news feeds.** A news feed that employs the Unix-to-Unix Copy (UUCP) program doesn't require direct Internet connectivity; you can use a modem to obtain the news feeds, but you'd be well advised to consider limiting the number of newsgroups you obtain.

To minimize costs, contact neighboring USENET sites to see whether they will give you a news feed. The newsgroup comp.mail.maps is a good source of information about USENET sites in your area. You can also post a message to news.admin.misc, with a distribution limiting the post to your region or state, asking for assistance. Be specific about what you're looking for—for example, a UUCP news feed using a 14.4 Kbps V.32 bis modem, and 30–35 newsgroups.

If you can't get a friendly neighbor to provide you with a news feed, you may have to obtain one from a commercial service provider (see Table 20-1).

TABLE 20-1. SERVICE PROVIDERS THAT OFFER USENET NEWS FEEDS

a2icommunications
1211 Park Avenue #202
San Jose, CA 95126
Data: (408) 293-9010 (v.32bis, v.32),
(408) 293-9020(PEP)
(login as "guest")
Telnet: a2i.rahul.net[192.160.13.1] (login as
    "guest")
info@rahul.net

Anterior Technology
P.O. Box 1206
Menlo Park, CA 94026-1206
Voice: (415) 328-5615
Fax: (415) 322-1753
info@fernwood.mpk.ca.us

CERFnet
P.O. Box 85608
San Diego, CA 92186-9784
Voice: (800) 876-CERF
help@cerf.net

Colorado SuperNet, Inc.
Attn: David C. Menges
Colorado School of Mines
1500 Illinois
Golden, CO 80401
Voice: 303-273-3471
dcm@csn.org

connect.com.au (Australia)
Attn: Hugh Irvine (hugh@connect.com.au)
Ben Golding (bgg@connect.com.au)
Voice: (613) 528-2239

Demon Internet Systems
internet@demon.co.uk

DM Connection
267 Cox Street
Hudson, MA 01749
Voice: (508) 568-1618
Fax: (508) 562-1133

ExNet Systems Ltd
37 Honley Road
Catford
London, SE62HY, UK
Voice: +44812440077
Fax: +44812440078
exnet@exnet.com or exnet@exnet.co.uk

Gordian
20361 Irvine Avenue
Santa Ana Heights, CA 92707 (OrangeCounty)
Voice: (714) 850-0205
Fax: (714) 850-0533
E-mail: uucp-request@gordian.com

Hatch Communications
8635 Falmouth Avenue, Suite 105
Playa del Rey, CA 90293
Voice: (310) 305-8758
E-mail:info@hatch.socal.com

HoloNet
Information Access Technologies, Inc.
46 Shattuck Square, Suite 11
Berkeley, CA 94704-1152
Voice: (510) 704-0160, Fax: (510) 704-8019,
Modem: 704-1058
Telnet: holonet.net
E-mail: info@holonet.net (automated reply)
Support: support@holonet.net

infocom Public Access Unix
White Bridge House
Old Bath Road
CHARVIL, Berkshire
United Kingdom
RG109QJ
Voice: +44[0]734344000
Fax: +44[0]734320988
Data: +44[0]734340055
E-mail: info@infocom.co.uk

Table 20-1. Service providers that offer USENET news feeds (continued)

Internet Initiative Japan, Inc.
Hoshigaoka Bldg.
2-11-2, Nagata-Cho
Chiyoda-ku, Tokyo 100 Japan
Voice: +81335803781
Fax: +81335803782
E-mail: info@iij.ad.jp

JvNCnet
B6 von Neumann Hall
Princeton University
Princeton, NJ 08543
Voice: (800) 35-TIGER
market@jvnc.net

MSEN, Inc.
628 Brooks Street
Ann Arbor, MI 48103
Voice: (313) 998-4562
Ftp:ftp.msen.com[148.59.1.2], see/pub/
    vendor/msen/*
info@msen.com

MV Communications, Inc.
P.O. Box 4963
Manchester, NH 03108-4963
Voice: (603) 429-2223
Data: (603) 429-1735 (login as "info"or "rates")
info@mv.mv.com

NEARnet (New England Academic and Research
    Network)
10 Moulton Street
Cambridge, MA 02138
Voice: (617) 873-8730
Fax: (617) 873-5620
nearnet-join@nic.near.net

Netcom-Online Communication Services
4000 Moorpark Avenue, Suite 209
San Jose, CA 95117
Voice: (408) 554-UNIX

Data: (408) 241-9760 (login as "guest,"
    no password)
Telnet:netcom.netcom.com[192.100.81.100]
(login as "guest")
E-mail:info@netcom.com

Northwest Nexus, Inc.
P.O. Box 40597
Bellevue, WA 98015-4597
Voice: (206) 455-3505
Data: (206) 382-6245 (login as "new")
Fax: (206) 455-4672
info@nwnexus.wa.com

Performance Systems International, Inc.
11800 Sunrise Valley Drive, Suite 1100
Reston, VA 22091
Voice: (703) 620-6651 or (800) 827-7482
Computerized info: all-info@psi.com
Human-based info: info@psi.com

Portal Communications Company
20863 Stevens Creek Boulevard
Suite 200
Cupertino, CA 95014
Voice: (408) 973-9111
Fax: (408) 725-1580
Data: (408) 973-8091 (V.32/PEP)
Telnet: portal.com
Email :CS@portal.com

SURAnet
8400 Baltimore Boulevard.
College Park, MD 20742
Voice: (301) 982-3214
Fax: (301) 982-4605
E-mail: news-admin@sura.net

TABLE 20-1. SERVICE PROVIDERS THAT OFFER USENET NEWS FEEDS (CONTINUED)

TDK Consulting Services
119 University Avenue East
Waterloo, Ontario
Canada N2J2W9
Voice: (519) 888-0766
Fax: (519) 747-0881
E-mail: info@tdkcs.waterloo.on.ca

UUNET Canada, Inc.
1 Yonge Steet, Suite 1400
Toronto, Ontario
Canada M5E1J9
Voice: (416) 368-6621
Fax: (416) 369-0515
info@uunet.caoruunet-ca@uunet.uu.net

UUNET Technologies, Inc.
3110 Fairview Park Drive, Suite 570
Falls Church, VA 22042
Voice: (703) 204-8000
Fax: (703) 204-8001
info@uunet.uu.net
AlterNet(networkconnectivity)info:alternet-
    info@uunet.uu.net

UUNORTH, Inc.
Box 445, Station E
Toronto, Ontario
Canada M6H4E3
Voice: (416) 537-4930 or (416) 225-UNIX
Fax: (416) 537-4890

WIMSEY
Attn: Stuart Lynne
225B Evergreen Drive
Port Moody, BC, V3H1S1
Voice: 604-93-7532
sl@vanbc.wimsey.bc.ca

Xenon Systems
Attn: Julian Macassey
7421/2 North Hayworth Avenue
Hollywood, CA 90046-7142
Voice: (213) 654-4495
postmaster@bongo.tele.com

OBTAINING AND INSTALLING THE SOFTWARE

You'll need the following programs to operate a USENET site:

- **Transport software.** Required to transport new articles to your site and send your subscribers' replies to the Net. This software must conform to the UUCP or NNTP protocols. If you want your readers to be able to send email replies, you'll also need mail software that conforms to the UUCP or SNMP mail protocols.

- **USENET server software.** Required to handle requests from newsreader programs to display newsgroups and articles. In addition, this soft-

ware deletes expired articles and performs other maintenance tasks.

- **Newsreader software.** Required to read the news, post articles, and send replies.

Unfortunately, installing and configuring this software isn't a trivial task; you'll need an experienced UNIX guru to pull it off.

REGISTERING YOUR SITE

Once you've obtained your feed and successfully installed the necessary software, you must register your site.

If you're linked to the net via UUCP, you do so by choosing a UUCP-compatible name and adding your site to the UUCP maps. For more information, see Grace Todino and Dale Dougherty, *Using UUCP and USENET* (O'Reilly and Associates), as well as the informational resources available from the comp.mail.maps newsgroup.

If you're linked to the net via NNTP, you'll want to register your site with the Domain Name Service (DNS). Chances are that your Internet service provider has already arranged this for you. In any case, this is a far from trivial matter, and it's beyond the scope of this book. For more information, see O'Reilly's *Connecting to the Internet*.

SUMMARY

If you just need a USENET connection, you don't need to become a USENET site, which requires a lot of work, computer resources, and (probably)

money. Develop a USENET site only if you decide that there's some compelling reason to do so, such as offering only a limited set of useful newsgroups for your firm's employees. To become a site, you'll need to obtain a feed, obtain and install the necessary software, and register your site with UUCP or the Internet (or both).

FROM HERE

- For an exploration of the issues facing USENET, see Chapter 21, "USENET issues and futures."

- For informaation on creating a newsgroup, see Chapter 19, "Creating a newsgroup."

USENET SERVER SOFTWARE

At UNIX sites, there are two USENET programs in common use: C News and INN. Both make extensive use of the Network News Transfer Protocol, introduced in 1986. In brief, NNTP allows Internet hosts to exchange USENET news via the Internet rather than the much slower UUCP connections. Additionally, sites with extensive local area networks can distribute the news internally without having to keep copies of all the articles on each of the machines.

C News (the successor, naturally, to the now-defunct B News) stems from work at the University of Toronto by Geoff Collyer and Henry Spencer. It's available from the official archive site at ftp.cs.toronto.edu:pub/c-news/c-news.tar.Z. C News requires NNTP.

InterNetNews (INN) was created by Rich Salz, and is specifically designed for large UNIX systems that employ socket interfaces. The program incorporates NNTP, making it easier to administer. It's available from the official archive site at ftp.uu.net in the directory/networking/news/nntp/inn.

Waffle is a USENET-compatible BBS system for IBM PCs and compatibles. It supports UUCP mail, UUCP, and USENET news. It's available in DOS and UNIX versions, although only the DOS version is available as an executable program. Both are distributed as shareware with a "try before you buy" period. Waffle is available by anonymous ftp from oak.oakland.edu in the directory pub/SimTel/waffle/waf165.zip.

21

USENET ISSUES AND FUTURES

USENET faces troubling issues, many of which are caused by its own burgeoning growth. Here's a sampler:

- The "anything goes" attitude that some system administrators have taken because they believe that disallowing certain types of posts or newsgroups constitutes censorship. As a result, postings that may break state and federal obscenity and copyright protection laws now exist in certain groups.

- The Net's aversion to blatant commercialism, coupled with its increasing inability to prevent outside advertisers from pelting newsgroups with unwanted commercial posts.

- The massive influx of millions of new users who know very little about the Net's traditions or behavioral expectations.

- The increasing prominence of antisocial behaviors and the vulnerability of USENET system software to manipulation by computer crackers.

- The controversy over anonymous postings, which can be used both to protect posters for legitimate reasons and also to abuse the network.

- The lack of a generally recognized system by which the authenticity of USENET postings can be determined.

The following sections discuss these issues in detail, but for now, it's worth pointing out that

USENET has faced equally serious challenges before and managed to surmount them. I wouldn't start taking bets on USENET's disappearance.

ANYTHING GOES?

You won't spend much time on USENET before you run across posts that could be construed to be illegal—especially by some politically ambitious prosecutor in a conservative area. It seems that some people seem bent on pushing the Net to the brink, as if they have something to prove by posting the most outrageous stuff they can find (or invent). In researching this book, I've found posts that could very well be construed to be obscene, in violation of copyright, or defamatory; I haven't run into anything seditious yet, but I'm sure I will, eventually. The following sections examine such posts and the issues they raise.

Obscenity

The courts have found it very difficult to define obscenity, the depiction of sexual acts in a way that the public finds indecent. It has long been agreed that obscenity does not constitute protected speech, that is to say, speech that is protected by the First Amendment of the U.S. Constitution; the problem has been to define what is obscene, and what is not (and therefore worthy of protected status).

Just what does "obscene" mean? A prior standard that a potentially obscene work should show some "socially redeeming value" turned out to be unworkable. In 1973, the U.S. Supreme Court ruled that obscenity could be judged only in culturally relative terms: To be judged obscene, a work had to violate prevailing community standards. What's considered obscene in San Francisco (if anything), then, is a very different matter from what's considered obscene in Muskogee. But the learned justices clearly weren't thinking of computer networks! The same USENET postings appear in San Francisco *and* Bible City, Texas. Does this mean that an entire global network must be held hostage to the values of a rural, fundamentalist Christian, Republican community? No one knows—but there's sure to be a test soon.

Cultural relativity doesn't apply to two kinds of pornography that have been specifically placed beyond the bounds of protected speech: The depiction of sexual acts involving children or anyone under 18, and the depiction of acts of sexual violence. It's apparent that USENET sites are courting disaster by carrying groups such as alt.sex.binaries.pictures and alt.sex.binaries.cartoons, which have recently had several posts that apparently fall into these unprotected categories. It is not beyond the realm of possibility that some or all of these posts were made by investigators planning a "sting" operation. Note that child pornography is flatly illegal (rather than just potentially "obscene") only if it involves the use of children (for example, in photographs or videos); written pedophiliac works may well be judged obscene, but it is not certain whether they are outright illegal in the sense of a video in which a child's innocence is exploited.

Employers struggling through the thicket of sexual harassment legislation and regulation must consider, too, whether the availability of pornography on USENET constitutes a form of sexual harassment. Experts on sexual harassment broadly agree that the open display of sexually oriented material at work creates the equivalent of a "men's locker room" and a hostile atmosphere for women workers. The courts have already ruled, in fact, that a worker's display of *Playboy* centerfolds constitutes sexual harassment; given such a view, a firm

could quite possibly find itself on the wrong end of a sexual harassment lawsuit should workers display erotica on office computer displays. Recognizing this fact, several organizations—including Apple Computer—have removed the alt.binaries.pictures.erotica.* and alt.sex.* groups.

The use of a corporate or university computer for the storage of sexually oriented material could well be judged inappropriate for an entirely different reason: misappropriation of resources. At the Lawrence Livermore National Laboratory of the University of California, for example, two workers were charged with misappropriation of state resources for maintaining a computer archive of some 91,000 erotic pictures, newspapers recently reported. The computer technician responsible for creating and maintaining the archive resigned after the charges were filed and faces maximum penalties of three years in prison for each of the two felony charges filed against him.

Will it take prosecutions to keep actionable erotica off USENET? An interim solution might involve more self-policing. USENET administrators have, in the past, remonstrated users for posting other illegal material, such as short stories retyped from science fiction magazines (and thus in outright violation of copyright), insisting that they remove such materials or face the loss of their accounts. But I doubt that most system administrators would like to set themselves up as judges of what's illegal and what's not when it comes to erotica/pornography; to do so would put them into the uncomfortable role of endorsing what's still on the Net. Given the political correctness craze still raging at most universities, where the largest sites are located, that could entail consequences ranging from public humiliation to job loss.

Copyright infringement

Any discussion of the excesses of alt.binaries.pictures.erotica.* should include an assessment of the perils posed by copyright infringement on the Net, since most of the graphics available have been scanned, without permission, from the likes of

AMATEUR ACTION BBS BUST MAY MEAN BIG TROUBLE FOR USENET SITES

In August, 1994, a jury in Memphis, TN, convicted a California couple, Robert and Carleen Thomas of Milpitas, CA, of 11 counts of transmitting obscenity through interstate telephone lines via their computer bulletin board system (BBS). Each count carries a penalty of up to five years in prison and a $250,000 fine. A Tennessee postal inspector subscribed to the BBS under a fake name and requested a number of explicit photographs and movies.

The convictions are based on the Supreme Court's standard specifying that to be judged obscene, erotica must be shown to be unacceptable to a particular community. The downloaded material probably would not have been judged obscene in California, but the jurors agreed that it would be judged obscene in Tennessee. Mike Godwin, an attorney for the Electronic Frontier Foundation (EFF), noted that this case "has one community attempting to dictate the standards for the whole country." Within hours after the conviction, a USENET article warned that should the case stand, "you can bet there will be a hell of a lot more prosecutions on the same basis in short order." Throughout the U.S., erotic BBSs were shutting down; one BBS operator said that staying in business amounted to "Russian roulette." Could the same be said of USENET sites that continue to carry alt.binaries.pictures.erotica?

Playboy and *Penthouse.* Copyright infringement is the duplication, without explicit written permission, of any intellectual work—for example, a text document, a computer program, a work of visual art. Since the U.S. became a signatory to the Berne Convention, an international agreement that governs the protection of intellectual property, any work that is not expressly placed in the public domain is considered to be copyrighted unless it carries an express notice that the author has deliberately placed it in the public domain. In general, though, the author of work cannot collect damages for copyright infringement unless the work carries a copyright notice and, more importantly, the author can prove that the infringement resulted in monetary or other tangible damages.

The rise of computer technology and advanced computer networking has deeply undermined intellectual property rights in general and copyright in particular—when you can duplicate a 500-page document or a high-resolution photograph with one press of a key and then distribute it worldwide, copyright violations are all but inevitable. When coupled with the computer community's strong values on the free exchange of information, it's all but guaranteed that copyright violations will become rampant on the Internet and USENET—and they are. John Barlow of the Electronic Frontier Foundation (EFF) put it in deliberately overstated terms: "Copyright is dead."

Computer users may feel that they honor copyright more in the breach than in the observance, but that doesn't mean their behaviors are right. The existence of copyright legislation stems from the conviction that writers, artists, thinkers, programmers, and other creative people will not bother to create works if they cannot hope to gain income from the sale or use of these works.

But the matter goes beyond morality: To avoid litigation, you'll be wise to avoid posting anything that's expressly copyrighted to USENET without first obtaining written permission. An exception: Copyright laws permit "fair use" for legitimate educational and research purposes, so long as the use of material is not excessive (a general guideline: Don't quote more than 5% of a written work) and no commercial gain is sought from the use of the excerpt.

Defamation

The term "defamation" refers to the injury of a person's good name or reputation by false statements, voiced for malicious purposes, that subject the person to public ridicule, social contempt, private shame, or even "mental anguish." Note that using vulgar language in a communication with a person isn't defamatory if it's intended as an insult. When a defamatory statement is written and published, it's called *libel*.

Most of what might appear to be libelous on the Net is probably protected speech. In general, you can defame public figures all you want, so long as the defamation isn't maliciously intended—but there's risk involved. What's a public figure? Government officials, certainly, but don't bet that the protections apply to famous private individuals. And what's "malicious" mean? Isn't all defamation malicious by definition? Perhaps, except when it's clearly bracketed as humor or satire.

It doesn't take long, though, before you run into a post that probably goes beyond the bounds of protected speech. An international USENET service provider recently provided a free USENET account to a Canadian freenet, only to withdraw the donation after posts appeared that described a Toronto priest using the terms "thieving," "Nazism," and "child molesting." Predictably, there were USENET participants who leaped to the freenet's defense, repeating the "anything goes" mentality that seems destined to get USENET into serious trouble: "Freedom of expression is freedom of expression," one told a newspaper. "There's no qualification, information is like water, it doesn't matter what's in the water. If they're going to start telling everyone what they can or cannot post, then they're going to have to start getting into the censoring business."

Unquestionably, an article posted to USENET that contains defamatory material could provide grounds for a lawsuit. Play it safe. Don't post anything to USENET that could be considered malicious defamation. If you really want to put somebody down, voice it in a humorous vein—lampoon and satire all you like. Anyone with a sense of humor (including the jury, one hopes!) will laugh it off.

Sedition

In the U.S., the courts have generally held that the freedom of speech does not protect advocates of the violent overthrow of the government—or even more broadly, saying anything that would threaten public order. Hypocritically, concern regarding sedition (and prosecutions) rarely occur except in times of war, when patriotism reaches its apex.

COMMERCIALISM

When USENET was primarily an academic network, using NFSNET for the bulk of its backbone traffic, commercial postings were not only unwelcome but in violation of the National Science Founda-tion's Acceptable Use Policy (AUP). According to this policy, the purpose of NSFNET—and by extension, any service that uses it, including USENET— is to advance research communication in and among U.S. research and educationalinstitutions. Business participation is restricted to non-proprietary uses carried out in a spirit of open scientific collaboration. The guidelines permit announcements of new products, but only if they pertain to research or instruction. Specifically excluded are uses motivated by profit or extensive use for private or personal business.

But NSFNET, and its Acceptable Use Policy, has become increasingly irrelevant. An organization called the Commercial Internet eXchange (CIX), a consortium of regional service providers, provides an AUP-free alternative to the NSFNET backbone. These networks do not restrict commercial use and are expected to play a significant role in the growing use of the Internet for business purposes. The transition is well underway. In 1993, there were almost as many sites in the com (business) domain as in the edu (university and research) domain. It's not surprising that, after examining USENET, someone decided that it would make a very nice, low-cost mass advertising medium.

April, 1994. In more than 5,000 newsgroups, there it was: An advertisement from a couple of Arizona lawyers offering to assist aliens in obtaining their "green card"—an official Bureau of Immigration and Naturalization certificate entitling them to permanent resident status in the U.S. With the aid of a program called Masspost, the two lawyers—a husband and wife team named Laurence Canter and Martha Siegel—had posted the article to more than 5,500 newsgroups.

Canter and Siegel's spam broke just about every rule in the book. The ad had nothing to do with the topics under discussion in almost all of the newsgroups, and what's more, some were quick to allege that the ad was a scam: The information that the two lawyers offered was publicly available, it was said, for the price of a 29-cent stamp. Predictably, the net.police went to work, bombarding Canter and Siegel's email account with flames and spams of their own, the objective being to drive the couple off the net. The amount of incoming traffic was so voluminous that it repeatedly crashed the computer system of the couple's Internet service provider, Internet Direct of Phoenix, AZ. Subsequently, Internet Direct cancelled the couple's account, only to find itself threatened with a lawsuit. Although Internet Direct's contract forbids the use of the service for advertising, Canter and Siegel had never returned a signed copy of the contract and argued that they were therefore not bound by its provisions. The suit didn't materialize, but Canter and Siegel remained defiant. In a subsequent *New York Times* interview, Canter denied that the couple had done anything wrong and vowed to return to USENET with more mass advertising. They pointed out that they had received many positive responses among the 30,000 flames and gloated that they had pulled off the impossible—advertising to an audience of millions for a matter of mere pennies. Provocatively, Canter also announced his intention to sell his services to anyone who would like to advertise on USENET.

Evidently, Canter and Siegel haven't had much luck finding another avenue back to the Net.

Another service provider, Netcom, announced that they had refused the couple an Internet connection; its position was that the service is like a public restaurant where a customer, out of concern for the health, safety, and comfort of other customers, can be refused service for not wearing a shirt or shoes. Anyone who has clearly stated an intention to persist in behaviors that disrupt USENET can and should be refused service, the announcement said. In a meantime, dozens of talented computer programmers and hackers have gone to work devising programs that will detect the couple's posts and cancel them.

The Green Card episode shows that blatant advertising violates USENET norms and will, for any firm that cares about its public reputation, prove counterproductive. Obviously, ethical concerns will not prevent crooks, scam artists, bogus investment counselors, fad diet firms, or the terminally clueless from attempting mass advertising campaigns on USENET—but that's just the point. A firm that cares about its reputation and image will think very long and hard before writing its own "masspost" program.

Peddlers—I think this term sums up their public image—will continue to spam USENET groups. What can be done to stop this practice? Dave Kristofferson, manager of the bionet newsgroups, suggests the following:

- Don't give the person more publicity by quoting and reposting their article.

- Complain to the postmaster at the site where the message originated (see Chapter 17, "Dealing with USENET problems").

- Write a short note to the offender noting that you will never purchase any of their firm's products.

FLUXERS

The massive expansion of USENET, especially as on-line services such as Delphi, CompuServe and America Online bring millions of new users on-line, brings with it the threat that the newbie influx—always a problem with each class of college freshmen—might overwhelm USENET's traditions. Worse, the new generation of users, accustomed to graphical user interfaces (GUI), might not possess the technical sophistication—or the educational background—to grasp the way USENET works, leading them not only to commit the usual newbie errors, but to continue making them and thus to alter or even destroy the character of USENET newsgroups. That's the concern of Jason M. Ruspini, of the University of Pennsylvania, who's coined a term for the new entrants: *fluxers*. A fluxer, in Ruspini's definition, is not only part of a massive influx of new users, but will also cause USENET to change as their repeated and unrelenting errors and insensitivity to USENET traditions continue to undermine the quality of USENET discussions.

Not everyone agrees with Ruspini's negative assessment of fluxers. Mitch Kapor, director of the Electronic Frontier Foundation (EFF), dismisses the old-timers' aversion to newbies as little more than the *hauteur* expressed by the passengers on the Mayflower to the passengers on the *second* boat. And, to be sure, each wave of newbies has generated aversive reaction, coupled with predictions of the Net's demise—but it hasn't happened. One distinguishing feature of the Fluxer invasion, however, is that Fluxers are using ineptly designed newsreaders—America Online's is a case in point—that actually prevent them from adopting good practices (such as replying to the newsgroup specified in the Followup-to: line of an article's header).

Recognizing the limitations of on-line services and GUI newsreaders, Ron Newman of MIT's Media Lab believes that the Fluxer deficiencies should not be attributed to their lack of knowledge of UNIX or general ignorance, but rather to the deficiencies of the software they're using. He has proposed a "Good Net-Keeping Seal of Approval for USENET Software," containing a series of design guidelines for anyone who's thinking about revising or updating a newsreader program. According to Newman, a good newsreader should do the following:

- Display all essential header information so that the user knows who sent the message and where a follow-up article should be posted.

- Clearly separate commands for posting, follow-up, and email replies so that users don't post follow-ups when they should be sending email replies.

- Implement crossposting so that users can crosspost an article when doing so is appropriate. If crossposting isn't available, users will work around this by posting the same article manually to separate groups, which wastes bandwidth and defeats automated features in some newsreaders that hide a crossposted article in any newsgroup after it has been read in one newsgroup.

- Allow users to edit the headers in follow-up articles so that they can change the subject to reflect subject drift or post the reply to a different newsgroup, if the drift of the discussion warrants this.

- Automatically direct follow-ups to the newsgroup listed in the Follow-up line, if such a line exists, rather than posting the follow-up to a long series of crossposted newsgroups.

- Direct email replies to the actual sender of the message (whose email address might be listed in the Reply-to line if the article has been forwarded).

- Quote text automatically in follow-up articles and set this quoted text off in some way, such as by indenting or beginning each line with an identifiable character.

- Insert an attribution along with the quoted text and allow the user to edit this attribution so that "I didn't say that!" controversies can be eliminated.

- Allow users to cancel their own articles, but no others.

NET.ABUSE

It was once thought that the development of USENET would bring an end to mailing lists. Although mailing lists provide a useful means for linking small "birds of a feather" communities, they have one enormous drawback: Each contributed letter goes to the electronic mailbox of every subscriber. With as many as 50 messages coming in each day, it's hard to find your personal mail amidst the noise and clutter of mailng list messages. USENET solves this problem by keeping the messages in newsgroups, away from your mailbox.

But mailing lists haven't died away—in fact, they're thriving. And here's one reason. Virtually every time that the members of a mailing list consider moving their group to a newsgroup, many argue—and usually with success—that doing so would be a terrible idea: Flamers and trollers would ruin the group.

Are antisocial behaviors becoming more common on USENET? The answer is almost certainly yes, but it's far from certain that their activities will necessarily ruin USENET discussions. Much of the aversion that mailing list members show to moving the group to USENET probably stems from elitism, the conviction that the Great Unwashed out there really don't have anything valuable to say about their subject. For many highly specialized or technical subjects, that's probably true. After all, there's a logical division of labor between a small, sharply focused mailing list of 25 to 50 people, who are all involved in research in a technical or scientific area, and a general discussion group concerning issues of interest to thousands. Mailing lists will continue to serve the needs of small research communities, and justifiably so.

As for the impact of net.abusers, you don't have to let them ruin your enjoyment of USENET. Here are some practical strategies for keeping them off your screen:

• Use a newsreader that can kill articles by author and subject. If the newsreader lets you specify initially which subject words you want to kill, add all the epithets you can think of, plus a generous sprinkle of four-letter words. This will serve to delete a good proportion of the garbage that would otherwise come across your screen. You might repeat this exercise yourself, and add the authors of any post containing these subject words to your kill file.

• Consider adding the site anon.petit.fi to your kill settings. This site broadcasts anonymous posts (see the next section for more discussion of anonymity). To be sure, some of them are worthwhile posts by writers who wish to remain anonymous for legitimate reasons, but the site has recently been used by spammers whose only objective is to destroy the thread of communication in newsgroups that they feel have overly "cute" subjects, such as rec.pet.cats.

• Avoid newsgroups that have a high crossposting percentage (see the statistics in Chapter 18, "USENET's best: the top newsgroups reviewed"). Although some high-frequency crossposting is explicable in other terms, it often indicates that the newsgroup has become a favorite target of trollers, spammers, and cascaders. In particular, avoid any group with the word "flame" in the title, as well as alt.bitterness, alt.mcdonalds, alt.evil, alt.religion, alt.kibology, alt.stupidity, alt.feminism, and talk.bizarre.

• If your newsgroup is being persistently attacked by flamers, spammers, and trollers, contact the postmaster at the offending sites. For more information, see Chapter 17, "Dealing with USENET problems."

ANONYMITY

Many USENET users tend to react negatively to the very concept of anonymous posts (see Chapter 17, "Dealing with USENET problems"), believing that one should stand behind one's word. And there's no question that anonymous posting services have been badly abused. Anonymous posting services have been used to send death threats and false allegations of drug use to employers. In a famous incident, somebody anonymously posted to sci.astro an alleged transcript of the *Challenger* crew's desperate dialog in the moments following the explosion. A posting appeared (again anonymously) from an ostensible relative of one of the deceased crew members, fueling an outcry against anonymous posting. The "transcript," of dubious authenticity anyway, turned out to have been published a year previously in a New York tabloid. The "*Challenger* transcript" deepened the resolve of many news administrators to put an end to anonymous posting in general and to the chief anonymous posting service, anon.petit.fi, in particular. The administrator of that Finnish site has steadfastly resisted pressures to control the content of posting emanating from his site or to reveal the identity of individuals who have used the site to abuse the net. What has angered site administrators the most, however, is his refusal to limit postings to the alt.* hierarchy; anonymous posters can use this service to post articles to the standard hierarchies as well.

In 1993, a news administrator named Dick Depew announced that he had written a program called Automated Retroactive Minimal Moderation (ARMM) that would automatically scan all incoming articles and remove from the sci.* hierarchy any coming from anon.petit.fi. It's one thing to implement such a program on one computer system, but Depew threatened to distribute the program throughout USENET if the anon.petit.fi operator did not agree to limit distribution of anonymous postings to the alt.* hierarchy. The operator refused to cooperate. In a subsequent flame war that attracted international press attention, Depew was accused of "censorship" and withdrew his program.

AUTHENTICATION

Anonymity, discussed in the previous section, has a flip side—authentication, that is, some means of verifying that a given message is actually from the person listed on the From: line. It's easy to forge articles (see Chapter 17, "Dealing with USENET problems"). Every April Fool's Day (April 1st) sees a spate of forgeries, with outrageous messages posted in the name of net.personalities. Don't believe anything you read on USENET on or near April 1!

April Fool's forgeries are all in good fun, but many forgeries have malicious intent. A recent example: An advertising spam hit many USENET newsgroups recently, giving as the return address an electronic mailbox that turned out to belong to the creator of a famous World Wide Web program, called Mosaic. A possible justification for this prank was the programmer's widely publicized decision to leave his position at the non-profit National Center for Supercomputer Applications (NCSA) and launch a for-profit firm—but nobody knows for sure.

In response to authentication concerns, security-minded USENET posters sometimes employ digital signatures using the Pretty Good Privacy algorithm, a public-domain security system that uses public key cryptography techniques. Briefly, public key cryptography is method of encrypting a message that does not require the sender to convey a key (the code used to decode the message) to the recipient. In public key cryptography, the encryption key differs from the decryption key. People can and should make their encryption keys private. This key is needed so that the sender can encrypt the message. When the message is received, the receiver uses the sender's *public* decryption key to decode the message.

Here's an example of a digital signature. To decode the signature, you'd need the sender's public key—which, when applied to the ciphertext, would reveal information that attests to the message's authenticity:

```
-----BEGIN PGP SIGNATURE-----
Version: 2.6

iQCVAgUBL1L/iWV5hLjHqWbdAQFV7AP/VBSa9Bi
    RfTuoBonJdkwTVC8fNGW8aI7n
QctOh+GrDaGl26rqtRjxtYTabAo+4B+sw6Dqz5o
    1OipKF/NuK7PFMzITdGMh940+
```

```
MXqOPCSLfDIwNzRzIHYQV/93jeJsixFZu/6j76m
  MxB6xrETXmswxIRicwm/QUxC1
0jbZEBrb/ug=
=u7IY
-----END PGP SIGNATURE-----
```

TIP: An excellent PGP program is copyrighted but freely redistributed from MIT. To obtain the software within the United States, follow these instructions:

1. Obtain and read ftp://net-dist.mit.edu/pub/PGP/mitlicen.txt. You must agree to the conditions in this document.

2. Obtain and read ftp://net-dist.mit.edu/pub/PGP/rsalicen.txt. Again, you must agree to the conditions in this document.

3. Telnet to net-dist.mit.edu and log in as getpgp.

4. Answer the questions and write down the directory name listed.

5. Quickly end the telnet session with ^C and ftp to the indicated directory on net-dist.mit.edu (the directory name will resemble /pub/PGP/dist/U.S.-only, followed by a four-digit number).

6. Obtain the distribution files. For DOS and Windows, get pgp26.zip pgp26doc.zip. For UNIX systems, get pgp26src.tar.gz. For Macs, get MacPGP2.6.sea.hqx and MacPGP2.6.src.sea.hqx.

USENET TOMORROW

Any network experiencing rapid growth inevitably runs into *scale-up problems* (the difficulties posed by growth far beyond that which was initially envisioned). You'll run into signs of USENET's phenomenal growth in the newsgroups that receive so many posts that it's impossible to read their subjects, let alone the articles themselves. Technical innovations such as threaded newsreaders and the hierarchical naming system help to reduce the clutter, but USENET still presents the reader with an overwhelming avalanche of information.

Future USENET technologies will help readers cope with the deluge of postings and organize information more efficiently. Future newsreaders, for example, will be able to create "virtual newsgroups" by scanning all incoming articles based on criteria you specify, and ordering them so that you can read them conveniently.

But the real innovations in USENET's future won't be technological; they'll come from USENET people. What transforms a mediocre newsgroup into a great one, as Chapter 18 demonstrates, is the human resolve to contribute to FAQs, to create databases of topic-related information, and to post substantive, informative articles that raise the level of discussion. If this book provides USENET users with the tools they need to improve USENET's quality, then this book will have admirably fulfilled my aims.

SUMMARY

USENET faces many problems, many of which reflect deep disagreements about social issues that transcend computer networking. The "anything goes" philosophy of many USENET posters, coupled with the Libertarian presumption that any interference with free speech constitutes censorship, virtually guarantees that USENET will become the focus of legal wrangles regarding censorship and copyright protection. Commercial advertising on USENET is less of a problem than some fear, since no responsible firm would risk its public reputation by joining the ranks of the peddlers who spam the Net. Hordes of new users, oblivious to USENET traditions, may prove incapable of learning them—but a greater enemy is the poor quality of the software they're using. Abuse of USENET seems to be on the rise, making kill capabilities a virtual necessity in any newsreader program. Anonymous posting services can mask identity for valid reasons, but also for posters who use the cloak of anonymity to harass and intimidate other users.

Appendix

A

NEWSGROUPS
WITH INFORMATION
RESOURCES
ARCHIVED AT
RTFM.MIT.EDU

alt.2600
alt.binaries.pictures
alt.binaries.pictures.ascii
alt.binaries.pictures.d
alt.binaries.pictures.erotica
alt.binaries.pictures.erotica.blondes
alt.binaries.pictures.erotica.d
alt.binaries.pictures.erotica.female
alt.binaries.pictures.erotica.male
alt.binaries.pictures.erotica.oriental
alt.binaries.pictures.erotica.orientals
alt.binaries.pictures.fine-art.d
alt.binaries.pictures.fine-art.digitized
alt.binaries.pictures.fine-art.graphics
alt.binaries.pictures.utilities
alt.binaries.sounds.d
alt.binaries.sounds.midi
alt.binaries.sounds.misc
alt.binaries.sounds.music
alt.bonsai
alt.books.reviews
alt.books.technical
alt.activism
alt.aldus.pagemaker
alt.anarchism
alt.angst
alt.answers
alt.aquaria
alt.archery
alt.arts.ballet
alt.ascii-art
alt.astrology
alt.atheism
alt.atheism.moderated
alt.backrubs

alt.bbs
alt.bbs.internet
alt.bbs.lists
alt.beer
alt.best.of.internet
alt.bigfoot
alt.binaries.multimedia
alt.binaries.pictures
alt.binaries.pictures.ascii
alt.binaries.pictures.d
alt.binaries.pictures.erotica
alt.binaries.pictures.erotica.blondes
alt.binaries.pictures.erotica.d
alt.binaries.pictures.erotica.female
alt.binaries.pictures.erotica.male
alt.binaries.pictures.erotica.oriental
alt.binaries.pictures.erotica.orientals
alt.binaries.pictures.fine-art.d
alt.binaries.pictures.fine-art.digitized
alt.binaries.pictures.fine-art.graphics
alt.binaries.pictures.utilities
alt.binaries.sounds.d
alt.binaries.sounds.midi
alt.binaries.sounds.misc
alt.binaries.sounds.music
alt.bonsai
alt.books.reviews
alt.books.technical
alt.buddha.short.fat.guy
alt.business.multi-level
alt.callahans
alt.chinese.text
alt.chinese.text.big5
alt.co-ops
alt.cobol

alt.coffee
alt.college.college-bowl
alt.comedy.british
alt.comedy.firesgn-thtre
alt.comics.superman
alt.comp.acad-freedom.talk
alt.comp.fsp
alt.config
alt.consciousness
alt.consciousness.mysticism
alt.conspiracy
alt.cult-movies
alt.cult-movies.rocky-horror
alt.culture.internet
alt.culture.tuva
alt.culture.usenet
alt.cyberpunk
alt.cyberspace
alt.devilbunnies
alt.dreams
alt.dreams.lucid
alt.drugs
alt.drugs.caffeine
alt.education.distance
alt.emulators.ibmpc.apple2
alt.emusic
alt.etext
alt.exotic-music
alt.fan.chris-elliott
alt.fan.conan-obrien
alt.fan.dave_barry
alt.fan.douglas-adams
alt.fan.dune
alt.fan.firesign-theatre
alt.fan.frank-zappa
alt.fan.greaseman
alt.fan.holmes
alt.fan.howard-stern
alt.fan.jimmy-buffett
alt.fan.lemurs
alt.fan.letterman
alt.fan.mst3k
alt.fan.pern
alt.fan.peter-hamill
alt.fan.pratchett
alt.fan.ren-and-stimpy
alt.fan.shostakovich
alt.fan.tolkien

alt.fan.tom-servo
alt.fax
alt.filesystems.afs
alt.folklore.college
alt.folklore.computers
alt.folklore.urban
alt.food.coffee
alt.games.frp.live-action
alt.games.gb
alt.games.tiddlywinks
alt.games.xpilot
alt.graphics.pixutils
alt.hackers
alt.hemp
alt.history.what-if
alt.housing.nontrad
alt.hypertext
alt.image.medical
alt.individualism
alt.internet.access.wanted
alt.internet.services
alt.internet.talk-radio
alt.irc
alt.irc.ircii
alt.irc.questions
alt.irc.undernet
alt.journalism
alt.locksmithing
alt.mag.playboy
alt.magic
alt.magick
alt.meditation
alt.music.a-cappella
alt.music.alternative
alt.music.bela-fleck
alt.music.billy-joel
alt.music.canada
alt.music.deep-purple
alt.music.enya
alt.music.filk
alt.music.james-taylor
alt.music.jewish
alt.music.karaoke
alt.music.machines.of.loving.grace
alt.music.pop.will.eat.itself
alt.music.progressive
alt.music.queen
alt.music.rush

alt.music.ska
alt.music.the.police
alt.music.tmbg
alt.native
alt.newgroup
alt.news-media
alt.online-service
alt.org.toastmasters
alt.os.multics
alt.out-of-body
alt.pagan
alt.philosophy.objectivism
alt.politics.datahighway
alt.politics.economics
alt.politics.libertarian
alt.politics.media
alt.politics.usa.misc
alt.polyamory
alt.privacy
alt.privacy.anon-server
alt.pub.coffeehouse.amethyst
alt.pub.dragons-inn
alt.quotations
alt.radio.internet
alt.radio.scanner
alt.rap
alt.rave
alt.religion.all-worlds
alt.religion.emacs
alt.religion.gnostic
alt.religion.islam
alt.religion.scientology
alt.revisionism
alt.rock-n-roll
alt.rock-n-roll.acdc
alt.rock-n-roll.classic
alt.rock-n-roll.hard
alt.rock-n-roll.metal
alt.rock-n-roll.metal.heavy
alt.rock-n-roll.metal.ironmaiden
alt.rock-n-roll.metal.metallica
alt.rock-n-roll.metal.progressive
alt.rock-n-roll.stones
alt.romance
alt.sci.astro.aips
alt.sci.physics.new-theories
alt.sci.planetary
alt.security

alt.security.pgp
alt.security.ripem
alt.sewing
alt.sex
alt.sex.bondage
alt.sex.fetish.fashion
alt.sex.pictures
alt.sex.pictures.d
alt.sex.pictures.female
alt.sex.pictures.male
alt.sex.stories.d
alt.sex.wanted
alt.sexual.abuse.recovery
alt.shenanigans
alt.ska
alt.skinheads
alt.society.civil-liberty
alt.soft-sys.tooltalk
alt.sources
alt.sources.d
alt.sources.mac
alt.sources.wanted
alt.sport.football
alt.sport.pool
alt.startrek.creative
alt.startrek.klingon
alt.suicide.holiday
alt.support.cancer
alt.support.depression
alt.support.diet
alt.sys.amiga.uucp
alt.sys.pdp8
alt.sys.sun
alt.tasteless
alt.thrash
alt.toolkits.intrinsics
alt.toolkits.xview
alt.tv.animaniacs
alt.tv.babylon-5
alt.tv.game-shows
alt.tv.mash
alt.tv.mst3k
alt.tv.mwc
alt.tv.nickelodeon
alt.tv.northern-exp
alt.tv.prisoner
alt.tv.red-dwarf
alt.tv.ren-n-stimpy

alt.tv.simpsons
alt.tv.snl
alt.tv.talkshows.late
alt.tv.tiny-toon
alt.uu.future
alt.visa.us
alt.war.civil.usa
alt.whistleblowing
alt.winsock
alt.zines
aus.comms
aus.computers
aus.general
aus.music
aus.net.aarnet
aus.net.access
aus.net.mail
aus.sf.star-trek
ba.general
bionet.announce
bionet.info-theory
bionet.software.acedb
bit.admin
bit.listserv.big-lan
bit.listserv.i-amiga
bit.listserv.muslims
bit.listserv.pagemakr
bit.listserv.pakistan
bit.listserv.pns-l
bit.listserv.transplant
bit.listserv.win3-l
biz.books.technical
biz.comp.services
biz.config
biz.sco.announce
biz.sco.general
biz.sco.opendesktop
ca.answers
ca.driving
ca.general
cl.bildung.hochschule
comp.ai
comp.ai.fuzzy
comp.ai.genetic
comp.ai.neural-nets
comp.ai.shells
comp.answer
comp.answers

comp.archives
comp.archives.admin
comp.archives.msdos.announce
comp.archives.msdos.d
comp.bbs.misc
comp.bbs.waffle
comp.benchmarks
comp.binaries.atari.st
comp.binaries.cbm
comp.binaries.ibm.pc
comp.binaries.ibm.pc.d
comp.binaries.ibm.pc.wanted
comp.compilers
comp.compression
comp.compression.research
comp.constraints
comp.databases
comp.databases.object
comp.databases.paradox
comp.databases.sybase
comp.databases.xbase.fox
comp.dcom.cell-relay
comp.dcom.fax
comp.dcom.isdn
comp.dcom.lans.fddi
comp.dcom.lans.misc
comp.dcom.modems
comp.doc.techreports
comp.dsp
comp.editors
comp.emacs
comp.emulators.announce
comp.emulators.apple2
comp.emulators.ms-windows.wine
comp.fonts
comp.graphics
comp.graphics.algorithms
comp.graphics.animation
comp.graphics.gnuplot
comp.graphics.opengl
comp.groupware
comp.home.misc
comp.human-factors
comp.infosystems
comp.infosystems.gis
comp.infosystems.gopher
comp.infosystems.interpedia
comp.infosystems.wais

comp.infosystems.www
comp.infosystems.www.misc
comp.infosystems.www.providers
comp.infosystems.www.users
comp.lang.ada
comp.lang.basic.visual
comp.lang.c
comp.lang.c++
comp.lang.clos
comp.lang.eiffel
comp.lang.fortran
comp.lang.functional
comp.lang.icon
comp.lang.idl-pvwave
comp.lang.lisp
comp.lang.lisp.mcl
comp.lang.misc
comp.lang.ml
comp.lang.modula2
comp.lang.modula3
comp.lang.oberon
comp.lang.objective-c
comp.lang.postscript
comp.lang.prolog
comp.lang.python
comp.lang.scheme
comp.lang.smalltalk
comp.lang.tcl
comp.lang.vhdl
comp.lang.visual
comp.lsi
comp.lsi.cad
comp.mail.elm
comp.mail.maps
comp.mail.mh
comp.mail.mime
comp.mail.misc
comp.mail.sendmail
comp.mail.smail
comp.mail.uucp
comp.misc
comp.multimedia
comp.music
comp.newprod
comp.object
comp.object.logic
comp.org.decus
comp.org.eff.talk

comp.org.fidonet
comp.os.386bsd.announce
comp.os.386bsd.apps
comp.os.386bsd.questions
comp.os.coherent
comp.os.geos
comp.os.linux
comp.os.linux.admin
comp.os.linux.announce
comp.os.linux.development
comp.os.linux.help
comp.os.linux.misc
comp.os.minix
comp.os.ms-windows.advocacy
comp.os.ms-windows.apps
comp.os.ms-windows.apps.comm
comp.os.ms-windows.apps.financial
comp.os.ms-windows.misc
comp.os.ms-windows.networking.tcp-ip
comp.os.ms-windows.nt.misc
comp.os.ms-windows.nt.setup
comp.os.ms-windows.programmer.memory
comp.os.ms-windows.programmer.misc
comp.os.ms-windows.programmer.multimedia
comp.os.ms-windows.programmer.networks
comp.os.ms-windows.programmer.ole
comp.os.ms-windows.programmer.tools
comp.os.ms-windows.programmer.win32
comp.os.ms-windows.programmer.winhelp
comp.os.ms-windows.setup
comp.os.ms-windows.video
comp.os.msdos.apps
comp.os.msdos.desqview
comp.os.msdos.mail-news
comp.os.msdos.misc
comp.os.msdos.pcgeos
comp.os.msdos.programmer
comp.os.os2.advocacy
comp.os.os2.apps
comp.os.os2.beta
comp.os.os2.misc
comp.os.os2.setup
comp.os.os2.ver1x
comp.os.research
comp.os.vms
comp.os.vxworks
comp.parallel
comp.parallel.mpi

comp.parallel.pvm
comp.periphs.scsi
comp.programming
comp.programming.literate
comp.protocols.dicom
comp.protocols.iso
comp.protocols.kerberos
comp.protocols.ppp
comp.protocols.snmp
comp.protocols.tcp-ip
comp.protocols.tcp-ip.ibmpc
comp.protocols.time.ntp
comp.realtime
comp.robotics
comp.security.misc
comp.security.unix
comp.society.privacy
comp.soft-sys.khoros
comp.software-eng
comp.software.config-mgmt
comp.sources.atari.st
comp.sources.d
comp.sources.misc
comp.sources.postscript
comp.sources.testers
comp.sources.wanted
comp.specification.z
comp.speech
comp.std.internat
comp.std.misc
comp.sys.3b1
comp.sys.acorn
comp.sys.acorn.announce
comp.sys.amiga.audio
comp.sys.amiga.datacomm
comp.sys.amiga.hardware
comp.sys.amiga.introduction
comp.sys.amiga.misc
comp.sys.amiga.networking
comp.sys.amiga.programmer
comp.sys.amiga.uucp
comp.sys.apple2
comp.sys.atari.8bit
comp.sys.atari.st
comp.sys.att
comp.sys.cbm
comp.sys.dec
comp.sys.hardware.hp

comp.sys.hardware.ibm
comp.sys.hardware.next
comp.sys.hardware.sgi
comp.sys.hardware.sun
comp.sys.hp.hardware
comp.sys.hp.hpux
comp.sys.hp.misc
comp.sys.hp48
comp.sys.ibm.pc.games.action
comp.sys.ibm.pc.games.adventure
comp.sys.ibm.pc.games.announce
comp.sys.ibm.pc.games.flight-sim
comp.sys.ibm.pc.games.misc
comp.sys.ibm.pc.games.rpg
comp.sys.ibm.pc.games.strategic
comp.sys.ibm.pc.hardware
comp.sys.ibm.pc.hardware.cd-rom
comp.sys.ibm.pc.hardware.chips
comp.sys.ibm.pc.hardware.comm
comp.sys.ibm.pc.hardware.misc
comp.sys.ibm.pc.hardware.networking
comp.sys.ibm.pc.hardware.storage
comp.sys.ibm.pc.hardware.systems
comp.sys.ibm.pc.hardware.video
comp.sys.ibm.pc.misc
comp.sys.ibm.pc.rt
comp.sys.ibm.pc.soundcard
comp.sys.ibm.pc.soundcard.advocacy
comp.sys.ibm.pc.soundcard.games
comp.sys.ibm.pc.soundcard.misc
comp.sys.ibm.pc.soundcard.music
comp.sys.ibm.pc.soundcard.tech
comp.sys.mac.apps
comp.sys.mac.comm
comp.sys.mac.games
comp.sys.mac.hardware
comp.sys.mac.misc
comp.sys.mac.programmer
comp.sys.mac.scitech
comp.sys.mac.system
comp.sys.mac.wanted
comp.sys.powerpc
comp.sys.sgi.admin
comp.sys.sgi.apps
comp.sys.sgi.bugs
comp.sys.sgi.graphics
comp.sys.sgi.hardware
comp.sys.sgi.misc

comp.sys.sun.admin
comp.sys.sun.announce
comp.sys.sun.misc
comp.text
comp.text.frame
comp.text.interleaf
comp.text.tex
comp.unix.admin
comp.unix.aix
comp.unix.aux
comp.unix.bsd
comp.unix.misc
comp.unix.pc-clone.32bit
comp.unix.questions
comp.unix.shell
comp.unix.solaris
comp.unix.sys5.r4
comp.unix.unixware
comp.unix.user-friendly
comp.unix.xenix.sco
comp.virus
comp.windows.garnet
comp.windows.misc
comp.windows.news
comp.windows.open-look
comp.windows.x
comp.windows.x.i386unix
comp.windows.x.intrinsics
comp.windows.x.motif
comp.windows.x.pex
de.admin.archiv
de.admin.lists
de.admin.mail
de.admin.misc
de.admin.news.announce
de.admin.news.groups
de.alt.admin
de.answers
de.comm.gateways
de.comm.internet
de.comm.isdn
de.comm.misc
de.comp.sys.amiga.misc
de.etc.lists
de.newusers
de.newusers.questions
de.rec.fahrrad
de.rec.music.misc

de.soc.studium
de.talk.chat
demon.ip.support.amiga
fidonet.aus.modem
fidonet.netcomm-support
fr.comp.text.tex
gnu.chess
gnu.g++.help
info.ph
lisa.lists.ats
maus.sys.amiga
misc.answers
misc.books.technical
misc.consumers
misc.consumers.house
misc.education
misc.fitness
misc.forsale
misc.forsale.computers.d
misc.forsale.computers.mac
misc.forsale.computers.other
misc.forsale.computers.pc-clone
misc.forsale.computers.workstation
misc.headlines
misc.health.diabetes
misc.invest
misc.invest.funds
misc.invest.stocks
misc.jobs.contract
misc.jobs.misc
misc.jobs.offered
misc.jobs.offered.entry
misc.jobs.resumes
misc.kids
misc.legal
misc.legal.computing
misc.legal.moderated
misc.misc
misc.writing
ncf.sigs.new.music
ne.general
news.admin.misc
news.admin.technical
news.announce.newgroups
news.announce.newusers
news.answers
news.groups
news.groups.questions

news.groups.reviews
news.lists
news.lists.ps-maps
news.misc
news.newusers.questions
news.software.anu-news
news.software.b
news.software.nn
news.software.nntp
news.software.readers
nj.general
nlnet.muziek
no.irc
ny.general
nyc.general
rec.answers
rec.aquaria
rec.arts.animation
rec.arts.anime
rec.arts.anime.info
rec.arts.ascii
rec.arts.bodyart
rec.arts.bonsai
rec.arts.books
rec.arts.books.marketplace
rec.arts.books.tolkien
rec.arts.comics.info
rec.arts.comics.marketplace
rec.arts.comics.misc
rec.arts.comics.strips
rec.arts.dance
rec.arts.disney
rec.arts.erotica
rec.arts.fine
rec.arts.int-fiction
rec.arts.manga
rec.arts.marching.drumcorps
rec.arts.movies
rec.arts.prose
rec.arts.sf.announce
rec.arts.sf.misc
rec.arts.sf.movies
rec.arts.sf.reviews
rec.arts.sf.tv
rec.arts.sf.tv.babylon5
rec.arts.sf.written
rec.arts.startrek.current
rec.arts.startrek.fandom

rec.arts.startrek.info
rec.arts.startrek.misc
rec.arts.startrek.tech
rec.arts.theatre
rec.arts.theatre.misc
rec.arts.theatre.musicals
rec.arts.theatre.plays
rec.arts.theatre.stagecraft
rec.arts.tv
rec.arts.tv.mstk
rec.arts.tv.soaps
rec.arts.tv.uk
rec.audio
rec.audio.car
rec.audio.pro
rec.autos.sport
rec.autos.sport.info
rec.aviation.answers
rec.aviation.military
rec.aviation.simulators
rec.backcountry
rec.bicycles.misc
rec.birds
rec.boats
rec.boats.paddle
rec.climbing
rec.crafts.brewing
rec.crafts.quilting
rec.crafts.textiles
rec.food.cooking
rec.food.drink.beer
rec.food.drink.coffee
rec.food.recipes
rec.food.veg
rec.food.veg.cooking
rec.gambling
rec.games.backgammon
rec.games.board
rec.games.board.marketplace
rec.games.bolo
rec.games.bridge
rec.games.chess
rec.games.corewar
rec.games.design
rec.games.diplomacy
rec.games.empire
rec.games.frp.announce
rec.games.frp.live-action

rec.games.frp.misc
rec.games.go
rec.games.hack
rec.games.miniatures
rec.games.misc
rec.games.moria
rec.games.mud.announce
rec.games.mud.diku
rec.games.mud.misc
rec.games.netrek
rec.games.pbm
rec.games.pinball
rec.games.programmer
rec.games.rogue
rec.games.roguelike.angband
rec.games.roguelike.announce
rec.games.roguelike.misc
rec.games.roguelike.moria
rec.games.roguelike.nethack
rec.games.roguelike.rogue
rec.games.trivia
rec.games.video.3do
rec.games.video.advocacy
rec.games.video.arcade
rec.games.video.atari
rec.games.video.classic
rec.games.video.misc
rec.games.video.nintendo
rec.games.video.sega
rec.gardens
rec.guns
rec.humor.funny
rec.humor.oracle
rec.mag
rec.martial-arts
rec.misc
rec.models.railroad
rec.models.rc
rec.models.scale
rec.motorcycles
rec.motorcycles.dirt
rec.motorcycles.harley
rec.motorcycles.racing
rec.music.a-cappella
rec.music.afro-latin
rec.music.beatles
rec.music.bluenote
rec.music.cd

rec.music.christian
rec.music.classical
rec.music.classical.guitar
rec.music.classical.performing
rec.music.compose
rec.music.country.western
rec.music.dementia
rec.music.dylan
rec.music.early
rec.music.folk
rec.music.funky
rec.music.gaffa
rec.music.gdead
rec.music.indian.classical
rec.music.indian.misc
rec.music.industrial
rec.music.info
rec.music.makers
rec.music.makers.bass
rec.music.makers.guitar
rec.music.makers.percussion
rec.music.makers.synth
rec.music.misc
rec.music.movies
rec.music.newage
rec.music.phish
rec.music.reggae
rec.music.reviews
rec.music.synth
rec.music.video
rec.nude
rec.org.mensa
rec.org.sca
rec.parks.theme
rec.pets
rec.pets.birds
rec.pets.cats
rec.pets.dogs
rec.photo
rec.photo.advanced
rec.photo.help
rec.puzzles
rec.puzzles.crosswords
rec.pyrotechnics
rec.radio.amateur.antenna
rec.radio.amateur.digital.misc
rec.radio.amateur.equipment
rec.radio.amateur.homebrew

rec.radio.amateur.misc
rec.radio.amateur.policy
rec.radio.amateur.space
rec.radio.broadcasting
rec.radio.cb
rec.radio.info
rec.radio.noncomm
rec.radio.scanner
rec.radio.shortwave
rec.radio.swap
rec.roller-coaster
rec.running
rec.scouting
rec.scuba
rec.skate
rec.skiing
rec.skydiving
rec.sport.baseball.college
rec.sport.basketball.college
rec.sport.disc
rec.sport.fencing
rec.sport.football.college
rec.sport.golf
rec.sport.hockey
rec.sport.misc
rec.sport.pro-wrestling
rec.sport.tennis
rec.sport.volleyball
rec.toys.lego
rec.travel
rec.travel.air
rec.travel.asia
rec.travel.europe
rec.travel.misc
rec.travel.usa-canada
rec.video
rec.video.cable-tv
rec.video.satellite
rec.woodworking
sb.hams
sbay.hams
sci.answers
sci.anthropology
sci.aquaria
sci.astro
sci.astro.fits
sci.astro.planetarium
sci.bio

sci.classics
sci.comp-aided
sci.cryonics
sci.crypt
sci.data.formats
sci.econ
sci.econ.research
sci.electronics
sci.engr.answers
sci.engr.semiconductors
sci.environment
sci.fractals
sci.geo.geology
sci.geo.meteorology
sci.image.processing
sci.lang
sci.lang.japan
sci.life-extension
sci.math
sci.math.num-analysis
sci.math.research
sci.med
sci.med.nursing
sci.med.occupational
sci.med.physics
sci.misc
sci.op-research
sci.philosophy.meta
sci.philosophy.tech
sci.physics
sci.physics.particle
sci.polymers
sci.psychology
sci.skeptic
sci.space
sci.space.alt.sci.planetary
sci.space.news
sci.space.policy
sci.space.science
sci.space.shuttle
sci.space.tech
soc.answers
soc.bi
soc.college
soc.culture.asian.american
soc.culture.australian
soc.culture.brazil
soc.culture.bulgaria

soc.culture.canada
soc.culture.cuba
soc.culture.esperanto
soc.culture.europe
soc.culture.filipino
soc.culture.french
soc.culture.german
soc.culture.greek
soc.culture.hongkong
soc.culture.indian
soc.culture.iranian
soc.culture.italian
soc.culture.japan
soc.culture.jewish
soc.culture.latin-america
soc.culture.lebanon
soc.culture.magyar
soc.culture.mexican
soc.culture.mexican.american
soc.culture.native
soc.culture.netherlands
soc.culture.nordic
soc.culture.pakistan
soc.culture.sri-lanka
soc.culture.thai
soc.culture.turkish
soc.feminism
soc.history
soc.history.war.world-war-ii
soc.motss
soc.net-people
soc.org.service-clubs.misc
soc.politics
soc.religion.bahai
soc.religion.christian
soc.religion.christian-bible-study
soc.religion.gnosis
soc.religion.islam
soc.religion.quaker
soc.religion.shamanism
soc.roots
soc.singles
talk.answers
talk.bizarre
talk.origins
talk.politics.crypto
talk.politics.drugs
talk.politics.misc

ucb.becmug
uk.bcs.announce
uk.bcs.misc
uk.misc
uk.net
uk.radio.amateur
uk.telecom
vmsnet.admin
vmsnet.announce.newusers
vmsnet.sources.d
zer.z-netz.bildung.uni
zer.z-netz.rechner.amiga.allgemein

abductions
alt.paranet.abduct
clari.news.crime.abductions

abortion
alt.abortion.inequity
talk.abortion

abstract
rec.games.abstract

abuse
alt.abuse.offender.recovery
alt.abuse.recovery
alt.abuse.transcendence
clari.news.crime.abuse

abuse partners
alt.support.abuse-partners

academic freedom
alt.comp.acad-freedom.news
alt.comp.acad-freedom.talk

a cappella
alt.music.a-cappella
rec.music.a-cappella

accelerators
sci.physics.accelerators

access
alt.internet.access.wanted

AC/DC
alt.rock-n-roll.acdc

acedb
bionet.software.acedb

acm
comp.org.acm

acorn
comp.binaries.acorn
comp.sources.acorn
comp.sys.acorn
comp.sys.acorn.advocacy
comp.sys.acorn.announce
comp.sys.acorn.tech

acoustic
rec.music.makers.guitar.acoustic

acoustics
alt.sci.physics.acoustics

act
alt.freedom.of.information.act

action
comp.sys.ibm.pc.games.action

activism
alt.activism
alt.activism.d
alt.activism.death-penalty
misc.activism.progressive

actors
alt.fan.actors

Ada
comp.lang.ada

Adams, Douglas
alt.fan.douglas-adams

Addams family
alt.fan.addams

addresses
bionet.users.addresses

administration
bit.admin

clari.net.admin
clari.net.talk.admin
comp.admin.policy
comp.archives.admin
comp.os.linux.admin
comp.sys.sgi.admin
comp.sys.sun.admin
comp.unix.admin
news.admin.misc
news.admin.policy
news.admin.technical
rec.games.mud.admin

admirers
alt.amazon-women.admirers

adoption
alt.adoption

ads
alt.bbs.ads
alt.personals.ads

adult education
misc.education.adult

adult movies
alt.sex.movies

advanced
rec.photo.advanced
sci.engr.advanced-tv

adventure
comp.sys.ibm.pc.games.adventure

advocacy
comp.os.ms-windows.advocacy
comp.os.os.advocacy
comp.sys.acorn.advocacy
comp.sys.amiga.advocacy
comp.sys.atari.advocacy
comp.sys.ibm.pc.soundcard.advocacy
comp.sys.mac.advocacy
comp.sys.next.advocacy
comp.unix.advocacy
rec.games.frp.advocacy
rec.games.video.advocacy

aeronautics
sci.aeronautics
sci.aeronautics.airliners
sci.aeronautics.simulation

Aerosmith
alt.rock-n-roll.aerosmith

aerospace
clari.tw.aerospace

Afghanistan
soc.culture.afghanistan

Africa
clari.world.africa
clari.world.africa.southafrica

African
soc.culture.african
soc.culture.african.american

African-American
soc.culture.african-american

africana
bit.tech.africana

Afro-Latino
rec.music.afro-latin

AFS (Andrew File System)
alt.filesystems.afs

afterlife
alt.life.afterlife

afternoon
alt.fan.disney.afternoon

aging
bionet.molbio.ageing
clari.news.aging

agriculture
alt.sustainable.agriculture
clari.biz.industry.agriculture
sci.agriculture

agroforestry
bionet.agroforestry

AIDS
clari.tw.health.aids
sci.med.aids

air
rec.travel.air

airliners
sci.aeronautics.airliners

aus.computers.amiga
comp.binaries.amiga
comp.sources.amiga
comp.sys.amiga
comp.sys.amiga.advocacy
comp.sys.amiga.announce
comp.sys.amiga.applications
comp.sys.amiga.audio
comp.sys.amiga.cd
comp.sys.amiga.datacomm
comp.sys.amiga.emulations
comp.sys.amiga.games
comp.sys.amiga.graphics
comp.sys.amiga.hardware
comp.sys.amiga.introduction
comp.sys.amiga.marketplace
comp.sys.amiga.misc
comp.sys.amiga.multimedia
comp.sys.amiga.networking
comp.sys.amiga.programmer
comp.sys.amiga.reviews
comp.sys.amiga.tech
comp.sys.amiga.uucp
comp.unix.amiga

Amiga UUCP
alt.sys.amiga.uucp
alt.sys.amiga.uucp.patches
comp.mail.uucp
comp.sys.amiga.uucp

anagrams
alt.anagrams

anarchy
alt.society.anarchy

Anderson, Laurie
alt.fan.laurie.anderson

andrew
alt.hurricane.andrew
comp.soft-sys.andrew

Andrew File System (AFS)
alt.filesystems.afs

Angband
rec.games.roguelike.angband

angst
alt.angst
alt.angst.xibo.sex

animals
alt.animals.badgers
alt.animals.dolphins
alt.animals.foxes
alt.animals.lampreys
clari.living.animals
talk.politics.animals

Animaniacs
alt.tv.animaniacs

animation
alt.animation.warner-bros
alt.ascii-art.animation
alt.drooling.animation.fandom
comp.graphics.animation
rec.arts.animation

anime
rec.arts.anime
rec.arts.anime.info
rec.arts.anime.marketplace
rec.arts.anime.stories

announce
alt.hope.announce
alt.irc.announce
alt.uu.announce
austin.announce
bionet.announce
biz.digital.announce
biz.oreilly.announce
biz.sco.announce
biz.zeos.announce
clari.net.announce
comp.ai.jair.announce
comp.archives.msdos.announce
comp.emulators.announce
comp.infosystems.announce
comp.networks.noctools.announce
comp.org.cpsr.announce
comp.os.bsd.announce
comp.os.linux.announce
comp.os.ms-windows.announce
comp.os.os.announce
comp.security.announce
comp.sys.acorn.announce
comp.sys.amiga.announce
comp.sys.atari.announce
comp.sys.ibm.pc.games.announce
comp.sys.mac.announce

AppleTalk
comp.protocols.appletalk

Application Visualization System
comp.graphics.avs

applications
bit.listserv.applicat
comp.sys.amiga.applications

apps
comp.apps.spreadsheets
comp.os.bsd.apps
comp.os.ms-windows.apps
comp.os.ms-windows.apps.comm
comp.os.ms-windows.apps.financial
comp.os.ms-windows.apps.misc
comp.os.ms-windows.apps.utilities
comp.os.ms-windows.apps.word-proc
comp.os.msdos.apps
comp.os.os.apps
comp.sys.hp.apps
comp.sys.mac.apps
comp.sys.sgi.apps
comp.sys.sun.apps
comp.windows.x.apps
sci.virtual-worlds.apps

aquaria
alt.aquaria
alt.aquaria.killies
alt.clearing.aquaria
rec.aquaria
sci.aquaria

Arabia
clari.world.mideast.arabia

Arabic
soc.culture.arabic

arabidopsis
bionet.genome.arabidopsis

arcade
rec.games.video.arcade
rec.games.video.arcade.collecting

arch
comp.arch
comp.arch.arithmetic
comp.arch.bus.vmebus
comp.arch.storage

archaeology
sci.archaeology
sci.archaeology.mesoamerican

archery
alt.archery

architecture
alt.architecture
alt.architecture.alternative

archives
aus.archives
comp.archives
comp.archives.admin
comp.archives.msdos.announce
comp.archives.msdos.d
rec.games.frp.archives

arena
alt.sports.football.arena

Argentina
alt.culture.argentina
soc.culture.argentina

Argic, Serdar
alt.fan.serdar-argic

arithmetic
comp.arch.arithmetic

Arizona
clari.local.arizona
clari.local.arizona.briefs

Arizona Spurs
rec.sport.football.pro.spurs

Arkansas
clari.local.arkansas

arms
soc.politics.arms-d

art
alt.binaries.pictures.fine-art.d
alt.binaries.pictures.fine-art.digitized

arthritis
alt.support.arthritis

articles
biz.digital.articles

Asia
clari.biz.market.report.asia
clari.world.asia.central
clari.world.asia.china
clari.world.asia.hongkong
clari.world.asia.india
clari.world.asia.japan
clari.world.asia.koreas
clari.world.asia.south
clari.world.asia.southeast
clari.world.asia.taiwan
rec.travel.asia

Asian
soc.culture.asian.american

Asian movies
alt.asian-movies

Asimov, Isaac
alt.books.isaac-asimov

Asprin, Robert Lynn
alt.fan.asprin

assembly language
alt.lang.asm
bit.listserv.asm
comp.lang.asm

asthma
alt.support.asthma

astrology
alt.astrology

astronomy
alt.sci.astro.aips
alt.sci.astro.figaro
alt.sci.astro.fits
sci.astro
sci.astro.fits
sci.astro.hubble
sci.astro.planetarium
sci.astro.research

AT&T
comp.sys.att

Atari
alt.atari
comp.binaries.atari.st
comp.sources.atari.st

comp.sys.atari.bit
comp.sys.atari.advocacy
comp.sys.atari.announce
comp.sys.atari.st
comp.sys.atari.st.tech
rec.games.video.atari

atheism
alt.atheism
alt.atheism.moderated
alt.atheism.satire

Atlanta Braves
alt.sports.baseball.atlanta-braves

Atlanta Hawks
alt.sports.basketball.nba.atlanta-hawks

attention deficit disorder
alt.support.attn-deficit

audio
comp.sys.amiga.audio
comp.sys.sgi.audio
rec.audio
rec.audio.car
rec.audio.high-end
rec.audio.marketplace
rec.audio.misc
rec.audio.opinion
rec.audio.pro
rec.audio.tech

Austin
austin.announce

Australia
clari.world.oceania.australia
soc.culture.australia

Australian
alt.flame.australian.net.cops
rec.sport.football.australian
soc.culture.australian

Austria
soc.culture.austria

Austrian
alt.culture.austrian

authorware
alt.authorware
bit.listserv.authorware

banjo
alt.banjo

banking
clari.biz.industry.banking

bar
alt.foo.bar

Barney
alt.barney.dinosaur.die.die.die
alt.christnet.dinosaur.barney
alt.tv.barney
alt.tv.dinosaurs.barney.die.die.die

Barry, Dave
alt.fan.davebarry
clari.feature.davebarry

baseball
alt.sports.baseball.atlanta-braves
alt.sports.baseball.balt-orioles
alt.sports.baseball.calif-angels
alt.sports.baseball.chi-whitesox
alt.sports.baseball.chicago-cubs
alt.sports.baseball.cinci-reds
alt.sports.baseball.cleve-indians
alt.sports.baseball.col-rockies
alt.sports.baseball.detroit-tigers
alt.sports.baseball.fla-marlins
alt.sports.baseball.houston-astros
alt.sports.baseball.kc-royals
alt.sports.baseball.la-dodgers
alt.sports.baseball.minor-leagues
alt.sports.baseball.mke-brewers
alt.sports.baseball.mke-brewers.suck.suck.suck
alt.sports.baseball.mn-twins
alt.sports.baseball.montreal-expos
alt.sports.baseball.ny-mets
alt.sports.baseball.ny-yankees
alt.sports.baseball.oakland-as
alt.sports.baseball.phila-phillies
alt.sports.baseball.pitt-pirates
alt.sports.baseball.sd-padres
alt.sports.baseball.sea-mariners
alt.sports.baseball.sf-giants
alt.sports.baseball.stl-cardinals
alt.sports.baseball.texas-rangers
alt.sports.baseball.tor-bluejays
clari.sports.baseball
clari.sports.baseball.games

rec.sport.baseball
rec.sport.baseball.college
rec.sport.baseball.fantasy

basement
alt.basement.graveyard

BASIC
alt.lang.basic
comp.lang.basic.misc
comp.lang.basic.visual

basketball
alt.duke.basketball.sucks.sucks.sucks
alt.sports.basketball.nba.atlanta-hawks
alt.sports.basketball.nba.chicago-bulls
alt.sports.basketball.nba.la-lakers
alt.sports.basketball.nba.miami-heat
alt.sports.basketball.nba.mn-wolves
alt.sports.basketball.nba.nj-nets
alt.sports.basketball.nba.orlando-magic
alt.sports.basketball.nba.seattle-sonics
alt.sports.basketball.nba.utah-jazz
alt.sports.basketball.nba.wash-bullets
alt.sports.basketball.pro.ny-knicks
clari.sports.basketball
clari.sports.basketball.college
rec.sport.basketball
rec.sport.basketball.college
rec.sport.basketball.misc
rec.sport.basketball.pro
rec.sport.basketball.women

bass
alt.guitar.bass
rec.music.makers.bass

Bass, Dale
alt.fan.dale-bass

Batman
alt.comics.batman

BBS
alt.bbs
alt.bbs.ads
alt.bbs.allsysop
alt.bbs.doors
alt.bbs.first-class
alt.bbs.internet
alt.bbs.lists
alt.bbs.lists.d

alt.binaries.pictures.erotica.d.
alt.binaries.pictures.erotica.female
alt.binaries.pictures.erotica.male
alt.binaries.pictures.erotica.orientals
alt.binaries.pictures.fine-art.d
alt.binaries.pictures.fine-art.digitized
alt.binaries.pictures.fractals
alt.binaries.pictures.furry
alt.binaries.pictures.misc
alt.binaries.pictures.supermodels
alt.binaries.pictures.utilities
alt.binaries.sounds-armpit.noises
alt.binaries.sounds.d
alt.binaries.sounds.misc
alt.binaries.sounds.music
biz.sco.binaries
comp.binaries.acorn
comp.binaries.amiga
comp.binaries.apple
comp.binaries.atari.st
comp.binaries.cbm
comp.binaries.geos
comp.binaries.ibm.pc
comp.binaries.ibm.pc.d
comp.binaries.ibm.pc.wanted
comp.binaries.mac
comp.binaries.ms-windows
comp.binaries.newton
comp.binaries.os

biology
alt.bio.hackers
sci.bio
sci.bio.ecology
sci.bio.ethology
sci.bio.evolution
sci.bio.herp
sci.bio.technology
bionet.biology.computational
bionet.biology.grasses
bionet.biology.n-fixation
bionet.biology.tropical

bio matrix
bionet.molbio.bio-matrix

biomedical
sci.engr.biomed

biophysics
bionet.biophysics

biotechnology
clari.tw.biotechnology

birds
rec.birds
rec.pets.birds

birthday
alt.happy.birthday.to.me

birthright
alt.birthright

bisexual
alt.personals.bi
soc.bi

BitGraph
comp.terminals.bitgraph

bitterness
alt.bitterness

bizarre
clari.living.bizarre
talk.bizarre

bizarro
clari.feature.bizarro

Black Adder
alt.comedy.british.blackadder

blacks
clari.news.blacks

blondes
alt.binaries.pictures.erotica.blondes

Bluenote
rec.music.bluenote

Blues Brothers
alt.fan.blues-brothers

Blues Traveler
alt.music.blues-traveler

Blumenthal, Dave
alt.fan.dave.blumenthal

board
rec.games.board
rec.games.board.ce
rec.games.board.marketplace

boats
rec.boats
rec.boats.paddle

Bobek, Nicole
alt.fan.nicole-bobek

body art
rec.arts.bodyart

bogus
alt.bogus.group

bolo
alt.netgames.bolo
rec.games.bolo

Bolton, Michael
alt.fan.michael-bolton

Bond, James
alt.fan.james-bond

bondage
alt.fax.bondage
alt.sex.bondage
alt.personals.bondage

bonehead
alt.bonehead.andy-beckwith
alt.bonehead.david-delaney
alt.bonehead.paul-hendry
alt.bonehead.tim-pierce
alt.bonehead.tom-servo

bonsai
alt.bonsai
rec.arts.bonsai

books
alt.books.anne-rice
alt.books.deryni
alt.books.isaac-asimov
alt.books.reviews
alt.books.stephen-king
alt.books.technical
alt.books.toffler
biz.books.technical
clari.living.books
misc.books.technical
rec.arts.books
rec.arts.books.marketplace
rec.arts.books.tolkien

boomerang
alt.boomerang

Bosnia
soc.culture.bosna-herzgvna

Boston Bruins
alt.sports.hockey.nhl.boston-bruins

bots
alt.cancel.bots

Bowie, David
alt.fan.david-bowie

bowling
alt.sport.bowling

boxing
rec.sport.boxing

Brady Bunch
alt.tv.brady-bunch

Brazil
alt.fan.nathan.brazil
soc.culture.brazil

brewing
rec.crafts.brewing

bridge
rec.games.bridge

brie
alt.fan.brie

Brisco County
alt.tv.brisco-county

British
alt.comedy.british
alt.comedy.british.blackadder
alt.politics.british
soc.culture.british

British accent
alt.fan.british-accent

broadcast
clari.nb.broadcast

broadcasting
clari.biz.industry.broadcasting
rec.radio.broadcasting

bsx
alt.mud.bsx

Bubble Gum Crisis
alt.fan.bgcrisis

Buddha
alt.buddha.short.fat.guy

Buddhism
alt.religion.buddhism.tibetan

Buffalo Bills
alt.sports.football.pro.buffalo-bills

Buffalo Roam
alt.comics.buffalo-roam

Buffalo Sabres
alt.sports.hockey.nhl.buffalo-sabres

Buffett, Jimmy
alt.fan.jimmy-buffett

bugs
alt.lucid-emacs.bug
comp.bugs.bsd
comp.bugs.bsd
comp.bugs.misc
comp.bugs.sys
comp.networks.noctools.bugs
comp.os.bsd.bugs
comp.os.os.bugs
comp.sources.bugs
comp.sources.games.bugs
comp.sys.next.bugs
comp.sys.sgi.bugs

builders
rec.music.makers.builders

Bulgaria
soc.culture.bulgaria

bungee
alt.sport.bungee

Burma
soc.culture.burma

bus
comp.arch.bus.vmebus

Bush
alt.politics.bush
clari.news.hot.bush

business
alt.business.import-export
alt.business.misc
alt.business.multi-level
alt.business.multi-level.scam.scam.scam
clari.nb.business
clari.world.americas.canada.business

C
comp.lang.c
comp.lang.scheme.c
comp.std.c

cable TV
alt.dcom.catv
alt.cable-tv.re-regulate
rec.video.cable-tv

cabling
comp.dcom.cabling

CAD
alt.cad
alt.cad.autocad
comp.cad.cadence
comp.cad.compass
comp.cad.pro-engineer
comp.cad.synthesis
comp.lsi.cad
sci.electronics.cad

cadence
comp.cad.cadence

cadet
alt.military.cadet

California
alt.california
clari.local.california
clari.local.california.briefs

California Angels
alt.sports.baseball.calif-angels

Callahans
alt.callahans

Callas, Maria
alt.fan.maria-callas

Campbell, Bruce
alt.fan.bruce-campbell

Chapman, Colin
alt.fan.colin-chapman

chat
alt.romance.chat

Chatsubo
alt.cyberpunk.chatsubo
alt.cyberpunk.chatsubo.d

chemistry
sci.chem
sci.chem.electrochem
sci.chem.organomet
sci.engr.chem

chess
alt.chess.ics
rec.games.chess

chia
alt.pets.chia

Chicago
clari.local.chicago
clari.local.chicago.briefs

Chicago Blackhawks
alt.sports.hockey.nhl.chi-blackhawks

Chicago Bulls
alt.sports.basketball.nba.chicago-bulls

Chicago Cubs
alt.sports.baseball.chicago-cubs

Chicago White Sox
alt.sports.baseball.chi-whitesox

child support
alt.child-support

Chile
soc.culture.chile

China
aus.culture.china
clari.world.asia.china
soc.culture.china
talk.politics.china

chinchilla
alt.chinchilla

Chinese
alt.chinese.text
alt.chinese.text.big

Chinese chess
rec.games.chinese-chess

chips
clari.nb.chips
comp.sys.ibm.pc.hardware.chips

chlamydomonas
bionet.chlamydomonas

Chomsky, Noam
alt.fan.noam-chomsky

chorus
comp.os.chorus

Christian
alt.religion.christian
rec.music.christian
soc.religion.christian
soc.religion.christian.bible-study
soc.religion.christian.youth-work

christnet
alt.christnet.bible-thumpers.convert.convert
alt.christnet.christnews
alt.christnet.crybaby.mine.mine.mine
alt.christnet.dinosaur
alt.christnet.dinosaur.barney
alt.christnet.evangelical
alt.christnet.games.ibm-pc
alt.christnet.manga
alt.christnet.philosophy
alt.christnet.religion
alt.christnet.second-coming.real-soon-now

christnews
alt.christnet.christnews

chrome
alt.chrome.the.moon

chromosomes
bionet.genome.chromosomes

Chrone's disease
alt.support.crohns-colitis

chronic fatigue syndrome
alt.health.cfids-action
alt.med.cfs
bit.listserv.cfs.newsletter

colitis
alt.support.crohns-colitis

collecting
alt.collecting.autographs
rec.collecting
rec.collecting.cards
rec.collecting.stamps
rec.games.video.arcade.collecting

college
alt.college.college-bowl
alt.college.food
alt.college.fraternities
alt.college.fraternities.sigma-pi
alt.college.fraternities.theta-tau
alt.college.sororities
alt.college.us
alt.folklore.college
alt.sports.college.ivy-league
clari.sports.basketball.college
clari.sports.football.college
rec.sport.baseball.college
rec.sport.basketball.college
rec.sport.football.college
soc.college
soc.college.grad
soc.college.gradinfo
soc.college.org.aiesec
soc.college.teaching-asst

college bowl
alt.college.college-bowl

Colombia
soc.culture.colombia

Colorado
clari.local.colorado

Colorado Rockies
alt.sports.baseball.col-rockies

colorguard
alt.colorguard

comedy
alt.comedy.british
alt.comedy.british.blackadder
alt.comedy.firesgn-thtre
alt.comedy.slapstick.-stooges
alt.comedy.standup
alt.comedy.vaudeville

comic strips
rec.arts.comics.strips

comics
alt.comics.alternative
alt.comics.batman
alt.comics.buffalo-roam
alt.comics.elfquest
alt.comics.lnh
alt.comics.superman
rec.arts.comics
rec.arts.comics.creative
rec.arts.comics.info
rec.arts.comics.marketplace
rec.arts.comics.misc
rec.arts.comics.strips
rec.arts.comics.xbooks

commodities
clari.biz.market.commodities

Commodore computers
comp.binaries.cbm
comp.emulators.cbm
comp.sys.cbm

Common Lisp Object System
comp.lang.clos

communication
comp.os.ms-windows.apps.comm
comp.sys.apple.comm
comp.sys.ibm.pc.hardware.comm
comp.sys.mac.comm

Communist
alt.politics.india.communist

compact disc
comp.sys.amiga.cd
rec.music.cd

compass
comp.cad.compass

compilers
comp.compilers
comp.compilers.tools.pccts

complex arrangement
alt.music.complex-arrang

components
comp.sw.components

compose
rec.music.compose

composition
comp.edu.composition

compression
alt.comp.compression
comp.compression
comp.compression.research

CompuServe
alt.online-service.compuserve

computational
bionet.biology.computational

computer
alt.computer.consultants
misc.forsale.computer
misc.kids.computer

computer aided
sci.comp-aided

Computer Professionals for Social Responsibility (CPSR)
comp.org.cpsr.announce
comp.org.cpsr.talk

Computer Underground Digest
comp.society.cu-digest

computers
alt.folklore.computers
alt.religion.computers
aus.computers
aus.computers.amiga
aus.computers.ibm-pc
aus.computers.linux
aus.computers.os
clari.tw.computers
misc.forsale.computers
misc.forsale.computers.d
misc.forsale.computers.mac
misc.forsale.computers.other
misc.forsale.computers.pc-clone
misc.forsale.computers.workstation

computing
alt.industrial.computing
misc.legal.computing

Conan
alt.fantasy.conan

concurrent
comp.sys.concurrent

conference center
alt.conference-ctr

conferences
news.announce.conferences

config
alt.config
biz.config
comp.software.config-mgmt
courts.usa.config
courts.usa.state.ohio.config
news.config

conflict
clari.news.conflict

Connecticut
clari.local.connecticut

cons
alt.fandom.cons

consciousness
alt.consciousness
alt.consciousness.mysticism
alt.consciousness.near-death-exp

conservatism
alt.society.conservatism

conspiracy
alt.conspiracy
alt.conspiracy.abe-lincoln
alt.conspiracy.jfk
alt.guinea.pig.conspiracy

constraints
comp.constraints

construction
clari.biz.industry.construction

consult
sci.stat.consult

consultants
alt.computer.consultants

consumer
clari.living.consumer

consumers
misc.consumers
misc.consumers.house

contents
bionet.journals.contents

contract
ba.jobs.contract
misc.jobs.contract

control
alt.control.test.test.test
biz.control
sci.engr.control

Control Data Corporation Computers
comp.sys.cdc

control theory
alt.control-theory

controls
comp.os.ms-windows.programmer.controls

Convex
comp.sys.convex

cooking
rec.food.cooking

co-ops
alt.co-ops

Corel
alt.soft-sys.corel.draw
alt.soft-sys.corel.misc

corewar
rec.games.corewar

corps
alt.peace.corps

correct
alt.politics.correct

corruption
alt.irc.corruption
clari.news.corruption

Cosmic Encounter
rec.games.board.ce

cough
alt.smokers.cough

counter
alt.revolution.counter

country
rec.music.country.western

country western
rec.music.country.western

couples
soc.couples
soc.couples.intercultural

courts
courts.usa.config
courts.usa.federal.supreme
courts.usa.state.ohio.appls-th
courts.usa.state.ohio.config
courts.usa.state.ohio.-supreme

covert
alt.politics.org.covert

CP/M
comp.os.cpm
comp.os.cpm.amethyst

CPSR (Computer Professionals for Social Responsibility)
comp.org.cpsr.announce
comp.org.cpsr.talk

crackers
alt.crackers

crafts
rec.crafts.brewing
rec.crafts.jewelry
rec.crafts.metalworking
rec.crafts.misc
rec.crafts.quilting
rec.crafts.textiles
rec.crafts.winemaking

Cray
comp.unix.cray

creative
alt.drwho.creative
alt.ql.creative
alt.startrek.creative
alt.tv.x-files.creative
rec.arts.comics.creative

soc.culture.colombia
soc.culture.croatia
soc.culture.czecho-slovak
soc.culture.ecsd
soc.culture.esperanto
soc.culture.europe
soc.culture.filipino
soc.culture.french
soc.culture.german
soc.culture.greek
soc.culture.hongkong
soc.culture.india
soc.culture.indian
soc.culture.indian.american
soc.culture.indian.info
soc.culture.indian.telugu
soc.culture.indonesia
soc.culture.iranian
soc.culture.israel
soc.culture.italian
soc.culture.japan
soc.culture.jewish
soc.culture.jewish.holocaust
soc.culture.korean
soc.culture.laos
soc.culture.latin-america
soc.culture.lebanon
soc.culture.maghreb
soc.culture.magyar
soc.culture.malaysia
soc.culture.mexican
soc.culture.mexican.american
soc.culture.mexico
soc.culture.misc
soc.culture.native
soc.culture.nepal
soc.culture.netherlands
soc.culture.new-zealand
soc.culture.nordic
soc.culture.pakistan
soc.culture.palestine
soc.culture.peru
soc.culture.polish
soc.culture.portuguese
soc.culture.romanian
soc.culture.scientists
soc.culture.singapore
soc.culture.slovenia
soc.culture.somalia

soc.culture.soviet
soc.culture.spain
soc.culture.sri-lanka
soc.culture.sri-lankan
soc.culture.swiss
soc.culture.taiwan
soc.culture.tamil
soc.culture.thai
soc.culture.turkish
soc.culture.ukrainian
soc.culture.uruguay
soc.culture.usa
soc.culture.venezuela
soc.culture.vietnamese
soc.culture.yugoslavia

current
rec.arts.startrek.current

current events
alt.current-events.clinton.whitewater
alt.current-events.korean-crisis
alt.current-events.la-quake
alt.current-events.net-abuse
alt.current-events.net-abuse.c-n-s

cyber
rec.games.frp.cyber

cyberpunk
alt.cyberpunk
alt.cyberpunk.chatsubo
alt.cyberpunk.chatsubo.d
alt.cyberpunk.movement
alt.cyberpunk.tech

cyberspace
alt.cyberspace

cybertoon
alt.cybertoon

cyberworld
alt.mud.cyberworld
cyb-sys
alt.cyb-sys

cytonet
bionet.cellbiol.cytonet

Czech Republic
soc.culture.czecho-slovak

Denny's
alt.food.dennys

dentistry
sci.med.dentistry

Denver Broncos
alt.sports.football.pro.denver-broncos

depression
alt.support.depression

Deryni series
alt.books.deryni

Desert Storm
alt.desert-storm
alt.desert-storm.facts

design
rec.games.design

desktop
comp.text.desktop

Desqview
comp.os.msdos.desqview

Detroit Tigers
alt.sports.baseball.detroit-tigers

development
comp.os.bsd.development
comp.os.linux.development
comp.society.development

Devo
alt.fan.devo

diabetes
misc.health.diabetes

diapers
alt.sex.fetish.diapers

dice man
alt.fan.dice-man

diet
alt.support.diet

digest
comp.sys.ibm.pc.digest
comp.sys.mac.digest
sci.psychology.digest

digital
alt.digital.dcu
alt.radio.digital
biz.digital.announce
biz.digital.articles
rec.radio.amateur.digital.misc

digital communications
alt.dcom.catv
alt.dcom.telecom
alt.dcom.telecom.ip
comp.dcom.cabling
comp.dcom.cell-relay
comp.dcom.fax
comp.dcom.isdn
comp.dcom.lans
comp.dcom.lans.ethernet
comp.dcom.lans.fddi
comp.dcom.lans.hyperchannel
comp.dcom.lans.misc
comp.dcom.lans.novell
comp.dcom.lans.token-ring
comp.dcom.modems
comp.dcom.servers
comp.dcom.sys.cisco
comp.dcom.sys.wellfleet
comp.dcom.telecom
comp.dcom.telecom.tech

Digital Equipment Corporation (DEC)
alt.dec.athena
biz.dec
biz.dec.decnews
biz.dec.ip
biz.dec.workstations
biz.dec.xmedia
comp.sys.dec
comp.sys.dec.micro

Digital Imaging and Communications
comp.protocols.dicom

digital signal processing
comp.dsp

digitized
alt.binaries.pictures.fine-art.digitized

diku
rec.games.mud.diku

draw
alt.soft-sys.corel.draw

dreams
alt.dreams
alt.dreams.lucid

drink
alt.mcdonalds.drink
rec.food.drink
rec.food.drink.beer
rec.food.drink.coffee

drinking age
alt.politics.drinking-age

drinks
alt.drinks.kool-aid

drivers
comp.os.ms-windows.programmer.drivers

driving
rec.autos.driving

drosophila
bionet.drosophila

drugs
clari.news.drugs
talk.politics.drugs

drum corps
alt.drumcorps
rec.arts.marching.drumcorps

dry goods
clari.biz.industry.drygoods

Dune
alt.fan.dune

Dylan
comp.lang.dylan

Dylan, Bob
rec.music.dylan

dynamic systems
comp.theory.dynamic-sys

dynamics
alt.engr.dynamics

early music
rec.music.early

earnings
clari.biz.earnings

Earth First
alt.org.earth-first

Earth Observation System (EOS)
sci.geo.eos

earthquake
alt.current-events.la-quake
clari.news.hot.laquake

eastern
clari.world.europe.eastern
soc.religion.eastern

Eastern Europe
bit.listserv.e-europe
misc.news.east-europe.rferl

Eckankar
alt.religion.eckankar

ecology
sci.bio.ecology

economics
alt.politics.economics
alt.education.ib.econ
sci.econ
sci.econ.research

economy
clari.biz.economy
clari.biz.economy.world

Eddings, David
alt.fan.eddings

editorial
clari.nb.editorial

editors
comp.editors

education
alt.education.bangkok
alt.education.bangkok.planning
alt.education.disabled
alt.education.distance
alt.education.email-project
alt.education.ib
alt.education.ib.econ
alt.education.ib.tok

English
alt.usage.english
misc.education.language.english

Eno, Brian
alt.music.brian-eno

entertainment
clari.living.entertainment

entrepreneurs
misc.entrepreneurs

entry
misc.jobs.offered.entry

environment
clari.tw.environment
sci.environment
talk.environment

Enya
alt.fan.enya
alt.music.enya
alt.music.enya.puke.puke.puke

EOS (Earth Observation System)
sci.geo.eos

epilepsy
alt.support.epilepsy

equality
alt.politics.equality

equestrian
rec.equestrian

equipment
rec.radio.amateur.equipment

erotica
alt.binaries.pictures.erotica
alt.binaries.pictures.erotica.bestiality
alt.binaries.pictures.erotica.blondes
alt.binaries.pictures.erotica.cartoons
alt.binaries.pictures.erotica.d.
alt.binaries.pictures.erotica.female
alt.binaries.pictures.erotica.male
alt.binaries.pictures.erotica.orientals
rec.arts.erotica

erotica
alt.sex.stories

Esperanto
alt.uu.lang.esperanto.misc
soc.culture.esperanto

ethernet
comp.dcom.lans.ethernet

ethics
alt.magick.ethics
alt.soc.ethics
bit.listserv.ethics-l

ethnicity
clari.news.ethnicity

ethology
bit.listserv.ethology
sci.bio.ethology

Eunice
comp.os.eunice

Europe
alt.politics.ec
alt.politics.europe.misc
alt.satellite.tv.europe
clari.biz.market.report.europe
clari.world.europe.alpine
clari.world.europe.balkans
clari.world.europe.benelux
clari.world.europe.central
clari.world.europe.eastern
clari.world.europe.france
clari.world.europe.germany
clari.world.europe.greece
clari.world.europe.iberia
clari.world.europe.ireland
clari.world.europe.italy
clari.world.europe.northern
clari.world.europe.russia
clari.world.europe.uk
clari.world.europe.union
rec.travel.europe
soc.culture.europe

European Community (EC)
alt.politics.ec

European economic union
clari.world.europe.union

evangelical
alt.christnet.evangelical

evolution
bionet.molbio.evolution
sci.bio.evolution

exhibitionism
alt.sex.exhibitionism

exotic music
alt.exotic-music

Explorer
comp.graphics.explorer
comp.sys.ti.explorer

explosives
alt.engr.explosives

export
alt.business.import-export

facts
alt.desert-storm.facts

fairs
alt.fairs.renaissance

family
clari.news.family

fan
alt.fan.actors
alt.fan.addams
alt.fan.alok.vijayvargia
alt.fan.amy-fisher
alt.fan.art-bell
alt.fan.asprin
alt.fan.barry-manilow
alt.fan.ben-elton
alt.fan.bgcrisis
alt.fan.BIFF
alt.fan.bill-gates
alt.fan.billcunningham
alt.fan.blues-brothers
alt.fan.brie
alt.fan.british-accent
alt.fan.bruce-becker
alt.fan.bruce-campbell
alt.fan.bugtown
alt.fan.cecil-adams
alt.fan.chris-elliott

alt.fan.colin-chapman
alt.fan.conan-obrien
alt.fan.cristina.morela.yamaguchi
alt.fan.dale-bass
alt.fan.dan-quayle
alt.fan.dan-wang
alt.fan.daphnes-corner
alt.fan.dave-williams
alt.fan.dave.blumenthal
alt.fan.davebarry
alt.fan.david-arkstar
alt.fan.david-bowie
alt.fan.david-lawrence
alt.fan.david-sternlight
alt.fan.debbie.gibson
alt.fan.devo
alt.fan.dice-man
alt.fan.dick-depew
alt.fan.dimitri-vulis
alt.fan.disney.afternoon
alt.fan.don.no-soul.simmons
alt.fan.douglas-adams
alt.fan.dr-bronner
alt.fan.dragonlance
alt.fan.dragons
alt.fan.dune
alt.fan.eddings
alt.fan.egham-hills
alt.fan.enya
alt.fan.eric.oehler
alt.fan.firesign-theatre
alt.fan.frank-zappa
alt.fan.furry
alt.fan.furry.muck
alt.fan.g-gordon-liddy
alt.fan.gene-scott
alt.fan.gooley
alt.fan.goons
alt.fan.greaseman
alt.fan.greg-kinnear
alt.fan.hello-kitty
alt.fan.hofstadter
alt.fan.holmes
alt.fan.howard-stern
alt.fan.howard-stern.fartman
alt.fan.itchy-n-scratchy
alt.fan.ivor-cutler
alt.fan.james-bond

alt.fan.jeff-wheelhouse
alt.fan.jello-biafra
alt.fan.jen-coolest
alt.fan.jen-kleiman
alt.fan.jeremy-reimer
alt.fan.jesus.monroy.jr
alt.fan.jimmy-buffett
alt.fan.jiro-nakamura
alt.fan.joel-furr
alt.fan.john-palmer
alt.fan.john-winston
alt.fan.john.line
alt.fan.jwz
alt.fan.karla-homolka
alt.fan.kent-montana
alt.fan.kevin-darcy
alt.fan.laurie.anderson
alt.fan.lemurs
alt.fan.letterman
alt.fan.lightbulbs
alt.fan.lila-feng
alt.fan.madonna
alt.fan.maria-callas
alt.fan.matt.welsh
alt.fan.meredith-tanner
alt.fan.michael-bolton
alt.fan.michael.deignan
alt.fan.mike-dahmus
alt.fan.mike-jittlov
alt.fan.monty-python
alt.fan.mstk
alt.fan.mts
alt.fan.naked-guy
alt.fan.nancy-kerrigan.ouch.ouch.ouch
alt.fan.nathan.brazil
alt.fan.nicole-bobek
alt.fan.noam-chomsky
alt.fan.oingo-boingo
alt.fan.oj-simpson
alt.fan.owain-vaughan
alt.fan.penn-n-teller
alt.fan.pern
alt.fan.peter.hammill
alt.fan.piers-anthony
alt.fan.pratchett
alt.fan.q
alt.fan.ren-and-stimpy
alt.fan.ricking-ball
alt.fan.riscos

alt.fan.robert.mcelwaine
alt.fan.ronald-reagan
alt.fan.rumpole
alt.fan.rush-limbaugh
alt.fan.sam-raimi
alt.fan.schwaben
alt.fan.serdar-argic
alt.fan.shedevil
alt.fan.shostakovich
alt.fan.shub-interne
alt.fan.skinny
alt.fan.spinal-tap
alt.fan.steve-lewis-aka-slash
alt.fan.sting
alt.fan.suicide-squid
alt.fan.surak
alt.fan.tammy-tanner
alt.fan.ted.thearp.dough.dough.dough
alt.fan.teen.idols
alt.fan.teen.starlets
alt.fan.thunder-thumbs
alt.fan.tna
alt.fan.tolkien
alt.fan.tom-robbins
alt.fan.tompeterson
alt.fan.tony-white
alt.fan.tonya-harding.whack.whack.whack
alt.fan.tuan
alt.fan.u
alt.fan.vejcik
alt.fan.vic-reeves
alt.fan.warlord
alt.fan.wedge
alt.fan.wodehouse
alt.fan.woody-allen
alt.uu.fan.newgroup.jyrki.jyrki.jyrk

fandom
alt.drooling.animation.fandom
alt.fandom.cons
alt.fandom.misc
alt.tv.tiny-toon.fandom
rec.arts.sf.fandom
rec.arts.startrek.fandom

fantasy
alt.fantasy.conan
rec.sport.baseball.fantasy
rec.sport.football.fantasy

financial
clari.news.usa.gov.financial
comp.os.ms-windows.apps.financial

fine art
alt.binaries.pictures.fine-art.d
alt.binaries.pictures.fine-art.digitized

Firesign Theater
alt.comedy.firesgn-thtre
alt.fan.firesign-theatre

First Class (BBS software)
alt.bbs.first-class

Fisher, Amy
alt.fan.amy-fisher

fishing
alt.fishing
rec.outdoors.fishing
rec.outdoors.fishing.fly
rec.outdoors.fishing.saltwater

fitness
misc.fitness
rec.fitness

fits
alt.sci.astro.fits
sci.astro.fits

flame
alt.flame
alt.flame.hall-of-flame
alt.flame.joe-hofmeister
alt.flame.landlord
alt.flame.mud
alt.flame.net-cops
alt.flame.parents
alt.flame.roommate
alt.flame.spelling

flash
clari.news.flash

Fleck, Bela
alt.music.bela-fleck

Fleetwood Mac
alt.music.fleetwood-mac

flight simulators
comp.sys.ibm.pc.games.flight-sim

Florida
clari.local.florida
clari.local.florida.briefs

Florida Marlins
alt.sports.baseball.fla-marlins

fluids
sci.geo.fluids
sci.mech.fluids

fly fishing
rec.outdoors.fishing.fly

FOIA (Freedom of Information Act)
alt.society.foia

folk dancing
rec.folk-dancing

folk music
rec.music.folk

folklore
alt.folklore.college
alt.folklore.computers
alt.folklore.gemstones
alt.folklore.ghost-stories
alt.folklore.herbs
alt.folklore.info
alt.folklore.military
alt.folklore.science
alt.folklore.suburban
alt.folklore.urban
comp.society.folklore

fonts
comp.fonts

food
alt.college.food
alt.food
alt.food.cocacola
alt.food.coffee
alt.food.dennys
alt.food.fat-free
alt.food.ice-cream
alt.food.mcdonalds
alt.mcdonalds.food
clari.biz.industry.food
rec.food
rec.food.cooking
rec.food.drink
rec.food.drink.beer

freehand
alt.aldus.freehand

freemasonry
bit.listserv.freemasonry

FreeNet
alt.online-service.freenet

French
soc.culture.french

functional computer languages
comp.lang.functional

funds
misc.invest.funds

funky
rec.music.funky

funny
rec.humor.funny

Furr, Joel
alt.fan.joel-furr

furry
alt.binaries.pictures.furry
alt.fan.furry
alt.fan.furry.muck

FurryMuckers
alt.fan.furry.muck

fusion
sci.physics.fusion

future
alt.uu.future
news.future

futures
alt.society.futures
comp.society.futures

fuzzy
comp.ai.fuzzy

Gabriel, Peter
alt.music.peter-gabriel

Galactic Bloodshed
alt.games.gb

galactic guide
alt.galactic-guide

gambling
alt.gambling
rec.gambling

game shows
alt.tv.game-shows

games
alt.christnet.games.ibm-pc
alt.games.doom
alt.games.frp.dnd-util
alt.games.frp.live-action
alt.games.frp.tekumel
alt.games.gb
alt.games.ibmpc.shadowcaster
alt.games.lynx
alt.games.mk
alt.games.mornington.cresent
alt.games.mtrek
alt.games.netrek.paradise
alt.games.omega
alt.games.pabu
alt.games.sf
alt.games.tiddlywinks
alt.games.torg
alt.games.vga-planets
alt.games.video.classic
alt.games.whitewolf
alt.games.xpilot
alt.games.xtrek
alt.video.games.reviews
aus.games
aus.games.roleplay
bit.listserv.games-l
clari.sports.baseball.games
clari.sports.football.games
comp.os.os.games
comp.sources.games
comp.sources.games.bugs
comp.sys.amiga.games
comp.sys.ibm.pc.games.action
comp.sys.ibm.pc.games.adventure
comp.sys.ibm.pc.games.announce
comp.sys.ibm.pc.games.flight-sim
comp.sys.ibm.pc.games.misc
comp.sys.ibm.pc.games.rpg
comp.sys.ibm.pc.games.strategic
comp.sys.ibm.pc.soundcard.games
comp.sys.mac.games

biz.zeos.general
clari.nb.general
dc.general

generation X
alt.society.generation-x

genetic
comp.ai.genetic

GEnie
alt.online-service.genie

genome
bionet.genome.arabidopsis
bionet.genome.chrom
bionet.genome.chromosomes
genome-program
bionet.molbio.genome-program

Geographic Information Systems (GIS)
comp.infosystems.gis

geography
bit.listserv.geograph

geology
sci.geo.eos
sci.geo.fluids
sci.geo.geology
sci.geo.hydrology
sci.geo.meteorology
sci.geo.satellite-nav

Georgia
clari.local.georgia
clari.local.georgia.briefs

GEOS
comp.binaries.geos
comp.os.geos

German
alt.mud.german
alt.usage.german
soc.culture.german

Germany
clari.world.europe.germany

ghost stories
alt.folklore.ghost-stories

Gibson, Debbie
alt.fan.debbie.gibson

gigantic
alt.flame.gigantic.sigs

GNO
comp.sys.apple2.gno

gnosis
soc.religion.gnosis

GNUPLOT
comp.graphics.gnuplot

Go
rec.games.go

golf
clari.sports.golf
rec.sport.golf

gone
alt.gorby.gone.gone.gone

good
alt.good.morning
alt.good.news

good news
clari.living.goodnews

goons
alt.fan.goons

Gopher
alt.gopher
comp.infosystems.gopher

gossip
alt.showbiz.gossip

gothic
alt.gothic

government
clari.news.usa.gov.financial
clari.news.usa.gov.foreignpolicy
clari.news.usa.gov.misc
clari.news.usa.gov.personalities
clari.news.usa.gov.politics
clari.news.usa.gov.statelocal
clari.news.usa.gov.whitehouse
clari.nb.govt

government documents
bit.listserv.govdoc-l

graduate school
soc.college.grad

hand-held computers
comp.sys.palmtops

handheld computers
comp.sys.handheld

handicap
misc.handicap

hangover
alt.hangover

hard rock
alt.rock-n-roll.hard

hardcore
alt.music.hardcore

hardware
alt.comp.hardware.homebuilt
biz.comp.hardware
comp.os.msdos.hardware
comp.publish.cdrom.hardware
comp.sys.amiga.hardware
comp.sys.hp.hardware
comp.sys.ibm.hardware
comp.sys.ibm.pc.hardware.cd-rom
comp.sys.ibm.pc.hardware.chips
comp.sys.ibm.pc.hardware.comm
comp.sys.ibm.pc.hardware.misc
comp.sys.ibm.pc.hardware.networking
comp.sys.ibm.pc.hardware.storage
comp.sys.ibm.pc.hardware.systems
comp.sys.ibm.pc.hardware.video
comp.sys.ibm.ps.hardware
comp.sys.mac.hardware
comp.sys.next.hardware
comp.sys.sgi.hardware
comp.sys.sun.hardware

Harley Davidson
alt.motorcycles.harley
rec.motorcycles.harley

Harris
comp.sys.harris

Hartford Whalers
alt.sports.hockey.nhl.hford-whalers

haven
alt.internet.talk.haven

Havens' rest
alt.pub.havens-rest

Hawaii
alt.culture.hawaii
clari.local.hawaii

headers
comp.mail.headers

headlines
clari.local.headlines
misc.headlines

health
alt.health.ayurveda
alt.health.cfids-action
clari.biz.industry.health
clari.nb.health
clari.tw.health
clari.tw.health.aids
misc.health.alternative
misc.health.diabetes

heavy metal
alt.rock-n-roll.metal.heavy

height
alt.sigma.height

Hello Kitty
alt.fan.hello-kitty

help
alt.lucid-emacs.help
alt.psychology.help
comp.os.linux.help
rec.photo.help

hemp
alt.hemp
alt.hemp.politics
alt.hemp.recreational

Hendry, Paul
alt.bonehead.paul-hendry

heraldry
alt.heraldry.sca
rec.heraldry

herbs
alt.folklore.herbs

Herman's Head
alt.tv.hermans-head

Hermes
comp.lang.hermes

Herzegovina
soc.culture.bosna-herzgvna

Hewlett-Packard
comp.sources.hp
comp.sys.hp.apps
comp.sys.hp.hardware
comp.sys.hp.hpux
comp.sys.hp.misc
comp.sys.hp.mpe
comp.sys.hp

Hewlett-Packard UX
comp.sys.hp.hpux

high technology
alt.toys.hi-tech

high-end audio systems
rec.audio.high-end

higher education
clari.news.education.higher

Highlander
alt.tv.highlander

Hindu
alt.hindu

historic
rec.food.historic

history
alt.history.living
alt.history.what-if
bit.listserv.history
clari.living.history
clari.living.history.today
soc.history
soc.history.moderated
soc.history.war.misc
soc.history.war.world-war-ii

HIV
bionet.molbio.hiv

hockey
alt.sports.hockey.ihl
alt.sports.hockey.nhl.boston-bruins

alt.sports.hockey.nhl.buffalo-sabres
alt.sports.hockey.nhl.chi-blackhawks
alt.sports.hockey.nhl.dallas-stars
alt.sports.hockey.nhl.hford-whalers
alt.sports.hockey.nhl.mtl-canadiens
alt.sports.hockey.nhl.nj-devils
alt.sports.hockey.nhl.ny-islanders
alt.sports.hockey.nhl.ny-rangers
alt.sports.hockey.nhl.phila-flyers
alt.sports.hockey.nhl.pit-penguins
alt.sports.hockey.nhl.que-nordiques
alt.sports.hockey.nhl.sj-sharks
alt.sports.hockey.nhl.tor-mapleleafs
alt.sports.hockey.nhl.vanc-canucks
alt.sports.hockey.nhl.wash-capitals
alt.sports.hockey.nhl.winnipeg-jets
alt.sports.hockey.rhi
alt.sports.hockey.uhf
alt.sports.hockey.vhf
alt.sports.hockey.whl
clari.sports.hockey
rec.sport.hockey
rec.sport.hockey.field

Hofstadter, Douglas
alt.fan.hofstadter

holiday
alt.suicide.holiday

holocaust
soc.culture.jewish.holocaust

home
comp.home.automation
comp.home.misc

homebrew
rec.radio.amateur.homebrew

homebuilt
alt.comp.hardware.homebuilt
rec.aviation.homebuilt

Homes not Jails
alt.org.homes-not-jails

Homolka, Karla
alt.fan.karla-homolka

homosexual
alt.homosexual

homosexuality
alt.politics.homosexuality

Hong Kong
clari.world.asia.hongkong
soc.culture.hongkong

hope
alt..hope.announce
alt..hope.d
alt..hope.tech

horror
alt.horror
alt.horror.cthulhu
alt.horror.werewolves

hot
clari.news.hot
clari.news.hot.bush
clari.news.hot.clinton
clari.news.hot.iraq
clari.news.hot.laquake
clari.news.hot.perot

hotrod
alt.hotrod

hot tub
alt.irc.hottub

house
misc.consumers.house

housing
alt.housing.nontrad

Houston Astros
alt.sports.baseball.houston-astros

Hubble Telescope
sci.astro.hubble

human
soc.rights.human

human factors
comp.human-factors

human interest
clari.living.humaninterest

humor
alt.humor.best-of-usenet
alt.humor.best-of-usenet.d
alt.humor.puns

rec.humor
rec.humor.d
rec.humor.funny
rec.humor.oracle
rec.humor.oracle.d

Hungary
bit.listserv.hungary

hunting
rec.hunting

hurricane
alt.hurricane.andrew

hydrogen
sci.energy.hydrogen

hydrology
sci.geo.hydrology

Hyperchannel
comp.dcom.lans.hyperchannel

hypercube
comp.hypercube

hypertext
alt.hypertext

hypnosis
alt.hypnosis

Iberia
clari.world.europe.iberia

IBM
alt.christnet.games.ibm-pc
alt.emulators.ibmpc.apple
alt.games.ibmpc.shadowcaster
aus.computers.ibm-pc
bit.listserv.ibm
bit.listserv.ibm-hesc
bit.listserv.ibm-main
bit.listserv.ibm-nets
bit.listserv.ibmtcp-l
clari.nb.ibm
comp.binaries.ibm.pc
comp.binaries.ibm.pc.d
comp.binaries.ibm.pc.wanted
comp.protocols.ibm
comp.protocols.tcp-ip.ibmpc
comp.sys.ibm.hardware
comp.sys.ibm.pc

Illuminati
alt.illuminati

image
alt.image.medical
sci.image.processing

image facility
alt.sci.image-facility

image processing
sci.image.processing

immigration
clari.news.immigration

immunology
bionet.immunology

import export
alt.business.import-export

important
news.announce.important

independent
alt.music.independent

index
alt.security.index
alt.sources.index
clari.nb.index

India
alt.india.progressive
alt.politics.india.communist
alt.politics.india.progressive
bit.listserv.india-d
clari.world.asia.india
soc.culture.india

Indian
alt.indian.superior
rec.music.indian.classical
rec.music.indian.misc
soc.culture.indian
soc.culture.indian.american
soc.culture.indian.info
soc.culture.indian.telugu

Indiana
clari.local.indiana
clari.local.indiana.briefs

individualism
alt.feminism.individualism
alt.individualism

Indonesia
alt.culture.indonesia
soc.culture.indonesia

Indonesian
alt.sci.tech.indonesian

industrial
alt.industrial
alt.industrial.computing
rec.music.industrial

industry
clari.biz.industry.agriculture
clari.biz.industry.automotive
clari.biz.industry.aviation
clari.biz.industry.banking
clari.biz.industry.broadcasting
clari.biz.industry.construction
clari.biz.industry.drygoods
clari.biz.industry.energy
clari.biz.industry.food
clari.biz.industry.health
clari.biz.industry.insurance
clari.biz.industry.manufacturing
clari.biz.industry.mining
clari.biz.industry.printmedia
clari.biz.industry.realestate
clari.biz.industry.retail
clari.biz.industry.services
clari.biz.industry.tourism
clari.biz.industry.transportation

inequity
alt.abortion.inequity

infertility
alt.infertility

infomercials
alt.tv.infomercials
alt.tv.infomercials.Don-LaPre.DIE.DIE.DIE

information
alt.folklore.info
alt.freedom.of.information.act
clari.net.info
rec.arts.anime.info
rec.arts.comics.info

Internet Amateur Mathematics Society (IAMS)
alt.math.iams

Internet Encyclopedia
comp.infosystems.interpedia

Internet protocols
alt.dcom.telecom.ip
biz.dec.ip

Internet Relay Chat (IRC)
alt.irc
alt.irc.announce
alt.irc.corruption
alt.irc.hottub
alt.irc.ircii
alt.irc.opers
alt.irc.ops.kiss.my.ass
alt.irc.questions
alt.irc.recovery
alt.irc.undernet

Internet Talk Radio
alt.internet.talk-radio

interviews
comp.windows.interviews

intrinsics
comp.windows.x.intrinsics

introduction
comp.sys.amiga.introduction

investments
misc.invest
misc.invest.canada
misc.invest.funds
misc.invest.real-estate
misc.invest.stocks
misc.invest.technical

Iowa
clari.local.iowa
clari.local.iowa.briefs

Iran
clari.world.mideast.iran

Iranian
soc.culture.iranian

Iraq
clari.news.hot.iraq
clari.world.mideast.iraq

Iraqi
alt.iraqi.dictator.bomb.bomb.bomb

IRC (Internet Relay Chat)
alt.irc
alt.irc.announce
alt.irc.corruption
alt.irc.hottub
alt.irc.ircii
alt.irc.opers
alt.irc.ops.kiss.my.ass
alt.irc.questions
alt.irc.recovery
alt.irc.undernet

Ireland
clari.world.europe.ireland

Iron Maiden
alt.rock-n-roll.metal.ironmaiden

ISDN (Integrated Services Digital Network)
comp.dcom.isdn

ISIS
comp.sys.isis

Islam
alt.religion.islam
soc.religion.islam

ISO (International Standards Organization)
comp.protocols.iso
comp.protocols.iso.dev-environ
comp.protocols.iso.x
comp.protocols.iso.x.gateway

ISO Development Environment
comp.protocols.iso.dev-environ

Israel
clari.world.mideast.israel
soc.culture.israel

issue
clari.news.crime.issue

Italian
soc.culture.italian

Italy
alt.politics.italy
clari.world.europe.italy

Ivy League
alt.sports.college.ivy-league

Jacksonville Jaguars
alt.sports.football.pro.jville-jaguars

Japan
bit.listserv.japan
clari.world.asia.japan
comp.research.japan
sci.lang.japan
soc.culture.japan

Japanese
alt.japanese.text

Jarf
alt.philosophy.jarf

jet ski
alt.sport.jet-ski

Jethro Tull
alt.music.jethro-tull

jewelry
rec.crafts.jewelry

Jewish
alt.music.jewish
soc.culture.jewish
soc.culture.jewish.holocaust

Jews
clari.news.jews

JFK (Kennedy, John Fitzgerald)
alt.conspiracy.jfk

Jittlov, Mike
alt.fan.mike-jittlov

jobs
aus.jobs
ba.jobs.contract
ba.jobs.offered
bionet.jobs
bionet.jobs.wanted
biz.jobs.offered
dc.jobs
misc.jobs
misc.jobs.contract
misc.jobs.misc
misc.jobs.offered
misc.jobs.offered.entry
misc.jobs.resumes

Joel, Billy
alt.music.billy-joel

jokes
aus.jokes
aus.jokes.d

Journal of AI Research
comp.ai.jair.announce
comp.ai.jair.papers

journalism
alt.journalism
alt.journalism.criticism
alt.journalism.gonzo

journals
bionet.journals.contents
bionet.journals.note

juggling
rec.juggling

juvenile
clari.news.crime.juvenile

Kansas
clari.local.kansas

Kansas City Royals
alt.sports.baseball.kc-royals

karaoke
alt.music.karaoke

Karnataka
alt.culture.karnataka

karting
alt.autos.karting

Kennedy, John Fitzgerald (JFK)
alt.conspiracy.jfk

Kentucky
clari.local.kentucky

Kerala
alt.culture.kerala

Kerberos
comp.protocols.kerberos

Kermit
comp.protocols.kermit

ketchup
alt.ketchup
alt.mcdonalds.ketchup

kettle
alt.brian.saunders.pot.kettle.black

Khoros X11
comp.soft-sys.khoros

kids
misc.kids
misc.kids.computer
misc.kids.vacation

kids talk
alt.kids-talk

killies
alt.aquaria.killies

kindness
alt.society.kindness

king
alt.elvis.king

King, Rodney
alt.rodney-king

King, Stephen
alt.books.stephen-king

Kinnear, Greg
alt.fan.greg-kinnear

kiosks
comp.infosystems.kiosks

kites
rec.kites

Kleiman, Jen
alt.fan.jen-kleiman

Klingon
alt.shared-reality.startrek.klingon
alt.startrek.klingon

kooks
alt.usenet.kooks

kool-aid
alt.drinks.kool-aid

Korean
soc.culture.korean

Korean crisis
alt.current-events.korean-crisis

Koreas
clari.world.asia.koreas

krunk
alt.krunk

Kuwait
alt.culture.kuwait

LA Law
alt.tv.la-law

labor
clari.news.labor
clari.news.labor.layoff
clari.news.labor.strike

Lake Wobegon
rec.arts.wobegon

lampreys
alt.animals.lampreys

landlord
alt.flame.landlord

language
alt.language.urdu.poetry
misc.education.language.english
sci.lang
sci.lang.japan

languages
alt.lang.apl
alt.lang.asm
alt.lang.awk
alt.lang.basic
alt.lang.ca-realizer
alt.lang.cfutures
alt.lang.focal
alt.lang.intercal
alt.lang.ml
alt.lang.sas
alt.lang.teco
alt.uu.lang.esperanto.misc
alt.uu.lang.misc
alt.uu.lang.russian.misc
bit.lang.neder-l
comp.lang.ada
comp.lang.apl
comp.lang.asm
comp.lang.basic.misc
comp.lang.basic.visual

LEGO
rec.toys.lego

lemmings
alt.lemmings

lemurs
alt.fan.lemurs

Letterman, Dave
alt.fan.letterman

Libertarian
alt.politics.libertarian

libraries
soc.libraries.talk

library
comp.internet.library

licensing
comp.software.licensing

Liddy, G. Gordon
alt.fan.g-gordon-liddy

lies
alt.lies

life
alt.life.afterlife
alt.life.internet
alt.life.sucks
sci.life-extension

life extension
sci.life-extension

light bulbs
alt.fan.lightbulbs

lighting
sci.engr.lighting

Limbaugh, Rush
alt.fan.rush-limbaugh
alt.rush-limbaugh

Lincoln, Abraham
alt.conspiracy.abe-lincoln

Line, John
alt.fan.john.line

lingerie
alt.clothing.lingerie

Linux Operating System
alt.uu.comp.os.linux.questions
aus.computers.linux
comp.os.linux.admin
comp.os.linux.announce
comp.os.linux.development
comp.os.linux.help
comp.os.linux.misc

lisp
comp.lang.lisp
comp.lang.lisp.franz
comp.lang.lisp.mcl
comp.lang.lisp.x
comp.std.lisp

lisp users
comp.org.lisp-users

lists
alt.bbs.lists
alt.bbs.lists.d
news.lists
news.lists.ps-maps

literate
comp.programming.literate

literature
alt.appalachian.literature

Liverpool
rec.sport.football.pro.liverpool

living
alt.history.living
clari.living
clari.living.animals
clari.living.arts
clari.living.bizarre
clari.living.books
clari.living.celebrities
clari.living.consumer
clari.living.entertainment
clari.living.goodnews
clari.living.history
clari.living.history.today
clari.living.humaninterest
clari.living.movies
clari.living.music
clari.living.tv

magazines
alt.mag.playboy
alt.sex.magazines
biz.sco.magazine
rec.mag
rec.mag.fsfnet

Maghreb
soc.culture.maghreb

magic
alt.magic

magick
alt.magick
alt.magick.chaos
alt.magick.ethics
alt.magick.sex

magnetic resonance imaging
sci.techniques.mag-resonance

Magyar
soc.culture.magyar

mail
aus.net.mail
comp.mail.elm
comp.mail.headers
comp.mail.maps
comp.mail.mh
comp.mail.mime
comp.mail.misc
comp.mail.multi-media
comp.mail.mush
comp.mail.pine
comp.mail.sendmail
comp.mail.smail
comp.mail.uucp

mail news
comp.os.msdos.mail-news

Mail User's Shell (MUSH)
comp.mail.mush

Maine
clari.local.maine

Malaysia
soc.culture.malaysia

male
alt.binaries.pictures.erotica.male

malicious
alt.hackers.malicious

management
alt.management.tech-support
alt.office.management

managers
comp.sys.sun.managers

managing
alt.managing.techsupport

manga
alt.christnet.manga
alt.manga
rec.arts.manga

Manilow, Barry
alt.fan.barry-manilow

manufacturing
alt.manufacturing.misc
clari.biz.industry.manufacturing
sci.engr.manufacturing

maps
comp.mail.maps
news.lists.ps-maps

marching
rec.arts.marching.drumcorps
rec.arts.marching.misc

Marillion
alt.music.marillion

market
ba.market.vehicles
clari.biz.market.commodities
clari.biz.market.misc
clari.biz.market.news
clari.biz.market.report
clari.biz.market.report.asia
clari.biz.market.report.europe
clari.biz.market.report.top
clari.biz.market.report.usa
clari.biz.market.report.usa.nyse

market failure
alt.technology.mkt-failure

sci.med.occupational
sci.med.pharmacy
sci.med.physics
sci.med.psychobiology
sci.med.radiology
sci.med.telemedicine
talk.politics.medicine

meditation
alt.meditation
alt.meditation.quanyin
alt.meditation.transcendental

Melrose Place
alt.tv.melrose-place

Members of the Same Sex (MOTSS)
alt.sex.motss
soc.motss

memetics
alt.memetics

memory
comp.os.ms-windows.programmer.memory

men
soc.men

Mensa
rec.org.mensa

Mentor Graphics
comp.sys.mentor

mergers
clari.biz.mergers

mesoamerican archaeology
sci.archaeology.mesoamerican

messianic
alt.messianic

metabolic regulation
bionet.metabolic-reg

metal
alt.bbs.metal
alt.rock-n-roll.metal
alt.rock-n-roll.metal.death
alt.rock-n-roll.metal.gnr
alt.rock-n-roll.metal.heavy
alt.rock-n-roll.metal.ironmaiden

alt.rock-n-roll.metal.metallica
alt.rock-n-roll.metal.progressive

Metallica
alt.rock-n-roll.metal.metallica

metalworking
rec.crafts.metalworking

metaphysics
alt.paranet.metaphysics
sci.philosophy.meta

meteorology
sci.geo.meteorology

Mexican
soc.culture.mexican
soc.culture.mexican.american

Mexico
clari.world.americas.mexico
soc.culture.mexico

Miami Dolphins
alt.sports.football.pro.miami-dolphins

Miami Heat
alt.sports.basketball.nba.miami-heat

Michigan
clari.local.michigan
clari.local.michigan.briefs

microbiology
bionet.microbiology

microscopy
sci.techniques.microscopy

Microsoft Access
comp.databases.ms-access

Microsoft Windows
comp.windows.ms
comp.windows.ms.programmer

Microsoft Windows
comp.binaries.ms-windows
comp.emulators.ms-windows.wine
comp.os.ms-windows.advocacy
comp.os.ms-windows.announce
comp.os.ms-windows.apps
comp.os.ms-windows.apps.comm
comp.os.ms-windows.apps.financial

rec.models.rockets
rec.models.scale

modems
comp.dcom.modems

moderated
alt.atheism.moderated
misc.legal.moderated
misc.test.moderated
soc.history.moderated

Modern Language Association (MLA)
bit.listserv.mla-l

Modula
comp.lang.modula3
comp.lang.modula2

molecular biology
bionet.molbio.ageing
bionet.molbio.bio-matrix
bionet.molbio.embldatabank
bionet.molbio.evolution
bionet.molbio.gdb
bionet.molbio.genbank
bionet.molbio.genbank.updates
bionet.molbio.gene-linkage
bionet.molbio.gene-org
bionet.molbio.genome-program
bionet.molbio.hiv
bionet.molbio.methds-reagnts
bionet.molbio.news
bionet.molbio.proteins
bionet.molbio.rapd
bionet.molbio.yeast

molecular models
bionet.molec-model

Monkees
alt.music.monkees

monster movies
alt.movies.monster

Montana
clari.local.montana

Montana, Kent
alt.fan.kent-montana

Montreal Canadiens
alt.sports.hockey.nhl.mtl-canadiens

Montreal Expos
alt.sports.baseball.montreal-expos

Moody Blues
alt.music.moody-blues

Moria
rec.games.moria
rec.games.roguelike.moria

morning
alt.good.morning

Mother Goose
alt.mothergoose

Mother Jones
alt.motherjones

mother-in-law
alt.motherinlaw

Motif
comp.windows.x.motif

motor
clari.sports.motor

motorcycles
alt.motorcycles.harley
aus.motorcycles
rec.motorcycles
rec.motorcycles.dirt
rec.motorcycles.harley
rec.motorcycles.racing

MOTSS (Members of the Same Sex)
alt.sex.motss
soc.motss

movement
alt.cyberpunk.movement

movies
alt.movies.monster
alt.sex.movies
clari.feature.movies
clari.living.movies
rec.arts.movies
rec.arts.movies.reviews
rec.arts.sf.movies
rec.music.movies

MPE computers
comp.sys.hp.mpe

MS-DOS
alt.msdos.programmer
comp.archives.msdos.announce
comp.archives.msdos.d
comp.msdos.programmer
comp.os.msdos.dos
comp.os.msdos.apps
comp.os.msdos.desqview
comp.os.msdos.hardware
comp.os.msdos.mail-news
comp.os.msdos.misc
comp.os.msdos.pcgeos
comp.os.msdos.programmer
comp.os.msdos.programmer.turbovision

MUD (Multi-User Dungeons)
alt.flame.mud
alt.mud
alt.mud.bsx
alt.mud.cyberworld
alt.mud.german
alt.mud.lp
alt.mud.tiny
rec.games.mud
rec.games.mud.admin
rec.games.mud.announce
rec.games.mud.diku
rec.games.mud.lp
rec.games.mud.misc
rec.games.mud.tiny

multi-level marketing
alt.business.multi-level

Multi-trek
alt.games.mtrek

multics
alt.os.multics

multimedia
alt.binaries.multimedia
comp.mail.multi-media
comp.multimedia
comp.os.ms-windows.programmer. multimedia
comp.os.os.multimedia
comp.publish.cdrom.multimedia
comp.sys.amiga.multimedia
misc.education.multimedia

multiple sclerosis
alt.support.mult-sclerosis

mumps
comp.std.mumps

muppets
alt.tv.muppets

murders
clari.news.crime.murders

music
alt.binaries.sounds.music
alt.music.a-cappella
alt.music.alternative
alt.music.alternative.female
alt.music.amy-grant
alt.music.awk-jam
alt.music.beastie-boys
alt.music.bela-fleck
alt.music.big-band
alt.music.billy-joel
alt.music.blues-traveler
alt.music.brian-eno
alt.music.canada
alt.music.complex-arrang
alt.music.danzig
alt.music.deep-purple
alt.music.ebm
alt.music.enya
alt.music.enya.puke.puke.puke
alt.music.filk
alt.music.fleetwood-mac
alt.music.from.the.hearts.of.alt.config
alt.music.hardcore
alt.music.independent
alt.music.james-taylor
alt.music.jethro-tull
alt.music.jewish
alt.music.karaoke
alt.music.kylie-minogue
alt.music.les-moore
alt.music.machines.of.loving.grace
alt.music.marillion
alt.music.misc.why.not.duplicate.the.entire
alt.music.monkees
alt.music.moody-blues
alt.music.nin
alt.music.nirvana
alt.music.pat-mccurdy
alt.music.paul-simon
alt.music.pearl-jam

alt.music.peter-gabriel
alt.music.pink-floyd
alt.music.pop.will.eat.itself
alt.music.pop.will.eat.itself.the.poppies.a
alt.music.prince
alt.music.progressive
alt.music.queen
alt.music.roger-waters
alt.music.rush
alt.music.sed-jam
alt.music.ska
alt.music.smash-pumpkins
alt.music.sonic-youth
alt.music.sophie-hawkins
alt.music.synthpop
alt.music.techno
alt.music.the-doors
alt.music.the.police
alt.music.tmbg
alt.music.todd-rundgren
alt.music.u
alt.music.weird-al
alt.music.world
alt.music.yes
aus.music
clari.living.music
comp.music
comp.sys.ibm.pc.soundcard.music
dc.music
rec.music
rec.music.a-cappella
rec.music.afro-latin
rec.music.beatles
rec.music.bluenote
rec.music.cd
rec.music.celtic
rec.music.christian
rec.music.classical
rec.music.classical.guitar
rec.music.classical.performing
rec.music.compose
rec.music.country.western
rec.music.dementia
rec.music.dylan
rec.music.early
rec.music.folk
rec.music.funky
rec.music.gaffa

rec.music.gdead
rec.music.indian.classical
rec.music.indian.misc
rec.music.industrial
rec.music.info
rec.music.makers
rec.music.makers.bass
rec.music.makers.builders
rec.music.makers.guitar
rec.music.makers.guitar.acoustic
rec.music.makers.guitar.tablature
rec.music.makers.marketplace
rec.music.makers.percussion
rec.music.makers.piano
rec.music.makers.synth
rec.music.marketplace
rec.music.misc
rec.music.movies
rec.music.neil-young
rec.music.newage
rec.music.phish
rec.music.reggae
rec.music.rem
rec.music.reviews
rec.music.synth
rec.music.video

musicals
rec.arts.theatre.musicals

music makers
rec.music.makers
rec.music.makers.bass
rec.music.makers.builders
rec.music.makers.guitar
rec.music.makers.guitar.acoustic
rec.music.makers.guitar.tablature
rec.music.makers.marketplace
rec.music.makers.percussion
rec.music.makers.piano
rec.music.makers.synth

Mutant Universe (Marvel Comics)
rec.arts.comics.xbooks

mutual funds
misc.invest.funds

mycology
bionet.mycology

mysticism
alt.consciousness.mysticism

mythic animals
alt.mythology.mythic-animals

mythology
alt.mythology
alt.mythology.mythic-animals

nachos
alt.os.nachos

nanotechnology
sci.nanotech

national
alt.national.enquirer

National Basketball Association (NBA)
alt.sports.basketball.nba.atlanta-hawks
alt.sports.basketball.nba.chicago-bulls
alt.sports.basketball.nba.la-lakers
alt.sports.basketball.nba.miami-heat
alt.sports.basketball.nba.mn-wolves
alt.sports.basketball.nba.nj-nets
alt.sports.basketball.nba.orlando-magic
alt.sports.basketball.nba.seattle-sonics
alt.sports.basketball.nba.utah-jazz
alt.sports.basketball.nba.wash-bullets

National Cash Register (NCR)
comp.sys.ncr

National Enquirer
alt.national.enquirer

National Hockey League (NHL)
alt.sports.hockey.nhl.boston-bruins
alt.sports.hockey.nhl.buffalo-sabres
alt.sports.hockey.nhl.chi-blackhawks
alt.sports.hockey.nhl.dallas-stars
alt.sports.hockey.nhl.hford-whalers
alt.sports.hockey.nhl.mtl-canadiens
alt.sports.hockey.nhl.nj-devils
alt.sports.hockey.nhl.ny-islanders
alt.sports.hockey.nhl.ny-rangers
alt.sports.hockey.nhl.phila-flyers
alt.sports.hockey.nhl.pit-penguins
alt.sports.hockey.nhl.que-nordiques
alt.sports.hockey.nhl.sj-sharks
alt.sports.hockey.nhl.tor-mapleleafs

alt.sports.hockey.nhl.vanc-canucks
alt.sports.hockey.nhl.wash-capitals
alt.sports.hockey.nhl.winnipeg-jets

National Information Infrastructure (NII)
alt.politics.datahighway

National Public Radio (NPR)
alt.radio.networks.npr

National Security Agency (NSA)
alt.politics.org.nsa

native
alt.native
soc.culture.native

natural language
comp.ai.nat-lang
comp.edu.languages.natural

NBA (National Basketball Association)
alt.sports.basketball.nba.atlanta-hawks
alt.sports.basketball.nba.chicago-bulls
alt.sports.basketball.nba.la-lakers
alt.sports.basketball.nba.miami-heat
alt.sports.basketball.nba.mn-wolves
alt.sports.basketball.nba.nj-nets
alt.sports.basketball.nba.orlando-magic
alt.sports.basketball.nba.seattle-sonics
alt.sports.basketball.nba.utah-jazz
alt.sports.basketball.nba.wash-bullets

near-death experiences
alt.consciousness.near-death-exp

Nebraska
clari.local.nebraska
clari.local.nebraska.briefs

necktie
alt.necktie

Necromicon
alt.necromicon

Nepal
soc.culture.nepal

net
alt.net.personalities
aus.net.aarnet
aus.net.acsnet
aus.net.directory

aus.net.directory.osi-ds
aus.net.mail
aus.net.news
aus.net.status
clari.net
clari.net.admin
clari.net.announce
clari.net.answers
clari.net.info
clari.net.newusers
clari.net.talk
clari.net.talk.admin
clari.net.talk.news
comp.sys.ibm.pc.net

net abuse
alt.current-events.net-abuse
alt.current-events.net-abuse.c-n-s

net cops
alt.flame.net-cops

net games
alt.netgames.bolo

Nethack
rec.games.roguelike.nethack

Netherlands
soc.culture.netherlands

net people
soc.net-people

Netrek
alt.games.netrek.paradise
rec.games.netrek

network
clari.nb.network

Network File System (NFS)
comp.protocols.nfs

Network News Transport Protocol (NNTP)
news.software.nntp

networking
comp.os.ms-windows.networking.misc
comp.os.ms-windows.networking.tcp-ip
comp.os.ms-windows.networking.windows
comp.os.os.networking.misc
comp.os.os.networking.tcp-ip

comp.sys.amiga.networking
comp.sys.ibm.pc.hardware.networking

networks
alt.radio.networks.npr
comp.networks.noctools.announce
comp.networks.noctools.bugs
comp.networks.noctools.d
comp.networks.noctools.submissions
comp.networks.noctools.tools
comp.networks.noctools.wanted
comp.os.ms-windows.programmer.networks

neural nets
comp.ai.neural-nets

neuroscience
bionet.neuroscience

Nevada
clari.local.nevada
clari.local.nevada.briefs

new
alt.test.my.new.group

new age
rec.music.newage
talk.religion.newage

newbie
alt.newbie

New England
clari.local.newengland

New England Patriots
alt.sports.football.pro.ne-patriots

New Hampshire
clari.local.newhampshire

New Jersey
clari.local.newjersey
clari.local.newjersey.briefs

New Jersey Devils
alt.sports.hockey.nhl.nj-devils

New Jersey Nets
alt.sports.basketball.nba.nj-nets

new media
clari.tw.newmedia

New Mexico
clari.local.newmexico

New Orleans Saints
alt.sports.football.pro.no-saints

new product announcements
biz.next.newprod
comp.newprod

Newsbytes
clari.nb
clari.nb.apple
clari.nb.broadcast
clari.nb.business
clari.nb.chips
clari.nb.dos
clari.nb.editorial
clari.nb.education
clari.nb.general
clari.nb.govt
clari.nb.health
clari.nb.ibm
clari.nb.index
clari.nb.law
clari.nb.network
clari.nb.online
clari.nb.pc
clari.nb.pda
clari.nb.pen
clari.nb.review
clari.nb.summary
clari.nb.supercomputer
clari.nb.telecom
clari.nb.top
clari.nb.trends
clari.nb.unix
clari.nb.windows

newsgroups
news.announce.newsgroups

new sites
news.newsites

news media
alt.news-media

new theories
alt.sci.physics.new-theories

new users
clari.net.newusers
news.newusers.questions

New–York
clari.local.newyork
clari.local.newyork.briefs

New York City
clari.local.nyc
clari.local.nyc.briefs

New York Giants
alt.sports.football.pro.ny-giants

New York Islanders
alt.sports.hockey.nhl.ny-islanders

New York Jets
alt.sports.football.pro.ny-jets

New York Knicks
alt.sports.basketball.pro.ny-knicks

New York Mets
alt.sports.baseball.ny-mets

New York Rangers
alt.sports.hockey.nhl.ny-rangers

New York Stock Exchange
clari.biz.market.report.usa.nyse

New York–upstate
alt.culture.ny-upstate

New York Yankees
alt.sports.baseball.ny-yankees

New Zealand
clari.world.oceania.newzealand
soc.culture.new-zealand

Newton
comp.binaries.newton
comp.sys.newton.announce
comp.sys.newton.misc
comp.sys.newton.programmer

NeXT
biz.next.newprod
comp.next.misc
comp.sys.next
comp.sys.next.advocacy
comp.sys.next.announce
comp.sys.next.bugs
comp.sys.next.hardware

comp.sys.next.marketplace
comp.sys.next.misc
comp.sys.next.programmer
comp.sys.next.software
comp.sys.next.sysadmin

NeXTStep
comp.soft-sys.nextstep

NFS (Network File System)
comp.protocols.nfs

NHL (National Hockey League)
alt.sports.hockey.nhl.boston-bruins
alt.sports.hockey.nhl.buffalo-sabres
alt.sports.hockey.nhl.chi-blackhawks
alt.sports.hockey.nhl.dallas-stars
alt.sports.hockey.nhl.hford-whalers
alt.sports.hockey.nhl.mtl-canadiens
alt.sports.hockey.nhl.nj-devils
alt.sports.hockey.nhl.ny-islanders
alt.sports.hockey.nhl.ny-rangers
alt.sports.hockey.nhl.phila-flyers
alt.sports.hockey.nhl.pit-penguins
alt.sports.hockey.nhl.que-nordiques
alt.sports.hockey.nhl.sj-sharks
alt.sports.hockey.nhl.tor-mapleleafs
alt.sports.hockey.nhl.vanc-canucks
alt.sports.hockey.nhl.wash-capitals
alt.sports.hockey.nhl.winnipeg-jets

nice
soc.singles.nice

Nickelodeon
alt.tv.nickelodeon

Nine Inch Nails (NIN)
alt.music.nin

Nintendo
alt.super.nes
rec.games.video.nintendo

Nirvana
alt.music.nirvana

nitrogen fixation
bionet.biology.n2-fixation
bionet.n2-fixation

nn newsreader
news.software.nn

NNTP (Network News Transport Protocol)
news.software.nntp
NOC tools
comp.networks.noctools.announce
comp.networks.noctools.bugs
comp.networks.noctools.d
comp.networks.noctools.submissions
comp.networks.noctools.tools
comp.networks.noctools.wanted

noise
alt.noise

nomad
alt.arts.nomad

non-profit
soc.org.nonprofit

non-smokers
alt.support.non-smokers

non-US
alt.mcdonalds.nonUS

noncommercial magazines
alt.zines

noncommercial radio
rec.radio.noncomm

nonlinear
sci.nonlinear

nontraditional housing
alt.housing.nontrad

Nordic
rec.skiing.nordic
soc.culture.nordic

North Carolina
clari.local.northcarolina

North Dakota
clari.local.northdakota

northern
clari.world.europe.northern

Northern Exposure
alt.tv.northern-exp

Northstar
comp.sys.northstar

oldies
alt.rock-n-roll.oldies

OLE
comp.os.ms-windows.programmer.ole

Olympic sports
clari.sports.olympic

Olympics
alt.olympics.medal-tally
rec.sport.olympics

Omega
alt.games.omega

online
clari.nb.online

online service
alt.online-service
alt.online-service.america-online
alt.online-service.compuserve
alt.online-service.delphi
alt.online-service.freenet
alt.online-service.genie
alt.online-service.portal
alt.online-service.prodigy

Ontario
clari.local.ontario.briefs

Open Desktop (Santa Cruz Organization)
biz.sco.opendesktop

Open Look
comp.windows.open-look

operating systems
alt.os.bsdi
alt.os.multics
alt.os.nachos
alt.uu.comp.os.linux.questions
aus.computers.os
comp.binaries.os
comp.os.aos
comp.os.bsd.announce
comp.os.bsd.apps
comp.os.bsd.bugs
comp.os.bsd.development
comp.os.bsd.misc
comp.os.bsd.questions
comp.os.chorus

comp.os.coherent
comp.os.cpm
comp.os.cpm.amethyst
comp.os.eunice
comp.os.geos
comp.os.linux.admin
comp.os.linux.announce
comp.os.linux.development
comp.os.linux.help
comp.os.linux.misc
comp.os.lynx
comp.os.mach
comp.os.minix
comp.os.misc
comp.os.ms-windows.advocacy
comp.os.ms-windows.announce
comp.os.ms-windows.apps
comp.os.ms-windows.apps.comm
comp.os.ms-windows.apps.financial
comp.os.ms-windows.apps.misc
comp.os.ms-windows.apps.utilities
comp.os.ms-windows.apps.word-proc
comp.os.ms-windows.misc
comp.os.ms-windows.networking.misc
comp.os.ms-windows.networking.tcp-ip
comp.os.ms-windows.networking.windows
comp.os.ms-windows.nt.misc
comp.os.ms-windows.nt.setup
comp.os.ms-windows.programmer.controls
comp.os.ms-windows.programmer.drivers
comp.os.ms-windows.programmer.graphics
comp.os.ms-windows.programmer.memory
comp.os.ms-windows.programmer.misc
comp.os.ms-windows.programmer.multimedia
comp.os.ms-windows.programmer.networks
comp.os.ms-windows.programmer.ole
comp.os.ms-windows.programmer.tools
comp.os.ms-windows.programmer.win
comp.os.ms-windows.programmer.winhelp
comp.os.ms-windows.setup
comp.os.ms-windows.video
comp.os.msdos.dos
comp.os.msdos.apps
comp.os.msdos.desqview
comp.os.msdos.hardware
comp.os.msdos.mail-news
comp.os.msdos.misc
comp.os.msdos.pcgeos

Orlando Magic
alt.sports.basketball.nba.orlando-magic

outdoors
rec.outdoors.fishing
rec.outdoors.fishing.fly
rec.outdoors.fishing.saltwater

out-of-body experiences
alt.out-of-body

owning
rec.aviation.owning

Pabu
alt.games.pabu

packet
aus.radio.packet
rec.ham-radio.packet

paddle
rec.boats.paddle

pagan
alt.pagan

PageMaker (Aldus Corporation)
alt.aldus.pagemaker
bit.listserv.pagemakr

Pagesat
biz.pagesat
biz.pagesat.weather

paintball
alt.sport.paintball
rec.sport.paintball

painter
alt.fractal-design.painter

Pakistan
bit.listserv.pakistan
soc.culture.pakistan

paleo-anthropology
sci.anthropology.paleo

Palestine
soc.culture.palestine

Palmer, John
alt.fan.john-palmer

panic
alt.support.anxiety-panic

pantyhose
alt.pantyhose

papers
comp.ai.jair.papers

paradise
alt.games.netrek.paradise

Paradox (Borland database)
comp.databases.paradox

parallel
aus.parallel
comp.parallel
comp.parallel.mpi
comp.parallel.pvm

Paranet
alt.paranet.abduct
alt.paranet.metaphysics
alt.paranet.paranormal
alt.paranet.psi
alt.paranet.science
alt.paranet.skeptic
alt.paranet.ufo

paranormal
alt.paranet.paranormal
alt.paranormal
alt.paranormal.channeling

parasitology
bionet.parasitology

parents
alt.flame.parents

parents of teenagers
alt.parents-teens

particle physics
sci.physics.particle

party
alt.party

Pascal
comp.lang.pascal

patches
alt.sources.patches
alt.sys.amiga.uucp.patches

patents
comp.patents

philosophy
alt.christnet.philosophy
alt.philosophy.jarf
alt.philosophy.objectivism
alt.philosophy.zen
comp.ai.philosophy
sci.philosophy.meta
sci.philosophy.tech
talk.philosophy.misc

Phish
rec.music.phish

Phoenix Cardinals
alt.sports.football.pro.phoe-cardinals

phonics
alt.recovery.phonics

photography
aus.photo
rec.photo
rec.photo.advanced
rec.photo.darkroom
rec.photo.help
rec.photo.marketplace
rec.photo.misc

photon
alt.sport.photon

photosynthesis
bionet.photosynthesis

physics
alt.sci.physics.acoustics
alt.sci.physics.new-theories
alt.sci.physics.plutonium
alt.sci.physics.spam
sci.med.physics
sci.physics
sci.physics.accelerators
sci.physics.electromag
sci.physics.fusion
sci.physics.particle
sci.physics.plasma
sci.physics.research

piano
rec.music.makers.piano

Pick
comp.databases.pick

pictures
alt.binaries.pictures
alt.binaries.pictures.cartoons
alt.binaries.pictures.d
alt.binaries.pictures.erotica
alt.binaries.pictures.erotica.bestiality
alt.binaries.pictures.erotica.blondes
alt.binaries.pictures.erotica.cartoons
alt.binaries.pictures.erotica.d.
alt.binaries.pictures.erotica.female
alt.binaries.pictures.erotica.male
alt.binaries.pictures.erotica.orientals
alt.binaries.pictures.fine-art.d
alt.binaries.pictures.fine-art.digitized
alt.binaries.pictures.fractals
alt.binaries.pictures.furry
alt.binaries.pictures.misc
alt.binaries.pictures.supermodels
alt.binaries.pictures.utilities
alt.fractals.pictures
alt.sex.pictures
alt.sex.pictures.female
alt.sex.pictures.services

piloting
rec.aviation.piloting

pinball
rec.games.pinball

Pine
comp.mail.pine

Pink Floyd
alt.music.pink-floyd

pipes
alt.smokers.pipes

pirate
alt.radio.pirate

Pittsburgh Penguins
alt.sports.hockey.nhl.pit-penguins

Pittsburgh Pirates
alt.sports.baseball.pitt-pirates

planetarium
sci.astro.planetarium

planetary
alt.sci.planetary

polymers
sci.polymers

pool
alt.sport.pool

population biology
bionet.population-bio

portable computers
comp.sys.mac.portables

porting
comp.os.os.programmer.porting

Portuguese
soc.culture.portuguese

postdoctoral research
sci.research.postdoc

postmodernism
alt.postmodern

PostScript
comp.lang.postscript
comp.sources.postscript

poverty
clari.news.poverty

Power PC
comp.sys.powerpc

Powerbuilder (PowerSoft)
comp.soft-sys.powerbuilder

PPP (Point-to-Point Protocol)
comp.protocols.ppp

Prairie Home Companion
rec.arts.wobegon

president
alt.president.clinton

Presley, Elvis
alt.elvis.king
alt.elvis.sighting

Pretty Good Privacy (PGP)
alt.security.pgp

Prince
alt.music.prince

printers
comp.periphs.printers

print media
clari.biz.industry.printmedia

prisoner
alt.tv.prisoner

prisons
alt.prisons

privacy
alt.comp.acad-freedom.news
alt.comp.acad-freedom.talk
alt.cyberpunk
alt.hackers
alt.politics.org.nsa
alt.privacy
alt.privacy.anon-server
alt.privacy.clipper
alt.security
alt.security.pgp
alt.security.ripem
alt.whistleblowing
comp.org.eff.news
comp.org.eff.talk
comp.security.misc
comp.society.privacy
sci.crypt
talk.politics.crypto

Prodigy
alt.online-service.prodigy

production
rec.video.production

products
rec.aviation.products

professional engineers
comp.cad.pro-engineer

professional wrestling
rec.sport.pro-wrestling

programmers
alt.msdos.programmer
alt.sb.programmer
comp.msdos.programmer
comp.os.ms-windows.programmer. controls
comp.os.ms-windows.programmer.drivers
comp.os.ms-windows.programmer.graphics
comp.os.ms-windows.programmer.memory
comp.os.ms-windows.programmer.misc

comp.os.ms-windows.programmer. multimedia
comp.os.ms-windows.programmer.networks
comp.os.ms-windows.programmer.ole
comp.os.ms-windows.programmer.tools
comp.os.ms-windows.programmer.win
comp.os.ms-windows.programmer.winhelp
comp.os.msdos.programmer
comp.os.msdos.programmer.turbovision
comp.os.os.programmer
comp.os.os.programmer.misc
comp.os.os.programmer.oop
comp.os.os.programmer.porting
comp.os.os.programmer.tools
comp.sys.amiga.programmer
comp.sys.apple.programmer
comp.sys.ibm.pc.programmer
comp.sys.mac.programmer
comp.sys.newton.programmer
comp.sys.next.programmer
comp.unix.programmer
comp.windows.ms.programmer
rec.games.programmer
rec.games.xtank.programmer

programming
comp.programming
comp.programming.literate

programming languages
alt.lang.apl
alt.lang.asm
alt.lang.awk
alt.lang.basic
alt.lang.ca-realizer
alt.lang.cfutures
alt.lang.focal
alt.lang.intercal
alt.lang.ml
alt.lang.sas
alt.lang.teco
comp.edu.languages.natural
comp.lang.ada
comp.lang.apl
comp.lang.asm
comp.lang.basic.misc
comp.lang.basic.visual
comp.lang.c
comp.lang.clos
comp.lang.clu
comp.lang.dylan
comp.lang.eiffel

comp.lang.forth
comp.lang.forth.mac
comp.lang.fortran
comp.lang.functional
comp.lang.hermes
comp.lang.icon
comp.lang.idl
comp.lang.idl-pvwave
comp.lang.lisp
comp.lang.lisp.franz
comp.lang.lisp.mcl
comp.lang.lisp.x
comp.lang.logo
comp.lang.misc
comp.lang.ml
comp.lang.modula
comp.lang.oberon
comp.lang.objective-c
comp.lang.pascal
comp.lang.perl
comp.lang.pop
comp.lang.postscript
comp.lang.prograph
comp.lang.prolog
comp.lang.python
comp.lang.rexx
comp.lang.sather
comp.lang.scheme
comp.lang.scheme.c
comp.lang.sigplan
comp.lang.smalltalk
comp.lang.tcl
comp.lang.verilog
comp.lang.vhdl
comp.lang.visual

Prograph
comp.lang.prograph

progressive
alt.india.progressive
alt.music.progressive
alt.politics.india.progressive
alt.rock-n-roll.metal.progressive
misc.activism.progressive

Project Gutenberg
bit.listserv.gutnberg

Prolog
comp.lang.prolog

prophecies
alt.prophecies.nostradamus

prose
alt.prose
alt.prose.d
rec.arts.prose

proteins
bionet.molbio.proteins

Proteon
comp.sys.proteon

protocols
comp.protocols.appletalk
comp.protocols.dicom
comp.protocols.ibm
comp.protocols.iso
comp.protocols.iso.dev-environ
comp.protocols.iso.x
comp.protocols.iso.x.gateway
comp.protocols.kerberos
comp.protocols.kermit
comp.protocols.misc
comp.protocols.nfs
comp.protocols.pcnet
comp.protocols.ppp
comp.protocols.snmp
comp.protocols.tcp-ip
comp.protocols.tcp-ip.domains
comp.protocols.tcp-ip.ibmpc
comp.protocols.time.ntp

providers
comp.infosystems.www.providers

PSION personal computers
comp.sys.psion

psychoactives
alt.psychoactives

psychobiology
sci.med.psychobiology

psychology
alt.psychology
alt.psychology.help
alt.psychology.personality
sci.psychology
sci.psychology.digest
sci.psychology.research

pub
alt.pub.cloven-shield
alt.pub.coffeehouse.amethyst
alt.pub.dragons-inn
alt.pub.havens-rest

publish
comp.publish.cdrom.hardware
comp.publish.cdrom.multimedia
comp.publish.cdrom.software
comp.publish.prepress

pulp
alt.pulp

punishment
alt.personals.spanking.punishment
clari.news.punishment

punk
alt.punk
alt.punk.straight-edge

puns
alt.humor.puns

puzzles
rec.puzzles
rec.puzzles.crosswords

Pyramid
aus.pyramid
comp.sys.pyramid

pyrotechnics
rec.pyrotechnics

Python
comp.lang.python

Python, Monty
alt.fan.monty-python

Q
alt.fan.q

Quaker
bit.listserv.quaker-p
soc.religion.quaker

Quantum Leap
rec.arts.sf.tv.quantum-leap

Quanyin
alt.meditation.quanyin

435

recipes
rec.food.recipes

recovery
alt.abuse.offender.recovery
alt.abuse.recovery
alt.irc.recovery
alt.recovery
alt.recovery.catholicism
alt.recovery.codependency
alt.recovery.phonics
alt.recovery.religion
alt.sexual.abuse.recovery
alt.usenet.recovery

recreational
alt.hemp.recreational

Red Dwarf
alt.tv.red-dwarf

Reeves, Vic
alt.fan.vic-reeves

reform
alt.politics.reform

reggae
rec.music.reggae

Reimer, Jeremy
alt.fan.jeremy-reimer

releases
rec.video.releases

religion
alt.christnet.religion
alt.recovery.religion
alt.religion.adma
alt.religion.all-worlds
alt.religion.buddhism.tibetan
alt.religion.christian
alt.religion.computers
alt.religion.eckankar
alt.religion.emacs
alt.religion.islam
alt.religion.kibology
alt.religion.monica
alt.religion.sabaean
alt.religion.satanism
alt.religion.scientology
alt.religion.shamanism

alt.religion.skibology
alt.religion.zoroastrianism
aus.religion
clari.news.religion
soc.religion.bahai
soc.religion.christian
soc.religion.christian.bible-study
soc.religion.christian.youth-work
soc.religion.eastern
soc.religion.gnosis
soc.religion.islam
soc.religion.quaker
soc.religion.shamanism
talk.religion.misc
talk.religion.newage

R.E.M.
rec.music.rem

Ren and Stimpy
alt.fan.ren-and-stimpy
alt.tv.ren-n-stimpy

Renaissance fairs
alt.fairs.renaissance

renewable energy
alt.energy.renewable

repair
sci.electronics.repair

report
clari.biz.market.report
clari.biz.market.report.asia
clari.biz.market.report.europe
clari.biz.market.report.top
clari.biz.market.report.usa
clari.biz.market.report.usa.nyse

reproduction
clari.news.reproduction

reptiles and amphibians
rec.pets.herp
sci.bio.herp

republican
alt.politics.usa.republican

research
alt.education.research
comp.compression.research
comp.graphics.research

Rogue
rec.games.rogue
rec.games.roguelike.angband
rec.games.roguelike.announce
rec.games.roguelike.misc
rec.games.roguelike.moria
rec.games.roguelike.nethack
rec.games.roguelike.rogue

role-playing games
alt.games.frp.dnd-util
alt.games.frp.live-action
alt.games.frp.tekumel
rec.games.frp
rec.games.frp.advocacy
rec.games.frp.announce
rec.games.frp.archives
rec.games.frp.cyber
rec.games.frp.dnd
rec.games.frp.live-action
rec.games.frp.marketplace
rec.games.frp.misc

roller coaster
rec.roller-coaster

Rolling Stones
alt.rock-n-roll.stones

romance
alt.romance
alt.romance.chat
dc.romance

Romanian culture
soc.culture.romanian

roommate
alt.flame.roommate

room sharing (USENIX conference)
comp.org.usenix.roomshare

roots
soc.roots

Roseanne
alt.tv.roseanne

roses
rec.gardens.roses

rowing
rec.sport.rowing

Royko, Mike
clari.feature.mikeroyko

rugby
rec.sport.rugby

rumors
talk.rumors

Rumpole
alt.fan.rumpole

Rundgren, Todd
alt.music.todd-rundgren

running
rec.running

rural
misc.rural

Rush
alt.music.rush

Russia
clari.world.europe.russia

Russian
alt.uu.lang.russian.misc

Saint Louis Cardinals
alt.sports.baseball.stl-cardinals

saltwater
rec.outdoors.fishing.saltwater

saltwater fishing
rec.outdoors.fishing.saltwater

sample
biz.clarinet.sample

samples
biz.americast.samples

San Diego Padres
alt.sports.baseball.sd-padres

San Francisco 49ers
alt.sports.football.pro.sf-ers

San Francisco Bay Area
clari.local.sfbay
clari.sfbay.misc

San Francisco Giants
alt.sports.baseball.sf-giants

San Jose Sharks
alt.sports.hockey.nhl.sj-sharks

Santa Cruz Organization (SCO)
biz.sco.announce
biz.sco.binaries
biz.sco.general
biz.sco.magazine
biz.sco.opendesktop
biz.sco.wserver
comp.unix.xenix.sco

satellites
alt.satellite.tv.europe
alt.satellite.tv.forsale
rec.video.satellite
sci.geo.satellite-nav

satire
alt.atheism.satire

Saturday Night Live
alt.tv.snl

Saved by the Bell
alt.tv.saved-bell

SCA (Society for Creative Anachronism)
alt.heraldry.sca
rec.org.scah

scale
rec.models.scale

scanner
alt.radio.scanner
rec.radio.scanner

Scheme programming language
comp.lang.scheme
comp.lang.scheme.c

science
alt.folklore.science
alt.paranet.science
clari.tw.science
misc.education.science
rec.arts.sf.science
sci.space.science

science fiction
alt.games.sf
aus.sf
aus.sf.star-trek
rec.arts.sf.announce

rec.arts.sf.fandom
rec.arts.sf.marketplace
rec.arts.sf.misc
rec.arts.sf.movies
rec.arts.sf.reviews
rec.arts.sf.science
rec.arts.sf.starwars
rec.arts.sf.tv
rec.arts.sf.tv.babylon-5
rec.arts.sf.tv.quantum-leap
rec.arts.sf.written
rec.arts.sf-lovers

science resources
bionet.sci-resources

scientists
soc.culture.scientists

Scientology
alt.religion.scientology
alt.scientology.scam.scam.scam

scooter
alt.scooter
alt.scooter.classic

Scott, Gene
alt.fan.gene-scott

scouting
rec.scouting

SCSI (Small Computer System Interface)
comp.periphs.scsi

scuba
rec.scuba

searchlight
alt.bbs.searchlight

Seattle Mariners
alt.sports.baseball.sea-mariners

Seattle Seahawks
alt.sports.football.pro.sea-seahawks

Seattle Supersonics
alt.sports.basketball.nba.seattle-sonics

security
alt.security
alt.security.index
alt.security.keydist
alt.security.pgp

alt.security.ripem
comp.security.announce
comp.security.misc
comp.security.unix
misc.security

Sega Genesis
alt.sega.genesis
rec.games.video.sega

Seinfeld
alt.tv.seinfeld

self-improvement
alt.self-improve

self-organizing systems
comp.theory.self-org-sys

semiconductors
sci.engr.semiconductors

sendmail
comp.mail.sendmail

Sequent
comp.sys.sequent

servers
comp.dcom.servers

service clubs
alt.org.toastmasters
soc.org.service-clubs.misc

services
alt.internet.services
alt.sex.pictures.services
biz.comp.services
clari.biz.industry.services

setup
comp.os.ms-windows.nt.setup
comp.os.ms-windows.setup
comp.os.os.setup

sewing
alt.sewing

sex
alt.magick.sex
alt.politics.sex
alt.sex
alt.sex.bondage
alt.sex.exhibitionism

alt.sex.fat
alt.sex.femdom
alt.sex.fetish.diapers
alt.sex.fetish.fashion
alt.sex.fetish.orientals
alt.sex.fetish.startrek
alt.sex.fetish.watersports
alt.sex.intergen
alt.sex.magazines
alt.sex.masturbation
alt.sex.motss
alt.sex.movies
alt.sex.not
alt.sex.pictures
alt.sex.pictures.female
alt.sex.pictures.services
alt.sex.spanking
alt.sex.stories
alt.sex.strip-clubs
alt.sex.voyeurism
alt.sex.wanted
alt.sex.wizards
alt.sexual.abuse.recovery
aus.sex
clari.news.crime.sex
clari.news.sex

sexual abuse
alt.sexual.abuse.recovery

SGML (Standard Generalized Markup Language)
comp.text.sgml

Shadowcaster
alt.games.ibmpc.shadowcaster

Shamanism
alt.religion.shamanism
soc.religion.shamanism

shared reality
alt.shared-reality.startrek.klingon

Shazam
comp.soft-sys.shazam

shells
comp.unix.shell
comp.ai.shells

shenanigans
alt.shenanigans

smoking
alt.support.stop-smoking
clari.news.smoking

snail mail
alt.snail-mail

sneakers
alt.clothing.sneakers

SNMP (Simple Network Mail Protocol)
comp.protocols.snmp

snowboard
rec.skiing.snowboard

snowboarding
rec.sport.snowboarding

snowmobiles
alt.snowmobiles

soap operas
rec.arts.tv.soaps

soaring
rec.aviation.soaring

soccer
rec.sport.soccer

socialism
alt.politics.socialism.trotsky

society
alt.society.anarchy
alt.society.civil-disob
alt.society.civil-liberties
alt.society.civil-liberty
alt.society.conservatism
alt.society.etrnl-vigilanc
alt.society.foia
alt.society.futures
alt.society.generation-x
alt.society.kindness
alt.society.resistance
alt.society.revolution
alt.society.sovereign
comp.society
comp.society.cu-digest
comp.society.development
comp.society.folklore
comp.society.futures
comp.society.privacy

Society for Creative Anachronism (SCA)
alt.heraldry.sca
rec.org.sca

sociology
alt.sci.sociology

software
bionet.software
bionet.software.acedb
bionet.software.gcg
bionet.software.sources
bit.software.international
biz.comp.software
comp.publish.cdrom.software
comp.software.config-mgmt
comp.software.international
comp.software.licensing
comp.software.testing
comp.sys.next.software
news.software.anu-news
news.software.b
news.software.nn
news.software.nntp
news.software.notes
news.software.readers

software engineering
comp.software-eng

software systems
alt.soft-sys.corel.draw
alt.soft-sys.corel.misc
alt.soft-sys.tooltalk
comp.soft-sys.andrew
comp.soft-sys.khoros
comp.soft-sys.matlab
comp.soft-sys.nextstep
comp.soft-sys.powerbuilder
comp.soft-sys.ptolemy
comp.soft-sys.sas
comp.soft-sys.shazam
comp.soft-sys.spss
comp.soft-sys.wavefront

Solaris
comp.unix.solaris

Somalia
alt.culture.somalia
soc.culture.somalia

Spain
soc.culture.spain

spanking
alt.personals.spanking
alt.personals.spanking.punishment
alt.sex.spanking

specification
comp.specification
comp.specification.z

spectroscopy
sci.techniques.spectroscopy

speech
comp.speech

spelling
alt.flame.spelling

spina bifida
alt.support.spina-bifida

Spinal Tap
alt.fan.spinal-tap

spreadsheets
comp.apps.spreadsheets

SPSS
comp.soft-sys.spss

squash
alt.sport.squash

Sri Lanka
soc.culture.sri-lanka

stagecraft
alt.stagecraft
rec.arts.theatre.stagecraft

stamps
rec.collecting.stamps

Standard Generalized Markup Language (SGML)
comp.text.sgml

standards
comp.std.c
comp.std.internat
comp.std.lisp
comp.std.misc
comp.std.mumps
comp.std.unix
comp.std.wireless

standup comedy
alt.comedy.standup

Star Trek
alt.sex.fetish.startrek
alt.shared-reality.startrek.klingon
alt.startrek.creative
alt.startrek.klingon
aus.sf.star-trek
rec.arts.startrek.current
rec.arts.startrek.fandom
rec.arts.startrek.info
rec.arts.startrek.misc
rec.arts.startrek.reviews
rec.arts.startrek.tech

Star Wars
rec.arts.sf.starwars

Starfleet
alt.starfleet.rpg

state courts
courts.usa.state.ohio.appls-th
courts.usa.state.ohio.config
courts.usa.state.ohio.supreme

statistics
sci.stat.consult
sci.stat.edu
sci.stat.math

step parents
alt.support.step-parents

Stern, Howard
alt.fan.howard-stern
alt.fan.howard-stern.fartman

Sternlight, David
alt.fan.david-sternlight

Sting
alt.fan.sting

stocks
clari.tw.stocks
misc.invest.stocks

stolen
biz.stolen

storage systems
comp.arch.storage
comp.sys.ibm.pc.hardware.storage

Surak
alt.fan.surak
alt.fans.surak

surfing
alt.surfing

surrealism
alt.surrealism

surveys
alt.usenet.surveys

sustainable agriculture
alt.sustainable.agriculture

swap
rec.radio.swap

swimming
rec.sport.swimming

Swiss
soc.culture.swiss

Sybase
comp.databases.sybase

symbolic mathematics
sci.math.symbolic

symphonic rock
alt.rock-n-roll.symphonic

syntax
alt.syntax.tactical

synthesis
comp.cad.synthesis

synthesizers
rec.music.makers.synth
rec.music.synth

synthpop
alt.music.synthpop

system administration
comp.sys.next.sysadmin

systems
comp.sys.ibm.pc.hardware.systems
sci.systems

tablature
alt.guitar.tab
rec.music.makers.guitar.tablature

table tennis
rec.sport.table-tennis

tactical
alt.syntax.tactical

tadpole
biz.tadpole.sparcbook

Tahoe
comp.sys.tahoe

Taiwan
alt.taiwan.republic
clari.world.asia.taiwan
soc.culture.taiwan

talk shows
alt.internet.talk.shows
alt.tv.talkshows.daytime
alt.tv.talkshows.late

tall
alt.support.tall

Tamil
alt.culture.tamil
soc.culture.tamil

Tampa Bay Buccaneers
alt.sports.football.pro.tampabay-bucs

Tandy
comp.sys.tandy

Tanner, Meredith
alt.fan.meredith-tanner

Tanner, Tammy
alt.fan.tammy-tanner

tarot
alt.tarot

taxes
misc.taxes

Taylor, James
alt.music.james-taylor

TCP/IP protocols
comp.os.ms-windows.networking.tcp-ip
comp.os.os.networking.tcp-ip
comp.protocols.tcp-ip
comp.protocols.tcp-ip.domains
comp.protocols.tcp-ip.ibmpc

teaching assistants
soc.college.teaching-asst

technical
alt.books.technical
biz.books.technical
misc.books.technical
misc.invest.technical
news.admin.technical

technical reports
comp.doc.techreports

technical support
alt.management.tech-support

techniques
sci.techniques.mag-resonance
sci.techniques.microscopy
sci.techniques.spectroscopy
sci.techniques.xtallography

techno music
alt.music.techno

technology
alt.clearing.technology
alt.cyberpunk.tech
alt.hope.tech
alt.sci.tech.indonesian
alt.techno-shamanism
alt.technology.misc
alt.technology.mkt-failure
alt.technology.obsolete
alt.technology.smartcards
bit.listserv.tech-l
bit.tech.africana
comp.dcom.telecom.tech
comp.sys.acorn.tech
comp.sys.amiga.tech
comp.sys.atari.st.tech
comp.sys.ibm.pc.soundcard.tech
rec.arts.startrek.tech
rec.audio.tech
rec.autos.sport.tech
rec.autos.tech
rec.bicycles.tech
sci.bio.technology
sci.philosophy.tech
sci.space.tech
techno-shamanism

teens
alt.fan.teen.idols
alt.fan.teen.starlets

Tekumel
alt.games.frp.tekumel

Telebit
biz.comp.telebit
biz.comp.telebit.netblazer

telecommunications
alt.dcom.telecom
alt.dcom.telecom.ip
alt.sect.telecom
clari.nb.telecom
clari.tw.telecom
comp.dcom.telecom
comp.dcom.telecom.tech

telemedicine
sci.med.telemedicine

Teletype terminals
comp.terminals.tty

television
alt.satellite.tv.europe
alt.satellite.tv.forsale
alt.tv
alt.tv.animaniacs
alt.tv.antagonists
alt.tv.babylon-5
alt.tv.barney
alt.tv.beakmans-world
alt.tv.beavis-n-butthead
alt.tv.bh
alt.tv.brady-bunch
alt.tv.brisco-county
alt.tv.dinosaurs
alt.tv.dinosaurs.barney.die.die.die
alt.tv.fifteen
alt.tv.game-shows
alt.tv.hermans-head
alt.tv.highlander
alt.tv.infomercials
alt.tv.infomercials.don-lapre. die.die.die
alt.tv.kids-in-hall
alt.tv.la-law
alt.tv.liquid-tv
alt.tv.lois-n-clark

alt.tv.mad-about-you
alt.tv.mash
alt.tv.max-headroom
alt.tv.melrose-place
alt.tv.mstk
alt.tv.muppets
alt.tv.mwc
alt.tv.nickelodeon
alt.tv.northern-exp
alt.tv.nypd-blue
alt.tv.prisoner
alt.tv.real-world
alt.tv.red-dwarf
alt.tv.ren-n-stimpy
alt.tv.robocop
alt.tv.robotech
alt.tv.rockford-files
alt.tv.roseanne
alt.tv.saved-bell
alt.tv.seinfeld
alt.tv.simpsons
alt.tv.simpsons.itchy-scratchy
alt.tv.sn
alt.tv.snl
alt.tv.snl.snl.snl
alt.tv.talkshows.daytime
alt.tv.talkshows.late
alt.tv.time-traxx
alt.tv.tiny-toon
alt.tv.tiny-toon.fandom
alt.tv.twin-peaks
alt.tv.wiseguy
alt.tv.x-files
alt.tv.x-files.creative
alt.tv.xuxa
clari.living.tv
rec.arts.sf.tv
rec.arts.sf.tv.babylon-5
rec.arts.sf.tv.quantum-leap
rec.arts.tv
rec.arts.tv.mstk
rec.arts.tv.soaps
rec.arts.tv.tiny-toon
rec.arts.tv.uk

Telugu
soc.culture.indian.telugu

Tennessee
clari.local.tennessee

tennis
alt.tennis
clari.sports.tennis
rec.sport.tennis

tenured
alt.grad-student.tenured

terminals
comp.terminals
comp.terminals.bitgraph
comp.terminals.tty

terrorism
clari.news.terrorism

test
alt.test
bit.listserv.test
bit.test
biz.test
comp.test
misc.test
misc.test.moderated
news.test

testers
comp.sources.testers

testing
comp.lsi.testing
comp.software.testing

TeX
aus.tex
bit.listserv.tex-l
comp.text.tex

Texas
clari.local.texas
clari.local.texas.briefs

Texas Instruments
comp.sys.ti
comp.sys.ti.explorer

Texas Rangers
alt.sports.baseball.texas-rangers

text
alt.chinese.text
alt.chinese.text.big
alt.japanese.text
alt.text.dwb

top news stories
clari.biz.market.report.top
clari.biz.top
clari.nb.top
clari.news.crime.top
clari.news.top
clari.sports.top
clari.tw.top
clari.world.top

TORG
alt.games.torg

Toronto Bluejays
alt.sports.baseball.tor-bluejays

Toronto Maple Leafs
alt.sports.hockey.nhl.tor-mapleleafs

tourism
clari.biz.industry.tourism

toys
alt.toys.hi-tech
alt.toys.transformers
rec.toys.lego
rec.toys.misc

transcendence
alt.abuse.transcendence

transcendental
alt.meditation.transcendental

Transformers
alt.toys.transformers

transgendered
alt.transgendered
soc.support.transgendered

transportation
clari.biz.industry.transportation

Transputer
comp.sys.transputer

travel
alt.travel.road-trip
bit.listserv.travel-l
rec.travel
rec.travel.air
rec.travel.asia
rec.travel.cruises
rec.travel.europe

rec.travel.marketplace
rec.travel.misc
rec.travel.usa-canada

trends
clari.nb.trends

triathlon
rec.sport.triathlon

trivia
rec.games.trivia

tropical
bionet.biology.tropical

Trotsky, Leon
alt.politics.socialism.trotsky

TTY terminals
comp.terminals.tty

Turbovision
comp.os.msdos.programmer.turbovision

Turkey
clari.world.mideast.turkey

Turkish
soc.culture.turkish

Twin Peaks
alt.tv.twin-peaks

U2
alt.fan.u-2
alt.music.u-2

Ukrainian
soc.culture.ukrainian

Undernet (Internet Relay Chat)
alt.irc.undernet

unidentified flying objects (UFOs)
alt.paranet.ufo

Unisys Corporation
alt.sys.unisys
comp.sys.unisys

United Kingdom (UK)
alt.floors.uk
alt.radio.uk
clari.world.europe.uk
rec.arts.tv.uk

451

USENET
alt.culture.usenet
alt.usenet.kooks
alt.usenet.offline-reader
alt.usenet.recovery
alt.usenet.surveys
news.lists.ps-maps

USENIX
comp.org.usenix
comp.org.usenix.roomshare

user friendly
comp.unix.user-friendly

user groups
comp.org.usrgroup
comp.sys.apple.usergroups

users
alt.foolish.users
bionet.users.addresses
comp.infosystems.www.users

Utah
clari.local.utah
clari.local.utah.briefs

Utah Jazz
alt.sports.basketball.nba.utah-jazz

utensils
alt.plastic.utensils.spork.spork.spork

utilities
alt.binaries.pictures.utilities
comp.os.ms-windows.apps.utilities

uupcb
alt.bbs.uupcb

vacation
misc.kids.vacation

vampires
alt.vampyres

Vancouver Canucks
alt.sports.hockey.nhl.vanc-canucks

vaudeville
alt.comedy.vaudeville

Vaughan, Owain
alt.fan.owain-vaughan

Vectrex
rec.games.vectrex

vegetarian
rec.food.veg

vehicles
ba.market.vehicles

Venezuela
soc.culture.venezuela

Verilog
comp.lang.verilog

Vermont
clari.local.vermont

veterans
soc.veterans

VGA Planets
alt.games.vga-planets

VHSIC Hardware Description Language (VHDL)
comp.lang.vhdl

video
alt.games.video.classic
alt.video.games.reviews
alt.video.laserdisc
comp.os.ms-windows.video
comp.sys.ibm.pc.hardware.video
rec.games.video
rec.games.video.do
rec.games.video.advocacy
rec.games.video.arcade
rec.games.video.arcade.collecting
rec.games.video.atari
rec.games.video.classic
rec.games.video.marketplace
rec.games.video.misc
rec.games.video.nintendo
rec.games.video.sega
rec.music.video
rec.video
rec.video.cable-tv
rec.video.production
rec.video.releases
rec.video.satellite

Vietnam
alt.war.vietnam

Washington Redskins
alt.sports.football.pro.wash-redskins

water polo
rec.sport.water-polo

Waters, Roger
alt.music.roger-waters

waterski
rec.sport.waterski

Wavefront software system
comp.soft-sys.wavefront

weather
biz.pagesat.weather
clari.news.weather

wedding
alt.wedding

Wellfleet
comp.dcom.sys.wellfleet

Welsh, Matt
alt.fan.matt.welsh

werewolves
alt.horror.werewolves

West Virginia
clari.local.westvirginia

what-if
alt.history.what-if

Wheelhouse, Jeff
alt.fan.jeff-wheelhouse

whistleblowing
alt.whistleblowing

white collar crime
clari.news.crime.whitecollar

White House
clari.news.usa.gov.whitehouse

White, Tony
alt.fan.tony-white

Whitewater scandal
alt.current-events.clinton.whitewater

Whitewolf
alt.games.whitewolf

Wildcat (BBS software)
alt.bbs.wildcat

Williams, Dave
alt.fan.dave-williams

windows
alt.windows.cde
alt.windows.text
clari.nb.windows
comp.os.ms-windows. networking.windows
comp.windows.garnet
comp.windows.interviews
comp.windows.misc
comp.windows.ms
comp.windows.ms.programmer
comp.windows.news
comp.windows.open-look
comp.windows.suit
comp.windows.x
comp.windows.x.announce
comp.windows.x.apps
comp.windows.x.iunix
comp.windows.x.intrinsics
comp.windows.x.motif
comp.windows.x.pex

windsurfing
rec.windsurfing

wine
comp.emulators.ms-windows.wine

winemaking
rec.crafts.winemaking

WinHelp
comp.os.ms-windows.programmer.winhelp

Winnipeg Jets
alt.sports.hockey.nhl.winnipeg-jets

Winsock standard
alt.winsock

Winston, John
alt.fan.john-winston

Wired (magazine)
alt.wired

wireless
comp.std.wireless

yeast
bionet.molbio.yeast

Yes
alt.music.yes

Young, Neil
rec.music.neil-young

youth work
soc.religion.christian.youth-work

Yugoslavia
soc.culture.yugoslavia

Z
comp.specification.z
comp.sys.zenith.z

Zappa, Frank
alt.fan.frank-zappa

zebrafish
bionet.organisms.zebrafish

Zen
alt.philosophy.zen
alt.zen

Zenith
comp.sys.zenith
comp.sys.zenith.z

Zeos
alt.sys.pc-clone.zeos
biz.zeos
biz.zeos.announce
biz.zeos.general

Zima
alt.zima

Zoroastrianism
alt.religion.zoroastrianism